International Relations in the Nuclear Age

International Relations in the Nuclear Age

One World, Difficult to Manage

Henry L. Bretton

State University of New York Press

Other Books by the Author

Stresemann And The Revision of Versailles (1953)
Power and Stability in Nigeria (1962)
The Rise and Fall of Kwame Nkrumah (1966)
Power and Politics in Africa (1973)
The Power of Money (1980)

Books Authored in Collaboration With Others

Germany Under Occupation (1949)
German Democracy At Work (1955)

Published by
State University of New York Press, Albany
© 1986 State University of New York
All rights reserved
Printed in the United States of America
No part of this book may be used or reproduced in any manner whatsoever
without written permission except in the case of brief quotations embodied
in critical articles and reviews. For information, address State University
of New York Press, State University Plaza, Albany, N.Y., 12246.

Library of Congress Cataloging in Publication Data
Bretton, Henry L., 1916–
International Relations in the Nuclear Age.
Bibliography: p.
Includes index.
1. International Relations. 2. International
Economic Relations. I. Title.
JX1391.B67 1986   327   85-30354
ISBN 0-88706-040-4
ISBN 0-88706-041-2 (pbk.)

10 9 8 7 6 5 4 3 2 1

Contents

PART ONE: FUNDAMENTALS OF INTERNATIONAL RELATIONS

PART TWO: THE CONDUCT OF INTERNATIONAL RELATIONS: CHANNELS AND INSTRUMENTALITIES

PART THREE: MANAGING THE WORLD ECONOMY

PART FOUR: MANAGING MILITARY POWER

EPILOGUE: PREVENTING WORLD WAR THREE
AND BEYOND   431

Preface

Five major considerations led to the decision to produce this book in its present form. First, neither I nor my students are satisfied with contemporary international relations texts. Those not outdated tend to overload textual material and references with detail more appropriately relegated to advanced courses. The transformation of international relations is discussed without adequate reference to its formation. Efforts to accommodate, in limited space, the many contending theories and approaches to the study of international relations leave beginning students confused and bewildered, diminishing the credibility of the discipline and of this particular field of study. In the process of compressing divergent material into their texts, some of the authors include illustrations and offer generalizations which neither fit into their narratives nor are consistently accurate.

The second reason is my conviction that the increasingly important political-economic dimension is not effectively handled in available texts. Among the leaders, those which seriously and competently address that dimension either do so to the exclusion of all else or they present economic material too abruptly, at too advanced a level to be of use to students who typically are not trained in the fundamentals of economics. Some of the latter tend to reproduce un-critically, often arbitrarily, and as currently relevant, formulations offered by economists whose views have long been overtaken by events. Also, while per-spectives of other "worlds" are increasingly reflected in newer texts, the accent remains rather heavily on First World views, problems arising within the other worlds either being inadequately treated or ignored. Economics and political economy, to be fully understood and appreciated by students lacking training in economics, cannot be presented and discussed in disjointed fashion, under topical headings having little or no bearing on actual economic relationships. Subjects like global monetary management, trade, finance, or economic develop-ment must be approached systematically, leaving intact logical economic con-nections and processes. In that regard, while economic and military dimensions of world politics are in the present book accorded the prominence they deserve, other aspects are also given appropriate attention.

The third rationale for this book stems from my firm belief that the nuclear threat *is* the overriding issue of our time, if not invalidating then certainly overshadowing much of traditional theory of international relations and war-ranting therefore special emphasis in a text on contemporary international relations. Unless a nuclear war can be prevented, nothing this or the next generation of faculty or students may study or discuss will matter, for a radically different world will emerge from a nuclear holocaust. Among other likely consequences, many issues currently attracting worldwide attention—no matter how urgent they may seem to their proponents—will pale in significance in the aftermath of a nuclear war. For example, problems of underdevelopment, poverty, and disease in the Third World, human rights violations, monetary imbalances, social injustice, and instability will under postnuclear war conditions be aggravated far beyond the most pessimistic forecasts. Most likely, similar conditions will materialize if the arms competition between the world's major camps continues unabated.

If the nuclear and similarly catastrophic threats are to be averted, they must be understood. This calls for a realistic approach. Such controversial yet essential topics as war planning, preparation, and fighting must be covered adequately, critically, and candidly. The overwhelming military preponderance of the two superpowers in these respects must not be underestimated nor obscured by sometimes spectacular but on balance insignificant third party challenges. Likewise, the inhumanity of contemporary military postures must not be downplayed or overlooked for it is that lack of sensitivity to the human factor which has opened the door to the contemporary apocalyptic threat. Especially important in that respect is a pronounced realization that elements in both superpowers and among some of their allies and associates propose to save humanity by destroying it. If humanity is to be spared, the human factor must be placed at the center of our concern above state, above nation, above ideology, above anything likely to detract from its central importance.

The fourth rationale arises from the realization that too often in the history of the world wars have been started as a means of conflict *resolution.* But few conflicts are ever totally resolved; they are most certainly not resolved by war. Given the world as it is, not as one would like it to be, for some time to come if a planetary catastrophe is to be avoided ways and means must be found to *manage* conflicts. It is for that reason that this book's central theme is *management,* not resolution, of the more basic hence more intractable and potentially explosive conflict situations.

Finally, considering my somewhat unique personal and professional-academic background and experiences which span several epochs and "worlds," it seems appropriate and timely for me to offer my own contribution to the discipline of international relations. Born in Europe during the First World War, I grew up in the turbulent postwar era which saw one world crumble and another rise, experiencing first-hand the rise of Fascism and Communism and the clash between these ideologies and political democracy. Living and working under totalitarian rule in Nazi Germany and fascist Italy, I saw these systems prepare for the Second World War. Following emigration to the United States, I fought World War Two on the American side, reversing my father's military experience . . . he had been a German soldier in World War One. From these vantage points developed a heightened sensitivity to questions of war, peace, and human rights.

My undergraduate and graduate studies and subsequent academic career coinciding with the transition from conventional to nuclear weaponry span the rise and fall of entire schools of thought on international relations and world politics. While on the faculty of the University of Michigan and of the State University of New York I conducted field research in Western Europe and Sub-Saharan Africa. My publications deal with such topics as foreign policy, political economy, comparative government, direct foreign investment, patron-client relations, psychopathology and political leadership, language and politics, and human rights. Research and a two-year tour of teaching duty in West and East Africa provided the opportunity to experience again first-hand the pressing problems confronting former African colonies during their transition "from empire to nation" and subsequently as independent states, part of the Third and Fourth Worlds. Added most recently was a tour of the Far East.

The Structure of the Book

Part One focuses on fundamentals of international relations including a summary overview of the origins, basic characteristics, and current state of the global community of nations, power and its sources, and structure and processes of foreign policy. Part Two deals with the channels and instrumentalities states utilize in the conduct of international relations. Parts Three and Four examine systematically and in detail the most critical problems and issues arising with respect to management of world economic and military affairs. The Epilogue suggests courses of action to prevent World War Three and, beyond, to advance the cause of peace. It concludes with a review of the contributions the study of international relations has made to world peace and world order.

I am greatly indebted to the State University of New York College at Brockport, especially Donna Byrd of Brockport's Document Preparation Center; to Diane Whalin, who typed the first draft; Norm Frisch and James Dusen, whose artistic work provided the illustrations; to the Publisher and staff of the State University of New York Press; and to the members of my family, whose encouragement and moral support was essential.

List of Figures

List of Tables

List of Boxes

Comprehensive Table of Contents

Part One
Fundamentals of International Relations

Chapter 1
A Community of Nations

The Evolution of the Global State System

Political and legal organizations with some attributes of what today we call states existed in some parts of the world at least 4000 years ago. But states with clearly defined boundaries, firmly established internal authority and administration, claiming exclusive jurisdiction over every square inch of their territory, insisting upon absolute sovereign control and independence and equipped to enforce it, are more recent sixteenth- or seventeenth-century phenomena.

Whatever their form or internal consistency, states or state-like entities have from earliest times formed alliances and leagues, or entered into less formal agreements, for defensive or offensive purposes. They allocated to themselves spheres of influence and sought to balance each other's power potential by diplomacy or, if that failed, by war. Conquests, subjugation, or total destruction of the losers frequently resulted, followed by realignments among the survivors and formation of new systems.

The most incisive changes during the evolution of state systems coincide with major technological advances, concomitant changes in methods of warfare, changes in the mode of production and distribution of wealth, and the repercussions from that—first regional then global economic interdependence. The event, if one may call it that, which sharply accelerated all of this was the industrial revolution.

Prior state systems were shaped by land armies, gradually reinforced by naval power, enforcing the will of monarchs, oligarchies, or Popes. On the European continent, a succession of states or combinations of imperial domains played dominant roles: first Greece and Rome, then the Holy Roman Empire, then its successors, France, Austria, Spain and Portugal, and numerous smaller splinter entities. Eventually, again following a series of armed conflicts, the more powerful continental successor states found themselves challenged from the periphery by Great Britain (England) from the west, by Russia from the east, and from the center of Europe by what initially did not seem much of a threat but eventually developed into the German Empire.

The industrial revolution and its technological, social, and political consequences influenced the evolution of the global state system in several ways.

1

Starting in Europe, it enabled the powers who emerged victorious from a series of land and naval encounters between the sixteenth and nineteenth centuries to assume positions of dominance vis-à-vis all other states and all other civilizations in the world. Eventually the original world powers, Spain and Portugal, were replaced by Great Britain, France, and Germany. Aided by superior naval power and advanced military technology and by improvements in economic productivity made possible by more effective internal social and political organization, the new masters carved empires of their own out of defenseless regions on the continents of Asia and Africa, leaving the Western Hemispheric remains of the Spanish and Portugese empires to fend for themselves until the emergence of the United States to world power status. Of considerable consequence for later years, Japan was left intact. Regarding Russia, France under Napoleon Bonaparte made an attempt at conquest but failed, likewise setting the stage for emergence of yet another world power.

Naval power enabled Great Britain to play a decisive role in the development and domination of alliance systems on the European continent until it lost that advantage and its power as a result of World War Two. In the middle of the nineteenth century, in the wake of Napoleon's defeat and the decline of France as a continental power, Prussia, under the leadership of its Chancellor Prince Otto von Bismarck, forged by skillfull diplomacy and by war the greater German Empire from a collection of kingdoms, duchies, and principalities. In the process, another continental power was eclipsed, the Empire of Austro-Hungary. In 1914 and again in 1939 Germany attempted to challenge Great Britain and her ally France in the West and Russia in the East, failing each time. The defeat affected adversely the fortunes of her allies, Turkey and Austro-Hungary in World War One and Italy in World War Two. Japan's drive to replace Europe in the Far East by military conquest succeeded briefly from the early 1930s to the early 1940s but ended in her decisive defeat in 1945.

Several major developments contributed to the shift of world power from the Western European center to the periphery: the rise of the United States and of the Soviet Union to military and economic military power status, the collapse of the colonial empires, and the discovery of nuclear power.

Toward the end of World War Two, in February of 1945, the leaders of the three major allies opposing the so-called axis powers of Germany, Japan, and Italy, namely Roosevelt, Churchill, and Stalin, met at Yalta (a Russian Black Sea resort) to engage in a time-honored practice of victors in wars—the distribution of spoils. Their plan was to impose on the world a new order. Their three countries would reallocate and rearrange territories, allocate to themselves spheres of influence, and establish neutral zones over which no single power was to seek hegemony. That grand design, like others before it and probably all others to follow, was doomed to failure, for several reasons. Foremost were the economic, military, and social consequences of World War Two. With the collapse of Germany at the center of Europe and of Japan in the Far East, critical vacuums developed in each region. Great Britain and France, exhausted from that war, themselves in need of support, were unable

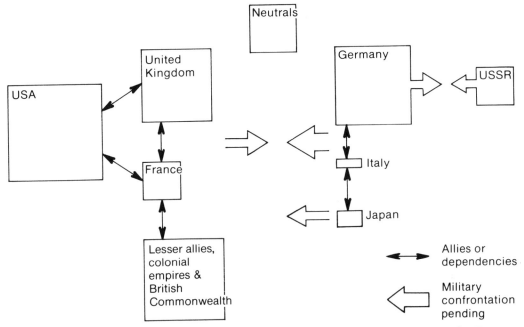

Fig. 1-1a. World Power Distribution On The Eve of World War Two. Scale: Per capita National Income x Potential Military Capacity 1938/1939, based on *UN Statistical Yearbook* 1949–1950.

to fill the void. The Soviet Union had the potential but now the heir to Western European world dominance, the United States, stood in its path.

The first formal postwar conference, at Potsdam in 1945, likewise failed to reflect reality.* Although Soviet armies had penetrated to the Elbe River in the center of Germany and deep into southeastern Europe, the Western Allies envisaged the reestablishment of a chain of independent, noncommunist states separating the Soviet Union from Western Europe. The reality of the situation prevented the Western Allies from interfering with the eventual conversion of once independent states, from the Baltic to the Black Sea, into provinces or client states of the Soviet Union.

A basic premise upon which the postwar settlement, especially that of Potsdam, was to rest was retention by the United States of its monopoly of nuclear power attained with the explosion of the two devices over Hiroshima and Nagasaki in 1945. When Soviet acquisition of nuclear capability in the 1950s terminated that monopoly, giving birth to a bipolar global power pattern, the old order envisaged by the Western component of the World War Two alliance had come to an end. Now the Soviet Union could strengthen and secure its hold on the newly acquired territories, reinforce its claim on adjacent spheres

---

* Principal participants were President Harry S. Truman, United States; Winston Churchill, later Clement Atlee, successive Prime Ministers of the United Kingdom of Great Britain and Northern Ireland; and Joseph Stalin, Soviet Dictator. The conference was held shortly after the end of the war in Europe, at Potsdam, near Berlin, then the capital of defeated Germany; the central purpose of the meeting was to determine the latter's fate.

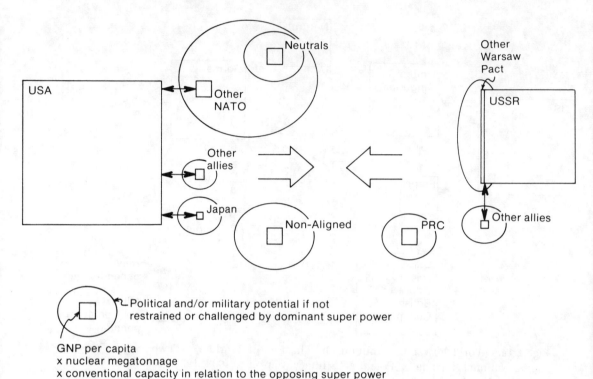

Fig. 1-1b. World Power Distribution: Post-1960. Based on *World Bank Atlas 1983*, IISS(1983/4), *SIPRI Yearbook 1982*, *U.S. Statistical Abstract 1984*.

of influence—Finland, Central Europe, Afghanistan, even the Middle East, and parts of the Far East—and pursue its own grand design, advancement of socialist or communist world revolution.

Hastened by the insistence of the Soviet Union and the United States as well as by the imperial powers' own sins of omission and commission, the colonial empires soon were liquidated by one means or another. From their remnants or their ruins arose yet another "world," a Third one, joining the capitalist, United States and Western Europe-centered First, and its challenger, the Second, the product of the 1917 Russian Revolution. The fervent desire of this new world to recover lost identities and lost opportunities provided yet another opportunity for the Soviet Union to press forward with its plans for a new and radically different world. But the emergence of that new world provided new opportunities also for the western powers.

The old order was rendered obsolete when military technology, already revolutionized by nuclear power, attained globe-girdling potentialities with the development of intercontinental ballistic missiles—potentialities soon extended into space by earth-orbiting satellites. Finally, for a variety of reasons which we shall explore in subsequent chapters, most if not all nations of the world found themselves brought ever closer, though to varying degrees, by the inexorably expanding interdependence of national economies.

At the end of World War Two, Roosevelt, Churchill, and Stalin had posed for the world a plan of their own. The alternative is still in process of formation. It is the central purpose of this book to trace and analyze the nature and dynamics of international relations since that time. From the Treaty of West-phalia (1648), generally regarded as the birth of the modern state system, to Yalta and Potsdam, the point when a new order was to begin but failed almost immediately, important precedents were created and the roots of much of what we face today were established. Where appropriate therefore, this book will refer to these earlier events. In the main, however, it is an introduction to the modern system—which differs from those which preceded it in numerous rather fundamental respects. Before we proceed with our analysis of the substance of international relations, it is necessary to examine more closely the basic unit, the nation-state.

It is no doubt advantageous to view the subject of the relations among nations from a lofty, space traveller's perspective permitting a broad overview to identify patterns of conduct, trends, and prospective developments. But too broad a perspective, or one too far removed from reality, can be misleading. It certainly will not facilitate discovery of the inner dynamics of the nation-state or of the processes and mechanisms which actually determine foreign policy conduct and which can explain what is and what is not done in the name of the state and why. Perhaps most important, if the *nation-state* upon which the entire *inter-nation-al* systemic structure rests has undergone significant changes (and we shall argue that this is the case) it is even more important to take a closer look. We shall begin therefore with an analysis of three basic components of the system—the state, the nation (the force credited with its dynamism, development, and virulence), and nationalism.

State, Nation, and Nationalism

Nation or Nationality?

It should be stated at the outset that the term *nation* has two distinctly different uses. In a legal sense it is synonymous with the state as a whole, regardless of the number of different ethnic or national groups—nationalities—contained within it. In that sense, one speaks of nation and means state. In another mainly social sense, the term nation and the related term nationality are typically applied to groups having the following characteristics: a common heritage and history, a common geographic origin or location, common cultural values, and a common language. In those contexts the difference between nation and nationality is in the main a question of group self-perception. One can say that nationality reflects the previously mentioned basic characteristics in a narrower, more explicit sense, whereas nation may actually comprise several nationalities. Typically, in the early formative stages of a newly established state the claim to nation-status is more declaratory than descriptive. Frequently a civil war has to be fought before a nation, which actually may consist of several different and distinct religio-ethnic-cultural groups, can truly claim to be one nation in the nation-state sense. Even then national minorities who lost out in the struggle for supremacy may continue to press their demands for separate status or even complete independence, for example, the Ukrainians and Central Asian Moslem nationalities in the Soviet Union, the Croats of Yugoslavia, the Catholics of Northern Ireland, the Armenians in Turkey, the Kurds in Iraq, Turkey, and Iran, or the Basques of Spain. The fact that many of these distinct groups are not formally recognized as nation-states under international law (or that we choose to define nation to exclude from that status nationalities not yet formally recognized as full-fledged claimants to independent statehood) does not by itself carry enough weight to deny such entities the right to claim separate status as nation-states. Here is one of the major sources of tension and conflict in the world today.

The question therefore of what constitutes a valid basis for independent nation status is difficult to answer with precision in the majority of cases; in the case of most newly independent states, emerging from the wreckage of the great colonial empires, and in some more established cases, claims to one-nation status are subject to challenge on one premise or another. In the final analysis the ability to advance and sustain a claim to separate national existence rests not so much on definitions or logic as on the force of arms a national government, a dictator, or a political party bureaucracy can muster against challengers from within; and it depends on the magnitude of the threat—real or perceived— which the state faces from outside. Thus, for many years following its independence Lebanon was able to exist as a distinct nation-state in a highly unstable regional setting, in spite of the fact that the country actually was a composite of numerous religious and ethnic subgroups or nationalities hostile toward each other and toward the state as a whole. However, when challenged politically and militarily by forces within and from outside (the latter resulting from the large-scale influx of Palestinians, displaced from what used to be called Palestine) Lebanon came close to total collapse. Other states, similarly divided and challenged, survive intact, usually by arranging compromises among the contending groups. Canada, for instance, in the face of determined and continuous challenge mainly from the French-speaking people in the province of Quebec, has so far succeeded in maintaining its integrity as a Canadian nation-state. States newly formed in the twentieth century have a harder time resisting nation-destroying forces inherited from colonial antecedents, partly because not enough time has elapsed for disparate ethnic, linguistic, or religious entities to fuse into solid units. But whether or not a particular national unit is recognized internationally as a separate state, nationalism and the particularism which it represents remains a factor in international relations.

The Origins of States

States then have varying origins. Some are the result of voluntary compacts among nationalities, races, or other groupings; some are the result of conquest, subjugation, and suppression. In theory, statehood rests on the principle of self-determination of "nations" or of "peoples." In practice, in the vast majority of cases the right to self-determination is by force denied to millions of people throughout the world. Obviously, if any kind of order is to prevail on earth, not every group claiming the right to self-determination, hence to independent statehood, can be accommodated. Indeed, although the term self-determination is widely used, no consensus exists regarding the criteria to be used in the determination of which groups are entitled to separate and independent status.

Since neither legal-constitutional nor racial, cultural, religious, or ideological tests can be devised which could satisfy all circumstances and all conditions, international law generally relies on *recognition*. A group of claimants is granted status as a sovereign and independent state if recognized as such by other states. Reasons why states recognize others vary greatly. A relatively small political faction may be granted recognition and thereby statehood for purely opportunistic and pragmatic reasons, over the objections of numerous other claimants within the very same geographic confines. The United States for instance, in 1903, desiring a separate state in the area where the Panama Canal was to be constructed, first encouraged a rebellious group in Colombia to seek separation from that state and then recognized it as the independent Republic of Panama. In the 1930s, Western European powers chose to confer statehood upon a rebellious military faction which, with the help of German and Italian intervention, had risen against the sovereign and independent Republic of Spain and before it had totally overcome the republican forces. These same powers, joined by the United States, refused for more than a decade, in spite of the fact that it controlled all of the Chinese mainland, to recognize the Chinese Communist regime under Mao Zedong, on the fictitious grounds that the Nationalist Chinese forces which had fled to the offshore island of Taiwan were more truly representative of all of China. As a result of a deal among the powers dominating the United Nations at the outset of its existence, two entities undeniably very much a part of the Soviet Union, namely the Ukrainian and Bylorussian Soviet Socialist Republics, were accorded full membership status in the UN, hence were technically recognized as sovereign and independent states complete with diplomatic status and privileges by all member states of that organization. The capricious approach to this problem manifested itself more recently when, as a result of pressure from the controlling coalition in the General Assembly of the United Nations, that organization conferred full *de facto* recognition as a state (therefore entitled to the many privileges accorded the other member states in the UN) upon a loosely organized, faction-ridden organization claiming to represent all Palestinians in the Middle East.*

Actually, a very substantial number of states currently recognized as such in the UN lack most of the essential ingredients commonly associated with in-

---

* Recognition was only *de facto* (in fact) and not *de jure* (in law) because under the UN Charter legal membership status can be conferred only by the Security Council where the United States would be expected to cast its veto; on the latter point, see Chapter 10.

dependent state- or even nationhood: ethnic homogeneity or consensus among diverse nationalities to live together in one state; capacity to maintain their independent status in all essential respects; economic viability; and ability to meet all obligations members assume upon entry into the organization, including the capacity to implement decisions voted upon by them and others within the UN.

Some states have fewer people than can be found during rush hour in a major department store in a city on the Chinese Mainland, but in the General Assembly of the UN they have the same voting rights as the People's Republic of China. The boundaries of some states are wholly, others partially, the product of negotiations conducted between colonial powers in Europe more than a century ago. Some states, arising from the ruins of the colonial empires, were no more than administrative subdivisions lacking any of the distinct characteristics normally associated with independent nation- or statehood—for example, Upper Volta, Chad, Niger, Togo, or Cameroon in Africa.

Tests of statehood based on criteria other than pragmatic recognition open a pandora's box. For example if one were to test member states in the UN for constitutionality or legitimacy of their respective government the majority would fail to qualify, as more and more states are ruled by usurpers who seized power in violation of existing constitutions. Tests based on the degree to which a government can claim to represent the majority of its subjects would pose similar problems since an increasing number of governments dispense with secret or free elections. Cultural affinity, common language, territorial propinquity of groups composing a state, all would fail to sustain claims to statehood in numerous instances. States like Pakistan, Israel, North and South Korea, and East and West Germany, are the product of partition imposed by outside forces and therefore exist on territory more or less disputed. On occasion, several states merge or fuse. Some of these, Yugoslavia for instance, remain intact. Others break up soon after the act of union—the Syrian-Egyptian United Arab Republic (1958); several Libyan-instigated, purely declaratory mergers, with Syria and Tunisia, for example; the Ghana-Guinea-Mali Union (1958-60); or the Senegal-Mali Federation (1959).

Whatever the legitimacy of a state may be, it is clear that the legal framework which validates statehood in the eyes of the other members of the "community of nations" tends to overshadow the human component of the system. While prevailing international law recognizes that individual human beings or persons have rights, the same law will as a general rule accommodate claims reflecting these rights only with the consent of recognized state authorities. Significantly, living by certain codes of conduct designed to sustain their claims to authority, sovereignty, and independence, governments are inclined not to offend or embarrass fellow governments or ruling elites by questioning their authority over their own subjects. Consequently, they tend to exercise great caution before questioning the right of other governments to do with their subjects as they please, including infliction of indignities, torture, or mass murder. While this attitude may tend to reinforce and stabilize the state system, it also renders it less responsive to fundamental human needs. It may actually be a major source of instability in the world.

Appeal to nationalistic impulses is attractive to governments or rulers hard pressed to solve intractable domestic issues and eager therefore to distract restless supporters at home by adventures abroad or by ethnocentric posturing vis-à-vis actually or merely allegedly hostile or competing states. Most important, appeal to the national conscience of people tends to overcome or obscure, for the moment at least, divisive ethnic, religious, language, or other cultural particularisms found within individual nation-states—states which actually are comprised of more than one unit, each of which can truly describe itself as a distinct national entity.

The "National Character"

Recognized or not, viewed as a positive or a negative force on the international scene, what is the intrinsic quality, the consistency, of what is described as "the national character" of a group? Is it an unchanging attribute which exercises a hold over the individual for life, or is it a superficial attribute which can be shed easily if more desirable values come into play? Do all Germans and all people of German origin, regardless of citizenship or domicile, share the same national characteristics? Do all persons of Jewish faith or of Jewish background subscribe to essentially identical goals in world affairs? Do all persons of Chinese, or Japanese, background, no matter where they make their home, have essentially the same characteristics, share the same values? Or is the "national character" mainly the product of membership in a firmly delineated, physically and politically consolidated state?

Culture, religion, language, tradition, all are extremely important to the individual but fade quickly in importance if physical and material human needs are not met by any one or all of these social means of reinforcement of the basically weak individual. While people ordinarily do not leave the country of their birth, several conditions can trigger mass migration and abandonment of citizenship. Social revolutions force the migration of members of the former ruling social classes. Ethnicity- or religion-driven suppression, mass killings, or threats of genocide cause threatened minorities to seek refuge elsewhere. Those who find acceptance and economic opportunities in their new domicile are known to shed their former national characteristics relatively quickly—leaving aside ritual or purely social manifestations, which are more a matter of nostalgia than of a fierce, politically significant commitment to separate existence.

The Romans had a term for it: *Ubi bene, ibi patria* (Where I am well off, there is my fatherland). As a general rule—as in all things, there are exceptions— the way a person or a family makes a living, or expects to make its living, tends to determine their allegiance to a given state or political system. Ethnic identity or national character are said to be unalterable in a person's lifetime. Actually, upon close analysis conflicts long represented as centering on ethnic or religious issues turn out to be primarily economic in nature, centering in all probability on questions of equitable access to the means of subsistence. Where such access is denied under one pretext or another, religion, ethnicity, and language may become central issues contributing to the development or strengthening of the long-standing characteristics of the group. Facilitate such access, increase the share of a state's wealth available to members of an ethnic, religious, or tribal minority, and the need for group identity begins to wane noticeably.

One reason for the relative prominence of ethnic, religious, tribal, or generally national character theories in historical and political analysis is the tendency to selectively focus on crisis and conflict situations which by their nature highlight and emphasize particularistic tendencies or commitments. But the same history usually is replete with examples of ethnic, religious, tribal, or other particularistic conflicts having been overtaken by cooperation and commensurate reduction if not loss of separate identities.

Evidence is overwhelming that not all Protestants and Catholics need to be locked in bitter and deadly conflict as are members of these groups in Northern Ireland. Not all racial groups need to view each other, and hence their own kind, as do whites and blacks in the Republic of South Africa. Jews and non-Jews have more often than not lived together in peace and harmony; so have Moslems and non-Moslems, including Jews in Palestine prior to Jewish mass immigration into the territory.

In short, while ethnicity, religion, nationalism, and tribalism relate to basic human instincts, they become virulent only under certain conditions. As focal points for conflict, they are not products of a mind at ease, at peace with itself and its environment. They are fed by fears, phobias, beliefs, superstitions, and irrational appeals. Though undoubtedly sources of international conflict, they do not by and of themselves precipitate confrontations. Something must be added for these states of mind to be converted into violent action. Major catalysts of internecine violence then are economic deprivation, denial of access to the means of subsistence, denial of a reasonable share of the wealth available in the larger community, or, at the other end of the spectrum, threats to physical existence emanating from possible physical extermination or serious personal injury. Why do any of these threats arise in the first place? Usually because the dominant or rival group, consciously or unconsciously, explicitly or implicitly, views the target of denial or extermination as an economic rival.

Nationalism in the Nuclear Age

We noted the interrelationship of group security and group identity. Prior to the development of means of mass destruction of entire states if not entire civilizations, the sense of group security was enhanced, or believed to be enhanced, by national defense, which in turn reinforced the sense of national or group identity. What will be the effect of the loss of that sense of security on nationalism?

A glance at some of the international and some of the civil wars waged today indicates that nationalism, and thereby the commitment to separate sovereign statehood, has survived the first explosion of the atom bomb and the subsequent development of intercontinental ballistic missiles and is still virulent in some parts of the world even though the arena of human conflict is now being extended to outer space. Will it survive the succeeding stages of technological development? Will it survive in the face of ever more intense and extensive intertwining of national interests within an ever tighter net of global inter-dependence? Can national borders and jurisdictions long remain meaningful in an age where, in the process of attaining cruising speed, planes and missiles are likely to cross several sovereign nation-states? Can nationalism survive the space age with its globe-girdling satellites?

Ironically, the principal reason why nationalism may continue to play a role in international affairs is the existence of the nuclear stalemate between the only world powers capable of policing the world and containing nationalistic outbursts likely to threaten world peace, namely the Soviet Union and the United States. The nuclear umbrella spread over the world by the two super-powers to protect their respective spheres of interest acts as a shield behind which lesser nations can continue to press their claims, secure in the knowledge that nuclear weapons or superior conventional armed forces may, in spite of warnings to the contrary, actually not be used against them. We shall address that issue in Chapter 19.

The process of nation-building which commenced on a large scale following World War Two, spurred on by the disintegration of the great colonial empires, has not yet lost its momentum. Neither has the concomitant process of nation-destroying, the result mainly of ethnic and racial particularism and irredentism. Nationalist fervor among the Poles is fanned by Western powers intent on dismantling the Soviet domain, while nationalism in Latin America, Central America, Asia, and Africa, is encouraged by the Soviet-socialist bloc nations to weaken the Western bloc militarily-strategically as well as economically. Actively encouraged by radical states or by the example of the new states emerging from colonial status, secessionist and irredentist movements redouble their efforts to break away from older established nation-states, the Basques, for example, from Spain, Irish Catholics from British Northern Ireland, Kurds from Iran and Iraq, Puerto Ricans from the United States, French Canadians from Canada.

But as we shall show in our discussion of contemporary economic issues (Part Three), insistence on national identity and particularism can be exceed-ingly costly in this age of global economic interdependence. Thus, one of the major issues arising is the clash of nationalism and economic reality. As the costs of duplication, redundancy, and waste resulting from stubborn adherence to the luxury of particularism in the face of global economic interdependence rise, resentment sets in against forces and factors which hard-pressed political leaders are prone to blame for their own shortcomings. To escape public pressure, one accentuates nationalism by appeals to national pride, self-esteem, and identity. This sets in motion another cycle of "protective" measures, such as nationalization of whatever segment of the economy has not yet been so treated, threats of limited military action, or war.

On balance the purported rationale for establishment of separate and independent groups of people under the nation-state banner, protection and preservation of lives and property, threatens to become an anachronism in the age of global interdependence and in the face of the threat of nuclear war. For numerous smaller and poorer nations, pursuit of narrow, local interests is a luxury neither they nor their financial backers in the wealthier more advanced countries can continue to afford. The more powerful and richer nations can indulge in that pursuit for longer periods but they too will feel the effect of rising costs of independence and particularism. Gradually it will become apparent that neither lives nor property, human rights nor human dignity, nor indeed the achievements of human civilization, can be protected if nationalism is not curbed. The attempt to reinforce the nation-state by acquisition of nuclear weapons (nuclear proliferation) will alone bring that fact home to many.

Until the great imperial powers lost their ability to constrain the war-making propensities of nationalist aspirations—as noted, mainly camouflaged economic aspiration—or at least contain wars fought over conflicting, allegedly nationalistic goals, world wars were avoided. This era came to an end in 1914 when one particular strategically sensitive caldron of conflicting nationalisms, the Balkans in southeastern Europe, finally exploded, mainly as a result of intervention by the great powers. One overriding issue today is containment of such conflicts; put differently, the issue is management on a global scale of nationalism and its corollaries particularism and ethnocentrism.

The Question of Sovereignty

The term sovereignty has its origin in the rule by individual monarchs, that is, the sovereign. As sovereign rulers monarchs were exempt from the laws promulgated by themselves. Seventeenth-century scholars developing the then embryonic body of international law—which intended to regulate conduct between emerging nation-states—extended that concept to apply also to the sovereign ruler's relations with his equals, other rulers and their states. If the ruler was sovereign at home then he also had to be sovereign abroad. If he was above the law at home, then he also had to be above the law abroad. Subsequently the concept became a doctrine and was extended to apply to the state as such.

Today, when authorities on international law say that a state is sovereign, they merely acknowledge its independence from the *direct* rule or dictate by another state. Put differently, the sovereign state is *in law* not a dependency of another sovereign state. But *law* covers only one segment of the totality of international relations. While a state may not be a dependency of another state in the legal sense, as we have seen, it may actually be heavily dependent on one or more states in economic or military respects, its most critical economic means may be substantially under the control of another state, or its defenses may wholly or critically depend upon another state's good will and armed force.

Like everything else in human affairs, and no matter how fervently international law authorities and national governments may argue the point, the doctrine of sovereignty is subject to steady erosion and atrophy; consequently state authority atrophies, and eventually so does the state itself. Any number of combinations of forces may diminish or undermine sovereignty: technological change, including change in weapon technology, exhaustion of critical raw materials, industrialization, and the progressive interdependence of what once were independent national economies. The sovereignty of a state may also be undercut or even destroyed as a result of internal or combined internal-external forces. We cited the case of Lebanon earlier. That country was first torn apart by internal strife between armed Christian and Moslem factions, then converted into an international battleground between the armed factions of the Palestine Liberation Organization (PLO), the Syrians, and the Israelis. We already referred to countries divided or separated from territory and people they claim, as the result of wars. Other states are deprived of sovereign control over part of their territory as a result of foreign-induced rebellion or secession—Yemen, for instance, which currently is split into North and South Yemen.

The free market economies of the Western countries, foremost the United States, find their sovereignty diminished or undermined by business and financial interests in search of higher returns on their investment and cheaper raw materials or labor. As the ability of large, perhaps even super-corporations, including banks, to act independently grows—a result of accumulation of monetary resources large enough to challenge the resources at the disposal of their respective home governments—they transfer part of their operations abroad, outside the sovereign jurisdiction of their home government or state—beyond the sovereign's reach. When that happens the abstract quality of the concept of sovereignty becomes most apparent; it may under certain conditions be challenged, evaded, and defied by superior means, finance in this case.

What is challenged is the notion that sovereignty carries with it absolute control over an area, over people, over resources. Soviet lawyers do not understand the Western approach to sovereignty. To them, the state is sovereign by definition and must remain sovereign if it is to survive. Therefore the power of those acting on behalf of the state to exercise all necessary controls must be absolute.

To a critical extent, states' foreign relations reflect their internal conditions and the internal conflicts and interests these generate. As states become less and less governable, they become less stable internally, a condition which transfers itself onto the international scene. Put differently, aside from their "national" protective or security function, states essentially are mechanisms or systems designed to manage and reconcile conflicts among diverse and divergent interest and pressure groups. To the extent a state fails to perform that function—for whatever reasons—will it contribute to instability of the community of states.

A Community of Nations?

Binding Principles

Whatever form an international grouping of states may assume for the foreseeable future, and not withstanding its progressive obsolescence, the state will remain in all essential respects the controlling unit. All configurations, associations, or organizations of two or more states will continue to depend for substance, durability, and effectiveness on the cooperation and consent of the participating states. In so far as a community of nations exists at the regional, interregional, or global level, it is held together mainly by two factors: the law of reciprocity and the laws of economic and military interdependence. We will in subsequent chapters examine these and related factors in greater detail. Here only a few brief identifying comments are in order.

The law of reciprocity reflects at the international level the same principle as at the interpersonal or social level. A state, or a person, should behave toward others in such a manner as to allow that behavior to be adopted universally as the maxim governing the behavior of every person in a community, or of every state. Simply put, the rule is: do unto others as you wish them to do unto you. No explicit code of law, no formal set of rules of conduct is required for that general principle to be applied in most instances; failure to act accordingly will sooner or later bring retribution. The casual observer of the behavior of states may gain the impression that this general rule is violated or ignored most of the time. That would be an illusion. What catches our attention and that of historians, or of the media in search of high drama, is the act of defiance, the exception to the rule. Routine compliance with general rules of conduct in everyday affairs is not news.

Every day of every year, for centuries, travellers of all nations have crossed and continue to cross international borders; as a rule citizens of all nations, friend and foe, are allowed innocent passage through third countries. Letters, parcels, and commercial shipments are granted transit rights through territories of sovereign states without being opened or destroyed. Radio, television, and other signals are allowed to be transmitted, as a rule without interference, through the airspace of third parties. Unless they break criminal law in host countries, and however unpleasant or annoying their activities may be to their hosts, diplomats are permitted to conduct their affairs without undue hindrance on the part of host country authorities. Even if local criminal law is violated, diplomats are granted certain courtesies and privileges by governments to whom they are accredited. Trade, aid, and financial transactions flow across national boundaries; ships ply the seven seas; planes, now also satellites, move through the skies, high above dozens of sovereign states. To be sure, international law addresses and covers all of these transactions and occurrences. Our point however is that it is the imperative of self-interest rather than the existence of explicit international legal prescriptions or prohibitions which in the main motivate states to behave the way they do.

As we shall point out in Chapter 9, international law performs an important function in these respects—it provides universally understood guidelines and norms to facilitate international cooperation. But international law is not *the source of* reciprocity. It merely benefits from its observance. Indeed, it can be said that the validity of international law *rests on* reciprocity. Without the latter, the former is reduced to a collection of dead letters.

Economic and military interdependence stems from two major conditions, one being the function of reciprocity, the other a function of need, the latter reinforcing the former. That is of course the condition on which any community is formed. In the case of economic relations, the element of reciprocity arises from an inadequacy of a state's capacity to meet basic economic requirements from its own national resources. Compelled to draw on other state's resources, a state develops an import dependency. But states also find it necessary to export, which creates yet another form of dependency: to export requires access to markets abroad. To be able to sell, one is required to buy. That condition alone has been a major factor in the formation of a sense of community among the nations of the world.

Rivalling economic interdependence as a binding element, or at least a close second, is military interdependence, likewise a state of affairs arising from the inability of most states to protect themselves militarily by means of their own material and human resources. To compensate for that deficiency, states enter into military alliances. Today the solidity of a given formal or informal international grouping depends principally on the degree to which economic and military interdependence have developed and are recognized as such by the participating states.

Following World War One, the ancient concept of collective security was formally recognized. Now its prime objective was prevention of another conflict of the magnitude of that war. The concept found its first formal expression in the *Covenant* of the League of Nations (1920-1945). Under the terms spelled out in the *Covenant*, member states committed themselves to employ specified peaceful means of conflict resolution before resorting to war; in the event a member of the organization elected to wage war in disregard of the terms set forth in the *Covenant*, all other members were obligated to combine their resources to secure the peace against the violator. All members were likewise obligated to participate in collective security actions against a nonmember who resorted to military aggression against a member state. At the core of this undertaking was the age-old principle of one for all, all for one. This experiment in collective security came to an end with the outbreak of World War Two in 1939, and what there had been in the way of an international community of nations broke up once again into warring sections. The League, and with it the principle of collective security—enshrined in numerous other international agreements as well—had failed because neither the *Covenant*, nor the treaties signed in accordance with its terms, had succeeded in curbing the principal nemesis of the concept of a community of nations—the sovereign state.

A second attempt to endow the community concept and the principle of collective security with concrete meaning and thereby put an end forever to global war brought the victorious allies of World War Two together in the United Nations. As we shall see in subsequent chapters, that experiment also fell far short of expectations. The prevention of World War Three thus far has been more the result of what has become known as the balance of terror than of efforts by the United Nations. Since 1945 the principle of collective security has been invoked from time to time but never on a global scale. The United States succeeded in persuading some of its military allies to contribute token forces to what was essentially its own war in defense of South Korea between 1950 and 1953 and again in its war to defend South Vietnam between 1954 and 1975. As an expression of a global community of nations the principle of collective security has yet to be realized.

It is now the hope of a growing body of public opinion throughout the world that the threat of a nuclear holocaust will at long last bring the nations of the world to the point where a genuine planetary sense of community, and hence of planetary collective security, will finally advance from pious wish to concrete reality.

Communities of Interest

Thus the economic and the related military self-interests of states continue to shape the structure and form of what there is in the way of a global community. For the present therefore and for the foreseeable future, the nature of such a community is more declaratory than substantive. In place of one global entity we have at best several major and some lesser regional and inter-regional groupings sharing economic or military interests or a combination of both. But these too are not exempt from the gravitational pull of the nation-state.

We referred to the three "worlds" on this planet, the First, Second, and Third. One can also distinguish major socioeconomic systems. The three-world concept poses serious definitional and classificatory problems as soon as one proceeds from the vague to the specific. The First World, committed to capitalism, arose from the industrial revolution and today is said to consist in the main of states located in the North Atlantic-West European area and Japan. Some of these states have mixed capitalist-socialist economies but all accept the principles of private property and private enterprise. Today all also practice political democracy.

The Second World emerged from the Russian Revolution of October 1917 and is founded to a lesser or greater extent on the socioeconomic principles of Marxism and Leninism. Subjecting state and society, including economy, to the closest possible central planning and control, it consists principally of the Soviet Union, the other members of the Soviet economic and military bloc (mainly located in Eastern and Southeastern Europe) and Cuba. Several other socialist states are associated with that grouping.

The majority of the Third World countries rose from the wreckage of the great colonial empires and became nominally independent following World War Two, the largest bloc in the 1960s. They are located mainly, though not exclusively, in Southeast Asia and Africa and in the regions of the Western Hemisphere south of the United States. Their economies and their political systems and practices are markedly less developed than are those of the First and Second Worlds. Their political and economic practices vary greatly, ranging from private enterprise capitalism to mixed economies and to forms of total-itarian socialism or communism. At the time of writing, countries in the latter grouping constitute the largest bloc among the 158 member states in the United Nations. But already a Fourth World has been identified, an offspring of the Third. This latest world shares one characteristic: the development of its members is lagging decisively behind other Third World countries primarily because they manifestly lack any prospect of generating by any known means the economic wherewithal required to sustain their independence.

The three- or four-world classificatory scheme does not provide a reliable index of mutuality of interest, hence of communal spirit or dedication, within any one of these worlds. To be sure most of the Second World countries are held in check by Soviet military power. But signs have increased in recent years that, aside from pro-Soviet regimes installed and protected by Soviet power, the people in this bloc are far from united. Moreover all three, or even all four, Worlds identified so far include countries which may fit the criteria of two or more of them. For example, Albania, in southeastern Europe, though socialist, is not part of the Soviet-led bloc; neither is Yugoslavia. The latter has since its inception been politically and diplomatically more identified with the Third than with the Second World. The People's Republic of China (PRC), by sheer industrial strength ranks far above several of the First World countries. The PRC, and North and South Korea, though the first two nominally part of the Second, the latter by general orientation either classifiable as belonging to the First or Third World, cannot really be placed in any of these. Then there are, within the Third World, the oil-rich but still less developed states in the Middle East. They, and to an extent also Venezuela and Mexico, can hardly be considered part of a World comprised also of countries situated at the very end of any scale measuring economic viability, per capita share of Gross National Product (GNP), prospects of attaining a level of economic growth sufficient to sustain political independence, or attaining minimal stand-ards of living or of quality of life for their people.

Thus, in a world still divided into diverse hence conflicting constellations and groupings of interest, a certain structural fluidity must be accepted as the norm. If a degree of stability and permanence prevails nevertheless, this is partly because reciprocity and interdependence at least on occasion prove stronger than the divisive national interest and partly because of the vastly superior military power of the United States and the Soviet Union.

There remains the community of interest of states desiring on principle to maintain their distance from either of the superpowers—the nonaligned—and the community of interest of permanent neutrals, states committed to stay out of any and all wars or military actions short of war unless they themselves are under attack. Neutral states can be divided into those neutral wholly by their own choice and those neutralized by international fiat or dictate. Since 1945 Finland, for instance, has been compelled on Soviet insistence to observe neutrality between the Western and Soviet-led blocs; Austria had to pledge neutrality between East and West in exchange for retreat from its soil of Soviet and Western Allied forces in 1955, following occupation in the wake of Germany's defeat in World War Two. Neutrals of their own volition, at least in modern times, are Sweden and Switzerland.

Regarding nonaligned states, their status falls short of neutrality in one critical respect. Whereas the permanently neutral state abjures all forms of warfare, except in self-defense, the purely nonaligned merely eschews formal military alliances only with the great power blocs.

Finally, the world is said to be divisible into North and South, the former comprised of the more highly developed, the latter of the less developed states. There are several problems with that classification. Some of the less developed countries (for example those of black Africa and Southeast Asia) are north of highly developed ones (for example the Republic of South Africa, Australia, and New Zealand). Similarly, Japan, a highly developed country, is south of Mongolia and opposite East Asia. Singapore, Taiwan, and North and South Korea are somewhere in between. However, precise geographic locational problems aside, it is generally understood that to an extent shared interests separate the majority of the more developed, more industrialized countries generally north of the Equator, from those less developed, less industrialized, generally located south of that line.

Who Relates to Whom?

The term inter*national* implies that the basic unit constituting the global community is the nation or, better, the nation-state. In one sense, this certainly is so. The United States, the Soviet Union, Nigeria, India, Brazil, or the People's Republic of China, all identify themselves and are identified in common usage as nations. But if we ask precisely who relates to whom, which are nations relating to each other, and which are states, we find that what we choose to call international relations may more realistically be a matter of holders of power or of state authorities relating to one another.

To be sure, all of the latter insist that they are authorized to act on their nation's behalf, and many of them in fact do so. But upon close inspection of the claims of a growing number of heads of state and of government—regime is a more accurate term—we discover that they have usurped or seized power illegally, that they represent mainly themselves and a small clique of supporters, and that the overwhelming majority of their people have no voice whatever in affairs of state. In such cases the legality or legitimacy of the regime derives not from internal sources but is conferred by other governments or regimes interested in maintaining what is in effect a convenient fiction or myth. Of the more than 160 states recognized as such today, no more than about three dozen have governments who base their authority to act in international affairs on the entire nation's behalf on what we in the United States would recognize as a constitution. Only a minority of the world's rulers have such a constitutional mandate to represent their subjects in international affairs. Even fewer can claim that their policies, domestic as well as foreign, reflect the will of a majority of their subjects, expressed in secret elections, on the basis of universal suffrage. In the majority of states today, naked military or police power is either thinly masked by inoperative or bogus constitutions or randomly, often capriciously, exercised by decrees formulated and issued at will by individuals lacking legitimacy as well as legal authority as these terms are understood in Western democracies.

Fortunately for the peace of the world, the majority of leaders are responsible and rational individuals. For the present, those who are not are subject to external constraints of sufficient persuasive quality to discourage outrageous, inflammatory, or reckless acts, one of which might some day precipitate a global conflagration. But a specter is haunting the world: the maverick firebrand, head of a thoroughly destabilized, conflict-ridden, ungovernable country, or the small determined and desperate band of terrorists, in possession of a nuclear device. . . .

Suggested Questions and Discussion Topics

What major historical forces and events shaped the global state system as we know it today?

What kind of an arrangement did the victorious allies of World War Two envisage for Central and Eastern Europe and what did actually emerge? What "communities of interest" confront each other in Europe and throughout the world?

Define *nation, nationality,* and *nation-state;* what forces tend to reinforce, what forces tend to weaken cohesion of a nation-state?

What are the basic qualifications for statehood and what circumstances or conditions render claims to independent, sovereign statehood questionable in some instances?

Normally, under international law, all states are said to be equal. Offer contrary argument.

In what respects and how does the nuclear age affect nationalist aspirations?

What are the prerequisites of national sovereignty and what tends to diminish that status for most if not all nominally independent states today?

Chapter 2
Power and Its Sources

The subject of power of humans over humans, of groups over other groups, and of states, has occupied the minds of philosophers and of political and social theorists since antiquity. Power is studied because of its bearing on human behavior and the behavior or conduct of states. Power analysis also enables us to construct a hierarchy or pecking order within organizations, institutions, or states, or, in the present context, within the broader community of nations such as it is. We focus on power because of all factors which might shed light on the behavior of states, the element of power—principally of the economic and military, less so of the psychological variety—explains the essence of international relations most satisfactorily. And we refer to states as "powers" because it is power that determines a state's standing in the world rather than quality of life, cultural achievements, the beauty of its landscape, the moral fibre of its people, or seniority among the nations of the world. "Great powers" are those able to overcome all lesser powers. "Middle powers" are stronger than the lesser but weaker than the great.

In contemporary international relations the absence of effective legal and moral constraints on the behavior of states places a premium on the possession of power, principally military and economic reward and coercive power, the essential means to ensure survival and to advance a state's interests in a highly competitive setting. States lacking the means of self-assertion and self-preservation are, as a rule, condemned to accept the status of clients of more powerful states. The clients are like satellites moving in the gravity sphere of a major or superpower.[1]

The theory of international relations identifies many sources of power. Obviously not all of these need to play a decisive role in all instances. Of real significance are only those which in critical situations may generate sufficient strength to spell the difference between state survival and state destruction, or, in less fateful situations, between prevailing in a dispute or confrontation and having to abandon a desired goal.

Population

Ironically, although people should matter most in international relations, in the aggregate, counted as "population," they tend to be a liability in all respects

Table 2-1. GNP, GNP Per Capita, and Population of Selected States[a]

	GNP at market prices (million US$)		GNP per capita (US$)		Population (million)	
Denmark	67,190		13,120		5.1	
Belgium	117,510	340,450	11,920		9.9	29.2
Netherlands	155,750		11,790		14.2	
People's Republic of China	299,770[b]		300		991.3	
Indonesia	78,750		530		149.5	
Nigeria	76,170		870		87.6	
Poland	135,450 (1979)		3,900 (1980)		35.9	
Egypt	28,160		650		43.3	

SOURCES: World Bank, *World Development Reports*, 1982, 1983, and *World Bank Atlas*, 1982 and 1983.

[a] 1981 data except where otherwise indicated

[b] GDP/GNP data on the PRC vary widely; the CIA's GNP estimate for 1981 was $568.69 billion (*Handbook of Econ. Statistics*, 1981, p. 15), and for 1982 $350 billion (*The World Fact Book*, 1983, p. 43). The 1985 *U.S. Statistical Abstract* (p. 846) shows $622 billion for 1981. British estimates for 1981 were $276.47 billion (IISS, 1983, p. 83).

but two: they furnish humanpower for conventional warfare, and they constitute a source of labor. Aside from that, as a matter of national policy states value not numbers so much as they do skills and productivity. Population translates into consumers who must be fed and clothed; while this may be an economic stimulant, it also is a drain on scarce resources. Consumers demand attention and, depending on the political system, generate pressure on governments to aggressively pursue policies designed to satisfy demands for goods and services.

One might assume that, all other things being the same in the case of any two states or regions, the one with a substantially larger population thereby has a power advantage. But this is not necessarily so. It may not seem just to them but the regions with the largest population also are at the lower end of the power scale. Likewise, a ranked listing of the countries of the world by population, shows, among the top ten, the two superpowers (the United States and the Soviet Union) and Japan. The People's Republic of China (PRC), ranking first with a population more than twice that of the two superpowers and more than five times that of Japan, ranks well below all three in current power potential.

If population alone were a determinant of global power, small states like Denmark, Belgium, or the Netherlands should rank below the PRC, Indonesia, Nigeria, Poland, or Egypt in all respects. But the economies of these three Western European states are relatively so strong that on a list based on that factor (per capita GNP for example) the three are well above a number of states with populations several times greater than those of the three states combined. (See Table 2-1.)

The entire African continent including South Africa, with a population of 516 million (mid-1983), has an overall Gross National Product (GNP) about 13 percent of that of the United States with a population less than half of that of Africa. Or Japan, with a population around 118 million or about 12 percent of that of the PRC, has a GNP per capita about 32 times that of its neighbor on the Chinese mainland. GNP of course generates the economic and necessary military wherewithal of international power status.*

When statesmen thought in terms of huge armies moving over land, large populations in hostile or potentially hostile countries filled them with fear; around the turn of the century Western European leaders and geopolitical strategists viewed the Asian masses as the greatest peril threatening their civilization. Following two wars with Germany, one French leader complained that there were about "twenty Million Germans too many." His concern was misplaced. Several decades later, a relatively small German armed force, but equipped with superior weapons and brilliantly led, defeated the numerically superior French armed forces in a few weeks.† Today, Soviet Russian strategists will view with alarm the one billion Chinese south of their 5000 mile border with the PRC. For the time being, the Soviet Union's nuclear strength suffices to keep that threat in check. That situation may change to Soviet disadvantage when and if the PRC acquires nuclear capacity sufficient to deter the Soviet Union from resorting to that weapon in the event of war. In that event, the numerical superiority of PRC forces could tip the balance. But this too is problematic, as the PRC still has far to go to equal Soviet technical and economic proficiency.

Under modern conditions, technological means can be employed to compensate for numerical disadvantage to a far greater extent than was possible several decades ago. On the other hand, large population remains an impediment, especially if highly concentrated in relatively narrow urban areas. In the event of impending nuclear war, a state must find ways and means of evacuating tens of millions of people within hours, at best within two to three days. Inability to achieve this objective could be decisive in choosing whether or not to resist a nuclear threat.

On balance, only steady expansion of economic (including agricultural) and technological support bases can cope with increasing population. Even then, under ideal conditions, governments are less and less inclined to view unhindered population growth as an asset. Should it turn out to be correct that the world's resources are steadily diminishing—and there is as yet no unanimity on this point among experts—unrestricted population growth could prove disastrous for many countries. There may be moral or religious arguments against birth control, but no government facing a burgeoning population and concerned with

---

* GNP—The total value of all goods and services produced nationally plus income accruing to domestic residents arising from investments abroad.

† To compensate for manpower deficiencies in anticipated land wars, Nazi Germany encouraged German women to produce more children, if necessary out of wedlock. Mussolini, whose military ambitions were boundless, introduced a system to honor and materially reward Italian mothers who increased their families beyond the then current norm of six children. In the 1930s France, experiencing a steadily declining birthrate and fearing another German assault, sought to compensate for the deficiency by constructing the presumably impenetrable Maginot Line along the entire Franco-German border.

power status is today disinclined to resort to birth-control measures. In the PRC for example, where currently over 20 percent of the world's population are concentrated on less than 6 percent of the earth's land, failure to proceed that way will simply defeat at the outset that government's efforts to enhance China's power status in the world.

Social and Political Organization and Cohesion

It should be apparent, from our discussion in Chapter 1, that to play any significant roles at all in international affairs, indeed to prevail in the universal struggle for existence, a state requires a degree of inner strength matching at the very least any and all forces arrayed against it or likely to threaten its vital interests or its existence at some time in the future. One source of that strength is the social fabric, another the political organizational framework for allocation and distribution of power, and the machinery for *peaceful* resolution of conflict or conflict management. In short, the relative strength of a state is a function of the solidity of its social and political structure and the quality of the social and political product—social justice, equity, and fairness in the distribution of wealth and opportunity for advancement. A critical part of this equation is the degree to which the social and political product satisfies the basic demands and expectations of the majority of the people. Social and political cohesion are functions also of a system's ability to reconcile conflicting interests of economically and militarily potent contenders for power.

A question has fascinated mankind ever since the first philosopher noted the difference between democratic and authoritarian rule: which generates more strength internally and externally, a state based on participatory democracy or one governed by a leader or ruling elite, to whom the people have delegated either voluntarily or as a result of coercion all or most of the elements of power? The matter is exceedingly complex and this is not the place to attempt a full examination. By all indications, Soviet Russia's totalitarian rule, especially under Stalin, who bloodily suppressed large sections of the population and decimated by mass executions the higher ranks of the armed forces shortly before Nazi Germany's military onslaught in 1941, should have spelled weakness to the point of impotence. Yet, once the initial attack and accompanying losses had been absorbed by the system, the state and the people rallied to defeat the enemy, proving as unfounded universally shared expectations of total collapse. In this instance, the ingredient generating requisite social and political cohesion may have been patriotism, backed up by even more brutal force.

Another facet of this problem complex is a state's dominant political culture; that is, its dominant mode of expectation regarding form of government, role and function of political institutions, and mode of political behavior. Political culture defines and prescribes the role of the individual citizen in governance, formulation of public policy, and decision-making in the public domain. What kind of a political culture enhances a state's external power potential, what kind spells weakness? Again, a glance at the two superpowers and their detrimentally opposing political systems suggests that the answer is inconclusive. For example, in the Soviet Union participatory democracy never struck roots and may therefore not be acceptable to a majority of the people as an alternative to totalitarian rule. Its absence, in the West widely regarded as a source of weakness, may actually be a source of strength. While undoubtedly large numbers of the Soviet people are known to be dissatisfied with the social and economic products of that system, a majority may well be incapable of conceiving of an alternative, preferring a familiar system of government to one unknown— preferring one which relieves the individual of the burden of political choice, ensures social and political order and stability, and distributes a sufficiently large share of the national wealth to a sufficiently wide segment of the population to minimize, if not eliminate, the risk of total personal or family disaster.[2]

Geography

A Factor of Strength and Weakness

From earliest times, control of a piece of land strategically situated, a hill for example, or a mountain top, a mountain pass, a defensible position from which one could block passage of commercial goods, travellers, armies, or ships, was highly prized as a power base. Failure to secure such positions became a source of weakness. Advances in technology, coupled with the emerging states' propensity to expand, extended the power-political significance of geographic location from relatively narrow topographic features to broader geospatial dimensions. Now entire coastlines, mountain ranges, sea passages, strategic islands, and straits connecting navigable bodies of water became objects of power struggles throughout the world. The British empire, for example, could be constructed and defended from the relatively small British isles only because a twenty-mile wide channel, controllable by the British Navy, for centuries constituted an effective barrier against invasion from the continent of Europe. In addition, with the aid of the same powerful naval forces Britain could seize and hold strategic islands, straits, and land positions controlling the sea passages from Europe to the Far East, via the southern tip of Africa and later via the Mediterranean.

By the same token, gaps between mountain ranges, waterways easily fordable, long coast lines difficult to defend, or shorter coastlines with wide and gently sloping beaches, became sources of weakness, unless compensated for by armed force and by unassailable fortifications. Over the centuries, the wide open plains of Eastern Europe and the mountain gaps of Southeastern Europe, the unobstructed coastal strips of North Africa, or the wide open northern borders of China facilitated periodic invasions which continuously altered power constellations, destroying some empires, occasionally entire civilizations, facilitating the construction of new empires only to see these falling to yet other forces. Other sources of weakness derived from geospatial features are land-locked status which deprives a state of access to the sea, making it dependent on the good will of neighbors who control the land route to the nearest port, or a national territory featuring a narrow waist or forming a long, thin strip both of which can be cut relatively easily by hostile forces, a condition of grave concern to the modern state of Israel.

Climate is another geographic factor profoundly influencing international power status. For centuries, a most inhospitable climate posed virtually impenetrable barriers to potential invaders of West Africa. When European forces attacked from the sea, the once forbidding rainforest with its miasma of diseases became strategically irrelevant. Today, that climate constitutes one of the major impediments to development throughout the tropics.

Geographic location, coupled with geological accidents or configurations, places some countries over immensely rich mineral resources while others must eke out an existence on virtually barren soil. We address that aspect under strategic resources below and in Chapter 16. Suffice it here to recall a wistful comment by the late Israeli Prime Minister, Golda Meir: "What if Moses had led the Israelites east instead of north, into what today is Saudi Arabia?"

Geopolitics

Different emphasis in geographic-strategic thinking and different power bases and relationships have for centuries been depicted by varying types and forms of maps. Today, we have maps depicting power relationships based on raw material deposits, financial means, economic productivity, per capita income, population and birth rate, military potential, and strategic location in naval and maritime respects (location at or near strategic sea lanes). Other maps demonstrate the vulnerability of states to attack by nuclear missiles or the advantageous position of states in the equatorial region with respect to launching missiles for peaceful space exploration or for military strategic purposes.[3]

Prior to and during World War Two, the military strategies of Germany and the Western Allies, and to an extent those of Japan also, were in part based on what aspired to become a science, geopolitics. One of its founders, Sir Halford Mackinder, impressed by the relationship between land and sea power, offered a thesis reflecting these concerns.* As he saw it, the center of political and military power was located in a *Pivot Area,* the *Eurasion Heartland* (see Figure 2-1). Immediately adjacent to that area was the *Inner Marginal Crescent,* or *Rimland,* containing Western Europe, parts of Eastern and Southeastern Europe, the Arabian, Middle Eastern desert lands, and the Asiatic monsoon lands. At the western extremity of that *Crescent* lay Great Britain, at the eastern extremity, Japan. Ranging from Canada and the United States, facing the Atlantic seaboard, through South America, Africa, Australia back to the Pacific regions of Canada, lay the *Lands of Outer Insular Crescent.* According to Mackinder,

---

* He obviously was deeply impressed by British sea power and was concerned lest it give way to land power organized against Great Britain, or British interests, somewhere within the Eurasian landmass.

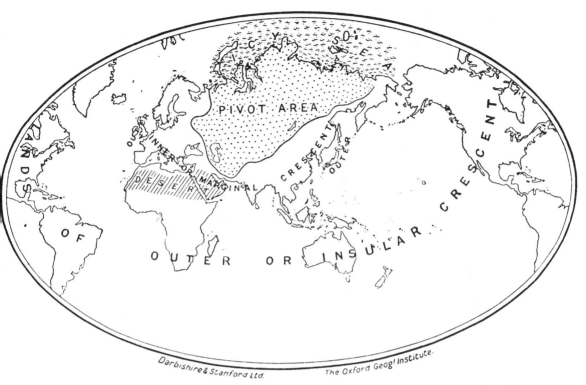

Fig. 2-1. Mackinder's Projection. (By permission *The Geographical Journal*, Vol. XXIII, 4 (April 1904), p. 435.)

he who controlled the *Rimland* or *Inner Marginal Crescent,* controlled the *Heartland* and thereby the world.[4]

On that premise, before the outbreak of World War Two and in view of the emergence of the United States as a world power, the security of the Western world (the Western Hemisphere and Western Europe) hinged on the ability of the United States and Great Britain to maintain sufficient naval strength—augmented by air power, both reinforced by skillful diplomacy—to prevent any one state or combination of states from dominating the *Heartland.* In 1939, the principal contender for that role, of course, was Germany. Today, the Heartland (the Soviet Union) is itself a center of world power and the science of geopolitics may appear to have joined other theoretical constructs which have, in their contemporary application at least, been overtaken by events. But adjusted and updated, the Mackinder thesis draws attention to the danger facing the Western Hemisphere should a Heartland power, the Soviet Union or a Sino-Soviet combination, succeed in overcoming and dominating Western Europe and Japan.

The Mackinder concept also demonstrates the essence of the Balance of Power mechanism, operated by Great Britain during its rise to world power status. The design was to prevent any one European state, or any combination of states, situated in or near the *Pivot Area,* from utilizing the Heartland to

Great Britain's and the British Empire's disadvantage. The principal objective was to prevent hostile forces from challenging British naval power from the numerous port facilities along the coasts of the Atlantic, the Mediterranean, the Indian Ocean, or the Pacific. A World War Two extension of the Mackinder thesis, advanced by Nicholas Spykman, urged as a matter of vital interest for the United States, "that no overwhelming power be allowed to develop Europe and the Far East."[5] This became the foundation of post-World War Two policies and strategies of the United States and possibly, in reverse, of the Soviet Union.

A contemporary version of geopolitics would add air and space power, including missiles and satellites, to land and naval power. It would represent the world as two hostile armed camps, one centering on the United States, the other on the Soviet Union. But the areas of conflict between *Rimland* and *Inner and Outer Crescent* would remain essentially the same as those outlined by Spykman.[6] The frontier, so to speak, would run from Norway, cutting Europe in half, along the southern boundaries of the Soviet bloc system, along the northern frontier of other Mideast countries (Iraq, Iran), along the northern limits of the Indian subcontinent and of Southeast Asia, to the west of Japan and the Philippines, and ending in the Arctic region near the Bering Sea. Should the Middle East be lost to the Western grouping, the frontier would run along the North and East African coastlines. This may well be the picture formed by Soviet leaders and may be the source of their concern, or even conviction, that it is the outer grouping which threatens the Heartland with encirclement and defeat. Figure 19-1a reflects that perspective.

Updated, such a map would lift out and mark especially the area of the Warsaw Pact and a crescent of less developed but well armed countries committed to a socialist orientation or potential, ranging from Cuba in the Western Hemisphere through socialist-leaning countries on the African continent, at this time foremost Libya, Ethiopia and Angola, Syria, South Yemen, Iraq, possibly Iran, Afghanistan, Vietnam, Laos, and Kampuchea. The People's Republic of China would be a source of greatest concern in that respect to both the West and the Soviet Union.

In the 1980s countries located in the steadily widening desert belt, from the Sahara to the Gobi, seem condemned to perpetual poverty, millions of their people facing starvation. Should contemporary world food production and distribution facilities prove to be inadequate to support the world's growing population, countries unable to purchase from abroad what their own soil cannot produce will be consigned to the end of the lengthening queue of petitioners for some form of global charity. But this need not always be so. There are indications that what today we know as the African Sahara, by current appearance a hopeless desert, a long time ago bloomed and supported substantial populations. It may do so again. Already geological mapping from space has expanded our knowledge of what may lie beneath the desert and beneath the Arctic and Antarctic icecaps. Advances in drilling and mining technology promise to provide access to subterranean and submarine wealth currently beyond our reach. The tropical rainforest, the Siberian tundra, and some mountain ranges can be made productive with the aid of science and technology. With such advances, the geopolitical power structure on earth could once again undergo significant changes.

Nuclear and solar power coupled with other scientific and technological breakthroughs, the development of the microchip, the laser beam, and the long-range weapon-guidance system, for example, may significantly alter the patterns of political power envisaged by Mackinder and Spykman. As we shall see in subsequent discussion of military developments, geographic, geopolitical or geo-strategic concepts which once were the basis for strategic military and diplomatic power calculations may have given way to radically different concepts, reflecting radically different spatial perspectives. Under conditions of conventional land, air, and sea warfare, traditional geostrategic defensive and offensive concepts remain valid, at least to an extent. But considering that weapons now have attained global reach and are on the verge of adding outer space as well, Rim, Heartland, Inner or Outer Crescent may decline in power-political significance and so most certainly will terrestrial fortifications, forbidding coastlines, mountain ranges, or strategic islands. Technologically, some states are now able, within hours or even minutes, to project their military power thousands of miles away, over and across so-called buffer states once thought to provide effective protection from invasion.

The Economy

Economic Viability

In national political rhetoric, power in international affairs is said to spring from such things as "national will," the alleged "racial purity" of a people, the degree of religious fervor and devotion, or the alleged superiority of a political system. To be sure, if well organized and effectively channelled and articulated, such claims can generate a certain degree of strength; but they are no substitute for the primary ingredients of power, the national economy, its product, and the military muscle it generates and supports.

Prior to World War Two, Italy's dictator Benito Mussolini had persuaded himself that it was his destiny to recreate the Roman empire by bringing the entire Mediterranean littoral under Italian control. Actually, Italy's armed forces at that time were no match for any conceivable combination of enemies, partly because Italy's economy could not support the kind of armed forces Mussolini needed to pursue his overly ambitious foreign policy goals. In other words, military ends and economic means were at odds. Before long, Italy became wholly dependent on its powerful ally, Nazi Germany, and within a few years Italy lay prostrate, militarily defeated at every front and economically bankrupt. To enable students to appreciate fully the relative importance of economics in international affairs, especially in international politics, we begin with a concise summary of some of the more fundamental aspects of economics, domestic as well as foreign—the two spheres being thoroughly intertwined and interdependent. In that connection, we distinguish between (1) the comparatively free, open market, free enterprise economies of the West, based essentially on accumulation and use of privately owned and controlled finance capital and private property generally, (2) the closed economies of socialist (communist) states, such as the Soviet Union, where all basic means of production and distribution of wealth including finance capital, land, and other resources, are state owned, and their uses planned, directed, and controlled by the state bureaucratic and political leadership, and (3) the mixed socialist-capitalist, highly experimental economies of the less developed, newly independent countries of the Third and Fourth worlds.

Economies constitute the substance from which states are fashioned and without which they would not be states but mere assemblages of helpless human beings, easy prey to anyone with a design on their territory, their property, or their lives. Economic forces largely determine whether a state is to be taken seriously as a power factor on the international scene or whether it must resign itself to be a mere onlooker or victim. Economies produce the revenue (including taxes) which makes government and administration possible and which enables the latter to provide certain public services which people expect routinely, such as health, welfare, education, police, and armed forces. Economies provide opportunities for gainful employment which in turn produces the goods and services needed to keep the economy going and which the people expect and need to maintain, or if possible improve, their standard of living. The same processes provide the surpluses required to pay for research and development— to secure the future—for expansion of the armed forces at times of crisis or in preparation for war, to build up reserves of the means of payment for goods and services from abroad (foreign exchange reserves). Surpluses are needed especially to assure continuing supply of goods and services which their own economy cannot provide, or could provide but at too high a cost; for example, food, medicine, or critical raw materials. Increasingly, because of the high cost of modern arms production, arms sales abroad have become an integral part of the defense economy of industrial states, partly to assure additional income to replace funds absorbed by the military, partly to reduce per unit cost of arms and equipment for defense.

Responsible governments are constantly under pressure to maximize their country's economic potential, because standing still invites disaster in the face of rising birthrates and inflation. Coincident are ever-rising expectations of better or more consumer goods and more as well as improved public service. Then there are the pressures generated by mounting debt services—paying interests on domestic and foreign loans—expanding social service obligations, and for a growing number of rich as well as poor countries, ever more complex and sophisticated, hence costly, defense establishments.

If a state's economy is sufficient to satisfy the people's most fundamental needs and demands for goods and services, while meeting also all pressing international obligations, the economy is said to be viable. Economic viability is diminished if, in order to fulfill its obligations at home and abroad, a government must borrow heavily either from internal or external sources. The situation turns critical if debts are beyond its capacity to pay interest and repay the principal on time. Reliance on others, on powerful allies for instance, is no substitute for lack of viability. Even a state well organized, brilliantly led, politically stable and cohesive, capable of generating the martial spirit necessary to field a large army, the majority of its people prepared to make great sacrifices in the interest of national security or even national expansion, will be in jeopardy if the economic means available do not suffice to sustain such efforts. Twice in the twentieth century, Germany took on a combination of world powers, and, all feats of individual and collective heroism on the part of their own and allied military and civilian elements not withstanding, the economic odds against Germany were overwhelming. The combined raw material, industrial, and financial resources of the United States and of the British and French empires in World War One, and of the Western Allies and the Soviet Union in World War Two, simply outweighed the best that Germany and her allies could bring to the fields of battle.

As illustrated by such otherwise weak states as Switzerland, Saudi Arabia, and Libya, possession of substantial financial resources alone can assist in overcoming basic economic deficiencies, augmented of course by other factors, such as the topography and strategic location of Switzerland or the temporary strategic value of Saudi Arabian and Libyan oil reserves. Certainly, the over-whelming financial resources generated by its economy in the past enables the United States to wield influence in world affairs on that basis alone. However, if the United States wishes to maintain its superpower status, its economy must demonstrate a renewed capacity to support that status and all that this entails, for decades to come, and *at a steadily increasing rate.* As shall be shown in Part Three, a key factor in that regard is the value of the U.S. dollar in relation to the currencies of the world's major trading powers.

Generally most political leaders and ruling elites and their supporting bur-eaucracies, motivated to devise more responsible solutions of national problems, are extraordinarily sensitive to economic considerations, not only because their nation's international power status, prestige, and security depend upon a viable economy but because their own personal political survival may hinge on how successfully they can manage their own national economies. Be they democratic, autocratic, or totalitarian, rational leaders know almost instinctively that a viable economy improves their own chances of retention of office, while economic failure invites unrest or even riot and insurrection at home, leaving the country open to aggression from abroad.

Strategic Resources

Aside from technological deficiencies, nothing affects a state's power status and capabilities as dramatically as a serious shortfall in economically or militarily essential resources for which no substitute exists. Most sensitive in that regard are coal; mineral oil, and nuclear fuel; basic minerals, metals, and alloys such as chrome, manganese, tungsten, and platinum; certain technologies; food, and medicine. These and similar resources are called strategic because if they are not available in sufficient quantities the economy including the defense industry of a country could be crippled. Along with possession goes the ability to deny enemies or competitors access to them. That ability can provide the margin between diplomatic or even military victory and defeat. By the same token, relatively weak or middle-level powers, like the Republic of South Africa, have been able to enhance their international status substantially on the strength of possession of strategic materials needed by the United States and other industrial powers.[7]

In recent years the most striking manifestation of this increment of power has been the Organization of Petroleum Exporting Countries (OPEC). Solely on the strength of enormous mineral oil deposits, in the space of a few years the organization was able to force the world's leading industrial powers to concede sharp price increases per barrel of oil and, following that, endow many of its member states with power and influence on the international scene far beyond their basic economic and military capabilities.

Economic Power Applied: Summary

Following this enumeration and analysis of the major components of economic power, a few comments regarding its application are in order. In particular, attention needs to be drawn to (1) the distinction between power-in-being and power-in-use, and (2) the degrees of certainty, reliability, and precision of knowledge with respect to economic power.

Power-in-being is less effective and less visible than power-in-use, but both forms are at work all of the time, one blending into the other, one reinforcing the other. For example, state A reminds state B of its capacity to deny B access to a vital resource, oil for instance, or state C notifies state D that if certain steps are taken by D the latter will be denied access to C's market. In both instances we are dealing only with threats; the economic power in question is merely cited, it is not applied. In any case the condition which might trigger overt application of that power has yet to materialize. Power-in-being is most effective if it is as manifest and as overwhelming as is that currently enjoyed by the United States; power of that magnitude converts into leverage whether or not it is actually used.[8]

Attempts have been made to express economic as well as other manifestations of power on the international scene through mathematical equations. Yet, only the general nature, general direction, the magnitude in aggregate terms—the broad-scale effects—can be assessed and only very cautiously and tentatively. The extent and effects of economic power can be at best only estimated. We are after all talking only of the sum total of myriads of economic forces, many of which work at cross purposes. We are dealing with an infinite array of human and material variables in a growing number of states. Often we are speaking only of abstractions, even though, being economic, they may have all of the appearances of hard facts. The effects of a given power play are typically long in coming, sometimes delayed for many years, or they are negated altogether by contrary moves on the international scene. Moreover it is not always possible to separate fact from fiction. The effects of a given application of power against a nation may deliberately be misrepresented or completely concealed from the public and from scholars by a government fearing adverse publicity. Or the intent is misrepresented. By the same token the closing of an industrial plant or depression experienced by an entire industry in the target country may be attributed by a hardpressed government to a foreign economic conspiracy, the result of a "hostile act," when it should have been attributed to internal shortcomings, a policy error, inefficiency on the part of management, obsolescence of plant or equipment, high taxation, or loss of a foreign market because of poor performance of the nation's exporters or superior performance by a competitor.

Nor is it always possible to determine reliably which of several possible effects of an act by a foreign government impresses the target country more. For one, economic theories differ radically within the capitalist and socialist camps, so do methods of analysis, definition of problem areas, and prescriptions for solutions. What is of greater sensitivity, unemployment, depression in one industrial sector, high prices for certain imports, a drop in the price of an export, or loss of a market abroad? Or does an economic power play by a foreign government acquire sensitivity only if the results affect directly and massively national security, for example depriving the target country's defense industry of a critical raw material?

A complete inventory of the economic sources of power a nation needs today to qualify for superpower or even middle power status would be too long and, because of its length, imcomprehensible. To provide a meaningful index of economic power we restrict the list to the most essential components.

1. Quantity and quality of raw material including energy resources actually available or with access assured, to maintain the economy and assure adequate national defense
2. Productive land together with an adequate supply of skilled and/or trainable labor and a population base large enough to support the country's productivity
3. Agriculture sufficient to supply adequate quantities of food, at low cost, for the population
4. A basic infrastructure sufficient to support national economic productivity and growth, for example roads, waterways, railways, ports, and transportation and communication systems
5. Capacity to produce within national boundaries needed supplies of steel, concrete, chemical and biochemical products, electricity, and most capital goods
6. Availability of up-to-date technology

7. Volume, value, and liquidity of finance capital sufficient to support ongoing and future needs; share of GNP invested annually to promote growth; magnitude of external public debt
8. Capacity to produce industrial and agricultural surpluses to support internal development and foreign trade objectives
9. Volume of trade adequate to support domestic and foreign policy objectives, terms of trade, and balance of payments favorable over an extended period

Force

In addition to being the product of economic processes, power, it is said, "grows out of the barrel of a gun."[10] Or, as a Central American revolutionary Calypso refrain puts it, "What is wrong and what is right, will be decided with dynamite." Both observations reflect a fundamental aspect of human behavior and of politics—national as well as international—if all else fails, the ultimate means of conflict resolution is force. This suggests in turn that, peaceloving or not, if a nation wishes to safeguard its independence and territorial integrity, pursue objectives beyond its boundaries, or generally lend weight to its membership in the international community, it must dispose of sufficient force to cope with all conceivable eventualities. Universally, this task is performed by the military or armed forces, augmented in some cases by militia or other auxiliary units.

To be effective, this component of a nation's reservoir of power must have certain minimum characteristics or qualities: (1) *Organization,* cohesion, and integration; (2) *weapons or arms,* equipment, and provisions (including arms *production,* distribution, replacement, and repair capacities); (3) *defense* to secure home and supply bases and secure supply lines to its fighting units; (4) kill and damage capacity, or, in modern terms, *fire and explosive* power; (5) *projection capacity;* and (6) *mobility and speed* in mobilization and deployment of fighting units. In addition there are the equally important *intangibles.* In fundamental respects, this list is today as valid as it was centuries ago. What has changed dramatically are scope and magnitude of the force component, the forms it has assumed, and the priority it claims among nations' internal and external policy choices, especially with respect to resource allocation.

Basic Characteristics

(1) *Organization:* Since the first commander of armed units discovered that command, control, and communication are linked and that forces must be organized and cohesive for these three essentials to function properly and effectively, organization has been a basic in all military thinking and planning. For roughly the first four thousand years of recorded history, military conflict was confined to land and sea. On land, armed force progressed from disorganized rabble to tightly massed, highly visible foot-soldier or cavalry formations to

systematically dispersed, camouflaged, virtually self-contained units combining infantry, armor, and artillery. Since World War One these forces have been augmented by air support, since World War Two by airborne and parachute contingents. In naval terms, nations still maintain organized coastal defense forces and offensively they continue to gather their naval units in fleets or flotillas. With the development of nuclear-powered vessels, including aircraft carriers and submarines, and with vastly improved satellite-relayed communications, it is now possible to conduct naval and air operations far from the main units. Air defense and attack forces are grouped in flights or squadrons, or air arms. Because fighting units can no longer be expected to supply or maintain themselves, armed forces today are closely integrated with rear echelon servicing and provisioning units.

(2) *Production of weapons, arms, equipment, and provisions.* Early humans required little more than their own muscle power to achieve their ends. Throughout antiquity to the Middle Ages, individual soldiers, even individual fighting units, at times entire armies, were expected to provide their own weapons and equipment and procure their own provisions by foraging among friendly or enemy populations. Advances in military technology and strategy gradually shifted the responsibility for armed forces support to the state.

The first notable shift occurred when reusable arms such as the sword and the lance gave way to the rifle, requiring ammunition which destroyed itself in use. Expansion of rifle-equipped armed forces and the development of the machine gun, the mortar, and artillery called for redoubled production capacities. Introduction of motorized armor, including the tank, fighter and bomber planes and expansion of naval forces, all expending unending rounds of ammunition, thousands of tons of explosives, and consuming millions of gallons of fuel as well as ever-increasing quantities of steel and other raw materials, led to the creation of military-industrial production sectors within individual national economies. This need was further accentuated as changing strategies called for greater reliance on massed artillery, mass bombing, massed motorized armor, and large-scale submarine warfare, not to speak of ships, planes, and rail stock to transport all that was needed for combat.

Before the onset of nuclear competition, several dozen states still managed to provide for their own military needs. The development of nuclear military technology and all that it requires changed this drastically. Soon the number of states fully capable of providing for their own and their allies' defenses from their own industrial base was reduced to two, the United States and the Soviet Union.

In recognition of the virtual intertwining of military force capability with industrial capacity, the United States and the Soviet Union, though the latter far more so than the former, assigned to their respective armed services direct responsibility over arms production and supply. Today, these problems are exacerbated by inflation, ever more rapidly changing technology and sophistication of weapons and weapons systems, especially with respect to the voracious, resource-consuming nuclear warfare sector. Consequently, today indicators of a nation's force capability are not only its standing armed forces and the quality and quantity of their equipment and supplies, including ammunition, but also its industry, its financial means, its technological acumen, and its willingness and capacity if necessary to shift scarce resources from other high priority needs to the military sector.

From this it follows that states lacking one or more of the essential ingredients, unable to correct such deficiencies by their own means, must ally themselves with those who possess what is needed. Or if they do not wish to enter into formal alliance they must borrow, lease, or otherwise procure the essentials for defense. The primary purpose of military alliances has always been supplementation of deficiencies in manpower or material. Obviously, to the extent to which such formal or informal linkage renders the recipient dependent on the donor, to that extent the power potential of the former is diminished.

(3) *Defense:* The concept of fortification protecting the home base, the national territory, and military outposts abroad, remained unaltered in essential respects until the advent of saturation and blockbuster bombing in World War Two. For centuries the fortified castle constituted the power base for warlords, knights, and robber barons. The Romans erected the Limes, an earth and stone wall protecting their conquests in Western Europe; the Chinese built the Great Wall to provide protection against Mongol invaders. Each advance in fire and destructive power led to stronger defenses and fortifications, which in turn led to further increase in destructive power to overcome improved defenses. The earthen wall, the stone wall, the reinforced concrete pillbox of World Wars One and Two, or the fortified town or military base, have now been replaced by super-hardened silos protecting defensive and offensive nuclear weapons with reinforced steel and concrete walls and covers ten or more feet thick, withstanding more than 100,000 pounds of explosive pressure per square inch. Moreover, to breech enemy defenses today calls for explosive power sufficient to cover not just isolated air bases and antiaircraft defense installations as in World War Two, but silos, mobile missile launchers, submarines, and other military targets scattered over dozens or even hundreds of square miles. The quintessential defense sought today, the ultimate guarantee that a nation's force potential can survive an attack, is the integrated, computerized, antiballistic defense system which seeks out, locks onto, and destroys each and every hostile nuclear delivery vehicle approaching the outer defense perimeters from any direction.

(4) *Kill and destructive (explosive) power:* Weapon effectiveness has undergone radical change, first with the discovery of explosive powder, then with the discovery of nuclear fission, followed by fusion. But again, a significant magnitudinal change did not occur for the first four thousand years of man's attempt to kill fellow human beings and destroy their defense works, homes, and property.

No significant increase in kill and destructive capacity occurred as humanity "progressed" from rock, to lance, to spear, to catapult, to crossbow, to iron bullet, to cannon ball. The invention of gunpowder, the handgun, the rifle, and explosive artillery shells enhanced destructive capacity. Numbers of casualties increased sharply with massed artillery as in the American Civil War and in World War One. The introduction of the repeat-fire rifle and of the hand-cranked Gatlin gun and its successor, the automatic machine gun, added new dimensions to kill and injure capacity—fire power. In one respect, the concept of fire power was not new. The desire to direct at an opponent more and more rapid destructive force than he can use in response gave rise to the massed spear and arrow assault formations and the phased muzzle loader firings which subjected an opposing force to continuous volleys. In siege operations, destructive capacity increased gradually from the catapult capable of throwing large rocks to breech fortifications to the siege guns of World War One and Two which could deliver shells large enough to penetrate the strongest reinforced steel and concrete fortifications then in existence. Destructive capacity experienced a sharp upward turn with the development of the nuclear weapon, soon to be followed by the mass-produced, nuclear, long-range missile.[11] (See Fig. 2-2.)

Now destructive capacity, already increased sharply by the massed bomber formations of World War Two—which in a single attack could cause deaths in the tens of thousands, one hundred thousand in at least one case—was extended to what today we call megadeaths, that is, casualties in the millions, tens of millions, or even, in worst-case scenarios, hundreds of millions.

(5) *Force projection:* To defend or attack effectively, to interdict attacking enemy forces, to attack and destroy their lines of communication and supply, and if possible attack and destroy their industrial support bases, calls for capacity to project force far beyond national boundaries. Since antiquity, naval forces performed that function; since World War One, surface vessels have been augmented by the submarine, then also by the airplane. When the latter first made its appearance in World War One, it was used mainly to observe enemy positions and movements. World War Two introduced new dimensions and capabilities with the tactical attack plane projecting fire power well ahead of advancing or defending ground forces and the bomber carrying its loads for hundreds of miles over land and sea. Launched from aircraft carriers, which themselves extended military capabilities far beyond maritime nations' territorial limits, fighter aircraft and bombers could protect naval forces thousands of miles from their home ports and carry the war to places like Pearl Harbor, believed by naval and airforce experts to be totally secure against such threats. It was airpower, of course, which significantly contributed to the victory of Anglo-American forces over Germany, Italy, and Japan partly by reaching and destroying strategic industries producing such essentials as ball bearings, synthetic rubber, and gasoline, located well behind the lines.

Before its defeat, toward the end of the war, in lieu of a bomber force which had become ineffective once British air defenses had measured up to the task, the Germans resorted to the V-weapon, the first self-propelled combat missile, fired from continental Europe at targets mainly in and around London. Since that time, we have had generations of far more powerful, far wider-ranging descendants of that weapon, the latest being the nuclear-tipped, multiple independently targetable reentry vehicle (MIRV) travelling six thousand miles or

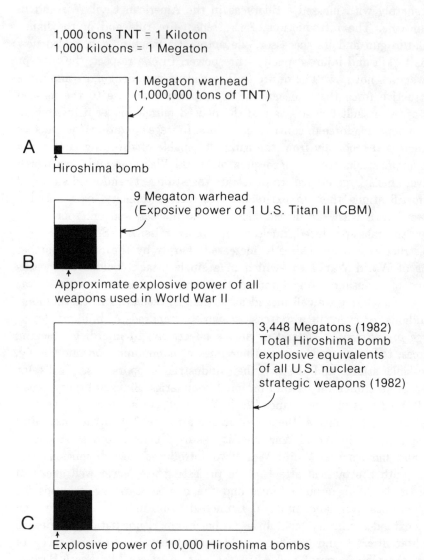

1,000 tons TNT = 1 Kiloton
1,000 kilotons = 1 Megaton

1 Megaton warhead
(1,000,000 tons of TNT)

A

Hiroshima bomb

9 Megaton warhead
(Exposive power of 1 U.S. Titan II ICBM)

B

Approximate explosive power of all
weapons used in World War II

3,448 Megatons (1982)
Total Hiroshima bomb
explosive equivalents
of all U.S. nuclear
strategic weapons (1982)

C

Explosive power of 10,000 Hiroshima bombs

Fig. 2-2.   Explosive Power of Nuclear and Conventional Weapons. (U.S. Congress, 98th, 1st, *The Consequences of Nuclear War* (1983); *SIPRI Yearbook,* 1982.)

more, across oceans and continents. Guiding and directing these, in addition to their own inner guidance and control systems, are the modern versions of the American Civil War and World War One observers, who, armed with binoculars, reported on enemy positions and movements from balloons suspended near enemy lines: we now have the earth-orbiting, spy-in-the-sky satellite.

Box 2-1. Current U.S. Conception of Requirement For Effective Naval Power Projection:

—Aircraft carriers with fighter bombers and associated escorts and "underway" replenishment units.

—Amphibious landing forces (such as Marines) and their transport and close support.

—Airborne forces designed to be dropped into hostile territory against armed opposition.

—Airforce tactical aviation wings (to provide air support for ground forces).

—Strategic airlift forces and air-to-air refueling tankers to enable the short-range tactical fighters to reach distant operation zones.

Foreign Policy
#33, p. 10

Further improving projective capacity are airborne and parachute divisions, as well as special forces, combining land, air and naval units which can swiftly be transported and rapidly deployed to engage in combat thousands of miles from home. With intercontinental missiles poised to reach targets on the other side of the globe and satellites surveying, photographing, and reporting on everything that moves or looks suspicious anywhere on earth, projective capacity has reached its terrestial limits. Now only outer space—already traversed by reentry vehicles—remains to be exploited for combat purposes. Already satellites are believed to be deployed there to attack and destroy hostile satellites upon command. We shall examine the full range of military strategic and political implications of these developments in Chapters 17 and 18. (See Box 2-1.)

(6) *Armed force mobility and speed:* These qualities did not improve significantly from the time when foot soldiers slogged along the ground until the arrival of cavalry; the horse drawn chariot was faster than the foot soldier but only by a few miles per hour. The availability of railway, motor car, and truck for troop transport improved mobility and increased speed with which forces could be deployed. The fast-moving tank and other armored vehicles linked and directed by two-way radio replaced the crudely charging cavalry and made possible the form of attack which became famous when in World War Two the German armies surprised and broke through enemy defenses, outflanking entire lines of fortification and divisions in swift blitzkrieg (lightning war) maneuvers. More recently, Israeli armor replicated these feats, most notably during the 1967 Six-Day War against overwhelming Arab Forces. Today planes

travel at twice the speed of sound and missiles can cover thousands of miles within minutes.

Intangibles

All other things being the same, each individual factor, down to the legendary lowly nail in the shoe of the king's horse, can of course spell the difference between success and failure. But it is most unlikely that all other things ever will be the same. In the final analysis, a nation's force potential is the product of a mix or combination of all or most of the qualities and characteristics enumerated. For example, as was shown earlier, numerical superiority is not an absolute requirement.* Nor are great wealth or superior quantities of arms and equipment. Such factors as quality of personnel, their individual skill and their morale, the quality of planning of strategy and logistics, or capacity of an intelligence service to penetrate enemy defenses and learn vital secrets— breaking a military code, for example—all can compensate for deficiencies in one or more of the other respects.†

(1) *The economics of force.* From the Middle Ages to early modern times, although armies and navies steadily have grown more expensive, it was possible to raise whatever was required in the way of war finance from confiscations, forced levies, current revenue, or borrowings usually from the banking sector. With the inception of total warfare in World War One, maintaining the nation's force capacity at required levels called for drastic adjustments in the economy and a shift from reliance on current financial resources to borrowing against the future.

As far as reliance on current resources is concerned, basically two schools of thought have emerged. One subscribes to the finite or zero-sum economy concept where domestic consumption, including social services, must contract if military expenditures are to be increased—the "guns *or* butter" proposition. This is countered by the kinetic economy concept, which sees sufficient elasticity and expandibility in an advanced economy to simultaneously support *both,* the production of guns and of butter. Whether one subscribes to the finite or the kinetic concepts, or one relies on current deficit spending at the expense of

---

* A flagging birthrate is of course not the only impediment. Today Soviet bloc armies far outnumber opposing Western forces in Western Europe and potentially in other theaters of war, mainly because of the ability of totalitarian regimes to do what political democracies are unable or unwilling to do in peacetime, namely impress large numbers of military-age men and women into the armed forces partly by manipulation of the economy, partly by rigidly enforced draft. To counter this apparent advantage, Western military planners rely more heavily on mechanization and automation and on nuclear and space technology. Ironically, Soviet planners face a similar situation in reverse, in the Far East, where more than a billion Chinese provide an inexhaustible manpower reserve for the PRC.

† See Lewin, (1978) and A. C. Brown (1975). The full extent to which Allied military successes in World War Two were attributable to the ability of their intelligence services to read top secret German, Italian, and Japanese military and economic messages has yet to be assessed adequately. The yield was staggering.

future generations, industrially advanced major and middle powers increasingly experience economic, social, and political strains as a result of the by now spiraling arms races. Weapons design as well as quantity must increasingly take into account current as well as future costs and the limits to military expenditure dictated by internal social and political requirements. It is now a well established fact of life that a weapons system which initially was expected to cost x billion dollars, may, with updating, testing, and the inevitable missteps in the early production phases, by the time it is ready for use by the armed force—about ten years later—require several multiples of the original cost estimate. To this must be added the effects of spiraling inflation and what some economists call opportunity costs but others may call greed of arms manufacturers and middlemen.* Although socialist economies dispense with the latter encumbrances, their lower GNP and overall production deficiencies combine to impose similar limits on their competitive position in military respects.[12]†

The transition from convention to nuclear weapons has profoundly altered the relationship between the powers. Richly endowed with natural resources, able to develop the needed industrial base and technology, the two superpowers have far outstripped the rest of the world in total power projection and destructive capacity. Earth-orbitting satellites, intercontinental ballistic missiles, and supersonic planes now reduce the opportunity for small powers to convert strategic location into economic or military leverage in international politics. On the other hand, given sufficient financial means, reinforced by alliances and mutual military aid and assistance treaties, states incapable of raising a conventional army, navy, or airforce on their own can now purchase these instruments of power on the open market. While this will not place them in contention for world power status, it can convert a desert kingdom such as Saudi Arabia or an otherwise militarily impotent military dictatorship such as the one in Libya into a contender for regional political supremacy. Reducing this potential, indeed increasing the dependence of the recipients of such military means on the suppliers, is the constant need to maintain ever more complex weapons systems at a level of technological proficiency superior to that of any combination of forces likely to be arrayed against them.

(2) *The obsolescence of military power.* We encountered the phenomenon in our earlier discussion of force projection: each time a state devises a means of

---

* A 1983 study by the Heritage Foundation showed "that for 28 weapons systems conceived [by U.S. planners] in the 1970s, the Pentagon estimated that inflation would increase costs from 9 to 100 percent. In reality, inflation and design and program changes, plus the added costs of unstable production, increased costs many times that estimate, from a minimum of 92 percent to as much as 400, 500, or even 800 percent." *The New York Times* (January 12, 1983).

† Wars and arms competitions have since antiquity been financed by surreptitious means, including confiscation of privately owned wealth and its transfer into governmental coffers. Nazi Germany financed its war machine in part from current production not only of Germany herself but of all of the conquered as well as allied peoples of Europe. To an extent the war was financed also by borrowing against the future. The contemporary version of such methods is the ballooning deficit the U.S. incurs over its efforts to more than match the armament of the Soviet Union.

improving its defensive or offensive capabilities, another state will improve on that. A premium is placed on discovery of the precise moment when a state's force no longer suffices to attain its military objectives. Until nuclear force made its appearance, discovery that one or another weapon or weapons system had become obsolete was not necessarily fatal. For instance, when in 1940 British air defenses turned out to be inadequate to ward off massive German bombing raids on British cities, the valor of inexperienced but indomitable British and Commonwealth pilots served to tide Britain over until more effective air and ground measures could be devised. Initial technological inferiority of Soviet forces, though disastrous during the first year of Nazi Germany's assault, did not prove fatal. Eventually Soviet determination to survive, reinforced by strategic reserves and by improved artillery, armor, and aircraft, offered more than a match for German arms. Today, loss of technological superiority in one or more critical respects can fatally undermine a nation's ability to prevail in political and military competition.

Often the margin between victory and defeat in war has been provided by a single timely invention, for example, the stirrup, the crossbow, gun powder, the steam engine, the machine gun, the internal combustion engine, the tank, the airplane, the submarine, the proximity fuse, and now the ever more sophisticated components of the nuclear-powered arsenal. Now high technology has become a factor but, by its nature, an exceedingly precarious, unstable one. A nation which can with a high degree of assurance reach an enemy's nuclear weapons accurately, reliably, and at precisely calculated times may be able to render the opponent entirely or at least substantially defenseless. Never before in history has it been more true that victory goes to the swift. Never before has fear of technological obsolescence so dominated military planning.

(3) *Relevance.* To be considered a valid element in a nation's power position, force must be relevant to whatever tasks confront the nation. As a sledge hammer may prove inadequate to kill mosquitos, so entire armed forces have proved well nigh useless when assigned tasks they were not created to perform. Germany's vaunted military machine, trained for swift breakthroughs prior to World War One, proved barely able to hold its own in prolonged trench warfare on the Western front. Similarly, a quarter of a century later, highly mobile, superbly coordinated German armored columns were unable to dislodge stubborn Soviet fighters in bitter house-to-house and street fighting at Stalingrad, nor could these forces defeat resourceful partisans striking from secure hideouts in the mountains of Yugoslavia. Britain's superior naval power proved irrelevant during the first few years of the Second World War when decisive battles in Europe, Africa, and Asia were fought mainly on land. Germany's airforce, designed to provide close support for ground forces and engage only in close-range bombing missions, was useless against the United States until the latter confronted German armies on the ground, by which time it was too late. By then Germany's airforce had ceased to be a threat. No matter how gallant and courageous, Poland's horse cavalry was no match for German tanks in 1939. United States conventional and nuclear might proved irrelevant in jungle warfare

against Viet Cong guerilla units and their North Vietnamese support. Today, the question is being asked: how relevant is nuclear overkill capacity as a means to deter or stop a conventional attack?

(4) *Strategy.* Weapons and strategy designed to use these are not necessarily in harmony. This for several reasons. Weapons, strategies, and tactics are not necessarily planned and designed by the same people.[13] Indeed, they might not be developed by the same generation. Furthermore, one or the other or both might be the product of incompetent leaders. Typically generals and admirals have always been prepared to fight the last war, the one they were most familiar with, over again.[14] Stalin and Hitler, one without any formal military training, the other a former corporal, imposed their personal wisdom on their respective armed forces, at enormous costs in manpower and materiel.

Unless fully automatic and perhaps even then, weapons design must take into account the limitations of the human element. But the latter is all too frequently not up to the task set by overall strategy. Weapons design depends heavily on available technology, financial resources, and raw materials, as well as on the human skills needed to operate increasingly sophisticated equipment. Strategy and tactics are not similarly restricted or limited. They can follow free flights of imagination or blind ambition.* Frequently, military strategies, sometimes even tactics, are set to accord with political calculations while competent weapons design must conform with laws of physics and military science. Furthermore, by nature sweeping and comprehensive, grand military strategies cannot readily be adjusted to accommodate changes in weapons design and production, should tests under simulated or actual battle conditions reveal critical deficiencies.

The importance of the latter point cannot be overestimated. As noted in our discussion of technological obsolescence, revolutionary breakthroughs in weapons design are a constant threat. When they occur, strategies and corresponding tactics, thoroughly ingrained and drilled into the rank and file of the armed forces, cannot readily be changed. This oversight cost the lives of tens of thousands of French and British soldiers during the first few months of the First World War, when traditional infantry charges against German lines were met by the then novel, rapid firing machine gun. Similarly, Japan's territorial defenses proved totally useless when the first nuclear device exploded over Hiroshima. Which raises the question: how much of modern strategy being

---

* In 1939, Polish cavalry units, exhorted by their leaders to advance to the heart of Germany and capture Berlin, got no further than the first line of German armored vehicles. Also during the Second World War, Italy's Navy, built by Mussolini to contest British and French naval supremacy in the Mediterranean, was partially destroyed before it ever left port; units which managed to join battle went down to ignominious defeat, and Italy's combined naval and air arms proved unable to wrest from British control the tiny island of Malta, located just off Italy's southern region. More recently Argentina's military leaders, having devised a strategy to capture from Britain the contested South Atlantic Falkland (Malvinas) Islands, managed to capture their objective only to lose it again when strategy proved woefully out of line with military capability. See also Kaldor (1981), Chapter 6.

devised at this moment, will prove relevant by the time today's weapons encounter tomorrow's response?

The question arises whether today's or tomorrow's military technology may not prove too much even for the relatively sophisticated command, control, and communication (C^3) structures now being developed by the opposing camps. Will these structures be able to process in timely fashion the tidal wave of information produced during the first few hours of modern war? If computers are key components, can these be relied upon to function amidst chaos? What are the probabilities that grand strategic designs will be implemented under these conditions? For example, if strategy calls for measured response to a conventional attack, first with limited "theater" nuclear weapons then with the full nuclear panoply, will the command control machinery remain in command and in control? One now speaks of "decapitation," that is, destruction or incapacitation of a nuclear combatant's top C^3 echelons by weapons especially designed for that purpose. It is conceivable that in a nuclear war the colossal forces assembled by both sides will—far from executing well-coordinated pre-planned strategic missions—seek to destroy each other like headless monsters reduced to lashing out in spastic convulsions.[15]

(5) *Quality of leadership, training, and logistics.* A few years before the outbreak of World War Two, at a time when Germany's military power posed a direct threat to the Soviet Union, Stalin decimated by execution and dismissal the ranks of the Soviet Union's officer corps, from Marshal and Admiral down to lowest lieutenant. He thereby deprived Soviet armed forces of experienced leadership. The effect of these events on the Soviet Union's international power position was devastating. It lowered her value to the Western Allies, forcing a temporary compromise with Hitler, and eventually cost the Soviet Union millions of lives and almost its existence as an independent state.

Effective leadership goes with effective organization. One is useless without the other, especially in times of war when command and leadership may spell the difference between victory and defeat. An officer corps composed of untrained political appointees will quickly dissipate the best armed forces in the world. Where top command positions are filled solely or primarily by reference to social status, ideological conformity, or partisan loyalty, a nation's armed forces may in effect be leaderless.

One reason why Germany's armed forces were so successful between 1939 and 1943, when the fortunes of war began to turn, was the availability at the outbreak of hostilities of what was then probably the world's best trained corps of professional military leaders.*

The quality of training and fitness of command elements at all levels, overall literacy and intelligence of leadership cadres, combat readiness, and quality of

---

* The Treaty of Versailles, imposed upon Germany by the victorious allies in 1919, following World War One, stipulated that the defeated nation's armed forces could not exceed 100,000 men. Germany promptly proceeded to train all of these to highest levels of proficiency, ready to assume command positions as soon as the Treaty terms could be scrapped and the armed forces expanded.

logistics (military planning and overall management of military personnel, material, and facilities) are essential to maximize a nation's power potential. Conventional armed forces, in essential respects engaged in conventional war, continue to require leadership, training, planning, and management qualities which have characterized armed forces for centuries. But modern forces, built around highly sophisticated nuclear and electronic arms and equipment, now extended into outer space, require far higher degrees of technical proficiency as well as overall intelligence on the part of key personnel in all services, at all levels. Critical in these respects is the general population pool from which these elements must be drawn. Equally important, care must be taken that, once recruited and trained, this now skilled resource is not lost to higher paying civilian positions. This problem is quite manageable in totalitarian states where both military and civilian sectors are under central government control, but it poses serious threats to military potential in societies where individuals are free to choose careers.

(6) *Appearances.* In earliest times, the Germanic hordes, seeking to magnify their strength to frighten the Roman legions, augmented their inadequate weaponry with their women's terrifying yells. In the early 1930s, when Nazi Germany's political leaders sought to strike fear in the hearts of their future victims but before German forces actually had been developed to full strength, they had their airforce engage in an interesting maneuver. Moving invited foreign observers like the American Colonel Lindbergh from airbase to airbase, they showed identical flight squadrons over and over again, conveying the desired impression of airpower sufficient to overcome any known opposition in Europe. Today enormous missiles and other paraphernalia of modern war are paraded annually through Moscow's Red Square. Perhaps they are as potent as they look, perhaps not. In any case, for obvious reasons they are eagerly reported as potent by foreign military observers anxious to inflate the threat, enhancing in the process the Soviet Union's power position by several degrees.

Nuclear Force Compared to Other Forms

(1) *Technical differences.* We have already referred to some of these differences above. Summarized, they extend to relationship between technology, shape and form of weapons, the components needed to service, arm, and trigger them, and to strategy. Unlike conventional weapons, where failure to reach and hit a target need not be fatal, nuclear weapons must be delivered reliably, accurately, and at greatest possible speed. Nuclear weapons must be ready at all times for instant action. Unlike conventional weapons which are tested constantly in peripheral wars, nuclear missiles cannot be tested fully and so far have not been tested in earnest. At best their combat performance can only be tested under simulated conditions.

(2) *Power potential.* Until now, no conventional armed force and no combination of such forces has ever been sufficient to force the surrender of another fully armed state, or, short of total surrender, compel another fully armed state

to comply unconditionally with an aggressor's demands. Only where superior armed force confronted no force at all or greatly inferior force could the former unequivocally coerce or subdue the latter, as, for example, when Nazi Germany confronted a virtually defenseless Austria in 1938 or a totally defenseless Denmark in 1940. As noted by one of the United States arms control negotiators, the cataclysmic potential of nuclear power directed in massive quantities at densely populated cities and regions has brought about a decisive change. Today, demonstrable nuclear superiority—and we have noted the problem with demonstrability of such weapons—once established in the minds of the leadership of a targeted stated, constitutes "a force of overpowering influence—the ultimate instrument of coercion and intimidation."[16] We shall examine this proposition in greater detail in Part Four.

Nonmilitary Technology

Our previous discussion of the economic and force components of power highlights the increasing importance of technology generally, in the overall scheme of things. Invention or discovery of the lever, the wheel, and the pulley added considerably to the muscle power of man. The catapult which breeched fortifications, the fast sailing ship which overtook the galley, and the steamship which overtook the clipper extended by far the power and the reach of nations, diplomatically and militarily. Today deficiency in one or two critical nonmilitary technological respects, even a mere time lag of a year or two, can militarily prove fatal for a nation. Similarly, prior to the advent of nuclear power and the computer age, technology tipped the scales in economic competition. Today (as argued so persuasively by Servan-Schreiber) technology has the potential of altering the power position not only of individual nations but of entire continents.[17]

Power Increment by Diplomatic Means

A state's power position may be enhanced or another state's position weakened by alliances, including military defense treaties, or military or economic assistance programs. For example, state A seeking to prevent state B, or a combination of states B and C, from attaining preponderance of power in a given region, allies itself with state D. (See Fig. 2-3.)

The Chemistry of Power

When all is said and done, all elements of strength having been added up, all deficiencies subtracted, the margin needed by one nation to prevail over another may be a combination of statistically ascertainable known factors and of unknown intangibles, a function of the chemistry of power. Are cultural factors, such as ethnicity, religion, literacy, life style, the popularity of a regime, social customs, and morale, hard determinants of power or are they soft myths?

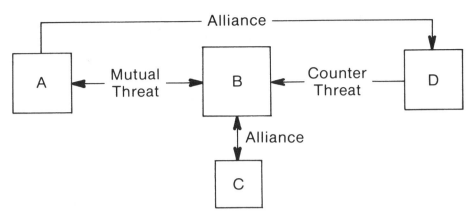

Fig. 2-3. Balance of Power.

The history of Germany, Great Britain, Japan, Russia, France, the United States, and China shows that a convincing case can be made for either interpretation. Each of these, at one time or another, qualified for world power status, but each also offers evidence in its history of tendencies toward both peace and war, aggressiveness and conciliation, militarism and pacifism, even militant war resistance, ethnocentrism as well as a desire to interact peacefully and cooperatively with strangers, of egocentrism and of unparalleled altruism. German, Russian, French, British, Japanese, and American cultural traditions reveal both a desire to rely on economic and military power to a maximum possible and the opposite, profound skepticism on that point and a manifest desire to achieve foreign political goals by peaceful means. Religion appears to have no decisive bearing on a nation's power potential. Japan's Shinto, Russia's Greek-Orthodoxy, Germany's Protestantism and Catholicism, and Britain's Episcopal and Presbyterian faiths, Israel's Judaism, Arab Islam, and Spain and Portugal's deep commitment to Roman Catholicism, all at one time or another were intimately associated with massive power plays including war and at other times with determined efforts to resolve human conflict peacefully. It would seem to be difficult to construct, from such matter, reliable foundations for accurate predictive assessment of a nation's international power potential.

The same can be said of political idea systems. While forms of fascism propelled Germany and Italy into World War Two, the Spanish version did not. Communism in Yugoslavia appears to assume a totally defensive posture, the Soviet original far less so, in the view of some the opposite. During the Second World War, political democracy in Great Britain and the United States permitted degrees of mobilization of manpower and material in wartime, and foreign policy flexibility, at least equalling if not exceeding that of totalitarian Germany, fascist Italy, and authoritarian Japan.[18] Argumentation to the contrary typically is based on highly selective examination of historical fragments, that is, whatever one wishes to prove about a country's tendencies can be proven. Still, all the luck and all the fortunate circumstances in the world cannot generate power in the absence of certain basic ingredients. Even where these are present, they must be skillfully combined by effective leadership which must succeed in bringing to the fore and applying effectively whatever tangible and intangible assets are called for. Here surprise can compensate for weakness.

The chemistry of power certainly is enhanced by basic resources, skills, knowledge, and technology. In addition to leadership, morale can be critical; so can social discipline, social and political cohesion, organization and stability, and character. Detracting from maximal realization of a nation's power potential are such neutralizing or debilitating influences as corruption, lethargy, over-extension, and mismanagement or depletion of available resources by waste and inefficiency. The importance of this aspect is perhaps best exemplified by the situation prevailing on the eve of World War Two. We noted already that in terms of sheer military potential, in 1938 or even 1939 the Western Allies together with the Soviet Union clearly disposed of sufficient military and economic strength to block the military ambitions of German, Italian, and Japanese rulers. If during the opening phases of that war the aggressors succeeded, beyond the wildest dreams of generations of their predecessors, this was a function primarily of the chemistry of power. France, for example, was militarily and economically powerful but unprepared to fight that war. Great Britain's leaders deluded themselves into believing that if a threat existed it was not directed at the British Isles. As for Japan, it was accepted strategic doctrine in the West that "these little people with thick lenses" would not dare challenge the British and U.S. navies combined, a belief conveying a false sense of security to Britain and the United States. Stalin appeased Hitler, calculating that the Soviet Union would benefit if, instead of being forced to attack the Soviet Union, Germany's military might could be enticed first to attack the avowedly anti-Soviet Western powers. Exhausted from that struggle, Germany would then be a more pliable partner or a victim. Eventually, the inability of Germany's and Japan's leadership to adjust to realities and reduce their ambitions, coupled with the willingness of their enemies to harness to maximum possible advantage all of their human and material resources, determined the final outcome.

Thus, what the chemistry of power will generate in a given situation is beyond accurate assessment or prediction.* The combined resources and other elements of strength at the disposal of a nation can be mobilized to the fullest by tapping such intangibles as spirit, fervor, enthusiasm, or patriotism; or they

---

* For instance, when in 1967 Israel went to war against the numerically superior armed forces of Egypt, Syria, and Jordan, plus several lesser enemies, who would have predicted that this tiny state would emerge the victor after six days of fighting? Here was an example of a state combining to maximum advantage all of the ingredients of power—human and material resources, skills, technology, administrative know-how, leadership, and morale. Regarding the latter quality, Karl von Clausewitz, one of the world's greatest military theorists, wrote: "When we speak of destroying the enemy's forces, we must emphasise that nothing obliges us to limit this idea to physical forces. The moral element must also be considered." *On War* (Princeton, N.J.: Princeton University Press, 1976), p. 97.

can be wasted by incompetence, ideological pedantry, and internal dissent; or they can be cancelled out by treason.

Suggested Questions and Discussion Topics

Discuss why population may or may not enhance a state's power potential and what steps some states have taken to compensate for deficiency in that respect.

Why can one speak of strength as well as weakness with regard to a state's geographic or geopolitical location?

What is the central theme of Mackinder's thesis and what are its implications for world politics today? (This question may be raised again after Chapter XIX has been read).

Which deserves higher priority in the assessment of a state's power potential—geography, population, economy, or (armed) force—in what order, and why?

What are the most essential economic components of a state's power potential?

Enumerate and discuss the basic characteristics or ingredients and the intangibles of a state's (armed) force component?

Chapter 3
Foreign Policy

The National Interest

A fundamental principle guiding the foreign policies of all states is said to be "the national interest." The widely held presumption is that this interest relates to a state's geographic, strategic-military and strategic-economic positions in the region where it is located and in the world generally. Because these aspects of a state's existence rarely change and if they do change only gradually, over extended periods of time, a further presumption is that whatever is said to be "the national interest" is indisputably an integral part of a state's heritage, passed on from generation to generation and adhered to more or less faithfully, more or less successfully, by anyone entrusted with the planning, formulation, and conduct of the state's foreign policies. At the same time, because the world does not stand still, it is conceded that adjustments must be made from time to time to align the "national interest" with changed circumstances abroad and at home. However, because the "national interest" is rarely defined in precise terms, it is usually possible to claim that a national consensus exists on what that interest is or ought to be in any given respect. In a very broad sense, superficially viewed, these presumptions seem valid. But they do not stand close examination.

Objective analysis reveals quite frequently that what is alleged to be in the national interest turns out to be quite the opposite, and the motivations of government officials enunciating foreign policy objectives, claiming these to be in full accord with the interest of the entire nation, may in fact not always reflect the general will. They may in fact be entirely self-serving.

History is replete with examples of governments leading their nations to disaster in pursuit of foreign policy goals claimed to be in the best interest of people and state. Sometimes the state as such may survive but the social and political order which the architects of the "national interest" policies sought to preserve collapses, often giving way to the very antithesis of what they sought to protect.* Typically those in charge of the foreign policy machinery

* Outstanding examples of this are the losers of World Wars One and Two, first
Imperial Germany, Austro-Hungary, the Ottoman Empire, Czarist Russia, and Italy, then,
a generation later, Nazi Germany, Bulgaria, Romania, Hungary, Fascist Italy, and
Imperial Japan.

are thoroughly convinced that their policies are designed to ensure national survival and the preservation of the social and political order of which they are a part. One reason for this is that leaders typically act out scenarios with which they are familiar, even though these may actually have been developed a generation or more earlier under substantially different conditions. Advice given by experts may be quite up to date, but the odds are that it cannot overcome the resistance of powerful heads of state whose minds are deeply rooted in a world long overtaken by events.*

More often than not, what is proclaimed as being in the national interest is actually no more than a reflection of the interest of a particular faction, interest, or pressure group, or of the personal prejudice of a single powerful ruler. In Western political democracies, "the national interest" may reflect little more than planks in a political party's election platform. In totalitarian states, it may reflect no more than the factional interests of a small band in control of the dominant party's bureaucracy and of the secret police apparatus. At times, "the national interest" is in fact no more than the personal formulation of a powerful secretary of state or foreign minister serving a monarch, a president, or prime minister who is particularly weak, vacillating, or uninformed.† Of course, to be rendered palatable to government and people, such factional or individualized policy formulations typically and without proof of any kind are couched in terms suggesting a far-reaching "national consensus."

Formal Foreign Policy Machinery

To enable the state to respond to foreign affairs crises in an effective, coherent manner, especially in the face of a threat to national security, and to satisfy certain international legal requirements, states typically assign ultimate responsibility for the *conduct* of foreign relations, including economic, political and military aspects, to the central, national government. Differences, some quite significant, appear with respect to allocation of responsibility and authority for foreign policy *formulation and control.* In that connection, we can distinguish between the following systems of government:

---

* This condition is almost always fatal under dictatorships because free discourse and debate on controversial policy matters is anathema to leaders who must rule by force. Stalin's failure to promote free discussion on policy questions nearly lost the war against Germany. On the other hand, the relative longevity of the post-Stalin Soviet regime suggests that today's Soviet leaders have developed a more constructive consensus mechanism.

† Notable examples of officials overshadowing nominal rulers or at least implanting their personal biases and prejudices onto their nation's foreign policies, are Prince Otto von Bismarck (Imperial Germany), Metternich (Imperial Austria), and Talleyrand (France). In modern times, Hitler's Foreign Minister von Ribbentrop and Eisenhower's Secretary of State John Foster Dulles shaped foreign policy far more than did their nominal employers. Presidential advisors Henry Kissinger and Zbigniew Brzezinski, neither a Bismarck or a Metternich, nevertheless shaped the foreign policies of their employers (Nixon and Carter) more than the other way around.

(1) Established political and social democracies whose governments are constitutionally obligated to submit periodically to electoral processes.
(2) Established totalitarian systems (the socialist "people's democracies" for example), whose governments must rely more heavily on force and are constitutionally assigned total control over state and society.
(3) Established authoritarian regimes who also rely on force but whose control over state and society is limited.
(4) Emerging systems of government, mainly in the less developed countries; these systems contain elements of all three of the above.

The first category, generally referred to as "Western democracies," constitutionally distribute responsibilities for foreign policy formulation and control rather widely, gathering the reigns tightly at the national center of government only with respect to execution and implementation. In the other three categories, a certain facade is maintained, formal processes and responsibilities are prescribed and assigned to various subordinate offices but are allowed to be effectuated by these only in marginal respects, in management of foreign service for example. In all critical aspects, that is whenever it appears to be "in the national interest" to do so, formal processes and procedures are summarily bypassed.*

Foreign Affairs Reality and Rhetoric

Regardless of the form of government a state may adopt, all systems experience a wide gap between what their foreign policy *appears to be* and what it actually is. Several factors account for this. The world is not as orderly and as easily manageable as some historians and some statesmen would want us to believe. It took a former U.S. national security adviser-academician, out of office and out of power, to reveal the true state of foreign affairs:

> My overwhelming observation from the experience of the last four years [during the Carter Administration] is that history is neither the product of design nor of conspiracy but is rather the reflection of continuing chaos. Seen from the outside, decisions may often seem clear and consciously formulated; interrelations between governments may seem to be the products of deliberately crafted, even if often conflicting, policies.
> But one learns, in fact, that so much of what happens . . . is the product of chaotic conditions and a great deal of personal struggle and ambiguity.[1]

Understandably, a head of state or of government, a prime minister, or a secretary of foreign affairs, wishing to mobilize public opinion behind a certain foreign policy design and desiring to leave to posterity an image of purposefulness, craft, and statesmanship, will as a rule not share with that public the

---

* The Soviet Constitution grants some nominal foreign affairs functions to the constituent Republics; this in no way affects the central Soviet government's prerogative to conduct foreign policy for the Soviet Union as a whole, very much as it sees fit.

sense of chaos so vividly described by Brzezinski. It is relatively easy to present chaotic and exceedingly complex international conditions and unstructured, often rash or ill considered, foreign policy responses as integrally related parts of a carefully prepared design, partly because the public and the media prefer to have things presented in an orderly simplistic fashion, partly because foreign affairs are relatively remote from the general public's everyday concerns. In addition, there is the unavoidable element of secrecy.

Foreign affairs may touch upon exceedingly sensitive national security matters which should perhaps never be made public or not be released prematurely. For example, while delicate international negotiations are in progress, premature disclosure of a plan, or a position may jeopardize the outcome. The public demand for full disclosure is far less insistent in foreign than in domestic affairs, primarily because in the latter instance the public is involved more intimately and is as a rule far better informed; foreign affairs failures as well as successes are therefore not examined or evaluated as closely as are failure or success in domestic public finance, social welfare, or in other respects affecting the lives of citizens more immediately.

One might think that in the relatively open "Western" societies the gap between apparent and real foreign policy is quite narrow whereas in the relatively closed totalitarian societies the gap should be substantial. Actually, the veil of secrecy can easily and legitimately be drawn to conceal real foreign policy objectives from the general public in any society, under any system of government. It can safely be assumed that secret or open foreign affairs tasks are generally approached by leaders and other government officials in a responsible manner, in good faith. But leaders are human and therefore fallible. Some leaders are incompetent, some venal and corrupt. Occasionally a ruler, a dictator appointed for life for example, may turn out to be mentally unbalanced. Some leaders are competent, honest, diligent, but catastrophically mistaken about their own country's best interests, or about another country's intentions. In these cases, secrecy can have devastating consequences. Unfortunately, in foreign far more than in domestic affairs, rhetoric and propaganda can be employed to convey the appearance of public disclosure when in fact the intent is to conceal foreign policy moves which cannot stand close public scrutiny because they are ill conceived or tragically mistaken.

The danger that foreign policy secretly conceived and secretly conducted serves purposes other than the best possible national interest is real and ever present. Because they are always hard-pressed to achieve success at home but are frequently unable to do so, leaders may seek successes by "escaping forward," that is, they try their luck in foreign affairs. Secrecy promises the opportunity to conceal the attempt until crowned with success and the error until the policy's author has retired from office. Meanwhile, even a relatively minor or in the long term highly questionable but in the short term dramatic foreign policy "success," can be touted at home as a significant accomplishment, especially if embellished by invocation of patriotic themes.*

Roman emperors resorted to circuses to distract their subjects from the shortage of bread. Modern leaders may provide similar entertainment by provoking a verbal altercation with a foreign government, thus distracting their public at least for a brief period from the grim realities at home, immediately preceding an election for example. Some leaders are known to have embarked upon foreign policies in the fashion of riverboat gamblers, staking the very existence of the state they were elected or appointed to protect on what at times were wild guesses, their attitude summarized by the comment attributed to one of their kind: *Après moi, le déluge* ("After me, the flood").

It is said that "lies have short legs." But in foreign affairs, secrecy and rhetoric may combine to extend the lifespan of a horrendous foreign policy hoax for years, at times for decades. Unlike domestic affairs, foreign affairs can escape cost or performance tests. Hence, a colossal foreign policy fiasco can for years be represented as a resounding diplomatic success. In systems where reality can easily be concealed behind nebulous ideological formulations, leaders can engage in empty posturing without ever having to deliver anything in the way of concrete results.†

Foreign Policy Decision-Making

"Rational" and "Irrational Man" Models

Franklin Delano Roosevelt, on his way to the momentous conference with Churchill and Stalin at Yalta in 1945, carried with him boxes filled with documents and position papers prepared to guide him and members of his delegation on matters experts had expected to be raised. Nothing less than the fate of the postwar world hinged on the outcome of these deliberations. Yet,

---

* Governments generally do not permit public access to classified documents and papers until decades have passed; in some instances such papers were not released, and even then not in their entirety, until half a century later.

† Decision-makers often dabble in foreign affairs rather than struggle with intractable domestic issues. As one writer put it, U.S. presidents "find foreign affairs less challenging because the standards of success in conducting them are vague." Nicholas von Hoffman, *The New York Review of Books* (June 25, 1981), p. 24. Perhaps the most striking examples of this are the two "great dictators," Hitler and Mussolini, who triggered World War Two while their respective nations careened toward economic and eventually military disaster. Writes D. M. Smith about Mussolini at a time when Europe was on the brink of war: "He now seemed bored with domestic matters: his time, he said, was more than ever taken up with foreign affairs—that is, with devising means of imposing his own views on other countries" (1982), p. 205. Significantly this occurred at a time when according to many of his closest associates the dictator had lost touch with reality. Another example was the leader of Ghana, a tiny West African republic, Kwame Nkrumah, who in 1966 travelled to the People's Republic of China on a quixotic mission to bring an end to the war in Vietnam; upon arrival in Beijing he learned that he had been overthrown, mainly because he had totally neglected management of the home economy. Bretton (1966), pp. 171-177.

Roosevelt preferred to rely on his own political instincts and intuitions, both proven of course only in domestic politics in the United States. Hitler is known to have disdained written briefs. Eisenhower is said to have held a low opinion of any matter brought to him for his decision, if it required more than one page to be presented. Stalin read briefs but usually followed his own instincts, influenced increasingly by paranoia.[2] All of these practices inevitably distorted reality. Yet many historical accounts of foreign affairs convey a sense of near perfection.

Theory on decision-making in general, and on foreign policy decision-making in particular, distinguishes between two major types: the "rational" and "the irrational man" models. Decisions or nondecisions have been defined as choices between or among alternative courses of action by a decisional unit, one of which is the individual decision-maker. The "rational *economic* man model" postulates that decisions are made by a person—or persons—who are aware of all possible alternatives, understand all possible consequences of each of these, and can arrive therefore, in theory at least, at a clear hierarchy of values or preferences regarding them. A modification of this model focuses on activity that considers alternatives sequentially until one that satisfies is identified and adopted.[3]

Harold Lasswell's seven functional categories correspond to the chronological stages through which decision-makers are presumed to proceed on their way to executive decisions:

process	*outcome*
information	problem identification
recommendation	proposal alternatives
prescription	selection of alternatives
invocation	general enforcement
application	specific enforcement
appraisal	review
termination	conclusion[4]

Such orderly models are undoubtedly of value in creating order out of apparent chaos, but, as noted above, chaos, chance, and gambling instinct may have as much to do with foreign policy outcomes as do orderly processes or logic.

Another model distinguishes three basic components of the process: the occasion for the decision, the individual decision-maker, and the organizational context in which the decision is made. This model has much to commend itself.[5] It makes allowance for improvisation and even more important for consideration that in a particular case chaos may indeed reign at the center of decision-making, that the decision-maker may be a wholly irrational individual, that he or she may be surrounded by incompetent advisors, ignorant of the most elementary pertinent facts, and that the entire machinery may be bogged down for technical reasons or because it simply is unable to cope with an unfolding crisis.

Regarding the entire process, certain critical factors must be noted above all else. The occasion for the decision is affected, often decisively, by the extent to which the decision-makers were able to anticipate a given event or crisis. This determines the decision-time or the time-to-task ratio; that is, how much time is available for what magnitude or difficulty of decision. Put differently, knowledge of the occasion for the decision informs us whether there was sufficient time for *all* theoretical or prescribed processes for all parts of the policy machinery to be activated and involved.

As suggested earlier, the occasion for the decision is not necessarily shaped by objective facts or by events presenting themselves automatically and fully to the decision-maker but, far more likely, may be the product of manipulation abroad or at home. Information available to the decision-maker is always incomplete. It is a matter of luck if the missing piece turns out to be unessential. For these reasons, the decision may be occasioned less by the objective event occuring in a distant place than by the coming together of sufficient information to permit formation of a clear and reliable picture of what it is that needs to be addressed. In the absence of such information, the occasion for a decision may be a misreading of a single report or it may be a complete fabrication. For example, President Nixon's decision in 1970 to invade Cambodia was based on information correct only in part; however, it was the incorrect part which proved to be decisive. In the president's mind, the invasion was necessary to close a North Vietnamese supply route and locate and destroy a major North Vietnamese headquarters, reportedly located on Cambodian soil and from there directing and coordinating attacks on U.S. and South Vietnamese forces in Vietnam. That target turned out to be a small group of men moving about on trucks.*

History has known statesmen who were rated "great" in their time and who turned into veritable giants after their death. In modern times, this applies to Bismarck, Disraeli, Wilson, Franklin D. Roosevelt, Hitler, Stalin, Mao Zedong, Churchill, and de Gaulle. Others who might be viewed in that light were Sukarno, Nehru, Nkrumah, Nasser and Sadat. Modern historiography, drawing on psychology and psychiatry, reinforced by cliometric methods of data collection and analysis, tends to reduce many of these leaders to normal size.[6]

A specialist in mental health recently reported on a series of experiments with a frog.[7] The experiment's object was determination of the animal's response to "information input overload." The experiment consisted of administering a series of electric shocks to sensitive points on the animal's body, at a steadily increasing rate. The animal's responses—voluntary and involuntary reflexes by head, skin, and limbs—were recorded and measured.

* The incident is discussed in Powers (1979, pp. 276-279). It seems that U.S. military intelligence had identified what they believed to be North Vietnam's military headquarters for South Vietnam, dubbed COSVN. The president ordered the invasion to "put COSVN out of business." Comments Powers: "The United States was about to invade a non-belligerent country in order to destroy COSVN and no one knew where it was." (p. 279) The invasion took place and COSVN, of course, was never located. Shortly after the supply route was bombed it was back in operation.

A pattern became apparent, reflecting steadily decreasing ability on the animal's part to cope with the mounting information flow until, when overload was reached, the animal ceased to cope altogether. The response pattern revealed the following behavioral manifestations beginning with responses at normal input rate and ending with the highest shock frequency:

1. omission
2. error
3. approximation
4. queuing
5. filtering
6. use of multiple channels
7. escape

During phase one, the animal begins to omit responses; it next commits errors—that is, it responds with one limb when normally it would have responded with the other. Next, it approximates the frequency of stimuli or shocks, responding to clusters rather than to each and every input. Then it delays responses, storing or queuing, selecting some stimuli for response, ignoring others. Next it employs multiple nerve channels, including some normally not used for such purposes. Finally, when the input load reaches unbearable proportions, it ceases to respond rationally and seeks to escape.

Anyone familiar with what actually transpires in a modern, major power foreign policy decision-making center will find the results of this experiment very familiar. Applied to contemporary international relations, the final response phase could mean the end of civilization as we know it.[8]

We know that one part of the human mind can be alienated from the other. The process may be gradual, not readily ascertainable. Its occurrence need not be regarded as pathological. It may merely be a case of deliberate exclusion or suppression of a memory, a set of facts, or a set of values. Pathological or not, with respect to foreign policy decision-making what are the chances that the condition is diagnosed in time and corrective action taken? Typically, the central or principal decision-maker dominates the immediate environment and selects aides and advisers who tend to reinforce personal prejudices and aggravate the condition to be corrected. This is true of leaders in our type of political democracy as it is of dictators. Neither the advisory nor the broader consti-tutional, institutional, or procedural safeguards which legal and political theorists and constitutional lawyers have devised offer guarantees in this respect.

The triple level model which we prefer ends with the organizational context in which the decision is made. We addressed this component earlier, noting that a wide gap separates reality from rhetoric or myth in this respect as in all others. One can generalize that if one or more decision-makers determine that the existing organizational context should be circumvented or ignored, they will find ways and means to do so. Constitutionally, the United States is endowed with one of the world's most balanced foreign policy machineries. Still, the Senate, constitutionally required to be consulted on treaties, has been circumvented, the Congress frequently sidestepped, and the Supreme Court importuned to the point where it too had no choice but to acquiesce.

Soviet leaders, nominally restricted by a Constitution, actually rely on the implied power broadly assigned to the Communist party and do very much as they please. Indeed, decision-makers everywhere employ legal advisers and speechwriters, and as of late image-makers, to assist them in finding legal constitutional or other plausible rationales for illegal, unconstitutional, or generally questionable acts or decisions; which returns us to the most convenient escape clause, used universally, "the national interest."

"Rational" and "Irrational" Interests

If a nation's official foreign policy is viewed as the governing rationale, then deviation from that position may be viewed as irrational. While totalitarian and authoritarian regimes have ways and means to prevent significant departure from official policy by special interest groups, or on public demand, the more open and permissive political democracies are more vulnerable in that respect. There public pressure, usually generated by impatience or frustration, has on occasion "wrecked attempts at balanced strategy," and the increasingly powerful and assertive multinational corporations frequently contravene official policy.[9]

Foreign Policy Formulation

Feliks Gross, in his classic *Foreign Policy Analysis,* offers a comprehensive analytical framework which accounts for all of the major influences shaping a country's foreign policy. Gross suggests that these influences bear on foreign policy in the order presented. In theory, this may be so. In the real world, as we have shown, influence over policy acts is less orderly, less predictable. Hence the schemes presented below are adaptions of Gross' model:

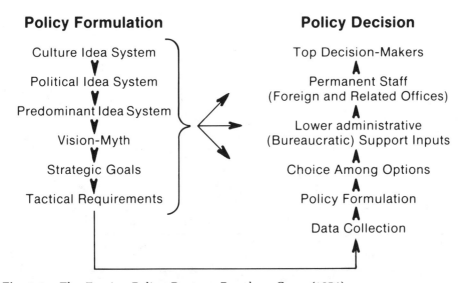

Policy Formulation

Culture Idea System
↓
Political Idea System
↓
Predominant Idea System
↓
Vision-Myth
↓
Strategic Goals
↓
Tactical Requirements

Policy Decision

Top Decision-Makers
↑
Permanent Staff
(Foreign and Related Offices)
↑
Lower administrative
(Bureaucratic) Support Inputs
↑
Choice Among Options
↑
Policy Formulation
↑
Data Collection

Fig. 3-1. The Foreign Policy Process. Based on Gross (1954).

Any one of the influences identified in Figures 3-1 and 3-2 as part of the foreign policy formulation process may directly or indirectly make itself felt at any one of the stages or at none. All can be encountered in any state's foreign policy process.

Summary

Reflecting the overall emphasis underlying this book, a priority ranking of forces, factors, or influences, likely though not necessarily shaping foreign policy formulation, decision-making, and conduct, might be as follows:

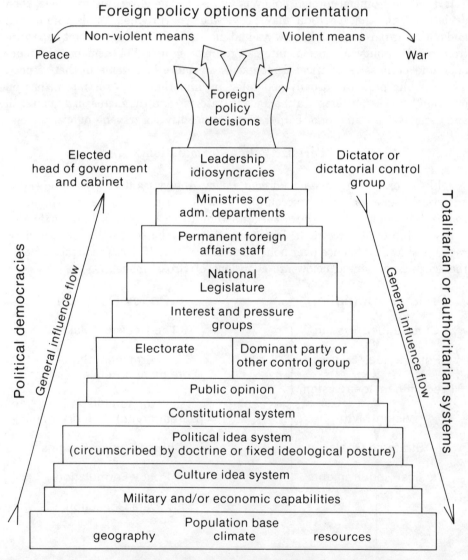

Fig. 3-2.   The Foreign Policy Structure. Based on Gross (1954) Table IV, p. 90.

1. Economic Resource Availability and/or Costs.
2. Military Security Considerations and Capabilities.
3. Internal Partisan-Political Considerations and Constellations.
4. Predominant Ideas in Cultural, Political, Ideological Respects as Modified by Doctrine or Fixed Ideological Positions.
5. The Nature and Effectiveness of Organization and Quality of Political Leadership.
6. The Nature, Disposition, and Quality of Top Decision-Makers.

Suggested Questions and Discussion Topics

In what respects do formulation of "the national interest" and of foreign policy generally differ among the world's major political systems and in what respects are they similar?

Is there a difference between foreign policy rhetoric and reality and, if so, why?

Identify and discuss the several foreign policy formulation and decision-making models discussed in this Chapter. What do these models tell us about international relations and international politics in particular?

Outline and discuss Feliks Gross's foreign policy formulation model.

Suggested Readings for Part One: Fundamentals

Chapter 1

Bull, Hedley. *The Anarchical Society. A Study of Order in World Politics.* New York: Columbia University Press, 1977.

Frankel, Joseph. *International Relations in a Changing World.* New York: Oxford University Press, 1979.

Kohn, Hans. *Nationalism. Its Meaning and History.* Revised Ed. New York: Van Nostrand, 1965, Part I.

Northedge, F.S. *The International Political System.* London: Faber and Faber, 1976.

Chapter 2

Claude, Inis L. *Power and International Relations.* New York: Random House, 1962, Chapters 1 and 2.

Cochran, Arkin, and Hoenig. *Nuclear Weapons Databook,* Vol. I Cambridge, Mass.: Ballinger, 1984, Chapter II "Factual Information on Present Nuclear Arsenals."

Brodie, Bernard, and Fawn M. Brodie. *From Cross Bow to H-Bomb.* Bloomington, Ind.: Indiana University Press, 1973.

Knorr, Klaus. *Power and Wealth. The Political Economy of International Power.* New York: Basic Books, 1973.

United Nations, Centre for Disarmament. Publication No. A/35/392. *Comprehensive Study on Nuclear Weapons.* New York: U.N., 1981, Chapter Two "Nuclear Weapons Primer."

Chapter 3

Bloomfield, Lincoln P. *The Foreign Policy Process. A Modern Primer.* Englewood Cliffs, N.J.: Prentice Hall, 1982.

Frankel, Joseph. *The Making of Foreign Policy. An Analysis of Decision Making.* London: Oxford University Press, 1967.

———. *International Relations in a Changing World, op. cit.,* Chapter 7.

Gross, Feliks. *Foreign Policy Analysis.* New York: Philosophical Library, 1954.

Jacobson, Harold K. and William Zimmerman. *The Shaping of Foreign Policy.* New York: Atherton Press, 1969.

Knorr, Klaus. *Power and Wealth, op. cit.,* Chapter 2.

Tuchman, Barbara W. *The March of Folly—From Troy to Vietnam.* N.Y.: Knopf, 1984; especially Part Five and Epilogue.

Wilkinson, David O. *Comparative Foreign Relations: Framework and Methods.* Belmont, Cal.: Dickinson, 1969.

Part Two
The Conduct of International Relations:
Channels and Instrumentalities

Chapter 4
Communication and Information

Clearly, an essential ingredient of relations among nations is communication: without communication there can be no relations. Myriads of contacts are made daily and routinely across national boundaries, between governmental and non-governmental agencies, between private groups or individuals acting with governmental knowledge and support, officially and unofficially, formally and informally, openly and secretly. Most of these contacts go unnoticed by the general public and probably are not even recorded anywhere. If recorded, most can be traced only by a diligent detective, scholar, or determined archivist. The general public and the world generally become aware of certain transactions mainly when something goes awry.

Of the various forms of international communication, diplomacy occupies the highest level. Narrowly defined, the term covers representation, gathering and dissemination of information, exchange of messages, and negotiation. More broadly defined it covers all official and some unofficial direct and indirect contacts between governments and their representatives abroad. It is also widely used to describe conduct of foreign policy generally. Along with everything else on earth, diplomacy is changing at a faster rate now than ever before.

Official Diplomacy

Levels, Functions, and Responsibilities

In their official relations, states, or more exactly heads of state acting in a state's behalf, are represented abroad by diplomatic missions.* For diplomatic ties to be established, missions to be opened, and diplomats to begin performing their official duties, the sending state must recognize the receiving state and be recognized in return. Under an *agrément,* the name and official function of each individual diplomat must be on a list submitted to the receiving state and each must be acceptable to that state. If not acceptable, diplomats are

---

* In the case of the United Nations, these missions are accredited to that body and are located at or near UN Headquarters in New York City.

declared *persona non grata;* if already in the receiving state, they must leave; if not yet there, they may not be sent.

The principal diplomat representing a head of state abroad is normally the ambassador. That officer heads the entire diplomatic mission of a country located in the receiving state's capital and all consulates located in major cities outside the capital. Under the ambassador—aside from purely administrative and support staff—are deputies and other officers in charge of political, commercial, military, and cultural affairs. Consular officers extend these functions to outlying areas. They also serve citizens of their own country who may be in need of assistance and issue visas to citizens of the receiving state and to others who wish to travel to the sending state.

In the event tension develops between two countries, several steps may ensue. First, one or both ambassadors may be "recalled for consultation," to be returned or not depending on the circumstances. If the ambassador remains absent or none is appointed, a chargé d'affaires is designated to take charge of the mission. If diplomatic relations are severed entirely, usually following outbreak of war or in response to an unusually grave affront, the entire mission is terminated. In that case, each of the two countries involved in the break ask third countries of their choice to look after their interests.

Many diplomatic missions also provide cover for secret service—persons officially assigned a diplomatic function actually may be secret agents engaged in espionage, counter-espionage, or acts of subversion.* It should be noted, however, that since one of the functions of diplomacy is to gather information about the receiving state and report the results to the home government, the line dividing legitimate and inappropriate diplomatic activity is not always easy to establish.

Among legitimate activities, also normally under the ambassador, are special missions a state might undertake abroad, such as foreign assistance programs— the United States Peace Corps, for example—or educational, cultural, and scientific programs.

Providing overall direction, supervision, and control over all of a country's diplomatic missions, the corps of diplomats and foreign service personnel generally, is a foreign office or ministry, for example, the Department of State in the United States, the Foreign Office in Great Britain, or the Ministry of Foreign Affairs in the Soviet Union. Individual diplomats are accredited by presenting their credentials to the appropriate officer in the receiving state, ambassador's always to the head of state, others to lower officials. To enable them to carry out their official duties, and provided that they do not exceed those, persons on the diplomatic list, including the ambassador's immediate

---

* If caught in an illegal act, such persons are usually expelled. If the expellee's home government disputes the charge of illegality, the practice is to expel a diplomat of corresponding rank; if more persons are expelled, retaliation may, if feasible, extend to the identical number.

family and retinue, are granted immunity from certain laws of the receiving state. For the same reason, embassy and consular grounds, all official diplomatic premises and the ambassador's residence, are considered inviolable, meaning that agents of the receiving state may not enter these premises without the ambassador's or his deputy's permission. Similarly, diplomatic baggage and pouches are ordinarily exempt from search and seizure. Both privileges may be temporarily suspended if authorities in the receiving state have reason to believe that a criminal act has been or is about to be committed.*

When in 1979 a group of Iranians seized the United States Embassy in Teheran, occupied it, and held captive large numbers of the diplomatic staff, six major international treaties and conventions were violated, not considering the basic principles of diplomatic immunity and exterritoriality which states including Iran had voluntarily accepted, as a matter of reciprocity, ever since the world emerged from the dark ages. Indeed, the greatest protection of diplomats abroad is not international law so much as reciprocity. States generally are reluctant to violate diplomatic immunity, or exterritoriality,† for fear that the safety of their own diplomats and their families and the integrity of their files and records will be equally endangered. Beyond that, even the most radical revolutionary regime must recognize that once the twin principles of diplomatic immunity and exterritoriality are placed in jeopardy all contacts between nations are endangered, all channels of communication are imperiled.‡

Diplomats engage in various forms of official conduct: they initiate and conduct discussions and negotiations, either formally recorded or summarized by a *note verbale* left behind, or by an *aide-mémoire,* also a summary of what was discussed or was agreed upon between the parties. They make representations, forcefully or discreetly. They engage in a *demarche* when their state has been victimized by acts of omission or commission on the part of the host state's government or its citizens. Examples are violation of the embassy grounds by a mob or by a single policeman, an insult published in a government-controlled newspaper, victimization of citizens of the sending state by local authorities—their rights violated or ignored or subjected to indignities, or military or some other hostile action.

---

* Treatment, prevention, and immunities of diplomats are covered, among other treaties and conventions, in the Vienna Convention on Diplomatic Relations of 1961, the Vienna Convention on Consular Relations of 1963, and the Convention of 1973 on the Prevention and Punishment of Crimes against Internationally Protected Persons, including Diplomatic Agents. The latter instrument was a response to a rash of physical attacks, including kidnappings and assassinations mainly of Western diplomats, partly instigated if not aided and abetted by certain revolutionary governments, partly the result of acts by self-serving terrorist groups. While it is difficult if not impossible to prevent all such attacks, the Convention attempts to discourage them by ensuring international cooperation in the identification, apprehension, and punishment of the perpetrators.

† Partial exemption of embassy grounds and buildings from local jurisdiction.

‡ It is significant that aside from the Iranian delegate all nations represented in the United Nations condemned the act. See U.S. Department of State (December 1979).

The form and language of diplomacy is generally expected to be respectful, courteous, and mindful of the feelings, sensitivities, self-perception, and customs of foreign governments and people. As a rule, diplomats are expected to be accurate, reliable, and trustworthy; however neither their own governments nor the governments to which they are accredited expect diplomats to be entirely candid. It is for that reason that one definition describes the diplomat as "a person sent abroad to lie for his [her] country."

Diplomacy takes place at various levels: at the state-to-state level already discussed, between states and international organizations or agencies such as the United Nations and its organs, within international organizations and agencies, and at international meetings called for special purposes. Normally, regularly appointed and accredited diplomats are used; if binding treaties or commitments are expected to be signed, a special envoy may be appointed and granted special powers as Ambassador Extraordinary and Plenipotentiary. Diplomacy may be conducted bilaterally (between two states) or multilaterally (involving a greater number).*

Typically, lengthy and protracted discussions precede formal international negotiation and agreement. Initially, lower-ranking officials, usually below the rank of ambassador, lay the groundwork. As agreement approaches or seems within reach higher officials are brought into the process. In the event a major breakthrough or even a treaty is in sight, the principal cabinet officer in charge of foreign affairs, for example the secretary of state or foreign minister, may participate or take over the negotiations. Or the heads of state or heads of government themselves may choose to meet "at the summit" to formalize the agreement.†

* Coincident with the creation of international organizations, such as the United Nations or the European Economic Community, a new class of diplomat has come into existence, the international civil servant. These persons are expected to practice diplomacy even-handedly vis-à-vis all states and governments encompassed within the organization which employs them. The administrative head of such organizations usually is the Secretary General, who is selected, or elected and appointed by the member governments. Given the central purposes of the United Nations, it is reasonable to regard the Secretary General of the UN, together with the leading members of his staff, as the core of a planetary diplomatic service whose members are expected to be committed to global rather than narrowly nationalistic or ethnocentric causes. International legal provisions protecting these diplomats and their support staffs are similar to those protecting diplomats representing individual states. However, the Secretary General must be mindful of the coalition of states which voted for him, and lesser officials must carefully reconcile the sensitivities and vital interests of their own governments with their presumably overriding international commitments and obligations.

† Some heads of state have purely ceremonial or at best highly limited executive functions. In such cases, for example Great Britain or West Germany, the prime minister or chancellor plays the more active role. A notable instance of such second-level summitry was the highly productive and intimate diplomacy practiced by West German Chancellor Konrad Adenauer and French Foreign Minister Robert Schuman in the late 1940s and early 1950s, a relationship instrumental in the creation of the European Coal and Steel Community, eventually leading to the European Common Market. See also the cordial personal diplomacy conducted in the late 1920s between German Foreign Minister Gustav Stresemann and his French counterpart, Aristide Briand. See Bretton (1953).

Because it always conveys a sense of high drama, and gives rise to great expectations, the subject of summitry warrants special consideration as perhaps the ultimate consummation of diplomacy, which in the final analysis is inter-action between heads of state.

The critical question regarding summitry is whether it serves any useful purpose. Is it worth the time and effort of a presumably busy monarch or president—who is usually not trained in foreign affairs or may be barely conversant with the issues under discussion—to travel to distant places, or should there not be reliance instead on professional diplomats already in place? If a special envoy has to be sent, should that person not always be an experienced diplomat? Opinions vary; some analysts argue that, meaningful or not, summit meetings between highly visible heads of state have symbolic value. They can clear the air, facilitate confidential exchange of views, or convey personal assurances where such may be called for to head off or at least minimize a conflict. If a workable agreement can be formalized at such a meeting, then no damage is done. If it cannot, then an appropriately worded communique can cover up any disagreement, leaving room for further negotiation at lower levels. Besides, so the argument runs, even if no concrete results materialize, an opportunity will have been provided for two or more highly placed individuals to become acquainted, open new channels of communication, or unblock old ones. At the very least, such meetings can contribute to a relaxation of tensions. (In the words of Winston Churchill, "It is better to jaw-jaw than to war-war.")

Skeptics stress the enormous complexity of contemporary world affairs, a function partly of steadily expanding and interlocking national and international political, economic, and military problem complexes, and partly of the rapidly spreading intrusion into foreign affairs of complex financial, scientific, and technical subject matter, calling for knowledge and skills few of these leaders possess. The argument is that, more often than not, uninformed, poorly prepared, naive, or overly enthusiastic heads of state may agree to terms which eventually defy implementation, produce new problems, and should therefore better have been left undone.*

Open and Secret Diplomacy

When only absolute monarchs and their personal representatives or emissaries conducted foreign affairs, when masses were not yet allowed to participate in the political process, the press had not yet attained independence from the

---

* Occasionally, a meeting at the summit may be the only effective channel. Thus, in 1977, to stage that dramatic act needed to break a long-standing diplomatic log jam, to cut through layers of accumulated hatred, animosity, and mistrust, Anwar Sadat, president of Egypt, undertook his historic journey to Jerusalem, disputed capital of Israel. A similarly justified occasion was the 1972 journey by United States President Richard Nixon to overcome nearly twenty-five years of hostility separating the U.S. and the People's Republic of China. Summitry may be the only feasible mode of contact, as between dictators for example, who may trust no one, or in time of war when highly secret negotiations must be restricted to narrowest possible circles.

sovereign, and at any rate did not yet wield the degree of power and influence enjoyed by today's mass media, diplomacy was generally regarded as a private, confidential, or secret matter. The general public became aware only of the more dramatic consequences of such doings, transfer of their homes and lands to another sovereign, for example, or war and destruction. To some statesmen and some historians, World War One was brought on partly by secret understandings and treaties secretly negotiated. Pledged to prevent a recurrence of that catastrophe, Woodrow Wilson, president of the United States, approached the peace settlement and the ordering of the postwar world determined to commit himself and his country to nothing but "open covenants, openly arrived at." The pledge did not stand close examination. Implemented as intended, it would have meant widespread publicity accompanying all stages of international discussion and negotiation. It would have opened the doors wide to public posturing and propaganda by interested parties, premature disclosure of cautious inquiry preparatory to submission of a formal offer, embarrassment, even riots and demonstrations while negotiations, for settlement of a dispute for example or toward creation of an unpopular military alliance, were under way. Beyond that, military alliances could not be very effective if their terms had to be shared with all and sundry. That of course was the intent; but in the world as it really is, military alliances will be indispensable for some time to come, and premature disclosure, public debate, and discussion, especially of the more sensitive aspects of such agreements, will remain something to be avoided.

Generally statesmen keep each other's secrets if obtained through diplomatic channels. Without that it would be impossible to maintain an atmosphere of trust and confidence. Likewise, ambassadors do not as a rule seek to disclose publicly information conveyed to them in confidence. Violation of that rule would undermine their own or their government's ability to conduct negotiations in the future.

Style and Quality of Diplomacy

For the greater part of the period when nations conducted their relations through diplomatic channels, diplomats typically belonged to the upper classes, identifying themselves consequently as members of an international socially exclusive elite. This sense of social affinity shaped form and tone of diplomacy for centuries. Traditionally, diplomatic conduct is to be characterized by utter discretion, subtlety, and indirection—it is "undiplomatic" to candidly speak one's mind or to come to the point too directly or too bluntly. As a rule, ambassadors and their principal aides are expected to refrain from commenting on or interfering with the receiving state's internal affairs. If espionage is an objective, it is expected that it be conducted as discreetly as possible, so carefully in fact that in the event of detection or of an agent's capture the ambassador and his or her government can plausibly deny having had anything to do with the person or the act.

Use of diplomacy to promote dissent if not insurrection and overthrow of a government or system probably traces back to the French Revolution, whose leaders saw themselves and their cause isolated in a sea of hostile, counter-revolutionary regimes. On the other hand, the prudent, skillful, and farsighted diplomat always was expected to establish and maintain contacts with future, usually opposite leaders. Benjamin Franklin proceeded that way, but most cautiously and discreetly. The Russian Revolution intensified the use of diplomats for revolutionary purposes. Today, efforts to establish contacts with tomorrow's leaders is common practice, though not necessarily for seditious purposes. One of the United States' most successful diplomats, Warren M. Christopher, criticizing United States practice in particular, wrote: "We must guard against the tendency to identify so narrowly with the personalities in power that we neglect crosscurrents of opinion taking sway among the people they rule."[1] To an extent, the tendency to restrict contacts to approved channels is a matter of prudence, but it also is a reflection of the status quo-orientation so characteristic of Western diplomacy. Representatives of revolutionary regimes tend to have fewer compunctions in these respects. Local conditions permitting, they assiduously seek to establish contact with what they term "representatives of the working class." Indeed, in the lexicon of social revolution diplomacy is the frontline of the struggle against the prevailing order.

In a way, World War One was a watershed when traditions were broken, diplomacy assumed new and different functions, and diplomats began to practice different styles. Beginning with the first envoys sent abroad by the young Soviet government shortly after the Revolution, continuing with the unorthodox official conduct as well as rude personal demeanor manifested by representatives of fascist Germany and Italy, to the often bizarre behavior of contemporary diplomats from such countries as revolutionary Libya or Iran, the profession has changed significantly.*

Technology, International Interdependence, and Diplomacy

Two hundred years ago, when it took several months for an ambassador's report to reach the home office, much depended upon the personal skill and resourcefulness of the individual envoy and his very small staff, if he had a staff. A good part of the time, connections between home government and embassy were for practical purposes nonexistent, some governments not hearing from their envoy for a year or more. Under the circumstances, instructions given to ambassadors had to be held sufficiently vague and flexible to remain

---

* In 1935, before walking out, the Nazi German delegates to the League of Nations cocked a snook at the diplomats assembled in plenary session. More recently Libya's Head of State, Colonel Quadhafi, instructed his "diplomats" to dispense with formalities and act abroad as representatives of "the revolutionary masses," each Libyan embassy abroad to be renamed "Bureau of the People's Jamharyia." The Libyan government also either permitted or instigated direct attacks in Libya's capital on embassies of countries of whose foreign policies the Colonel disapproved.

valid until a series of messages had been sent, returned, and sent once again to offer new and different guidelines. By then, the situation abroad and possibly also at home had probably changed significantly.

Today's globally interlocked, nearly instantaneous, computerized communication links, telephone lines which can be kept open for hours, even days, enabling a home office to participate directly in conferences with personnel in one of its embassies half-way around the world, have altered the role, function, and importance of diplomats and their mission. Ambassadors still yearn for a certain degree of independence from the bureaucracy at home. But the latter, aided materially by ever faster airplanes and telecommunications, now tend to inject themselves increasingly into the diplomatic process. Vastly improved communications now permit the most minute instructions to be transmitted around the globe if necessary to dozens of embassies within minutes, hours at most. These instructions can be updated to reflect rapidly changing conditions. The same technology of course also tends to render redundant the embassy as such, as the sole or even prime source of information on the receiving country. The spy-in-the-sky can in one sweep gather more information on a country's military condition than could an embassy in a year of diligent cultivation of sources or scouting on the ground.

In a sense, that same technological revolution has contributed to the diminution of the ambassador's role from another direction. The progressive intertwining and interlocking of financial, commercial, and economic affairs generally with political and military affairs which as we noted earlier so frustrates foreign policy makers in general now also threatens to overwhelm diplomacy. No longer can the affairs of one country be viewed in isolation. They must be viewed in the context in which they unfold, a context which is far beyond the range of observation of an individual ambassador or even a well-staffed embassy, which mandates even greater reliance on the home base where all relevant information flows together. This tips the scales even more in favor of the home bureaucracy and tends to reduce the ambassador progressively to the role of carrier of messages between governments, an "errand boy" as Soviet Premier Khrushchev once described the foreign minister of the Soviet Union. At best, today's ambassadors tend to function mainly as high level administrators of diplomatic communication and information facilities located abroad.

Unofficial Diplomacy

On occasion, in quest of specific objectives requiring absolute secrecy, governments find it convenient or politic to utilize informal channels of communication. United States presidents and other Western leaders have used prominent businessmen, bankers, or industrialists, high ranking members of the Catholic Church hierarchy, labor leaders, members of their family, or other personal confidants to transmit messages, to help break a diplomatic impasse, to make discreet inquiries, and to convey assurances. Sometimes before a matter is considered officially, a counterpart is sent; high ranking military officers talk to their opposites, members of a secret intelligence service to theirs, or lower-ranking bureaucrats explore a given situation at their level. Such informal modes are highly favored as a means of contact between "fraternal" governments within the Soviet-led socialist bloc.

Increasingly, distinctions between official and unofficial diplomacy, between representation of a universally recognized sovereign state and a group merely claiming such status, are allowed to become obscured for political reasons. As we have seen, the Palestine Liberation Organization (PLO) for example, denied official legal recognition as a state or as a government, has been permitted nevertheless by some governments and by the United Nations to quietly assume that status by a fudging of the rules governing diplomatic relations. When in 1972 the United States decided to establish formal diplomatic relations with the Chinese People's Republic, it became necessary to downgrade the status of Taiwan, the island claimed by the PRC as part of China. Accordingly, the United States in 1974 downgraded Taiwanese representation in the United States as well as U.S. representation on Taiwan to "liaison offices;" however, both countries continue to extend the usual privileges and protections to their respective diplomats.

Similar problems confront the Soviet Union and its allies in their relations with so-called national liberation movements. The commitment to support such movements in Asia, Africa, and South and Central America, while maintaining formal diplomatic relations with states against which the movements are directed, has led the Soviet Union to develop a dual standard following approximately the *de facto/de jure* dichotomy in international law. Relations with representatives of liberation movements are conducted in Moscow, Prague, or Havana as though the former enjoyed official diplomatic status; agreements are negotiated with them and are executed while the official diplomatic representatives profess ignorance.

The machinery for conduct of foreign relations of the Soviet Union and similar systems permits role changes very much as the ruling party directorate desires. Thus an apparently low-ranking official at a Soviet embassy may in fact be the most influential person because he may be an officer in the Soviet secret police, the KGB. On occasion members of the Politburo, the highest organ of the Communist party, are sent abroad to conduct or conclude negotiations. Such procedures are unlikely to be followed by Western countries because of legal or internal political constraints. A strong U.S. secretary of state, for example, would object strenuously to a secretary of defense or commerce or a high-ranking official in the political party in power conducting negotiations with a foreign government. Incidentally, U.S. law prohibits any U.S. citizen, regardless of rank or official status, to conduct negotiations or even give the appearance of conducting foreign relations with a foreign government without authorization by the appropriate body of the U.S. government.*

Unofficial diplomacy has certain distinct advantages over formal representation, especially in tense situations. Sending an unofficial emissary saves face. Both sides can deny that any discussions took place. Sensitive and delicate matters can be discussed in complete candor without hindrance or restriction by rules of diplomatic protocol. Western diplomats and government officials, legally and politically accountable to legislators at home, may not wish to touch upon certain subjects or violate certain political taboos, such as discussing the opening of diplomatic relations between the United States and Communist China prior to 1972. Private individuals need to have no such compunctions. Likewise, whereas officials may be prohibited by law or by political fiat from meeting with officials of another country, or with representatives of proscribed political movement such as the Palestine Liberation Organization, or of the Communist party of Albania, for example, private individuals, especially if they conduct such talks on neutral territory, need have no such inhibitions.

The Product of Diplomacy

As a rule, the aim of diplomacy is fulfillment of a country's foreign policy goals as set by its political leaders. Its end product may be peace or war, success in a given foreign policy venture, or defeat, or even an end to the existence of the state. Normally, the aim is maintenance of correct, if possible cordial and mutually reassuring relations with friend and foe. As the sending country's eyes and ears, at least until electronic devices began to replace them, a major objective of diplomats was to open and maintain two-way channels of communication and information in all directions, in all conceivable respects. Treaties, conventions, alliances and pacts are negotiated and, if concluded successfully, implemented, new arrangements and understandings formulated, and where appropriate, preparation made for improvement of trade, commerce, military, technical, or scientific cooperation or cultural exchange. If formal pacts or alliances are not feasible, a less binding arrangement such as an *entente* may be sought.†

Sometimes the task confronting diplomacy is to induce another government to change its foreign policy stance, to dissuade it from pursuing a course not in the best interest of the sending state, or to assume a neutral position regarding a specific conflict. In the face of such efforts the diplomatic response

---

* Nevertheless, nothing can prevent a private person from lending his services to a government wishing to use unofficial rather than official channels. Soviet governments, beginning with Lenin, have endowed certain private individuals from Western countries with quasi-diplomatic status, granting them easy access to highest levels of government, and using them for informal messages to foreign governments, for example Dr. Armand Hammer, Chairman of the Board of Occidental Petroleum, one of the world's major multinational corporations.

† *Entente*, a nonbinding understanding between governments to cooperate diplomatically or even militarily. *Entente* may find formal expression in treaties.

of the receiving country is defense of its position, explanation of its goals to all interested parties, and justification of its measures taken in pursuance of these goals.

Among secondary products are conveyance to government and people in the host country of the most favorable impressions possible regarding the sending country's intentions, its quality of life, and its reliability and credibility as a negotiating partner, ally, or antagonist. Diplomats also provide opportunities for their counterparts from third countries to acquaint themselves with the sending state's foreign policies. The same channels, of course, are available to transmit messages from states with whom the sending state does not maintain diplomatic relations.*

Information

Serving Humanity?

The presumption, at first glance a justifiable one, must be that the more information we can obtain about each other, at the individual as well as at the international level, the better off we must be. Expansion of the frontiers of knowledge obviously depends on improved communication. Toward the end of the twentieth century, humanity appears to have succeeded in these respects beyond the dreams of our ancestors, though not of our seers. The vistas opened by breakthroughs in computer science and technology and in telecommunication are limitless. Along with "robotics," we now speak of "informatics," that is, continuous expansion of information flows resulting in steady increases in computer capacity to replace human functions and thereby expand enormously the range of intellectual and scientific inquiry.[2] Not least important in this regard is the impact of the information explosion on the interdependence of peoples and nations. Does all of this constitute a promise or a threat?[3] Is humanity facing yet another insoluble dilemma? The momentum of scientific and technological discovery is far from spent. Each day, somewhere on earth, probably in a laboratory in Japan or in the United States, someone succeeds in scoring yet another breakthrough to meet spiralling demand for ever faster, ever more voluminous communications to keep up with parallel advances in related technology, especially automation. With every innovation the flow of information increases exponentially, a spur to yet additional efforts at improvement. One question must not be allowed to go unanswered: Will human capacity to receive, digest, and intelligently act on what is received be able to keep pace? The answer to this question may well determine whether burgeoning

---

* Prior to resumption of normal diplomatic relations between the United States and Communist China, the respective ambassadors to Poland, meeting for years on a regular basis in their respective embassies in Warsaw, served as the principal links between the two countries. Similarly, at the UN Israeli and some Arab diplomats whose governments did not recognize Israel were indirectly brought into contact via third party envoys also accredited to the UN.

international conflict can be managed and its companion threat, nuclear war, averted.

Projecting Information Abroad

George Orwell in his not so futuristic, in some respects prophetic, *1984* drew attention to the problem: not all information is intended to inform; some is designed to do the opposite. Still, nations expend increasing amounts of money and much effort to inform others about themselves, most of the time in a straightforward manner with no sinister motives or hidden intent. It stands to reason that the more a government can project to the world outside a favorable yet reasonably accurate and complete image of itself, of its foreign policy objectives, and of the people and society it represents, the more credible will be its future efforts in these regards, the more effective should be its efforts to gain the confidence of others.

Image building has not always been high on the agenda of governments and did not always call for the kind of financial outlays it now demands. For centuries, when government was the exclusive preserve of a mere handful of royalty and aristocrats, a letter or personal representation from one ruler to another was all that was needed to convey an assurance, assuage hurt feelings, or remove a suspicion. The people did not play a role in statecraft. They did not matter. But given the dynamics of human nature this was not to last.

Beginning with the French Revolution of 1789, the long established order in Europe began to crumble, its dissolution hastened by the Napoleonic wars (1800–1815), the war of 1914–1918, and, most decisively, by the Revolution in Russia in 1917. Soon the waves of revolutionary discontent reached other continents. Simultaneously, partly contributing to these events, partly gaining momentum because of them, the industrial revolution began to make inroads on the incidence of illiteracy, thereby extending the benefits of education to millions who had been virtually if not totally ignorant of the world beyond their immediate environment. The effects first made themselves felt in Western Europe, translating into ever more insistent demands for popular participation in government, democratization of the political processes, and, in international relations increased sensitivity of ever widening circles to events abroad. Among other things, this meant insistence that rulers account to the people for their acts, including their foreign policies, and for the results obtained.

During and shortly after World War Two, spurred on largely by the ideas of Marx and Lenin, to a lesser degree but still noticeably inspired by the example of the American Revolution, and actively encouraged and promoted by the governments of the United States and the Soviet Union, forces pent up for centuries, hidden from view by imperial rule in parts of Europe, Asia, Africa, and South America, now clamored for recognition and joined the march against the existing order. Weakened by the 1939–45 war, unable to stem the tide, the great empires collapsed. Suddenly, what had been relatively docile, disorganized, inarticulate masses now entered the global competition for resources, wealth, and power in the form of dozens of newly independent states, more often than not ruled by dictators.

In the industrialized world, the new order meant that instead of small circles of august personalities, literally millions of people had to be considered, placated, persuaded, as well as informed, if a given foreign policy was to succeed. The age of mass persuasion, mobilization and communication of public opinion, public relations, public opinion polls, and "public diplomacy" had arrived.

As far as the newly independent countries are concerned and some of the older ones as well, not every one weighs heavily in the scales of international politics or seems worth great efforts at persuasion. Some of the new states are still too weak to attract much attention. Others, strong, worth courting, or potentially dangerous, prove utterly inhospitable to communications from abroad. Although great strides have been made in the reduction of illiteracy, wide segments of the world's population remain functionally illiterate, that is, they are not yet able to master some elementary skills and functions.* Of those capable of using press or radio, millions remain outside the reach of either, because access to such media is controlled, restricted, or denied by their respective governments or simply because they are too poor.

Consequently, for some time to come the most intensive public relation and information campaigns will be directed at the masses in the industrially advanced countries, mainly at interest groups in position to influence their governments.† Next in line are the more limited circles of intellectuals, bureaucrats, and other politically sensitive and active groups under totalitarian rule. Last is an even smaller number of worthwhile targets in a few power-politically marginal but strategically important less developed countries.

In normal times, the greatest share of international informational exchange is taken up by constructive, inoffensive pursuits such as promotion of trade and tourism, presentation of cultural subjects through government-sponsored lecture tours, exhibits artistic performances and educational exchanges, or guided tours for influential personalities or opinion leaders from selected countries. If permitted, books, periodicals, newspapers, magazines, films, and tapes are made available to foreign audiences by free, direct distribution or through libraries, reading rooms, or information offices attached to diplomatic missions. Wealthy countries, for instance the United States, the West European states, the Soviet Union, Japan, and Saudi Arabia, offer direct financial contributions and informational materials to institutions of higher education, or to cultural organizations, or they endow professorial chairs in the hope or expectation that

---

* Approximately half the world's people are functionally illiterate; nearly three-quarters live in low-income countries. *World Bank, Development Report 1983*, p. 145.

† The new style of diplomacy received formal recognition on January 14, 1983 when President Reagan signed National Security Decision No. 77, setting up a special group to equip the United States for the new "public diplomacy." The central purpose of the decision of course was to compete more effectively with Soviet propaganda designed to win over the masses in the industrial democracies and other key states throughout the world.

accurate, objective (preferably of course favorable) information about the donor is made available in the receiving country.

At times of international tension, in the face of imminent threats in conjunction with an impending war, or to avert war, or lately, in conjunction with the arms competition, communications between nations increase markedly in volume and intensity. Covert flow—including defensive measures—begins to rival overt exchanges; straightforward diplomatic, commercial, or cultural information assumes a more militant if not military coloring. Instead of promotion of one's own image, increasing efforts and funds are expended to tear down or discredit the opposition. Almost imperceptibly, information blends into propaganda, disinformation, psychological warfare, and subversion until eventually peaceful and warlike information efforts become indistinguishable.

Propaganda

The Origins of Modern Propaganda

If ordinary information services may misrepresent the truth occasionally, propaganda in its modern form does little else.* Propaganda clearly has an aggressive, destructive edge. If ordinary information services may deviate occasionally from their basic objective, to present information for information's sake, propaganda typically has ulterior motives; usually it is designed to serve specific strategic-political, -military, or -economic ends. If aboveboard programs may occasionally be guilty of deliberate selectivity or even exaggeration, it is the very essence of propaganda to select what serves its purposes and to delete or suppress or blatantly deny what is not and generally replace the truth with artful products of distortion, falsification, misrepresentation, and, if need be, complete fabrication. Because no effective internal checks exist to challenge them, totalitarian regimes and other forms of dictatorship are prone to conceal

---

* Colin Cherry (1971), p. 113, reminds us that "The word propaganda was first used as an ecclesiastic term, being the name given the Committee of Cardinals in the Roman Curia 'Congregatio de propaganda fides' (congregation for the propagation of the faith), a committee charged with 'care and oversight of the foreign missions' of the Church." Van Dyke (1957), p. 340, outlines a modern version. Propaganda, he writes, involves informational efforts "to influence another state to follow, or not to follow, a specific course of action, without challenge to the existence or integrity of the other state and without challenge to its fundamental values and basic institutions." In time of war, or in preparation for war, continues Van Dyke, propaganda's purpose is "to bring about some kind of fundamental change which the government in the target state opposes—perhaps the overthrow of that government or the overthrow of the whole economic and political system within which it operates."

their banal, drab, often brutal and criminal side behind a propaganda facade of glittering but empty social myths.*

Propaganda was elevated to the status of prime instrument of national and international politics by the Fascist regime in Italy, by the Soviet rulers working partly through the Communist International, and eventually by the German National-Socialist regime under Adolf Hitler. Copying techniques employed by Lenin, Stalin, Mussolini, and (according to his diaries inspired also by American advertising techniques) Hitler's Minister for "Propaganda and People's Enlightenment," Dr. Joseph Goebbels, completely perverted the meaning of the latter term: whatever else Goebbels did, he certainly did not enlighten. Indeed, his most effective technique was first to assert, then brazenly defend, a lie so stark, so horrendous, as to be beyond belief that it was a lie.[4] Bringing under his control nearly all of Nazi Germany's public and private communication and information facilities, most of the press, all radio, the arts, writers, motion picture and theatre producers, and most actors, he and his associates proceeded to orchestrate continuing assaults on the minds and souls not only of the German people but of millions in other countries, including many of Germany's future victims and their leaders. The machine fashioned by Goebbels succeeded all too well in substantially misrepresenting to audiences at home and abroad the character and intentions of Nazi rule, maligning the motivations of Germany's antagonists and discrediting governments which stood in Hitler's way.

Working in tandem much of the time, fascism and communism raised propaganda to levels which some traditional political leaders may have aspired to attain but could never hope to reach. Eventually, the escalation brought on by the stridency and cynical abandon typical of revolutionary movements, coupled with their characteristic militancy and aggressiveness, made it most difficult on occasion to distinguish between legitimate information, political education and enlightenment, propaganda, and psychological warfare. The outbreak of the Second World War, and only that, awakened the Western democracies to the need for an appropriate response, but directed only at fascism, Nazism, and Japan. It was not until the Cold War in the late 1940s that systematic efforts were directed at communism and the Soviet Union.

Totalitarian rule by its very nature must deny its subjects free access to information likely to pose a challenge to its survival. Consequently, unable to deliver its message to the vast majority of the people of Eastern Europe and the Soviet Union by any other means, the United States and to a lesser extent

---

* It has been a time-honored propaganda device to discredit an opposing political system or government by impugning its motives. A favored method is to label any information emanating from that source as propaganda. For example, right-wing extremists in the U.S. are prone to regard as propaganda *any* information from Soviet sources, including for example an entirely accurate and faithful rendition of current communist political thought. Extremists in the Soviet Union return the compliment by describing as propaganda, for instance, a wholly accurate account of positive aspects of life in the United States.

its Western allies rely most heavily on shortwave broadcasts. A first step is to gain the attention and the confidence of the potential audience. This is accomplished by providing the news-starved listeners in Eastern Europe and the Soviet Union with a steady supply of accurate information about their own domestic as well as foreign affairs and generally about the international scene. Having gained their attention and hopefully also their confidence, they do more.

By such means as Radio Free Europe, later Radio Liberty, and the Voice of America (more through the former than the latter) United States announcers, aided by emigres from behind the Iron Curtain, analyze, dissect, and expose ideological weaknesses in Marxism, Leninism, and Stalinism, emphasizing the inadequacies and failings of contemporary socialist rule. In the main the aim is to counter regime efforts to conceal their shortcomings from their people, but occasionally broadcasts go over to militant attack.

In the early 1950s, U.S. broadcasts, conducted in part by the Central Intelligence Agency (CIA), actively encouraged listeners in Hungary, East Germany, and Poland to revolt. Indeed, listeners in Hungary actually understood the United States government to offer military assistance in the event of a successful overthrow of communist rule. Similar messages, though less explicit and eschewing any suggestion of military intervention, were directed at Poland in the early 1980s. Understandably, target regimes spare no efforts to interdict the flow of that type of information. But more on that later.

The Soviet Union, and to a lesser extent its associates in the Socialist bloc, lead the world by a wide margin in resources expended on propaganda, which should not be surprising as propaganda is of course one of the mainstays of totalitarian rule.* Serving the same or at least similar purposes, the cause of communism is propagated throughout the world by the international network of communist and affiliated political parties, associated movements, organizations, and interest groups, further augmented by front organizations, front publishing houses, bloc-owned banks, and other seemingly nonpolitical enterprises financed by the Soviet government or by its allies.†

* In 1981 the CIA estimated that the Soviet Union spends $700 million a year on the operating budget of Radio Moscow, which was broadcasting 2000 hours weekly in 82 languages over 285 high-powered transmitters. By contrast, the combined operating budgets of the Voice of America (VOA) and Radio Free Europe/Radio Liberty for fiscal year 1981 totalled approximately $200 million. At its peak, VOA broadcast in 46 languages and Radio Free Europe/Radio Liberty in 6 major languages of Eastern Europe and 15 languages of the Soviet Union. The Heritage Foundation, "Mobilizing the Airwaves . . ." *Backgrounder* No. 156 (November 13, 1981); see also Adelman (1981), pp. 913-936. In 1984, VOA broadcast directly 989 hours per week compared with 2,148 by the USSR.

† The East German Democratic Republic (DDR), for example, established a front organization in Luxembourg to finance the publishing house of the Greek Communist Party. Western intelligence officials believe that the same organization was also being used by the Soviet Union and other Eastern European states to further their interests by means of publicity placed in Western newspapers. *The New York Times* (October 7, 1982); see also Bretton (1980), p. 267.

Beginning with the 1917 revolution and until the middle of World War Two, the world communist network was organized by and directed tightly from Moscow through the

Communist regimes regard their own propaganda as the logical response to attempts by "the capitalist ruling classes" to undermine socialist rule, undo the achievements of the Revolution, and thus eliminate the only force capable of resisting and eventually defeating capitalism. Regarding their own systems as superior, they suspect that Western rulers wish to keep that fact from their own people. They see no reason to be apologetic about their efforts since the Western nations have numerous advantages in the propaganda contest. The contention is that as a result of centuries of indoctrination by deeply rooted, continuously and powerfully reinforced organized religion, by firmly entrenched educational systems and well financed private press, radio, and now television, and by a powerful capitalist global network of commerce, finance, and industry, the West can afford to be less obvious and militant in spreading its messages. Viewed from Moscow, the socialist camp has far to go before it can fully match these assets. To Lenin, religion was the opium of the masses. Now, from the socialist perspective, consumerism numbs people's ideological senses and slackens the revolutionary fervor of the masses, thus endangering the achievement of the Revolution and delaying further Marxism/Leninism's "scientifically" predicted victory.

The Soviet view tends to be born out by the record. Considering the extent and intensity of Soviet propaganda efforts ever since 1917, relatively little progress has been made. Indeed, the trend appears to be in the opposite direction. Everywhere, the campaign to capture for the Soviet Union at least the ideological leadership of twentieth-century revolutionary movements seems to have failed. It appears that in the war of words the same maxim applies as in the military version: attack requires greater effort than defense. Whereas communist and socialist propaganda everywhere faces an uphill struggle, its opponents need only reaffirm and reinforce existing traditions, values, and beliefs. For example, in the 1950s and 1960s, the Central Intelligence Agency, in an effort to counter increasingly aggressive Soviet propaganda in Western Europe, Africa, and parts of South America, secretly financed or subsidized cultural organizations, magazines, newspapers, and labor unions, without insisting that any of them endorse United States foreign policy objectives in every respect.*

The East–West conflict is of course not the only communications contest in the world. But whatever the issue, radio far outstrips all other media as far as the overwhelming majority of mankind is concerned. Although illiteracy is on

Communist International (Comintern). Following the Comintern's dissolution, the Communist Information Bureau (Cominform) was to coordinate worldwide propaganda efforts; the plan had to be abandoned in the wake of Soviet suppression of independent Communist movements in Hungary and Czechoslovakia in 1956 and 1968 respectively. Today, a less centralized mechanism still appears to be in operation, restricted mainly to propagation of Warsaw Pact policies and proposals, coordinated loosely by the Soviet Foreign Office and the KGB.

* Outstanding examples of such relatively independent bodies, on occasion even expressing views contrary to official U.S. positions, were the European Congress for Cultural Freedom and *Transition*, a high quality periodical serving as an outlet for the emerging Third World intelligentsia.

the wane—at least so it appears from official United Nations and World Bank statistics—the vast majority of people on earth neither read newspapers and magazines nor possess television sets; but most are in all probability within range of shortwave broadcasts. Now, thanks to the transistor the radio receiver has become affordable to the multitude. However, radio receivers, and to an extent the airwaves, are in many parts still under government control, and there has resulted the "cassette revolution."

In 1979 the Shah of Iran, with the aid of a highly efficient and brutal secret police network, seemed firmly in control of all means of internal and external communication in Iran. Yet highly inflammatory revolutionary messages demanding his overthrow, taped in exile by his principal opponent the Moslem leader Ayatollah Khomenei, reached the masses. Smuggled by cassette into Iran and there reproduced and distributed en masse, the Ayatollah's word eventually triggered a popular uprising, forcing the Shah's departure. The success inspired the Ayatollah's followers now in power to attempt to replicate the feat by introducing similar messages, for similar purposes, into neighboring Moslem states.*

The Structure of Propaganda

Professionals distinguish between three types of propaganda: white, gray, and black. The first conveys straightforward, mainly objective, though of course selective, information; the source is correctly identified. To establish and main-

---

* Interesting examples of propaganda both strikingly successful and acting as a boomerang were reported by the former high-ranking South Vietnamese Communist leader Truong Nhu Tang, commenting on the betrayal of his South Vietnamese "Liberation Movement" by the North Vietnamese. While confronting powerful U.S. forces, the Communists established the myth that theirs was a war of national liberation to free the people of South Vietnam from any and all foreign oppression. However, with victory over U.S. and South Vietnamese anti-Communist forces assured, the Communist leadership of North Vietnam ordered the Southern National Liberation Front (NFL) dissolved, terminating all talk of Southern liberation. A propaganda myth had triumphed only to be shelved at the first opportunity.

Earlier, there had been the celebrated Tet offensive, an all-out assault, mainly by NFL forces, on the anti-Communist South Vietnamese and United States positions. According to Tang: "Unfortunately the Tet offensive also proved catastrophic to our [NFL] plans. It is a major irony of the Vietnamese war that our propaganda transformed this military debacle into a brilliant victory, giving us leverage in our diplomatic efforts, inciting the American antiwar movement to even stronger and more optimistic resistance, and disheartening the Washington planners." "The Myth of a Liberation," *The New York Review of Books* (October 21, 1982), p. 32.

In 1963, the then foreign minister of the PRC, Chou En-Lai, mainly to outdo Soviet propaganda, announced upon his arrival in Kenya that Africa was "ripe for revolution." This positively terrified the majority of the newly established, exceedingly unstable regimes throughout the continent. As a result, the PRC suffered a decisive defeat in its propaganda war against the Soviet Union. Similarly, tons of Chinese Communist propaganda material featuring translations from "Chairman Mao's 'Little Red Book,'" presented as gifts "to the African peoples," rarely if ever were distributed by the governments so honored. These materials became wholly counterproductive with Mao Zedongs death and disgrace.

tain its credibility, this type occasionally offers the unvarnished truth. White propaganda "conforms to the policies of the government for which it speaks."[5] The black variant misrepresents its true source, has clearly subversive intent, is not committed to present the truth but seeks to achieve its objectives by legitimate means or by deceit, "and is disowned by the government using it."[6] The gray version may or may not present true accounts but in any case leaves the listener or reader guessing as to the source. Propaganda and psychological warfare specialists utilize all forms, mixing them up on occasion for better effect.*

All propaganda, white, gray, or black, like all routine information activities generally, tends to reflect national, ideological, cultural, or other prejudices and perspectives. Thus official communications originating with Western governments, for example the government of the United States, are likely to speak of "free world," "democracy," "free enterprise," as though these terms conveyed precise meaning. Western military measures serve world peace, Soviet measures constitute aggression. Communications originating with Soviet bloc regimes are likely to propound the virtues of "socialism," "people's democracy," "wars of national liberation," "people's government" or "the people's will." Hitler was an expert in the use of the disarming word "peace" and so are Soviet rulers when they advocate "peaceful coexistence" with the West but mean that the United States and its allies are not to attack the Soviet Union while the latter remains free to support "wars of national liberation" wherever and whenever these occur or are encouraged to occur, by Soviet propaganda.[7] U.S. propaganda regarding Latin America, for example, tends to identify friendly regimes as democratic, or at worst authoritarian but anticommunist: while the Soviets and Radio Havana in Cuba identify regimes or forces friendly to them as "peace-loving" or "people's national liberation" fronts. From that perspective, Western forces aiding the anti-Soviet Afghans in their effort to remain outside the Soviet sphere are "imperialists."†

In short, the "double-speak" of Orwell's *1984* does indeed serve the propaganda efforts of most governments today. "Free" may mean captive or at best dependent. "Liberation" in all probability is a prelude to suppression. The demand for "one man, one vote" does not invariably usher in democracy. It means instead: one man, one vote, *once,* and the "people's democracies" exist not so

---

* Sometimes this confuses the originating government as well, as for example when agents of the CIA beamed broadcasts into Ethiopia from a ship stationed off the East African coast, pretending that these originated with a rebel group inside that country. The broadcasts seemed so genuine that another U.S. agency, the Federal Broadcast Information Service (FBIS) disseminated transcripts to all interested agencies in Washington; on the distribution list was of course the CIA which at first was not aware that the purported Ethiopian rebel movement was a phantom of its own making. Marchetti and Marks (1974), pp. 159-160.

† Soviet armed forces, assassinating the Afghan head of state Hafizullah Amin in 1979, then invading the country outright, bringing along a pro-Soviet government, are merely "extending assistance to the legitimate government," aiding a "fraternal people in their struggle against imperialism." Western plans to resist such moves are routinely labeled by Soviet organs as "aggressive imperialist designs to oppress and exploit."

much for the benefit of the people as for the benefit of a small band of political party bureaucrats. At the other end of the political spectrum, corrupt, murderous rightwing dictators in Latin America or in racist South Africa, for example, unhesitatingly represent themselves as the benefactors of the masses and their genuinely aggrieved opponents as communists, terrorists, or, at best, as traitors. In that respect, they are no different from communist leaders who routinely and without offering proof of any kind refer to themselves as "representatives of the working class," although it should be noted that they at least, in their constitution and official pronouncements, concede—however hackneyed that phrase may be—that theirs also is a dictatorship albeit "of the proletariat."

Psychological Warfare*

We noted earlier that ancient Germanic tribes, partly to frighten their enemies, partly to give themselves courage, immediately before as well as during battle often emitted terrifying howls enhanced by blowing horns and screaming women drawn up behind battle formations. Modern versions of this type of assault are more sophisticated, of course. But whether employed in conjunction with war or in preparations for war, psychological warfare has one major objective, to influence civilian as well as military audiences within enemy territory or within territories soon expected to be hostile. By written and spoken word, by pictorial display or poster, by music and other art forms, and by steady drumbeat using all available means of communication, an attempt is made to adversely affect a hostile or nonhostile but projected target state's capacity to resist or sustain its war effort. (Matching efforts to enhance one's own capacity to wage and sustain war is the responsibility of home front counterpsychological warfare which promotes confidence in ultimate victory by exaggerating or misrepresenting military events favoring one's own side and downplaying or falsifying enemy successes.)

Preparing for its all-out assault on Poland, and subsequently on Belgium, the Netherlands, and France, the Nazi psychological war effort between 1939 and 1940 succeeded in undermining the self-confidence and belief in their military capacity on the part of key civilian and military personnel in all target countries. In this effort—not to be confused with ordinary propaganda—they used to maximum advantage radio broadcasts and films shown to selected foreign audiences in target countries. For example, following the defeat of Poland and the destruction of Warsaw in 1939, films of the systematic destruction of Warsaw were shown to audiences in the West, graphic depiction of agony, death, and destruction enhanced by insertion into the soundtrack of mechanically induced scream effects of "Stuka," planes especially designed to bomb accurately as well as terrify.

---

* Although conducted occasionally by uniformed members of armed forces, psychological warfare in the main is the product and responsibility of civilian personnel and agencies; hence it is more appropriately discussed here. Strictly speaking it is not a military operation.

On the allied side, psychological warfare was described by one of the United States' most successful practitioners, William J. Donovan, as being aimed at "persuasion, penetration, and intimidation . . . the modern counterpart of sapping and mining in the siege warfare of former days."[8] During World War Two, the list of "black" psychological warfare operations considered or actually executed by the "Morale Operations Branch" of the Office of Strategic Services (OSS–MO) included: Spreading of false rumors, operation of "freedom" radio stations in enemy territory or outside but so as to be able to convey the impression that the station is located in enemy territory, dropped leaflets and false documents, the organization and support of fifth column activities by grants, trained personnel and supplies and the use of agents, "all for the purpose of creating confusion, division and undermining the morale of the enemy."[9] During that war, especially toward the end, the Morale Operations Branch conducted "white" and "black" warfare, interchangeably. For instance, the "black" operation would spread unfounded rumors of an impending appearance by Hitler at a rally; when Hitler predictably failed to appear, "white" sources explained his nonappearance, which was once again followed by "black" suggesting mysterious reasons, that he was dead, that he was insane, that serious divisions were rending the party asunder—all of these rumors, fabrications, and speculations being promptly and faithfully reported by "white."*

"Disinformation" and Other Deceptions

Whereas psychological warfare is primarily designed to disorient, confuse, demoralize, and destabilize an enemy population or elite, the aim of "disinformation" and other deceptions is primarily to discredit actual or potential enemies mostly by operations in third countries.† Although the United States Department of State suggests that this form of informational warfare is a uniquely Soviet device, all countries actually engage in such practices more or less, probably few however on the scale practiced by the Soviet government, a regime, as we noted earlier, thriving on secrecy and maintaining itself largely with the aid of propaganda.[10]

The principal Soviet instrument in this and similar covert undertakings is the KGB (Committee for State Security). Unlike its principal counterpart, the

* U.S. War Department (1976), pp. 217–218. Another illustration of World War II psychological warfare, mixing white occasionally with black, was the "Soldatensender West," an Anglo-American venture. A powerful sender, it offered German armed forces straightforward nonpropaganda entertainment of the highest quality, designed to attract and hold listeners. In addition, however, a political cabaret very popular in Europe offered subtle Allied propaganda for ten months during the final crucial phases of the war. *Ibid.,* p. 219.

† These measures may also be employed to soften public opinion in third countries, rendering them more conducive to the manipulator's foreign policy objectives. Massive deception was practiced by the Allies in World War Two to prevent the Germans from discovering that Allied intelligence was reading their top-most secrets. As Churchill put it: "In war-time, truth is so precious that it should always be attended by a bodyguard of lies." A.C. Brown (1975), p. 10.

American CIA, the KGB combines secret police, espionage and counter-espionage functions, is accountable only to the Politburo, itself a totally secret body, and can if need be rely on two sets of external supports, all overt and covert foreign facilities available to the other members of the Soviet bloc, including their secret police and secret services and most communist parties abroad. Also available to a lesser extent are the previously mentioned political, commercial, and cultural front organizations. Through these channels, a range of what the Soviet calls *active measures* are undertaken in a massive effort to undermine the United States' standing in allied and neutral countries, discredit U.S. diplomatic and especially military initiatives directed against the Soviet Union, and generally sow division and discord among Western allies. According to the U.S. Department of State, "The approaches used by Moscow include control of the press in foreign countries; outright and partial forgery of documents; use of rumors, insinuation, altered facts, and lies; use of international and local front organizations; clandestine operation of radio stations; exploitation of a nation's academic, political, economic and media figures as collaborators to influence policies of the nation."[11]

Specifically, the Soviet Union is accused of placing falsely attributed press material into the media of foreign countries, forging letters designed to embarrass the U.S. and purporting to have been sent by the president of the United States or other high-ranking officers to foreign governments, spreading rumors, for example that the United States was behind the seizure of the Grand Mosque of Mecca in late 1979, or insinuating that the presence of a high-ranking U.S. official in a given country presaged a coup against the government there. The State Department further charged that the "active measures" campaign is waged largely through organizations which are probably unaware of being used. However, if the enemies of the Soviet Union fail to match its efforts in these respects, it is not for want of trying.

Each and every one of the accusations cited by the State Department can be levelled against the United States and many of its allies. Although far less powerful than the KGB, the CIA and to an extent the secret services of Great Britain, Canada, the United States, France, West Germany, and Japan, can rely on channels, organizations, and facilities far more numerous, far better established, and more representative of the majority of the people in target states than can be said of most of the means available to the Soviet Union and its allies.[12]

Restricting the Flow of Information

The efforts by totalitarian rulers to erect a protective screen around their subjects and to control the outflow of information is not new. In the 1920s and 1930s, the two fascist regimes, the German more than the Italian, imposed strict limits on what their people could read, listen to on the radio, see on stage or at exhibits, or even think. The Nazi regime for instance ordered the removal of shortwave bands from radio receivers available to the public, imposed heavy penalties to discourage listening to the British Broadcasting Corporation's or Radio Moscow's international broadcasts, imposed general censorship of all internal media, and restricted the supply of foreign newspapers and magazines sufficiently to minimize the danger of mass contamination from these sources. Both regimes also imposed strict controls on what foreign journalists could report about their respective countries, especially about political events there and about the leaders. Foreign journalists were importuned, cajoled, enticed, bluntly threatened, or bribed to refrain from reporting news unfavorable to the regime, or to serve the regime by reporting only what was favorable. Used as instruments of coercion were deportation, threats of deportation, and extension or refusal of special favors such as permits or grants of newsworthy sought-after interviews likely to produce journalistic scoops.[13]

More recently, the totalitarian Soviet bloc nations have begun to impose draconic penalties to prevent their own citizens from transmitting to foreigners, in any form whatsoever, what the regimes term "state secrets" but much of which would in open societies be regarded as legitimate information which all people should be entitled to share. To cast the net as widely as possible, prohibitions are held sufficiently vague to inhibit all contacts with foreigners, which in effect restricts information outflow to official channels. It is interesting that the flow of information is censored and controlled also between "fraternal" socialist states within the Soviet bloc, especially when one of them, like Poland in 1981, shows signs of wanting to break from the fold.

Equally sensitive are the chronically insecure rulers of unstable newly in-dependent states. One of their principal concerns centers on what they regard as a tendency in Western coverage of events in the non-Western world to give vent to racial, ethnic, cultural, or political prejudice. They also complain of a lack of understanding and appreciation on the part of the Western press of the special circumstances under which long neglected, underdeveloped countries must be ruled and administered. Correspondents from Western countries, of course, view things differently. To them, authoritarian or totalitarian rule is anathema, suppression of human rights, corruption in government, or economic mismanagement are newsworthy and they report accordingly; but proponents of dictatorship of one kind or another are in the majority today and together they can, in theory at least, impose on the world their own version of freedom of the press.*

* At the 1976 General Conference of UNESCO, a coalition of Soviet-led and Third World states supported a resolution entitled "Declaration of Fundamental Principles Governing the Uses of the Mass Media in Strengthening Peace and International Understanding and in Combating War, Propaganda, Racism, and Apartheid." To the Western powers this had all the markings of an attempt to impose on the world the Soviet prescription for world peace through social revolution, establishment of dictatorships of the proletariat, totalitarian rule, and its mainstays police state control and censorship. To the U.S. it looked like an attempt to exclude Western journalists from Third World countries and include Soviet bloc journalists. United Nations *Chronicle*, Vol. XX, No. 1 (January 1983), pp. 40–44.

In the rapidly intensifying competition between the relatively open and the relatively closed societies, mainly between East and West, the latter is under a distinct disadvantage in yet another potentially damaging respect. In the United States, for example, legislation like the Freedom of Information Act enables not only United States citizens but the world generally—by simply acting through sympathetic U.S. citizens, probably lawyers—to obtain information which in the Soviet Union, East Germany, or the People's Republic of China could be obtained only at enormous risk, including the penalty of death. Even without special legislation, political democracies either because it is constitutionally mandated or because of a commitment to free market economies, hence to free exchange of information, place no restrictions whatever on vital statistics, economic data, most technical information, or data pertaining to public political processes. Thus any agent of any one of the 160states in the world, including agents of the totalitarian regimes, can openly purchase from the government printing offices in Washington, London, Paris, or Bonn what it would require a secret agent to purloin at great personal risk from government agencies in Moscow, East Berlin, Warsaw, Prague, or Beijing. Moreover, in the United States, provided they register with the federal authorities and properly identify their product, agents of most countries are allowed to lobby for their respective governments and openly disseminate their propaganda. Restrictions are imposed only on the basis of reciprocity, the U.S. insisting that agents as well as diplomats from other countries be granted the same or similar privileges and opportunities as their respective regimes are inclined to grant to representatives of the United States.

Suggested Questions and Discussion Topics

What are the several levels, the responsibilities, and the functions of diplomats?

How do technological advances affect diplomacy and diplomats' roles?

What are diplomacy's principal products?

What is the central purpose of propaganda in contemporary international relations and what are the major instrumentalities governments employ in this regard?

Compare and contrast information, propaganda, psychological warfare, and disinformation.

Chapter 5
Monetary Policy and Finance*

In order to introduce the reader to the fundamentals of international economics, Chapter 2, although devoted to *sources of power,* of necessity also touched upon some aspects of international financial and trade *relations.* However, in a general discussion, critical specifics are easily overlooked. To provide an overview of the more essential *instrumentalities* nations employ in their economic relations, we shall summarize here what was broached in an introductory context in the previous discussion and present more adequately what was not.

A brief explanation is also in order regarding the distinction between normal economic relations and economic warfare. Anyone familiar with economics knows that most if not all economic transactions have a sharp edge, and that especially under capitalism—though increasingly also under socialism—economics tends to be a zero-sum game, a matter of survival of the fittest. What then is the distinction between what we call normal economic relations and economic warfare? Where does one end and the other begin? As generally understood, economic warfare reflects unfriendly or even hostile large-scale, substantive, deliberate state action involving one or more economic measures intended to achieve a particular *noneconomic* diplomatic, political, or military objective. One should regard as entirely normal sharp competition even occasional retaliatory acts, as long as they serve only or at least principally economic ends. Inevitably some acts will straddle the dividing line.

---

* Monetary Policy "is that part of [public] economic policy which regulates the level of money and liquidity in the economy in order to achieve some desired policy objective, such as the control of inflation, an improvement in the balance of payments, a certain level of employment, or growth in the Gross National Product." Graham Bannock, R.E. Baxter, and Ray Reed. *The Penguin Dictionary of Economics.* (Hammondsworth, Middlesex, England: Penguin Books, Ltd., 1972), p. 286. Finance "is the provision of money, when and where required." *Ibid.,* p. 163. Balance of payments is a tabulation of the credit and debit transactions of a country with foreign countries and international institutions. *Ibid.,* p. 26.

The International Monetary System

Although the reader is at this point aware of the existence of an international monetary system, it should be helpful if we were to summarize its essential characteristics.*

Basically, international monetary transactions are between private individuals, public and private commercial and financial enterprises, individual organizations, or combinations of these. Private or public, because national economies are invariably affected, governments are always interested parties in any such transactions. If intervention is required government always can fall back on regulatory powers. Financial transactions are by means of instruments conveying a specific purchasing power. Some transactions may be by notes, promises, or pledges and most utilize one or more currencies—that is to say they use whatever nations issue as their money. Virtually all nations have their own distinct currency, partly as a matter of prestige but mainly to safeguard national sovereignty and independence.†

Working in the opposite direction, away from the imperative of national sovereignty toward international interdependence, is the imperative of international trade. Because national currencies may fluctuate widely in their value relative to other currencies, some integrative mechanism must exist to facilitate exchanges between *national* money systems.[1] That mechanism is the *international* monetary system. The latter is the natural product of trade, but this does not apply to the international monetary *order*. As formulated by Cohen: "The international monetary order . . . is the legal and conventional framework within which this mechanism of interchange operates—the set of governing procedures to which the system is subject, either explicitly or implicitly. Control [over the system] is exerted through policies implemented at the national level and [through] interacting at the international level. Formally or informally, the monetary order specifies which instruments of national policy may be used and which targets of policy may be regarded as legitimate."[2] Such an order may cover a limited number of countries within a specific trade zone or geographically limited region for example, or a political bloc, or it may span the globe.

Because all orders or suborders and all systems to a greater or lesser degree interact in monetary as well as in all other respects, all systems, local and international, large and small, and all international orders must be viewed individually as well as in relation to each other. Of special interest to the student of international relations are the reasons why rates of exchange (foreign exchange rates) between the world currencies fluctuate and what bearing this has on international politics.

* Benjamin J. Cohen (1977), p. 3, uses the following definition of a system: "An aggregation of diverse entities united by regular inter-action according to some form of control."

† As we shall see, that is one of many illusions: where economies are interdependent, the moment a new currency is issued, or an old one traded abroad, sovereignty is thereby diminished.

Money performs several basic functions; foremost it is a measure and a means of storage of value, a means of settling debts. It takes various forms—currency (principally coin and paper money), bank deposits, credit, checks in circulation, and so forth. Today, issuance, circulation, rate of increase, and decrease of its supply within a nation are the responsibility exclusively of national governments or institutions to whom that responsibility is delegated; typically it is the responsibility of the central banks. Total money supply at any given time is calculated in the aggregate and regulated by estimating the requirements of the national economy, including its obligations abroad. But data are inexact, unknown variables affecting the economy abound, and not all of the known ones can be accurately assessed.* For our purposes most important is the fluctuation of value of a given currency in terms of currencies of major trading partners.†

The reasons for normal fluctuations vary. Is a given currency in over-supply; that is, does the economy for whose benefit it is issued show too much money available and not enough goods and services to buy? In that event, foreign holders of that currency will try to dispose of it, driving down its value vis-à-vis other world currencies. Or has a given nation assumed a greater debt than it can service, through excessive imports for example? Is its government unstable or economically incompetent? On the other hand, a currency's value in terms of other currencies rises with increased confidence in the issuing state's ability to manage its finances and economy and to balance its trade with other nations. That currency is most valuable which can easily and readily be converted either into gold—which was the case when nations were using the gold standard or,

---

* In 1983, economists estimated that $100 billion "is disappearing from the books of the world economy [annually]." The U.S. alone showed a shortfall of $41 billion in 1982. Peter T. Kilborn, *The New York Times* (July 29, 1983). That alone introduces an element of uncertainty and imprecision into economic analysis and forecast.

† Periodically, fluctuations of foreign exchange rates exceed the capacity of corrective mechanisms available to governments. In that event, governments, financiers, and traders speak of foreign exchange crises. A crisis may be the result of deliberate manipulative action or inaction by one or more governments, or it may arise more or less accidentally from one or more countries' domestic politics or economics, or it may be the unintended by-product of an international event.

Among internal nonmanipulative causes, the following may produce a foreign exchange crisis: 1) advent of a government proposing seemingly unsound economic, financial, or monetary policies; 2) advent of a government hostile to business interests; 3) adoption by a government of an economically damaging and inhibiting tax; 4) advent of an unstable government or destabilization of a previously stable one; 5) unpopularity of a government, causing resistance to its measures; 6) threat of or actual civil war; 7) failure of a government to keep its economy in order, discharge its debts, or service its obligations. Among external, international developments, the following may precipitate a foreign exchange crisis: 1) significant pressure or an attack by traders, investors, or speculators, or by other governments on a dominant world currency, like the U.S. dollar; 2) an abrupt transnational shift of substantial deposits or holdings of a major world currency from one country to another; 3) a sharp upturn in an arms race or deterioration in relations between two or more major powers or between their allies; 4) war or threat of war. The foregoing list is adapted from Einzig (1968), pp. 99ff. In the way of a historical note, a relatively minor movement on international money markets can trigger a major foreign exchange crisis. On the other hand, the outbreak and course of World War One did not upset the world's monetary equilibrium; World War Two, however, did.

as in the case of the United States until 1971, declared their readiness to so convert it—or can be exchanged at favorable and predictable rates into raw materials, manufactured goods, or needed services.*

The gold standard came into use around 1870 partly to cope with the consequences of trade imbalances, partly to provide an internationally acceptable standard of value. The rules of the gold standard were primarily expected to accomplish two objectives, first to bring a degree of stability to trade among nations and second to prevent any one nation from gaining too great an advantage over its competitors. At the root of this problem complex is the balance of payments, that is, the balance between the funds a nation takes in as a result of exports and the funds it owes others as a result of imports (technically, the balance between the credit and debit transactions of a country with foreign countries and international institutions). A nation enjoying a favorable balance of payments can with the increase in financial strength expand its economy, partly by attracting funds fleeing from states already disadvantaged, in search of higher interest rates or more lucrative investment opportunities. This in turn tends to cause a rise in unemployment and political repercussions in the disadvantaged countries, threatening to set off chain reactions throughout the world. Without an agreed upon standard, adversely affected countries would try to defend their economies by drastic measures, which would further disrupt international trade. Under the gold standard, participating nations were expected to hold the value of their national currencies firm in terms of the price of gold—with only minor variance—exchange their national currency for a set amount of gold upon demand, and expand or contract their own domestic money supply in direct proportion to inflow or outflow of gold resulting from their international commercial or financial transactions.

The standard worked reasonably well until about the eve of World War One. The exigencies of war preparation, the war itself, and its catastrophic aftermath proved too much. By 1931 political reality caught up with economic theory. The standard's utility was undermined when participating nations insisted that, all rules of the game notwithstanding, they should remain unalterably sovereign and independent, free to cope with the vagaries of national and international economics as their respective governments saw fit. Partly giving rise to this position, partly flowing from it, was the growing diversity of economic and political systems and of economic and political objectives based on these.

---

* Why is convertibility important to international trade? In the course of trade, nations accumulate holdings of other countries' currencies; especially favored are those of countries with a strong production potential, for example the United States, Great Britain, West Germany, or Japan. If a government has publicly declared a commitment to exchange any units of its currency for, let us say, gold (or for another hard currency [see note p. 92 below]) countries are prepared to risk holding more of the latter than they may be able to use on a short-term basis. The moment convertibility is restricted or terminated, confidence in the issuing country's word and credit drops. Moreover, holders of that country's currency try to dispose of all or most of their holdings, driving down its value, upsetting trade balances, and triggering yet other economically unsettling consequences.

Simultaneously, reflecting the free market philosophy dominant in Western democracies and contravening insistence on national sovereignty, holders of large accumulations of finance capital remained free to shuttle their funds from nation to nation in search of higher return, upsetting in the course of these financial peregrinations the economic, political, and social objectives of their respective home governments and disrupting international trade in the process.

Furthermore, social change and in some countries social revolution broadened the base of government, rendering national, let alone international, economic and financial management ever more difficult and the economies ever less controllable. The demise of the gold standard seemed imminent when a decade prior to World War One, to meet the costs of armament and of the then anticipated military conflict, the leading trading nations removed all restraints on increase of their own national currency supply. The Russian Revolution, the Great Depression, the fascist upheaval in Germany (a key trading nation), and eventually World War Two and its consequences finally removed any premise upon which a revived gold standard could be based.

Desiring to retain some functions of the precious metal while freeing themselves from the excessive rigors of the gold standard, the world's financial leaders devised the modified *gold-exchange* standard. Under this system, the exchange of currency for gold on demand was dropped. Instead, central banks of participating countries agreed upon demand to exchange their own currency for "hard currency," that is, currency backed by gold, foremost the U.S. dollar, the British *pound,* the French *franc,* the German *mark.* The gold-exchange standard also was the linchpin holding together the international monetary (Bretton Woods) system developed after World War Two.* That system collapsed in 1971, starting a search for workable alternatives.

The volatility of the post-Bretton Woods means and mechanisms of settling international accounts necessitated special defensive measures by the major trading nations. Gold standard or not, as a rule imports must be paid for in currencies acceptable to the exporter, who may be a private individual or a corporation but whose government always is an interested party. Exporters will accept payment only in values they recognize, either the equivalent in goods or services or, more likely these days, in currency no longer backed by gold but convertible nonetheless into other desirable currencies or at least acceptable to sellers with something of value to sell. Under the new dispensation, realistically viewed, acceptable "hard" currencies are those which are internationally transferable, issued by countries capable of high productivity of goods and enjoying a degree of economic, hence social and political, stability likely to allow their

---

* As we shall show in detail in Chapter 11, the system performed well mainly because it rested, in the final analysis, on the strength and potential of the U.S. economy and the overall soundness of the dollar as a substitute, or as a reserve currency, taking the place of gold. For the system to function properly the U.S. dollar had to be exchangeable for gold.

currency to remain valuable in the eyes of major business and financial interests in the trading capitals of the world.*

Still a maxim of economic policy throughout the world is the notion that the strength of a state to a large extent is a function of its financial independence. This conviction is strongest in times of national peril, where an international crisis threatens for example or shortly before and during a war. Partly to prepare for such contingencies, partly to ward off lesser threats, governments are under constant pressure to acquire and maintain a reserve in the currencies of their major trading partners or in a world reserve currency, such as the U.S. dollar. A state whose government allows its foreign exchange reserve to dwindle below minimal national requirements must either cut back sharply on imports or it will be at the mercy of its creditors and competitors.†

The major trading nations, foremost the U.S., Western European countries, and Japan, require reserves in each other's currencies for defensive reasons of yet another kind. Once currency values are free-floating, that is, depend on supply and demand, a major trading nation's international economic position (and if export accounts for a significant portion of that, its domestic economy as well) ride more than ever on its ability to defend its currency; this is so mainly because a state's export capacity depends to a critical extent on the value of its currency in terms especially of its principal competitors. If for example the U.S. dollar increases in value vis-à-vis the British pound, it requires more of the latter to buy the same amount of U.S. goods. At the same time, because fewer dollars buy the same amount of British goods, U.S. importers prefer to "buy British." In that event, U.S. exports decline, unemployment in the U.S. increases. When the reverse occurs, the British economy suffers and the U.S. economy prospers. To defend their own currencies and improve their country's economic position, central bankers in New York, London, Bonn, Paris, Zürich, or Tokyo may offer to buy or sell substantial amounts of their competitor's currency on the world financial markets. An offer to buy will tend

---

* "Hard" currencies are traded internationally and are consistently in great demand mainly because they are issued by states with high performance economies, which tends to guaranty stable exchange-rates. "Soft" currencies, on the other hand, are not much in demand—some not at all—mainly because they are issued by states plagued by unstable or exceedingly weak economies, which tends to subject these currencies to frequent, often sharp exchange-rate fluctuations. Leading "hard" currencies, in addition to the U.S. dollar, are the Japanese *yen*, the British *pound*, the French *franc*, the Swiss *franc*, and the West German *Deutschmark*. Blocked currencies are those which may not be exported from the issuing country and cannot therefore be used to settle international accounts, hence are not subject to international monetary valuations or fluctuations. Their value vis-à-vis other currencies is artificially set or "pegged" by government decree. The Soviet *ruble* is a prime example.

† Absence of an adequate foreign exchange reserve has several additional consequences. Other states, aware of the deficiency, are reluctant to trade with such a state for fear that their bills will not be paid; the state has become a poor risk. This can be serious as critical needs arise, urgent acquisition of spare parts for key industrial plants for example, or medical supplies to combat an epidemic, or arms and other military supplies for defense. Availability of ample foreign exchange reserves also enables states to stockpile critical raw materials when prices are low.

to stimulate a rise of its value vis-à-vis other currencies, an offer to sell may have the opposite effect.*

International Finance and Development

Most of the world's less developed countries (LDC) experience great difficulty balancing the costs of imports with the proceeds from exports. These countries find it even more difficult to build up and maintain sufficient foreign exchange to cover contingencies such as a catastrophic drop in the world market price of their principal, sometimes sole, export commodity.† Whatever the state of their foreign exchange reserve, it must be subjected to firm government control, mainly to prevent squandering of that precious resource by private interests capriciously satisfying personal tastes and needs at the expense of national development or security goals; an example would be purchase of luxury goods and other consumption priorities urged upon them by high pressure salespersons from the advanced industrial countries. Since most of the LDCs have yet to create an adequate industrial capacity, they are compelled for decades to come to import first of all the machinery and technology needed to extract or produce their principal export commodities, typically raw materials. Next they need to import rails and rolling stock, fertilizer to increase production of agricultural commodities and keep up production of food for their own increasing population; they need road-building equipment, construction material for housing, manu- facturing or processing plants for hydroelectric power stations and dams. For one or another reason many governments feel compelled to add to the list arms and equipment, including planes, ships, and costly missiles, and more recently also the wherewithal for production of nuclear energy.

Among special controls imposed are strict limitations on the amount of foreign currency a citizen may hold; also, all foreign trade is conducted through

* Another way of looking at this: When a currency let us say of country A falls in value vis-à-vis one or more other currencies, let us say of countries B and C, the goods and services of country A become less expensive—it takes less of country B or C's currency to buy a given good or service from A. Conversely, it requires more of A currency to buy from B or C, which is to say that exports from B and C become more expensive. Country A tends to benefit from this state of affairs, B and C do not. Currency A may have dropped in value because of deliberate measures by its government—it may have wished to increase exports and thereby employment, or decrease imports by making them more expensive, or both. In any case, where an international agency exists to adjust such imbalances, the governments of B and C would insist that A's currency not deviate in value more than permitted by international agreements—it is to stay within a certain "band." In the absence of such an agency, or firm international agreement, the governments of B and C, through their respective central banks which are in charge of such matters, will quickly seek to buy up sufficient quantities of A's currency to signal to currency markets of the world that they are prepared to buy, hence drive up the price. These are defensive measures designed to prevent B and C from losing ground in economic competition against A.

† They suffer, in other words, from adverse "terms of trade," that is, the ratio between the index of prices they receive for their exports and the index of prices they must pay for their imports shows the latter higher than the former.

government agencies whose permission must be obtained before export or import are allowed. If permission is granted to import, only the stated equivalent in foreign currency will be released for that specific purpose. Citizens who earn foreign currencies through export are obliged to turn these in at the central national bank in exchange for the national currency, at an official rate set by the government. Typically, that rate is set to maximize government revenue and does not reflect the currency's true international exchange value. In many instances the latter may be very close to zero. As a result, exporters resort to subterfuge in an attempt to retain in secure foreign banks as large a share of the sales price as possible. By the same token, lacking confidence in their own national currency, citizens tend to smuggle large quantities to neighboring countries, there to be exchanged if at all possible for "hard" foreign currencies, at heavily discounted rates. Who will buy such currency, at discount? Speculators and foreigners who must do business in the country in question. To interdict this illicit traffic, governments impose drastic penalties for unauthorized export of their own national currency and unauthorized import of that of others.*

Finance as an Instrument of International Politics

Today, though many political leaders and public officials still are unable to grasp national let alone international finance in all of its ramifications and implications, few fail to recognize that without plentiful, ready-to-use or liquid finance the state cannot long survive. What is adequate finance? Theoretically, each state has a minimum threshhold—more a broad band than a fine line, of course—below which its financial means may not drop. If financial resources—currently available liquid resources as well as reserves—are allowed to fall below that level, unemployment increases, the economy falters, some sectors may fall into irreversible disrepair, social and political instability increase, national defense is endangered, and the nation's standing in the world deteriorates. Traditionally, governments look to the balance of payments for indications of trouble. If all financial transactions with foreign countries and international institutions show an excess of credits over debits, or inflow of foreign funds exceeds outflow, the balance of payments is said to be favorable and the international facet of the economy is believed to be sound. But in today's progressively complex world that may well be an illusion.

In theory, the world might be blessed with unlimited resources and infinitely expandable production and consumption capacities. Realistically, all indications

---

* The following are common reasons for currency smuggling: Currency of country A may not inspire confidence because too much is being printed too readily, frequently to enable the government to pay for frivolous or unproductive projects. Or the economy of country A is steadily growing weaker, is unstable, or the country is unstable as a whole. Holders of that currency tend to fear that unless they transfer it promptly, selling it for other currencies, even at a loss, they may end up holding nothing at all. Aside from many less developed countries, totalitarian countries like Nazi Germany (1933–1945) and all contemporary socialist countries whose economies are centrally planned and controlled practice tight foreign exchange control, imposing severe penalties for currency smuggling.

are that at least some of the earth's more essential resources and capacities are limited, some are finite, and in any case, problems are mounting and it is not possible, therefore, for all nations to achieve and maintain a favorable balance of payments. Someone's favorable balance translates into a negative balance somewhere else in the world; someone's economic success spells someone else's failure. To an extent this has always been the case, but it is rapidly becoming more apparent by the steadily progressing interdependence of the world's economies. Enlightened statesman today are inclined to accept the principle that to live in today's world also means to let live; in other words, to pile up financial resources at the expense of others can be self-defeating. Still, logical or not, rational or irrational, internal pressure impels individual governments in their foreign policies to place domestically attractive but dubious, possibly self-defeating short-term interests above what in the long term may actually be of advantage to them as well as their trading partners.

However inclined in that regard, governments feel compelled, aside from the power to create money and regulate its circulation, to retain a degree of control over all foreign financial and trade transactions likely to affect their national monetary position. We saw that the totalitarian systems can accomplish this more readily and more thoroughly than can the relatively permissive, free-trade, free market oriented political democracies. By the same token, if at all feasible all major powers seek to establish and maintain direct or indirect control, or at least secure a dependable degree of leverage, over the monetary policies, including currency valuation and banking and investment practices of the weaker among their trading partners.

If the target proves recalcitrant or uncooperative, governments resort to combinations of indirect measures to achieve their objectives. While most of the free market currencies were tied to the gold standard, there was the option of forcing a currency adjustment elsewhere by threatening to unilaterally raise or lower the value of the national currency in terms of the price of an ounce of gold. Today, when the foreign exchange rates of free market currencies are allowed to float upward or downward, depending on the flow of trade, there is the threat of expanding or contracting national supplies of monetary instruments in circulation. We recall that, all other things remaining essentially unchanged, expansion tends to lower a currency's value vis-à-vis competing currencies while contraction tends to have the opposite effect.[3] Alternatively, as noted earlier, governments may intervene in international money markets by offering to buy or sell substantial amounts of their own or a competitor's currency, depending on the circumstances.* Centrally planned and controlled socialist systems, their currencies' foreign exchange rates fixed by government decree and insulated

---

* To reiterate, the effect of selling large amounts of one's own currency, or that of a competitor, lowers the relative international exchange value, thereby improving the issuing country's export position. The opposite result obtains in case of massive buying of a given currency. Currencies are also sold because its holders anticipate a drop in their exchange value and wish to cut their losses, or they are bought in anticipation of rising rates.

against outside influences and incidentally also against outside manipulation, do not ordinarily participate in these activities. An exception is the Soviet Union.

From time to time, mostly to obtain hard currency to pay its import bills and meet its defense requirements, the Soviet Union sells substantial quantities of gold on the world market. Although the gold standard as such has been abandoned, a certain linkage remains between the world's major trading currencies, the available world supply of gold, and its world price, partly because possession of quantities of that precious metal continues to be a fall-back position for governments as well as private investors, as a protection against a precipitous downward trend of the world economy or as a hedge against one of the perennial foreign exchange crises. Indeed, in the face of adversity people have seemingly always turned to gold. By treating gold production data as a state secret, the Soviet Union, estimated to be the world's second largest gold producer, prevents its own gold from depressing the world price as much as might be the case if precise information on Soviet gold holdings were available. Equally important, as long as the price of gold and the world's currencies remain linked, however tenuously and indirectly, the Soviet government also retains a measure of influence over the world's money markets.*

Other means of influencing currency standards or supplies, hence the flow of trade and investment, include bi- and multilateral transfers of funds, in the form of loans or investment in public or private enterprises some of which is done on a government-to-government basis, some by governments acting through private bankers and investors.† Or, needed foreign exchange amounts are "swapped" to provide temporary relief for a government under pressure and increase international liquidity. Under such an arrangement, one central bank lends a given amount in its own currency to another central bank in exchange for an equivalent loan in that bank's national currency. For example, the Federal Reserve Bank of New York extends to the Bank of England credit to the amount of $100 million. In exchange, the latter credits the British account of the Bank of New York with the equivalent in British pounds (£67 million in 1983). As noted by D.P. Whiting, "in this way international liquidity is increased by $200 million, as the U.S. can make use of $100 million worth of sterling and the [United Kingdom] can make use of $100 million in dollars."[4] Both countries have improved their position to settle their international accounts. The exchange is to be reversed, as soon as both countries by exports or by

---

* Robert G. Kaiser (1976), p. 243, reports that among topics Soviet newspaper censors are instructed to keep from being published are "calculations of the relative purchasing power of the ruble and the hard currency of foreign states." See also, Timothy Green, (1973), pp. 93–95.

† Because international lending has not reached levels and risks beyond the capacity of even the larger public and private banks, lending operations increasingly are conducted through multibank, multicountry consortia. In 1982, for example, a five billion dollar loan to Mexico, supported by the United States and other Western countries, ultimately involved 1500 banks throughout the Western world, including Yugoslavia. *New York Times* (January 19, 1983).

other means have acquired sufficient reserves, the United States in pound sterling, the UK in dollars.

Alternatively, credits can be extended, enabling a country experiencing foreign exchange difficulties to postpone expenditure of scarce foreign exchange reserves to acquire urgently needed goods and services, thereby restore its financial viability, improving its "liquidity" position and stabilizing its currency as a result. Badly needed foreign exchange may also be obtained in the form of direct loans or "drawing rights" from international sources such as the International Monetary Fund (IMF).*

Indicative of worldwide economic setbacks, a steadily rising share of international finance is taken up by debt servicing (payment of interest on loans and credit) and the costs of scheduling and rescheduling of delayed repayment of the principal. Also increasing are remittances of corporate or individual earnings from abroad to their home countries. A lesser though also increasing share is directed to induce or support economic development in the large number of newly independent, less developed countries.

Occasionally, monetary and financial objectives are achieved by strong-arm measures, although one cannot classify such acts as forms of economic warfare. For example in the 1930s, in an effort to expand its influence into southeastern Europe, Nazi Germany, hinting at military consequences, insisted that client states like Romania and Hungary adjust the value of their currencies to the Reichsmark at a rate favoring the latter. To facilitate this, a scheme was devised which worked as follows: Germany contrived to arrange transfer of the bulk of client state's principal export commodities to Germany in return for a promise to deliver whatever manufactured goods Germany happened to have in excess. The value of the items exchanged—it actually was a form of barter— was to be calculated in German Reichsmark. The value of that currency was then artificially set at three times its real worth; that is, at three times the value it would have attained had free market conditions been allowed to operate. By that arrangement, the Germans secured three times of what they would otherwise have been entitled to, while Romania and Hungary realized from the exchange only a fraction of what they could have obtained had they traded with their traditional customers, France, Italy, and Great Britain. Once caught in a web of this kind, states find it difficult, if not impossible, to extricate themselves. Today, the Soviet Union employs similar means to protect its interests in Eastern and Southeastern Europe.†

* Special Drawing Rights (SDRs) were established by the IMF to provide a means of international financial assistance to states short of other means of paying their bills or meeting other outstanding obligations. This became necessary when the U.S. dollar lost its virtualy exclusive global reserve position and a reasonably stable means of settling international accounts had to be created to take its place. See Part Three and Banks, *et al., Economic Handbook of the World, 1981,* pp. 17–21.

† In addition to financial losses incurred by the weaker or client states, the latter frequently also incur qualitative losses, for whatever the patron state may have to sell the client state may not need. The Nazi Germans for example forced their then captive customers, mainly in southeast Europe, to accept inordinate quantities of aspirin, mouth organs, and glass eyes.

Various forms of currency control, if not outright dictation and manipulation of internal finance generally, characterizes colonial relationships. Great Britain, France, Belgium, and Portugal, for example, in addition to military occupation and control, held sway over their possessions simply by retaining in their hands total control over the monetary and banking systems. In one form or another these controls survived initial grants of political independence for many years, for decades in some instances.

To an extent, during the first so-called independence decade from 1960 to 1970, the collection of states succeeding the colonies of France was held together mainly by financial means. However, France, now dealing with less docile partners and facing external competition, found that the relationship had to be rendered more attractive. Accordingly, though thereby actually strengthening the dependency relationship, the government of France assumed direct responsibility for part of the client state's national budget, assumed a share of the new state's national debt—a debt incurred by the colonial power—and added such perquisites as annual payments to colonial veterans of France's wars. France also underwrote a share of the new states' current administrative expenses, granted loans on favorable terms, and pegged the exchange rate of the client's currency in relation to the French franc, substantially above its intrinsic economic worth.

The United States, in the formal sense not as colonial a power as were its European friends and allies, nevertheless dominated the monetary systems, including all aspects of national currencies, in many parts of Central and South America, in Liberia, and in the Philippines. What became known as dollar diplomacy consisted partly of monetary policy control, partly of at times subtle, at times blunt application of the money weapon through trade and financial aid as well as outright bribery. Dollar diplomacy exchanged United States financial contributions to an economy in need of such infusion for some *quid pro quo:* accession to a treaty, concessions in a particular trade deal, or rejection of an initiative from a non-U.S. state. In one instance, described as "the frank enlistment of finance to bolster foreign policy," dollar diplomacy meant enlistment of major U.S. investment houses to entice the Central American Republic of Nicaragua to permit the U.S. to determine which of several political factions should rule that country.[5]

Actually, every major power and most middle-level powers have at one time or another in their history engaged in that kind of "diplomacy," bribing foreign heads of state or other key military or civilian administrators, currying favor with factions in other countries, hastening the downfall or overthrow of a regime by refusing to release funds for its support, or, the reverse, saving a regime by timely provision of needed finance including transfers satisfying a monarch's or a dictator's personal financial needs. States offering or floating bonds especially in wealthy countries to finance their own industrial development or strengthen their defenses find the door open only if the accomodating governments can expect something in return.

Independent Legitimate and Illegitimate Finance*

In the 1930s, or at least so some economists and historians believe, the governments of the United States, Great Britain, France, and Germany held in their hands the fate of nations, mainly because they also controlled the largest blocks of finance needed to sustain the world's economies. Their and their leading bankers' decisions and nondecisions could save or bring down governments almost at will.[6] Today, though less arbitrarily and more subject to influences from a wider circle of financial powers, U.S. treasury officials, central and private bankers, and financiers, working in cooperation with their counterparts now from 10 other major trading powers, still have a controlling voice in international finance. However, the international order is in disarray; signs of potentially permanent disorder, if not anarchy, are mounting.[7]

Two major factors have combined to diminish the controls and discretionary powers over monetary policy and finance generally which governments insist are essential and in the national interest. One is the inordinate growth in size and global expansion of multi- or transnational corporations, the other, in part resulting from the foregoing, is the progressive internationalization of finance capital. One consequence of this trend is the gradual loss of discretionary powers on the part of individual governments to employ, for foreign political purposes, and as their national interests demand, the multiple financial instrumentalities which in theory or even in law are supposed to be at their disposal.

It can be argued that the root of the problem is capitalism's intrinsic commitment to free trade and free movement of capital across national boundaries, both clearly accruing to the advantage of mankind as a whole. However, some multinational corporations (MNCs), and other independent financial forces breaking away from or circumventing national constraints, now threaten to acquire momentum and rationales all of their own. Increasingly they pursue objectives detrimentally opposed to those of countries whose currencies they use. To Marxist critics of capitalism, the apparent contradiction inherent in free-wheeling financial interests tilting against the interests of their home economies is but one of many signs of capitalism's decay and eventual collapse. Be that as it may, the problems and the consequences are quite real.[8]

Whether legitimate or illegitimate the incentives for independent finance capital seeking an escape from national economies and nationally restrictive legislation are essentially identical; both forms are in search of financial gain and security from governmental control and interference. The only difference is that the former can cross most international boundaries in full view whereas the latter is compelled, at least initially, to remain concealed. Legitimate finance, accounting by a wide margin for the greater share of global totals, because it

* "Legitimate" in this context refers to government approved, "illegitimate" to transactions with either are secret or clandestine, or open, but in neither case bear an official stamp of approval. Inevitably some transactions straddle the dividing line, creating snarls only batteries of accountants and lawyers can unravel. See Bretton (1980), Chapter 11.

is respectable can utilize official channels and enter into open discussions with heads of state, treasury officials, or bankers. Proceeds from its transactions can be remitted to the owner across national boundaries, again entirely in the open; not so, the other kind.

Materialized most likely from shady or illegal operations, illegitimate finance is most likely transacted in secret, anonymously, through third parties pledged to secrecy. Typically it is in flight from prosecution—the proceeds of embezzlement, outright theft by public officials from national treasuries either while securely in office or shortly before being deposed, drug traffic or other criminal operations, corruption and bribery, and tax evasion. Commensurate with the intensity of regional or global conflict, ever greater amounts are transferred internationally by the world's major secret service organizations, principally the CIA of the United States and the Soviet Union's KGB Funds from these sources, while awaiting specific assignment, are known to have been invested under spurious ownership in legitimate banks or enterprises, for profit.[9] Either at the behest of specific governments or their respective secret services, or spontaneously and independently, various terrorist organizations, some exceedingly well financed, likewise avail themselves of these channels and opportunities. All funds of dubious origin and provenance must surface eventually if they are to be of any use at all. Therefore, somewhere along the line they must be "laundered", that is, they must be sluiced through a legitimate bank or business to obscure all traces. Somewhere between legitimate and illegitimate international enterprise are the speculators who conceals their funds to escape currency control or the income tax collector.

The economic and political effects of such transfers or maneuvers vary in direct proportion to the ratio between the inflow and the target country's GNP. For obvious reasons because they are respectable and far greater amounts are involved, legitimate transactions far outweigh the others in political influence or power generated, especially if applied in heavy concentration. In such cases, sudden transfer or withdrawal can set off repercussions in the economy from which they originate or into which they are injected. As we noted earlier massive outflow or inflow of large funds, for whatever purpose, causes foreign exchange values of affected currencies to fluctuate. Likewise, in the case of weak or temporarily weakened economies, timely and substantial financial infusion can save a government; in the case of nearly bankrupt countries, it can help save the entire economy, and in the case of LDCs, who are chronically short of externally useable funds, financial transfusions are needed on a continuing basis, to prop up perpetually unstable regimes, pay current bills (especially for army, police, and government apparatus), cover essential imports, and generally support the country's credit worthiness. Typically, all countries, large and small, find the bulk of their liquid funds tied up or obligated, current revenue insufficient to cover current and future expenditures, deadlines looming constantly for repayment of loans or payment of interest.

Because it must avoid close scrutiny, the shady variety of international finance tends to gravitate at least initially toward smaller, poorer, hence weaker countries, favoring especially those prepared to accommodate funds of questionable origin by offering secret bank accounts and other protection.*

Large or small, legitimate or not, the cumulative effect of all of these extra-governmental transactions has been a steady weakening of control over certain widely traded currencies by their respective issuing authorities. Because both types, legitimate as well as illegitimate, are most comfortable in countries whose governments show no direct interest or are permissive because it serves their interest to accumulate foreign funds, they tend to flow together, giving rise to ever increasing but also ever more destabilizing "expatriate" accumulations in the most favored currencies, beyond the supervision and control of the authorities, most notably the government of the United States, who are ultimately responsible for their exchange value.[10]

The bearers of financial assets—the big ones in all countries, the smaller only in small-scale economies—are welcome not only because of their largesse. They also commend themselves to ruling circles because of the contacts they represent. By its very nature, international finance represents a network of interdependent interests which in turn create most valuable contacts in key places in government, business, and industry as well as in financial circles, a feature which attracted the special attention of rulers since the Middle Ages. From the legendary banking house of Fugger in Medieval Germany to the equally legendary house of Rothschild to the multinational banking conglomerates and consortia of today have come key domestic as well as foreign policy advisers to governments, irrespective of religious, ideological, or partisan political considerations. Also, by its nature, involvement in international finance provides insights into some of the most vital secrets of governments and nations. Such knowledge, rulers long ago discovered, makes excellent cabinet officers and ambassadors, special emissaries and trouble-shooters. The fact that throughout history bankers and financiers have aided monarchs, dictators, presidents, prime ministers, and other government officials to augment their personal fortunes is not insignificant in that regard.†

Foreign Investment

Private interests, individual and corporate, and governments invest surplus funds abroad for a variety of reasons: high rates of interest, currency fluctuations, financial stability, or, in the case of private investors, flight from income tax

---

* Not weak but traditionally most accommodating in these respects is Switzerland; see Ferris, Chapter 7. Other havens for finance capital in flight are Liechtenstein, the Bahamas, and several Central and South American states. Lebanon served as one before turmoil ruined it.

† The often decisive role of legitimate "high" finance—i.e. involving large sums transferred at highest levels—is brought out in Fritz Stern's account of the relationship between the architect of German might in Central Europe in the latter half of the nineteenth century, Prince Otto von Bismarck and his banker (1977); see also Bretton (1980), p. 22. For a Soviet view, see Stadnichenko (1975).

collectors. Capital importing countries use such funds to modernize or expand their industries, start new industries, or develop other sectors such as agriculture.

Governments of less developed countries regard foreign investment as a mixed blessing. On the one hand they welcome it as a support of their weak if not ailing economies. On the other hand they are suspicious of the power and influence that comes with it, especially the control over aspects of their internal affairs when foreign investment takes the form of direct ownership of key industrial or agricultural enterprises.[11] A major source of discontent in that regard has been the conduct of large multinational corporations.

A U.S. congressional study found that the growth of direct investment abroad and the rise of the multinational corporation have been two of the major economic developments of recent times. The U.S. is the world's largest capital exporter, direct foreign investment accounting for the greater share.[12] But as the U.S. dollar gained against the major competing currencies in the first half of the current decade level of more than $800 foreign investment in the United States reached a billion, further evidence of the growing economic interdependence of nations.

Suggested Questions and Discussion Topics

What basic functions does money perform in international economics? What is foreign exchange? Why are foreign exchange fluctuations important? Why must sharp fluctuations in foreign exchange values be avoided?

What causes foreign exchange crises?

Why is convertibility of a state's currency important in international trade and commerce?

What was the role of gold in international trade when the world's major trading nations were on the gold standards? What brought on the end of that standard and what took its place?

What are "hard," what are "soft" currencies, and what is the significance of each with respect to international trade?

Why are foreign exchange reserves important to states? Why do some states impose strict foreign exchange restrictions?

What is "dollar diplomacy?"

How and why are funds transferred among nations?

Chapter 6
Trade and Aid

Trade

The Foreign Trade Imperative

Nations feel compelled for a variety of reasons to engage in trade beyond their borders. The emergence of national economies—the successors to feudal and city-state economies—in the latter part of the seventeenth and early part of the eighteenth centuries, burgeoning international trade, and the rising merchant class in the dominant trading nations of Western Europe spawned the mercantilist school of thought whose central argument was that international trade had one overriding purpose: accumulation of national wealth. To that end, government was to apply its energies toward maximization of any and all available opportunities to engage in international trade to national advantage. Results were to be measured in amounts of precious metal which a nation could garner from trade with others. In other words, the wealth of a nation was to be gauged foremost in terms of its gold and silver hoard. Underlying that notion was a conviction that in the final analysis the strength of an economy depended on the availability, in the coffers of national treasuries, of sufficient wealth to cover all national requirements for peace or war.

If such belief seems simplistic, the latter part of the eighteenth and the nineteenth century saw veritable revolutions in economic thought, a consequence in part of the industrial revolution and the profound social and political changes which occurred in its wake. But it was not until the outbreak of the first World War that economic theorists became aware of a basic flaw in mercantilist thought, an awareness not shared by all policy and decision-makers in all of the trading nations today.

Mercantilism had urged nations to sell as much of their product abroad as the traffic would bear and import as little as possible, hoarding the proceeds to cover all eventualities. Now it is realized that this tended to impoverish the very economies which were to produce the funds needed to pay for the exports. In other words, mercantilism tended to impoverish one's best customers. Overlooked in nation-centered economic thought was the element of reciprocity, a dominant consideration in most of today's national and international economic planning.

Today some trade is initiated solely to obtain foreign exchange for purchase of an essential raw material, a commodity, or a service, some to gain additional flexibility and a widening of options regarding alternate suppliers. Constant pressure to reduce costs and increase production provides an incentive to rely to an ever greater extent on the benefits of international specialization or division of labor; the aim is to capitalize on the comparative advantage which arises from producing at home what can be produced there most efficiently and at least expense and to import from others what they can do better, at less cost.*

Trade also is pressed to gain access to advanced technology, two outstanding examples being Japan between the two world wars and the Soviet Union and its associates today. Another spur to trade is the need—attributed by socialist writers exclusively to capitalist economies—to dispose abroad of goods the

Table 6-1. World Trade (1981 in million US$)

	Imports (c.i.f.)[a]	Exports (f.o.b.)[b]
World[c]	2,024,952	1,967,122
Developed Market Economies[d]	1,353,771	1,239,535
Developing Market Economies	483,588	545,346
OPEC	143,294	280,038
28 Least Developed Countries	15,686	7,156
Centrally Planned Economies	187,593	182,243

SOURCES: U.N. *Statistical Yearbook 1981*, Table 178, pp. 886–887.
[a] c.i.f.—cost, insurance and freight or charged-in-full
[b] f.o.b.—free on board
[c] excluding trade between the P.R.C., the Mongolian People's Republic, and the Democratic Republic of Korea (North Korea)   \
[d] including trade between the Federal Republic of Germany and the German Democratic Republic (D.D.R.)

* The law of comparative costs was first formulated by David Ricardo (1772–1823) in his *Theory of International Trade*. According to Ricardo, trade follows cost differences. If wine is less expensively produced in country or location A than in B, and cloth less expensively in B, then A will tend to specialize in wine and B in cloth, and trade will be conducted between the two to mutual advantage. Trade will also result if both commodities can be produced at less cost in either A or B but one is relatively more costly to produce than the other within one country:

| | Man-Hours Per Unit of Output | |
Country	Wine	Cloth
A	120	100
B	80	90

Assuming cost of labor being the same in both countries, A devotes more man-hours to production of wine than to cloth and B does the reverse. Therefore, A stands to gain by exchanging cloth for wine, while B benefits by exchanging wine for cloth.

Comparative (cost) advantage results from any one of several factors, foremost greater efficiency, such as more efficient use of plant, material, and labor, more efficient farming, or lower standards of living for workers and farmers.

exporting state's own consumers cannot afford to buy in sufficient quantities to make domestic sales worthwhile. A century or so ago, this certainly applied to the industrially advanced countries of Western Europe. Today, it applies more to the newly industrialized countries whose people still lack the purchasing power to absorb all that is being produced at home or which are in need of foreign exchange to further their development.

In response to pressure from an increasingly more demanding electorate, the modern political democracies of the West tend to orient their foreign trade more to serving the home market. However, there still is a dimension to capitalism which favors foreign over domestic trade without necessarily benefiting the home economy. In certain economic spheres, and regardless of domestic needs or conditions, profits tend to be greater abroad than at home.

Today it is recognized that if a state wishes to export it must as a rule also import. If it wishes to secure best available ("most favored") terms from its trading partners, it must extend best available terms to the partners as well. Imposition of prohibitive costs on foreign goods seeking entry, that is, imposition of prohibitive import duties or tariffs, most likely results in retaliation by countries affected. Similarly, restrictions—such as import or migration quotas—imposed on imports of goods and services, including foreign labor, bring in their wake similar action by others. One major difference between the era when mercantilism could flourish and today is the complexity of the modern nation state, which tends to reduce governments' freedom of action at home and abroad. In the open free market states, "the merchant class" has given way to numerous conflicting pressure and interest groups some of which have a vested interest in export, some not. Organized labor tends to favor protection of national industries and jobs by reduction of imports, while powerful multinational corporations, with extensive holdings and investments abroad, pull in the opposite direction. Even in the centrally controlled socialist economies, export-oriented state enterprises compete for central government support with those depending on foreign supplies. The progressive interdependence of nations exhausting their own nonrenewable resources or encountering increasing scarcity of such resources throughout the world alone renders mercantilism, or its modern counterparts autarky and across-the-board protectionism, obsolete. Economic interdependence and international trade are further accentuated by the confluence of two factors: the uneven international distribution of capital for finance of industrialization and development and the fact that finance capital is the prerequisite, facilitator, and driving force of all trade. Thus, if unemployed finance capital is to expand commensurately with expanding need and if it is to be directed where needed, only international cooperation and coordination in trade *and* finance can ensure maximalization of trading opportunities throughout the world.*

---

* One of the complications is the matter of credit. Credit is always required to finance trade at a stage when either seller or buyer, exporter or importer, is short of funds. Reliance on credit is endemic with less developed countries whose finances are likely to be inadequate to sustain trade for decades to come. See Chapter 14, below.

Economists differ regarding future prospects for international trade, the difference of opinion arising over varying assessments of the consumption potential of regions not yet fully opened to foreign trade or otherwise not yet fully developed. Whatever the truth, adverse trade balances resulting from an excess of imports over exports produce certain economic and political repercussions for the disadvantaged country. For one, imports tend to cause unemployment in the sector producing the same or similar goods. Potentially, unemployment causes social and political unrest; at the very least it increases demands for retaliation, for example reduction of imports by one means or another. For these reasons among others, when the monthly trade balance figures are released, governments, especially those subject to popular approval through election, do not welcome news of a substantial trade deficit. (See Fig. 6-1.)

Promotion of Trade and Investment

To promote one's goods and services in another country can be a rather sensitive undertaking. After all, what is really being proposed is replacement of products or services in the target country with presumably less expensive or higher quality substitutes from abroad. For that reason governments prefer to advertise their trade offers and opportunities, be they from private or public sources, discreetly. Preferred methods are promotion through contact established by commercial attaches assigned to most embassies and through consular staff. Occasionally exhibits are organized abroad or foreign dignitaries as well as potential private or public buyers are invited to tour specific industrial or agricultural sectors whose products they might buy. Arms sales are promoted

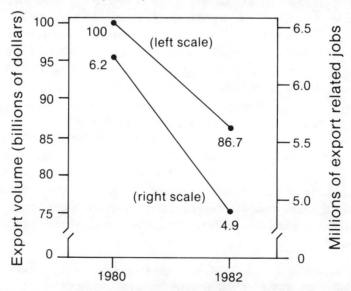

Fig. 6-1. U.S. Exports and Jobs for American Workers. (*Business America*, Vol. 6, 13, June 27, 1983, p. 4.)

by demonstration of weapons at airshows or during maneuvers to which potential military as well as civilian buyers are invited.*

To attract foreign investors, guaranteed markets are offered for their products for limited periods of time. In the same vein states offer concessions or special advantages, 5 to 10 year moratoriums on taxes for instance or establishment of duty or tax-free zones. A common vehicle for trade promotion is a treaty of commerce, friendship, and consular relations, negotiated between two or more states, usually containing a *Most Favored Nation* clause (MFN) under which all parties extend to each other any and all favorable trade terms extended to yet other nations, terms which either are already in force or are to be negotiated in the future. Given the size of their respective economies, by offering MFN privileges the United States, Japan, or West Germany can and do obtain diplomatic or political advantages as well.†

Trade Blockage or Disruption

To achieve their internal economic or foreign trade objectives in the face of opposing trends or forces, states may resort to internal or external defensive measures, or they may go over to the attack.

Defensively—though the targets may consider such measures offensive—states have for centuries sought to protect themselves by erecting barriers against imports likely to be detrimental to "the national interest," most likely to whichever interest group has the government's ear. The most common barrier consists of tariffs imposed to regulate import of specific goods and reduce overall levels of all or most imports by making them more expensive to consumers than comparable domestic products. Tariffs also may be imposed to safeguard the national interest by protecting "infant" industries, pending development of their full competitive capacity, or basic industries or sectors essential to national defense such as ship-building or steel production.‡

Less visible, less dramatic, but potentially just as effective as direct tariffs are so-called Non-Tariff Barriers (NTBs). Some of these are natural products of an environment, some are imposed deliberately to serve the same ends as tariffs. Some NTBs reflect attitudes more than specific discriminatory acts. Whatever their provenance or purpose, the effect of tariffs and NTBs is essentially the same; both interfere with the free flow of trade and narrow choices open to customers.

Most widely used are the following NTBs: Government procurement and discrimination in government purchases and contract awards at home and

---

* Exporters and investors are encouraged to venture into unstable foreign situations by their respective governments assuming the major share of the risk through overseas investment insurance programs.

† MFN is the central feature of GATT; see p. 181 below.

‡ Tariffs may also be imposed solely to raise government revenue; in that event, comparable domestic products may be taxed an equal amount. Preferential tariffs single out a particular country; nondiscriminatory tariffs are applied uniformly.

abroad with intent to favor domestic over foreign suppliers; payment of subsidies, extension of tax credits or relief to strengthen domestic producers against foreign competition, or surcharges, levies, taxes or fees for administrative services are imposed on importers or their foreign suppliers; payment of an export subsidy to cover the difference between the price an exporter would have to charge abroad to stay in business and the price he must charge to undersell a foreign competitor; imposition of exaggerated quality tests or health standards with an eye to favor domestic over foreign manufacture or commodities; customs procedures sufficiently cumbersome to delay and thereby discourage certain imports; imposition of quotas, that is, restrictions on the quantities imported or on the share of the total market an import may attain. In addition, myriads of national, state, or local rules and regulations, and licensing arrangements and permits can be combined to make life very difficult for an importer or other competitor trying to gain a foothold in the protected economy.[1] Among attitudinal social or psychological barriers likely to block trade or slow it down are consumer tastes, traditional practices or habits favoring use of domestic over foreign products—for example popular belief in the efficacy of a domestic medicine or remedy—all of which, depending on a government's inclination, can be countered or mitigated or encouraged and reinforced.

To drive competition from desirable markets or prevent competitive producers or industries from making inroads at home or abroad, goods may be "dumped," that is to say sold abroad below home market prices or below cost. Competing sea and air transport services may be countered by price cutting for passengers or freight. Regulations may require that certain categories of imported goods contain parts produced in the receiving nation. To force prices up, production of goods, commodities, or primary products and raw materials may be reduced or held up, or, under exceptional circumstances, surplus commodities may actually be destroyed. Brazil burnt tons of coffee on several occasions, and Ghana attempted to hold up sale of cocoa in the early 1960s.[2] The reverse side of this coin is stockpiling of nonperishable commodities and raw materials by consumer states in order to reduce dependency on unreliable or untrustworthy sources of supply, hence vulnerability to economic blackmail or dictation on that account. Stockpiling also may be instituted to depress the price of a particular commodity or resource. On occasion, export of a particular item may be curbed to conserve scarce supply or protect a technological advantage.

States faced with a chronic unfavorable balance of trade, balance of payments, or both, in need therefore of either increasing exports, decreasing imports or ceasing imports of all nonessential goods altogether at least for a while, and endowed with the requisite will and organizational as well as political capacity, have on occasion moved in the direction of total self-sufficiency, or autarky. In that event, the economy is directed to function as far as possible without recourse to foreign sources of supply. Typically, this strategy is employed to cope with severe and chronic shortfalls in foreign exchange reserves or to prepare for war.

Another severely disruptive measure is nationalization of foreign enterprise, be that gradual or phased, all accounts equitably settled, or sudden, inadequately settled, or without any compensation. This step is taken for a variety of reasons. The immediate objective may be nothing else but enrichment of a ruling elite; in some instances the beneficiary is the head of state. This has been a pattern in some LDCs where an economically unhealthy share of earnings from the seized operation is simply skimmed off and invested abroad. More likely, the rationale is a desire, dictated by necessity, to transfer command points in the economy from foreign control to indigenous hands. Most likely targets of such measures are basic sectors, such as mining, transport including shipping, communications, or banking and insurance. Whatever the reason or circumstances, inevitably for extended periods thereafter—in some cases for decades—the volume and quality of trade is adversely affected, sometimes disastrously so.

Sometimes what may have the appearance of trade promotion, advanced in the name of free trade, may have the opposite effect. Ever since they attained world power status, the great maritime states, foremost the United States and Great Britain, have favored free over restricted trade. But that was the case only because they were powerful enough, militarily and economically, to compel weaker states to trade on their terms, a point Soviet writers tend to stress.[3] Actually, behind the facade of a commitment to free trade these and other free trade proponents practice restriction whenever and wherever their national interests so demand. To be sure, insofar as they were and still are dependent on foreign sources of supply and overseas markets, serious disruption of world trade threatens to undermine at least segments of their economies. However, the "have-nots" of the world have long regarded unrestricted free trade as a weapon used by the rich and strong to exploit the poor and weak. To an extent this confrontation contributed to the outbreak of the first, possibly also the second World War.[4]

Less developed countries, as we have seen, still largely tied to the former colonial powers and dependent generally on assistance of all kinds from abroad— we shall address their problems in detail in Part Three—tend to disrupt established patterns of trade in an attempt to diversify markets and suppliers. Thus Ghana in the 1960s attempted to break away from Western, mainly British and United States, economic ties by shifting its trade to the Soviet bloc and to the People's Republic of China. The attempt came to an end with the overthrow of the president who had initiated the move.[5] France, on the other hand, succeeded in retaining the loyalty of most of her former possessions by providing guaranteed profitable markets for their major foreign exchange-earning exports. There also were equally attractive monetary policy arrangement.

Foreign Aid

What Is Aid?

Charles P. Kindleberger notes that trade and aid are inextricably linked.[6] But aid is also linked to politics, domestic as well as foreign, to military strategy, and to war. Indeed, aid rarely serves just one purpose. Viewed from the donor nation's perspective, it reflects unselfish dedication to the advancement of peace and prosperity in the world. As seen by critics, foreign aid runs the gamut from simple prelude to trade, to Trojan Horse designed to subvert, to a hook sunk deep into the body politic or a state about to be enslaved. Whatever the motivation, foreign aid typically is skimmed off the economy of a state enjoying a surplus and is conveyed to a state in need. It involves transfer of goods, services (including technical assistance), or finance, either directly by a government agency or by nongovernmental bodies acting at a government's behest and using funds provided from the public treasury. The major share of all aid is transferred openly, but some aid is conveyed covertly, well concealed under labels suggesting something else to spare the donor government embarrassment at home, or enable the recipient to save face.*

Aid may be offered as a gift or as a loan, or it may be in the form of lend-lease, as were fifty old destroyers transferred from the U.S. Navy to Great Britain in the early stages of World War Two. It may be a one-time transaction or it may be continuous, over years or even decades as, for example, U.S. aid to Israel and Soviet aid to Cuba. Aid may be offered unconditionally or it may have strings, that is, the recipient is expected to perform a political, economic, or military act or transfer something of value in return. The presence or absence of strings is one of the more controversial aspects of foreign aid. Strictly speaking, strings signify a dependency relationship analogous to that of puppet to puppet master. In reality it is less compelling. In most instances terms are flexible, leaving the question of compensation or return favor to the recipient government's discretion.

Some aid is said to have been tendered without strings of any kind. Aside from outright but typically very modest gifts, that is most unlikely. If nothing else, donors may at the very minimum expect aid to be applied responsibly in a manner likely to obviate continuation at a point not too distant in the future.

Specifically, Why Is Aid Given?

The Humanitarian Rationale. All nations with wealth to spare respond to emergency situations, such as natural disasters, epidemics, or massive dislocation of people as a result of war, civil war, revolution, or persecution. Still, even in this respect political judgments tend to interfere as capitalist nations are limited in what they can do for people in need inside the Soviet-led bloc, and the latter tend to regard humanitarian aid to people within the capitalist sphere

* Rulers of newly independent less developed countries, having told their followers that independence means standing on one's own feet economically, are reluctant to admit that the opposite may actually be the case. To accommodate such states, France devised elaborate budgetary categories to conceal various forms of aid to her former colonies in Africa, for example assuming the costs of teacher and technician training, paying war service bonuses to African veterans of French wars, or covering salaries of French civil servants on loan to the newly established governments.

of influence as exclusively the responsibility of the capitalist system. Socialist governments outside the Soviet sphere are not so inhibited.

As the world's wealthiest nation, the United States has led the world in dispensation of foreign aid. In its original form, U.S. aid was an outgrowth of the missionary spirit to assist people in desperate need; however until 1945 it was not unrelated to the fact that the recipients more likely than not were ethnic kin of influential segments of the American electorate. Since the emergence of the Third World, U.S. aid has assumed a racially and ethnically more universal character. Humanitarian aid was sent by the people of the United States to the victims of the civil war following the Russian Revolution, to Germany in the 1920s to mitigate the suffering, especially among the very young, resulting from the Allied blockade of Germany during and shortly after the First World War, and to famine victims in drought-stricken regions on the African continent. Since their recovery from the second World War, the nations of Western Europe and Japan have joined in the effort to alleviate human suffering on a global scale. Reluctant to become entangled in ideological or purely political struggles or confrontations, neutrals like Sweden, Austria, and Switzerland prefer humanitarian to all other forms of aid, except of course aid related to trade. Obviously all governments prefer to present their foreign aid activities in the most favorable light possible, but one need not examine the ostensible humanitarian explanations too thoroughly, to uncover an economic, political, or military rationale. However moving it may be, suffering of people far away has a relatively low priority when it comes to allocation of public funds. Indeed, this is true of all foreign aid and assistance showing no visible returns.

The Economic Rationale. The economic rationale for foreign aid may be inner- or outer-directed. An example of the former is aid sent abroad by the United States mainly to dispose of wheat and other food surpluses which, in the absence of such a measure, would depress prices and thereby farm income at home.[7] Outer-directed aid is intended to open up new markets for the donor's goods and services, create new opportunities for investment, or regain old markets subject to restrictions or rendered inaccessible for other reasons. Aid may be given to help out a trading partner in need, stabilize a weak or tottering economy, help to reverse an adverse balance of payments, develop an economy or one of its sectors, or help to reconstruct an economy shattered by war.

When after 1945 the United States' Western European allies stood in danger of internal collapse, the cornucopia of U.S. farm products, manufactured goods, and war-swollen financial resources was tapped to support West Europe's economic, social, and political, eventually also military reconstruction. The first manifestation of that effort was the Marshall Plan, a program eventually reaching a total of 51 billion dollars. Described by some as the greatest act of altruism in history, it was denounced by others as just another imperialist design on the wealth of weaker nations. Objectively viewed, the Marshall Plan was no exception to the rule; it did have a distinct political edge. In its main thrust, it was conceived to shore up Western Europe against the threat posed by aggressive communism.

In its most blatant form, aid is an instrument of domination of donor over recipient. Offers are carefully designed to render the recipient more or less dependent upon the donor. One means of accomplishing this is design of an aid package—funds, goods, and services—in such a manner as to reinforce consumption or production patterns favoring the donor's economic interests or create such patterns where none existed before. Foreign aid can extenuate export patterns, that is, the recipient economy is conditioned to direct its exports to the donor of industrial plant or processing equipment, partly to ensure steady supply of spare parts and replacements, technicians, and technical expertise. A lesser form of dependency results from foreign aid's demonstration effect. Donation of certain food or beverages or of certain commodities may encourage development of consumption habits and tastes, if not addiction, to ensure spiralling demand when aid is terminated and trade begins.*

The Political Rationale. In its simplest form, politically-oriented aid is intended to create good will for the donor and nothing else. A stark application of that is aid-for-show-only, for example a spectacular gift of a sports stadium, a magnificent but uneconomically burdensome exhibition or conference hall, or a wholly uneconomic hotel. Stunningly elaborate airports have been built under aid programs where more modest facilities would have sufficed, national airlines were developed where neither local resources nor passenger or freight demand justified such ventures. Not too infrequently, a major project is facilitated by foreign aid primarily for political effect, against persuasive technical and financial expert advice. The Soviet-built Aswan Dam in Egypt may be one example, and the railroad built by the Chinese People's Republic to link Zambia to the Indian Ocean port of Dar-es-Salaam may be another.

Or aid is given with full knowledge that purported economic objectives can under no conditions be attained. Perhaps the outstanding example is aid conveyed by the oil-rich Arab states, principally Saudi Arabia, to maintain Egypt's military potential in the anti-Israel front, prevent the Palestine Liberation Organization (PLO) from directing its militancy toward the donors and discourage Black Africa from assuming a neutral, or worse, pro-Israeli stance in the Arab-Israeli confrontation. Israel, on the other hand, herself a recipient of considerable aid from the United States, sought to defeat the latter strategy by offering a wide variety of aid programs to any black African state willing to accept it. Especially important in that regard was aid to Nigeria, Africa's most populous and predominantly Moslem state. Keeping Nigeria from joining the Arab anti-Israeli front, promised to counter Arab efforts to mobilize world Islam on their behalf.† Alas, oil money succeeded at least temporarily in defeating

---

* Critics of this tactic, commonly associated with neoimperialism or neocolonialism, both modern versions of classic patterns of domination or conquest, point specifically to introduction of alcohol and tobacco where religious strictures forbid their consumption.

† Between the late 1950s and the Six-Day War of 1967, when many Third World countries severed diplomatic relations with her, Israel's foreign aid was responsible for keeping the large bloc of black African states from voting solidly with the Arab states against Israel in the United Nations.

that purpose, a design reversed once again, at least partially, when the oil-rich aid donors simultaneously tripled and quadrupled the cost of oil for energy-starved recipients of their largesse.

Conceivably, the highly visible wealth and conspicuous consumption patterns in the United States, Western Europe, and now the oil-rich Arab states in the Middle East generate a sense of guilt. It suggests voluntary sharing through aid and assistance programs to counter the image of parasites feasting on a world progressively poorer because of their greed.

Aid, or its reverse denial of aid, can be said to be politically motivated when the purpose is to induce a government to comply with certain provisions of international law or principles of morality or social justice; examples are denial of U.S. aid to states guilty of gross violations of human rights or of aiding and abetting introduction of dangerous drugs into the United States.*

Straddling the dividing line between economic and political rationales is aid to specific groups or organizations. We referred to such assistance in our discussion of propaganda. Capitalist, socialist, and communist governments have channeled aid to support incipient labor unions in less developed countries, partly to correct imbalances in wage structure and working conditions—accruing to the detriment of trade—partly to strengthen their respective favorites among groups contending for power, the West favoring democratic labor movements, the East favoring Marxists or communists. Both camps provide aid to shore up weak or shaky governments, influence the outcome of elections, and generally create a political climate favorable to their side. Much of U.S. aid is directed to strengthen past or potential targets for political intervention by the Soviet Union or its proxies, for example Cuba or East Germany.

The Military-Strategic Rationale. As donor economies began to experience shortfalls of their own, inflation eroded the strength of their currencies, fatigue set in among their people who now grew tired of seeing highly visible shares of their national wealth flow abroad without ascertainable results. As the costs of arms production, acquisition, and maintenance skyrocketed, the attention of the world's leading sources of foreign aid shifted to military objectives. The major cause of the shift from civilian to military aid was of course the superpower rivalry. Under those conditions the politically marginal and militarily inconsequential less developed countries stood to fare poorly, unless they too had something of value to offer to the military planners of the major industrial nations. This aspect is discussed more fully in Chapter 19.

Bi- and Multilateral versus International Organization Aid. Aid programs are implemented bilaterally, multilaterally, or through international agencies or organizations. Obviously, strictly political aid does not lend itself to international administration. Military aid and assistance may be applied on an international basis only by an alliance system, such as the North Atlantic Treaty Organization

---

* On two different occasions, aid authorized by law to go to Bolivia was blocked by a U.S. administration because of its displeasure over Bolivia's refusal to curb drug trade involving Bolivian military leaders. *The New York Times* (September 24, 1981).

or the Eastern counterpart, the Warsaw Pact. Generally the major powers disdain the interference and loss of control associated with shared efforts and prefer therefore to handle the bulk of their programs under their own auspices.

On the other hand certain advantages accrue to the donor or group of donors, or generally the trading nations of the world, if trade, aid, and finance can be administered through relatively neutral or at least politically less committed international bodies, such as the International Monetary Fund or the International Bank for Reconstruction and Development, or World Bank. Similarly, the Soviet Union finds it more convenient to apply aid through the Council for Mutual Economic Assistance (CMEA/COMECON) as the Western or North Atlantic Group finds the Organization for Economic Cooperation and Development (OECD) more suitable for what they have in mind. Similar considerations have led to the creation of equivalent bodies elsewhere in the world to share costs, distribute burdens and risks more equitably, screen out historic grievances or hostilities, and reduce wasteful duplication and redundancies in aid programs and administration. However, aid still remains an instrument which governments prefer to use at their own sole discretion.

Multilateral Economic Relations.

Some of the reasons why nations resort to multilateral or international organizational aid also apply to economic relations generally. For instance, while not entirely shedding their fear of diminution of power through decision-sharing, the two superpowers continuously seek ways and means of minimizing their oppressive, all too apparently self-centered and foreboding preeminence in world affairs. Associating with middle and lesser powers in economic pursuits tends to reduce these effects. But more universally valid, more practical considerations lead nations normally inclined to bow to the imperative of economic self-interest to accept the principle of international economic cooperation, either through treaty networks or firmly established international organizations.

Foremost among the more practical rationales leading the majority of the nations of the world to create or accede to international economic constructs of one kind or another are the following: elimination of costly barriers to trade; pooling of scarce resources; reaping benefits of worldwide, or regional, division of labor and of the principle of economic comparative advantage; reducing costs of production; eliminating wasteful duplication and redundancies; generally, taking fuller advantage of the benefits flowing from economies of scale; and enhancing the competitive potential of regional groupings of nations. Last but certainly not least, while international economic cooperation cannot wholly eliminate causes of tension, conflict, and war, it tends—at least in theory—to minimize such obstacles to trade as ethnic hostilities and similar animosities rooted in the past and therefore intrinsically irrelevant to the achievement of economic objectives at another time, in another age.

On a very different plane, for entirely different purposes governments occasionally find it advantageous to join efforts not to advance but to restrict trade, drive up prices, force a dangerous competitor out of the market, or otherwise collude in pursuit of shared objectives at the expense of others. Toward the end of the Middle Ages, the North European Hanseatic League was formed partly for such purposes. In modern times, the giant oil companies, the "Seven Sisters," persuaded their respective governments, foremost Great Britain, the Netherlands, and the United States, to cooperate in order to protect lucrative production distribution and marketing arrangements throughout the world. The cartels and other protective organizational frameworks developed by the raw material producing states in more recent times, continue that pattern.[8] More constructive are banking consortia formed by private banks and finance houses, in cooperation with respective governments, to distribute the potential costs of high risk lending and investment ventures more equitably.

Economic Warfare

Prior to World War Two, the line separating peace and war was relatively clear. Since then the distinction has become blurred, peace blending into cold war with occasional hot encounters like the Korean and Vietnam wars, for example. Consequently, distinctions are difficult to draw between peaceful economic relations and economic warfare. What at one point may seem no more than a slight escalation of peaceful economic competition may at another justifiably be regarded as an outright hostile or warlike act. Thus, at times of crisis or in war we may encounter once again some of the practices described earlier under the heading 'trade blockage and disruptions'. Indeed, it is not uncommon to dub an incident in peaceful competition among friends and allies a war, for example the "Chicken War" over broilers between the United States and several of its Western European allies in the 1950s.* The issue was free trade versus protectionism, a frequent cause of economic warfare, but the contestants in this case were very much at peace. But there are forms of economic warfare which fall into a different category mainly because the antagonists are either in a state of hostility, are about to engage in a military confrontation, or are at war. Thus, when Soviet bloc countries undercut Western freight and shipping charges by extensive subsidies to their state-owned and controlled traders and shippers, or, the reverse, when Western trading nations hold up shipment of certain goods to the Soviet bloc, it is difficult to determine whether one is looking at a normal economic defense measure or at a hostile manifestation with martial under- or overtones.

On the other hand, one cannot always conclude that economic cooperation is ruled out among belligerents. During World War Two, in keeping with the

---

* Kindleberger (1979), pp. 120–121, reports that in that "war," U.S. "foreign service officers . . . awarded medals to each other for gallantry on the field of battle." At issue was a U.S.-developed technique of producing broilers in exceedingly short time, enabling U.S. exporters to capture a large portion of the European market. European producers persuaded their respective governments to block imports of this product long enough to allow local industries to copy and adopt that technique.

principle of reciprocity, the Western Allies and Nazi Germany continued to honor certain economic agreements and contracts, even though this would enable one or the other side to gain a military advantage as a result. Germany, for example, could not very well refuse payment of royalties to Allied concerns, paid through Switzerland, Argentina, or other neutrals, if her leading firms, like I.G. Farben or Agfa, expected their claims to royalties honored during and after the war in countries Hitler's war machine would be unable to subdue.

Limited Economic Warfare*

A range of economic weapons short of war are at the disposal of governments as a means of achieving political or diplomatic objectives. Among these are financial maneuvers to weaken the target country's currency or credit standing, freezing of its assets, sanctions (partial or complete cessation of all economic transactions, including shipment of certain goods or commodities), banning of all or some imports from the target country, or financial measures, boycotts and blacklistings, or stockpiling of raw materials or commodities which would otherwise have to be imported from the country affected. A few illustrations should suffice.

Following World War One, mainly to ensure compliance by defeated Germany with the financial and economic provisions of the Versailles Peace Treaty, France organized what amounted to a financial general staff, similar to the command echelon of its armed forces. That staff also had the responsibility to employ financial means to prevent Germany from ever again posing a military threat to France. Measures taken included maneuvers on international financial markets designed to weaken Germany's currency and prevent her from securing credits and direct financial aid from other Western countries, principally from Great Britain and the United States.[9] In the 1960s, French President Charles de Gaulle, partly to assert French independence from the United States, partly to show France's financial muscle, and partly to avenge himself for humiliations inflicted upon his person by U.S. leaders during the war, briefly entertained the thought of staging a raid on the gold hoard of the United States by abruptly demanding exchange of France's substantial dollar holdings for gold.[10]

Trade sanctions as a means of applying pressure have been used increasingly in recent years, by the United Nations in 1966 to compel the government of Southern Rhodesia (now Zimbabwe) to modify its racist stance toward its black population and by individual countries over several decades to achieve the same results in the Republic of South Africa. In 1980 the U.S. halted grain sales to the Soviet Union, followed by a ban on all agricultural products to express its displeasure over the Soviet invasion of Afghanistan. In 1982, similar action was taken by the U.S. over the establishment of military government to suppress

---

* Some nations, considering themselves at war, refrain nevertheless from overt military action. For example, member states of the Arab League have for decades considered themselves at war with Israel, hence several of their acts—boycotts, embargoes, and blacklists—could technically be regarded as measures attendant to latent military action.

the free trade-union movement in Poland. An import embargo was imposed in 1982 on all goods from Argentina by Great Britain and her European allies to effectuate the withdrawal of Argentine military forces from the Falkland Islands. Earlier, in response to the invasion of Ethiopia by Italian forces in 1935, the League of Nations imposed sanction on the aggressor.*

When in 1979 Iran permitted the seizure of the U.S. embassy in Teheran and the detention of diplomatic personnel as hostages, the U.S. imposed trade sanctions and ordered the freezing of all Iranian government assets in U.S. banks and their affiliates overseas. Writes President Carter in his *Memoirs:* "I thought that depriving them of about twelve billion dollars in ready assets was a good way to get their attention."[11] Britain took similar action in the Falkland case, but neither the U.S. nor Britain achieved their objectives solely by recourse to sanctions. The American hostages were released when the election of a hardline right-wing administration in the U.S. signaled to Iran that more direct measures might be taken, and Argentine forces had to be driven off the islands by military force.

At times sanctions are applied very selectively, care being taken to exempt certain exports or imports to limit damages to both sides, or because only one particular economic weapon is available. Thus, when in 1973 the Arab oil-producing states sought to compel the United States and several of her Western European allies to withdraw military support from Israel, an oil embargo was imposed only against selected countries, reinforced by the previously established blacklisting of companies trading with Israel. Neither action achieved its objective.†

In general history shows that sanctions by themselves are quite ineffectual.[12] Indeed, they have been said to be the equivalent of shooting oneself in the foot. Freezing of Iranian assets, for example, also penalized U.S. companies with claims against Iran and frightened oil-rich Arab governments and private investors who feared similar action against their holdings and deposits in U.S. banks in the event of some revolutionary developments in their own countries. It would seem that, to succeed, sanctions must be total, all of the target country's trading partners participating without reservation, without leaks, loopholes, or circumvention.[13]

One form of economic warfare falls between psychological, military, and political action, namely the inducement of a country's economic collapse by

* On recent experiences with sanctions, see Seeler (1982), pp. 7-10. Other instances were the 1941 U.S. embargo on export of pig and scrap iron to Japan to deter Japan from expanding her military actions in the Far East and the embargo on export of helium to Nazi Germany, instituted by the U.S. prior to the Second World War, to inhibit Hitler's war machine. The latter act compelled Germany to fill the dirigible Hindenburg with highly inflammable hydrogen instead, which caused, or at least contributed to, the 1937 air disaster at Lakehurst, New Jersey, when the airship was totally destroyed.

† Early in 1982, to register its displeasure over certain actions by Libya's ruler Colonel Quadhafi, the United States among other measures ordered a ban on oil imports from that country; on the role of oil in economic warfare, see Chapter 16 below.

precipitation of a major economic crisis. The classic case is that of Chile under the socialist government of Salvador Allende Gossens. Persuasive evidence exists to indicate that several U.S. administrations, over a ten-year period, funnelled several million dollars into Chile through the Central Intelligence Agency and through a number of private corporations to aggravate already difficult economic conditions in order to bring about Allende's overthrow.[14]

In preparation for national emergencies or for war, governments take steps to conserve and stockpile critical resources. The United States, for example, has been stockpiling the following raw materials or commodities for the eventuality of a major war: gold, oil, chromite ore, chromiumferro alloys, manganese, ferromanganese, vanadium, ferrovanadium, and platinum-group metals.[15] Similarly, in spite of the Nazi-Soviet Pact of 1939 Germany withheld from its treaty partner as many strategic goods as possible, in preparation for the planned invasion of the Soviet Union.[16]

Full-Scale Economic Warfare

When war turns hot and is declared as such, some economic objectives are pursued by direct military means, others continue to be addressed by economic means but on a more comprehensive if not total scale. The overall objective of course is to prevent the enemy from continuing the war; if that cannot be readily accomplished the aim is to cripple his war efforts.

Economic warfare measures are direct and indirect. Among the former are immediate seizure or impoundment of all enemy assets, including securities, bank deposits, corporate property, ships in port, and planes on the ground. Citizens are prohibited from trading with the enemy unless licensed to do so by the government. Indirect measures seek to dry up sources of material supply and finance located beyond the enemy's direct grasp. Intelligence ferrets out secret sources and points of departure of blockade running ships or planes preparatory to persuading nonbelligerent or neutral suppliers to desist from delivery. Where this is not feasible, preemptive buying of critical materials is an alternative.*

Because the Western Allies, principally the United States and Great Britain, were the leading naval powers in the 1914-1918 and 1939-1945 world wars, they based the weight of their economic warfare measures against Germany and Japan on their ability to effectively blockade shipping to and from both countries. That strategy had been successful during the Napoleonic wars a century earlier and was expected to have the same effect again. Germany, on the other hand, and to an extent Japan in the second world war, used their limited naval strength—principally submarines and fast cruisers or pocket battle ships—to interdict the allies' shipping and breech the blockade at least for

---

* During World War Two, once the leading neutral—the United States—had entered the war, the Allies exerted intense pressure on the remaining neutrals, foremost Sweden, Switzerland, Turkey, Portugal, and Argentina, to reduce or cease altogether their trade with Germany. See Milward (1979), pp. 306-307.

transport of the most critical strategic materials.[17] Naval blockades are instituted to interdict trade by compelling neutral or nonbelligerent suppliers to divert their cargoes away from the target country or, regarding enemy shipping, to seize ship and cargo as a prize or if that is not feasible to sink the ship.*

World War Two also saw strategic bombing attain the level of a science. Basing their strategies on economic and military intelligence analysis of Germany's economy, the Allies sought to attack and destroy assumed strategic bottlenecks, that is, segments of the German economy without which, it was assumed, that country could not continue the war, for example ball bearing, synthetic rubber, and fuel plants. Germany however was able to cope with the resulting damages by increasing trade with such neutrals as Sweden and by internal re-organization undetected by the Allies until after the war. The story was different with regard to aviation fuel. There, timely and strategic bombing virtually immobilized the German airforce and weakened German defenses for the critical 1944 Normandy invasion.

Postwar Economic Warfare

Since the beginning of recorded history, victors have demanded indemnities from the vanquished. Following the defeat of France in 1871, victorious Prussia extracted from France gold worth several billion dollars by today's prices. Half a century later, France along with her allies retaliated and demanded several times that amount in gold, as well as a long list of other economic and military transfers and territorial demands centering in part on rich mineral deposits. The intent in both instances was to prevent the defeated power from rising

---

* Germany's decision in 1915 to sink the Lusitania, carrying a large number of U.S. citizens, hastened the entry of the U.S. into World War One; similar acts directed at U.S. shipping in 1940 and early 1941 had the same effect, preparing the American public for U.S. entry into that war as well.

During the Napoleonic wars, and on other occasions in the past, naval blockades were executed by actual deployment of warships astride major trade lanes or outside key ports. During World War Two, the Allies relied mainly on strategic bombing and mining of narrow straights, channels, and ports. Because Germany was essentially a land power, and following the defeat of France in 1940 and the occupation of the Balkans in Southeast Europe, the German economy could be supplied from areas not subject to Allied naval power, for example Sweden, Turkey, and Portugal. That so-called neutral hole in the Allied blockade enabled Germany to prolong the war by many months. Landlocked Switzerland, obliged to obtain vital supplies by sea through the Allied blockade, was more susceptible to Allied pressure to reduce trade with Germany and Italy.

According to one source, it was in the Far East that economic warfare, based mainly on naval and air power, "achieved its greatest success," mainly because, aside from the Soviet Union—which until late in 1945 did not participate in the war against Japan—there were no neutrals in the area and, unlike Germany, Japan was an island. Most Japanese traffic from occupied territories therefore had to be by sea. Milward (1979), p. 317.

During World War Two, Germany and Japan sought to defend against Allied economic warfare measures by increasing the submarine arm, concentrating their naval power on blockade-running and breaking, by stockpiling, and "by ruthless acquisition" of needed materials from all territories their armies managed to occupy. *Ibid.*, p. 299.

again. History indicates that after 1871 France recovered quickly, posing an insurmountable obstacle to Germany's military ambitions in 1914, and within twenty years from the imposition of World War One reparations Germany was ready once again to invade France. Following World War Two, the Western Allies briefly entertained the thought of reducing Germany to an agricultural existence, abandoning that idea when it became apparent that this would only serve Soviet designs on Western Europe. The Soviet Union, partly to ensure Germany's pacification, partly to replace what German forces had destroyed in the Soviet Union, proceeded to dismantle most of Germany's industrial plants within the grasp of its occupation forces.

Imperialism and Colonialism as Forms of Economic Warfare

As long as humans have roamed the earth, the strong have sought to improve their living conditions at the expense of the weak. The earliest organized and institutionalized forms of that were slavery and feudalism. Then came the great empires of the European maritime powers, carved out of Africa, the Americas, and Asia. The common denominator was economic exploitation, a form of economic warfare. Simply put, the imperial power, by force of arms, stealth, and guile, either annexed territories outright as colonies or, indirectly "as protectorates," or rendered them dependent by other means. It then obtained from the victim whatever raw materials and commodities could be extracted, at lowest possible cost. At the same time, it secured for its industry markets for surplus products. To ensure uninterrupted flow of goods in both directions, the imperial power, through colonial administration, imposed on the overseas territory a regime which had all the marks of a military dictatorship. Laws and decrees were formulated and at times ruthlessly enforced to discourage or suppress any opposition to imperial rule, punish those who dared to challenge the imperial order, and prevent the captive economy from reaching a point from which it could hope to develop independently. Political, social, and cultural measures were likewise applied to strengthen the imperial hold. One notable characteristic of this form of economic warfare was racial degradation of the subject peoples, one of the last remaining vestiges of which is the Republic of South Africa in its relation to black populations in Southern Africa generally and in its midst.

Imperialism also took other, more subtle forms, many of which we encountered in our review of basic economic forces and of the modes of financial manipulation used by the powerful to subdue and exploit the weak. Originally identified by Lenin and others as exclusive traits of capitalism and its attendant evil, the social class struggle, certain aspects of both imperialism and colonialsm can today be found in the system imposed by the Soviet Union on Eastern and Southeastern Europe. However, certain important differences must be noted. Able to secure compliances by other means, the Soviet Union does not directly appropriate or annex all of its dependencies nor does it seek proprietary privileges abroad. We shall examine this relationship more closely in Chapter 13.

Since the end of World War Two, the economic warfare aspect of imperialism has lost its sharp edge. No longer are sources of raw material and cheap labor or overseas markets annexed. More subtle forms now are applied to the same or similar ends. Because these are to some extent reminiscent of the older forms, terms like neoimperialism and neocolonialism have been coined. But as we shall see in Chapters 14 and 15, the differences between the new relationship and its discredited past far outweigh the similarities.

Suggested Questions and Discussion Topics

Why must nations engage in foreign trade?

How is foreign trade promoted? By what means is it blocked or disrupted?

What is foreign aid and for what reasons is it given? What are some of the adverse effects of foreign aid on recipient states' economies?

Discuss some of the means and methods of limited and of full-scale economic warfare.

Why may imperialism and colonialism, and their contemporary versions, be regarded as forms of economic warfare?

Considering the contents of Chapters 5 and 6 together, show how finance, trade, and aid contribute to growing economic and political interdependence of nations on a global scale.

Chapter 7
Armed Force and Intelligence:
Nonviolent Aspects

Armed Forces

Force-In-Being

Force need not be applied; it can be quite effective just being there. Mere possession of overwhelming military power together with demonstrated ability and willingness to use it, ruthlessly if necessary, cannot but help impress a weaker state. Add to that the absence of an effective or credible counterweight, that is, another equally determined and equipped power ready to throw its weight into the scales, and we have an explanation of the relative quiescence among states situated in the immediate vicinity of the Soviet Union. Indeed, the noteworthy aspect of the recent history of Soviet military power is its repeated utilization not for conquest but to subdue, control, and intimidate— in other words force as a tool of "coercive diplomacy," a manifestation of "force-in-being," "demonstration of force," "show of force," "showing the flag," or "rattling the sabre."[1]

The common purpose of such indirect methods is to impress another government or people with the potential consequences of an act of omission or commission, to influence a government to cease and desist from a given course of action or to induce it to surrender without a struggle. To that end, a naval force may sail to a point within range of its guns, planes, or missiles, or planes may be moved closer to a border. Before the nuclear age, a relatively expensive but meaningful signal was partial mobilization of armed forces. Today, mobilization being too dangerous—a nuclear exchange could be precipitated all too readily—the alternative is to let it be known that the nuclear striking forces have been put on alert.*

---

* An alert, declared for demonstration purposes, is not to be confused with automatic alert in response to reports or signals indicating an impending or actual nuclear attack.

   Hitler, and to a lesser extent his partner, Mussolini, banking on the relative timidity of political democracies before they are aroused, were initially quite successful in relying on their own repeatedly asserted readiness to employ force to dissuade Great Britain and France from resisting what turned out to be preludes to World War Two. In 1935,

Probably the first effective demonstration of recourse to force-in-being in the nuclear age occurred during the Cuban missile crisis in 1962 when the United States, if not enjoying a nuclear monopoly at that time, unquestionably was in a position of nuclear preponderance, enabling President Kennedy to compel the Soviet Union to back down in the Caribbean without a shot being fired.*

Given the enormous destructive power of contemporary nuclear weapons and of yet more powerful ones still in the planning or experimental stages, not only Soviet but all military planners today are greatly concerned lest their country turn out to be a defenseless against blackmail based solely on implied use of one or another of these weapons.

Deterrence

An aggressor can be deterred only if the costs of an attack exceed the potential gains. Therefore, to be effective defense measures must be credibly sufficient to inflict the required damage. From earlier times a first deterrent step has been formation of alliances to balance any conceivable opposing combination of forces. Beyond that the usual method was erection of theoretically impenetrable fortifications along borders, deployment of forces in strategic places, periodic and highly visible military maneuvers, or display of particularly potent weapons on parade. Today, emphasis has been shifted to detonation and testing of nuclear weapons, ballistic missile tests, spacecraft maneuvers, development of ever more effective electronic defense systems, and dispersal and concealment of offensive as well as defensive bases to escape detection and premature destruction and to retain and maximize retaliatory capabilities.

An important difference between nuclear and conventional deterrents is that the former must of necessity be absolutely credible, leaving little room for doubt. In 1914 and again in 1939 Germany faced numerically and materially

ranting and raving, threatening apocalyptic horrors—the Germans call this posture "Schrecklichkeit"—moving armed forces toward the Austro-German border, Hitler obtained Austria's surrender without having to fire a shot. The dismemberment of Czechoslovakia, agreed to by Great Britain and France at Munich in 1938, likewise was exclusively the result of the demonstration effect exploited by ruthlessly aggressive leaders presumed to be ready to wage war to achieve their objectives. Since that time, Munich has become synonymous with appeasement.

* The means used in that instance was a naval quarantine, a measure designed to interdict shipment only of specific goods or weapons as distinct from a full-fledged blockade which attempts to seal off all traffic in both directions; on the Cuban missile crisis of 1962, see Allison (1971); on the blockade action, *ibid.*, Chapter 6.

Under international law, to be respected a blockade must be effective; that is, the blockading power's vessels must be capable of physically enforcing the blockade. Unwilling to cast a net throughout the Caribbean wide and tight enough to physically prevent all Soviet ships carrying missiles to Cuba from reaching their destination, the U.S. merely declared a quarantine, announcing to the world that any vessel carrying certain types of weapons would be searched and, if found to carry the prohibited military hardware, turned away. Ultimately, the deciding factor was not the effectiveness of the naval measures but the nuclear force known by Soviet leaders to be at the disposal of the United States and sufficient at that time to enable the latter to prevail in a showdown.

superior military combinations. Her high commands were not deterred from launching attacks, because they were confident that opposing combinations lacked sufficient cohesion to be effective during the early decisive phases of each war and could therefore be brushed aside, circumvented, or overcome. Today the sting of a retaliatory nuclear capability, however modest it may be, is bound to be felt at once and with unpredictable consequences by an aggressor employing nuclear force. In the event of a nuclear-backed conventional attack, the potentiality of a nuclear reaction cannot be ruled out under all circumstances.

Firmness, determination, and clarity of purpose are major ingredients of deterrence. Construction of an incomplete defense system, its weapons pointing in only one direction, virtually invited Hitler's armies to attack France through Belgium and the Netherlands in 1940 and the Japanese to attack the British naval fortress of Singapore by land. Similarly, a firm line on the map, indicating to an aggressor precisely at what geographic point and over which territorial move a military response must be expected, is considered a *sine qua non* of deterrence. Failure on the part of the United States to draw such a line on the Korean peninsula prior to 1950 is said to have been interpreted by North Korea as a signal that an attack on South Korea would not precipitate a U.S. military response. Likewise, ambiguous signals to Hitler from London and Paris regarding the Allies' military intentions permitted him to test their determination again and again until finally his attack on Poland in September of 1939 forced them to take a stand, albeit far too late to prevent a second worldwide conflagration.

Arms-building programs are widely believed to have deterrent qualities. For example, expansion of a naval construction program or a shift from one weapons system to one more lethal may cause an aggressor to hestitate or reconsider. So might a well publicized announcement of a breakthrough or improvement in weapon designs, for example an aircraft carrier capable of launching long-range bombers equipped with radar evading or detecting multi-warhead missiles, or a more silent, more far-ranging missile-carrying submarine. Allies are reassured if certain types of weapons are developed, tested successfully, and deployed and opponents are warned. The virtual absence of a timely and effective armament program on the part of the United States in the 1930s certainly encouraged Germany and Japan in their aggressive designs in Europe and the Far East. By the same token, the existence of such a program in the United States and the Soviet Union, on a scale unparalleled in history, has so far caused a number of smaller aggressors in peripheral areas and the two superpowers as well to be most circumspect in their recourse to armed force.

Conversely, acting as a negative deterrent are efforts to keep an antagonist or a combination of antagonists at a numerical or qualitative disadvantage. Between 1921 and 1936, the United States, Great Britain, and France, their naval superiority challenged by Japan, Italy, and Germany, sought to contain the threat by limiting the six navies to certain types of ships and armament based on ratios reflecting the prevailing naval strength. The complex system, enshrined in a series of interrelated bi- and multilateral treaties and agreements, was bound to fail because it omitted taking into account the underlying causes of Japanese, German, and Italian aggressiveness and because no world power will at any rate accept an implication of second- or third-class status.[2] These lessons the world was to be taught again, scarcely forty years later, when the Soviet Union began to insist on military parity with the West. The result of that challenge was the series of treaties, agreements, and continuing negotiations considered in detail in Chapter 18.

A more decisive deterrent of course is to disarm a potential enemy totally or, at the very least, deprive him of the more destructive and lethal weapons. Following Germany's defeat in World War One, the victorious Allies, in the Treaty of Versailles (1919), aside from numerous other punitive and restrictive measures imposed on the defeated nation strict limits on her military threat potential. Her naval strength was severely circumscribed, airplane construction was restricted to commercial craft, and her land army was not to exceed 100,000 men. Germany also was forbidden to construct or operate any kind of submarine, and there were to be no armored forces of any kind.[3]

Following their defeat in World War Two, Germany was briefly treated as a power to be permanently disarmed and Japan was prohibited from acquiring anything except a modest internal defense force. With respect to Germany the illogicality of confining disarmament to industrially advanced nations on a selective, discriminatory basis became apparent within a little more than a decade after the peace treaty of 1919 and again within less than five years following World War Two. In the first instance Germany brushed aside all restrictions, emerging once again as a major threat, and in the second, except for nuclear armament, the Allies reversed their position on their own account, rearming Germany as rapidly as they could, in fact incorporating her in their military alliance. Japan and her erstwhile conqueror, the United States, became close military partners and Japan's arms limitations likewise came under review.

The ultimate deterrent, of course, would be disarmament on a universal scale. While the need for disarmament on a global scale has in principle been recognized since the turn of the century, each and every concrete proposal toward that objective has so far manifestly failed. The reasons for that are many but one stands out: during each cycle of universal disarmament discussion and negotiation, the uncertainty surrounding so far-reaching and complex a task, compels even the most dedicated supporters of the principle among world leaders, to cling to armament just in case. It is conceivable that the threat of a nuclear holocaust will at long last move the cause of universal disarmament from more or less ritual exercise to at least partial realization.

Arms Transfers

In recent years, transfers of arms by sale or by gift have mushroomed throughout the world.* What are the underlying causes, what place does this aspect of international relations occupy on states' foreign policy agendas?

* The politically most salient issues arising from that development are discussed in detail in Chapter 19.

Whether sold for cash or transferred on soft credit terms or as a gift, arms win friends and influence people. All nations, or nearly all, feel threatened from some direction and prefer therefore to have at their disposal certain deterrent capabilities. The universal drive is to acquire weapons superior to those available to actual or potential enemies or hostile combinations: faster planes, speedier, more mobile tanks, more destructive and more accurate missiles. One major spur to international arms transfers in recent years has been the changeover from manual, human-directed to automatic, electronically computer-controlled and directed weapon systems. This has driven the costs as well as the technical dimensions of arms production beyond the means of all but a handful of countries. At the same time, it accelerates technological obsolescence, accentuating the need for constant modernization and replacement. The other major incentive for arms transfer is of course the spiralling arms competition between the superpowers.

Law and Order Support and Peace-keeping

On occasion, states place units of their armed forces at the disposal of states unable to cope with natural, political, or military emergencies. Armed land, sea, and air contingents have been transferred to assist other governments to prevent riots, insurrection, or civil war.* U.S., French, Italian, and British troops and troops from states uncommitted in the East-West confrontation furnished directly or under United Nations auspices have been employed to keep the peace between warring factions and foreign armies in Lebanon. U.S. troops alone were assigned to the border between Israel and Egypt. Armed units from neutral and nonaligned countries have participated in peacekeeping operations under UN auspices in numerous trouble spots throughout the world, and units of African states have served similar purposes on the African continent. Unarmed U.S. and Soviet military transport planes are used frequently to ferry troops and emergency supplies as well as military equipment for governments in many parts of the world whose own transport facilities are inadequate.

Foreign Intelligence†

The primary reason for existence of foreign intelligence services is not conduct of clandestine operations abroad or infliction of "dirty tricks" on foreign

---

* U.S. involvement in Vietnam started with internal police support, a continuation of a practice which has involved U.S. armed forces in the Caribbean and Central America for the greater part of the twentieth century. Soviet, Cuban, and East German forces perform similar services for "fraternal" socialist regimes in many parts of the world, a first step usually being provision of secret police cadres. France has protected friendly regimes in her former colonies with the aid of an "intervention force" created for that purpose; Great Britain has done the same, but more discreetly, in her former colonies in the Caribbean and Central America.

† Foreign intelligence is to be distinguished from internal intelligence, which usually is associated with internal police or national security investigation. The two spheres blend and often come into conflict in Western democracies over the issue of counterespionage. In the Soviet Union the two functions are combined within the KGB.

governments, but enhancement as well as protection of their own countries' military capabilities. In those respects, they are engaged in a war of sorts against their counterparts in opposing countries who will try to defeat their efforts and against foreign agents in their own backyard who will seek to penetrate their defenses and steal their military secrets.

The typical organizational approach is to openly establish separate, strictly military intelligence and counterintelligence services for the armed forces as a whole or attached to army, navy, and air force or hide all or some of such bodies in some recesses of an executive branch. There usually is a central agency to coordinate the total information flow—which, incidentally, involves numerous nonmilitary departments and agencies—as well as conduct its own intelligence activities over and above those required by the specialized military services. Primary responsibilities are collection by overt and covert means of intelligence pertaining to foreign military establishments and capabilities, analysis and interpretation of what has been collected, planning and execution of operations at home and abroad in furtherance of national security, including counterintelligence and counterespionage.* A coordinating or central agency's principal responsibility is to ensure that relevant information is directed to appropriate government agencies in a timely fashion.†

The bulk of intelligence gathered by all agencies is procured by overt means, consisting of inherently nonsensitive information readily available to the general public in most countries. (We noted earlier the proclivity for secrecy characteristic of totalitarian regimes). The military significance of much of such information becomes apparent only upon expert analysis and interpretation and through collation with related fragments from different sources, collected at different times. As a matter of course, the greater the military significance of a given item, the more determined will be its guardians to protect it from

---

* The two terms are often used interchangeably but, strictly speaking, while counterespionage concerns itself with the activities of foreign spies and their witting and unwitting tools, counterintelligence seeks to uncover, penetrate, and neutralize the foreign organization behind them.

In totalitarian systems, control over all communications and security processes being essential to regime survival, foreign intelligence functions are not only centrally coordinated and controlled but are combined with internal secret police functions, placing them at an advantage over open societies with respect to counterintelligence and counterespionage, for example Nazi Germany's RSHA (Reichssicherheits-hauptamt or State Security Central Office) and the Soviet Union's *Komitet Gosudarstvennoi Bezopasnosti* (hence KGB) or Committee for State Security, successor to Cheka, GPU and NKVD.

The Cold War, coupled with the theoretical and technical imminence and potential finality of a nuclear attack, has accentuated the need for constantly alert, technically up-to-date, comprehensive and aggressive intelligence capability certainly in the U.S. and the USSR, but increasingly also on the part of their respective allies. In addition, the conventional, narrowly military orientation of intelligence has been expanded to encompass a wide range of political, economic, technical, and scientific as well as social subjects all of which are now considered to be germane to a nation's military capability.

† The CIA was specifically created for that purpose, mainly in response to the surprise attack on Pearl Harbor on December 7, 1941. See Cline (1976), pp. 93ff; Jeffreys-Jones (1977), Chapter 14.

unauthorized disclosure. It is at this point that intelligence resorts to covert means, employing undercover agents or spies to steal, blackmail, bribe, seduce or murder to gain access to vital secrets or at least secure details, fragments, or snippets of information believed to relate to an actual or potential enemy's military capabilities or plans. Or efforts are directed to penetrate opposing services, uncover their methods, identify or render harmless or even recruit or "turn around" their agents or spies, and subvert other key military or civilian personnel and possibly recruit them also or at least persuade or force them by means of blackmail to cooperate.

Espionage is conducted on a short- or long-term basis, mostly by human but increasingly also by electronic means. Unless captured or otherwise rendered useless, spies and agents are withdrawn after relatively short periods of service. For long-term purposes, "moles" or "master spies" are recruited or planted deep in a target country's intelligence structure, military establishment, or in some other sensitive government office or agency. Or, carefully trained and programmed "sleepers" are insinuated into sensitive positions or are provided with a cover such as an entirely nonsensitive civilian occupation. Unlike the mole, who is expected to produce intelligence and generally facilitate his manipulator's espionage designs on a continuing basis, the sleeper is instructed to remain inactive unless needed earlier for some critical task. More likely, sleepers are held in reserve for real emergencies such as war.*

Foreign intelligence operations are conducted by "legals" and "illegals". The latter, spies and agents, are infiltrated by various means, smuggled across borders through underground contacts, landed from submarines, or parachuted, or they enter in the guise of travelling salesmen, businessmen, educators, students, scientists or are hidden in groups of artists or of athletes. "Legals" are inserted as members of diplomatic missions. They are given a bogus assignment at an embassy or consulate and if discovered claim diplomatic immunity, to be returned promptly to their homeland. Because all Soviet bloc countries and most dictatorships and authoritarian regimes exercise total control over their citizens, it is relatively easy for them to insert agents in the guise of tourists, journalists, airline employees, or members of trade missions or state corporations.

Mutually reinforcing advances in communications, electronics, space exploration and space craft operation, and computer science and technology, have

---

* The British intelligence official Kim Philby is perhaps the best known mole, who, for many years, until exposed and forced to flee to the Soviet Union, served Soviet intelligence in key positions within the Western intelligence network. For Soviet moles placed inside Nazi Germany and Nazi moles inside the Soviet Union before and during World War Two, see Trepper (1977), and A.C. Brown (1975). It is widely suspected that Mossad, the Israeli Secret Service, has moles in sensitive positions in all major and many lesser powers, and sleepers securely installed in a number of Middle Eastern countries with whom Israel has been or is expected at some future date to be at war. Günter Guillaume, an employee of the East German Democratic Republic's Ministry of State Security, for several years supplied his employer with West German and NATO secrets from his position as a personal assistant to West Germany's Chancellor Willy Brandt. Rositzke (1981), pp. 149-151.

enormously enhanced the capacity of industrially advanced powers to uncover safely, from a distance, in minutes if not seconds, what formerly would have called for high risk espionage efforts over a period of years. However the need for the human spy operating on the ground has not yet been obviated. For many espionage tasks there is as yet no substitute for the human touch and human ingenuity.*

The objectives of espionage change with changing circumstances. Always highly prized are order of battle of military units, weapons or weapon systems, military applicable technology, military strategy and tactics, war and defense plans generally, location and quality of defense installations, transportation networks and bottlenecks, ports and coastal waters, and the three C's, command, control and communication.† Regarding the latter, standard espionage objects have always been any and all materials relating to the production and use of secret codes such as code books, encoding and decoding machines, anything pertaining to construction of ciphers, and coded messages. It is generally conceded that successes in breaking German and Japanese secret codes materially contributed to the Allied victory in World War Two.‡

A major problem confronting all nations who have equipped themselves with ever more sophisticated and complex intelligence gathering facilities is management of what is being collected. Today it is a question largely of true intelligence against glut produced by legions of agents, feeding their often contradictory products through an infinite array of often conflicting and competing channels onto computers. Can computers discriminate the trivial from the significant, the militarily crucial piece of information from the wholly marginal? Will the inexorably expanding mass of information first completely

---

* The principal U.S. agency concerned with code cracking and other electronic and signal intelligence is the National Security Agency (NSA). It is believed to employ 95,000 people, classifies 50 to 100 million documents a year, and has an annual budget of close to $10 billion. Bamford (1982), Chapter 3, especially pp. 77–78. The National Reconnaissance Office (NRO) manages U.S. spy satellites. The NSA's British counterpart is the electronic intelligence center at Cheltenham, England, which was penetrated by the KGB for several years. *New York Times* (October 24, 1981). West Germany's central electronic and signal agency is the *Bundesnachrichtendienst* (BND)

† Because Soviet technology lagged considerably behind that of the U.S., the KGB, with the assistance of Soviet bloc sister services, mainly those of Poland and Czechoslovakia, embarked in the early 1980s upon an all-out effort to close the gap. Rapidly expanding its foreign industrial, technical, and commercial operations, the Soviet agency, according to U.S. intelligence estimates, succeeded in circumventing U.S. imposed restrictions on transfer of strategic goods to Soviet bloc countries, narrowing the gap from about ten to about two years by 1982. Methods employed ranged from traditional espionage and theft to acquisition of advanced technological products to the Socialist Bloc via third-country middlemen. See Rositzke (1981), pp. 188–190.

‡ See Lewin (1978) and A.C. Brown (1975), p. 38. Today's codes, enciphered or encrypted by computer, can confront expert cryptographers trying to break them with quadrillions of possible combinations. Yet it is said that the same computer technology can be used to try out every one of these "in less than a day." Powers (1983), p. 12.

satiate, then stymie or confuse key agencies, resulting in a final, fatal end-effect?*

Suggested Questions and Discussion Topics

How may armed forces be employed to achieve foreign policy objectives without recourse to violence?

What are the primary objectives of states' foreign intelligence services? How and by what means are these objectives pursued nonviolently?

---

* The sheer volume of intelligence generated these days, coupled with the uncertainties of ever more complex international relations, tends to rule out total accuracy and reliability in intelligence analysis; see Aspin (1981), and Ellsworth and Adelman (1979).

Chapter 8
Armed Force and Intelligence:
Violent Uses

A variety of domestic as well as foreign political considerations motivate governments to pursue some foreign policy objectives by violent means or accept violent action against their territory without recourse to formal declaration of war. Among the reasons for that reticence are fear of escalation, a desire not to activate alliance or collective security mechanisms designed to become operative automatically if war is formally declared, and, marginally but not unimportantly, a desire to escape the onus of aggressor or warmonger. To cover up the war-like character of this form of violence, numerous euphemisms are employed, such as "act of war," "armed conflict," "police action," or "liberation." Depending on the issue, the disposition of forces, and the circumstances, undeclared wars are fought at several levels and in several disguises, rarely however against major powers or against firmly established regimes. With very few exceptions, the target is an already unstable or militarily vulnerable state whose social, economic, or political fabric is to be further weakened by propaganda or disinformation methods discussed earlier, or by military means. Alternatively military intervention may be ordered to restore the status quo.

Armed Operations Short of War

Incursions, Surgical Strikes, and Hot Pursuit

Actions under this category can be subdivided into military engagements conducted by regular, irregular, or paramilitary forces entering a country openly or clandestinely by infiltration, induced rebellion or subversion, sabotage, terrorism, or assassination, all classifiable as acts of war if governments affected are so inclined. Forces employed may be the initiating state's own regular military formations (sometimes introduced in the guise of "volunteers"), those furnished by friendly states or dependencies (called proxies), nationals of the target state who have trained abroad and infiltrated, or they may be mercenaries (soldiers for hire). Alternatively, the instruments may be nationals of the target state fighting entirely on their own as guerillas or in formally identified revolutionary formations but armed, supplied, and directed or advised from abroad.

Actions by regular forces take the form of armed clashes or temporary incursions across borders into the target state's airspace or territorial waters, for demonstration purposes, as a warning, to provoke a military response, or perhaps to test a potential enemy's air, sea, or land defenses. Or military action may be ordered defensively in "hot pursuit" into adjacent territory of an actual or purported invading force, or a "surgical strike" may be conducted to eliminate a specific threat, a nuclear installation for example, or as a warning.* Of a similar nature would be dispatch of a strike force to disperse, disrupt, or discourage an attack by regular or irregular forces about to be launched from adjacent territory or in retaliation for such attacks in the past.†

Faced with a growing threat from "terrorists" and other illegal or illicit forces, including pirates, most states reserve the right to resort to armed force to protect their endangered nationals or their property, if governments responsible for their safety are unable or unwilling to act. Israel for instance in 1976 used its regular forces to rescue its citizens held hostage in Uganda, and United States forces were inserted in 1980 into Iran to rescue U.S. diplomats in an unsuccessful attempt to replicate the Israeli feat.‡

The 1968 invasion and partial occupation of Czechoslovakia by Soviet and other Warsaw Pact forces, the Soviet action against Hungary in 1956, and the invasion of Afghanistan in 1979 were each staged under pretext of an invitation to intervene. Not too dissimilar, the 1970 U.S. airstrikes, followed by invasion of nominally neutral Cambodia (now Kampuchea) from neighboring Vietnam, were justified as acts of self-defense, but the 1961 landing by U.S. organized, trained, and directed Cuban exiles at the Bay of Pigs with the intent to precipitate an anti-Castro uprising was clearly an act of war, and so, by international consensus, were the U.S. supported incursions and other military actions directed against the Sandinista government of Nicaragua in 1984 and 1985.

Insurgency

Irregular or paramilitary forces including mercenaries engage in insurgency to stage coups d'états, commit sabotage of critical installations, and subvert or dislocate segment of the target state's population. Some of these actions are

---

* In 1981, to prevent Iraq from acquiring nuclear military capability and to warn other Arab states in the region not to try, Israel destroyed by air-raid Iraq's nuclear reactor shortly before it was to become operational. Of a similar nature would be dispatch of a strike force to disperse, disrupt, or discourage an attack by regular or irregular forces poised to attack from adjacent territory or in retaliation of such attacks in the past.

† Israel's periodic incursions into neighboring Lebanon have served that and similar purposes. So have actions by regular forces of the Republic of South Africa against Angola and Mozambique in Southern Africa.

‡ In 1975 U.S. Marines were used to rescue the American freighter *Mayaguez* and its crew from Cambodian troops who had seized the vessel in the Gulf of Siam. Weston, Falk, D'Amato (1980), pp. 911–917.

of a hit-and-run nature, solely to keep an antagonist off balance. Others are intended to produce lasting results.*

Somewhere between overt state-sponsored military action, spontaneous revolutionary acts, and purely internal strife, are rebellion induced from abroad and terrorism. Indisputably not deserving credit for every revolution on earth, the Soviet Union is nonetheless openly committed to support "wars of national liberation" throughout the world. Seen from Moscow, this means liberation of peoples from "imperialist-capitalist oppression." Viewed from the opposing side, including incidentally the Chinese People's Republic, it is no more than another manifestation of a Soviet drive to world domination. Whatever the truth, the Soviet Union and her allies take that particular commitment most seriously. Common to all such "wars" as an ultimate objective is the overthrow of an established, usually pro-Western or genuinely nonaligned regime. All means and all methods are appropriate: direct or indirect action, introduction of outside-trained guerilla cadres, foreign advisers or technicians, and provision of arms and equipment, usually via Soviet allies such as Cuba, the East German Democratic Republic, North Korea, or Vietnam.

In pursuance of their interests, the Western allies are somewhat more inhibited. However, working with a distinct advantage derived from centuries of world dominance and experience, still enjoying the use of support bases throughout the world, they can afford to assume a loftier, essentially defensive position. When the need arises they can compete successfully in this twilight zone between peace and war.

International Terrorism†

To some, terrorists are bomb-throwing anarchists, to others a valiant freedom-fighters; yet others may view them as soldiers in an undeclared war. If an objective determination can be made on that subject, leaving aside acts committed for purely criminal or wholly vicarious purposes, *international* terrorism may be viewed as the weapon of the militarily weak or impotent against superior military and police power. It is the instrument of individuals, groups, or even governments who for one or another reason cannot hope to achieve their objectives by legal means within established national legal orders or in accordance with prevailing international law. Or it is the instrument of the strong who prefer not to use their military power. It covers the global ideological and

---

* Counterinsurgency operations consist of military and police measures designed to isolate invading forces, cut off their sources of supply, drive them back across the border or into the sea, or at least deny them access to strategic locations.

† Strictly speaking, a terrorist is a person who resorts to violence primarily "for the purpose of putting the public or any section of the public in fear." (From the Terrorist Order promulgated by British Authorities with reference to events in Northern Ireland and in England. Weston, Falk, D'Amato (1980), p. 495.) The term is often misused or misapplied. Here we are not considering acts of terror perpetrated by governments to control or suppress their own population or acts of terror committed by contending domestic factions in the course of a civil war.

political spectrum from one extreme to the other ranging from ideologically uncommitted nationalists, separatists, and irredentists* seeking political independence, separation, or transfer from fascist, capitalist, socialist, or communist systems, to social-revolutionaries pressing for radical social change, to counter-revolutionaries defending the established order, or to anarchists rejecting all forms of government. Some of these groups seek social justice and an end to economic exploitation, some defend wealth and social privilege, some seek to avenge a historic wrong or prevent a new one, like genocide. Some acts of terrorism emanate spontaneously from the masses, others are instigated if not staged on the initiative of revolutionary regimes or of unpopular or dictatorial ones seeking to root out and discourage regime opponents operating from abroad. Or they are ordered or sponsored by otherwise law-abiding governments preferring to dissociate themselves from the act. All forms of terrorism share one basic characteristic: either because their purpose or their sponsorship does not stand the light of day, because exposure would invite their physical or organizational destruction, or because their potential targets might be alerted, all prepare their strikes in secret.[1]

International terrorists prefer to stage dramatic and often spectacular attacks, directed at randomly selected vulnerable civilian or military personnel facilities or installations, for a variety of purposes: to press specific political demands, collect ransom to finance further attacks, compel release of prisoners, impair the ability of governments or of entire social or state systems to function, dramatize the inability of governments or of entire social or state systems to function, demonstrate the inability of a particular government to maintain order, undermine the existing international order as such, or simply to bring a particular cause or grievance to world attention.†

As shown in Fig. 8-1 by far the largest number of terrorist attacks, as defined by Western intelligence, are directed against nationals of the industrial democracies—which raises the question whether this fact reflects merely the relative vulnerability of Western political democracies or whether it supports the theory shared widely that international terrorism in its major thrust, is a hot instrument of the Cold War, directed mainly against the United States and its allies.[2]

---

* Separatism: an ethnically distinct group seeks separation from a state; irredentism: a similar group, by transfer of the territory within which they reside, seek to join their ethnic kin in an adjacent nation state.

† Recognizing that giving in to terrorist demands for ransom or for other concessions merely invites more terrorist acts, most governments now refuse to negotiate with terrorists. Because the majority of terrorist acts have been directed at U.S. citizens, officials, and property, the U.S. government now tends to view certain groups of terrorists and nations known to sponsor or support them as waging undeclared war against the U.S. It therefore considers itself legally justified to hold nations sponsoring anti-U.S. terrorists fully accountable for these actions, inviting overt or covert economic, political, or military retaliation; not ruled out are "pre-emptive strikes" against terrorist bases. Israel, the target of numerous acts of terrorism as part of Arab especially Palestinian warfare, treats both terrorists and their victims as quasi-military participants in a life and death struggle for survival.

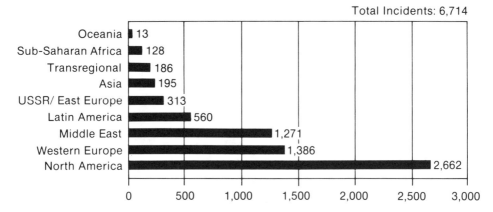

Fig. 8-1. Nationality of Victims of International Terrorist Attacks 1968–1980. (CIA, *Patterns of International Terrorism, 1980*, Fig. 6, p. 6.)

All terrorist groups operating internationally obviously require, at the very least, some government's passive indulgence, if for no other reason than that they are in need of training bases, places of refuge somewhere on earth, and funding, passports, transport, weapons, and equipment. In the West, belief is widespread that there is complicity to greater or lesser degree on the part of the Soviet Union, its principal allies, and such additional radical states as Libya, Syria, South Yemen, North Korea, and Cuba. Regarding Libya, there is no doubt that terrorism plays a part in the foreign policy plans of its radical revolutionary leader, Colonel Quadhafi.[3]* Soviet allies such as the East German Democratic Republic, Czechoslovakia, and Bulgaria are known to have maintained training bases and provided instructors, weapons, funds, and logistical support for groups associated with terrorist attacks, such as militant factions of the Palestine Liberation Organization (PLO) and some of the urban terrorist groups operating in Western Europe.

The case against the Soviet Union is not convincing. Ideologically Soviet authorities certainly show a consistent affinity for groups they deem "progressive" but which in Western eyes are classifiable as terrorist, by far the largest number of whom either are declared social-revolutionaries, or have sympathies

* Libya's leader received with open arms, as folk heroes, members of Palestinian commandos who machine-gunned civilians in Israel and the murderers of eleven Israeli athletes at the Munich Olympic Games in 1972 and is known to have supplied members of such groups as the Italian Red Brigade with sophisticated weapons to attack targets in Italy. To him, such attacks are legitimate responses to demonstrative application of superior military might by the United States and its allies, which he regards as a form of terrorism on the part of the strong against the weak. Revolutionaries like him, who emerged from militant struggle against foreign dominations of their homeland, are inclined to regard assassination and terror squads as legitimate counterparts of the forces which only half a century or so earlier executed leaders of national independence movements such as Omar Muchtar, revered Libyan Beduin leader hanged by Italian occupation forces in 1931, or which today support or sponsor terrorists seeking to overthrow socialist regimes or which support rightist dictatorships ruling by terror as the United States has done in Central America.

in that direction, but who in any case regard the Soviet Union as a friendly power and the U.S. as their principal enemy. Soviet foreign policy objectives are no doubt furthered by terrorist attacks on U.S. military personnel or installations, for example, or against pro-Western governments. Then there are "wars of national liberation," which to Western eyes in many instances are no more than terrorist attacks on established governments. However evidence directly linking Soviet authorities to specific acts of terrorism, though persuasive, is largely circumstantial, derived mainly from surmise and from alleged but secret and often unverifiable testimony obtained from defectors and from captives.[4]

Most likely the truth lies somewhere between extremes. It is doubtful that post-Stalin Soviet leaders consciously and deliberately encourage throwing of grenades into crowded market places or machine-gunning of innocent passengers waiting at a bus station or at an airport or that they regard such tactics as appropriate instruments of Soviet foreign policy. More likely they are caught on the horns of a dilemma of their own making. Committed as they are to world revolution, they cannot very well disassociate themselves from the tactics all revolutionary forces must of necessity employ in the face of overwhelming police and military power. Consequently Soviet authorities must continue, at the very least, to confer diplomatic or semiofficial recognition upon such groups even if these regard terrorism as a legitimate political instrument. By the same token, at international conferences or in international organizations, when the subject comes up, even if they should be so inclined Soviet bloc delegations cannot unreservedly join international efforts to curb or outlaw all forms of terrorism. All of this lends credence to the complicity theory. So does the often voiced Soviet confidence that theirs is the wave of the future, for today's terrorist often turns out to be tomorrow's prime minister of yet another pro-Soviet state.

Like the democracies who distinguish between just and unjust wars, Soviet leaders have convinced themselves that the struggles of most international groups identified by the West as terrorist are just and that in a just cause, ends justify means. Still, they are demonstrably cautious. Indications are that Soviet personnel have been observed in or near terrorist training camps only in surrogate countries, for example Cuba, East Germany, Czechoslovakia, Bulgaria, or South Yemen.

Evidence linking the United States to terrorist acts in many instances rests on similar assumptions and circumstances. For the greater part of the post-war period, the Soviet Union had to be content to support groups in opposition to established regimes whereas the United States had the majority of the nations of the world either on its side or at least uncommitted. From that position, recourse to terrorist tactics was not necessary.[5] This could be changing.*

---

* By National Security Decision Directive (NSDD) 138 of April 3, 1984, President Reagan directed U.S. government agencies to draft plans for "pre-emptive counterforce and military retaliation" against states known to sponsor terrorist acts against the U.S., or states suspected of such conduct. *Department of State Bulletin*, Vol. 84, 2086 (May

Whether or not U.S. authorities are directly involved, groups or individuals employing terrorist tactics but in causes supported by the United States—for instance against social-revolutionary regimes such as Cuba or Nicaragua—are considered by some not terrorists but "freedom fighters," akin to the patriots of the American Revolution. Likewise there is a widespread, though certainly not universally shared, tendency in U.S. government circles and U.S. public opinion to similarly regard anti-Soviet, anticommunist regimes who subject their own people, including exiles seeking refuge in the U.S., to police-state tactics, including terror.

It would seem that the major terrorist threat is perhaps posed not by the Soviet Union and its principal allies or by the United States but by certain radicalized LDCs, whose governments consider terrorist tactics less dangerous to themselves and less expensive than open warfare. But even they—while not overly concerned with the repercussions of terrorism on the existing international order—must realize eventually that terrorism is a two-edged sword. Once created and released, this genie cannot easily be recaptured. Awareness of the threat may account for the unusual display of universal solidarity in the United Nations Security Council when U.S. diplomats were held hostage in Iran.[6] Likewise, a sense of universal apprehension that attacks on one airliner can potentially affect all international air travel is responsible for the sharp reduction of politically motivated plane hijackings where the perpetrators utilize more than one country for planning, execution, and escape.

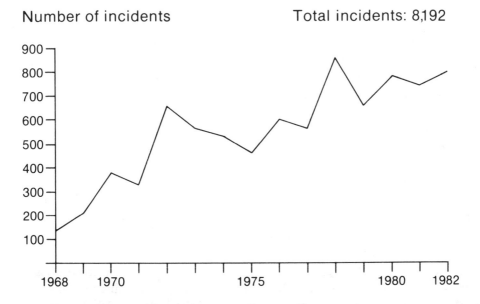

Number of incidents   Total incidents: 8,192

Fig. 8-2. Incidents of International Terrorist Attacks 1968–1982. (CIA, *Patterns of International Terrorism, 1980,* Table 1, p. 2 and *ibid, 1983.*)

1984), pp. 13–14. Included in such Counter-Terrorist (CT) measures were terrorist acts; see for example, the account of a CIA Primer entitled "Psychological Operations in Guerilla Warfare," *The New York Times* (October 17, 1984).

No government can remain insensitive to the greater threat, acquisition of nuclear weapons by terrorists and their use for blackmail purposes. It is unlikely therefore that any government will encourage or condone, let alone support materially, as an instrument of foreign policy or for other reasons, use of nuclear or biochemical weapons by terrorist groups.[7] All governments must fear coalescing of disparate terrorist groups into a consolidated international force under a unified command. Such a force could conceivably acquire nuclear weapons and could develop a momentum and direction entirely independent of its erstwhile sponsors.

Government-Sponsored Assassination
or Murder of Foreign Leaders

As is well known, the immediate incident sparking World War One was a political assassination traced to Czarist Russian designs on southeastern Europe. Two decades later, entertaining similar ambitions, Italian Fascism facilitated the assassination of Yugoslavia's King Alexander in France. But the most highly publicized case of government officials ordering assassination of foreign leaders is that of the United States, undoubtedly mainly because the subject was publicly aired and documents regarding it made publicly available. While no evidence was developed that any foreign leaders were actually assassinated by the hand of American officials, ample proof was presented that plots and plans had been under way within the Central Intelligence Agency against specific foreign leaders, including several who were eventually assassinated by someone and that in each case someone in authority in the U.S. government had either directly or indirectly given an order or a hint which could be interpreted as an order to eliminate the subject physically.[8]

Likewise well-known but of course not so well documented are the assassinations or murders of foreign leaders by Soviet secret services on Stalin's orders during that dictator's reign. Later, in 1956 following the Hungarian uprising, Hungarian Premier Imre Nagy was murdered and recently, in 1979, the communist Afghan President Hafizullah Amin, who had fallen out of Moscow's favor, was reportedly assassinated by a special Soviet squad. Political assassination or murder appears to be standard Soviet procedure to ensure removal of obstacles to Soviet foreign policy who cannot be removed by other means. Of course, all governments so inclined prefer to have the deed done by surrogates.[9]

So far the largest number of assassinations ordered by governments in conjunction with foreign policy objectives occur in the Middle East; most heavily involved are Syria, Iraq, and Iran. The deliberate assassination of Israeli diplomats by Palestinian commandos, mainly Al Fatah and the Black September group, and counterassassinations of PLO leaders by Israeli agents contribute further to an especially high toll in that region.*

* See CIA, *Patterns of International Terrorism, 1982,* Fig. 6, p. 7.

War

Definition and Typology of War

The traumatic impact of war on the human species and its frequency have produced an extraordinarily rich literature covering all spheres of intellectual and scientific inquiry and commentary. Historians, sociologists, psychologists, anthropologists, economists, and political scientists in particular have endeavored to discover commonalities regarding the causes of war, individual and group propensity to fight wars, modes of conduct, and conditions under which wars have been terminated. A major spur to inquiry and analysis of war has been the desire to prevent or at least to curb it.*

War or a state of war is said to occur when legally, sociologically, or politically well-defined entities engage *as such* in violent combat against each other. This can but usually does not include civil wars.†

Internationally war occurs when states *as such,* as distinct from mere segments of their armed forces, embark upon armed conflict either immediately or on a suspended basis at some point in the future. In times past the line separating war from peace was wholly juridical: to signal intent to cross that line, governments, pusuant to constitutional as well as international law, formally declared war on specified countries. Occasionally such formalities are still observed. However, several major developments have tended to drastically alter the juridical as well as the substantive nature of war.

Modern weapons technology, strategy, and tactics place greater emphasis on the element of surprise, that is on the need to inflict upon an enemy if at all possible decisive, paralyzing blows before he can rally his forces for defense. This renders formal declaration of war impractical for the aggressor in most instances; it most certainly renders it suicidal if nuclear weapons are to be employed initially against an enemy similarly armed.

Secondly, war changed from limited encounter between nation's armed forces to total war involving the nation as a whole when changes in weapons technology shifted from reliance on military manpower to reliance on industrial strength. The totality of war was further enhanced by the rapidly increasing destructiveness of modern weapons (see Figure 2-2).

The Causes of War

Under what conditions, for what reasons, under what circumstances do modern nations or their governments embark upon war? What might cause them to

---

* Estimates of the frequency of wars throughout recorded history depend of course on such varying criteria as definition of war, magnitude, scope, duration, intensity, and various legal considerations. Estimates of war occurrence from the beginning of recorded history range from several hundred major wars to well over fourteen thousand large and small ones since 3600 B.C. Singer and Small (1972), p. 11.

† Quincy Wright, in his classic *Study of War* (1965), p. 8, defines war as "in the broadest sense . . . a violent contact of distinct but similar entities." He defines modern war more narrowly as "the legal *condition* which equally permits two or more *hostile groups* to carry on a *conflict* by *armed* force."

avoid that option? Efforts are legion to identify causalities, characteristics, commonalities, or correlates and to develop analytical models or paradigms to provide answers to these and related questions. Unavoidably, given the expanded scope of modern war—as compared with local tribal battles, for instance—the focal points for such studies and the criteria selected tend to be rather diffused and disparate and so tend to be the conclusions. Western analysts have sought to attribute war to cultures, social and socioeconomic systems, religions, ethnic strains, ideologies, forms of government, diplomatic styles, alliance patterns or systems, or informal combinations of states, or to an infinite variety of beliefs, perceptions, inclinations, proclivities, or propensities of people, groups, and individuals. Marxist/Leninist analysis, on the other hand, focuses on social class, "historical materialism," and socioeconomic forces. Few of the approaches have advanced knowledge significantly on these vexatious questions. It is most doubtful that any can help us much with respect to the next conflict.[10]

Actually, if formulated broadly enough, the topic defies generalization or prediction. No two wars are sufficiently similar to support predictive generalizations. If two or more wars *appear* to be similar, like the two world wars for example, or a series of regional wars, this is merely an illusion, the by-product of an effort to provide intellectually manageable foundations for statistical compilation and analysis or for theoretical speculation. As we shall develop in Part Four, the task of war prevention in the nuclear age, now nearly a universal mandate, is advanced only by examination of currently as well as potentially available, flexible, original, and imaginative mechanisms of conflict resolution. Because history actually does not repeat itself, lessons from the past are instructive but irrelevant to questions of *war and peace in the nuclear age.**

One major source of confusion on the subject is the difficulty of separating basic long-range from immediate or short-range causes. Did the assassination of Archduke Francis Ferdinand of Austria at Sarajevo on the eve of the First World War have to be the spark that set in motion the mobilization machineries of the then major powers? Was Hitler's attack on Poland in 1939 the cause of World War Two, or did that conflagration start with the series of concessions made by Great Britain and France to satisfy his thirst for aggrandizement, or was it the mistake of the Treaty of Versailles which sowed the seeds of revenge in millions of German minds? Was the real cause of the Second World War the psychological state of Adolf Hitler, a state of mind which brooked no

---

* Mesquita (1981) believes that he has developed an analytical model with predictive value in the nuclear age. Quincy Wright (1965), p. 719, comments:

> *While it would be difficult enough to predict the future occurrence of war if the criteria for deciding what war is were constant, the solution becomes indeterminate when these criteria are changing. When the concepts, constituting the frame of reference of a problem, resemble rubber dollars or expanding yardsticks, they must be treated as parameters yielding indeterminate equations in any scientific formulation of the problem.*

Organski and Kugler (1980), p. 13, comment, "Despite the vast literature devoted to war, little is known on the subject that is of practical value," by which, presumably, they mean predictive value.

compromise, tolerated no contrary advice, and in matters of foreign and domestic policy proved capable of rejecting all normal human impulses?[11] When does an individual decision-maker's moral fibre suffice to impel recourse to yet another attempt to avert war and under what conditions will it prove insufficient? What is the balance in political leaders' minds between morality and immorality and at what point do humane dispositions give way to inhumane considerations?

One of the more tragic aspects of modern war is the acquiescence of otherwise reasonable human beings in courses of action totally at variance with everything they have been taught, have come to believe, or have practiced for a lifetime. The imminence or the excitement of war appears to eclipse if not wipe out deeply held commitments and terminate rationality, flooding the recesses of the mind with emotions. At that point, once the die is cast war fever develops a momentum of its own, more likely than not following a direction and producing results totally unplanned by the initiators.[12]

The following list is not intended to be exhaustive, and no attempt is made to differentiate between types of wars, magnitude, scope, duration or intensity. It is a selective list only of *major* causes of modern war. The list is confined to the most salient causes identified by capitalist, socialist, and Third World analysts as having contributed significantly to the outbreak of war in recent times and are likely to contribute to war in the forseeable future.

Major Contributory Causes of Modern Wars of Aggression

Economic and Socioeconomic Causes:

—economically motivated claims or designs on such objectives as natural resources, ports, waterways, sources of water, fertile lands, cheap labor, or outlets for presumed or actual population pressure;
—spheres, markets, or opportunities for export of goods or capital;
—unemployment;
—promise of loot or booty;
—differential rates of economic development or growth;
—dynamics of capitalism, imperialism, neocolonialism;
—socioeconomic class struggle;
—the dynamics of arms production

Military-Strategic Causes:

—improvement of a state's military-strategic position;
—acquisition of land, including islands, littoral, straits, ports, or land bases;
—removal of obstacles to future military action;
—preemptive action: destruction of a military threat, by direct attack, partition of a state or its permanent neutralization, or liquidation of a threatening alliance;
—shift in the balance of power;

—collective security obligations to an alliance or to an international organization;

—militaristic tendencies or propensities on the part of a particular leadership group or ruling elite;

—desire to test military strength or weapons.

Legal-Political Causes:

—attainment or promotion of national independence;

—secession from an existing state;

—irredentism;

—conflict over rights of succession to a state or other controlling authority;

—involuntary abandonment of control over a territory;

—unification of an ethnically or culturally homogeneous but legally divided or partitioned area or region.

Ideological, Social-Revolutionary, and Religious Causes:

—Overthrow of an established regime and its replacement with a revolutionary alternative;

—support or defense of an ideologically kindred regime or political system in danger of attack or overthrow;

—intervention in a civil war on the side of an ideologically kindred faction or intervention on behalf of a social class;

—wars of national liberation, that is, transfer or shift of a territory from Western capitalist to non-Western or socialist spheres of influence;

—imposition of a particular religious orientation on a people.

Purely Territorial Disputes:

—border disputes;

—reclamation of territory lost as a result of a previous war or under other forms of compulsion, for example a peace treaty or another international or national edict or agreement of disputed authenticity or authority.

Opportunity:

—development of a power vacuum, as a result of externally or internally induced changes in a state or region;

—belief that if action is not taken demographic, economic, or military balance in a state or region will shift to the aggressor's permanent disadvantage;

—diversion from severe internal problems.

Other:

—recovery or bolstering of prestige position;

—retaliation;

—revenge for actual or perceived historic wrongs;

—punitive action;

—psychopathological impulses on a leader's part.

Or any combination of the above.

The Question of Just and Unjust Wars

Understandably, no leader about to embark upon an act of aggression will concede that it might not be just.* But the answer to this question depends on more than an individual leader's personal inclinations or instincts. Indeed, the question has intrigued and challenged humanity ever since antiquity, as long as thought has been given to the why and wherefore of war, killing, and destruction. For one, numerous committees and commissions, working on the matter for decades, have so far been unable to arrive at a universally acceptable definition of aggression.[13] Beyond that, to some the just/unjust dichotomy is a question of morality, to others it is a matter of logic—the first inquiring whether it is moral to kill any human being under any circumstances or whether it is moral to kill even for a cause, the second concluding that a war is just if fought for a worthy cause.

As long as wars are fought in conventional ways, there is time for this and similar debates. Aside from fairly obvious invocations of justice, such as self-defense or national self-preservation, it has been argued that wars are just also if they promise to correct an injustice, for example oppression of a people, or if fought in accord with prevailing international law, to preserve "civilization" or "in the name of God."[14]

But it should be apparent that all of these and similar rationales are most subjective. All can easily be refuted. For instance, since wars have a way of not ending as initially conceived, could it at all be just to engage in physical destruction of a state solely to liberate an ethnic or religious minority from the majority? In the 1930s the German war machine was set in motion initially and allegedly to liberate ethnic Germans from several neighboring states. Many of those liberated from Czechoslovakia and Poland perished during the ensuing world war; those who survived were expelled from their homelands by the millions. All too frequently, wars deemed eminently and indisputably just by their initiators merely create new injustices, most likely far more than were addressed originally. Beyond that, one man's justice is another's injustice, one people's concept of civilization is another's barbarism, one people's concept of morality is another's immorality.

Nuclear war may collapse all approaches to this question into one: Is it just or unjust to invite or risk destruction of all forms of human civilization or, at

---

* In an attempt to cover up his aggression against Poland in 1939, Hitler's Secret Service dressed concentration camp inmates in Polish uniforms, had them attack a German radio station (at Gleiwitz), had the attack broadcast, then executed the witnesses to the deception. See Weston, Falk, D'Amato, p. 150, for a similar incident planned by Nazi German forces to justify aggression against Czechoslovakia in 1938.

the very least, destroy most of them and render vast sections of the earth uninhabitable for generations? It would seem, from ever more frequent public utterances by leaders in all parts of the world, that the majority of them are inclined to shy away from first use of nuclear weapons. Whether they also are convinced that any recourse to nuclear weapons is unjust to humanity as a whole is not yet certain.

While self-defense or self-preservation have universally been regarded as just causes, the technology of nuclear war and the "strategic wisdoms" based on that place even that premise in doubt. Today, few states if any can calmly wait until an enemy has fully mobilized his forces, dispatched his bombing planes, or armed his missiles. Faced with imminent attack, is a prior strike with nuclear weapons just? What if the assumed attack was misperceived? In the West the public debate on this point is intense and widespread. All Western leaders without exception have publicly declared that to start a nuclear war is insane. What of the Soviet leadership, who are ideologically committed to certain kinds of conventional war, any one of which can conceivably trigger a nuclear exchange with the United States?

The theoretical or ideological rationale for a decision by Soviet rulers to engage or not engage in war was provided by Lenin. With respect to conventional, prenuclear wars, he wrote that "an historical analysis of each war [is necessary in order] to determine whether or not *that particular* war can be considered progressive, whether it serves the interests of democracy and the proletariat and, *in that* sense, is legitimate, just, etc."[15] The "progressive" wars Lenin had in mind are what one of his successors later raised to the level of a sacred Soviet commitment, wars "of national liberation," "directed" in Lenin's words, "against foreign domination" and "just from the standpoint of the oppressed and [because they] have a progressive significance."[16] Lenin also considered just what he termed "revolutionary wars," which "*may* prove necessary *in the interest of socialism.*"[17]

Commenting on these thoughts, with particular reference to the likely consequences of such a war in the nuclear age, Tomashevsky ventured the following interpretations: "The death of hundreds and millions of people, above all working people, and the destruction of vast productive forces throughout the world would be too big a price for the world to pay for the destruction of capitalism, already doomed by history."[18] And "[a] thermonuclear war would not accelerate progress; it would, on the contrary, set back the movement of mankind towards communism."[19] On the other hand, the commitment to wars of national liberation remains, except that this type of war must most carefully be separated from the global holocaust:

> The aggressive policy of the reactionary forces are compelling the peoples who are struggling for national and social liberation to take up arms, inasmuch as they have no other way of satisfying their vital interests and national aspirations. The anti-imperalist wars that are developing out of popular struggles for national and social liberation, as Lenin noted frequently, are progressive and just. The Soviet Union, the CPSU [Communist Party of the Soviet Union] support such wars.[20]

Positions actually taken by statesmen outside the Soviet Union regarding their countries' and alliance system's problems reflect similar ambivalence.

Conventional and Unconventional Warfare
and the Decision to Go to War

History provides ample evidence that decisions to go or not to go to war at times are based on thorough, in-depth examination of a wide range of options and alternatives involving numerous agencies of government, laboring over extended periods. On other occasions however, the command was issued on one ruler's personal whim, on frivolous grounds, more or less on the spur of a moment. Sometimes, as we pointed out in our analysis of foreign policy decision-making, extensive, often agonizing examination of alternate options and of the cost-benefit aspects of a full-fledged war may have preceded the fateful moment; but the go-ahead itself is issued under complete disregard of everything that has gone on before. At the outset of the next to last decade of the twentieth century, only two governments were likely to be confronted with the choice between nuclear and nonnuclear war, the United States and the Soviet Union. Indications were that by the end of that decade if not earlier that number would increase.[21] That possibility suggests it might be useful to compare and contrast the basic aspects of conventional and unconventional nuclear war which are likely to influence the ultimate decision.

CONVENTIONAL WARFARE	**UNCONVENTIONAL WARFARE**
At the Point of Crisis	
Time-frame for decision may be weeks, days, or hours. Even after military action has been initiated, for example mobilization, room is left for diplomatic maneuvers, second thoughts, and negotiation.	All forces must be in a state of instant readiness. No time may be left for mobilization, only for a brief alert. Time-frame for decision may be minutes. Negotiations may be viewed as militarily dangerous.
Warzone	
Although in modern times civilian targets far behind military frontlines have been bombed almost immediately, most of the action has been confined to military forces at the "front."	All of the state's territory becomes at once part of the warzone, including centers of command. Military and civilian sectors, front and rear become totally indistinguishable as offensive weapons can be launched from any point on earth or in space.

Confidence in the Armed Forces and in Weaponry

Military tactics, personnel, and weapons have been tested for accuracy, reliability and endurance, most likely under actual combat conditions. Weapons have been tested against weapons. Defenses and warning systems have been tested. Margin for strategic and tactical error is considerable.

Neither tactics, nor personnel, nor certain critical weapons can be tested in earnest. At best, tests can be conducted only under simulated conditions.

Actual tests are prohibitively expensive and might reveal vital secrets to an enemy. None of the major weapons can be tested for destructive potential against other equally expensive defensive weapons systems. None of the weapons aimed by the superpowers against each other's territories can be tested over the anticipated wartime trajectory. No assurance that warning systems and defenses will function as planned. Margins for strategic error may be exceedingly narrow. There may be none.*

The Control Element

Human minds are in control at all times to abort an action, redirect forces, cancel a decision, slow down mobilization, and prevent escalation after hostilities have commended. Reserves need not be committed at once. Total war may be avoided.

Everincreasing reliance on computerized decisional processes and on automation may narrow the time-frame for command and control decisions to the point where human control has to be sacrificed for speed. Left in their silos, on the chance that a nuclear attack was intended to be limited, all reserve missiles may be destroyed if the attack turns out to be total.

The Aftermath

War fought with conventional weapons has been described as continuation of diplomacy, or politics, by other means. Following a war, affairs were expected to return to normal.

Nuclear war has an air of finality at best; at worst it could be the prelude to global anarchy.[22]

---

* Prior to World War One, all major belligerents tested their arms in actual combat in a series of local wars. Prior to the Second World War, Germany, Italy, and the Soviet Union tested some of their weapons and some of their combat tactics against each other during the Spanish Civil War (1936-1939); Germany and the Soviet Union had another opportunity during the first Russo-Finnish war in the winter of 1938-1939. Some tests of advanced but nonnuclear aerial combat tactics and some tests of modern fighter aircraft against electronically guided antiaircraft defenses were conducted in the 1970s and early 1980s in the course of military action in the Middle East when Israel's U.S.-supplied arms and equipment were matched against planes and anti-aircraft defenses supplied Syria by the Soviet Union.

An intriguing question arises: can the history of past wars tell us anything of value regarding a war fought with unconventional weapons? Can tomorrow's generals still learn something of practical value—as they did until recently— from an inspection of the battlefields of Carthage, biblical Palestine, Waterloo, or Gettysburg?* This is most doubtful. While, superficially viewed, certain similarities can be discerned and even some of the classic terminologies may seem applicable, magnitude, spatial and time dimensions, destructiveness, and accompanying social, political, and economic fall-out of nuclear war seem to suggest that reliance on classic strategy and tactics could have disastrous consequences. The battles of old may do for the nuclear commander what nursery building blocks do for the nuclear engineer.

Finally there are the questions of ethics, morality, and humanitariansim. The world has advanced, painfully slowly, but it has advanced, from utter barbarism to a measure of civilized behavior even in war. As we shall note in our following analysis of international law, at first glance neither ethics, nor morality, nor human instincts could spare the world the barbarism of World War Two. But they did have an impact. While neither Hitler nor Stalin appear to have had moral or ethical scruples, many of their commanders and many of their troops did observe certain legal, moral, and ethical concepts and rules. Churches, museums, art objects, and entire cities, were spared, if at all possible. Rome and Paris survived in spite of orders to destroy both. With the inevitable exceptions, prisoners of war were accorded certain protections and privileges by belligerents who had signed relevant international legal conventions. It was possible to negotiate through neutral channels, even at the height of the conflict, for the exchange of lists of prisoners and other understandings.

Yet, merely posing the question of what Hitler or Stalin might have done had they been in possession of the atom bomb and remembering of what an American president did do when he had it at his disposal suggest that consideration of ethics, morality, and humaneness, evolved through millenia, are but a very thin and fragile veneer. The victims of firestorms caused by conventional bombing in Hamburg and Dresden suffered as much and were as numerous as those killed by the nuclear bombs dropped over Hiroshima and Nagasaki. Employed in a noble cause or for evil, the nuclear arsenals now being built, and the probably far more sophisticated and less controllable ones of tomorrow, may leave no room whatever for observance of notions and rules of civilized conduct. After all, the only reason why gas was used in 1915 and 1916 during World War One was that the German High Command was confident that they could cope with retaliation. They were mistaken. Although available, gas was not used by Hitler against Great Britain and the Soviet Union only because he was certain that their air power aided by prevailing air-currents would tip

---

* U.S. General George S. Patton found the Norman campaigns in France and the ruins
of Carthage and the battlefields around them instructive for modern tank warfare;
General Moshe Dayan, the Israeli leader, learned some of his tactics successfully employed
against five Arab armies in 1967 by studying biblical campaigns; generals in both world
wars and since have found Gettysburg militarily instructive.

the scales in favor of the Western Allies. The threat of mutual annihilation is believed today to be an effective deterrent. But once that threshold has been crossed, indications are that war-induced descent to barbarism will be more precipitous than ever.

Occupation and Conquest

While a war is in progress, all territory overrun by armed forces is considered occupied and the territory, including its inhabitants, is treated accordingly— sometimes with humane consideration, sometimes brutally. But in any case wartime occupation is regarded as auxiliary to the military effort, its extent and duration determined solely by the fortunes of war.

Postwar occupation serves different purposes, its extent determined more by political than by military considerations. Most frequently enemy territory remains under occupation as leverage to influence the terms and conditions of a treaty of peace. If reparations for wartime damages are demanded, land and people in the occupied territory may be held hostage to guarantee delivery. Sometimes all or part of a defeated state may remain occupied pending restoration of law and order and of minimal defensive capabilities, especially if the defeat has created a power vacuum in the region and a direct threat to the victor's interests remains.

Or occupation may be ordered without formal declaration of war to prevent an ally from changing sides or surrendering, or to prevent a neutral from placing his territory at an opponent's disposal. Toward the end of World War Two, Germany's troops occupied the northern parts of its Italian ally's territory to prevent their loss to the British and American forces approaching from the south. Earlier, toward the end of the First World War, following the Bolshevik Revolution in 1917, forces of Russia's western allies briefly occupied Russian soil in an unsuccessful attempt to prevent a military collapse or surrender. Other occupations have taken place to stake out a claim, for example the occupation by Argentine forces of the British Falkland (Malvinas) islands in the South Atlantic in 1982, or the Turkish occupation in 1974 of the northern part of the island of Cyprus, purportedly to ensure protection of the Turkish minority.

Following the First World War in pursuance of terms of the peace treaty, Germany's principal industrial region, the Ruhr area, was occupied by French troops explicitly to compel payment of reparations; other areas along the Franco-German border remained occupied for many years to enforce their demilitarization. After World War Two, all of defeated Germany was occupied from the end of the war until 1949, the western regions by British, French, and American forces, the eastern half by the Soviet Union. Initially the common goals were liquidation of the Nazi regime, enforcement of Germany's total demilitarization, and, on the part of the Soviet Union, collection of reparations. Because the wartime alliance soon broke up—we shall review this development in Chapter 12—from 1949 on, occupation was officially terminated and changed to "military presence," each side anxious to prevent the other from uniting and eventually rearming partitioned Germany, then pointing it once again against the other.[23] In the Far East, the Soviet Union maintained its military occupation of several Japanese islands long after military occupation of the principal islands by U.S. forces had given way to supportive or defensive military presence; or the Soviets remained there because of that.

In the wake of the 1967 Six-Day War against her Arab neighbors, Israel occupied the western parts of the Sinai desert, the Gaza Strip, the territories on the west bank of the Jordan, and the Golan Heights mainly to enhance her overall military security. Eventually the Egyptian portion of the Sinai was traded for a peace treaty with Egypt.*

If conquest is the objective of war, the legal means is annexation, the *modus operandi* of aggressors since the beginning of organized society. In the main, the reasons for annexation are the reasons for war, although the idea has occurred to some governments while conflicts were under way and the opportunity presented itself.

The history of Poland is illustrative of conquest and annexation, as well as partition, and of the political purposes all of these measures serve. Three powers, Austria, Prussia, and Czarist Russia, in 1772, 1793, and 1795 respectively, partitioned that country, each annexing its part, it was hoped on a permanent basis. In 1918 the Western Allies, principally the United States, Great Britain, and France, anxious to contain a then threatening westward march of Bolshevism, reestablished Poland as an independent state consisting of undisputed Polish territory but also of areas containing a substantial German population. Russia, of course, did not accept loss of the territories it had annexed on previous occasions. Predictably, on the eve of World War Two Hitler and Stalin entered into a pact, partitioning the country once again. Russia also annexed— reclaimed, as Stalin saw it—the three small Baltic republics, Lithuania, Latvia, and Estonia. After Germany's defeat in 1945 Poland was reconstituted once again, but about 150 miles to the west, at Germany's expense, to permit the Soviet Union to improve its defensive position.

At the end of this discussion of one of humanity's most tragic tendencies, it is appropriate to note that abhorrence of mass violence and of the anarchy which always follows in its wake has been the principal spur of universal efforts to subject the totality of international relations to the rule of law.

Suggested Questions and Discussion Topics

Give examples of "Armed Operations Short of War."

---

* It is argued that Israel's policies and practices on the West Bank (of the Jordan River), that is on territory liberated or seized from Jordan during the 1967 war, including establishment of Jewish settlements, are in violation of international law which stipulates that no permanent changes may be instituted in occupied lands until and unless ratified by a peace treaty. Also of questionable legality is Israel's diversion of Jordan River headwaters. See Cooley (1984).

What are the root causes of international terrorism?

Discuss international terrorism in the context of the East-West conflict.

Why do some governments feel justified to treat acts of international terrorism directed against their citizens or armed services as the equivalent of war?

Give other examples of violent foreign intelligence operations.

Define war.

What are some of the major contributory causes of modern war and aggression?

Can any war be just? In the nuclear age, what is the moral problem with the proposition that a war may be just?

In the nuclear age, what considerations may influence decisions to engage or not engage in conventional and/or nuclear warfare?

Chapter 9
International Law

It is the purpose of this chapter not to trace the history of international law but to present its utility and disutility as an instrument of international relations, discuss its strengths and weaknesses in that respect, and assess its potentialities in the nuclear age and the degree of its success or failure in advancing the more fundamental aspirations of humanity.*

In its origins, like its counterpart domestic law, international law is the product of a universal human preference for containmnent of violence and establishment of some form of order. Inevitably, because the origin of modern international law coincides with the emergence of the sovereign state and the state-system, its subsequent development converted it essentially into an instrument of states as such and not of human civilization. This is as if domestic law, in the United States for instance, had been created primarily to serve the interests of the individual states and not the interests of the people for whose benefit the system was to have been created. To be sure, those who contributed to the development of international law were motivated partly by the belief that if law and order could be secured and maintained among states at the international level, all of humanity's basic interests would thereby be served as well. But judging by the record of performance this assumption has not at all been warranted. To the contrary, too often in the course of history have national sovereignty and principles as well as the letter of international law been used to justify indescribable brutalities and miscarriages of justice, providing protection not for the victims but for their persecutors.[1] On the other hand, international law has been instrumental in mitigating human suffering, securing a modicum of order among states, and thereby offering at least the promise of a better world.

---

* Western literature credits Hugo Grotius (1583–1645) with the first codification of international law, his major purposes being reduction or containment of the incidence of war, preservation of some form of order in the then incipient state-system, development of channels of communication among the sovereigns themselves, promotion and protection of trade, and extension of basic principles of civilization to the conduct of relations among ever more powerful and ever more contentious states. However, treaties incorporating concepts and provisions with which Grotius was concerned were negotiated and honored in the Middle and Far East long before the birth of Christ; see Schwarzenberger (1976), Chapter 4.

153

Is It Law?

All law can be regarded as sets of rules. To claim legal validity a rule need not be enforceable; hence lack of enforceability, a defect in international law quite apparent to the casual observer, does not by itself invalidate the legal standing of the body of rules making up international law. All that is required for a rule to qualify as law is that it can or will be enforced eventually in the majority of cases. Perhaps more important than the enforcement aspect is the willingness of persons or entities subject to such rules to accept them on principle, to abide by them, and to accept enforcement on terms and under conditions mutually agreed upon between subjects and rule-setting or law-giving authority. Beyond that, rules and law as such function partly as mere sets of guidelines or standards of behavior. As such they meet a basic social need. Thus, enforceable or not, universally accepted or not, international law has legal quality; it is law. As will be seen shortly, one of the more controversial aspects of international law is its binding force. But one need not resolve that problem totally to recognize that *some* aspects of international law are *optionally* binding with respect to governments willing to take up that option. That alone stamps international law as law.

Article 38 of the Statute of the International Court of Justice, the statement on that subject reflecting the widest international consensus, enumerates several categories of law which the Court is directed to apply:

   a. international conventions, whether general or particular, establishing rules expressly recognized by the contesting states;
   b. international custom, as evidence of general practice accepted as law;
   c. the general principles of law recognized by civilized nations;
   d. judicial decisions and the teachings of the most highly qualified publicists of the various nations, as subsidiary means for the determination of rules of law.

In addition, the Court is authorized "to decide a case *ex aequo et bono,* if the parties agree thereto."*

The first category stipulates that for conventions to have effect all states whose conduct is to be judged by the Court must expressly signal their consent, that is, the convention must have been ratified by all states who are parties to a litigation, in accordance with their respective constitutional requirements. Conventions of special importance are those which codify major segments of law such as the 1960 Vienna Convention of the Law of Treaties which addresses the central instrument by which states enter into relations with one another and which as such is regarded as a valid source of international law: the treaty. Earlier we referred to another universally accepted and basic instrument, the 1961 Vienna Convention on Diplomatic Relations.[2] International custom ac-

---

* *Ex aequo et bono* relies on "just and good" principles acceptable to contesting parties rather than on the letter of the law.

counts for a major portion of existing law and is itself based on practices and observances of conduct some of which have been recorded as early as two thousand years before the birth of Christ. Among other things, custom applies to mutual recognition and acceptance of the "sovereign rights of nations," to the freedom of the sea, to "good faith" and to the right of self-defense. One of the most firmly established and oldest customary rules directs ships at sea to come to the aid of other vessels in distress.

As one might expect, customary law is often vigorously disputed, especially if applied to questions of war and peace. The problem is exemplified by the post-World War Two Nuremberg and Tokyo trials of German and Japanese leaders for alleged war crimes, including "conspiracy to wage war of aggression," and "crimes against humanity." Although some of the offenses committed by the accused clearly were actionable under their respective domestic laws, the case against them on the "conspiracy" and "crimes against humanity" counts was quite tenuous. To make their case on those grounds, the victorious Allies— who were the sole judges in the matter—had to *establish* a custom, namely the prosecution and execution of civilian and military leaders for official acts which, at the time they had been committed, had as such not yet been defined as criminal under international law. It is not condoning the acts as such to say that the combination of biased judges and legal ambiguity undermined the deterrent qualities of this entire chapter in the development of international law.

But the potentially most controversial set of sources are "the general principles of law recognized by civilized nations." At the time this provision was incorporated in the Court's Statute, the term civilized really meant Western. While it did convey a sense of advanced cultural development, it also implied acceptance of the prevailing *status quo* in the world. In short, it signified acceptance of the body of international law as developed by the predominantly European, Judeo-Christian civilization. Especially important in this particular connection is the fact that modern ideas of what does and what does not constitute civilized conduct of international relations were developed over a 300 year period which coincided with the conquest and often brutal subjugation of defenseless peoples in all parts of the world. All too often, during that period, might rather than established law determined what was right. We shall return shortly to that source of law which really is a major source also of its weakness.

Equally controversial today is the reference to "most highly qualified publicists of various nations." During the most productive years in the development of modern international law, numerous outstanding jurists and legal scholars from China, for example, or South America were recognized as "highly qualified," hence their judicial decisions, writings, and teachings were generally accepted. But they were "qualified" only because they did not challenge the prevailing order, including acceptance of treaties and conventions imposed upon the world by a minority of states.*

Aside from judgments by established courts, among the most widely respected sources yet also most controversial and least enforceable are resolutions by international governmental organizations (IGOs). These sources are respected because they reflect as a rule a fairly wide if not universal consensus, especially now that the peoples of Asia, Africa, and of all of the Western Hemisphere have achieved a degree of equality under international law. Their enforceability is in doubt, ironically, for that very same reason: whereas under domestic law the minority is expected to bend to the will of the majority, provided of course that the latter respects the former, in the international setting no such assumption can as yet be made. Thus at that level, the dictum by a U.S. president speaking of a decision by the U.S. Supreme Court, "The Court has rendered their decision, now let them enforce it," applies even more to international law emanating from what in reality are political forums, for example the General Assembly of the United Nations.

A prime example of the product of all of the foregoing is the long-standing effort to define aggression. In 1974, following half a century of work by relays of international committees and commissions—the process started under the League of Nations—the United Nations passed a resolution defining aggression as "the use of armed force by a State against the sovereignty, territorial integrity or political independence of another State, or in any other manner inconsistent with the Chapter of the United Nations, as set out in this definition."[3] Almost at once, the East-West conflict injected itself into this matter, raising the question whether wars of national liberation, including military acts in support of such wars, constituted acts of aggression. Beyond that any reference to the Charter of the United Nations, itself the product of a compromise among diverging and divergent camps, is itself an invitation to conflicting interpretations. As Schwarzenberger points out, the bottom line in this as in most other legal questions is *political* not legal determination.[4] As a result, the solemn resolution notwithstanding, the ambiguities if not inconsistencies inherent in this as in numerous other UN resolutions opened the doors wide to pseudo-tribunals seeking to indict the United States for alleged aggressive acts in Southeast Asia and the Soviet Union for acts in Eastern Europe and Afghanistan. Indeed, whenever points of law are formulated by what Schwarzenberger terms "systems of power politics in disguise" such as the League of Nations or the United Nations—Schwarzenberger includes in this the Kellogg Pact system of Non-Aggression and the Outlawing of War—power politics bear as much on law as do strictly legal sources.[5]

---

* Schwarzenberger (1976), p. 6, notes a "basic distinction" in Article 38 between "law-creating processes" such as treaties, customary law and the general rules, and "law-determining agencies" such as the states themselves and courts and writers. Because the latter reflect contemporary political and ideological differences more than the former—"law-creating," after all, is a process century if not millenia old—we must see here another major source of conflict between opposing sources of legality.

Enforcement and Peaceful Settlement of Disputes

There are in the internal affairs of nations two major determinants of what is and what is not legal: the will and fiat of the dominant elite and the rule of law. This applies equally to the international scene where, depending on one's theoretical or ideological position, the former is represented either by economic or military power or by the authority of the sovereign state itself while the latter is represented by the body of international law. In either case, ultimately, and regardless of its universality or legitimacy, the *efficacy* of all law, including that of all agencies of adjudication and arbitration, is determined by the degree of certainty that violation of the law invites a penalty.*

To maintain law and order, domestic legal systems typically provide institutional and procedural opportunities for peaceful application of public law and for peaceful settlement of disputes. But always behind the legal authority of the state and behind the judges and the courts stands the element of force, ready to apply legal sanctions ranging from arrest and detention to trial, imposition of fines or prison sentences, or in extreme cases execution. While relatively fine points of the law may be argued or contested, the majority of the members of societies subject to such law tend to accept it, respect the judicial and other modes of settlement of disputes, and, with the possible exception of capital punishment, approve of the range of sanctions and enforcement mechanisms.

International law also has its institutional structure, including courts, tribunals, and commissions, and its sanctions and enforcement mechanisms, but with several major differences. To be regarded as legitimate and legally valid, all the instrumentalities of law must be formally and explicitly accepted and approved by all states to whom such law is to be applied; this includes potential or actual violators and all other parties to international disputes to be submitted to international adjudication or arbitration. Secondly, the element of force, always ready to be applied under state law, must under international law await the express consent of all states called upon to provide it. To be sure, some theorists insist that once a principle has been formulated and accepted by the majority of the members of the community of nations, its legitimacy and its enforceability are securely established. But in practice, as a matter of historic record, even where an aggressor state was a party to a convention outlawing wars of aggression, applicable international law has not always been invoked let alone enforced. Many reasons can be cited for this, the most pervasive being a general reluctance to go to war in order to stop a war.

All international law enforcement faces two exceedingly potent impulses on the part of violators: aggression or self-defense. The violator is either impelled to employ the full power of the state to pursue a particular objective at another state's expense or the motivation is to ensure national survival. In neither

---

* This has no bearing on the question posed earlier, whether international law is law. An affirmative answer to that question does not depend on enforcement.

case—certainly not where time is of the essence—is the violator prepared to allow international adjudication or arbitration to run its course.

Consequently, governments of aggressor states as well as of states genuinely fearing for their survival have proceeded in the past and will in all probability proceed in the future to violate as much of existing international law, including as many provisions of solemnly negotiated and ratified international treaties or conventions, as they deem necessary to achieve their purpose. Moreover, to conceal the illegality of an act or to render it palatable to potential challengers, possibly to prevent a collective security mechanism to be activated, aggressors have become quite skilled in the art of legal camouflage. As we pointed out in our earlier discussion of just and unjust war, what does constitute aggression has yet to gain universal agreement. Even an act of clearly unprovoked aggression can always be presented to the world as an act of self-defense. There are numerous additional loopholes permitting disregard of of international law, rendering enforcement doubtful if not illegal. For example, one of the foundation stones of international law, the principle that treaties must be honored (*pacta sunt servanda*), is voided by exceptions, such as *force majeure* or superior force, or by invocation of the *clausula rebus sic stantibus* by one of the parties to a treaty.*

International law recognizes a wide range of methods of peaceful settlement of disputes, the mode far more prevalent than actual enforcement. Most frequently disputes are settled by negotiation between two parties. To assist, third parties or an international organization may offer their *good offices* to bring the parties together, to mediate the dispute, or to conduct an inquiry merely to establish the facts. In these instances, the third party does not enter into the final decision, the terms of settlement being exclusively within the discretion of the disputants. These proceedings are also called nonjudicial. More formal are arbitration and judicial methods. There the third party, usually a tribunal or a court, is expected to formulate the terms of settlement or, in the event a violation is established, assess the compensation or the penalties.

Arbitration is defined as "the settlement of disputes between states by judges of their choice and on the basis of respect for law." Adjudication utilizes a permanent court or tribunal. Historically, arbitration was the function of a superior power, the head of the Catholic Church for example or a monarch enjoying the respect and trust of the disputants. In modern times, a Permanent Court of International Arbitration was established under the Hague Conventions for the Pacific Settlement of International Disputes of 1899 and 1907. Aside from regional attempts, the first full-fledged international judicial court with a reasonable claim to universality, the Permanent Court of International Justice, was established as part of the League of Nations structure in 1921. With the

---

* According to Article 62 of the Convention of the Law of Treaties the *clausula* permits voidance of a treaty or of one or more of its provisions in the face of "a fundamental change of circumstances which has occurred with regard to those existing at the time of the conclusion of the treaty, and which was not foreseen by the parties"; see Levi (1979) p. 229.

demise of the League during World War Two and its replacement by the United Nations, the International Court of Justice, more widely known as the World Court, continued the tradition.

International law permits a wide range of enforcement measures to be applied at two levels: universal or regional. Enforcement is effected either through permanent international organizations or through collective security mechanisms such as alliances. Or it may be executed by *ad hoc* application, in specific instances, under the doctrine of self-help by aggrieved or injured parties. If their statutes permit it, international organizations or agencies may resort to expulsion of an offending member or they may resort to armed force. Some, like the European Economic Community, are empowered to impose fines for treaty violations. Collective security avails itself of the entire range of armed actions, including threat of the use of force. Individual states, usually invoking the doctrine of self-help, may resort to *retorsion* or *reprisal;* an example of the former would be withdrawal of an ambassador, breaking diplomatic relations, or erection of trade barriers; an example of the latter would be seizure of a ship or bombardment of an offender's territory.

The ultimate sanction remains application of superior military force. It was that and not the weight of international morality which brought the leaders of Nazi Germany to justice. While the legal proceedings at the Nuremberg War Crimes Trials had been professionally unimpeachable, it is certain that the German and Japanese leaders who were tried, convicted, and sentenced to be hanged on several counts, one being "conspiracy to wage wars of aggression," went to their deaths convinced that their crime had not been to start such a war but lose it. Predictably, not all governments intent on aggression have been deterred by the Nuremberg or Tokyo precedents.*

What Does International Law Cover?

Because the sovereign state and not the individual is the primary constituent unit, international law accords highest priority to matters relating to the creation, existence, maintenance, and territorial integrity of states, and, should a state meet its demise, to matters of succession. Concomitant with that emphasis are rules and laws governing rights and duties of states in their mutual relations. Included in the latter category are individual rights and property of their citizens while outside their home states' jurisdiction.

The legal ramifications and exigencies of expanding international relations have required development of a substantial body of law governing the sending, acceptance, and treatment of diplomats and consular personnel, along with their families and property required to fulfill their mission. All persons and their

---

* Nor have the other counts, crimes against humanity for instance, deterred such crimes as genocide, in parts of Africa, Asia, and Latin America, for instance; see Epilogue. On the Judgment and its legal consequences, see Weston, Falk, D'Amato (1980), pp. 1467–162.

goods, mail, and other property are covered while in transit through third states.

The bulk of international law has developed to accommodate commerce. This in turn has generated law on boundaries, coastlines, territorial waters and the high sea, now extended to outer space in anticipation of increased travel and even commerce in that sphere. The extent of territorial waters and jurisdiction beyond coastlines, exploitation of the sea, fisheries and minerals in the sea and on the ocean floor, have of late spawned considerable debate and is about to create new law.*

International law addresses neutrality in peace and war, belligerency, treatment of civilians and prisoners of war, use of certain types of weapons and ammunition, collective security, peacekeeping, and the rights, duties and privileges of recognized international organizations and bodies.

Because only states are parties to international law, individual human rights are as yet inadequately covered. One reason of course, is fear on the part of governing elites that once the authority of international law can be invoked on behalf of individuals, they will be challenged too often over too many issues by too many of their aggrieved subjects. Of course, this fear is most pronounced in states ruled by arbitrary and brutal regimes.

The subject of diplomatic immunity and protection of foreign embassies demands special mention for two reasons. After several centuries of progress in these respects, terrorist attacks and mob actions against embassies and embassy personnel threaten to reverse a trend deemed essential to world peace and advance of civilized conduct among nations. Negligence if not complicity on the part of host governments in the seizure of the United States embassy in Iran, the burning of the U.S. embassy in Islamabad (Pakistan), three embassies in Tripoli (Libya), and similar actions directed against the diplomatic missions or diplomats of other countries, coupled with the inability of the United Nations to enforce relevant law, do not augur well for diplomacy, the key link in the communication chain the world must utilize if a nuclear catastrophe is to be avoided. Not conducive to advancement of law to protect diplomatic mission is the growing practice, especially on the part of the superpowers, their allies, and their proxies, to use diplomatic missions for purposes of espionage.†

Seeds of Change

Reaching as far back in history, ranging over as many civilizations and cultural eras, as it does, international law by its very nature is the product of

---

* See the Law of the Sea, Chapter 16, below.

† The shooting of unarmed demonstrators and a policewoman from inside the Libyan embassy in London, in 1984, coupled with insistence on the part of the clearly culpable Libyan government that the offenders be allowed to return home protected by diplomatic immunity, and that, on the same grounds, their baggage and the embassy premises not be searched for evidence, is illustrative of yet another dilemma facing the community of nations: governments, like that of Libya under Colonel Quadhafi, rely on international law to violate it.

change. All law arises from an admixture of social, political, cultural, and ideological ingredients. In practice, in their decisions on which law to accept and which to reject, and in their emphases, attitudes, and postures, governments have reflected such divergent positions as Confucian thought, the tenets and doctrines of the Roman Catholic Church, and the material requirements of modern capitalism. If now an increasing number wish to incorporate the principles as well as the doctrines of Marxism/Leninism, or the special needs and perspectives of former colonies and contemporary dependencies, an established tradition is merely being continued. International law is expected to do no more than accommodate changing values, as expressed by the *clausula rebus sic stantibus,* a basic feature of that law. This can best be appreciated by a brief review of the theoretical, philosophical, and pragmatic juxtaposition of international law positions arising from the interaction between the First, Second, and Third Worlds.

The Western Influence

The Judeo-Christian roots of contemporary international law are revealed in the naturalist-positivist dichotomy which splits First World legal scholars and theorists into two opposing camps. Historically, in its main thrust, the naturalist school (foremost Hugo Grotius 1583-1645) represents a reaction to the dominance of the Catholic Church over all intellectual trends during the Middle Ages. Naturalists viewed all law as arising directly from laws of nature which dictate survival, hence preservation of some form of order and maintenance of a society, and thereby ordain mutual accommodation. Applied to the community of nations, this meant acceptance of basic norms of legality by states, not only within their own domestic jursidiction but as a force regulating their mutual relations. The positivists countered that the legal and moral source of international law can only be the actual behavior of states, because all states are sovereign hence cannot be subjected to any force outside their jurisdiction, be that natural, divine, or human. Although it is not entirely clear, the presumption can be drawn from the record that the naturalist position proved especially attractive to writers and scholars rebelling against or simply questioning the then prevailing social order, a order based primarily on legal and moral dictates derived by authority of the Church from what it claimed to be divine dispensation. The positivist school on the other hand attracted supporters as well as advocates of the prevailing social and economic order. To an extent, positivism as well as naturalism legitimized lawlessness in international affairs by emphasizing the absence of an order superior to anything humans could or would devise. Originally this benefitted mostly monarchs, military leaders, empire builders, and commercial and financial interests in commanding positions. Eventually it contributed to the emergence of totalitarian rule and total war.

Likewise, both schools contributed to the suppression of humanitarian impulses in domestic and international affairs—ironically since both naturalism and positivism claimed as their prime objectives protection of humanity from the ravages of marauding, looting, and pillaging armies moving back and forth across entire regions for decades or more, frequently invoking divine authority to justify their acts. Eventually the doctrine of sovereignty became established, drawing from both naturalism and positivism the notion that to be sovereign is to be above the law, a notion most appealing to national and international predators.

Another dichotomy distinguished between monism and dualism, the former arguing that only one legal system existed in the world; that is, that international law and state law are concomitant aspects of one legal system, the latter contending that domestic legal systems and those serving the community of nations are intrinsically separate and distinct. Monism of course clashed directly with the concept of national sovereignty. In particular, all state authorities emphatically reject the assumption implicit in the monist position that any and all rights universally recognized as such apply directly to each and every of the sovereign state's individual subjects.

Communist/Socialist Theory and Practice

Since much of contemporary international law serves Soviet foreign policy purposes rather well, Soviet legal writing and practice have not assumed an outright rejectionist stance. But in theoretical expressions, Soviet perspectives differ significantly from those of the West. In consonance with Marxist insistence on the centrality of the class struggle in national and international affairs, Soviet and other communist writers argue that until revolutionary forces are strong enough to radically overhaul the entire structure, it is international law's prime purpose to serve and protect the achievements of the "October" Revolution. Until then, the principle of national sovereignty constitutes a first line of defense for the Soviet Union and its allies and must therefore be maintained at all costs. Likewise, the corollary principle that all international law depends on express agreement among all states protects the "Socialist Revolution" against capitalist "revisionism" and "reaction."* This, with one exception. When a class revolution occurs in one country, the new revolutionary ruling group is not bound by rules accepted on behalf of the old state by their "bourgeois" predecessors, if those rules existed solely for the latter's benefit.[6]

Soviet legal writing also does not follow Western lawyers who seek to accord individuals at least the same status as is claimed for states or, going beyond that, press for eminence of individual rights over those of states when acts ordered in the latter's name are in clear violation of valid international law, for example a violation of a legal principle established by the Nuremberg War Crimes Tribunal. One reason for that resistance is fear that concessions in that

* One Soviet legal writer attributed the post-1945 Western drive to establish the "pre-eminence" of international over national law as indicative of a "desire for world domination cherished by many in the imperialist countries." Academy of Science of the USSR, quoted in Weston, Falk, D'Amato (1980), pp. 164–165.

regard would provide an opening to undermine the dictatorship of the proletariat and undo the achievements of the Revolution.

We referred earlier to another product of Soviet legal thought, the distinction drawn between just and unjust wars depending on the bearing a conflict has on Marxist/Leninist revolutionary objectives and, of course coincidentally, on Soviet foreign policy goals. The same principle extends to just and unjust rebellions against or succession from "oppressive" rule, as it does to "justifiable" and "unjustifiable" intervention by one state in the internal affairs of another. Intervention, including invasion, on behalf of an "oppressed class" is just while intervention against the dictatorship of the proletariat is unjust, hence illegal.

Does contemporary international law have a special relationship to "imperialism?" From the socialist perspective it does in so far as it serves to maintain the *status quo*. But, as already noted, regarding that point the Soviet Union and socialist states generally are in a quandary. They too have a *status quo* to defend. The result is a curious ambivalence. If Western powers invoke international law in defense of their interests, Soviet bloc authorities define that as manifestation of arrogant "reactionary," "imperialist" behavior. If, on the other hand, Soviet bloc governments cite identical provisions to safeguard their interests, that is regarded as legitimate and wholly legal exercise of rights under international law. By that reasoning, efforts on the part of capitalist states to maintain world peace constitute threats to peace; they impede "social revolutionary progress." Active intervention, including armed aggression, by socialist forces, are by definition legitimate exercises of obligations under international law. Put differently, socialist intervention in the internal affairs of a state which is under imperialist-capitalist influence serves the cause of peace because it removes a major threat to peace, namely "capitalist oppression."*

* Concern over the nuclear threat to world peace appears to have spawned a new theme in Soviet writing, namely the divergence between "bourgeois" and "progressive" approaches to the resolution of international conflict and crisis. The argument is that the former urges separation of foreign from domestic policy whereas the latter, in accord with basic principles of Marxism/Leninism, stresses the inseparability of the two policy spheres. Academy of Science of the USSR (1972). "Bourgeois" theory, so the argument goes, insists on the separation in order to detach from the study of international relations the deeper social and economic causes of conflict and crisis, causes which socialist writers recognize as constant features, as givens, in contemporary international affairs. The point of the argument is that by refusing to be diverted, socialist theory of international politics as well as law is enabled to uncover the capitalist roots of the global nuclear threat. Tomashevsky (1974), pp. 27-28.

This ambivalence toward international law extends as a matter of course to international law on international commerce, financial transactions, including investment, and property rights. Because neither the Soviet Union nor her allies claim property rights abroad or have foreign investments—in the financial sense of that term—to protect, they tend to side with the former colonies when it comes to such measures as the Charter of Economic Rights and Duties of States (1974), the Law on Protection of Foreign Investment, or generally to all disputes concerning expropriation or nationalization of foreign holdings in "Third World" countries. Weston, Falk, D'Amato (1980), pp. 730-733.

Third World Perspectives

Not unlike their Soviet counterparts, writers espousing the cause of the world's less developed countries recognize that, poor and weak as they are, newly independent states must of necessity hang on to existing international law as their first line of defense. At the same time, all aspects of that law must be subjected to review. Like Soviet theorists, the more radical among Third World writers stress that no genuine representatives of their world perspective participated in the development of international law in its present form; therefore, unless it clearly and specifically aids them in their struggle for equality, newly independent countries should not be held accountable under that law. They feel justified in taking this position as history is replete with examples of Western governments, then in the driver's seat, bending the letter as well as the spirit of *their* law to suit *their* purposes.* Accordingly, the "Third World" coalition, supported by the Socialist bloc, have ever since the end of World War Two pressed for revision of those aspects of international law which in their opinion adversely affect their independence or hinder their development and growth.† The People's Republic of China, for example, rejects as invalid leases, treaties, transfer of territory, or concessions attained in violation of domestic Chinese law or imposed on China under "unequal" conditions. It is for these reasons that they insisted on renegotiating the status of Hong Kong. (See Chapter 13 below)

Predictably, given the world's inclination to ambivalence regarding law and anarchy and the absence of alternate law, this position tends to open the door to rebellion, international terrorism, numerous minor wars, hostage-taking, and attacks on alien's property and on diplomatic premises throughout the world.

* See the response by the Government of Iran to the Complaint by the United States in the Hostage Case, U.S. Department of State (1979), p. 12. Prior to World War One, Russia, Great Britain, France, Germany, and the United States, on rather specious grounds, claimed a right to intervene in the internal affairs of China. Their position seemed to be that governments whose territories offered attractive trade opportunities to outsiders were thereby obligated to maintain peace within their borders. Alternatively "they had to submit to foreign control." F.J. Goodnow, cited in Sheng (1981), p. 220.

† One focal point in that effort is the law on aliens which about a century ago gave rise to the *Calvo Clause*. In its origins that clause was a product mainly of the clash between the United States seeking special privileges for its citizens in Latin American countries and the latter insisting upon equality between foreigners and their own nationals. Specifically, the U.S. took the position that its citizens in conflict with local law in host states were to be treated in accordance "with ordinary standards of civilization," meaning of course standards to which U.S. citizens were accustomed. In response to refusal by local authories to comply, U.S. troops repeatedly intervened. It was the intent of the Calvo Clause in treaties of commerce to prevent foreign intervention by compelling aliens to renounce their asserted right to appeal to their own government for support. While the need for the clause itself was obviated as military intervention ceased to be employed in such cases, the basic problem remains. According to Levi (1979), p. 178, "Communist states reject the 'ordinary standards' principle as a disguised imposition of bourgeois legal principles upon the world, and as a tool employed by 'imperialist' states to guarantee a superior status for their citizens and corporations abroad."

Enduring Qualities of International Law

To summarize: dramatic though they are, massive violations of law, spectacular acts of defiance, and significant failures do not quantitatively outweigh the far greater number of instances when governments find it useful or convenient to avail themselves of the advantages of international law. By their very nature violations of law are more noteworthy than acts of observance. Overlooked and forgotten are myriads of instances throughout the world when provisions of international law are respected, are instrumental in averting a war somewhere, provide protection for some human beings, and generally serve the cause of world peace somewhere on earth.

As we suggested in Chapter 1, sovereignty is today not what it used to be. The universal nuclear threat, the power and range of modern weapons generally, economic interdependence, advances in technology, transportation, and communications, and ever widening networks of treaties, conventions, and pacts provide daily reminders even to the most independent minded rulers that theirs is not the only state on earth. At the same time, commitments and beliefs in absolute sovereignty being what they are, international law is attractive because it is flexible, open to amendment and change, and incapable of exercising the tyranny domestic law can and does exercise in many countries. This contributes to a relaxed atmosphere, removing the sense of urgency, compulsion, even desperation which so often incites the subjects of domestic law to seek recourse to violence.

Second, since international law is based largely on custom, breaking such law creates a precedent, a new custom perhaps, but one which may come to haunt the violator. In other words, most governments are reluctant to create a snare in which some day they themselves might be trapped. Closely linked to this consideration is the element of reciprocity: governments are motivated generally to respect a body of law which they themselves may have occasion to rely upon at some future date, or they expect their compliance will set a precedent for others to follow. With respect to such comities as diplomatic immunity, which we encountered earlier, governments generally act and anticipate that others will act lawfully and in good faith, most of the time.

Third, unlike citizens residing in a given state, nations cannot move around, changing their location at will, selecting their own neighbors, their own environment, and their own opportunities for advancement through mobility. They are bound—some for centuries, some for millenia—to remain where they are, live next to each other, as a rule tolerate even the most odious and obnoxious neighbor, learn to get along, and devise ways and means of settling conflicts peacefully. If under these conditions an atmosphere of mutual trust and confidence, of live and let live, can be created, so much the better, and international law is the most highly developed, most suitable instrument developed for that purpose so far.

Fourth, it can be most costly if a state acquires the reputation of an outlaw. Commercial contracts and assumption of long-range debt or credit obligations call for mutual trust, confidence, and dependability. A government willing to renege on its commitments, including those undertaken by its predecessors, or even conveying a hint of such inclination, may find it increasingly difficult to satisfy its needs on international money markets, to cite but one potentially costly consequence.

The majority of states currently recognized as such are economically and militarily weak. They therefore owe their continued recognition, their independence, in some cases even their very existence, to international law. That law protects their boundaries, it assures land-locked states access to the sea— if the Law of the Sea, to be discussed in Chapter 16, is ratified they can expect even more—provides some protection for their citizens abroad, and assures uninterrupted safe transit of their goods across other states' territory or on the high sea. We saw that governments of some newly independent states favor drastic revision of existing international law. But pending implementation of that wish no state is prepared to repudiate what is in effect the only legal foundation of its existence.

In conclusion, addressing the socialist and Third World challenges to existing international law but only those, Schwarzenberger argues that this really is not a new development. There always have been entities whose rulers had reason to be discontent with existing law or rules. Since its inception, international law has by its very nature reflected prevailing social and political pressures and interests. Rules of conduct between sovereigns have therefore always and will forever face obsolescence. They will of necessity always lag behind changing social, political, economic, technological, and military realities.* Although it is true that some legal scholars, and a larger number of political leaders, resist adaptation of the letter and the spirit of the law to changing conditions, the fact that certain principles have survived for centuries may also suggest that something in international law has enduring qualities.

Suggested Questions and Discussion Topics

Is "international law" law?

What are the principal sources of international law?

Cite some of the loopholes aggressor nations exploit to circumvent international law.

---

* Schwarzenberger (1976), p. 54, sees the process as one of repetition rather than continuation. Certain rules are "adopted again and again because they correspond to stereotyped needs of societies which are motivated by the quest for power rather than law and based on the coexistence of entities which consider themselves as ends rather than means."

What sanctions are available to enforce international law?

What are the most salient First, Second, and Third World positions regarding existing international law and why are these positions taken?

Chapter 10
International Organization

It has been said that "international *organization* is a process; international *organizations* are representative aspects of the phase of that process which has been reached at a given time."[1] As a process, international organization has had its ups and downs, its efficacy depending largely on the degree to which the effort to bring together a number of states or private interest groups to common purpose is in accord with the vital interests of the dominant powers, or combinations of such powers, in the areas covered, which may be limited to a region or may encompass the globe.

International organizations may be formed either by governments (international governmental organizations or IGOs) or by private or semipublic bodies (international nongovernmental organizations or INGOs).* As a process, international organization seeks to advance international cooperation to promote peace, prosperity, and general well-being, or, on a more limited scale, it seeks to resolve a particular conflict, dispute, or problem. Whatever the organizational format or geographic context, all such organizations are but instruments serving the interests of their members, all are subject to severe political constraint. Furthermore, while organization rhetoric and diplomatic conventions may seek to convey a sense of unity of purpose and of equality of members, the principle of national sovereignty, coupled with conflicting and often divergent military, economic and social interests and orientations, determines the actual concrete functions and set the limits of all international bodies. Politically, international organizations are microcosms of the world in which they operate.

As long as individual monarchs personified nation-states, international conferences and congresses, the forerunners of permanent international organizations, were convened on their personal initiative, reflecting principally their personal preferences and priorities. As the emphasis shifted from monarch to

---

* Jacobson (1984), p. 9, offers the following definitions: "International non-governmental organizations share with IGOs the three characteristics of having regularly scheduled meetings of representatives of membership, specified procedures for decision-making, and a permanent secretariat . . . their members are individuals or private associations, or perhaps a combination of both, from two or more countries, rather than states themselves, and INGOs must have been created by some means other than agreement among governments."

state, diplomacy by "great powers" rather than emperors and kings became the established pattern.[2] From that point until 1945 international organizational efforts throughout the world served mainly the interests of the dominant Western European powers and the United States, joined briefly to a limited extent and only until the Russian Revolution by then heavily Europe-oriented Czarist Russia. Although they were nominally associated with such efforts as the 1899 and 1907 Hague Peace Conferences, the Paris Peace Conference (1919) following the First World War, and the League of Nations which sprang from it, the republics of Latin America, China, and rapidly rising Japan, plus a sprinkling of other non-Western states, were unable to challenge European and North American dominance of the international organizational network until after World War Two. The Russian Revolution, other destabilizations in the wake of the First World War, and the eventual collapse of the great empires after 1945 ushered in a new phase. With the proliferation of nations from the theretofore neglected, exploited, and under-represented continents, international diplomacy and consequently international organization took on substantially different forms.

International Governmental Organizations (IGOs): General Characteristics

A generalized typology of IGOs groups them by purpose, degree of integration of national, legal and political systems, and geographic scope. (See Box 10-1.)

Aside from serving great powers as instruments of their foreign policies, IGOs are designed to serve a wide variety of broader, more far-reaching ends ranging from entirely open-ended, unrestricted, general purpose goals to precisely defined, restricted and specific military, monetary, customs, postal service, or health-related functions, for example. Integration may involve little more than periodic exchange of views or it may extend to states ceding to a common organization segments of their sovereignty, the right to assess penalties for noncompliance with organizational mandates, for example, command powers over joint military forces, or, in more advanced cases, legislative and judicial powers. Organizations nominally open to all nations of the world need not and most do not include all states in existence at any given time.

Most prominent among non-integrated universal IGOs are the League of Nations (1920-1945) and the United Nations system founded in 1945. Declared by its founders to be a world organization, for the greater part of its brief existence the League actually did not include all of the then known great powers: the United States never was a member, and Germany and the Soviet Union were barred for a number of years. Furthermore, most of the peoples of Africa, Asia, and the Middle East had yet to achieve independence—they were represented only indirectly, and without their consent, by the colonial powers. The League's claim to universality therefore was debatable. The founders of the United Nations undertook to correct this deficiency from the outset.

Box 10-1. Typology of International Governmental Organizations[a]

Purpose/Degree of *Integration*	*Universal or Global*	*Regional or Inter-Regional*
I Political/ Diplomatic Non-Integrated	League of Nations United Nations	Council of Europe Organization of African Unity Organization of American States (British) Commonwealth Arab League ASEAN (Association of Southeast Asian Nations)
II Functional Non-Integrated	UN Specialized Agencies, UNCTAD, IMF, IBRD	Andean Group OECD European Payments Union (EPU) Economic Commission of West African States (ECOWAS) Arab Monetary Fund
III Functional Partially Integrated	International Court of Justice (ICJ) Permanent Court of Arbitration	European Economic Community (EEC) North Atlantic Treaty Organization (NATO) Warsaw Treaty Organization Council for Mutual Economic Assistance (CMEA/COMECON) Caribbean Community and Common Market (CARICOM)

[a] Examples

By the terms of their constitutions—the League's Covenant and the UN's Charter—the two organizations were committed to make the world safe from the calamities which had given birth to them, World War One and Two respectively. But the League's collective security mechanism to prevent aggression—and if not prevent then punish it—had obviously failed to deter the Japanese, Italian, and German military machines from overrunning parts of Asia, Africa, and all of continental Europe beginning in the 1930s. From the vantage point of that experience, the founders of the UN designed a more ambitious, more far-reaching, hopefully more effective collective security system, backed by an equally elaborate system for conflict resolution to prevent disputes from turning into armed clashes and war. If that combination failed, the Charter provided for an organizational military capability to keep the peace by policing troubled areas and intervening if necessary. In addition, recognizing that the League's approach to war prevention had been rather superficial, the UN was endowed with powers to address some of the more important underlying social and economic causes of conflict and war.

The outstanding example of a universal, functionally restricted, partially integrated IGO is the International Court of Justice or World Court. While governments are free to decline acceptance of the Court's jurisdiction, the Court as such of necessity is constituted as one integrated body. The judges are expected to set aside national, political, and other loyalties and commitments, relying instead on their professional legal skills and judicial expertise, applying international rather than national law in the interest of the community of nations as a whole.

Organizations limited to a particular region or subregion enjoy several distinct advantages over more comprehensive universal bodies. Because they need to satisfy fewer members whose interest are likely to coincide in more numerous respects, they can be more specific and concrete, hence more effective. Regional efforts range from creation of formally constituted complex and comprehensive organizational structures, the European Common Market for instance, to free associations of states tied together only by a vaguely worded charter or treaty, like the Organization of African Unity (OAU) or the Organization of American States (OAS). Some are solid bodies dedicated to performing specific and entirely manageable tasks; some are little more than declaratory entities, existing more in name than in substance. Many, like the OAU or the intra-regional Commonwealth of Nations, once associated with the British Empire, encompass too wide a spectrum of cultural, ethnic, and religious orientations to permit anything more than vague generalizations: opposition to racism and colonialism on the African continent in the case of the OAU or defense against encroachments from outside the Western Hemisphere in the case of the OAS. For these reasons such organizations, at their meetings tend as a rule to take up matters only if a consensus can be taken for granted in advance. At the opposite end of that spectrum is the tightly reined East European Council for Mutual Economic Assistance (CMEA/COMECON). It does not deviate in significant political and economic respects from Soviet foreign policy requirements.

Thus it can be expected that the solidity, manageability, and purposefulness of international organizations increase in inverse proportion to the diversity and numbers of assigned functions and membership. Degree of integration is of some consequence but, as will be shown in the discussion of intra-European relations (Chapter 12), even the most advanced case of integration remains afflicted by the national sovereignty virus. Still, the progress made by Western European nations in voluntarily overcoming ancient and deep-seated hostilities and fashioning, in the course of little more than a decade, a network of concrete and fully operational interrelated regional organizations is remarkable. Engaged not too long ago in internecine battles, the region now features organizational facilities expressing a common will, exercising policy and decision-making powers over member states in economic, military, and judicial respects. We shall return to that subject shortly.

IGOs: The United Nations System

Organizational Structure

Today, the focal point of global international organization is the United Nations. With its six basic organs and its committees, commissions, and specialized agencies it influences all international organizational activity directly or indirectly in all corners of the globe. But a careful reading of its Charter and, equally important, of the negotiations leading up to its adoption, clearly reveals two potentially troublesome, perhaps even fatal, limitations: (1) Article 2, paragraph 7 prohibits the organization from interfering in the "internal affairs of member-states;" (2) Charter provisions coupled with certain historic understandings bar the organization from *taking any action* which could threaten, directly or indirectly, or affect adversely the vital interests of any one of five states accorded special veto powers, the so-called permanent members—the United States, the Soviet Union, Great Britain, France, and [the People's Republic of] China. If the five could agree, the sky is the limit; if they cannot, as indeed they do not on most issues, the potential of the entire system, especially its collective security and war prevention provisions, is placed in jeopardy.[3]

In a way, the veto provision acknowledges power-political reality. No matter how overwhelming a majority vote in the Security Council may be, if an order by the Council regarding questions of peace and war, collective security, or any other sensitive issue is to have any practical effect at all, the unanimous support of the world's leading economic and military powers is of the essence. In the absence of that unanimity, Security Council intervention in a crisis can only complicate matters. Accordingly, Article 27, paragraph 3 of the Charter stipulates that in addition to "an affirmative vote of nine members" the "concurring votes" of all five permanent members are required if a decision by the Council on *substantive* matters is to have legal effect.* Fig. 10-1 shows the basic structure of the United Nations.

The hub of the organization is the General Assembly, where all states including the permanent ones have only one vote. The Assembly has five major functions: deliberative, supervisory, financial, elective, and constituent. Because all states have equal voting power, states or groups of states confident of a majority but fearing a big power veto in the Security Council have taken their cases to the

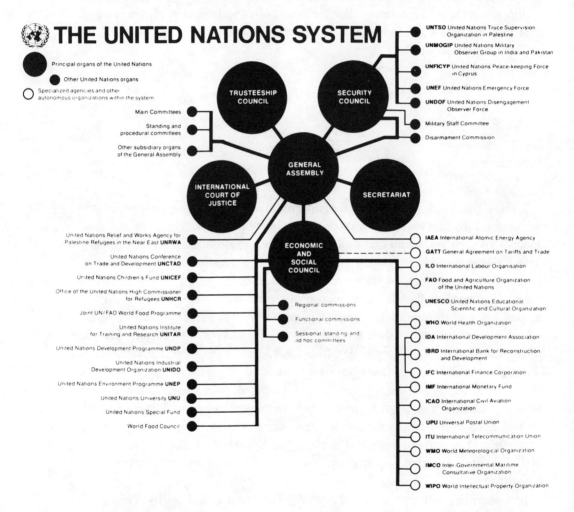

Fig. 10-1. Basic Structure of the United Nations. (U.S. Department of State. *The United States and the United Nations.* Publication No. 8875 (1976).)

* The UN derives its power, authority, and its finance from member states. Only states can be voting members. Aside from the special provision under Article 27, all states have only one vote. The veto applies only to substantive not procedural matters. Its most important application has been in the spheres of military and economic measures such as sanctions against states accused of violating the Charter or UN-initiated peace-keeping missions, questions of membership, and declaratory resolutions likely to result in concrete action.

Assembly. To be sure, unlike the Security Council the Assembly can only recommend action to member states; but where a majority is sympathetic all that might be required is a resolution to recommend action to members willing and able to act.

The Security Council is the executive organ of the system, charged as its name implies with maintenance of world security. To ensure that a majority, acting spontaneously or at a rival's behest, could not at some future date, over their objection, institute action against their vital security interests, the major powers stipulated under Chapter VII of the Charter that only the Council was to be empowered to act on such matters. But in 1950, anticipating repeated Soviet vetos to prevent the Western powers from activating the UN's collective security functions in opposition to communist acts of aggression, the United States, then enjoying majority support in the General Assembly, caused that body in effect to amend the Charter. Under the "Uniting for Peace Resolution," the General Assembly could recommend collective security measures, if the Council was unable or unwilling to *act*.*

Joining the five permanent members on the Council are ten members elected by the General Assembly for two year periods. By general agreement these ten seats are apportioned as follows: five for Africa and Asia, two for Latin America, one for Eastern Europe—understood to go to another Soviet bloc member or to Yugoslavia—and two for Western Europe and other Western-oriented states.

As noted, the manifest failure of the League of Nations to prevent World War Two, together with the traumatic experiences and memories of that conflict, led to a broadening of the mandate given to the successor organization. Accordingly the UN was to concern itself not only with imminent military threats to world peace but also with the underlying causes of tension and conflict. Primary responsibility in these respects was assigned to the General Assembly. Under its general supervision and that of the Economic and Social Council (ECOSOC), a number of committees, commissions, and specialized agencies were to address such problem complexes as health, illiteracy, poverty, starvation and malnutrition, care of refugees and of children, status of women, human rights, and working conditions.

---

* In 1950, in the wake of the attack by Communist North Korea on South Korea, the U.S. succeeded in obtaining Security Council approval of military action in South Korea's defense only because the Soviet delegation, whose government is believed to have encouraged North Korea, had "walked out." In anticipation of future Soviet vetoes should another such attack take place, the U.S. initiated the Resolution which was passed by the General Assembly that same year. To be sure, the General Assembly could only *recommend* military action, relying on resolution sponsors to *act* and provide the military wherewithal. Nevertheless, it can be argued that the Resolution violates an understanding central to the entire collective security structure of the UN, namely that no *action* was to be taken under UN auspices against the wishes of any one of the five permanent members. However urgent the invocation of the Charter's collective security provisions appeared to a majority in the Security Council or in the Assembly, the veto could legally not be circumvented. If it was in fact circumvented, the permanent power whose veto was being sidestepped could not legally be expected to accept or honor such action nor could it legally be compelled to help cover expenses. See Claude (1964), Chapter 8, and (1967), pp. 16–17, 40, and 42.

Combinations of UN bodies and specialized agencies were to deal with problems afflicting the world economy, in particular trade and finance as well as economic development. Foremost among these were the Economic and Social Council itself, the International Bank for Reconstruction and Development (IBRD), and the International Monetary Fund (IMF), the United Nations Conference on Trade and Development (UNCTAD)—concerned in particular with the General Agreement on Tariffs and Trade (GATT)—the set of regional Economic Commissions for Europe, Asia and the Far East, Africa, and Latin America, and numerous other bodies.

The Trusteeship Council was to supervise the progress of former colonies toward independence and the International Court of Justice was to adjudicate disputes among nations which accepted its jurisdiction and matters pertaining to the interpretation of or conflict under the UN Charter. The Secretariat, headed by the Secretary General of the United Nations, administered the system, the Secretary General to perform such special tasks as the Security Council or the Assembly assigned to him.

Although intended and expected to be part of the UN system, the specialized agencies enjoy legally and administratively autonomous status. Several considerations led to this arrangement. First, several of these agencies, the International Labor Organization for instance, had come into existence independently of the UN, their membership therefore not necessarily coinciding with that of the larger organization. Second, majority rule, the principle governing all UN bodies except the Security and Trusteeship Councils, was not deemed appropriate for such agencies as IBRD or the IMF where, if the organizations' financial viability was to be ensured, voting would have to be weighted according to financial contributions. Third, it was felt that such relatively nonpolitical, technical cooperative undertakings as world health care (WHO), food and agriculture (FAO), or civil aviation (ICAO) should be separated from the UN's anticipated involvement in highly sensitive disputes in conjunction with its collective security, military peace-keeping, and conflict resolution functions.

Balance Sheet of the UN: Liabilities

Unlike the League of Nations which in essential respects was the instrument mainly of a homogeneous combination of Western powers, the United Nations was the product of a temporarily expedient alliance between status quo-oriented capitalist democracies and revolutionary totalitarian communism. With the defeat of Germany, Italy, and Japan in 1945, the raison d'être for the wartime alliance evaporated. Thus at its very inception the UN structure was enfeebled by a chasm which widened with every passing year. The steadily worsening confrontation between the superpowers and their allies adversely affected all aspects of the organization: military, economic, and social. In particular, the split endangered from the outset the collective security function as well as the planned campaign against the more basic causes of war and human suffering. It almost immediately inhibited and eventually paralyzed the Security Council, critically impaired potentialities of the International Atomic Energy Agency and the Disarmament Commission and undercut efforts to advance basic human rights. Its failure to play a decisive role in world affairs curtailed financial contributions, denying the organization the means to carry out its assigned tasks in these and related respects at levels likely to produce meaningful results.

Because the organization can no longer be relied upon to act swiftly and decisively in the face of indisputable acts of aggression or in response to other crises, victims of aggression or states who feel compelled to resort to military force for other reasons have tended to rely on the so-called right to self-defense, granted under Article 51 of the Charter. Under that article, invocation of that right must cease as soon as the Security Council "has taken the measures necessary to maintain international peace and security." However, more often than not measures taken by the Council fall far short of what might be considered "necessary" to stop the shooting and killing, leaving scholars and jurists to note that the Charter is being violated while wars increase in number.* One obstacle to effective Council action, of course—but not the only one—is the veto.

Once the Security Council was prevented from meeting its collective security and conflict resolution responsibilities, the weight of responsibility in these respects was bound to shift to the General Assembly and the Secretariat. But the General Assembly was subject to rule by a majority lacking the means to implement or enforce its decisions and the Secretariat had to exercise special care not to offend any of the permanent members. Moreover neither the Assembly, nor any of its committees and commissions, nor the Secretariat, could guarantee let alone protect military secrets, a mandatory requirement for resolution of conflicts involving the vital interests of major military powers.

In any case, very few if any of the more pressing issues facing the world are likely to be settled by majority vote. The will and desires, even the vital interests, of the majority of the world's nations may be morally unassailable. But they pale in significance in a setting where two superpowers have acquired the means of destroying each other several times over. Faced with near instant and total annihilation, or believing that the threat is real, neither of the superpowers and few of the lesser powers are prepared to commit their national security interests to majority rule or to the Secretariat which by itself lacks any effective security enforcement apparatus.

The inherent weakness of the UN with respect to some of the more pressing world peace and collective security issues was compounded as the organization's membership expanded from the original fifty-one to more than three times that number by 1985. Now the majority includes microstates little larger than the top of a volcano but exercising the same voting power as the Soviet Union covering an area of more than 8.6 million square miles. States with a population of one or two million equal the voting privileges of the People's Republic of China with now more than one billion people.

---

* In 1983, at least 45 nations were directly involved in external armed conflict of one kind or another.

The world's ten leading industrial powers can be outvoted by any eleven economically feeble, militarily impotent states. The Maldives with a GNP of $30 million equals the voting power of the United States with a GNP of nearly $3 trillion or the USSR with more than $900 billion, and militarily insignificant states can outvote the superpowers. Decisions made on these bases could not possibly produce results significantly related to the real world where finance, trading potential, and industrial capacity outweigh by a wide margin historical claims to greatness, actual or perceived injustice, or inequity. Under such conditions, power derived from the "one country, one vote" principle easily becomes separated from responsibility. One result is financial irresponsibility in proposing and voting predictably wasteful expenditures beyond known budgetary limits.[4]

Another liability is voting by blocs which actually have little in common. It is not unusual in any organization for weak members to enhance their position by entering into voting coalition or by trading votes. But normally the resulting combinations reflect a modicum of shared values. To an extent this does apply to the United Nations. Today the largest voting bloc encompasses the Soviet-led East European group, the more radical Third World states, and a changing assortment of opportunistic states. Ostensibly, the coalition is united more or less by opposition to racism, colonialism, rejection of the capitalist prescription for the solution of the world's ills, and advocacy of a New International Economic Order (NIEO), one objective of which appears to be redistribution of the world's wealth from the "haves" to the "have-nots." As we note throughout this study, in real terms the coalition partners represent in some respects diametrically

Table 10-1. Per Capita GNP (Gross National Product) and GDP (Gross Domestic Product) of Top and Lowest Ten Countries[a]

Group of Ten	Per Capita GNP (US$)	GDP (million US$)	Ten Lowest Income Countries	Per Capita GNP (US$)	GDP (million US$)
Belgium	10,760	85,240	Chad	80	400
Canada	11,320	289,570	Bangladesh	140	10,940
France	11,680	537,260	Ethiopia	140	4,010
Fed. Rep.			Nepal	170	2,510
of Germany	12,460	662,990			
Italy	6,840	344,580	Mali	180	1,030
Japan	10,080	1,061,920	Burma	190	5,900
Netherlands	10,930	136,520	Zaire	190	5,380 (1981)
Sweden	14,040	98,770	Malawi	210	1,320
United			Upper Volta	210	1,000
Kingdom	9,660	473,220			
United			Uganda	230	8,630 (1981)
States	13,160	3,009,600			

SOURCES: World Bank, *World Development Report 1984*, Table 1, pp. 218–219 and Table 3, pp. 222–223.
[a] 1982 data except where otherwise indicated

opposed positions. More important for the efficacy of the organization, whatever it is that brings the coalition together does not necessarily serve the cause of world peace. Just as the coalition of like-minded Western powers cannot expect to reduce international tension by ganging up against the Soviet bloc or the growing number of newly independent states, the new "radical" majority cannot expect to make real progress toward its objectives by brushing aside or overriding the vital interest of the still economically and militarily powerful forces supporting the status quo.* (See Tables 10-2, 3.)

Shortly after the UN had come into existence, the newspaper columnist Samuel Grafton wryly commented, "If all members of the animal kingdom were to receive certificates declaring them to be equal, squirrels would still be squirrels and elephants would still be elephants, and the squirrels would know it, and the elephants would know it." To some observers it seems that in recent years, on the strength of sheer numbers, the squirrels have taken over the organization. Pressing their numerical advantage,, they have succeeded in separating the United Nations from military and economic reality, discouraging super—as well as middle—powers from taking their more sensitive problems to the organization, encouraging them instead to confine their participation to exploitation of the organization and its agencies for propaganda purposes.†

---

* In recent years, a pattern appears to have developed. The more radical members of the group, frequently aided and abetted by the Soviet delegation and supported by bloc votes, seek to weaken the West's defenses by stretching the meaning or reinterpreting the intent of Charter provisions on such subjects as "threat to the peace" or "aggression." Originally intended to apply to direct or indirect *military* aggression, the Socialist bloc-Third World coalition now applies them, but only selectively, to social and economic practices and conditions meeting with their disapproval. Arguments by targets of their actions, by the Republic of South Africa, Israel, or the United States, for instance, that resolutions on race relations in South Africa, treatment of Arabs in Israel, or on Puerto Rican independence (decolonization is the preferred term), violate the domestic jurisdiction clause of Article 2 of the Charter are brushed aside. The resolutions, it is said, are in full accord with the "spirit of the Charter" which places social justice, human rights, and self-determination, as interpreted by the "people of the world," that is by the coalition partners, above national self-interest of defenders of the status quo.

† Concludes one analysis: "The U.S. faces a double handicap at the UN. Almost constantly outvoted in the General Assembly and in nearly every UN agency, the U.S. is also deprived of sufficient control of the administrative and policy posts to ameliorate anti-U.S. and anti-Western pronouncements and resolutions." The Heritage Foundation, *Backgrounder* No. 247, February 14, 1983, "Americans at the U.N.: An Endangered Species," A United Nations Assessment Project Study. The study also concludes that nationals from the U.S., the USSR, Japan, the Federal Republic of West Germany, and Israel are all under-represented in key administrative positions given their respective contributions to the budgets of the UN generally and its major associated agencies; see especially Tables I, II, and III, pp. 7-9; also Bernstein (1984) and U.S. Dept. of State, Report . . . on Voting Practices in the UN (1984). Regarding attempts to reinterpret the letter and the spirit of the UN system, the general thrust of the endeavor, abstractly viewed, may seem entirely reasonable and just. However, in the form in which such resolutions usually are advanced in the General Assembly, in such agencies as UNESCO and in a broad spectrum of specialized committees and commissions, they must be wholly unacceptable to the very powers whose full cooperation is required if any of the problems addressed in those resolutions are to be brought nearer to solution. Equally detrimental to the cause of international cooperation is the tendency on the part of the more radical

Balance Sheet of the UN: Assets

Great powers have not in the past prevented and will not in the future prevent small, intermediate, and great wars. Therefore, in a world by all indications once more heading toward global catastrophe, notwithstanding all of its faults and record of abuses the availability of a global organization comprised of most of the world's great, middle, and lesser powers cannot be unwelcome. Indeed one can identify many positive contributions by the UN to world peace and human progress.

As shown earlier, communication is of the essence in the resolution of conflict. From time to time, and in some cases all of the time, states do not or their leaders dare not communicate with one another. The existence of an organization where all parties to a dispute may be represented facilitates discussion of the issues, on neutral ground, while all disputants may actually be in the same building. Beyond that, progressive global interdependence, especially in economic respects, and the constant threat of war make it imperative for machinery to exist where views can be exchanged, informally, without invocation of cumbersome rules of diplomatic protocol, out of range of prying eyes and ears, without the risk of loss of face. It is clearly better for such machinery to exist, for instant use at times of need. The outstanding examples of this capacity are the UN's "peace-keeping" operations. (See Table 10-4.)

Under Chapter VII of the Charter, UN forces have on several occasions either intervened in armed conflicts or have been inserted between belligerents to observe, enforce, or supervise truce or armistice agreements, or pending such arrangements, separate or keep apart the opposing forces. To be sure, the peace-keeping machinery can be used legally and effectively only with the tacit or, better, express approval of all five permanent members of the Security Council. But the machinery is available and can be activated when and if a majority of the Council, including the five permanent members, are so inclined.[5]

The greatest potential of the organization lies in areas not directly impinging upon the vital military and economic interests of the world's leading powers. Potentially most promising are efforts to identify shared interests among the nations of the world, narrowing of cultural, religious, and ideological gaps through improved communications and cultural, educational, and scientific investigatory enterprises and exchanges, preparatory work toward narrowing the gap between the rich and poor nations of the world, eradication of disease, identification of major causes of social injustice and human suffering especially among children and refugees, and making inroads cautiously with respect to basic human rights.

With respect to the more sensitive areas of international trade, monetary affairs, and the arms race, although prevented from assuming a controlling

members of that group to politicize proceedings of essentially or wholly technical organizations, detracting from their assigned purpose organizations which otherwise could contribute to the amelioration of the world's pressing problems. We shall return to this subject in Chapters 14 and 15. See also The Heritage Foundation, U.N. Assessment Project (June 18, 1984) and Pines (1984).

Table 10-2. Distribution of Votes and Share of World Population in the UN

Groupings[b]	Number of Member States (1983)	Percent Votes in General Assembly (1983)	Percent World Population (1981)[a]
Mainly LDCs			
The Non-Aligned Group	99	62.6	58.8
"The Group of 77"	121	76.6	40.0
The African Group	50	31.6	9.3
The Asian Group	39	24.6	47.5
The Central and South American Group	33	20.8	7.3
The Islamic Conference	41	25.9	12.5
The Arab Group	21	13.3	4.2
The Association of Southeast Asian Countries (ASEAN)	5	3.1	5.3
Developed Countries			
The "West European and Other" Group	22	13.9	8.7
The Industrial Market Economies	19	12.0	14.6
The European Economic Community (EEC)	12[c]	7.5	6.5
The Nordic Group	5	3.1	.4
The East European Non-Market Economies	11[d]	6.9	8.1[e]

SOURCES: *World Bank Atlas*; U.S. Department of State. *Voting Practices in the UN* (1984).
[a] Estimated Total: 4,550,000 million
[b] Groupings by count of the U.S. Mission to the U.N.
[c] Including Spain and Portugal, Excluding Turkey
[d] Including Bylorussia, Ukraine, and Yugoslavia
[e] Excluding Bylorussia and Ukraine

position UN agencies can be credited with several important initiatives. The General Assembly and the Economic and Social Council succeeded in prodding the leading economic powers to negotiate and ratify the General Agreement on Tariffs and Trade (GATT) and the less productive but promising United Nations Conference on Trade and Development (UNCTAD). Critical needs have been identified among the less developed countries by the UN's various regional Economic Commissions. The sensitive issue of utilization of mineral resources on the ocean bed would not have been tackled had it not been for UN initiatives.[6]

Similarly, because of its extended and diverse membership the organization can provide relatively disinterested personnel to perform tasks too sensitive to be handled by the great powers or their allies. Questions of birth control, for example, are best addressed in India, Bangladesh, or Nigeria, by personnel from states whom the subject populations do not suspect of desiring the extermination

Table 10-3. Share of World Population and GNP in the World at Large

	Share World Population 1980	Share World GNP 1980
All LDCs	73.6	21.5
	73.9	22.9
High Income Oil Exporters	.3	1.4
All Industrial Non-Market Economies	10.7	12.4
	26.1	77.1
All Industrial Market Economies	15.4	64.7

SOURCES: IBRD. *World Development Report 1982; U.S. Statistical Abstracts.*

Table 10-4. UN Peacekeeping Operations

Designation-Area of Operation	Where Deployed	Date When Created
UN Military Observer Group in India and Pakistan (UNMOGIP)	Kashmir	1948 and 1949
UN Truce Supervision Organization (UNTSO)	Middle East; Between Egypt and Israel	1948
UN Emergency Force (UNEF) I and II	Middle East; Between Israel and Egypt	1956, removed in 1967, as UNEF II recreated in 1973
UN Observer Group in Lebanon (UNOGIL)	Lebanon	1958
UN Congo Operations (ONUC)	Congo	1960
UN Observation Mission in Yemen (UNYOM)	Yemen	1963
UN Force in Cyprus (UNFICYP)	Cyprus; Between Greek and Turkish Cypriots	1964
UN Disengagement Observer Force (UNDOF)	Middle East; Between Israel and Syria	1973
UN Interim Force in Lebanon (UNIFIL)	Southern Lebanon	1978

of non-white races. Likewise, persuading a financially unstable, generally poor and underdeveloped state to cut back on industrialization or postpone some of its cherished development plans is best not proposed by representatives from a former colonial power which may have contributed to these conditions in the first place and may now be suspected of planning to recapture its lost position.

On balance the League of Nations, far less pretentious than the UN, could not realistically have been expected to accomplish more than it did. The UN's mandate moreover went far deeper and was far more comprehensive. Given the limitations and restrictions written into the Charter, the organization cannot be faulted for failure to prevent the collapse of the wartime alliance, the keystone in its collective security or maintenance of peace structure. If cynical misuse of the Charter has become a pattern, this must be expected in an organization as large and as diverse as the UN. If today's anti-Western majority conducts itself irresponsibly, applying the provisions of the Charter inconsistently and selectively, then it must be recalled that when control of the international organization system was in Western hands, cynicism and selectivity also were the rule.

Revising the Charter

The threat of nuclear war has added an entirely new dimension to the tasks facing all international organizational efforts. If both superpowers remain incapable of bringing the threat under control, only the UN remains to do the job. Under the circumstances, whoever is in control of the UN structure bears a greater responsibility to strengthen the organization's credibility and enhance its political efficacy than has ever been the case in the history of international organization. Yet the UN is losing whatever precarious grip it held on the more critical issues confronting the world. One source of the problem is the voting system, especially in the Security Council but also in the General Assembly. Behind the facade of Soviet bloc–Third World unity, pressure is building against the concept of great power veto, still an absolute and sacrosanct requirement from Moscow's point of view. Third World states take the position that since none of them played a role in the foundation of the UN and the writing of its Charter, they have a right to demand that the rules be amended to accommodate their particular needs and aspirations. To press their demands under current rules, they are compelled to coalesce with whoever shares their interests. Ideally they would want to do away with the veto, to them a remnant of the imperial past.* At the same time the economically and militarily powerful but numerically outdistanced Western states are considering proposals to reduce the voting power of the dominant coalition. If unsuccessful these powers will have no alternative but to further reduce their reliance on the United Nations and shift the weight of their international organization efforts to specialized agencies, such as the IMF and the IBRD where voting is weighted to protect their particular interests.[7]

---

* The fact that the People's Republic of China, certainly a Third World Power, is one of the veto holders tends to disarm Third World advocates of the abolition of the veto. Sensitive to the problem, the PRC has so far exercised great care not to use the veto to the detriment of Third or Fourth World interests.

IGOs: Regional Systems*

Clearly, the most persuasive rationale for regional cooperation within firm organizational frameworks is war prevention, the prime motivation for creation of the post-World War Two integrated network in Western Europe. Not unrelated to that objective is the removal of causes of tension and conflict arising from unfair economic competition, shortage of critical raw materials, trade restraints and imbalances, and unemployment. Though no panacea, international economies of scale, resulting from expansion within a common framework of productive capacities of several theretofore separate economies, promise to bring down costs of production, thereby improving the region's position vis-à-vis large, extraregional competitors. As barriers to trade and to movement of goods and labor are lowered or removed altogether and customs and tariff policies coordinated to mutual advantage, the region's economies gain in flexibility and large-scale producers find it easier to locate needed investment capital. Most important, where basic resources are shared wars need not be fought to gain access to them.

As will be shown in our subsequent discussion of North-South and South-South relations, states facing an uphill struggle to escape poverty and underdevelopment are eager to enter into cooperative, if possible also integrative, ventures with their neighbors to eliminate drains on their scarce resources. Ironically, in that endeavor they must in many cases laboriously reconstruct colonial institutions abandoned or dismantled as a concrete expression of newly attained political independence. To their sorrow, the new regimes quickly learn that rebuilding cooperative structures or facilities or starting new ones is frequently far beyond their administrative and financial capacity.†

On occasion, regional organizational efforts reflect a mix of political and military-strategic as well as economic rationales. For example, shortly after the end of World War Two several West European leaders began to explore prospects of permanent pacification of their war-torn region through merger of key sectors

---

* Because organizations like the European Economic Community (EEC), and the Soviet-led East European Council for Mutual Economic Assistance (CMEA or COMECON), together with their military counterparts NATO and the Warsaw Pact, play a prominent role in intra-Western and intrasocialist relations, subjects covered in Chapters 12 and 13 respectively, only the most salient organizational features will be covered here.

† Many of the institutional and administrative frameworks and institutions inherited by many newly independent states from British, French, Belgian, Portuguese, and Netherlands colonial administrations in Africa, Southeast Asia, and the Caribbean were dismantled or fell into disuse solely because they were regarded as instruments of exploitative European capitalism. Development of substitutes or replacements, however, turns out to be possible only if the very same sources of capital can be interested. This is exemplified by the experiences of the Caribbean Community and Common Market (CARICOM), the Central African Customs and Economic Union (UDEAC), or the Economic Community of West African States (ECOWAS/CEDEAO). On the other hand, assuming that they can be revived, postcolonial integrative efforts can no longer be impeded by jealousies among the colonial powers and can therefore in theory address more directly genuine regional concerns and requirements.

of their national economies. But they had another objective. A consolidated Western European industrial complex would constitute an effective block to westward Soviet expansion. For that reason alone, and notwithstanding the evident fact that such a union posed a future threat to U.S. economic interests, the cause of European integration received substantial material support from the United States, whose foreign policy at the time had as a central theme the containment of communism.

As exemplified by the European Economic Community, diplomatic explorations precede first organizational steps and many years elapse before even these can be consolidated. In the European case, the germ of the structure was introduced when in 1944 three small states, Belgium, the Netherlands, and Luxembourg (BENELUX), laid the foundation for a customs union.* This was followed by the more dramatic creation of the European Coal and Steel Community (ECSC) in 1951. With one blow the ECSC removed one of the prime sources of friction in the region, Franco-German rivalry over control of rich coal deposits and steel production facilities theretofore separated by national boundaries and protective barriers. With that problem complex seemingly solved, a broader European Economic Community (EEC) became feasible. The Community was created in 1957 and, beginning in 1965, the existing sub-units were welded into one grand design.

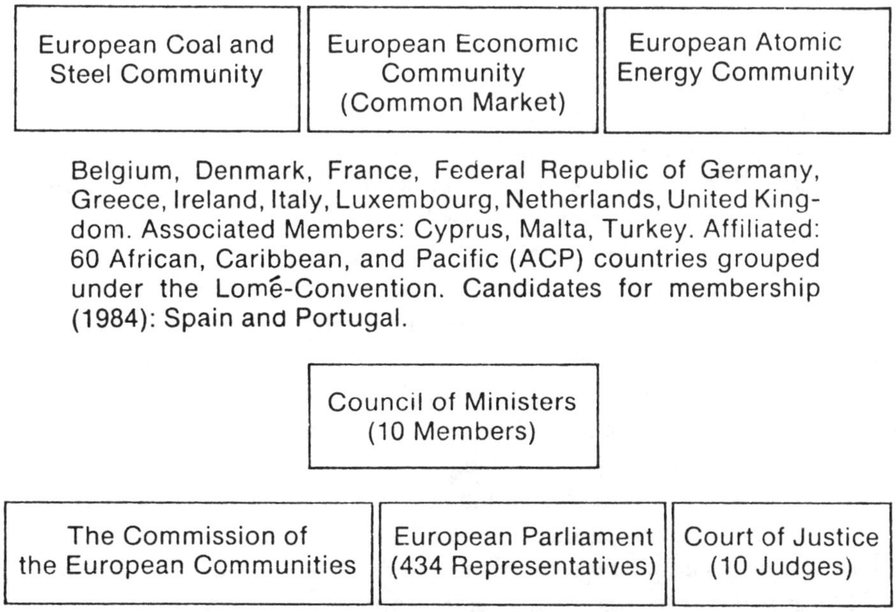

European Coal and Steel Community	European Economic Community (Common Market)	European Atomic Energy Community

Belgium, Denmark, France, Federal Republic of Germany, Greece, Ireland, Italy, Luxembourg, Netherlands, United Kingdom. Associated Members: Cyprus, Malta, Turkey. Affiliated: 60 African, Caribbean, and Pacific (ACP) countries grouped under the Lomé-Convention. Candidates for membership (1984): Spain and Portugal.

Council of Ministers (10 Members)

The Commission of the European Communities	European Parliament (434 Representatives)	Court of Justice (10 Judges)

Fig. 10-2. The European Community System

* A customs union of two or more states attempts to remove such barriers to trade as tariffs and quotas from governmental agendas within the group, while establishing a common set of barriers against nonmembers.

A European Free Trade Association (EFTA) was created in 1960 consisting of the so-called "outer seven", that is states existing along the periphery of the EEC and prevented from joining either by their own preference or because of their neutrality status. These were Austria, Iceland, Norway, Portugal, Sweden, and Switzerland. Finland, fearful of adverse Soviet reaction, cautiously joined as an associate member, and Spain was expected to join preliminary to becoming a member of the EEC.

As will be shown in our discussion of intra-Western relations (Chapter 12), it is not possible to predict whether the relatively advanced form of regional organization represented by the EEC will make further progress toward full integration and political union or whether it will falter and eventually disintegrate because of an inability to cope with residual internal conflicts and contradictions. Moreover, in a progressively ever more interdependent world, it becomes increasingly difficult to separate internal regional from broader international problem complexes. For reasons of military security alone, Western European integrational undertakings, therefore, must remain linked with the United States in the EEC's military counterpart, the North Atlantic Treaty Organization (NATO). For economic as well as political reasons, ties must also be maintained with other Western Hemispheric, African, Asian, and South Pacific associates of Great Britain and France, with Japan, and with an increasing number of nonaligned states seeking such association.[8]

The Soviet-led Council for Mutual Economic Assistance Soviet faces similar pressures and pulls. Organized initially as a bloc response to U.S. offers of massive economic aid to Europe under the Marshall Plan (1949), and the simultaneous formation of economic as well as military unions at its very doorstep, the Council now extends far beyond the immediate region it was to serve initially. While the core of the organization remains Eastern and Southeastern European, global strategic considerations have expanded its scope to include Cuba in the Caribbean and Vietnam in Southeast Asia.*

The major problem facing all regional organizations is the need to fight constantly the retrogressive influences emanating from nationalism and national sovereignty. Both act like weights attached to a swimmer. If he is to reach the opposite shore, he must continue to swim. If he pauses, he drowns. The treaty creating the European Common Market recognized the need for "progressive harmonization" of aims, objectives, and policies of member states. The emphasis is on *progressive.* The integrative momentum must be continuous and ever more comprehensive, lest national economic self-interest, ethnocentrism, historic antipathies, fears and phobias, together with divisive influences emanating from outside the region, combine to reverse the process.

The dynamics of economics alone dictate that to succeed integration must encompass, sooner rather than later, all sectors of all participating economies;

---

* Associated with the Council to a lesser extent are Afghanistan, Angola, Ethiopia, the Democratic People's Republic of [North] Korea, Laos, Mozambique, and the People's Democratic Republic of [South] Yemen.

each sector affects all others throughout a region. Partial economic integration has never succeeded unless maintained by artificial and costly means or by force. Even then, as exemplified by the system imposed on Europe by Germany, by Japan on East and Southeast Asia, and, more recently, by the East European model, the undertaking has a hollow ring.*

International Non-Governmental Organizations (INGOs)

As Harold K. Jacobson has noted, it is not always possible to draw clear distinctions between INGOs whose members are in all significant respects tightly controlled and directed by agencies of their respective national governments, those which may be so controlled only partially, and those entirely independent.[9] Certainly, even though they may nominally be dissociated from their respective governments, INGO members from totalitarian systems cannot in any meaningful sense be classified as nongovernmental. Even in the comparatively freer Western systems, organizations classifiable as INGOs may exist in the penumbra between public and private sectors, or may otherwise wholly or substantially be dependent on their respective national governments, a fact detracting from the nongovernmental status of their membership. In any case, the record indicates that when national interests so demand most governments find ways and means to bring their private citizens or their associations firmly back under national control.†

INGOs can be subdivided into several major categories. One is by membership, that is, universal or restricted; another is by manifest purpose or function, which may be very broad or very specific. An additional distinction may be drawn on the basis of geographic or political scope: some INGOs represent, though only informally to be sure, entire nations, national Olympic Committees for example; others, like academic and other professional organizations, grouped in the International Political Science Association for instance, or the International Commission of Jurists (ICJ), represent only members of a particular profession. As a rule, these bodies confine their activities to their specific professional needs and related concerns; the ICJ, for example, serves as an official advisory body to the UN regarding human rights.

In many respects, INGOs parallel, reinforce, and augment operations of IGOs. They expand and at the same time tighten the network of international cooperative and exchange ventures. They set up and develop informal channels of communication.

---

* See Chapter 13 below.

† In 1980, several national Olympic Committees decided to ignore their respective governments' requests to participate in a worldwide boycott of the Moscow Olympic games. Some scholars interpreted this as evidence of INGO autonomy, for example Kegley and Wittkopf (1981), p. 142, n. 25. Actually, the governments in question (Britain, France, Italy, and Australia), were divided on the issue and therefore refrained from applying the kind of pressure determined governments can apply "in the national interest."

Several developments have contributed to the proliferation of INGOs: the relative freedom of movement and of association granted citizens in relatively open Western societies, advances in transportation and communication, and the astronomical expansion of international capital movements, a function of both public and private enterprise. The latter factors in particular have compelled free economies to lower national barriers to foreign travel and banking arrangements, facilitating greatly the flow of personnel and funds needed to support their operations.

Foremost among politically highly influential INGOs falling somewhere between governments and nongovernmental origin and scope, are the Roman Catholic Church, subject to an extent to control by the Vatican, and the Socialist or Second International, representing the world's noncommunist socialist parties, many of which are in control of national governments and reflect on occasion official views.*

Seemingly among the most powerful and influential INGOs are the Multinational Corporations (MNCs), the most important ones of which are listed annually in *Fortune* magazine. Because of their phenomenal growth and ever more pervasive global reach, these entities have in recent years attracted special attention. Actually imposition of private commercial, financial, and industrial interests on public policy, nationally and internationally, is not new. Empires have been built with the active support of trading corporations whose interests and facilities spanned the globe, banking houses have since the Middle Ages served as agents and brokers, at times as partners in international financial undertakings involving monarchs as well as elected governments; notorious is the role played in international affairs by the "Seven Sisters," the major international oil companies.[10] Thus, a case can be made that this category of INGOs occupy a special place in the hierarchy of power. But this can be and has been exaggerated. Going by assets, annual product, network of subsidiaries, sources of supply and markets, and where appropriate by extent of monopoly and by their power as investors, many MNCs undoubtedly eclipse in power and influence governments, and in some cases entire countries. But these too can and, when the political chips are down, will be curbed.

Ranking MNCs along with countries by "annual product," it has been suggested that General Electric for example is more powerful than Israel or Egypt, the Ford Motor Company more powerful than Venezuela, and so on.[11] That is misleading. In developed countries MNCs are constitutionally, hence legally as well as politically and economically, subject to state control; states

---

* The Socialist International, a consultative body of the several component socialist parties, in 1983 passed a resolution supporting independence of Puerto Rico from the U.S., a demand officially pressed by numerous governments in the United Nations and elsewhere. *The New York Times* (May 6, 1983). Among the most productive sponsors of INGOs are the United Nations, in particular the Economic and Social Council (ECOSOC), the United Nations Educational, Scientific and Cultural Organization (UNESCO) and the regional organizations set up or sponsored by the UN to encourage more intensive and extensive transnational cooperation throughout the world; see Jacobson (1984), pp. 9–10.

or countries on the other hand are not in any way subject *to control* by corporations, individually or collectively. While some MNCs are known to have influenced some governments, individually none can influence entire countries; at best their power or influence is shared and partial; and all governments these days possess the means to discipline recalcitrant corporations, where vital national interests are at stake. In some notable cases MNCs have overshadowed governments, but only in weak and unstable less developed countries and only in cooperation with willing governments. Today opportunities for MNCs to play decisive roles in international affairs are diminishing. Even the weaker LDCs have learned how to tame even the largest MNCs in their midst. If they exceed what is considered tolerable, their assets can be nationalized, their possessions expropriated, their staffs expelled. Parent countries increasingly examine the impact on the national interest of MNC conduct at home and abroad.[12] Host countries find that increased international competition for their resources and markets enables them to bring troublesome MNCs to heel.

Suggested Questions and Discussion Topics

What three major categories of international organization reflecting degrees of integration can you name? Give three examples of each.

Outline the basic organizational structure of the United Nations.

What are some of the "liabilities" or weaknesses of the UN as a major instrument of conflict management in the world today? What are some of its more important assets in that regard?

What form have West and East European experiments with international organization taken?

Give some examples of INGOs and the reasons for the proliferation of this category of international organization since the end of World War Two.

Do INGOs help or hinder the cause of international peace?

Suggested Readings for Part Two:
Instrumentalities of International Relations

Chapter 4

Cherry, Colin. *World Communications: Threat or Promise?* London: Wiley, Interscience, 1971.

Herzenstein, Robert E. *The War That Hitler Won.* New York: Putnam's, 1978.

Whitaker, Urban G., Jr. *Propaganda And International Relations.* San Francisco, Cal.: Chandler, 1962.

Chapter 5

Bretton, Henry L. *The Power of Money.* Albany, New York: State University of New York Press, 1980, Chapter 11.

Hirsch, Fred. *Money International.* Middlesex, England: Pelican Books, 1969, Chapter 4, Section 4, pp. 113-122.

Spero, Joan E. *The Politics of International Economics.* Second Edition. New York: St. Martin's, 1981, Chapter 2.

Chapter 6

Cohen, Benjamin J. *The Question of Imperialism. The Political Economy of Dominance and Dependence.* New York: Basic Books, 1973, Chapters I-III.

Doxey, Margaret P. *Economic Sanctions and International Enforcement.* Second Edition. New York: Oxford University Press, 1980, Chapter 2.

Milward, Alan S. *War, Economy And Society 1939-1945.* Berkeley: University of California Press, 1977, Chapters 1 and 2.

Spero, Joan E., *op. cit.,* Chapter 3.

Chapters 7 and 8

Alexander, Jonah, and John M. Gleason, eds. *Behavioral and Quantitative Perspectives on Terrorism.* New York: Pergamon, 1981.

Brown, Anthony C. *Bodyguard of Lies.* New York: Harper and Row, 1975, Chapters 3 and 4.

Hoffman, Stanley. *Duties Beyond Borders. On the Limits and Possibilities of Ethical International Politics.* Syracuse: Syracuse University Press, 1981, Chapter 2.

Jeffreys-Jones, Rhodri. *American Espionage. From Secret Service to CIA.* New York: The Free Press, 1977.

Knorr, Klaus. *Power and Wealth. The Political Economy of National Power.* New York: Basic Books, 1973, Chapters 3-5.

Marxism-Leninism On War And Army (A Soviet View). Publ. Under the Auspices of the U.S. Airforce (Washington, D.C.: GPO; 1974).

Rositzke, Harry. *The KGB-The Eyes of Russia.* New York: Doubleday, 1981.

Stoessinger, John G. *Why Nations Go To War.* Second Edition. New York: St. Martin's, 1978, Chapter 7.

Wright, Quincy. *A Study of War.* Chicago: The University of Chicago Press, 1965.

Chapters 9 and 10

Akehurst, Michael. *A Modern Introduction to International Law.* Third Edition. London: Allen and Unwin, 1977, Chapter 1–3.

Bennett, A. LeRoy. *International Organization.* Second Edition. Englewood Cliffs, N.J.: Prentice-Hall, 1980.

Claude, Inis L., Jr. *The Changing United Nations.* New York: Random House, 1967.

———. *Swords Into Ploughshares.* New York: Random House, 1984.

Goodrich, Leland M. *The United Nations in a Changing World.* New York: Columbia University Press, 1974.

Jacobson, Harold K. *Networks of Interdependence. International Organization and The Global Political System.* Second Edition. New York: Knopf, 1984.

Levi, Werner. *Contemporary International Law: A Concise Introduction.* Boulder, Colo.: Westview Press, 1979, Part I.

Part Three
Managing the World Economy

Introduction

Since World War Two, management of the world economy has gone through two distinct phases. The first was concerned primarily with reconstruction and rehabilitation of war-ravaged national economies; the second, the postrecovery period, returned the world to old conflicts and rivalries and created new ones. Foremost among the latter has been the clash between the West and a militarily, economically, and diplomatically more aggressive East, and the economic tug-of-war between the less developed and the advanced countries.

As shown earlier, terms like East and West, while useful for approximate delineation, do not accurately identify the opposing camps. Nor do they point to the basic sources of conflict. Capitalism and socialism also are flawed as descriptive designations. There are many forms of socialism and one can argue, so far as the Soviet Union and the East bloc are concerned, that policy is determined not so much by orthodox socialist or Marxist thought as by the survival interests of the party, police, and military bureaucracies. On the capitalist side, to varying degrees the accent seems to be on free enterprise, accumulation of private capital, and free competition for profits and markets. There also is an emphasis on political democracy among the leading countries in that grouping. In contrast, totalitarian rule is preferred on the socialist side. Some writers distingush between market and nonmarket economies. This has some merit. Though not totally excluded from Soviet bloc or contemporary Chinese communist economic thinking, markets are not permitted to play the same role there that they do on the capitalist side.

Accordingly, while terms such as East and West, Western or Soviet bloc socialist and capitalist, or Western and non-Western, market and nonmarket (or central market) economies will be used where appropriate, the principal distinctions in this Part will be between free enterprise (Chapter 12) and centrally planned and controlled economies (Chapter 13), both understood to reflect only general orientation.* Chapter 12 examines the tasks of international economic management from the free enterprise perspective, while Chapter 13

---

* As will be shown, socialist or communist countries do allow or even encourage market forces to operate on a limited scale; what is not allowed in countries like the Soviet Union or the PRC is that market forces influence or shape the economy, and thereby state and society, in fundamental respects.

views the same problem from the other side of the great divide. "Advanced versus Less Developed" or "North versus South" are useable designations to identify the opposing sides in the other global rift. But as we have seen, geographic terms can be quite misleading and "development" is a condition characteristic of all countries on either side of that divide. First, Second, and Third World labels also fall short of the mark in this respect. For these reasons, Chapter 14 focuses on *economic viability* rather than development or geographic location.

Within these major categories, on the free enterprise side trade and finance are treated separately in spite of their being intertwined and mutually reinforcing. The reason is that although many countries may participate in one production process, international trade on the capitalist side typically is conducted on a bilateral basis; international finance, including monetary and currency operations are, of necessity, as a general rule conducted multilaterally, increasingly through international agencies or other forms of multinational cooperation. Regarding the socialist sector, finance not playing an independent or separate role, trade and finance are treated as two integral parts of the same system, the centrally planned and controlled economy. Another reason why Chapters 12 and 13 are structured differently is that the economically determined power-political options open to the Soviet Union and the bloc generally are quite limited compared to those available to the leading capitalist powers.*

---

* The *World Bank Development Report 1983* divides the world economy into six major groups: low income, middle income oil importers, middle income oil exporters, high income oil exporters, industrial market, and nonmarket economies. This classificatory scheme focuses on a single factor of critical importance to the world economy at a particular time. Should oil be replaced as a prime source of energy, other schemes may have to be devised.

Chapter 11
Postwar Recovery

For the first postwar decade, management of the world economy was the responsibility primarily of the United States, which had emerged from the war as the only free enterprise industrial democracy whose economy was intact. Two major tasks demanded immediate attention: emergency measures had to be devised to prevent social and political collapse followed by social revolution in war-torn Europe and Japan. Beyond that, world trade, finance, and related monetary affairs had to be reordered if another wrenching depression and another catastrophic war were to be prevented. Recovery of Western Europe and Japan was essential for another reason. The United States economy alone was not sufficient to sustain a reconstructed world economy. Only if recovery extended to all three centers could an economic engine be constructed powerful enough to drive the world economy to meet its next task: satisfying the rising expectations of hundreds of millions in Africa, Asia, and the southern section of the Western Hemisphere whose welfare had for so long been thoroughly neglected. Recovery once achieved of course had to be sustained at a steady rate without incurring runaway inflation.

Also at stake was the future of free enterprise, of capitalism, and of political democracy, the three foundations of the Western economic system. It was clear to the principal planners of the postwar period and to many of the Western leaders that capitalism would not survive another global war. Unless urgent rescue efforts were undertaken it would not even survive the last one. For that reason, the first item on the agenda was creation of a new monetary order.

Creating Monetary Order

Mindful of the catastrophic interwar experience, postwar planners set themselves four major monetary tasks. A mechanism had to be devised to: (1) grant loans on an emergency basis to countries encountering difficulties in paying current bills; (2) ensure cooperation among the major trading powers, eventually among all states, regarding their national monetary policies and coordination of these as well as of other internal measures likely to affect foreign exchange value of the world's major trading currencies, ideally of all such currencies; (3) establish and maintain fixed rates for the exchange of foreign currencies to avoid economically disruptive and politically unsettling payments and trade imbalances arising from erratic, precipitous, and wide fluctuations of rates of exchange; (4) augment national funds to provide liquidity in order to expand world trade.

With the production centers of Western Europe and Japan barely functioning, the U.S. economy, which had served as "the arsenal for democracy" during the war, now represented the world's major source of capital—and consumer—goods, raw materials, and food, as well as the critically needed finance capital. Coincidentally, the United States also was the only power strong enough militarily to shield the recuperating states of Western Europe and Japan from military or paramilitary pressure exerted by an aggressively expansionist and revolution-minded Stalinist Soviet Union. The fact that Germany, Italy, and Japan had been on the losing side in the just concluded war was of no consequence. They now were integral parts of the capitalist, freeenterprise order, or they had to be, if capitalism was to survive. It was with that in mind that the United States in cooperation primarily with Canadian and West European financial leaders and experts, proceeded to forge a new monetary order at a conference held at Bretton Woods, New Hampshire, in July 1944.

The centerpiece of the new structure was the International Monetary Fund. Voting within the fund was weighted in proportion to contributions or subscriptions, with the United States accorded the largest share of the total vote, followed initially by Great Britain and West Germany.* Tied to the size of contributions was a quota which determined the amount of foreign exchange or its equivalent that each member was entitled to withdraw from the Fund, the so-called "drawing rights." However, the entire structure depended more on the proper functioning of the system governing exchange rates than on the IMF as such.

Under the Bretton Woods Agreement, members were to assume responsiblity for their currencies' value vis-à-vis those of all other members. To that end, each currency was assigned a par value or "peg." Secondly, member governments were obligated to intervene in the exchange markets, that is, buy or sell their own or other nations' currencies in sufficient amounts to maintain their own currency's exchange value within a "band" no more than 1 percent above or below the par value. A currency's par value was determined with reference to the prevailing relationship between the U.S. dollar and the price of gold. If market operations did not align their currency's value with prevailing market conditions expressed in trade balances, governments were free to adjust the par value.†

* The U.S. had in effect veto power over Fund decisions. In 1983, the U.S. together with Great Britain and West Germany had 31.88 percent of the total vote. Whereas the leading financial powers had directors of their own on the Fund's Board of Executive Directors, the majority of member states, grouped by regions, had to share directors.

† Other features of the system were a set of rules governing the conduct of member governments in currency exchange and related matters and an institutionalized framework for periodic consultation among members; see Cohen (1977), especially pp. 89ff; for the background of the new monetary order, see *ibid.*, Chapter 3.

The Bretton Woods system survived for 27 years mainly because it had, in the United States, a leader with a vested interest in its success, disposing of an economy sufficient to maintain its own momentum as well as its contributions to the IMF and the IBRD while simultaneously producing and distributing to the world at large the enormous quantities of goods and services needed in the wake of the most destructive war in history. But most important, the trading partners of the United States, and the recipients of loans, grants and of foreign exchange transactions arising from the stationing around the world of large contingents of U.S. armed forces, were prepared to accept U.S. dollars and rely on their exchange value as a standard for their own national currencies. They did so because they had confidence that whenever they wished they could come to the "gold window" of the United States and exchange unneeded dollars for fixed equivalents of gold.

It should be noted at this point that at war's end the United States owned, securely deposited in its vaults, almost three quarters of the world's existing monetary gold.* The full-fledged gold standard, tying all major trading powers to that metal, had expired in 1914. Following several half-hearted efforts to revive it in modified forms, Bretton Woods modified it once more by creating a U.S. dollar-based *gold exchange* standard. The system depended on the willingness and ability of U.S. governments to maintain a dollar-gold relationship at precisely thirty-five dollars per troy ounce of gold. This placed the dollar in a straight-jacket and assumed that its real worth was not subject to external or internal pressures, a very questionable assumption. On the other hand (and again this explains why the system survived for so long) for decades it was in the interest of the U.S.'s trading partners to do all they could to keep the dollar at a steady rate.

The dollar had in fact become the principle "vehicle" or "top" currency for international trade and investment, the principal asset employed by the major trading powers' central banks to provide reserves for emergencies, and indeed a world currency of sorts. It was acceptable for all purposes to all peoples in all corners of the world, including states where trading in foreign currencies was a government monopoly, as in the member states of the Soviet-led bloc. The dollar served as "the universal solvent to keep the machinery of Bretton Woods running."[1] Unfortunately, to provide the liquidity the world needed the U.S. incurred ever increasing balance-of-payments deficits.†

---

* Gold produced for other purposes, industrial or private use for instance, was not included in the accounting system. At the end of 1982, the worldwide distribution of Official Holdings of Foreign Exchange, of the four major currencies, was as follows:

US $—53%

ECU—12.8%

West Germany's Deutschmark— 9.2%

Japan's Yen— 3.2%—IMF, *Annual Report 1983*, Table 15, p. 71.

† We recall balance of payments stands for balance of a country's international credit and debit transactions covering both current account merchandise export/import and capital account.

Providing Financial Stimulus

The West European countries had extensive balance of payments deficits vis-à-vis the United States and prospects were that these would grow larger. In 1946, the United States and Canada engaged in a large-scale monetary transfusion to alleviate the dollar shortage, especially in Great Britain. The medium were loans. When these proved insufficient, further loans were extended primarily by the US through the European Recovery Program between 1948 and 1950. The main thrust of that effort became known as the Marshall Plan, named after the U.S. Secretary of State General G.C. Marshall. To administer the aid, the Organization for European Economic Cooperation (OEEC) was formed.* Other sources of funding to prevent a worldwide liquidity crisis were the IRBD, the IMF, and an increasing flow of private investment primarily by U.S. and Canadian multinational corporations.

Reviving World Trade

It is said that the United States is committed unequivocally to free trade and open markets throughout the world. However, U.S. governments have restricted imports upon demand of special interest groups at home and also abroad, as for example in Imperial China before and around the turn of the century. Ever since, the U.S. proclaimed open market doctrine has had limited application. It was advanced primarily to ensure access to overseas markets for U.S. commercial interests. Once that seemed assured, closing of a market to others does not appear to have troubled U.S. governments. Indeed it is doubtful whether any power on earth is unreservedly dedicated to free and open trade. Thus, while some of the postwar planners undoubtedly sought to assure free trade absolutely, the reality called for construction of a framework for trade conflict resolution.

Awareness of this need is reflected, implicitly, in the United Nations Charter and explicitly in the economic structure which emerged from the wreckage of World War Two. That structure, emphatically capitalistic in conception as well as in practice, initially rested on three pillars: the economy of the United States, the General Agreement on Tariffs and Trade (GATT, 1947), and the trade supporting and regulating functions of the IMF and the World Bank (IBRD). By 1957, the European Common Market provided an additional support.†

---

* In 1960 this was replaced by the Organization for Economic Cooperation and Development (OECD), see Figs. 11-2 and 12-5. OECD expanded the scope of Western cooperation to include virtually all "free world" market economies.

† A portent of conflicts to come was the stillbirth of a proposed International Trade Organization (ITO) which was to have joined the other specialized agencies of the UN system, replacing GATT which was to have been a purely temporary measure. See Banks *et al., Economic Handbook of the World, 1981,* pp. 544-547. The less formal, hence less effective open-ended GATT remained the sole regulatory instrument governing world trade, mainly because special interests in the United States found the more binding ITO concept unacceptable.

GATT's principal purpose is to reconcile conflicting trade objectives and regulate and promote world trade through tariff reductions negotiated at periodic conferences or "rounds," usually extending over a period of months or even years. Like all other global economic undertakings of the postwar world, if it is to be reasonably effective GATT must remain in accord with the capitalist system and on that basis accommodate also the special needs of the less developed countries. The Agreement's prime targets are unfair trade practices and individual country trade policies likely to inhibit reasonably free and fair trade relations throughout the world.*

The Post-Recovery Economic Power Structure

Explicitly recognized or not, a global political economy had come into existence once the recovery period had run its course. Of course periodic setbacks were unavoidable. New conflicts and new problems demanded attention continuously. But a consensus appears to have been reached to the effect that global economic interdependence was now a fact of life no country could afford to ignore. It certainly was true of the Western powers, their associates, and their client states throughout the world. The conviction appears to have been shared also— though none would admit it officially—by members of the Soviet and Non-Aligned blocs.

While the capacity of noncapitalist, non-Western states to challenge Western leadership militarily and diplomatically increased steadily, economically the gap separating the Big Ten and the other industrial democracies from the rest of the world was widening. But still at the helm was the United States, its economy still acting as the world's principal engine. With its $3 trillion plus economy, accounting for more than 30 percent of the world's total output and consumption of goods and services, with more than $500 billion in annual imports and exports, its trading influence remained unsurpassed.† A 5 percent drop in U.S. imports could still affect 50 percent of a single developing country's exports, a potentially catastrophic effect. It still was true, as the saying went, that if the U.S. sneezed, the rest of the world caught a cold.

If an economic challenge of that position was likely, it would come from the bloc of states united, to an extent, in the European Economic Community. Consolidated, its 10 members (as of 1985), with roughly 270 million discriminating and demanding consumers and one of the world's largest industrial complexes, constituted one of the most lucrative and powerful markets on the

---

* "The General Agreement establishes international norms of responsible trade policy against which the national trade policies of its member states can be evaluated." Walters (1983), p. 13. By 1983, seven major tariff-reduction conferences had been held under GATT auspices, the most productive ones being the Kennedy Round (1964-1967), so named because the round had been initiated under President John F. Kennedy, and the Tokyo Round (1976-1979). By 1983, eighty-eight states had acceded to the Agreement, including several members of the Soviet bloc. Thirty additional countries applied the GATT rules without formal accession.

† 1983 data.

globe. Together they also imported and exported more goods than the United States and Japan combined. The United States, enjoying a comparatively higher standard of living, retained its lead with its approximately 230 million population and a still vibrant industrial base. But a shift of power was in the wind. Over the horizon was the challenge from Japan and the New Industrial Countries (NICs).*

Economically the bloc of nations led by the Soviet Union had for the time being only sporadic, mostly negative, manipulative influence on world economic conditions. This was true even more of the well over 100 less developed nations, with the exception of course of the high income oil exporters such as Saudi Arabia and Kuwait. For strategic reasons the Soviet bloc chose not to enter the mainstream of global trade and finance, while the low income LDCs were ever more deeply involved and in a steadily worsening, disadvantageous position. Combining their voices in several international organizations, they could press their demands for readjustment or even redistribution of the world's wealth. But given their individual and collective weaknesses, they could, for the time being, do little more than press demands, and their options were diminishing steadily.

The Collapse of the First Postwar Managerial Structure

Many explanations can be offered why the structure hammered out at Bretton Woods collapsed eventually, but, whatever the reasons, the history of that experiment in global economic management foreshadows the shape of problems to come. Benjamin Cohen traces the event to a bargain between the United States and its principal allies and trading partners. At the birth of Bretton Woods, writes Cohen, "America's allies aquiesced in a hegemony system that accorded the US special privileges to act abroad unilaterally to promote US interests. The United States, in turn, condoned its allies' use of the system to promote their own economic prosperity, even if this happened to come largely at the expense of the United States."[2] According to that view, the collapse became inevitable when the bargain either was not or could not be kept. In other words, the monetary order prevailed only so long as U.S. leadership was regarded as essential by the trading powers of the world, and provided that both the leader and the led were prepared to follow a live and let live policy— a difficult proposition for economically competing systems, to say the least.

Another interpretation traces the system's collapse to the unworkability of the gold exchange standard, according to that view an essentially fictitious arrangement based on an illusion. The argument was that, realistically, U.S. gold stocks could not keep pace with the volume of dollars being accumulated abroad, the "dollar overhang" or Eurodollar pool, so named because most of these dollars reposed in Western European banks. Instead of being supported

---

* In addition to the NICs listed in Fig. 11-2, Argentina, Brazil, Mexico and Yugoslavia are challenging the older industrial powers.

by convertability of overseas or "expatriate" dollars into U.S.-held gold, a resource always to be available in sufficient quantity, the system actually rested on the willingness of U.S. taxpayers and their political representatives to accept constantly increasing balance of payments deficits.* Public acceptance of such deficits, with their adverse effects on the home economy, especially employment, was certainly not an unlimited commodity. As the "overhang" grew to gigantic proportions (in 1979 it amounted to over $600 billion) the world's leading bankers, treasury officials, investors, and speculators realized that U.S. liabilities exceeded by a wide margin gold stocks actually available to meet the obligation to convert.[3] (See Fig. 11-1 and Table 11-1.)

The "overhang" was initially not allowed to cascade down upon the U.S. economy, for several reasons. (1) A run on the dollar would force the U.S. to adjust the gold-exchange standard and increase the price of gold. As more dollars would be needed per ounce of gold, the exchange value of foreign dollar holdings would be reduced. (2) If the United States attempted to live up to its obligations as long as gold stocks available for that purpose held out, dumping "expatriate" dollars back into the U.S. economy would a) cause a world-wide liquidity crisis, b) bring down the value of the dollar, and c) induce the U.S. government to review its foreign commitments, including military ones, across the board.†

Two sets of events, interrelated to an extent, caused a shift in the relationship between the United States and its allies: the "miraculous" recovery of West Germany and Japan, and the Korean and Vietnam wars, one mainly the other exclusively U.S. undertakings. Recovery of the two allies lessened their dependence on imports from the United States, reducing their needs for U.S. dollars. At the same time, as their own export capacity rose sharply their currencies rose in value against the dollar. Inevitably increased exports brought more, now unneeded, dollars into their coffers from a world already saturated with that

---

* U.S. balance-of-payments deficits resulted from an excess of dollar outflows, a consequence in part of foreign aid and assistance programs and of military operations, mainly the Korean and Vietnam wars. From 1950 to 1957, the annual U.S. balance of payments deficits average $1.3 billion. Over the same period the official reserves of industrial Europe (excluding the United Kingdom) rose from $5.1 billion to $12.6 billion, while the U.S. gold stock remained virtually unchanged at about $22 billion. Between 1958 and 1961 the U.S. balance-of-payments deficit widened, running at more than double the average annual rate of the preceding eight years, U.S. gold stocks now being steadily reduced. United Nations, UNCTAD (1972), p. 8. In addition to being reduced as a result of some conversions and other official uses, not all gold held in U.S. vaults was available for current transactions in any case. A reserve had to be retained for national security purposes, a national nest egg for times of war or universal economic breakdown.

† According to a U.S. authority, "Liquidity represents access to funds on short notice to meet unexpected payments. Liquidity is made up of cash, assets that can be readily liquidated (liquidity thus depends intimately on the functioning of markets), and ready access to borrowing from either official or private sources. One can view the adequacy of liquidity either from the point of view of an individual country or from the point of view of the world as a whole. The latter perspective involves how well the system as a whole functions under strain. In 1931 it was the system of liquidity that collapsed, not merely access of individual countries to funds." Cooper (1980), p. 1.

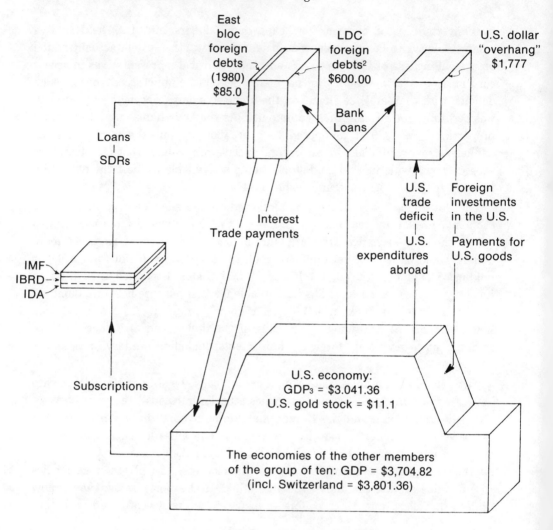

Fig. 11-1. LDC and Soviet Bloc Debts, World Trade and Finance[1]

SOURCES: *U.S. Statistical Abstract 1984*; Morgan Guaranty Trust Co., *World Finance Markets* (1984); IMF, *International Financial Statistics* (1984); *OECD Observer* (1984)

[1] 1984 data unless otherwise indicated; debts estimated; all amounts in billion US$.
[2] Oil-importing LDCs only   [3] GDP=Gross Domestic Product

currency. The two wars, one following on the heels of the other, overheated the U.S. economy, mainly through war-goods production and other war-related expenditures. The resulting inflation was promptly transferred abroad via the Bretton Woods system, which prevented downward adjustment of the dollar now necessitated by the weakening economic position of the United States.*

---

* Under the Bretton Woods Agreement, participants were obligated to defend the pegged rates of their own currencies by buying, with their own currencies, excess amounts of foreign currencies flowing into their economies. Consequently, buying U.S. dollars at

Table 11-1. U.S. Gold Reserves and External (U.S. Dollar)
Claims Against the U.S. (billion US$)

	1965	1972	1977	Aug. 1984
External Claims	12.25	17.42	92.56	442.17
Gold Reserves	14.07	10.49	11.72	11.10

SOURCES: IMF, *International Financial Statistics*; Morgan Guaranty Trust Company, *World Financial Markets*, p. 11; *U.S. Statistical Abstract*. By March 1985 the total external debt of the U.S. was reported to have reached $900 billion.

Pressure now increased on governments in Paris, Bonn, Tokyo, and elsewhere to rid themselves of the dollar burden. France initiated the reverse process. Looking for ways to discipline the United States not only economically but also politically, French President Charles de Gaulle in 1965 ordered conversion of its outstanding dollar balances into gold.* The U.S., aware of the problem, warned that should a massive return of dollars demanding conversion into gold actually take place, the "gold window" might have to be closed. That step had to be taken eventually, but for another reason. On August 15, 1971, in response to domestic political pressures, Nixon ordered the "window" closed, thereby terminating the fiction of dollar convertibility and causing the Bretton Woods system to collapse. The action released the dollar from its shackles, permitting it to find its own true value, which, indications were, would be lower than that of the leading competitive currencies. Coupled with other measures, this step promised to benefit the U.S. economy by reviving U.S. exports, reducing the balance-of-payments deficit, and reducing unemployment. However, from the broader perspective of world trade an era had come to an end, with no signs that a workable alternative was available.

Without the security and stability provided by the dollar-gold anchor, however tenuous and circumscribed its functions may have been, the world monetary system, the leading currencies, and with that the trading system as a whole were cast adrift. For the moment, the motto was *sauve qui peut* (everyone for himself). Soon the major trading powers found themselves in conflict with one another.

the pegged rate, participants pumped more of their own currency into their respective economies than should have been the case given the dollar's real value. The result, as many of Washington's partners saw it, was inflation "made in the United States."
  * Actually, as noted earlier de Gaulle had contemplated a more massive run on U.S. gold stocks but was dissuaded by his advisors who feared the consequences for the Western alliance system; see Cohen (1977), p. 103. In 1968, the Big (financial) Ten—the U.S., Belgium, Canada, France, West Germany, Italy, Japan, the Netherlands, Sweden and the United Kingdom—created the Special Drawing Rights (SDRs), a world fiduciary reserve asset—paper money it was called—to reduce reliance on U.S. financial support by the world monetary system. The SDRs were rights funded by contributions from members of the IMF and allocated on the basis of need, mainly payments imbalances and liquidity shortfalls.

Robert Gilpin reminds us that "the modern world economy has evolved through the emergence of great national economies that have successively become dominant. . . . Every economic system rests on a particular political order; its nature cannot be understood aside from politics."[4] This view conforms with the prevailing Soviet position except that their experts, contemplating events since 1945, are inclined to insist that what the West prefers to call "order" actually amounts to manipulation of the world economy in the interest primarily of one "monopoly-capitalist" state, namely the United States. From that perspective, Bretton Woods was but a device to assure the U.S. advantages over its capitalist competitors.*

The Leadership Question

It would seem elementary, in a contentious yet interdependent world where consensus on vital matters is possible only on a piecemeal basis and then only on generalities, that leadership by one state, willing and able to provide it, is an absolute necessity. Today the common interest of an overwhelming majority of states can be frustrated, almost at will, by individual governments, some of whom are compelled to comply with the erratic wishes signaled periodically by unpredictable electorates, some free to do as they please. Under the circumstances, only the power of persuasion of a superior economy backed by matching military capability can prevent the system, such as it is, from being pulled down by its component parts.†

Next to the very questionable proposition of leadership by a consortium of powers, the Group of Ten perhaps, no alternative is in sight to the United States continuing in that role. But, as in the past, this solution will give rise to controversy. Can effective world leadership be provided by a power whose motivations are questioned, which is viewed simultaneously by some governments as life support, gratefully remembered for its generous postwar aid and

---

* Invited to join the system, the Soviet Union refused, suspecting proposed membership to be a trap set by the United States. Undoubtedly, when Poland after having borrowed extensively from Western banks in the 1970s experienced severe internal disturbances— the Solidarity Crisis—Soviet leaders reproached their Polish counterparts with a "we-told-you-so." On the other hand, the dollar "overhang" probably had its origin in Soviet preference to keep dollars earned from foreign trade transactions throughout the world— by sale of gold for instance—out of the hands of U.S. authorities who, it was feared, might seize them at times of political or military crisis. Depositing their dollars in interest-paying Western European banks seemed to be more secure; it also facilitated camouflage of Soviet-initiated international market operations. For a Soviet assessment of the overhang's power-political implications, see Stadnichenko (1975), p. 101.

† Although they may not publicly admit it, even the more radically inclined leaders of economically dependent less developed countries, perhaps even leaders in Warsaw, Prague, or Budapest, realistically may not be able to conceive of an alternative to continued "free-world" leadership by the United States. Although the economic power of the EEC as a whole approaches that of the U.S., the former still is far from matching the consolidated power generated by an economy managed, and to a degree controlled, by one single government serving one nation. On the rise and decline of U.S. hegemony and of the "international regime" it helped to create, see Keohane (1984).

```
                        ┌─────────────────────┐
                        │    US Economy &     │
                        │ Major Allied Economies │
                        └─────────────────────┘
```

Group of Ten
  Belgium
  Canada
  France
  Germany, Fed. Rep. of,
  Italy
  Japan
  Netherlands
  Sweden
  United Kingdom
  United States
  Associate Member:
    Switzerland

```
┌──────────────────────┐
│ UN System:[1]        │
│ UN-IMF-IBRD-GATT     │
│ UNCTAD, UNCLOS etc.  │
└──────────────────────┘
```

OECD[2]
  Group of Ten plus
  Australia
  Austria
  Denmark
  Finland
  Greece
  Iceland
  Ireland
  Luxembourg
  New Zealand
  Norway
  Portugal
  Spain
  Switzerland
  Turkey

EEC[3]
  Belgium
  Denmark
  France
  Germany, Fed. Rep.
  Greece
  Ireland
  Italy
  Luxembourg
  Netherlands
  United Kingdom
  Candidates for
  Membership:
    Spain
    Portugal

East Asian NICs[4]
  Hong Kong
  Korea, Rep. of,
  Singapore
  China, Rep. of,
  (Taiwan)

OPEC[5]
  Pro-Western or
  Non-Aligned:
  Saudi Arabia
  other OAPECs[5]
  Venezuela
  Indonesia
  Nigeria, etc.

Fig. 11-2. The Capitalist World's Economic Management Structure, 1985.

[1] U.N.-sponsored or associated
[2] Organization for Economic Cooperation and Development; Yugoslavia is a Special Status member.
[3] European Economic Community. Spain and Portugal are scheduled to join on January 1, 1986.
[4] New Industrial Countries; Hong Kong, though still a British colony, warrants separate listing as a NIC.
[5] Organization of Petroleum Exporting Countries; Organization of Arab Petroleum Exporting Countries (see Chpt. 16)

assistance, and by others as the imperialist arch- or class-enemy? As a close ally of all of the former colonial powers, itself a colonial power of sorts in the Western Hemisphere, can the United States distance itself sufficiently from culpability for some of imperialism's worst excesses? Can it convincingly convey a sense of solidarity with the growing number of low income economies struggling for survival while its people enjoy one of the highest standards of living in the world, thanks in part to consumption of a third of the world's exportable resources?

The answer to the question of world leadership comes down to this: The less developed countries cannot hope to escape poverty unless the economy of the United States is at their disposal as a market and as a source of financial support. The allies of the United States, while the military threat from the Soviet Union persists, cannot assume the full costs of their defense. Therefore, "decoupling" from the United States or repudiation of its leadership has for them distinctly suicidal implications.

To be effective, world leadership must offer more than military strength and diplomatic persuasion. With the gold standard abandoned and not likely to be revived, any conceivable alternative still requires a strong and relatively stable currency of global respectability and value. Even a combination of currencies, assuming that agreement on such an alternative can be reached, still requires the binding force of a single dominant currency enjoying worldwide confidence.*

What must be the characteristics of such a currency and of the economy upon which it is based? What must be the responsibilities of the leader with respect to its management? (1) The key currency must be freely convertible, that is, any state finding itself with an excess balance in that currency must be able to convert it without loss into gold or some other monetary unit of universally recognized worth. (2) The leading nation's political, financial, and business policies and practices, at home and abroad, must be outer-directed. The leading nation cannot obstruct the vital interests of allies, nor can it ignore the vital interests of its principal opponents. Among other measures, this calls for support of a price structure and internal banking and lending policies within the leading country which do not contravene external commitments. Keeping government spending and interest rates down must be high on such an agenda. (3) The lead currency must be backed by an economy resilient and powerful enough to meet all domestic and foreign commitments in peace as in war. (4) Regardless of contrary domestic pressures, the leading economy must be open to exports, on reasonable terms, from trading partners experiencing payments difficulties and from other countries compelled to break into the established market as a matter of survival. (5) Mindful of capitalism's scourge, wildly swinging cyclical fluctuations, the leader must be prepared to intervene "to flatten out" the swings and cushion the impact on the system's weakest members. (6) At times of severe economic crisis, it must be prepared to act as lender of last resort, backing with its financial power the banking and lending structures of all of its trading partners. It must, in other words, assume the role played for over a hundred years by Great Britain acting through the Bank of England.†️ (7) Essential for leadership to remain effective and in control over time is the availability of a very substantial, very elastic cushion, a margin to draw upon in the event of a crisis not susceptible to resolution by ordinary financial means. Cohen, quoting Hirsch, points out that until World War Two Great Britain managed its imperial system at the expense of its weakest members, the peripheral mostly underdeveloped members of the Empire and Commonwealth, whose treasuries reposed in London and could therefore be tapped on command to buttress financial transactions and support financial rescue operations of

* For some time the European Common Market has rested its monetary system on a "basket" containing the average exchange rates of all market currencies; the value created by that means is called the European Currency Unit or ECU.

† It must be noted that this institution was not subject to close parliamentary scrutiny and oversight, hence it was relatively insulated from conflicting pressures today's political democracies tend to impose on their monetary policy makers and financiers, to the detriment of both national and global economic requirements.

immediate interest to the imperial center.[5] Therein lies an important lesson for the contemporary leader. Now that the periphery has acquired numerical as well as a degree of marginally significant political power, in the aggregate at least, successful management of the world economy will have to take into account not only the interests of economies at the center but also of those along the periphery.

Misalignment of Economic and Military Power and Responsibility

It has been argued that the existence of the gold standard was the principal reason why the world economy functioned as well as it did during the nineteenth and early twentieth centuries, until it broke down under pressure of preparation for World War One. That calamity ushered in an era of competing currency blocs, principally those based on the British pound, the French franc, and the U.S. dollar. One consequence of this was the replacement of the governor of the Bank of England by a consortium of directors of the now competing central banks of Great Britain, France, and the United States, who soon were joined by the central bank directors of Germany, Japan, Sweden, Switzerland, Italy, and Brazil, among others. The result was financial and economic chaos which if it did not by itself spark the Second World War certainly contributed to its genesis.

Imperfect though it was, ridden with social injustice and other inequities and anomalies, a global political economy existed and survived between 1815 and 1914, mainly because supreme economic and military power were concentrated at one center, aligned and in harmony. British financial controls spanned the globe and so did the reach of the British navy as a controlling force. Economic interests in maintaining what had become known as *Pax Britannica* coincided with military capacity to enforce it. The upheaval in the wake of World War One terminated that order, creating a vacuum into which stepped the fascist dictatorships and imperial Japan. The ascendancy of the United States to sole world power status restored once again the alignment of global interest, power, and responsibility—or so it seemed.

Within two decades, the recovery of Western Europe and Japan converted Western economic leadership into a tripolar arrangement, a partnership at best. Simultaneously, its growing military power enabled Moscow to press forward with its claims, and those of its allies, on world resources, without however a corresponding commitment to safeguard or maintain the existing global economic order. If Moscow's aim was to hasten the collapse of the capitalist order or at least cause it to break up in disarray, nothing could have furthered that objective more than the proliferation of newly independent yet economically and militarily impotent, politically and socially unstable, states, all demanding a voice in the management of the world economy. This problem was compounded by the spreading intrusion of the military in the domestic and foreign policies of these critically underendowed countries. As scores of civilian governments were overthrown in military coups, in far too many instances, the relative inexperience of the ousted rulers gave way to total ignorance. Professional soldiers generally are strangers to the intricate world of public and private finance, international trade, and economic development. In a world already destabilized, their presence in position of power can be an invitation to disaster.

To some observers, the giant multinational corporations (MNCs) now extending their tentacles across the globe pose a similar threat to world stability. Alleged to pursue their own foreign policies, frequently in contravention of the foreign policies of their respective home governments upon whose resources they draw to a considerable extent, they have been likened to "cannons loose on the deck" or to "rogue elephants," defying national as well as international norms of conduct, powers onto themselves. It is said that it is they who have succeeded in reversing a century-old trend by holding national "sovereignty at bay."[6] Frustrating the will of all established governments, their own as well as those who admit them into their midst, they are accused of contravening international agreements, treaties, and unwritten understandings. Through their subsidiaries on foreign soil, beyond supervision and control by their home government, they manage enormous funds, buy and sell foreign exchange on international markets in volume well in excess of financial resources at the disposal of many sovereign states, and even speculate against their own base currency, all in pursuit of corporate objectives.[7]

A contrary view sees in the MNCs the logical product of global economic interdependence, the ideal instrument to spread prosperity, reduce poverty, and assure stability in an ever more tightly integrated world.[8]

Of Sovereignty and Economic Interdependence

At first glance, there seems to be a clear incompatibility between national sovereignty and global economic interdependence. Yet, if they are to be successful the managers of the world economy cannot afford to ignore either. To the rulers of the Soviet Union, for example, as to most other rulers in the Soviet bloc and those in charge of the People's Republic of China, the protective walls of national sovereignty constitute a primary defense against what they perceive as capitalist designs on socialism. Also, noted earlier, socialist rulers fear becoming entangled in the "boom and bust" contraction and expansion cycles characteristic of capitalist economies.* To incompetent, corrupt, and brutal civilian or military dictatorships, on the other hand, national sovereignty is the first line of defense against accountability. Unfortunately for the world, this carries over into economics. It is difficult for such regimes to insist that wanton murder or brutal suppression of one's own people is an internal matter, a right covered by the sovereignty principle under international law, and at the same time permit inspection of chaotic budgets or confused accounting

---

* They are aware, as Lawrence B. Krause notes, that interdependence works in two opposing directions: "It spreads prosperity when the world economy is expanding and it spreads recession when [it] is contracting." (1983), p. 4.

procedures by a delegation from the International Monetary Fund or the World Bank. Yet, the trend away from undivided, absolute exercise of sovereignty toward interdependence continues. There will be setbacks and reversals, but all signs indicate that in broad historical terms the process is irreversible.[9]

Suggested Questions and Discussion Topics

Why was it necessary, following World War Two, to create a monetary order? What was the organizational centerpiece of that order? What other major economic steps were taken by the Western Allies to make the postwar world secure for their purposes?

Why did the first postwar monetary management structure collapse? In particular, what was the role of the United States before, during, and after the collapse?

Why may one speak of "misalignment of economic and military power and responsibility" as one of the causes of the contemporary global economic management crisis?

Chapter 12
The Advanced Capitalist Sector:
A House Divided Against Itself

The State of "Western" Unity

Compass directions do not adequately or accurately identify the world's major economic or military groupings. Neither do terms like "freedom-loving," "free world," or "democratic." Such attributes point to certain commonalities but in their rather expansive sweep they also tend to obscure important differences. The members of the so-called Western coalition certainly share certain values. All rely to a greater or lesser extent on private capital accumulation as a source of economic energy. For that reason all oppose, though to varying degrees, radical forms of socialism, foremost the seemingly aggressive Soviet variety. The majority of capitalist states are basically committed to political democracy, the rule of law, and free, secret, and periodic elections.* They have similar economies, including modes of production and distribution of wealth and of income, and respect private property within certain constitutional bounds; they also generally share a concern in principle for basic human rights. They permit private capital to move freely within and across their national boundaries and from one internal economic sector to another. Most encourage and recognize free trade unions and collective bargaining as well as free competition for resources and markets at home and abroad. If the electorate is so inclined, they permit shifts to socialist practices including nationalization of some basic means of production, always—unlike totalitarian regimes—retaining the option of changing direction once again.

In recent years, West European and some of the Far Eastern systems have shown an accelerating trend toward wholly or partially state-owned enterprise, the result of large-scale nationalization programs either to rescue failing key

* Contrary to widespread belief, endorsement of capitalism *as such* does not necessarily mean commitment to individual freedom, social justice, or even political democracy. Since World War One, the capitalist "world" or system has included, tolerated, propped up, or actively encouraged fascist and other authoritarian regimes, military dictatorships, and feudal monarchies. See Lindblom (1977), Chapter V; Bretton (1980), pp. 233–234; and Pisar (1979), pp. 241–247. Communist leaders are similarly flexible if that serves their purpose.

enterprises or just extend government control to improve the economy's foreign competitive position. While private enterprise today still constitutes the core of economies currently classified as free enterprise and market-oriented, the trend suggests the presence within the Western system of an ever more assertive blend of socialism and a move away from unqualified reliance on domestic and world markets. For one, unlike genuinely private firms, wholly or partially state-owned enterprises can draw on the public purse to overcome market-related shortfalls. In the context of international politics, this trend suggests two major consequences. It may further weaken free enterprise capitalism by sharpening the conflict and competition within the Western group, pitting against each other the still relatively free enterprise and market-oriented economies and those steeled by government ownership and subsidies against the vagaries of the open market. In the main this could widen the split between the United States and its Western allies. Or as U.S. government intervention broadens to cope with the threat, capitalism may generally be strengthened in its struggle against the more emphatically nonmarket oriented economies operating under total government control.[1]

The core Western group includes states as far apart geographically as the United States, Western Europe, and Japan. It includes the members of the North Atlantic-Western European military alliance, which in turn also includes Turkey and Greece, both situated in the Eastern Mediterranean region, and demilitarized Japan, as well as permanently neutral Sweden and Switzerland. The periphery, including several former colonies, extends from the southern and central sections of the Western Hemisphere to southwestern and south-eastern Europe, the Middle East, Africa, through Southeast Asia to the Southern Pacific and the Philippines. Increasingly active and influential are such New Industrial Countries (NICs) as Taiwan, Hong Kong (still a British colony), South Korea, and Singapore. In the Middle East, oil-rich Arab states, locked in seemingly permanent struggle with Israel, share with their antagonist reliance on U.S. economic and military power.

While some states along the periphery insist that they are "nonaligned" vis-à-vis the two major power blocs, their economies remain linked to the capitalist system as suppliers, processors of manufactured goods, or customers. Although their governments are reluctant to acknowledge this publicly, many of these "nonaligned" states attribute their continuing independence to the core group's military strength.

The core group is held together partly by fear of Soviet power, partly by a commitment to prevent a rebirth of aggressive militarism in Germany and in Japan. One way to avert the latter threat is to tie the Western half of Germany and Japan firmly into a network of contractual military and economic obligations. So far, West Germany, reduced to second-rate military status, and Japan, prohibited by treaty and its constitution from acquiring a defense force of more than modest proportions, have willingly accepted membership in Western military and economic systems designed in part to obviate their remilitarization. There is however a degree of apprehension on all sides that the unity achieved so far can rather suddenly be disrupted. No one can entirely rule out a defection of either or both, the result of concessions offered to these powers in particular by the Soviet Union intent on breaking up the Western alliance. On their part, the two former axis partners—though another, greater Germany was then involved—are sensitive to the possibility, however remote, that the United States may once again turn isolationist.

Of potentially greatest consequence for the survival of the Western system is the future of Western European union. The notion that all of Western Europe should really be united originates with the Holy Roman Empire. More recently, the Pan-Europe concept proposed to extend the union to the entire sub-continent.[2] To an extent, in its contemporary form the unity between the Western European nations strengthens the Western system, to an extent it renders it more precarious. An effective union between major industrial and financial powers, at the doorstep so to speak of the Soviet bloc, poses a clear obstacle to westward Soviet expansion. On the other hand, driven by capitalist forces still in the thrall of national sovereignty and self-interest, the several members of the union seem to be unable to resist the temptation to profit from superpower rivalry. There also is the notion, gaining popularity throughout Europe, of creating a third force between the militarily and sociopolitically threatening Soviet bloc and a friendly, but economically overpowering United States. Indeed, in the minds of some of Western Europe's contemporary leaders is the hope, perhaps even the expectation, that if Western Europe could demonstrate to the Soviet Union a certain detachment from the United States, some or all of the states of Eastern and Southeastern Europe could be pried out of the Soviet Union's grip.

Militating against any neutrality or third force posture for Western Europe or Japan is the threat of blackmail by a Soviet Union freed of fear of United States involvement in the defense of either region. Such a turn of events, some predict, could result in the neutralization ("finlandization" is the term used) of Western Europe, Japan, and possibly all of Southeast Asia. Or it could invite military expansion of Soviet power to the English Channel, into the People's Republic of China, and beyond.*

Cracks were also becoming noticeable in the Western Hemisphere. The long standing harmony between the United States and Canada could not prevent mounting friction, caused partly by the weaker partner's fear that it was being drawn into global conflicts over issues unrelated to its own best national interests. Binding Canada, the United States, and much of South and Central America was still a mutual commitment to maintain continental or hemispheric integrity vis-à-vis outside influences or intervention. But this too was crumbling in the wake of social revolutionary unrest and civil war throughout Central America.

---

* "Finlandization" would replicate the condition imposed upon that Scandinavian country by the Soviet Union, calling for abstention on Finland's part from any military alliance with the West and generally a neutral posture with respect to the East-West conflict. Finland is however allowed to maintain economic ties with both East and West; Robert G. Kaiser, (1976), pp. 524-525, offers a less alarmist assessment of that threat.

Also, with U.S. military power matched by Soviet power and Western Europe and Japan challenging U.S. economic dominance, individual Latin American states like Argentina, Brazil, Venezuela, and Mexico feel encouraged to pursue commercial policies independent of the United States.

Capitalism's Enduring Utility and Strength

Marxists are inclined to argue that capitalism has failed or at best has now entered the twilight of its existence.[3] Even capitalism's most optimistic defenders see difficulties ahead. Still, whatever the prognosis capitalism will remain a potent force in world affairs for decades to come. Abstractly, intellectually, on primarily humanitarian grounds appealing, the socialist alternative—especially the eviscerated bureaucratized totalitarian Soviet model—has not demonstrated a capacity to cope with national let alone worldwide economic problems. But capitalism remains a formidable force in world affairs for yet other reasons. Developed over many centuries, its products, techniques, attitudes, mores, and tastes having penetrated and still permeating all parts of the globe, it now has established roots deep and resilient enough to survive even social revolution. Neither Stalinism nor Maoism, including the Cultural Revolution, succeeded in extirpating all vestiges of capitalist thought or practice in the Soviet Union or the PRC. Today, as bearers of essential finance capital and goods, and provided they leave their arms at home, representatives of capitalist enterprise and their diplomatic representatives as well encounter hospitable political climate even in the most virulently radical societies. Furthermore, capitalist enterprise has acquired extensive experience, even familiarity, with varied economic systems and modes of production throughout the world, enabling it to outbid and outperform most competition from the Socialist bloc. It is aided in that respect by a worldwide network of interlocking interests, linking banking, industrial, transportation (especially shipping), marketing, and distribution systems of all capitalist states. Described as "imperialist" or "neocolonialist" by its detractors, the network constitutes a force to be reckoned with for some time to come. While causing some disorder, the multinational corporations reinforce the network.

Capitalism's Principal Weaknesses

One need not be a Marxist to recognize that many characteristics and features of capitalism detract from its capacity to manage the world economy successfully. Our previous discussion of the foundations of international trade and finance touched upon some of the impediments. Perhaps foremost is the fact that inherent in the free enterprise variant of capitalism are two diametrically opposing values. At one and the same time, free enterprise facilitates the unfolding of the individual's maximal potentialities and ruthless entrepreneurial egotism of a potentially brutal kind. Capitalism can be viewed as a zero-sum game; one party's gain must be another party's loss.[4] The profit motive, one of capitalism's mainstays if not its driving force, manifestly enhances certain endemic human frailties resulting in usury, fraud, corruption, and criminality.

A system prizing accumulation of capital in the hands of private winners of economic contests inevitably creates and intensifies social class distinctions, causing pockets of great wealth, security, and privilege to coexist with large-scale unemployment, grinding poverty, squalor, destitution, and despair. Food surpluses pile up amidst hunger and starvation. Emphasis on tight and highly efficient organization within capitalist enterprises contrasts outside with social permissiveness, moral dissolution, and disintegration of the social environment, including the effects of urban sprawl, to the detriment of capitalism's avowed objectives in safeguarding the foundation stones of society: church, marriage, and the family.*

For these reasons, whatever its merits the gospel of free enterprise capitalism encounters vigorous opposition in certain cultures and societies, providing grist for the propaganda mills of powers with a vested interest in undercutting Western, especially U.S., managerial leadership of the world economy.[5] It is difficult to defend capitalism against the charge that it is permanently afflicted with the "boom and bust" syndrome.

* Urbanization-out-of-control adds to capitalism's managerial problems by creating powerful political pressures which at one and the same time depend on its success, that is, its continuous economic growth, and suffer from its success by becoming ever less manageable as political entities. The table below illustrates another source of pressure and instability.

Unemployment
Group of Ten plus Switzerland

Countries	1974	1976	1978	1979	1980	1981	1982	1982 Dec.	1983 March
			annual averages, in percentages of labor force						
United States	5.6	7.7	6.1	5.9	7.2	7.6	9.7	10.8	10.3
Canada	5.3	7.1	8.4	7.5	7.5	7.6	10.8	12.8	12.6
Japan	1.4	2.0	2.2	2.1	2.9	2.2	2.4	2.4	2.6
Germany....	2.7	4.6	4.4	3.8	3.9	5.6	7.7	8.5	9.3
France......	2.3	4.3	5.3	6.0	6.4	7.8	8.8	8.9	8.8
United Kingdom....	2.6	5.2	5.5	5.1	6.5	10.2	12.0	12.7	13.0
Italy........	5.4	6.7	7.2	7.7	7.6	8.4	9.1	9.8[a,b]	—
Netherlands	3.3	5.5	5.1	5.1	5.9	9.0	12.3	14.1	16.5[c]
Sweden	2.0	1.6	2.2	2.1	2.0	2.5	3.1	3.4	3.6
Belgium	2.6	5.7	7.0	7.2	7.9	9.4	11.0	11.6[b]	12.2[b]
Switzerland	0.0	0.7	0.3	0.3	0.2	0.2	0.4	0.7	0.8

SOURCE: Bank for International Settlements, *Fifty-Third Annual Report,* Basle (June 13, 1983), p. 27.
[a] First week in January 1983
[b] Not seasonally adjusted
[c] New series from January 1983

Managing World Trade

Some writers speak of world trade dilemmas, having in mind the vexatious problems confronting theorists as well as world leaders in their efforts to reconcile apparently irreconcilable conflicts between capitalism and socialism and between the advanced and less developed countries. But a characteristic of a dilemma is that one loses inevitably if one choses either of two options; there is no third option. Yet, no such situation exists in the real world, politically or economically.[6] All issues are open-ended, offering an inexhaustible array of alternative solutions. This is true especially of world trade. World trade, therefore, is not a question of dilemmas but of astute, prudent, imaginative conflict management, a question not of articulating contradictions but of reconciling conflicting interests. Given their aggregate power, most challenging are the conflicts between the leading industrial market economies, who at the time of writing are still allied. (See Fig. 12-1.)

Trading Among Allies

*The United States versus Western Europe:** The normal friction inherent in relations among capitalist countries has been exacerbated with the formation of the European Economic Community (EEC). To be sure, as signatories to the General Agreement on Tariff and Trade (GATT) the allies are nominally and to an extent legally obligated to avoid instituting measures designed to impede free and fair trade. Yet, as is the case with all such agreements, enough escape clauses are provided to defeat their purpose if a state or group of states are so determined.

A major source of conflict among the allies has been the production and sale of food. On several occasions food became the issue over which the U.S. and EEC nearly fought a war, albeit one with subsidies and tariffs not with bullets.[7]

Food and farmers became an issue because on both sides of the Atlantic the political influence of farmers is out of proportion to their numbers, about 3 percent of the population in the United States and about 10 percent in Western Europe and Japan. Farmers are influential partly because food is a strategic commodity, partly because food accounts for 15 percent of the $2,000 billion

* The following table, showing opposite growth trends, reflects a major source of friction between the U.S. and its Western European economic partners and allies.

Comparative Economic Growth
(GNP at current prices and exchange rates in billion US$)

	1980	1981	1982	1983
U.S.	2,599	2,924	3,041	3,282
The Western European Members of OECD (19)	3,513	3,113	2,990	2,901

SOURCES: *OECD Observer; World Bank Reports.*

annual volume of world trade (as of 1981–82), and partly because multibillion
dollar agrobusinesses and related service industries have grown around agriculture in the U.S., Western Europe, and Japan. Western European and Japanese
farmers compel their respective governments to subsidize them through artifically
high food prices imposed upon consumers. In the United States, subsidies are
paid also but at taxpayers' expense. One consequence is that European farmers,
principally in the agriculturally least efficient member countries of the EEC,
tend to be more protection-oriented than their counterparts in the U.S., who
generally favor free trade and aggressive export policies.[8]

As a result of pressure from agricultural lobbies in several member states,
the EEC in 1967 instituted a Common Agricultural Policy (CAP), partly to
settle disputes within the Market, partly to gain foreign trade advantages.
Complained an American Deputy Secretary of State in 1983, after about a year
of falling U.S. agricultural exports:

> The EEC's common agricultural policy [CAP] has artifically boosted prices on some
> key commodities to double those in the United States, encouraging high production.
> The resulting surplus [the butter mountains and wine lakes] is then exported with
> the aid of massive subsidies. This practice has helped European farmers to expand
> their share of third-country markets at the expense of the American farmers.[9]

To which U.S. Secretary Shultz added, when justifying the U.S. decision to
retaliate by selling subsidized wheat flour to Egypt, traditionally a European
customer: "When all the world is mad, 'tis folly to be sane."*

Trade wars threaten the alliance over other commodities as well. The EEC's
policy to distribute Market resources in such a way as to strengthen (protect
is another term) the weakest economic sectors within the system led to payment
of subsidies to the steel industries of France, Italy, and Belgium. In addition,
the British government subsidized its own steel industry. The West Germans
did likewise but at a lesser rate. Together, to the chagrin of U.S. steel makers,
the five European countries, plus Romania from the socialist side, proceeded
to sell—U.S. steel manufacturers would say "dumped"—heavily subsidized steel
in the United States at prices as much as 41 percent below what U.S. government

---

* Dam (March 21, 1983), p. 3. In response, the Europeans reminded the United States
that U.S. farmers still led the world's food exporters and regularly maintained "a
handsome surplus in agricultural trade with the ECC." Paul Lewis, "Europe's Farm
Policies Clash With American Export Goals," *The New York Times* (February 22, 1983).
In any case, they pointed out, the U.S. had in the past never allowed GATT provisions
to stand in the way of accommodating its own lobbies. Moreover, in its Domestic
Industry Sales Corporation (DISC), the U.S. maintained its own taxpayer-subsidized
export support machinery. Finally, the Europeans pointed out that in accord with GATT
requirements to observe "traditional export interests," the EEC group had actually
carefully adjusted its export pricing practices so as not to compete unfairly with the
United States in its own backyard, Latin America and the Far East. They expected the
U.S. to reciprocate by respecting West Europe's traditional interests in Africa, the Middle
East, and Eastern Europe. Hence they protested vigorously when the U.S. proceeded to
undersell mainly France in Egypt, for instance. With Spain and Portugal joining the EEC
in 1986, the U.S. expects to have its exports to Western Europe further reduced.

Table 12-1. Share of World Trade of Selected Countries and Groupings
(1980 Data, Percent)

	Export	Import
World Total	100 %	100 %
United States	13.3	11.5
Belgium	3.0	3.0
Canada	2.8	3.7
France	6.0	5.0
Germany, Fed. Rep.	8.1	9.5
Italy	4.5	4.0
Japan	6.9	7.5
Netherlands	3.4	3.6
Saudi Arabia	1.8	6.5
Sweden	1.4	1.4
Switzerland	1.5	1.4
United Kingdom	5.2	5.2
Soviet Union	3.8	4.3
Non-Industrial Countries	33.6 (1981)	32.1 (1981)

SOURCES: U.S. *Statistical Abstract, 1984*, Table 1530, pp. 879–880. *Finance and Development*, Vol. 20, No. 1 (March 1983), p. 39.

authorities regarded as fair market value. Threatened with retaliation, the exporters reconsidered but the matter was not clearly or neatly resolved. The imbroglio over steel was another illustration of the problem facing the allies; the choice confronting the U.S. and West European governments was not "between protectionism and free trade, but rather between degrees and kinds of protectionism."[10]

Given the dynamics of trade among allies industrially as powerful as the United States, Western Europe, and Japan, there really is no limit to sources of conflict. Should the military ties of the alliance ever weaken, the increasing dependence of all members of the alliance on certain essential raw materials for defense as well as economic survival could trigger a conflict far more severe than "wars" fought over chicken, food exports, or steel.*

Within the EEC: The European Community's current difficulties were not difficult to predict at the time of its birth. If integration did not progress

---

* In 1983, a full-page ad was placed in U.S. newspapers by the United Steel Workers of America, warning stockholders of "American Steel Companies" in banner-headline: The British Are Coming, The British Are Coming . . . And America's Steel Independence Is Going." *The New York Times* (May 19, 1983), p. D 13. The cause for the alarm? U.S. Steel Corporation was about to import from Britain steel theretofore produced in one of its U.S. plants about to be closed.

Here the increasing number of nationalized outright state-owned or heavily state-subsidized corporations in Western Europe, Southeast Asia, and Japan warrant special attention. Expanding their role in such markets as aerospace, steel, ship-building and automobile production, chemicals and pharmaceuticals, and now in electronics and computers, British, French, West German, Portuguese, or Japanese companies, able to accumulate losses at taxpayers' expense, are outbidding even some of the larger American privately owned multinational corporations on their home grounds. See R.J. Monson and Kenneth D. Walters, *Nationalized Companies* (New York: McGraw-Hill, 1983). In 1985 the U.S. responded by offering prospective buyers of U.S. products such inducements as cut-rate credit disguised as foreign aid.

steadily, encompassing eventually all economic sectors, public finance, labor policies, and even social policies, the inevitable political pressures building up within member states would tend to roll back whatever had already been accomplished.[11] To be sure, accomplishments are many and they are impressive. Since 1957, when the Treaty of Rome was signed, the Community has progressed from a mere design to a concrete Common Market, including coordination of some economic and social policies, a customs union, a payments union, and a rudimentary monetary system. But deep and abiding fissures remain, giving rise to frequent confrontations.

Joining the American–European "chicken war" in the annals of trade confrontations, the Common Market has had its disputes over the price of a leg of lamb, imported from Great Britain to France, the price and quality of wine crossing the Franco-Italian border, or the price of butter being sold by any one of several dairy product-exporting states. Inevitably, trade disputes raise more fundamental questions regarding the value of the entire integrative enterprise. In 1983 the British Labor Party, as an election campaign issue, pledged to take Britain out of the Common Market.* France and West Germany had strong words for each other over trade-related money matters, and numerous lesser trade disputes broke out like rashes as the world recession deepened and unemployment rose in Europe to all-time heights.

It became clear that unless the Market proceeded from partial to comprehensive economic, social, even political integration, internal and external pressures would combine to bring the experiment to a potentially tragic end. In the absence of political integration, member states find themselves unable to institute the fundamental structural changes required. Instead, they rely on superficial procedural adjustments or "gimmicks" as the skeptical former French President de Gaulle termed some of the Community's impressive sounding but ineffective institutional innovations.

Even measures taken by the Community to avoid internecine trade wars give rise to conflicts. In the early 1980s under CAP more than two-thirds of the Common Market's annual revenue was devoted to subsidies and to storing and selling the aforementioned "butter mountains and wine lakes," benefiting mainly France, Italy, and Greece. Rather than permitting the price of excess commodities to drop within the Community, the Market stored surpluses, then proceeded to sell them on the world market, at a loss, making up the differences out of Common Market funds. With Spain and Portugal about to become members, prospects were that soon the Market's entire budget would be absorbed to maintain a butter and wine glut. The budget was derived mainly from a 1 percent share of members' sales taxes. Great Britain and West Germany, major food importers, objected to their contributions flowing into other members' dairy and wine sectors without commensurate benefits returning to them— support for their own ailing industries for example—making them the only net contributors to the economic fund. By 1984 this and other problems had brought

---

* Labor lost resoundingly and the issue was shelved temporarily.

the Market to a point where only drastic reforms and structural adjustments could save it.*

The United States and Canada. Aside from cultural and ethnic affinities, the strongest bond between the two countries is the imperative of co-existence on one continent in a world predominantly nondemocratic and noncaucasian. The two are also each other's principal trading partners, Canada being the United States' leading market by a wide margin and its leading supplier. In 1985, Canadian investment represented the third largest investment bloc in the U.S. and the economies of the two countries are becoming ever more intertwined and interdependent. Of necessity, the two countries must maintain joint military defenses. Still, as must be expected when an economic giant and an economically weaker partner are compelled to coexist, friction is unavoidable. Dominant ever since it replaced British capital and influence, especially in the English-speaking sections of Canada, increasingly controlling in certain sectors of the Canadian economy, the United States has become a target of nationalistic demands for greater independence from the colossus to the south. Pressure has mounted in recent years to reduce U.S. presence in commerce, industry, and finance, in particular ownership or management of key industries, and to free Canada's foreign economic policies by reducing dependence on U.S. finance and markets. In that connection Canada has attempted to develop a stance toward the Third World, especially the Caribbean and Central and South America, somewhat detached from U.S. policy. Talk of protectionist measures has been heard on both sides of the otherwise extraordinarily peaceful border; on occasion, injured interests on both sides have pressed for economic retaliation.[12] Fishing rights have been one source of friction, acid rain another.

The Western Allies and Japan: Simply stated, Japan irritates its allies by what appears to be excessive zeal in pushing exports over imports, not caring much what methods are to be used. But as with all trade issues this is not a simple matter. There are at least three positions, those of the Western partners, the view from Tokyo, and the objective truth.

At first glance, Japan appears to have no alternative but to press exports to the limit. Overpopulated, with insufficient acreage for food production, more dependent for its energy and industrial raw materials on outside sources of supply than any other industrial power, Japan constantly faces one of the highest import bills. (In 1982, her oil self-sufficiency rating was 15 percent as against 86 percent for the U.S.) It would seem that only a higher rate of exports

---

* Also pressing for changes in CAP, in addition to the U.S., were Australia and Argentina, whose traditional markets were being invaded. In 1982 Britain attempted to use its veto to block farm price increases. By 1984 London had succeeded in reversing the trend. With respect to the then projected accession of Spain and Portugal, France in particular appeared to drag its heels, causing the two Iberian candidates for membership to ask whether "the European idea is a matter of civilization, politics, and common history or of wine, vegetables, cheese, and potatoes." *The German Tribune,* No. 1071 (February 6, 1983), p. 6. Another specter facing the EEC was the massive influx of Turkish migrant labor. *Ibid.,* No. 1027 (March 1982).

can feed the population, keep industry going and prevent large-scale unemployment. But Japan has done more than meet its bills.

From a low point in 1945 Japan has reached a position where it ranks only below the United States and the Soviet Union in GNP; it is now estimated that by the year 2000, Japan will overtake the United States in per capita GNP by a wide margin. That would have been acceptable, had it not been for the fact that Japan's advances appear to the allies to have been accomplished in the past, and sustained now and in the future, at their expense. For example, for some years the interallied balance of trade has been lopsidedly in favor of Japan, a condition widely and persistently attributed by Japan's competitors to unfair Japanese practices at home and abroad.*

Be that as it may, as a competitor Japan appears to enjoy several advantages over the other leading industrial powers. The Japanese state and society certainly are more cohesive than is true of Western Europe and the United States.† Labor-management relations in Japan are comparatively more harmonious, restraining wages and salaries, reducing absenteeism, causing fewer strikes, increasing productivity, and permitting more rigorous quality control. Japan's consumers are less demanding, freeing for export goods and resources which otherwise would have to be directed toward home consumption. Personal savings are the highest among the leading industrial societies, making more capital

Table 12-2. Economic Strength of Three Powers

	Population mid-1981 In Millions	GNP at Market Prices 1980 In US $ Millions (1980 Dollars)	GDP 1981 In US $ Millions	GNP Per Capita 1981 US $
Japan	117.6	1,152,600	1,129,500	10,080
US	229.8	2,614,100	2,893,300	12,820
USSR	268.0	1,423,800	n.a.	3,700– 4,000

GNP = Gross National Product
GDP = Gross Domestic Product
SOURCES: World Bank Atlas 1980, 1983 World Bank Reports 1982, 1983

* Between 1976 and 1981, the U.S. incurred a cumulative merchandise trade deficit with Japan of some $56 billion. In 1980, the annual deficit was $9.9 billion, approaching $40 billion in 1985.

† For one explanation of Japan's presumed advantage, see Trezise (1983), p. 13. Hofheinz and Calder (1982), pp. 22 and 26, reject the notion, widely held in Western business circles, that Japan is really one giant state-corporation, "Japan Inc.," governed by MITI (Ministry of International Trade and Industry). Instead, they contend, it is the combination of statist, corporate, and spiritualist strength and solidity (they term it "synergy"—producing more together than separately) which lends Japan, indeed all of "Eastasia," a competitive advantage over the West. They see other qualities, such as "lean government," Table 3-1, p. 34 or "work not welfare," Table 3-2, p. 35; government *directs* or moves the economy not leaving direction to laissez-faire, as is the case in the West, p. 37. They note that the U.S. has 500,000 lawyers, Japan only 12,000.

available for investment and providing an additional spur for greater productivity. Japan's GNP per acre is ten times that of the United States.

Western sources point out that in 1981 the U.S. spent 5.8 percent of its GNP on defense, Great Britain 5.0 percent, West Germany 4.3 percent, France 4.2 percent, and Japan a mere 0.9 percent. Japan's aid to less developed countries was not proportionate to her comparative GNP standing among the world's leading powers.[13] It is conceded in Western circles that the peace settlement imposed upon Japan by the victorious Allies after World War Two virtually mandated low defense expenditures on Japan's part. Nonetheless, it is argued that this constitutes a distinct, perhaps even unfair, advantage calling for commensurate concessions on Japan's part vis-à-vis those who in effect must bear the oppressive burden of defense in the nuclear age.[14]

Japan's production costs were said to be well below those for comparable goods exported by Japan's competitors not only because of labor peace but also because of artificially depressed living standards, a condition enabling Japan to engage in "social dumping."* Then, there was the complaint of the "dirty float." Japan, it was charged, rendered Japanese exports less expensive on the world market by artificially keeping the yen's exchange value low in violation of GATT and other international understandings. Most flagrant in that regard were instances of collusion between the Japanese authorities and exporters to circumvent domestic law in order to improve Japan's competetive position on the world market.†

Japanese authorities also were accused of dragging their feet in implementing promised reforms of a bewildering national system of tariff and other obstacles to imports from abroad. Tokyo appeared to be inordinately slow in carrying out agreements negotiated during the so-called Kennedy and Tokyo Rounds under GATT auspices. Especially objectionable to frustrated potential importers were literally hundreds of non-tariff barriers (NTBs), some going back to the Middle Ages, and a byzantine distribution system based on long-time social links which naturally militated against foreign products.‡

---

* Wilkinson (1983), p. 203. "Social dumping" refers to artificial lowering of costs, thereby improving one's competitive edge, by depressing the standard of living of one's own working population.

† The allegation was that Japan's financial managers deliberately failed to institute needed reforms in their banking and investment practices and intervened with less than required speed when foreign exchange trends called for support of the falling yen. *Ibid.,* p. 200. Japan disputed the allegation but took steps to accommodate what Tokyo considered to be reasonable requests.

‡ Termed "backdoor protectionism," these practices include such arbitrary measures as insisting that American cars be repainted or reassembled, purportedly for reasons of safety. Or Japanese authorities insist that public agencies or the national universities use only computers made in Japan. Or elaborate testing and inspection procedures are instituted to discourage the sale of such U.S. products as pharmaceuticals and food additives. In November 1982, France retaliated over a similar annoyance, decreeing that all videotape recorders imported from Japan had to be cleared through a tiny inland customs station at Poitiers. For a while, that measure virtually stopped the flow of Japanese video-recorders into France.

The Japanese conceded some points and made adjustments, but they rejected others as unreasonable. They also registered complaints of their own. They pointed out that some demands for reduction or removal of some tariffs would inflict severe injury upon economically vulnerable groups.* They pleaded for time, pointed to their comparatively desperate situation regarding energy, for instance, and noted that protectionism was a universal practice. Moreover, unlike the United States, which protected older industries long after they had lost their competitive edge on world markets, Japan, so they argued, only protects its "infant industries" until they become internationally competitive. Demands that Japan increase its defense outlays from a 1982 percentage of 0.9 to 2 percent of its GNP in five years were described as unreasonable as that would call for annual increases in defense outlays at a rate several times its maximal annual GNP growth rate of about 4 percent, assuming no recession.[15]

Regarding the burgeoning U.S. trade deficit, Japanese as well as U.S. and West European analysts offered different explanations.† A report by the EEC Commission, for example, attributed Japan's advantage to such qualities as "hard work, discipline, corporate loyalties, and management skills of a crowded, highly competitive island people." Western Europe, it was argued, had fallen behind because "the Protestant work ethic has been substantially eroded by egalitarianism, social compassion, environmentalism, state intervention, and a widespread belief that working hard and making money are anti-social."[16]

On balance, it should be noted that the U.S. trade deficit, reflecting as it does increased earnings by America's allies and a number of LDCs, thereby strengthens the Western economic system and aids numerous Third World countries to climb out of their depressed position. On the other hand, in as much as the deficit is caused in part by the high exchange value of the U.S. dollar, a development contributing to sharply rising costs of oil and other imports throughout the world, the U.S. must bear part of the blame if the benefits from increased trade within the Western system and between North and South do not accrue to all participants. (See Fig. 12-1.)

The New Industrial Countries and the "Eastasia Edge": A new confrontation was shaping up, especially in such intensive industries like textiles and electronics, between the older established industrial democracies and the East Asian NICs, or "New Japans," the People's Republic of China, Hong Kong, Taiwan, the Philippines, South and North Korea, and Singapore. Unless the North

---

* For example, reduction of tariffs on leather imports—high on the list of allied demands—was said to be socially inadvisable. It was said to hurt a group known as the *burakumin,* outcasts, who due to Buddhist prohibition against slaughtering animals had become the only people in the tanning business and therefore had now no alternative source of income.

† Japanese analysts, incidentally, did not accept U.S. balance of trade or account figures. See an editorial in *The Wall Street Journal,* "Trade Is Aid" (January 31, 1984). Furthermore nearly two-thirds of Japan's currency surplus was returned to Western European and U.S. economies in the form of private Japanese investments. *Ibid.,* (August 27, 1984). By 1985 that flow was at a rate of $50 to $100 billion a year rivaling the flow of "petrodollars" following the 1973 oil price increase, (see Chapter 16, pp. 309ff).

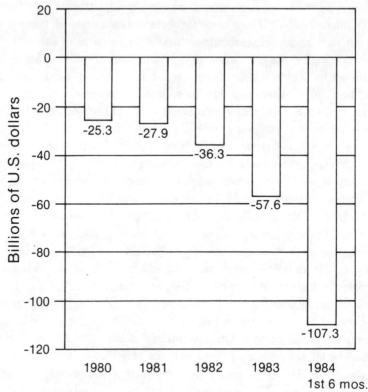

Fig. 12-1. U.S. Trade Deficit. (*Business America*, Vol. 6, 13 (June 27, 1983), p. 5.)

Atlantic-West European group saw its way clear to accommodate the exploding export capacity of the newcomers, and not press Japan too severely, the old and the "New Japans" together could capture and defend against the western allies the potentially enormous markets of East Asia, including China.* (See Table 12-3.)

Trading Across Ideological Divides:
The View From the West

If the volume of East-West trade, as compared to overall world trade, is relatively low, ideology as such does not appear to be one of the reasons.† If

---

* Regarding Hong Kong's future disposition see Chapter 13. p. 258. Hofheinz and Calder (1982), p. 3, contend that the U.S. now "depends more on 'Eastasia' economically than it does on Western Europe." Other predictions are that "Eastasia" will outstrip the Atlantic region economically by the 1990s, East Asian NICs accounting for 20 percent of world output by the end of the century, that of the Atlantic region probably declining. A U.S. recession would of course reverse the trend. By 1983 U.S. trade with the Asian Pacific region amounted to approximately 40 percent of its entire export-import business.

† The "East" in this context consists of three distinct groups or countries: 1) the Soviet Union and the European CMEA members who account for the by far greatest share of trade within the grouping, and 2) the non-European members or associates like Cuba, Vietnam, and 3) the People's Republic of China.

Table 12-3. The U.S. and East Asia: GNP Per Capita (1982) Selected Countries

	U.S. $	Average Annual Growth Rate (Per cent) (1960–1982)
United States	13,160	2.2
Japan	10,080	6.1
Korea, Republic of	1,910	6.6
Hong Kong	5,340	7.0
Singapore	5,910	7.4
Taiwan	1,700 (est.)	4.0 (est.)[a]
Korea, Democratic Republic of	1,200 (est.)	4.0 (est.)

SOURCES: *World Bank, World Development Report 1984; World Bank Atlas 1980.*
[a] Taiwan's annual GDP growth rate for 1984 has been estimated at 9.5 percent, that of the Republic of Korea at 8 percent. Morgan Guaranty Trust Co. of New York, *World Financial Markets,* October/November 1984, Table 6, p. 4.

Table 12-4. Wheat Export-Import: Leading Sellers and Buyers
(in '000 of metric tons, 1982)

Export		Import	
United States	40,522	20,900	Soviet Union
Canada	19,205	14,707	PRC
France	10,736	5,713	Japan
Australia	10,912	4,224	Brazil

SOURCES: *U.S. Statistical Abstract, 1985,* Table No. 1501, p. 858.

profits can be made, critical raw materials obtained, and unemployment reduced, Marxist, Leninist, or even Maoist pronouncements do not seem to deter capitalists. Even the ideologically most rigid administration in U.S. history, under President Reagan, was relieved if it could sell U.S. farm surpluses, especially grain, to the Soviet Union. When, to make a political point, the U.S. chose not to sell, or sold less than usual, an emphatically anticommunist regime like the now deposed Argentine military Junta eagerly filled the gap to relieve pressure on their shaky economy. (See Table 12-4.)

West–Soviet Bloc Trade*

The obstacles to East-West trade appear to be more of a practical nature. The Soviet Union is relatively self-sufficient, hence not under pressure to risk making its economy dependent on the West.[17] On the whole, trade is impeded by the structural rigidity characteristic of centrally planned and controlled

---

* For the view from the East, see Chapter 13. For a map of NATO and the Warsaw Pact see Fig. 13-1.

economies.* Many Western businessmen find negotiating with totalitarian bur-
eaucracies not worth the effort. Lastly, East-West trade is impeded by military
security considerations which assume greatest importance in trade between
members of the NATO group and the Soviet bloc.[18] But serious differences of
opinion have arisen in recent years between the NATO partners even on that
subject. More on that shortly. (See Table 12-5.)

Once a deal is struck, communist regimes actually are among the world's
most reliable customers and suppliers. For example, no country can match the
Soviet Union's record in having the same political party in control for two-
thirds of a century. Soviet client states, somewhat less reliable, are as a general
rule back-stopped by the Soviet Union in the event of default. This, and the
potential market offered by the bloc, has given rise to a thesis that Soviet
power can through trade be contained or even rendered less aggressive. Entice
Moscow with attractive offers into two-way trade, it is argued, and it may
modify its revolutionary zeal, agree to arms control, and generally help advance
the cause of peace.[19] West Germany, through its *Ostpolitik,* presses trade with
the Soviet bloc *(Osthandel)* partly to improve prospects of German unification,
calculating that an economically satisfied Soviet regime has less of an incentive
to keep apart the two halves of a once threatening enemy.†

Countering political, diplomatic, and economic rationales most persistently
are concerns, most strongly expressed by U.S. military and ultra-conservative
circles, that trade with bloc countries but most of all with the Soviet "enemy"
accrues to the latter's military advantage. Proceeding from the premise that
"the Soviet economy, its government, its foreign policies, and its military
apparatus are one integrated whole," it is argued that "any Soviet economic
gains can readily be transformed into strategic benefits."[20] It has that effect,
it is contended, because trade with the other members of the CMEA tends to
diminish the Soviet Union's obligations toward its client states, enabling it to
divert the savings to further augment its armed forces. The positions for and
against East-West trade, within the Western alliance, came into sharp focus
over the Soviet offer in 1981 to increase the supply of natural gas to an
economically depressed Western Europe via a new gas pipeline to be constructed
with Western financial, technical, and material assistance.‡

---

* A common complaint by Western businessmen is that commercial negotiations with
totalitarian regimes will pit competing and divided entrepreneurs against monolithic
totalitarian buyers and sellers. See, for example, Thomas G. Corcoran, "The Myth of
China Trade," *The New York Times* (September 19, 1976). A German industry
spokesman noted that the "Soviets deal different cards to different partners to keep them
all in the dark." *The Wall Street Journal* (November 16, 1983), p. 34. Another complaint
centers on Soviet refusal to release essential economic data, on mineral reserves for
instance.

† A diplomatic loophole in the Treaty of Rome permits the (East) German Democratic
Republic (DDR) to export to EEC member states without incurring import duties, on a
reciprocal basis. This makes the DDR a *de facto* member of the EEC.

‡ Under the plan the Soviet Union was to provide an annual flow of 40 billion cubic
meters of gas, starting in the mid 1980s; in return Western European suppliers were to
furnish the Soviet Union 6 million tons of steel pipe. Financing was to be arranged
through a consortium of West European and other banks.

The Soviet offer came at a time when a more emphatically anticommunist U.S. administration was determined to tighten existing curbs on transfer of strategic goods from NATO members to the Soviet bloc. High on the list was "critical technology," especially advanced computers and electronics, fibre optics, semiconductors, a variety of metallurgical processes, goods designed for peaceful purposes but containing strategically valuable technology, strategically useful plants built by Western firms in East bloc countries, and training of personnel in skills likely to enhance East bloc military capabilities. The interallied instrument to enforce the ban was the Coordinating Committee on Export Controls or Cocom, an informal body attached to NATO though not organizationally linked to it.*

To U.S. authorities, the gas-for-pipeline deal had all the appearances of a Soviet strategic move to drive a wedge into the Western alliance and develop a degree of West European dependency on the Soviet Union, while yielding for the Soviet Union eventually substantial financial gain. There was also concern that delivery of steel pipe and compressors by West European manufacturers would give the Soviet Union access to sensitive technology developed by U.S. concerns and made available to the Western allies through licensing agreements. U.S. government spokesmen and congressional leaders also contended that by extending credits to the Soviet Union toward construction of the steel pipes and compressors on relatively easy terms, Western governments were subsidizing Soviet military construction, since in the absence of such credits valuable foreign exchange would have to be expended by the Soviet government, leaving less available for military purposes.† The allies responded that they would not render themselves dependent on the Soviet Union, as they intended to develop their own natural gas deposits and increase their strategic reserves. Credits granted the Soviet government, the allies argued, did not aid its military efforts, because the Soviet regime was powerful enough to extract from the Soviet economy whatever it thought was needed for its military. In any case Soviet gold supplies were quite sufficient for these and related purposes. But the strongest objections were raised over Washington's decision to bar European licencees of American firms using these licenses to produce essential components of the pipeline project abroad. This, the allies argued, implied an "extraterritorial extension of United States jurisdiction . . . contrary to international law."[21]

---

* Established in 1949, the Committee includes 14 of the 15 NATO countries. Only Iceland does not participate. France, though formallly outside NATO, is a member. Controls, monitored at the U.S. end by the Department of Commerce's Office of Export Administration and abroad by the Committee, to apply to the Soviet Union, the Warsaw Pact members of Eastern Europe and the Asian communist countries of Laos and Vietnam. The PRC is not included among target countries.

† In 1983, former Secretary of State Henry Kissinger ruefullly noted that "Lenin's dictum that capitalists would compete to sell the rope with which they are to be hanged is coming true with a vengeance . . . but Lenin never guessed that Western governments would provide the money to buy the rope and subsidize the price to facilitate the purchase." *The New York Times* (May 22, 1983). By 1984, the Soviet Union alone owed Western banks $28.7 billion, ranking high among the major borrowers of the world.

Table 12-5. East–West Trade of OECD Countries

	Exports to East as % of GNP	Share of total OECD exports to East		Share of East in country's total exports	Exports to East as % of imports from East		
	1982	1970–80	1982	1982	1970–79	1980–81	1982
Finland	7.83	5.4	10.4	28.8	82	100	100
Austria	2.62	5.0	4.8	11.1	116	80	80
Iceland	2.30	0.2	0.2	8.4	69	67	59
Germany[a]	1.14	23.8	20.9	4.3	145	106	97
Belgium-Luxembourg	1.09	3.0	2.5	1.7	115	78	49
Greece	0.84	1.1	0.9	7.7	77	72	63
Sweden	0.84	3.5	2.3	3.0	87	77	52
Switzerland	0.80	2.9	2.2	3.1	141	70	71
Netherlands	0.72	3.2	2.8	1.5	85	55	30
Italy	0.71	7.6	6.8	3.3	82	52	47
Canada	0.71	2.7	5.7	3.0	315	736	1,156
New Zealand	0.60[b]	n.a.	n.a.	2.0[b]	n.a.	391	n.a.
Turkey	0.57	0.8	0.8	5.3	57	54	76
Australia	0.53	2.1	2.4	3.8	708	996	892
France	0.52	10.0	7.8	3.0	128	72	65
Denmark	0.45	1.1	0.7	1.6	56	61	34
Japan	0.42	8.7	12.4	3.2	140	173	241
Norway	0.39	0.9	0.6	1.2	77	69	37
Portugal	0.39	0.2	0.2	2.1	50	35	62
Ireland	0.38	0.1	0.2	0.8	30	72	49
United Kingdom	0.31	5.7	4.2	1.6	70	101	76
Spain	0.25	1.1	1.2	2.1	78	83	51
United States	0.12	10.7	10.0	1.7	285	275	337
OCED	0.47	100.0	100.0	3.1	118	99	91

SOURCE: *OECD Observer*, No. 128, (May 1984), p. 15.
[a] Federal Republic; excluding intra-German trade.
[b] 1981.

The matter came to a head when the U.S. announced that any foreign company failing to honor its embargo on sales of American pipeline technology to the Soviet Union could be barred from access to U.S. products or technology.

Also troubling U.S. allies was the fact that only ten years earlier U.S. energy experts had briefly considered the possibility of a similar deal between the Soviet Union and the United States. Moreover, at the time when Washington sought to prevent the West European-Soviet gas-pipeline deal the United States had extended a grain contract with the Soviet Union plus another under which New Zealand butter was to be processed in the United States before it was sold to the Soviet Union. To the West Europeans and Japan, once the military security concerns could be laid to rest there really was no difference between deals they wished to consummate with the Soviet Union and those Washington was prepared to pursue.

Sanctions, Strategic Embargoes, and Technology Transfer

The evidence tended to support the allies' argument. United States efforts to slow down the Soviet arms build-up and discourage Moscow's military aggressiveness by economic means appeared to have been unsuccessful. A grain embargo did not remove Soviet troops from Afghanistan, and other economic sanctions against Poland did not force Warsaw to permit free trade unions. The long-standing policy to deny the Soviet bloc goods and technology of military-strategic value likewise fell short of its objectives. Thousands of items embargoed by the U.S. under the strategic restrictions plan were in fact not denied to the Soviet Union. Many were easily acquired from close allies like France, West Germany, or Japan. Or they were smuggled out of the United States under false invoices, through third neutral or non-aligned countries. Some, it turned out, could even be obtained from within the Soviet bloc, from the East German Democratic Republic for example. Contracts from which U.S. firms were compelled to withdraw were in numerous instances promptly taken up by U.S. allies.

In the United States, hard-liners vied with doves, each seeking to place their stamp on U.S. economic policy. The former insisted that, leakages and allied competition notwithstanding, restrictions on trade with the Soviet bloc were bound to have some effect, even if only temporarily. The other side countered that while economic warfare clearly was necessary in support of military actions, in peacetime it was tantamount to shooting oneself in the foot. Cut-offs of wheat, soy beans, and corn, over such issues as the Afghanistan invasion and the Polish crisis, may temporarily reduce Soviet meat production and slightly alter Soviet armed forces' diet, but shortfalls were always quickly made up from other sources, for example Argentina, Canada, or Australia. Some restrictions, those regarding oil-drilling equipment for example, if implemented fully would work to prevent the Soviet Union from developing its own oil resources, forcing it onto the world market eventually, there to compete with the Western world.*

Trade with the People's Republic of China

It would seem that the potential is enormous: over one billion potential consumers of Western goods and services, some 400,000 industrial establishments in need of technological modernization, vast and as yet untapped natural

---

* Requests by American firms for exemptions from the Cocom embargo list increased from 1.6 percent of the total list in 1962 to 25.6 percent in 1970 and to 62.5 percent in 1978. U.S. Congress, Senate, 96th, 2d (1980), *Transfer of Technology to the Soviet Bloc*, p. 69. In 1984, the Reagan Administration lifted the ban on all goods which the bloc countries could readily obtain from other sources. *The New York Times* (March 7, 1984), p. D 1. See also Friesen (1978), pp. 22-24, 143 and Luttwak (1983), p. 91.

resources, and tightly controlled labor-management relations. But the obstacles to significant expansion of trade are formidable. In 1980, the PRC's share of world merchandise exports was 0.9 percent.[22] The PRC still is a critically underdeveloped country steeped in poverty. Its overall foreign exchange earnings still are precariously low, limiting imports to dire necessities. Deeply rooted in China's past is a high degree of xenophobia, a consequence in part of centuries of conquest and subjugation by Mongols, Russians, Japanese, British, Germans, and Americans.[23] That the latter four invaded China during the nineteenth and early twentieth centuries in pursuit of commercial and financial gain, and that the United States stubbornly refused for more than two decades to accept the communist conquest of the mainland carry over into trade relations with these states today.

Several factors suggest possible improvement following a period of adjustment necessitated by a sharp turn away from the radicalism and lawlessness promoted by Chairman Mao and "the Gang of Four" during the—for China disastrous—Cultural Revolution (1966-1976). Soon after order was restored, the post-Mao regime embarked upon a program to modernize agriculture, industry, science and technology, and defense, proceeded to relax bureaucratic and party controls, introduced production incentives in agriculture and industry and began cautiously to experiment with market economies.[24] Part of the incentive program was a dramatic reversal of Maoist deemphasis of consumer goods production for domestic consumption. "Anti-foreignism" began to wane following the resumption of diplomatic relations with the United States in 1972.*

Table 12-6. China and the Other Major Powers: GNP Per Capita
(1982 in US$)

PRC	USSR	German Fed. Rep.	U.S.	France	Japan	United Kindgom
310	4,550 (1980)	12,460	13,160	11,680	10,080	9,660

SOURCE: World Bank, *Development Report 1984*, Table 1, pp. 218–219 and *ibid*, 1982, Table 1, pp. 110–111.

* Liao, *op. cit.* in Liao (1981), pp. 20–28. To attract private investment, and with it advanced technology, Special Economic Zones were created in Southern and Eastern China, offering rents, wages, and taxes well below those available in Hong Kong for instance. The PRC also increased borrowing from the World Bank and began to grant credits to foreign purchasers of PRC goods. *Standard Chartered Review* (May 1982), pp. 16-17; see also U.S. Dept. of Commerce (1982), pp. 15-16. Deteriorating relations between the PRC and the Soviet Union encouraged the United States to "play its China Card," in the hope of countering Soviet pressure in Europe as well as in the Far East. One consequence of this was extension to the PRC of Most Favored Nation (MFN) status beginning in 1980, placing the PRC in the same category as two other potential defectors from the Soviet sphere of influence, Hungary and Romania. U.S. Dept. of Commerce (1982), p. 20.

In 1983 the U.S. even considered placing the PRC into an export category which would qualify it to receive sophisticated equipment and technology normally denied states whom

Still, expert assessments of the level of trade one can expect from the PRC over the next decade remain on the pessimistic side. Tremendous internal difficulties have to be overcome before the new regime's ambitious plans can be brought to fruition. Always possible is a rapprochement between Moscow and Beijing. Continuing support of the *de facto* independence of Taiwan by the United States and several of its allies remains a thorn in China's side, and prospects are not good that the issue can soon be resolved. For one, U.S. trade with Taiwan still far outweighs trade with the PRC. Disputes also break out occasionally over such issues as alleged "dumping" of Chinese textiles in the United States, a policy defended by Beijing as fair, given its status as a Third World country. Conceivably, given the best of likely circumstances trade between the PRC and the West could surpass that between the NATO powers and the Soviet Union by 1985 or 1986, reaching about half the 1980 volume of NATO trade with the entire Eastern bloc.[25] On the Far Eastern and Southeast Asia sides of the "West," Japan along with the East Asian NICs will probably account for an increasing share of this rapidly expanding segment of East-West trade.

Managing World Finance

Major Obstacles to Effective Financial Management

As the world's leading sources of finance, the industrial democracies face several high-priority tasks: (1) finance normal world trade on as equitable a basis as possible; (2) provide sufficient liquidity to prevent sharp contractions of trade in key areas or collapse of key economies; (3) prevent bankruptcy or temporary insolvency of major suppliers of critical raw materials or of countries representing major export markets; (4) in the absence of an automatically adjustable global monetary system, provide emergency assistance to stabilize foreign exchange rates; (5) recycle, in a financially sound manner, the petrodollars, that is, the funds accumulated by oil-exporting countries in excess of what they can use for their own development; (6) apply their financial power selectively to political objectives in their own global political and military-strategic interests; (7) develop further international organizational facilities and procedures to reconcile the conflict between inner-directed national political systems and outer-directed internationalized finance capital.

Most financial operations are conducted swiftly, smoothly, and without controversy. Disruptions or disequilibriums are attended to and difficulties are overcome without special effort. Astronomical sums are quietly and almost instantly shifted electronically from one part of the world to another. Investments are made and withdrawn; if withdrawn, they are quickly replaced, unless

Washington regards as actually or potentially posing military strategic threats. This would designate the PRC as a "friendly, non-allied" nation, a category reserved for states like Yugoslavia and India, both of which maintained ties with the Soviet Union. In 1984, the U.S. took steps to share with the PRC technology for peaceful use of nuclear energy.

the world economy is in recession. Generally, the industrial democracies' top financial officers, the managers of central banks and other supervisory authorities, in close collaboration, manage the flow of world finance fairly successfully. On the other hand, given the magnitude of the funds and other assets involved, managerial lapses or misjudgments can have disastrous global consequences. So can ill-considered acts of commission or omission by political leaders.

Some impediments to successful management are intrinsic to a world economy composed of some 160 sovereign states; some, like the "boom and bust" expansion and contraction cycles, are intrinsic to capitalism. So is the conflict between rational management of scarce resources and the unbridled pursuit of profit. Further complicating matters are structural anomalies between highly complex and sophisticated industrial democracies and relatively crudely governed, less developed suppliers of critical raw materials and agricultural commodities. The different managerial styles and operational requirements of market and nonmarket economies and the suspicions, misunderstandings and tensions arising from these divergencies pose additional obstacles.

But the major upheavals putting the combined managerial talent of the world's bankers and financiers to the test in recent years were triggered by two developments: the quadrupling of the price of oil between 1973 and 1974, together with the second shock in 1979, and the ballooning of the Eurocurrency market. The former brought about a dramatic shift of the world's financial resources from oil-importing to oil-exporting countries. The latter served as a relatively uncontrolled waystation for a large share of petrodollars (so called because they are mainly dollars earned from the sale of oil), for funds shifted about solely for speculative purpose, and other private and public accumulation in search of profit or security. It was this combination which precipitated the global debt crisis of the 1980s.

The Debt Crisis of the 1980s: A Case Study in Global Mismanagement

The abrupt oil price increase beginning in 1973 brought on a dramatic increase between 1970 and 1975 and again between 1979 and 1980 in Current Account Balances* of "high-income oil *exporters*" and of a corresponding decrease or deficit incurred by all oil *importers.* Primarily to cushion their oil-dependent economies, the weaker among the oil importers, foremost the less developed ones, sharply increased their external borrowing.[26]

Inevitably several circumstances combined to produce a global crisis. The OPEC countries typically could not fully absorb the current account surpluses, which amounted to approximately $140 billion between 1974 and 1976 and somewhere between $100 and $120 billion for 1980 alone. Although they immediately began to apply as large a share of the windfall as was practical to their own development, large amounts had to be invested where they could

* Current Account Balance is the balance between national income and national expenditure, including visible and invisible expenditures such as debt services.

earn the highest possible returns, in the private banks and corporations and in real estate in the advanced industrial democracies.[27] At the same time, lining up for relief from the rising costs of energy were the oil-importing LDCs. It seemed reasonable, under the circumstances, to consider recycling to them funds extracted from them under duress. But desperate as they were they proceeded to contract debts well in excess of their capacity to service.

At the end of 1982, 21 of the major LDC borrowers had committed more than 70 percent of their export earnings to external debt service and repayment of principle (the debt-to-export ratio). (See Figs. 15–2a, b, c.) Argentina had committed 68 percent, Brazil 89 percent, Ecuador 69 percent, and Chile 65 percent, making repayment of loans most unlikely except on a rescheduled, very long-term basis. In some cases, total repayment was highly improbable under any circumstances.* According to some sources, private bank loans to non-oil LDCs reached approximately $500 billion, according to others $700 billion, in 1982. United States banks alone had lent over $140 billion to LDCs and countries in the Eastern bloc.[28]

Among the non-market economies following the pattern of increasing East-West trade, Czechoslovakia, Hungary, Romania, the East German Democratic Republic, Poland, and Bulgaria accumulated by 1980 a total debt to Western sources in the range of $63 billion, with Poland alone contracting for $26 billion.[29] Several reasons accounted for that development: increased costs of oil imported from the Soviet Union, the latter's poor harvest which reduced its lending capacity, and, in the individual bloc countries, internal shortfalls due to overextension. In the case of Poland, an ambitious program to modernize the economy and raise living standards—a strategy of simultaneous expansion and consumption—called for heavy borrowing.[30] In this instance as in some of the other cases, external borrowing was in part a means of covering up gross mismanagement and miscalculation.

To an extent, credits to East bloc countries had been made available at the urging of Western leaders who saw in the loan/credit connection diplomatic opportunities. West Germany, for instance, hoped for an opening in the wall separating the two Germanies and generally expected improved relations with traditional customers in east and southeast Europe. U.S. leaders, Henry Kissinger for example, interpreted East bloc overtures to Western capitalist institutions as a loosening of ties between the Soviet Union and some of its client states.[31]

On the other hand, Soviet readiness to apply for loans in the West and permit other COMECON countries to do so aroused suspicion in rigidly anti-

* Griffith (1983), pp. 30–31. Debt service accounted for 80 percent of Poland's hard currency earnings in 1982. If a debtor country declares inability to meet its schedule of servicing and repayment of external debt, lenders have two options. They declare the debtor in default or they agree to reschedule the debt. The debtor can accept the new service and/or repayment schedule or he can repudiate the debt, thereby virtually foreclosing any opportunity to receive credits or loans from the same or similar sources in the future. Given the world-wide influence—the global reach—of Western bankers, prospects of a defaulting country obtaining loans from any Western source are exceedingly slim. But see note on p. 237.

communist circles in the West, principally in the United States. Was capitalism living up to Lenin's prophecy that greed would lead capitalists to sell the rope with which communists would eventually hang them? Western military strategists were divided. Some, eager to disrupt strategic links and communications between the Soviet Union and its forward position in East Germany, hoped that a Poland linked to Western economies would eventually want to pursue independent foreign policies.* Others were concerned that East bloc borrowing simply would enable the enemy to devote more financial resources to the arms race. But Western bankers would not be denied.[32] Nor did Western diplomatic strategists committed to the soft-line approach to communism give up hope for a lessening of tensions. In any case, what was true of East-West trade also applied to finance: if one country or one bank consortium declined to deal with communist regimes, a dozen competitors were eager to take its place. Thus, debts grew and, to qualify for more, Hungary, Romania, Poland, and Yugoslavia as well applied for membership in the IMF, a step as we shall see viewed by Moscow with very mixed feelings.†

The debt crisis is a prime example of the effect on world politics of the internationalization of finance capital. Western banking houses have played key roles in international affairs for several centuries. But until the debt crisis broke upon the world, that role had not been associated with imprudence and recklessness. It was the seemingly inexhaustible cornucopia largely filled with petrodollars (the Eurocurrency market), which brought the banking world, the LDCs, and several East bloc countries together in ventures unequalled in the annals of international finance. The peculiarities of the Eurocurrency market go a long way to explain what happened.

In addition to being a waystation for petrodollars waiting to be recycled, the market constitutes the ideal haven for funds whose owners have reason to avoid control and supervision by their respective governments. The market is administered and assets traded largely through subsidiaries of some of the world's largest banks, through such places as Luxembourg, London, Hong Kong, the New York Free Trade Zone, or the Cayman Islands. There, reposing next to ill-gotten fortunes seeking refuge from income tax collectors, these funds are

---

* Words written by one of the United States' foremost financiers, Felix Rohatyn, at the height of the Polish crisis, tended to confirm the worst suspicions of Moscow's hardliners: "The weapon of capital is potentially one of the most powerful and least used in the Western world. Poland affords us a chance to use it. It might turn out to be our only effective way, in the long run, of bringing about change behind the Iron Curtain." *The New York Times* (January 11, 1982), Op. Ed.

† Relations between Western states and Yugoslavia have been excellent for several reasons. First, NATO's southern flank touches upon Yugoslavia, and, related to this, Yugoslavia is a near-Mediterranean power with maritime access to that sea from the Adriatic. Incorporation of that country into the Warsaw Pact military alliance system would place East bloc land, air, and naval forces in position to seriously impede NATO defenses in the event of a westward move by bloc forces. Second, intent on maintaining its independence, Yugoslavia has oriented sections of its economy toward the West. It enjoys Special Status Membership in the OECD. Another Communist member of the IMF is the PRC.

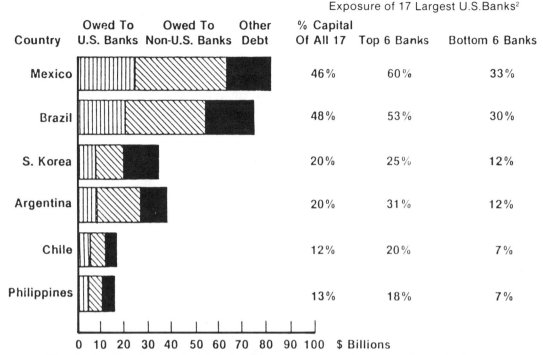

Fig. 12-2. The International Debt Crisis: Exposure of U.S. Banks. (U.S. Congress, Senate (1983) *Hearings*, International Debt, Chart 3, p. 367.)

completely uncoupled from domestic banking requirements, giving both lenders and borrowers greater flexibility.* There also are certain cost advantages to trading through the market. Especially enticing is the opportunity to earn unusually high fees and commissions. As the world recession mounted, many Western banks lost their traditional credit customers. The LDCs and the Soviet bloc, all starved for funds, offered attractive alternatives.

Illustrated here is an international management problem of unfathomable dimensions. Commented a former British Cabinet officer:

All the great banks of the world were drawn into this operation, and they have built a structure of debt that must surely be the largest and most remarkable

---

* See Ruggie (1981), pp. 139-154. Here is a prime example of economic forces acting like "cannons loose on the deck." According to Ruggie, "There are no minimum reserve requirements on Eurodeposits, so that the Eurodollar, and other Eurocurrency banking can both pay and charge more competitive rates than is possible domestically. For the same reason, Euro-banking tends to be more aggressive than banking in the United States." *Ibid.*, pp. 150-151. Politically significant is the fact that "about two-thirds of all credits granted to East bloc countries were without home government guarantees. One reason for this was bankers' confidence that the sound financial position of the Soviet Union could be viewed as a quasi-guarantor of the smaller East bloc nations. Jahnke (1982), p. 10. The New York Free Trade zone was created to cut the State of New York and thereby the U.S. into the trillion dollar lending business which had theretofore gone to other "off-shore" or overseas havens. See Robert A. Bennett, "America's Debut in Offshore Banking," *The New York Times* (November 26, 1981).

financial house of cards ever created. It still is not clear how the governments, the central bankers and the great private bankers themselves could ever have believed that this structure could endure.[33]

It seemed that sovereign independence was now truly held at bay. No major bank, and no government whose banking system rested on that precarious foundation, dared to remove one single card without putting another swiftly in its place. Loans which could or would not be repaid were promptly "rolled over," frequently someone else in the lengthening chain assuming responsibility and risk. If interest payments could or would not be honored on schedule, payments were "rescheduled." As the weaker banks began to withdraw from the competition, strains became noticeable in the intricate "interbank" market where, by 1982, more than $1 trillion had been lent by some banks to others, who had passed the risk onto yet others, moving the true measure of risks incurred by the entire network completely out of sight. (See Fig. 12-2.)

Cessation of this practice was out of the question. But even a slowdown in lending threatened to create a liquidity crisis in the borrowing countries, preventing them from meeting current trade obligations as well as compelling them to halt their internal development, all with unforeseeable economic and political consequences.* One predictable consequence of a credit slowdown certainly would be contraction of LDC imports from the developed countries, causing serious economic decline where LDC exports were going.[34] There also was an increasing probability of widespread political and social unrest if borrowing countries were to be compelled to cut back on social and economic benefits made possible by the credit explosion. Most disconcerting to the sensitive Western economies of course was the ever present threat of debt repudiation and default. Some of the world's largest banks were dangerously overcommitted. Their respective home governments, obligated by law to bail them out to an extent in the event of default, were beginning to perceive the full dimensions of the crisis. One of the world's leading financiers warned that mass default would not be ruled out.† If default, or long-term postponement

---

* By 1982, Argentina was $1.6 billion in arrears on its then nearly $37 billion debt. By 1984, confident that it had the banking community at its mercy, it was threatening to bring down the entire structure unless concessions were made, easing the burden. There were suspicions, however, that the major banking houses had artificially promoted a crisis, perhaps even encouraging Argentina in its recalcitrance, in order to nudge their respective governments into increasing their IMF contributions and aiding the bankers in other ways, so that the latter could more easily extricate themselves from a deepening morass. See, for example, *The Wall Street Journal* (April 27 and April 30, 1983).

† Wrote Felix Rohatyn: "It is, in my judgment, an illusion to think that no sovereign country will default on its external debt because it would become a pariah in the international financial community. Default or a repudiation of debt could occur as a result of radical political changes (as possible in literally any Latin American country) or geopolitical decisions (as might be the case in Eastern Europe.) of the $500 billion in loans to the poorer nations from the Western banking system, much will never come back." *The New York Review of Books* (November 4, 1982), pp. 6 and 8. See also the pessimistic scenario outlined in a lead article in the *Wall Street Journal* of November 10, 1982, summarized in Weintraub (1983), pp. 24–25.

of interest payments, or some other delay was not the immediate threat, argued one observer, the debtors should insist on more liberal access to creditor nations' markets so that they could earn the foreign exchange with which to honor their debts.

In the end, as counted on by many bankers, the IMF, together with the Big Ten, OECD, and Saudi Arabia acting in consonance with IMF policies, came to the rescue. But, whereas individual governments were disinclined or legally unable to impose firm discipline upon borrowers and lenders, the IMF had no such inhibitions. As a condition for support of the rickety debt structure, the IMF required among other things that borrowing countries develop and implement in some cases rather draconic economic adjustment programs. Included were institution of austerity measures such as a shift of import patterns from consumer goods to raw materials or capital goods useful for industrial development. Not surprisingly the IMF option was one of last resort for governments preferring less or no outside interference in their internal affairs. It was all the more remarkable that the otherwise secretive Polish, Hungarian, and Romanian Communist Party bureaucracies chose to apply for membership in so meddlesome an organization.*

Monetary "Order" or Management?

Finance and trade then go hand in hand and both are tied inextricably to global politics and to world peace. Although the first two are the foundations of the latter, if the world economy is to be managed successfully for the benefit of all both factors must be taken into account. Because it still predominates, the capitalist system bears prime responsibility for maintenance of some kind of world economic order. Within such an order, by general agreement the U.S. continues to bear a major share of that responsibility.

---

* Between 1982 and 1983, in return for a multibillion dollar loan from the IMF, Brazil agreed to continue its IMF-imposed austerity program which held down wages, curbed the rate of inflation (which always hurts some interest groups), raised cost of imports, and reduced government expenditures—all bound to produce internal political repercussions. Poland's attempt to comply with similar requirements to improve its external credit standing brought on the labor union crisis of 1980, which in turn led to imposition of martial law, followed by U.S. sanctions.

   In addition to the IMF, LDCs and some of the East bloc countries have available to them, though on a more modest scale, the resources of the World Bank, the Inter-American Development Bank, the Asian Development Bank, and the African Development Fund. The U.S. also assists through its Commodity Credit Corporation's "Overseas Lending Window" and the Exchange Stabilization Fund of the U.S. Treasury, partly to retain in its hand a degree of control over this politically sensitive aspect of foreign economic policy. A separate General Arrangement to Borrow was set up by the leading industrial nations, the Big Ten; there also is a back-up fund to support the IMF, and the Big Ten's Central Banks are available. Then there is the International Finance Corporation within the World Bank group, among other ad hoc and temporary institutional assistance programs. See U.S. Department of State, Bureau of Public Affairs, "Multilateral Development Banks," *gist,* (February 1982).

World liquidity can no longer be maintained by U.S. deficit spending.* That worked for a decade or so, but under post-Bretton Woods conditions it spells global financial instability and political discord among the major industrial powers. A strong dollar creates problems for the world as does a weak one: the first adversely affects advanced economies because it lures needed capital away from allies, the second tips the balance of world trade toward the U.S., which also disadvantages the other industrial economies. Therefore, if currency stability is to be achieved, although the dollar remains the core currency, the other leading world currencies must be integrated in the system.

As the world's economic leader the U.S. is obligated in all of its economic, political, and military actions to take into account the interests of allies as well as of major opponents insofar as these have the capacity to influence world affairs. For example, unless the arms competition is curbed the Soviet Union cannot be expected to play the supporting role East Europe's banker-creditors have presumed it will. Similarly, because Mideast oil is so essential to the West European allies and Japan the allies expect the United States to exercise greatest care lest its support of Israel leads to a military confrontation with the Soviet Union, a confrontation which might affect the U.S. less than it would its allies because the U.S. depends less on oil imports than do they.†

Clearly the debt crisis must be brought under control. But there are no easy solutions. To curb and eventually roll back inflation, one of the world's major scourges and a prime source of global economic instability, the U.S. tightened its money supply. The resulting scarcity drove interest rates up, making loan money more expensive and attracting, as we noted, capital from friendly economies already suffering from large-scale unemployment among other problems. Every other seemingly sensible "solution" of the world's economic ills is similarly double-edged.

Even if attempted on a limited regional scale, monetary stability is an elusive goal. Under the European Monetary System (EMS), based on a "basket" of Common Market currencies, any destabilizing development was to be countered at once by appropriate corrective measures initiated by whichever government appeared primarily responsible.‡ But ten of the most advanced diverse and divergent national economies, each subject to fragmenting and inhibiting do-

---

* It should be noted that in 1985 the United States, for the first time since 1914 became a debtor instead of a creditor nation; it was estimated that by 1990, the U.S. would owe the rest of the world about $1 trillion, more than the total owed by all developing countries, C. Fred Bergsten *The New York Times* (December 7, 1984).

† Meyer notes: "America's allies balk at joining an armament race that is bound to intensify their fiscal plight and heighten their economic and monetary subordination to the United States—a condition aggravated by their heavy reliance on fuel that is payable in dollars." Meyer (1982), p. 30.

‡ The system was initiated in March 1979 in the wake of the Bretton Woods collapse, mainly to stabilize the Eurocurrencies against the Dollar. The instrument was the European Currency Unit or ECU.

mestic pressures, can generate as much discord as can more than one hundred of the less complex and less sophisticated.*

It may be in the nature of the world that no degree of stability can be achieved with respect to currency values or with respect to the aggregate world economy generally. It may only be possible to *manage* crises, not *resolve* them. Candid assessment of all attempts to "solve" world economic problems indicates that as soon as one segment of the world economy is reasonably stabilized, another will unravel, most likely as a result of the success of the first. The situation may be compared to an attempt to submerge a very large air mattress in a body of water. It will not allow itself to be submerged completely, one or more of its corners will insist on popping out. If too much pressure is applied simultaneously on all corners and the center, the mattress most likely will spring a leak.

W.W. Rostow believes that because the world economy has grown more complex, in the coming decades more than ever before governments may have to intervene in the various processes by which finance capital is distributed throughout the world.[35] That may extend to the hitherto privately controlled investment flow which must be directed to compensate for shortfalls, resulting from technological setbacks in some parts of the world and advances in others.

Suggested Questions and Discussion Topics

What holds the Western economic bloc together? What tends to divide it? In particular, what are the major sources of economic conflict within the so called Western alliance system, that is, between the United States and Western Europe, between the United States and Canada, and between the North Atlantic-West European allies and Japan?

In the context of the East–West struggle, what aspects of capitalism tend to accrue to its advantage? What aspects tend to detract from its competitive strength vis-à-vis communism/socialism?

Give some of the reasons why East–West trade, and especially U.S. trade with the Soviet bloc and the PRC, are low relative to world trade generally.

What major factors contributed to the international debt crisis?

What other major obstacles to effective global financial management can you cite?

---

* In 1983, as the French *franc* was weakening rapidly against the dollar, French President Mitterand warned: "We have to develop a new system as we did at Bretton Woods. Monetary disorders fuel economic wars between friends." Leonard M. Glynn, *The New York Times* (May 8, 1983). See also Karl Otto Pohl, President of the West German Bundesbank, *The German Tribune* (March 13, 1983), p. 6.

Chapter 13
The Advanced Socialist Sector:
Unity or Fragmentation?

The "World Socialist System"

According to the rulers of the Soviet Union, there is only one legitimate world socialist system: the one led by the Communist party of the Soviet Union (CPSU), which is to say the Soviet bloc.[1] Objectively, the socialist world is split into three major groupings: (1) the Soviet bloc of socialist states and several "associates," mainly LDCs, whose governments accept the leadership of the CPSU, (2) Communist-led countries outside the bloc, for example the PRC, Yugoslavia, and Albania, and (3) a number of noncommunist socialist governments and political parties, including parties in opposition, all outside the Soviet bloc and gathered loosely in the Socialist International. Moving in and out of the latter grouping are various less developed countries whose leaders experimentally embrace, more or less seriously, one or another of the socialist models, only to abandon the experiment when a more attractive alternative materializes or when they are overthrown.

The Political Economy of the Soviet Bloc

The Bloc's Historic Roots

In essence, the bloc is the Soviet Union's shield against invasion from the West. Its roots are deeply embedded in the historic relationship between the Soviet Union and the individual states of Eastern and Southeastern Europe on the one hand and the rest of the European continent on the other. It is a history of invasions, great power manipulation, and economic exploitation. Poland, Czechoslovakia, Hungary, Romania, and Bulgaria—as well as the people now united in Yugoslavia, incidentally—for centuries served as pawns in great power struggles for European supremacy. Following the 1917 Russian Revolution, Poland, Czechoslovakia, Hungary, and Romania served as part of a buffer system created by Great Britain, France, and the United States to "quarantine" the Bolshevik "virus." Viewed from Moscow, these states were intended to serve as advance bases for capitalist/imperialist invasion of the Soviet Union when the time was ripe.* Following World War Two, taking advantage of the chaos and confusion in the wake of the collapse of Germany's military empire and determined to put an end to that threat, Stalin set out to construct what he envisaged as an impenetrable wall composed of solidly entrenched Soviet-type communist regimes from the Baltic to the Black Sea. Success seemed assured when he managed to install replicas of his own brand of Communist regime in Warsaw, Prague, Budapest, Bucharest, and Sofia. Only Yugoslavia, firmly ruled by Marshal Tito, and Albania escaped Stalin's net.† (See Fig. 13-1.)

Soviet Management of the Bloc Economy

The Council for Mutual Economic Assistance (CMEA/COMECON). The Council was created in 1949, partly in response to the Marshall Plan, to compensate

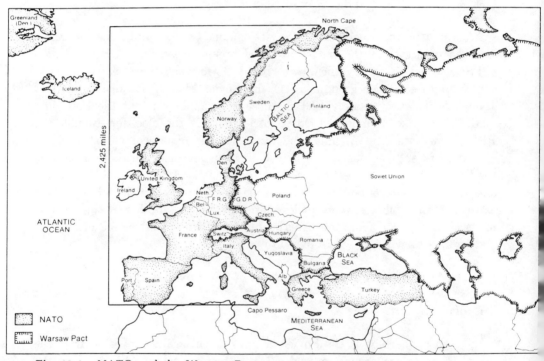

Fig. 13-1.   NATO and the Warsaw Pact.

SOURCE: United States Department of State, Bureau of Public Affairs, *Atlas of NATO,* 1985, p. 3. Not shown on the map, in the case of NATO, are the United States and Canada.

* Lithuania, Latvia, and Estonia were part of the same system. Situated along the eastern shores of the Baltic Sea, they were annexed by the Soviet Union in 1940 in the wake of the Stalin-Hitler Pact of 1939, a non-"aggression" treaty providing for the partition of Poland between Nazi Germany and the Soviet Union and relieving Germany, for the moment, of the threat of a two-front war. The U.S. does not recognize these acquisitions.

† In an effort to bring Yugoslavia to heel Stalin conducted economic warfare against that country from 1948 to his death in 1953. His purpose was frustrated in part by the West, which came to the aid of the stubbornly independent-minded Yugoslavs. See Holzman (1976), pp. 77–79.

bloc members for American aid which Soviet dictate prevented them from accepting, and partly to further solidify the bloc and institutionalize Soviet leadership. Its avowed formal purposes were promotion of intrabloc trade, scientific and technological exchange, and coordination of relevant internal and external policies. It is reported that some Marxist/Leninist strategists had visions of hastening capitalism's collapse if a Soviet-led trading bloc could deny Western economies access to East Europe's markets.[2] More likely the aim was restricted to no more than "the forced restructuring of the trade of all CMEA members away from the West and toward each other, particularly, of course, toward the Soviet Union."* Whatever the aim, Soviet management of the bloc economic system was steeped in controversy from the outset. As will be shown shortly, each of several major uprisings in bloc countries is traceable to widespread popular dissatisfaction with that management and its material consequences for Moscow's partners.

While Stalin lived the CMEA was virtually defunct, bloc relations being conducted almost exclusively by dictate from Moscow, administered faithfully by Moscow's surrogates in bloc capitals. After his death moderate relaxation of controls was followed by Soviet pressure, starting in the early 1960s, to endow the Council with supranational powers similar to those accorded the West European Common Market. Suspecting total loss of their hard-won independence—circumscribed and restricted as that was—bloc members balked. Their resistance was legitimized to a degree by the example of Yugoslavia's defiance and by the PRC's challenge, beginning in 1956, of what Beijing insisted on calling "Soviet hegemonism." The schism following the 1968 invasion of Czechoslovakia by Warsaw Pact forces—to stifle a revisionist, native form of "Communism with a human face"—shelved the proposal for the time being.[3]

Soviet authorities will insist that on balance the CMEA benefits all members equally; in their view the Soviet Union bears a disproportionate share of the burden. To East European members, the system leaves much to be desired. Some of the organization's difficulties stem from the basic incompatibility of transnational economic integration and central planning, one reason being that nothing can be traded that is not being produced according to plan. Indeed much of what is being traded appears to be virtually identical, for the same or very similar designs are used by identically or similarly oriented planning agencies. Planning generally leads to rigid, economically irrational pricing, for if the costs of a given item are too high or too low—in response to demand or supply, for instance—the difference can all too easily be erased or adjusted

* Holzman (1976), pp. 51 and 68. CMEA/COMECON membership, in 1981, included Albania (inactive), Bulgaria, Cuba, Czechoslovakia, the East German Democratic Republic (DDR), Hungary, Mongolia, Poland, Romania, the Soviet Union, and Vietnam. Yugoslavia was an Associate Member and Finland, Iraq, and Mexico were Cooperative Members. See also footnote above, p. 186.

by simple bookkeeping transactions.* On the other hand, proposals to phase out inefficient industries in some bloc countries in favor of more efficient ones elsewhere in the bloc encounter vigorous resistance, either on nationalistic grounds or from workers' councils who regard such decisions as anathema in a socialist republic.

Other problems result from Soviet insistence that trade be shifted from West to East, depriving bloc members of critical goods and technology which the Soviet Union either cannot or will not provide or provides inadequately, in many instances above world price.

A major source of discontent among Moscow's CMEA partners has been Soviet insistence on nonconvertibility of CMEA currencies into either foreign or other bloc currencies and on commodity inconvertibility in intrabloc trade.† The effect is that other CMEA members are prevented from taking advantage of currency and price fluctuations on the world market, something the Soviet Union can do with relative ease using its ample gold stock and hard currency reserves earned from trade outside the bloc. Moscow enjoys yet another advantage as the ruble, by sheer volume of transactions the dominant bloc currency, is pegged at an artificially high level, the inflated value then being reflected in exorbitant prices charged the Soviet Union's bloc clients.[4]

In defense of its policy Moscow argues that free convertibility is injurious to planning and central control of socialist economies, hence to socialism in general. Free convertibility would jeopardize carefully developed production and consumption goals as foreigners could use their currencies to drain the bloc of essential goods and commodities while bloc citizens might prefer more attractive, better quality foreign goods over the more expensive ones available within the bloc.‡ Moreover, the Soviets contend that since the system works both for and

* Holzman (1976), p. 62; Holzman, p. 60, also quotes a Polish source: "In a group of metal-working machines . . . 40 percent of all machines exported [by Poland] possess exactly the same characteristics as those we import and 87 percent of those we import have the same characteristics as our own . . . [yet] prices paid by Poland for imported metal-working machines are higher than those paid to her for exported machines of types which are similar in quality and technical performance. . . . Similarly, import prices paid by Poland for bearings are about 42 percent higher than the prices for Polish bearings on foreign markets." Rigid insistence by Moscow on "bilateralism" (that each bloc member must have a perfect balance of trade with each other member) prevents the more efficient ones from taking advantage of division of labor.

† Under the system "all CMEA trade had to be transacted through [the International Bank for Economic Cooperation (IBEC)] and the balances recorded there [paid for] in . . . so-called transferable (perevodnye) rubles. [These] rubles were called transferable because in theory a surplus of transferable rubles in trade with one CMEA nation could be used to pay off a deficit with another." However, even if a CMEA member accumulated a surplus of these rubles in the Bank it could not spend it on "unplanned imports from the other Soviet bloc nations." Holzman (1976), pp. 108–109.

‡ Spero (1981), p. 306, notes that "'Irrational' pricing in the East also makes inconvertibility necessary." Prices being planned, hence not related to market factors, cannot be allowed to rise and fall in response to fluctuating currency values. Certain products are subsidized, thus sell at low prices. "Convertibility would enable foreigners to purchase goods which are deliberately kept inexpensive and nationals [would purchase] abroad goods which are deliberately kept expensive."

against raw material exporters it offers relative stability: because world raw material prices fluctuate constantly, Soviet clients may lose occasionally but they will also gain.[5] In addition, if the ruble is assessed in terms of real world raw material prices it actually is undervalued, not overvalued, in terms of finished goods imported from CMEA partners, giving the latter a distinct advantage. Significantly that interpretation is shared by the CIA, not one of the Soviet Union's admirers.* On the other hand, indicative of a certain inconsistency in all outside assessments of Soviet cost accounting, the CIA estimated that Soviet subsidies to bloc countries amounted to roughly $70 billion between 1960 and 1982, 90 percent of which is traceable to oil exports to Eastern Europe at prices adjusted sharply upward in the wake of the 1974 explosion in world oil prices. In other words the Soviet Union was not prepared to forgive entirely the opportunity costs incurred by delivering oil to fraternal socialist trading partners at reduced prices, at a time when substantial profits could be made by selling high-priced oil to the enemies of the revolution.†

As the East-West arms competition heated up, the Soviet Union's defense burden and the CMEA partners' need for assistance mounted; Moscow was forced to relent and allow, perhaps even encourage, Eastern European countries to turn more frequently to the West for financial and other assistance. Simultaneously, Soviet assistance to and preferential treatment of CMEA partners experienced a decline. All of this of course contributed to the debt crisis discussed in the preceding chapter. It was during that period that Poland became the first Warsaw Pact nation to allow private monitoring of its economy by Western observers, to qualify for a $550 million loan from United States, British, and Canadian banks.[6]

The net effect of Soviet economic domination. Throughout its existence, the bloc has seen repeated internal uprisings, traceable in the main to popular dissatisfaction with Soviet domination and with the skewed distribution of wealth within the bloc. More immediately and directly, workers and farmers, led to expect much, now objected as both individual freedom and acceptable

---

* According to a CIA spokesman, "Eastern Europe's terms of trade vis-à-vis the Soviet Union are more advantageous than those that would prevail if Eastern Europe conducted that same trade with the non-Communist world." "In essence, the USSR sells energy, mainly oil, and other raw materials to Eastern Europe for less than world market prices and pays more than world market prices for manufactured goods it buys from Eastern Europe." CIA (December 1, 1982), p. 40.

† *Ibid.* Opportunity costs: the costs of not taking advantage of a profitable opportunity. Because it preferred to retain a degree of economic independence, Romania did not qualify for favorable economic treatment. But it was not subjected to unfavorable treatment either. For a different assessment of Soviet oil pricing policies, see Holzman (1976), pp. 100-103. He suggests that instead of driving for maximum gain, the Soviets "chose to trade off profits for popularity, economies for politics." For yet another assessment, by the conservative U.S. Heritage Foundation, see *ibid.* (February 17, 1981), p. 20. Among other points made in this study, it is noted that in 1979 "there was absolutely no Soviet economic assistance to Poland. The credits that had been offered through the Soviet bank in London (Moscow Narody) were never used by Poland, as their terms were worse than Poland could get at the Eurodollar market." See discussion of the Polish debt crisis, Chapter 12, p. 233.

living standards seemed to recede further from their grasp. The first major crisis occurred in 1956, in the wake of moderate relaxation of controls under Premier Khrushchev, a manifestation of the "de-Stalinization process" then under way in the Soviet Union. Disturbances broke out in East Germany, Poland, and Hungary; in the latter country, this resulted in the temporary replacement of the pro-Soviet regime with a Hungarian Communist alternative seeking independence from Moscow. Armed intervention by the Soviet Union brought this episode to an abrupt end. A decade or so later, Khrushchev's successors Brezhnev and Kosygin cautiously opened the door once more to reforms. When this led to yet another manifestation of nationalism within the bloc, the aforementioned Czechoslovak deviation, necessitating yet another invasion of a fraternal communist state by Soviet forces, Moscow decided to shift the responsibility for future suppressions of such revolts from itself to the entire bloc. The new concept was embodied in the first part of the now renowned Brezhnev doctrine:

> When the internal and external forces inimical to Socialism seek to influence the development of a Socialist country with the aim of restoring the capitalist system, when the threat to Socialism in this country becomes a threat to the security of the entire Socialist community, then this ceases to be a national problem. It becomes a general problem which must be a concern of all socialist countries.[7]

In effect, this statement informed all bloc members of the extent to which the Soviet Union was prepared to tolerate efforts by individual Communist regimes to accommodate national aspirations of their people, including economic openings to the West likely to compromise their ideological and bloc commitments.

In 1971, in response to persistent pressure from bloc members, the Brezhnev regime expanded the multilateral potential of the CMEA. The concrete result of that decision was the "Comprehensive Programme for the Further Extension and Improvement of Cooperation and the Development of Socialist Economic Integration."[8] The net effect was minimal. CMEA remained essentially "a form for the management of a series of bilateral trading agreements between the member states."[9] Slow growth and spiraling foreign debts intensified general disillusionment with the entire bloc concept. When Moscow moved the price of oil delivered to CMEA partners steadily closer to the OPEC price and reduced subsidies and credits, only the most stalwart ideologues, Communist party bureaucrats, and other beneficiaries of continued Soviet dominance remained completely loyal. It was in that setting that the Polish "solidarnøst" crisis erupted in November of 1980.*

---

* Solidarnøst was the name of the nationwide labor union, with emphatically Polish religio-nationalist orientation, which briefly challenged communist rule with cautious support from the Catholic Church, headed by a Polish Pope. In 1984, faced with rising oil-production costs and stagnating output, the Soviet Union began to cut back on subsidized oil deliveries to bloc members, risking yet another wave of disaffection among its allies.

On balance, the political economy of the Soviet bloc is most profoundly affected by the following factors: (1) The capitalist-socialist confrontation causes Communist party leaders and support cadres to fear for their political survival if too wide an opening is permitted to the West. A key element is consumer satisfaction; by their manifest willingness to flee Communist rule, vast numbers have demonstrated a preference for capitalist ways. (2) The Soviet Union continues to regard the military strategic security of bloc borders with the West a matter of highest Soviet national priority. For that reason Moscow will insist on retaining ultimate control over all bloc economies. (3) Favoring the Soviet position and thus countering the centrifugal tendencies of individual bloc members is the realization, still widespread throughout Eastern Europe, that, all of the disadvantages associated with Soviet domination notwithstanding, only Soviet military power can prevent a recurrence of the traumatic experience of World War Two when much of Eastern Europe was devasted by the German invasion and occupation. (4) The time when brute military power can be applied in Eastern Europe may have passed. (5) If conflicts within the bloc are to be reduced, integration of the bloc must proceed on mutually advantageous terms. To that end, (6) given the severe limitations of Soviet economic capacity, especially as long as that economy is strained by spiraling defense outlays, East-West trade and financial deals will increasingly be relied upon to overcome bloc deficiencies.

Trading with the Class Enemy: The View from Moscow

Theory

The official Soviet view regarding the world economy adheres rigidly to theories expounded by Marx, Engels, and Lenin. The position is that twentieth-century international relations generally and economic relations in particular are conducted in the shadow of capitalism's final effort to escape its fate. In its final throes capitalism poses a mortal danger to world peace. This places special responsibilities upon "the fatherland of socialism," the Soviet Union. Among other measures the Soviet Union a) must carefully insulate its own economy and that of its allies from the capitalist world economic system to defend against capitalist manipulation and encroachment, b) arm itself with the economic means to aid the victims of imperialist aggression and exploitation, c) exploit every opportunity to weaken capitalism, thereby hastening its demise. Capitalism's drive for profits provides one such opportunity; its sensitivity to monetary fluctuations provides another, at least in theory. It was with that in mind that Lenin advised his followers "the capitalists will sell you the rope with which to hang them," and the most effective way to bring them to their knees is "to debauch their currency" (undermine their currencies' exchange value).[10]

Communist leaders accept that their side still does not begin to match the combined economic power of the capitalist countries. But the socialist camp enjoys some advantages which skillful diplomacy and trade strategy can convert into effective bargaining chips in preparation for the ultimate showdown. For example, whether or not the capitalist countries are on the gold standard, that precious metal continues to be a keystone in the capitalist world economy and the Soviet Union is the world's second largest producer of gold. Beyond that, the Soviet Union's self-sufficiency in energy sources is expected to last well into the twenty-first century and its reserves in mineral resources required for industrial and military purposes in some cases match those of the capitalist countries, exceeding them in others.* (See Table 13-1.)

Considerable advantage in economic respects accrues to the socialist camp as a result of the capitalist world's high vulnerability to penetration by foreign agents, their actual production statistics and their industrial, technological, and commercial secrets wide open to espionage and theft.† On the other hand, because socialist economies are major weapons in the anticapitalist struggle, information regarding them is as tightly protected as are the socialist camp's military secrets. This is relatively easy as under socialism the means of pro-

Table 13-1. USSR: Estimated Reserves of Selected Fuels and Nonfuel Minerals[a]

	Size of Reserves	Share of World Reserves (Percent)	Years to Exhaustion (At 1980 Production)
Gas	30 trillion m³[b]	40	65
Coal	165.5 billion tons	27	230
Iron ore	63.3 billion tons	40	250
Manganese	2.5 billion tons	40	250
Chromite	271.2 million tons[c]	10[c]	80[c]
Copper	40.0 million tons	7	28
Nickel	11.3 million tons	18	48
Cobalt	100 million tons	n.a.	17
Lead	17 million tons	11	28
Zinc	22 million tons	10	24
Gold	200 million troy ounces	35	20
Platinum-group metals	90 million troy ounces	25	25
Tungsten	215 thousand tons	11	24

SOURCE: CIA, Rowen (December 1, 1982), Table 1.
[a] Corresponding to Western concepts of proven and probable reserves, exploitable at current prices with existing technology.
[b] Cubic meters.
[c] Other estimates are considerably lower; cf. Table 16-4 (this text).

* According to the CIA (December 1, 1982), p. 7, "the ability of the Soviet economy to remain viable in the absence of imports is much greater than that of most, possibly all other industrial economies." See also Fig. 16-3 below.

† In communist thought, theft of capitalist property, including secrets, is morally justifiable "expropriation" of ill-gotten gains.

duction are state-owned and the economy is planned and controlled by the central government, hence the resources and power of the secret political police are available to enforce that policy in economic as in military respects.* Soviet leaders generally seem to find it exceedingly difficult to shed the instinctive revolutionary conviction that counterrevolutionary influences inevitably accompany trade with the class enemy, a position not entirely unreasonable, incidentally, in light of their own as well as the Western practice of utilizing trade representatives for purposes of espionage. In terms of economic management, as one writer put it, "probably the major factor behind [Soviet] trade aversion is the desire of . . . central planners to minimize disturbances to their 'commodity' balance. They view foreign trade as inherently risky and are unwilling to depend on foreign sources of supply which are outside their direct control. . . ."[11] That position seemed borne out when the U.S., in retaliation for the invasion of Afghanistan and in response to Soviet military pressure on Poland, imposed an embargo on grain shipments to the Soviet Union. Trade aversion, it emerged then, had proved to be a viable defense against U.S. efforts to extract foreign policy concessions from the Soviet Union by means of export restrictions.†

Although opportunities to play capitalist countries against each other have increased in recent years, Soviet strategists accept that a degree of harmony continues to prevail among the capitalist ruling classes, enabling them to coordinate their aggressive plans and prolong the life of the world capitalist system. The primary agent making that possible is the United States, socialism's principal and most dangerous antagonist. Strange as it may seem, it appears that Moscow's leaders are genuinely surprised to find that this antagonism is mutual.

Although of dubious authenticity, the above cited comment by Lenin about capitalist—or imperialists—being so hungry for profits that they will sell Moscow the rope with which to hang them continues to arouse suspicion in Western

---

* In addition to the ability to maintain high levels of secrecy, thus gain an edge in bargaining and negotiation, the Soviet Union's political stability is an asset which no Western state can match. It has after all been governed by only one political party, the CPSU; leaving aside brief inter-regnums it has had only five effective heads of government between 1917 and 1985 (Lenin, Stalin, Khrushchev, Brezhnev, and Gorbachev. Brezhnev's successor, Andropov started out energetically but soon died and his successor, Chernenko soon passed away as well.)

† A contrary view was expressed in a U.S. Commerce Department (Census Bureau) study which found that "the long-held notion that Soviet foreign trade is unusually small for an industrial nation should be discarded. Foreign trade has clearly played an increasingly significant role in the Soviet economy." *The New York Times* (July 13, 1982). This was promptly challenged by critics who accepted the statistics but questioned the interpretation. *The New York Times* (July 15, 1982). On Soviet trade dependency, see *Business America*, Vol. 5, 15 (July 26, 1982) p. 22, which reports that Soviet imports increased from 8 percent of national income in 1960 to 20 percent in 1980; exports increased from 3.5 to 7 percent over the same period.

trading circles who fear that this is precisely what Moscow has in mind.* To which Soviet leaders retort that all capitalists in truth hope that their trade and financial deals with socialist regimes will enable them by one means or another to reduce the revolutionary threat to their existence. They can, of course, find support for that contention in Western official pronouncements as well as acts of omission and of commission. In any case, in recent years—in the wake of de-Stalinization and proclamations of peaceful coexistence and peaceful competition—the tone has been constructive and conciliatory. Now the official line is that "the development of trade between socialist and capitalist countries is an integral part of world politics, the general situation, and scientific and technical progress."[12] Put differently, it now seems to be the Soviet position that global economic interdependence has progressed to a point where traditional Soviet aversion to foreign trade may have to be modified further.

Practice

Indications are that in its secret deliberations the Soviet Politburo is fully aware that behind the brave rhetoric of socialism's ultimate victory over capitalism is a far less encouraging reality. While oil reserves, for example, appear to be adequate for the time being, demand anticipated from Soviet as well as client state industries is likely to exceed supply unless drilling can be stepped up significantly.[13] That requires access to Western, primarily United States and Japanese, technology, now a prime target for Soviet overt and covert procurement efforts. But until shortages materialize Soviet export policy in the energy field continues to be quite aggressive.

At this point, the estimate is that "the Soviet Union has about 40 percent of the world's proven [oil] reserves . . . the 30 trillion cubic meters under Soviet control exceed[ing] the reserves of all industrial nations combined."[14] While the world price of oil was relatively low, Soviet sales opportunities were few, except of course within the bloc. It would appear that it was to improve their position that Moscow counseled several OPEC states to assert their independence from the West and sharply increase the price of oil.[15] When they followed that advice, the Soviet Union benefited considerably, especially when the price increase was accompanied by a boycott of certain industrial states. Promptly, Soviet oil sales were directed to fill the storage tanks left empty by

---

* According to one source, the following passage was copied from Lenin's papers:

The capitalists of the whole world and their governments in their rush to conquer the Soviet market will close their eyes to [various diplomatic subterfuges by the Soviet government] and will thereby be turned into blind deaf mutes. They will furnish the credits which will serve us for the support of the Communist Party in their countries and, by supplying us material and technical equipment which we lack, will restore our military industry necessary for future attacks against our suppliers. To put it in other words, they will work on the preparation of their own suicide.

Letter to New York, Senator Daniel P. Moynihan (Washington, D.C., December 26, 1981). See Bretton (1980), p. 267.

that boycott. In some instances Moscow even resold oil it has received from Arab countries in return for military supplies and diplomatic support. It sold that oil below the level set by OPEC. In part, this drive to take advantage of an opportunity was made possible by shifting sales from CMEA customers to the West, the former being advised to go to the world market to make up their energy deficits.[16]

If oil embargoes, crises in the Persian Gulf, or other conditions producing shortfalls in the West fail to present Moscow with trade opportunities, its ample gold stock will. Ironically the crises over Afghanistan and Poland brought Moscow a veritable windfall as the tension-laden atmosphere caused a sharp rise in the price of gold and other precious metals. In other words, while the United States and its allies frantically cast about for ways and means to discipline the errant Soviet government for its invasion in one case and a threatened invasion in the other, the Soviet Union calmly took advantage of the opportunity to increase its foreign exchange holdings.*

Lenin's prediction that capitalists will compete for the privilege of selling their class enemies the means of their own destruction has not been borne out entirely in the sphere of strategic materials and technology transfer. Here capitalism's ardor for profit has not prevented the Western allies from imposing and enforcing some restrictions on the flow of strategic materials and sensitive technology. In response the Soviet Union, fully mobilizing its secret service embarked upon an intensive drive to obtain by stealth and deception what could not be obtained in open trade.†

Coming to Terms with the Class Enemy

Beginning with Lenin, Soviet leaders have quietly come to accept in practice what they once swore they would not tolerate. While Communist dogma serves as a useful guide to an indistinct future, it does not all serve well as a manual for management of a modern economy. Accordingly the Politburo has for some time now conceded that regardless of the motivations which capitalists may

* Although no hard evidence is available to support the contention, international financial circles have long been convinced that the Soviet Union and the Republic of South Africa, which together account for more than 75 percent of world gold production, are in collusion to keep up the price. See, for example, Marsh and Simon (1981). Soviet-South Africa cooperation also has for decades extended to control of the price and supply of diamonds, Epstein (1982), pp. 17-19, 38 and *ibid* Chapter 17, which suggests that East-West cooperation regarding the world diamond market may be coming to an end.

† By 1985 more than 100 Soviet and East European diplomats and agents had been deported from a number of Western countries, charged with unlawfully seeking to acquire sensitive technological information..

The drive to secure Western secrets was first signalled, rather innocuously, under the heading "new economic relations," in a paper entitled "Just Democratic Peace. For Security of Nations and International Cooperation," Moscow, 1973, cited in Kostyukhin (1979), pp. 137-138; see also Jacobson (1982) and Kempe, "Keeping Technology out of Soviet Hands. . . . *Wall Street Journal* (July 24, 1984)

Box 13-1. Countertrade

If trade between East and West has increased in recent years, this can be attributed in part to several forms of countertrade or compensation East bloc countries insist on as a *quid pro quo* for imports from the West. The main forms of that kind of trade are as follows:

Commercial Compensation. In return for imports from the West, East bloc nations demand compensation in the form of goods imported in return by Western exporters. This is accomplished in several ways:

Barter: Goods are exchanged directly, without transfer of funds.

Counterpurchase: By separate contracts or agreements, sales of Western goods to the East are balanced by sales of East bloc goods to the West.

Pre-compensation: The purchase of East bloc goods precedes the sale of Western goods to the bloc.

Industrial Compensation: East bloc goods are purchased by Western exporters corresponding to East bloc sales by the West of machinery, other industrial equipment, or "turnkey" factories. This takes several forms:

Buy-back Agreements: Exporters of machinery, equipment or factories contract to import from the bloc recipient, goods up to the value of goods delivered, either goods produced by that machinery, equipment or plant, or goods less directly related to the export in question.

Framework Agreements: Goods are exchanged for exports "the nature, timing, and value of which are determined by special renewable agreements."

Source: *OECD Observer* No. 114 (January 1982), p. 13.

bring to that task, if socialism is to be made to work in the Soviet Union and its client states, the financial and technical resources of capitalism as well as many of its methods may be indispensable. If reproached by die-hard ideologues in their midst, the reformers can always quote Lenin, who classified concessions to capitalism as "war on a new plane." They can of course also point to a consistent and successful strategy of never granting capitalism an opportunity to establish imperialist footholds on Soviet soil.

Whatever deals Western capitalists were offered, the Soviet government never relinquished control. Proceeding with extraordinary caution—some negotiations extended over several years—amidst characteristic secrecy, in the end both sides benefited. The Soviet side secured credits, technical know-how, processed or manufactured goods, or a public project ready to operate; the other side had its profits and trade, keeping its factories going. A favored instrument has been the joint-stock company or the turn-key project—a Western firm builds or assists in building a plant, turns over the keys to Soviet managers, and departs;

neither the ownership nor the control of the means of production and distribution of Soviet wealth are compromised in the process.*

While it is conceivable that Soviet utilization of capitalist know-how and channels may indeed be another form of warfare against the enemies of the revolution, it is more likely simply a manifestation of opportunism, a quality actually highly admired in capitalist circles.† Given the historic record of capitalism and imperialism, it is difficult to fault Soviet leaders when they are caught in acts of deviousness or in commercial maneuvers vis-à-vis capitalist negotiating partners. In any case the albatross of Communist orthodoxy coupled with the administrative impediments built into centrally planned and controlled economies, the lethargic tradition-bound if not archaic party bureaucracy, and the general stifling atmosphere generated by all forms of totalitarian rule tend to diminish the benefits from any successes Moscow may be able to score in the realm of foreign trade or finance.‡

Trading with the Class Enemy: The View from Soviet Client States

The perspective from the capitals of Soviet client states differs in one fundamental respect: none are self-sufficient and all, should their principal backer and supplier renege on its commitments, would have to engage in compensatory trade with the West. Furthermore some of the client states do not share Moscow's apprehensions regarding the intentions of the West as far as trade and finance are concerned. Consequently, following the Yugoslav example—and noting that this did not lead to the overthrow of Communist rule there—Poland, Romania, and Hungary have permitted "foreign equity participation" or "co-production agreements" in certain ventures.# The East German Democratic Republic, leaning on the Soviet Union more than all the

---

* The tendency to protract negotiations, especially when purchases of manufactured goods from the West are the object, coupled with insistence by Soviet negotiators on extraordinarily long and detailed lists of specifications they must see before placing an order, has given rise to suspicions that often they may be more interested in copying a product than buying it. Western businessmen also note that if they turn down an order they may have to wait years before they are given another chance. Soviet negotiators are said to have long memories.

† A manifestation of a form of kinship among executives of large-scale enterprises may be the special treatment accorded certain leading capitalists by individual Communist leaders. See, for example, Edward J. Epstein, "The Riddle of Armand Hammer," *The New York Times Magazine* (November 29, 1981), pp. 69ff or Jeff Gerth, "U.S. Entrepreneur's Soviet Ties," *The New York Times* (October 5, 1979).

‡ Robert G. Kaiser, (1976), p. 509, argues that the "Soviet economy does not support the hypothesis that after buying foreign technology for a transition period, [the Soviet Union] will suddenly blossom with new technological capacity of its own. On the contrary, foreign purchases allow the Russians to avoid confronting the structural reasons for their technological inferiority, and thus ensure that the inferiority will last." See also Pisar (1970), pp. 34–36.

For example, in the Romanian case Control Data Corporation invested $1.8 million worth of technology and equipment, receiving in return 45 percent interest in a $4 million Romanian enterprise producing and selling computer equipment.

others, follows Moscow's prescription closely and so does Bulgaria. Czechoslovakia, mindful of the 1968 Warsaw Pact lesson in bloc solidarity, is equally cautious. But none of the client regimes permit their readiness to do business with the class enemy to obscure their revolutionary vision or flagrantly provoke the big fraternal power to the East.

Should any of Moscow's client states try to stretch the leash—and attempts are made continuously—Moscow cannot really complain. If it is unwilling or unable to live up to its fraternal obligations, help its partners to pay their bills for instance, or service their debts—which, as we noted earlier have now reached staggering proportions in the case of Poland—Moscow cannot also insist that their clients reject the only remaining source of rescue, the West. After all the Warsaw Pact and CMEA are mutual assistance agreements: in return for assured security of its frontiers, Moscow assumed the obligation to provide criticial raw materials in sufficient quantities and at reasonable prices to render the fraternal Communist regimes at least as politically secure as the Soviet regime itself. To an extent, doubts along these lines contributed to turmoil in Poland in the late 1970s and in the 1980s causing mounting restiveness and tensions within the bloc generally.

Poland: Between Two Worlds

Poland may turn out to be the fulcrum of Moscow's economic diplomacy toward its client states and toward the West and of the West's economic policies vis-à-vis the Soviet bloc and through the bloc vis-à-vis Moscow. Among the client states Poland is the most important. Militarily, in the event of war in Central Europe it lies astride the Warsaw Pact's main line of communication to the front. Its armed forces are the second largest in the Warsaw Pact. Should Poland become politically unreliable, Warsaw Pact strategy based on deployment of ground forces in Central Europe at levels superior to those available to NATO in the West would be jeopardized if not entirely negated. No amount of pressure could persuade fiercely nationalistic Poles to fight if they are convinced that their country is exploited by the Soviet Union. Of some consequence in that connection is the fact that Poland, next to the Soviet Union the bloc's most populous country, is 95 percent Roman Catholic.

The opening to the West, created when economic shortfalls in several bloc countries compelled their governments to turn to Western bankers, eventually became far wider than Moscow could possibly have anticipated when the first requests for permission to turn to the West were submitted to the Kremlin. First Romania, then Hungary, both following the Yugoslav example, and then Poland opened to Western bankers financial records which had never before been made public let alone made accessible to the class enemy. Indeed prior to that step prison if not worse awaited any Polish citizen communicating mere fragments of such information to Westerners. By 1979 Poland's principal financial institutions reorganized themselves, made changes in top staff positions, and opened their records to Western bankers to qualify for IMF loans. In addition, the Polish government had to agree to changes in its import policies, currency valuation, and pricing policies, and to a reduction in subsidies, all in the face of mounting popular unrest over shortages and oppressive laws and regulations.

Ironically, when at the height of the debt crisis, in response to what Moscow perceived to be counterrevolutionary reformist activities—centering on a burgeoning independent labor union and the Catholic Church—Soviet armed forces commenced threatening maneuvers in and near Poland, Western bankers were not certain where their interests lay. Without Soviet military intervention in Poland that creditor could conceivably become totally insolvent, triggering a sharp deterioration of an already grave international financial situation. On the other hand, if the Soviet Union intervened it would eventually have to assume full responsibility for Poland's debt and Poland's creditors could hope to be eventually repaid.

The View From Beijing

Sino-Soviet Relations

The People's Republic of China occupies a unique position. It clearly is one of the more important components of the socialist world. But unlike the Soviet Union and most of its client states it also is a major constituent of the Third World. Yet it seems to be in a category all of its own. Manifestly, the PRC's geostrategic position vis-à-vis the Soviet Union differs in fundamental respects from that of most other socialist states. For one, the Soviet Union is only partially an Asiatic country. China is wholly so, which provides one of the sources of tension between the two colossi.

States like the DDR, Poland, or Czechoslovakia are of the utmost military-strategic importance to the Soviet Union. Perhaps during the Korean war, when U.S. troops fought in the immediate vicinity of the Soviet Union's Far Eastern region, some Soviet strategists, perhaps Stalin himself, saw in the PRC an ally against an American threat. This is doubtful though. More likely Moscow regarded the PRC, with its inexhaustible manpower supply, as a surrogate to tie American armed forces down in protracted struggle far from home, a tactic which was repeated soon thereafter, but without the PRC, in Vietnam.

China also differs from the Soviet Union's East European partners in that Soviet troops never attempted, let alone secured, a foothold in its vast reaches. Instead at least one million Soviet troops are believed to be deployed to guard the 5000 mile border with the PRC. Finally, not only does the PRC regard itself as part of the less developed world but it identifies itself as a victim of imperialist-colonialist exploitation, for which Beijing's leaders blame the neighbor to the North as much as they do Great Britain, Germany, France and the United States.

While insisting on their right to develop their own approach to communism, today's Chinese leaders, notwithstanding their willingness to experiment with modified forms of capitalism, manifest a degree of solidarity with the world's socialist front against Western capitalism. It is in that context, and that alone, that Beijing and Moscow are seen as sharing certain interests.[17] Also, the PRC's political system follows to an extent the Soviet model.[18] But if a full and lasting alliance is to be achieved between these two giants (at this point the PRC would be the weaker partner by far) a number of issues separating them will have to be resolved, or progress made toward their resolution. Foremost is the question of territories covering several hundred thousand square miles which China claims Czarist Russia seized illegally.* Also rankling is "the loss" to China of the nominally independent Republic of Outer Mongolia, now used by the Soviet Union to pose a direct military threat to the PRC's northern region, China's industrial heartland and an area where ethnic minorities continue to manifest centrifugal tendencies. According to the Chinese view of history, the territorial losses and other indignities, including extensive economic "concessions," were inflicted upon a defenseless country in a series of "unequal treaties" between the 1840s and the 1880s. Outer Mongolia was lost through "legalistic legerdemain" perpetrated by the Soviet Union at a time when China had not yet recovered from the ravages of World War Two, four years prior to the establishment of the People's Republic in 1949.[19]

Economically the PRC owes a great deal to the Soviet Union. Moscow provided generous assistance almost from the moment the Communist forces defeated the Nationalists in 1949. From 1950, when the Treaty of Friendship, Alliance, and Mutual Assistance was signed between the two countries, until the break in 1956, the Soviet Union aided China with substantial credits, initially about $300 million, with technical assistance in the development of petroleum and nonferrous metals, in the development of Chinese aviation, and in the form of numerous trade benefits.

For present purposes, it does not matter what triggered the break.† It may have been a quarrel between Stalin and Mao over leadership of the world socialist camp.[20] Or it may have been Moscow's reneging on an agreement to transfer to the PRC nuclear technology, thus enabling the Chinese to join the "nuclear club." Or the break occurred over Soviet Premier Khrushchev's attempt to steer the Soviet Union away from Stalinism, a development Mao Zedong may have perceived as a threat to his own position.[21] Whatever the root cause, the two countries drifted apart when Khrushchev began to withdraw promised economic support, renege on other treaty commitments, and generally provide Beijing with ample grounds to charge that Moscow now practices "superpower hegemonism," meaning arbitrary and arrogant application of superior economic

---

* Luttwak (1983), p. 91, notes that PRC claims on Soviet territory are not firmly pressed because Beijing finds it difficult to assert "claims of an imperial dynasty that was Manchu and not ethnically Chinese, over lands never seriously settled by the Chinese people."

† Mark N. Katz (1982), pp. 14–15, traces the bitterness separating the two powers to Stalin's decision in the 1920s ordering the Chinese Communist Party to support the Nationalist Kuomintang, who eventually turned against them.

and military power to serve its own interests at the expense of other socialist states.[22]

Moscow responded with an identical complaint: The PRC was guilty of anti-Soviet conduct by splitting the socialist front in pursuit of its own hegemonistic ambitions.[23] But Moscow's economic warfare was to no avail. Instead of following the East European example and surrender, the PRC decided to strike out on its own. It opened its borders to the West, developed diplomatic and economic ties with Moscow's East European client states, and embarked upon a campaign to identify itself more emphatically with the Third World, intent on replacing the Soviet Union as the champion of the world's poor and oppressed. Prospects for a rapprochement between the two receded in the early 1980s when discussions failed to resolve four outstanding issues: Soviet intervention in Afghanistan, Soviet support of the Vietnamese occupation of Kampuchea, continued massing of Soviet armed forces along the Sino–Soviet frontier, and continued Soviet domination of and military presence in the Mongolian People's Republic. Afghanistan was a sensitive issue as Soviet occupation of that country would extend the Soviet military threat to yet another region, China's Far West, another area where the PRC is experiencing problems with ethnic minorities. Soviet support of military operation in Kampuchea was viewed as a provocation as it was directed against a pro-PRC regime and occurred in an area China's rulers have traditionally regarded as within their sphere of interest.[24] Finally, radical reforms of the PRC's economic structure, adopted by the Central Committee of the Communist Party of China in 1984, featuring, among other revolutionary innovations, economic decentralization, financial incentives to efficient agricultural and industrial enterprises, and a nod toward free market economics, in effect constituted a shift away from if not an outright rejection of Soviet-style Marxist/Leninist economic theory and practice.*

Antihegemonism Extended

Until China emerges from its LDC status, it cannot expect to influence how or by whom the world economy will be managed. Even its capacity to exert political or economic influence within the socialist camp is severely limited. As noted, identification of the PRC with the Third World is high on Beijing's agenda. But that does not take China very far, given the marginal power position of all Third World countries combined. If Soviet "hegemonism" directed at the PRC is to be contained, the Third World can be of some use but more potent support will have to be secured in the more advanced world as well.

Indications are that from Beijing's perspective the utility of the United States lies mainly in its value as a counterfoil to the Soviet threat and as a source of finance capital and technology. This is true also of Western Europe and Japan, of some of Moscow's East European client states, and of North Korea,

* *The New York Times* (October 21, 1984); see also Wang Dacheng "Reforming the Foreign Trade Structure," *Beijing Review* Vol. 27, 43 (October 22, 1984), pp. 4–5

Romania, and Yugoslavia, socialist states who have manifested a degree of independence from Moscow. In general Beijing prefers a multipolar world to a bipolar one, because in a bipolar setting the Soviet Union is accorded the elevated status of a superpower along with the United States.* In a more decentralized multipolar international power constellation, the two superpowers along with their political dependencies would be regarded as the equals of Western Europe, Central and Southeast Asia, the grouping of free and non-aligned socialist and other non-Western states, the Third World or "the South."[25] For that reason, Beijing's trade policies can be expected in years to come to aim at making some of Moscow's client states more independent.

There is of course always the possibility that the two socialist powers are once again driven into a close partnership. This can occur as a result of serious foreign policy errors on the part of the United States, over the highly sensitive issue of Taiwan for instance, coupled with a more sensitive and more astute conciliatory posture on Moscow's part. Indicative that no change is imminent may be the fact that PRC–U.S. trade was expected to total about $6 billion in 1983 compared with an estimated $815 million between the PRC and the Soviet Union, though up from $300 million the year before, and another $818 million for the rest of the Soviet bloc.[26]

We referred earlier to Communist China's trade with the West through Hong Kong and, less visibly, through Hong Kong with Taiwan and South Korea. Here we want to review briefly the PRC's attempt to extend its brand of socialism to China's traditional sphere of interest, Southeast Asia. As soon as they had consolidated their power over the Chinese Mainland and until the end of the Cultural Revolution in 1977, China's Communist rulers had targeted specifically the five states then joined in the Association of Southeast Asian Nations (ASEAN), Indonesia, Malaysia, Philippines, Singapore, and Thailand.† The attempt was made partly through the "Overseas Chinese," emigrants from the Mainland now residing in these states, partly through indigenous Communist parties. The reconstruction necessitated by the Cultural Revolution, the requirements of the modernization drive initiated by the post-Maoist leadership in the wake of that disaster, and the continuing Soviet threat, now from three directions, caused Beijing to downgrade any revolutionary designs on Southeast and East Asia. The need to establish closer ties with Japan, the rapprochement with the United States, and generally the need for foreign capital, technology, and markets had much to do with that and similar decisions. When the modernization drive extended to decentralization of the economy, experiments with market economics and with limited forms of capitalism, the PRC's position in the region assumed an entirely different coloring.

An additional spur to moderation of Communist revolutionary ardor was Beijing's desire to achieve the return of Hong Kong and Taiwan by peaceful

---

* Machetzki (1981), p. 73, mentions "China's lasting interest in a European community 'strengthening itself through unity and common resistance to hegemony.'"

† Since then Brunei has become the sixth member.

means. Accordingly, in anticipation of the expiration of Britain's lease covering parts of the Hong Kong colony in 1997 and in the hope that this would reassure the people of Hong Kong as well as of Taiwan of the PRC's intentions, Beijing, in 1984, signed an agreement with Great Britain guaranteeing Hong Kong virtual autonomy after 1997 in all respects except foreign affairs and defense. Following the return of the colony to Mainland China it was to be designated a Special Administrative Region within the PRC with autonomy in such matters as international trade and finance, internal monetary and fiscal policies, free to pursue its capitalist ways from within the communist system.* The people of Hong Kong and Great Britain kept their fingers crossed. One fact, of course, tended to work in Hong Kong's favor: 3 percent of the PRC's foreign trade passed through the colony and it was unlikely that the PRC would soon be able to dispense with that facility.

Suggested Questions and Discussion Topics

What reinforces economic cohesion within the Soviet bloc? What acts as a divisive influence?

What arguments can Moscow offer in defense of its approach to intrabloc economic relations?

With respect to international *trade and finance* between East and West, discuss the difference between Marxist/Leninist theory and practice, and the rationale for the latter. In particular, regarding Moscow's approach to East-West *trade*, what are the major incentives, what are the major disincentives?

How does Beijing view Sino-Soviet relations politically and economically?

---

* "Sino-British Joint Declaration On the Question of Hong Kong," *Beijing Review*, Vol. 27, 40 (October 1, 1984), pp. I-XX.

Chapter 14
Closing the Viability Gap:
The Problem and Proposed Solutions

The issue here is a gap separating a few dozen of the world's rich and industrially advanced nations (developed countries or DCs) from well over a hundred whose economies range from poverty to seemingly permanent pauper status (less-developed countries or LDCs). The two groups or categories are commonly classified as developed and less-developed, and for purposes of identification we have used those terms. But within the developed–less-developed continuum, the question of economic viability appears to be most critical.

The Condition of Nonviability

Opinions differ on the root causes of the gap, although there appears to be universal agreement that imperialism and colonialism bear a heavy responsibility. It is partly for that reason that the issue has itself become an object in the East–West struggle. Another reason of course centers on the raw material riches currently being extracted from the less developed world or awaiting discovery and exploitation in the future.

Basically, viability is defined as a state's "ability to live, grow, and develop." Among indices of that ability some are more informative than others, depending largely on prevailing circumstances. Of foremost importance are GNP or GDP, total and per capita, per capita income, and foreign exchange reserves. One of the hallmarks of nonviability is excessive dependence on imports of essential goods and services including food. Another is inability to save a sufficient portion of the national product to finance initially unprofitable and costly projects essential for future growth and development.

At the time the typical LDC attains political independence, and for decades thereafter, the means to pay for needed imports are derived mainly if not exclusively from export to markets in the developed world. Typically, this centers on one or two commodities, usually agricultural products or minerals. In a few cases this yields sufficient hard currency to cover most essential imports. In most cases, however, earnings are insufficient, obliging the government to borrow from abroad. Of critical importance therefore is the purchasing power on world markets of the principal exports in terms of such essentials as energy, loan capital including interest, and manufactured as well as processed goods and commodities needed to maintain requisite export levels—fertilizer for example or agricultural machinery and implements. All this and more contribute to a country's rate of growth, another index of viability, or the capacity to make ends and means meet. If existing production facilities, especially food production, are to be modernized and industrialization is to be attempted, both being prerequisites of growth, the need for loan capital from abroad increases commensurately. It goes without saying that in addition export earnings must cover the costs of government and administration as the typical LDC economy is too weak to support even these sectors. These costs are disproportionately high in most LDCs.

The following illustrations depict the nature and extent of the viability gap.

Table 14-1. Profile of DC–LDC Economic Positions (Percent of World Total)

Population		GNP	
LDCs	DCs	LDCs	DCs
76%	24%	20%	80%
Low-Income LDCs 46%		Low-Income LDCs 4%	

GNP per capita: Ratio LDC to DC

1950	1980
1:23	1:39

SOURCE: *China and the World* Vol. 1, p. 25.

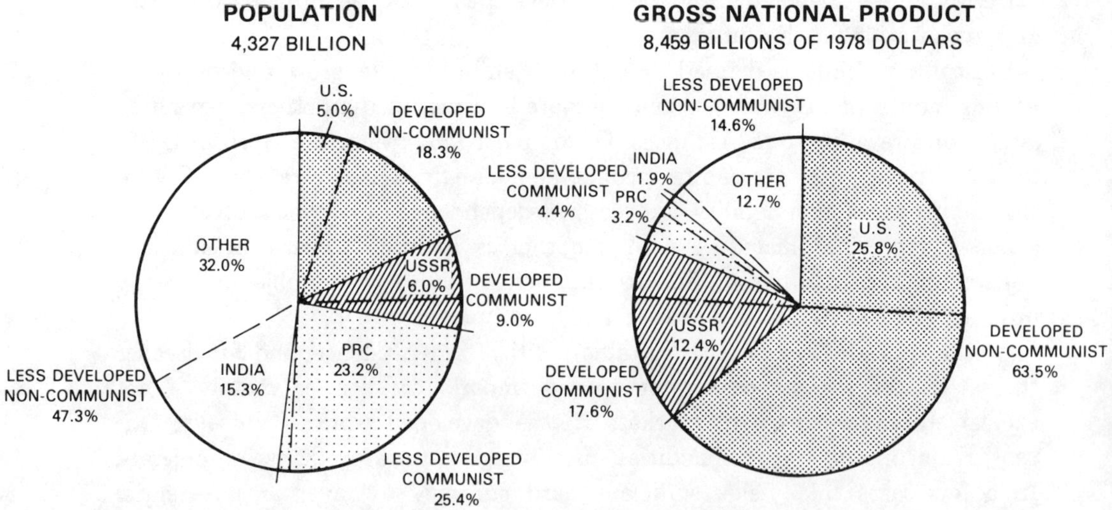

Fig. 14-1. World Population and World Output. (U.S. Department of State. *The Planetary Product.* Special Report No. 58 (1979), Chart II, p. 45.)

Whether requisite measures will be taken to narrow the gap depends to a considerable extent on the outcome of what commonly is called the North–South Dialogue. We shall address that topic shortly. But first a brief review is in order of the more representative perspectives and prescriptions which the principal parties bring to that dialogue, for it is from these perspectives that explanations evolve of how the condition arose in the first place, who or what should be held responsible, and what should be done to remedy the situation.

Total personnel (1980) = 3,756,100

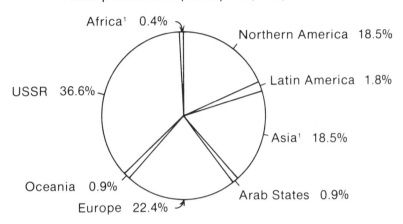

Total expenditure (1980) = U.S. $207,801 million

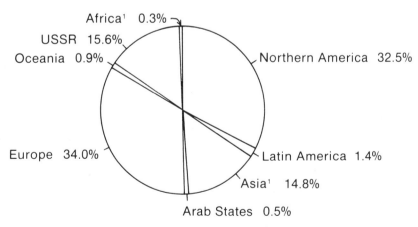

[1] Excluding Arab states

Fig. 14-2a. Research and Development: Personnel and Expenditure (1980). (From the *UNESCO Statistical Yearbook 1983*, p. V-20. © Unesco, 1983. Reproduced by permission of Unesco.)

Prescriptions, Perceptions, and Explanations

Recommendations on how to resolve the problems and dilemmas confronting the LDCs fall into several major categories: those reflecting the vital interests of the developed countries, those emanating from the LDCs, and proposals advanced by international bodies. Within these broader categories, sharp differences of opinion have arisen between capitalists and socialists, and within each of these among moderates, radicals, progressives, and traditionalists. At

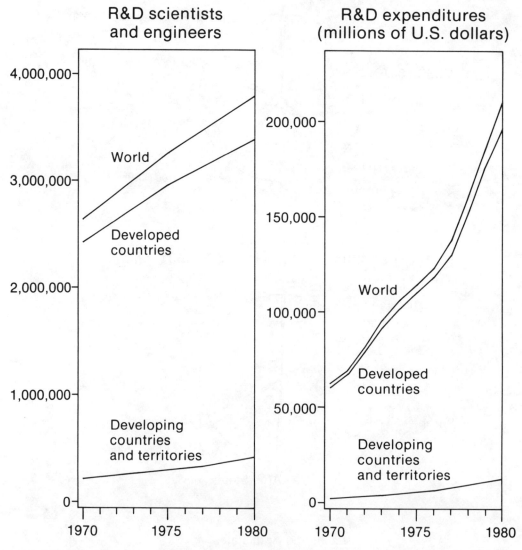

Fig. 14-2b. Research and Development: World Trends (1970–1980). (From the *UNESCO Statistical Yearbook 1983*, p. V-19. © Unesco, 1983. Reproduced by permission of Unesco.)

one extreme are advocates of unrestricted capitalist entrepreneurial initiative who brook no compromise, least of all with socialists or communists. At the opposite end of that spectrum are the radical proponents of social revolution who brook no delay and likewise accept no compromise. In the latter's view the lot of the world's poor will not improve until all vestiges of feudalism, colonialism, and capitalism have been removed from the underdeveloped world and all social and economic structures inherited from colonial days torn down and replaced by a new revolutionary order, by force if necessary. Within the LDCs progressives and traditionalists vie for power, the former eager to borrow, assimilate, and adapt whatever can be introduced from abroad to spur growth and development, the latter entertaining serious doubt whether growth and development are unmitigated blessings.* Few of these extreme positions are likely to be adopted except in theoretical formulations and in propaganda but a number of the more practical capitalist and socialist prescriptions are worth a closer examination.

The View from the North

The capitalist and "liberal" prescriptions: Capitalists, principally industrial and commercial interests or their supporters or representatives in government, are inclined toward pragmatism, cost effectiveness, and profit. Northern "liberals" take a broader view but are less representative of the power structure. Basically the capitalist position is one of gradualism. Recognizing that most LDCs must labor under severe handicaps, they recommend postponement of gratification, curbing of expectations, and adjustment of development and growth targets to available means. LDCs are counseled to be patient and to rely on free market mechanisms—with some assist from the developed countries—to earn sufficient foreign exchange to pay for essential imports at reasonable prices. The DCs will assist with aid carefully measured to accommodate sound economic projects. Wasteful expenditures on prestige projects for example will as a rule not be financed. Insofar as their own economic conditions allow, the DCs will modify tariff barriers to accommodate modest imports of manufactured goods from LDCs. Fundamentally the capitalist prescription posits economic prosperity in the advanced industrial countries as a prerequisite for closing the viability gap. To achieve that goal, the LDCs not the DCs must sacrifice. If sacrifices are made also by the developed countries both sides will lose; the LDCs will be deprived of export markets, the DCs subjected to internal social and political turmoil. Finally, as a condition for continued assistance and other concession on the DCs part, LDCs are expected "to put their own house in order" by instituting sound financial management and budgeting procedures, curbing ex-

---

* Opposition to growth and development takes various forms. Where it is linked to religious fundamentalism, as in contemporary Iran, it inevitably extends to suppression of other manifestations of modernity, such as equality of the sexes, individualism, human rights, and education.

cessive government spending on unproductive ventures, and curbing corruption which in LDCs consumes too large a portion of the national product.

The "liberal" prescription, more abstract, theoretical, and humanitarian, accepts a degree of responsibility for the condition the Third World is in, hence is prepared to make more concessions. The "liberal" position has little if anything in common with that espoused by Marxists, socialists, or communists.

The Socialist Approach

The Soviet bloc: Because prescriptions from that direction stress the need for establishment by the LDCs of absolute control over their internal affairs, they are understandably more popular with former colonial dependencies. But they have a wider appeal for yet other reasons. The Western capitalist model for development is suspect because of its intimate association with the colonial experience and its manifest lack of support for measures designed to render the former colonies genuinely independent. In addition, some of the mainstays of capitalism, private property for instance or free enterprise, are in practice far too weak and untried in LDCs to play the crucial role expected of them in capitalist theory. But similar objections can be raised with respect to Marxist/ Leninist theory, which likewise is applicable to less developed, primarily agrarian countries only in a fragmentary way. Central planning, for example, a critical feature of Marxist economic theory, in LDCs encounters greatest difficulties between conceptualization and implementation. Soviet bloc theoreticians' definitions of workers, peasants, or proletarians, drawn from nineteenth-century European and to a lesser extent prerevolutionary Russian experiences, are categorically rejected as irrelevant to LDC conditions by socialist revisionists, followers of the late Mao Zedong for example.

For a brief period during the first independence decade, perhaps the middle 1950s and the middle 1960s, Soviet social and economic theorists attempted to apply classical Marxist/Leninist theory directly and literally to the problems of the newly independent states. But soon they recognized that, far from carrying the socialist gospel to distant places, they were actually improvising on a basically irrelevant theme. Accordingly, allowance was made for the socialist world's temporary inability to furnish the financial wherewithal needed by the desperately poor states to prevent immediate collapse. Suspect as it might be, driven by ulterior motives, Western capital as well as material aid had to be tolerated, provided it was carefully controlled and supervised. One way to accomplish that was by formation of mixed capitalist-socialist enterprises. Where such compromise did not seem feasible or was rejected by the ruling group socialist recommendation called for more drastic measures.[1]

In its more mature form the Soviet bloc approach to the problem rests on several basic premises, all arguable but firmly advanced nevertheless by partisans of that persuasion. First, capitalism is said to be detrimental to the best interests of the LDCs because in order to prosper it must increase profits from the sale of its products to the poor and depress prices paid to them for their commodities.

To ensure permanent subservience to its interests capitalism must of necessity maintain colonial attitudes and mentality among the people in the nominally independent states, artificially promote and maintain a supporting class, the compradors, and so shape the client states' production methods and market conditions as to accommodate its customary needs. Viewed from that perspective adverse terms of trade (see p. 93n) are not an accident but a matter of design.

Second, to compensate for inherent or endemic weaknesses and contradictions, capitalism is compelled to acquire ever larger supplies of raw materials at lowest possible prices. To that end it will seek to keep supplier states politically pliant and economically dependent. Third, because capitalist systems can or will not provide their own people with the purchasing power needed to consume all that is produced at home, the burgeoning populations of the less developed world must be recruited as alternate consumers. That in turn calls for discouragement of LDCs plans to enter the world market as rival producers of manufactured goods.

Concretely, what has been Soviet bloc advice? Reduce trade dependence on the West by gradual shift to bloc suppliers and buyers. Begin to develop industrial capacities by import of heavy machinery, machine tools, even entire plants to be constructed by bloc state enterprises. Accept technicians and technical assistance from bloc countries. Bloc leaders persuade themselves that theirs is the more competent and relevant counsel because, as one Soviet development expert put it "[third world countries] have been convinced by the example of the socialist countries that it is possible to raise a backward nation to the modern level within the course of one to three generations." (The assumption, that viability will follow soon, is a debatable proposition, as most of the bloc states including the Soviet Union actually experienced their revolution when they had already reached an industrial plateau).[2]

The People's Republic of China: Although the PRC sees itself as a Third World power, part of the "South," it is useful to contrast its position on this question with that of the Soviet Union. Ever since the break with Moscow, Beijing has advised LDCs to reject not only "imperialist" and "colonialist" influence but also "Soviet hegemonism."* Beyond that LDCs should not even attempt to copy each other but embark upon development programs, especially improvement of production capacity, best suited to each country's capabilities. Contrary to the general thrust of Soviet recommendation, agriculture should not be neglected. The high living standards advertised by the West represent a benefit which capitalist models bestow only upon a minute elite and should therefore not be a first priority. Like the Soviet Union, the PRC recommends continued utilization of foreign, that is Western, capital provided it is received and applied under controlled conditions most favorable to the LDCs.

---

* Beijing's advice is that "Western patterns of capitalist economies are not appropriate for developing countries, nor is the Soviet lopsided development of heavy industry and all-round nationalization of the enterprises which the Soviet Union has peddled to them." Zhongyun (1983), p. 73.

Mixed capitalist/socialist approaches: Somewhere on the spectrum are approaches which fall into neither category. One of these is the so called "dependency theory."*

Dependency theory argues that to defend successfully against imperialist penetration and control, mainly by multinational corporations (MNCs), LDCs must reorient their economies from outward to inward emphasis, stress labor rather than capital intensive industrial development, retain capital within their own boundaries instead of permitting it to be exported or smuggled to safe havens abroad, and narrow the gap between rich and poor within their own countries. Viability must remain a distant goal if, as is the case in Latin America, about 2 percent of the population receive one-half of the total income. Approaching the problem from a somewhat different direction are the *structuralists,* the Swedish economist Gunnar Myrdal being one of the leading exponents of that school. Their contention is that the free market solution condemns the LDCs to perpetual backwardness because it favors the already well endowed while thwarting the less developed.[3] Therefore, coincident with certain reforms of capitalism—unlike Marxists, structuralists see no need to have capitalism abolished—certain changes must be allowed by the advanced countries in the structure of international trade and finance to accommodate the special requirements of the poorer states. Among these changes are tariff concessions, price adjustments, quota allowances, and reallocation of markets

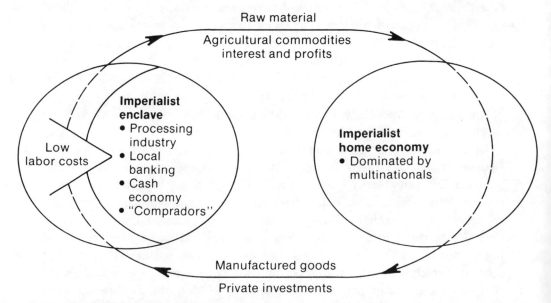

Fig. 14-3. The "Imperialist" System.

* Another is Liberation Theology, a prescription advanced by socially activist Catholic clergy for social and economic liberation of Latin America; see, for example, Gustavo Gutiérrez, *A Theology of Liberation,* Maryknoll, N.Y.: Orbis 1973; and the Vatican response, Sacred Congregation for the Doctrine of the Faith, "Instruction On Certain Aspects Of The 'Theology of Liberation,' " (Rome: Vatican Press, 1984).

and, to a limited extent, basic resources. A primary focus of this school is the impact of prevailing market patterns on the LDCs' economic structure. Like the dependency theorists, structuralists point to the existence in less developed countries of two economies, one based on exports, draining scarce resources from the country without adequate value replacement, the other, crippled by the first, serving domestic needs inadequately. With respect to the capitalist argument that foreign investment and lending will eventually work to close the viability gap, structuralists note that because risks are too high, investment capital tends to avoid LDCs; moreover the bulk of lendable finance capital available to LDCs tends to seek returns clearly above the borrowers' capacity to service or repay; (See Figs. 14a, b, and 15-2, b, c.)

In 1980 a commission headed by former West German Chancellor and socialist world leader Willy Brandt issued its Report entitled *North–South: A Program for Survival*.[4] Its recommendations focused on three main areas. First, international bodies like the International Monetary Fund, the World Bank, GATT, and the numerous lesser social and economic agencies of the United Nations created under its aegis had to be reformed mainly because when most of these were created the majority of the LDCs, with whose fate they were to be concerned, had yet to achieve political independence. Although the commission had not intended to go that far, this recommendation was welcomed especially by those in the Southern camp who demanded that all of the world's nations should be granted one vote in all matters pertaining to the world community, regardless of GNP, per capita income, or other standards traditionally applied. Predictably the notion was not popular among the Big Ten who command the lion's share of the wealth to be divided by such democratic methods. Secondly,

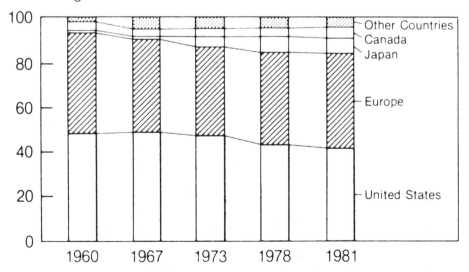

Fig. 14-4a. Direct Foreign Investment by Donor Country and Region. (*Business America*, Vol. 7, 16 (August 6, 1984), Figure 2, p. 9.)

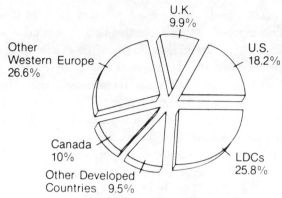

Fig. 14-4b. Direct Foreign Investment by Recipient Country and Region. (*Business America*, Vol. 7, 16 (August 6, 1984), Figure 3, p. 9.)

the current mode by which funds are transferred from the rich nations to the poor, solely at the former's discretion, was to be changed to automatic transfer by means of a form of global taxation. These taxes were to be raised from such sources as proceeds of seabed mining (itself a highly controversial issue), world trade, airline tickets, and similar international transactions. Finally, worldwide disarmament was to free funds to aid the world's poor, the burden to be apportioned according to current and projected arms expenditures.*

A follow-up report by the same commission shifted the emphasis to immediate financial emergency measures involving the IMF through the "General Arrangements to Borrow" and the "Fund's Compensatory Facility." Also to be tapped were the IRBD, the International Development Association, and the Bank for International Settlements.

The View from the South

Accepting for present purposes that "South" means poor or less developed and "North" the opposite, several problems still remain with that dichotomy. Neither designation actually represents a cohesive unit and one can therefore not speak of a dialogue.[5] Figure 14-5 illustrates the diversity of views and positions on either side. One can also not really speak of *prescriptions* coming from "the South" as such. More appropriate might be to speak of *demands,* formulated and advanced sometimes in full accord with reality, sometimes wholly polemical in intent. Indeed, if one wants to speak of a dialogue, one can say that on balance all exchanges between rich and poor from 1945 to this day resemble more a futile dialogue of the deaf than a productive discourse.

---

* According to Willy Brandt (1980), p. 4: "The military spending of half a day would finance the entire World Health Organization programme to eliminate malaria. Even less would be needed to wipe out onchocerciasis (river blindness), still a scourge for millions. . . . A modern tank costs about 1 million dollars. This money could improve storage facilities for 100,000 tons of rice and reduce spoilage by 4,000 tons a year. (A person can live on a pound of rice a day). The same money could also build 1,000 classrooms for 30,000 school children; the cost of a fighter plane (20 million dollars) could provide 40,000 village pharmacies; One percent of annual arms expenditure would buy all the agricultural equipment needed to improve the food deficit of the poor countries until 1990 and would even make them self-supporting in the food sectors."

Perhaps the most respected voices reflecting Southern perspectives are those of Raul Prebisch and Sir W. Arthur Lewis, the former a Latin American, the latter a West Indian. Prebisch, first secretary-general of UNCTAD, concedes that Northern liberals may have a point when they recommend that removal by the advanced countries of protective barriers against imports from LDCs would improve the latter's chances to catch up. But this measure, espoused by GATT, will alone not do the job. To him, the root of the problem is not the volume of exports from the poor to the rich but the price such exports fetch over time, and in this regard, argues Prebisch, the world economy remains rigged against fair pricing of raw materials from the less developed world. The LDCs, he contends, sell their coffee, copper, cocoa, sisal, tea, palm products, ground-nuts, and so forth, in highly competitive markets. On the other hand they must purchase abroad automobiles, earth-moving equipment, all or most construction materials, and other finished goods, in some cases everything required for urban existence and for commerce and needed to support their infant industries, all from sellers powerful enough to fix price levels. That, he explains, is one reason why LDCs receive less and less, pay more and more, or as one African leader put it: work harder and harder and get poorer and poorer. Put differently, steadily declining commodity prices cause ever increasing exports to pay for fewer imports.* (See Table 14-2 and Fig. 14-6.)

Lewis also stresses the terms of trade as the North–South conflict's primary cause and agrees with Prebisch and the structuralists in many respects. But

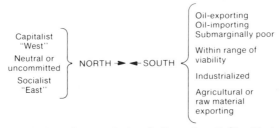

Fig. 14-5. Diversity Within the North-South Complex: Policy Postures and Interests.

* According to Prebisch a dilemma arises because ". . . productivity advances in advanced industrial states lead to wage and other input cost increases that keep prices constant or rising. In contrast, in less-developed countries productivity advances do not lead to wage increases and/or constant prices because of disguised unemployment and weak labor organizations. Instead they lead to price declines that are passed on to the consumers—predominantly located in rich states," Blake and Walters (1983), pp. 34–35.

Development economists point to the effect of Engel's Law *(Ernst Engel, 1821-96)* as one source of LDC poverty. That law states that given the same tastes and preferences, the proportion of income spent on food diminishes as income rises. The end-effect of this is reduced demand for primary products of LDCs as income rises in the advanced countries, accompanied by increased demand for manufactured goods in the now foreign exchange-poor LDCs. Prebisch and others refer to this as a structural bias in the world trade and production system, a condition not relieved by lowering or even abolition of barriers to trade. Instead, it is argued, the LDCs must industrialize behind protective tariff walls, while simultaneously the developed countries inject into the LDC economies a share of their capital commensurate with their margin of trade; this can be effectuated through grants or soft, i.e. low interest bearing loans. Critics point out that the declining terms of trade thesis typically focuses attention only on declining commodity prices and rising prices of manufactured goods, sloughing off reverse trends in some sectors in both categories.

Table 14-2. Purchasing Power of LDC Commodity Exports (1975–1982)

Copper for Crude Oil[a]	down by 63%
for Capital[b]	down by 44%
Cocoa for Crude Oil[a]	down by 70%
for Capital[b]	down by 45%
Coffee for Crude Oil[a]	down by 50%
for Capital[b]	down by 24%
Cotton for Crude Oil[a]	down by 64%
for Capital[b]	down by 46%

SOURCE: *Africa News*, September 20, 1982.
[a] Quantity of oil one ton of each commodity can buy.
[b] Capital in US$ for which one ton can cover debt service payments at prevailing rates.

he does not believe that the North can make the concessions required. For that reason the LDCs must redirect their efforts, reducing their dependence on exports in their development strategy. They should rely on their home market. A first step toward that goal is to modernize agricultural production, releasing manpower currently engaged in that sector for other purposes and eventually increasing the purchasing power of the labor force. Agricultural surpluses should soon be available to feed the growing urban population, reducing the need for expensive food imports, in turn freeing scarce foreign exchange to support a Southern industrial revolution. "International trade," argues Lewis, "became an engine of growth in the nineteenth century, but this is not its proper role. The engine of growth should be technological change, with international trade serving as lubricating oil and not as fuel."[6] Unfortunately, like so many other seemingly sound and reasonable proposals this one too is likely to founder on the shoals of political pride and prejudice. For one thing the aim of most developing countries is to narrow the gap immediately, at the very least within the lifetime of their leaders. For them the Lewis formula is far too slow.

Formation of a "Southern" Front

While most of what is now the Third World was in colonial bondage or otherwise controlled by imperial powers, few opportunities existed for future leaders to fully acquaint themselves with conditions in their respective territories and compare experiences, exchange information, and plan for the future on that basis.* The Third World or "South" assumed its first concrete organizational form under the banner of Afro-Asian Solidarity and antiimperialism at the Bandung Conference in 1955. Joan Spero sees the "Southern strategy" thereafter as "one of unity and confrontation."[7] While the record does bear this out, it also reveals that it is far easier to plan than implement such a

---

* If discussions took place among future Third World leaders, this was typically as students at foreign universities, in the context of the Pan African or similar movements, or at ideological training institutes in a number of socialist countries.

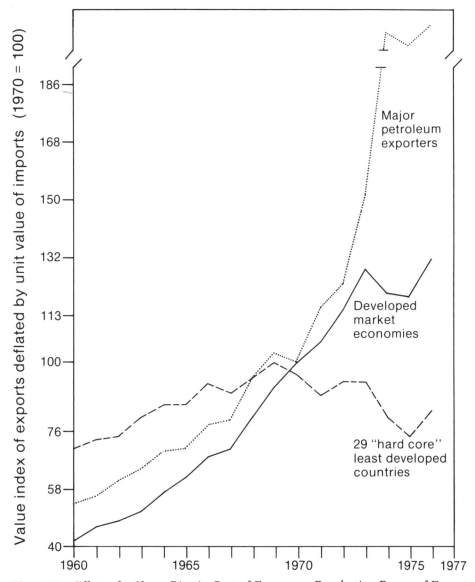

Fig. 14-6. Effect of a Sharp Rise in Cost of Energy on Purchasing Power of Exports. (*UNCTAD Handbook 1977*. Supplement.)

strategy. Although Bandung was followed by a series of meetings and a degree of unity was achieved on some of the more general aspects of the entire problem complex, disunity rather than unity characterized efforts to consolidate and mobilize the South.

Inevitably the Third World movement, such as it was, was swept up in the East-West confrontation. For reasons outlined earlier the Soviet bloc and generally the socialist side had at the very least the sentimental edge, a fact which did not contribute to the popularity of the Southern cause in the West. Consequently, many of the newly independent states were compelled to take

Box 14-1. Major Events in North–South Relations (1945–1983)

1939–1945	World War Two. Foundations of colonial empires crumble.
1945–1947	Independence of Indonesia (1945), Philippines (1946), and India (1947). Dissolution of colonial empires set in motion.
1947	General Agreement on Tariff and Trade (GATT) negotiated at Geneva (Switzerland).
1955	Bandung (Indonesia) Conference of Asian and African states.
1957	Asian-African People's Solidarity Conference at Cairo (Egypt). The pronounced pro-Soviet Communist orientation of this Conference contributed to the formation of the Movement of Non-Aligned States. First UN Conference on Law of the Sea (UNCLOS I).
1960	Charter of Organization for Economic Cooperation and Development (OECD) signed at Paris.
1961	Development Assistance Committee (DAC) of OECD becomes operational. Belgrade (Yugoslavia) First Conference of Non-Aligned States. Formal start of Non-Aligned Movement.
1964	First United Nations Conference on Trade and Development (UNCTAD I) held at Geneva. "Group of 77" founded. Cairo Conference of Non-Aligned States.
1966	United Nations Industrial Development Organization (UNIDO) established.
1968	UNCTAD II held at New Delhi (India).
1970	Lusaka (Zambia) Conference of Non-Aligned States.
1972	UNCTAD III meets at Santiago (Chile).
1973	Algiers (Algeria) Conference of Non-Aligned States. Sharp OPEC price increase. Third UN Conference on the Law of the Sea (UNCLOS III). (Second Conference, held in 1960, was unproductive).
1974	Special Session of the General Assembly of the United Nations to consider the plight of the LDCs. "Group of 77" forces through Declaration on the Establishment of a New International Economic Order. UN General Assembly adopts Charter of Economic Rights and Duties of States. UN World Food Conference meets at Rome (Italy)
1975	Lomé Convention signed between the European Economic Community (EEC) and the African, Caribbean, Pacific (ACP) states. Conference on International Economic Cooperation (CIEC) meets between 1975 and 1977.

Box 14–1. *(Cont'd.)*

1976	UNCTAD IV meets at Nairobi (Kenya). Advance Integrated Commodity Scheme. Colombo Conference of Non-Aligned States.
1979	UNCTAD V meets at Manila (Philippines). UN General Assembly calls for Special Session to conduct "global negotiations" on raw materials, trade and finance. Independent Commission on International Development (Brandt Commission) issues Report. Havana (Cuba) Conference of Non-Aligned States.
1980	Third General Conference of UNIDO meets at New Delhi. "New Delhi Declaration," drafted by the "Group of 77," sets confrontational course for UNIDO. UN General Assembly Special Session on Global Economic Matters. UN proclaims Third Development Decade (1981–1990) and New International Development Strategy.
1981	North-South Summit meets at Cancun (Mexico).
1982	UNCLOS III concluded, Law of the Sea signed.
1983	UNCTAD IV meets at Belgrade.
1984	Lomé III signed between EEC and G4 ACP states.

sides. In another embodiment the movement sought to confine itself to questions of development, as at Cairo in 1962 for example. Eventually, though in a very inchoate sense, a kind of "Southern front" emerged, meeting by meeting, issue by issue, beginning at Colombo in 1954, at numerous regional meetings thereafter, in the United Nations, and within regional bodies such as the Organization of African Unity.* Still, differences on rather basic issues far outweighed areas of agreement.

Against persistent delaying actions by the Western free-market wing of the North, a group of 77 LDCs (Group 77) succeeded eventually in bringing the UN General Assembly to endorse the Southern cause and take some definitive, concrete steps. The watershed year was 1964.† In that year, the United Nations Conference on Trade and Development (UNCTAD) came into existence as a Southern response to GATT.

Even though the Group of 77 eventually grew to 121 and at that level acquired a measure of influence and diplomatic clout, unity displayed at meetings failed to extend to the field of action. Behind a veneer of group solidarity, most effective as rhetoric, individual members of the group continued to compete bilaterally as well as multilaterally for favors from either East or West, many refusing to implement UNCTAD recommendations or recommendations from

---

* Key leaders at that time were Nehru of India, Sukarno of Indonesia, Nkrumah of Ghana, Nasser of Egypt, and Tito of Yugoslavia.

† The group originally numbered 75, constituting a caucus for LDCs on economic matters in the unfolding North-South debate. It was formally established as an action group, preparatory to UNCTAD I held in Geneva, Switzerland, March-June 1964.

the group as such. The root problem of course was the emergence of a Fourth, possibly even a Fifth, world, splitting those among the poor countries with good or better prospects of closing the viability gap from those lacking any such prospects whatsoever. And where does one place the oil-rich countries of the Middle East whose rhetoric exudes solidarity with the world's poor but whose financial posture resembles closely that of Western bankers?*

Southern Demands

Proposals advanced by various segments of the Southern front on various occasions fall into three major categories: Maximalist propositions formulated or inspired by Soviet bloc advisors or advanced by proxies, Cuba for example, mainly to score propaganda points against the West, principally against the United States; demands genuinely reflecting Southern concerns but tending to be hyperbolic, hence impractical; and third, minimalist demands carefully crafted by LDCs economists, administrators, or technicians, working in tandem with experts from advanced countries, Western as well as Eastern, and from international organizations.

The spearhead of the Southern front then was UNCTAD. Decisively influenced by Prebisch and by a large number of socialist-leaning states who soon represented a majority in the United Nations, a 1963 UN Resolution to prepare for the 1964 Geneva meeting of UNCTAD (UNCTAD I) outlined the basic strategy as follows:

1. Progressive reduction and early elimination of all barriers and restrictions impeding the exports of the developing countries, without reciprocal concessions on their part;
2. Increase in the volume of exports of the developing countries in primary products, both raw and processed, to the industrialized countries, and stabilization at fair and remunerative levels;
3. Expansion of the markets for exports of manufactured and semimanufactured goods from the developing countries;

---

* Perhaps the problem facing the South was best expressed by Richard Cooper, then under secretary of state for economic affairs:

One reason it is so difficult for developing countries to limit their attention to a few priority items is the wide diversity of interests among them. The poorest countries need increased official development assistance, middle-income countries want balance-of-payments support and improved conditions for commodity trade, and the wealthier developing countries are most concerned about access to markets, and to technology. Oil-importing countries want stable oil prices and help to pay for the oil; oil-exporting countries worry about industrial-country inflation and security of their financial assets. Policies which might help one group of developing countries are of limited value or even detrimental to others. This results in formulating a list of demands based on a maximum common denominator, which satisfies their collective political needs but limits their political effectiveness in dealing with industrial countries, and greatly complicates the overall dialogue. Cooper (May 15, 1980), p. 4.

4. Provision of more adequate financial resources at favorable terms so as to enable the developing countries to increase their imports of capital goods and industrial raw materials essential for their economic development, and better coordination of trade and aid policies;

5. Improvement of the invisible trade of the developing countries, particularly by reducing their payments for freight and insurance and the burden of their debt charges;

6. Improvement of institutional arrangements, including if necessary, the establishment of new machinery and methods for implementing the decisions of the Conference.[8]

New demands, variations of old themes, and refinements were advanced at succeeding meetings of UNCTAD, in the UN generally, and at ad hoc meetings where Third World countries predominated, for example at the periodic conferences of the Nonaligned Nations. Among focal points were an increased share of LDC control over commodity prices, greater price stability, and guaranteed prices for certain raw materials. The drive to improve the commodity exporters' position received its greatest impetus with OPEC's success in 1973 and 1974. If OPEC-like price-fixing cartels could not be formed for non-oil resources and commodities, then it was felt prices should at least be stabilized or guaranteed by means of integrated plans, supported by common funds, to finance buffer stocks* and promote the exploitation and processing of raw materials by the producers themselves. One proposal called for "indexing" of LDC exports similar to such indexing in inflation-ridden countries like Brazil.†

More radical proposals emanated from the United Nations Industrial Development Organization (UNIDO) created in 1966 to coordinate global cooperation to advance especially industrial development in the South. At its third meeting in New Delhi in 1980, the Group of 77 in coalition with the Soviet bloc and the PRC caused a declaration to be adopted which proposed creation of a global fund of $300 billion by the year 2000 for the benefit of the LDCs, the principal contributors of course being the industrially advanced countries of the West who, predictably, declined the invitation. The intention was to' replace the Western-dominated International Monetary Fund and the World Bank. Significantly, the Soviet bloc, although as usual voting with the majority, had reservations concerning technology transfer and sharing of skills.‡ Not unreasonable in that connection was the complaint that steadily worsening terms of trade, coupled with worldwide inflation and mounting energy costs,

---

* Buffer stocks are commodities held back from the world market to drive up prices or prevent precipitous price declines.

† Under such "indexing," wages and salaries as well as other incomes are tied to cost of living.

‡ At an earlier UNIDO conference in Lima, Peru, a plan was adopted "to help the developing countries increase their share in the world industrial output to 25 percent from 7 percent, by the year 2000," another practical impossibility as the gap between the two spheres, in that respect especially, is steadily widening. See Cooper (May 15, 1980), p. 4.

Table 14-3. DC–LDC Trade Positions (by commodity, 1980
Percent of World Total)ᵃ

	Origin of Exports		Destination of Exports	
Class Commodity	*DC*	*LDC*	*DC*	*LDC*
Allᵃ	63.2	28.0	67.3	23.2
Food, Live Animals, Beverages and Tobacco	64.6	28.2	61.7	24.4
Crude Materials, Oils and Fats (Fuels Excl.)	61.1	28.9	70.7	17.3
Minerals, Fuels, Lubricants and Related Materials	18.2	72.4	76.1	17.8
Chemicals	87.3	6.7	64.3	25.9
Machinery and Transport	85.5	5.3	60.4	28.9
Other Manufactured Goods	77.3	15.3	69.7	22.1
Percent Change 1970–1980	−12.1	+59.0	− 4.5	+24.7

SOURCE: United Nations, *Statistical Yearbook*, 1981, Table 181, p. 924.
ᵃ Percentages do not total 100 because of different accounting procedures, statistical deviations, and report shortfalls.

were eroding whatever financial and other assistance the North was making available. Under the circumstances, it was felt that it would only be fair if a compensatory fund could be established.

A constant refrain was the demand for recognition on the part of the developed countries of "sovereign control" over all natural resources and of economic activity generally within individual LDCs, both highly problematic demands in the age of global economic interdependence.[9] The principal sources of concern were the larger MNCs who, it was argued, were all too prone to intervene directly in host countries' internal affairs. Specifically, the MNCs were said to place their own corporate or home country interests above those of their hosts and generally evince a lack of interest in helping to narrow the viability gap. Although they claimed to favor advancement of indigenous production capacity, through training programs or technology transfer for instance, the record, it was charged, did not bear out the promise.[10]

Regarding technology transfer it was noted that the developed countries, foremost of course the United States, Western Europe and Japan, enjoyed a virtual monopoly in that respect, holding virtually all patents. If the position of the LDCs was to be improved, appropriate patents should be released to LDCs at costs commensurate with their ability to pay.*

---

* Technology transfer acquires special significance in the age of the microchip and the integrated circuit, as shown eloquently by Servan-Schreiber (1980). He predicted significant improvement in the LDCs "through computer power" prospects limited only by the "rigidity of our mental structure" (pp. 215 and 229). "Computerization," he predicted, "will free every human being to make the maximum use of his or her faculties" (p. 229) and "miniaturization . . . will make the computer one of the least

The North's Response to the South's Demands

That prospects of a satisfactory response were poor became more apparent with every passing year. In 1981, at Cancun, Mexico, leaders of fourteen developing nations met with eight from developed ones at a summit conference in the "North-South Dialogue" series, this one restricted to the leading Western and the more moderate Southern states, with China (the PRC) the sole representative of the orthodox Marxist position.* One of the agenda items was the perennial LDC request for a global bargaining round, on a one-nation-one-vote basis, analogous to the previously mentioned Kennedy and Tokyo Rounds sponsored by GATT. The plan was to endow that round with power to overrule decisions made by formally established bodies within which members of the Western group enjoyed built-in voting advantages, for example GATT, the World Bank, or IMF. The proposal was flatly rejected. So were proposals to regulate, through OPEC-like cartels if necessary, world prices of—among other commodities—aluminum, bauxite, cocoa, coffee, and zinc, tariff preferences to be accorded all manufactured goods imported into Northern countries from the South.†

Prospects of a satisfactory response were no better at UNCTAD VI, meeting in 1983 in Belgrade, Yugoslavia. Here rhetoric about redistribution of the world's wealth, creation of special funds, and other concessions by the rich to the world's poor had to compete with a reality of 32 million workers unemployed in the industrial countries, the consequence in part of a worldwide recession. Compounding these conditions were about $700 billion worth of debts, the bulk incurred by LDCs, which had to be restructured before serious consideration could be given to additional financial outlays on the part of the developed countries.[11]

Sometimes diplomatically, sometimes quite bluntly, at numerous international encounters and in well publicized addresses, Western leaders made it increasingly clear that demands for them to relinquish control over their financial resources and their own vital national interests were unacceptable. Global bargaining, on a one-nation-one-vote basis, would simply mean that the poorest and least responsible nations, probably encouraged by the Soviet Union, would then be in the global economic driver's seat. The eventual outcome of such a scheme

---

expensive technological objects of the world" (p. 208). The computer therefore will be the least expensive in the chain of technological breakthroughs that have revolutionized human kind and its social and political constructs. See also Hofheinz and Calder (1982), Chapter 10. A major obstacle to technology transfer has been and to an extent still is the West's near monopoly of certain patents, a position increasingly challenged by LDCs. See The *New York Times*, "U.S. and Third World At Odds Over Patents," October 5, 1982.

* In a way that meeting was one of a series begun in 1975 under the name Conference on International Economic Cooperation (CIEC).

† A counterproposal advanced by the U.S., whereby all LDCs were to avail themselves of GATT mutual tariff reduction benefits by acceding to the Agreement, was not taken up because under GATT terms such reductions were based on reciprocity and few LDCs were prepared to abandon their own tariffs imposed to protect their own infant industries.

would be transfer of substantial portions of wealth from the Western countries into a bottomless pit.

With respect to the South's assertion that much of the West's wealth had been "created" by the LDCs, the West pointed to their own industry, enterprise, economic prudence and foresight; their people's willingness to assume great risks; their readiness to postpone gratification for extended periods; and their proclivity to save and invest in the future as their side's contribution to what there was in the way of development in the South and wealth in the North. As for the generous recommendations of such bodies as the Brandt Commission, Western diplomats and development specialists asked what assurance there was that any of the funds diverted for the benefit of LDCs, and any of the funds saved in the event of disarmament, would in fact be put to the purposes of the commission envisioned. Further it was pointed out that proposals for large-scale transfers of funds typically fail to take into account the impact of such transfers on the source. For example, if one million dollars earmarked for a tank were instead transferred directly to improve storage of rice in India, what would be the economic effect of that transaction on the region where that tank would have been produced and what would be the impact of that shortfall on further financial aid to the South?[12]

Still, all skepticism notwithstanding, not all demands for a new economic order went unheeded. For instance, the Development Assistance Committee (DAC) of OECD, in its annual report for 1980, conceded that "the international economic order must undergo fundamental change."[13] As the committee saw it, the collapse of Bretton Woods had terminated one economic order without creating a new one, a condition not new in history but potentially explosive in the coming decades. The pressure building up could in this nuclear age jeopardize world peace. The problem was, and remains, how to improve conditions without causing irreparable damage to the economic engines upon which both developed and less-developed must rely.

As will become apparent from the following discussion theorists of all persuasions failed to foresee the debilitating effects on North-South relations, and on the South's capacity for self-help, of the East–West competition, especially its military dimension. In addition, it was mistakenly assumed that forward development of the former colonies was prevented solely by imperialism or neocolonialism. Overlooked, or underestimated, were the effects of indigenous shortcomings impeding social, economic, and political progress. While some of these undoubtedly were traceable to the neglect characteristic of colonial rule, many reflected willful acts by new leaders, too eager to reap the benefits of power.

Suggested Questions and Discussion Topics

What is the "viability gap," what are its principal causes, and what are its principal manifestations?

Characterize the theoretical "capitalist" and "liberal" prescriptions for closing the viability gap; then characterize the several "socialist" approaches to that problem.

How do analysts representing or reflecting the "view from the South" see the problem?

What constitutes the "Southern Front," what are its concrete recommendations and demands, and what has been the "North's" response to these demands?

In your opinion, what should be done in theory and what can be done in practice to narrow or close the gap?

Chapter 15
Closing the Viability Gap: Practice

The Capitalist Approach

Foreign Aid and Assistance

From euphoria to disillusionment: Under the most favorable circumstances, assuming the best intentions on the part of the donor and recipient, only a few of the LDCs already close to the viability threshold could hope—with massive infusion of aid—to overtake a few of the marginally viable DCs. The general prognosis among realists is that it will take at least 50 years for the majority of the newly independent countries to reach the level of development the more advanced countries attained a 100 years ago.[1] The collapse of the colonial empires and the emergence of dozens of politically and legally independent but economically nonviable states (eventually more than 100) was accompanied by an unprecedented flow of financial and material aid from the rich to the poor. But the expectation was not a closing of the viability gap. Indeed that was not at all the intent.

The former colonial powers, anxious to retain their economic control positions and protect their considerable investments, relied on aid partly to stabilize the still weak regimes but more importantly to ensure continued access to agricultural commodities, raw materials, and markets and generally to lay the foundations for future economic relations preferably on a more or less exclusive basis. The United States, along with other industrial powers who had no former colonies to tend, resorted to aid primarily to gain access to markets and to resources which the colonial powers had theretofore jealously protected from competing influences and now were striving to retain for their own benefit. Although not structured and not sufficient in other respects to significantly advance the recipients' viability, aid from these outsiders was generally more generous, less stringent, and more likely designed to modestly advance the recipients' economic independence. Initially, United States aid partly reflected a genuine humanitarian commitment, partly a desire to open more markets to free trade. But very soon both objectives were eclipsed by an overriding concern with what Washington perceived as a growing Soviet threat to U.S. security at home and abroad. Taking advantage of the opportunity, Many LDCs invited competitive

283

bidding for their favors—access to their resources or markets, permission to establish military bases on their territory, or supporting votes in the United Nations—in return for steadily increasing aid. At first the United States seemed quite ready to quell incipient defections with more aid offers, but soon disillusionment set in.

Actually, foreign aid had never enjoyed wide public support in the industrially advanced countries. Now adverse economic conditions, including large-scale unemployment, pushed different priorities to the fore, and outflow of scarce funds was viewed with outright hostility. As the popularly perceived viability goal receded out of sight—the ranks of the world's poor seemed to be swelling— a sense of futility began to spread, a feeling that aid was indeed being poured into a bottomless pit. When an increasing number of former and current aid recipients began to display a proclivity to join members of the Soviet bloc in attacks on the United States, while apparently finding no fault with Soviet policies or conduct, including Soviet refusal to increase its share of foreign aid, pressure mounted in the U.S. Congress to retaliate by cutting aid to ingrates to the bone. Similar reactions were registered in other political democracies.

At the outset of the next to last decade of the twentieth century, foreign aid was to undergo fundamental changes in philosophy as well as execution. Also, while worldwide inflation made the total appear to be greater, overall aid experienced a sharp decline in purchasing power. In addition many donor governments concluded that past emphasis on public sector aid had set them up too clearly as targets for criticism and attack, especially by the growing number of radical regimes among the LDCs. Attempts by donor governments to impose upon aid recipients a modicum of self-discipline regarding domestic spending, for example, were frequently attacked as presumptuous, domineering manifestations of imperialist intent. It seemed appropriate under the circumstances to turn the task of assisting the less developed over to politically less visible private enterprise and to international agencies.

In the early stages of the DC-LDC relationship, private enterprise could not be interested except in the most profitable investment opportunities. The risks were too great, the returns generally uncertain. In particular, the more basic public projects which had to be constructed first promised no financial yields for decades; many were most likely to be losing propositions forever. However, once the foundations for a modern reasonably well-functioning economy were laid, prospects for profitable involvement by private enterprise improved. Moreover, it was now realized that private sector participation in overseas development created jobs at home, a subject of mounting sensitivity in the industrial world. Consequently the emphasis in public sector aid was shifted to "create institutional and infrastructural preconditions for subsequent private sector cooperation."[2] The number of aid recipients was reduced, the weight shifted from the marginal or submarginal to those most likely to succeed. Increasingly, precautions were taken to render aid funds less accessible to corrupt elements in the receiving countries. Donors also began to posit, as a qualification, "efficient use" of aid by the recipients. Simultaneously, greater reliance was placed on consortia of private banks representing a mix of donor countries and on regional banks, in the expectation that expansion of the number of donors would serve to diffuse the inevitable reaction as conditions for aid were tightened and demands for greater discipline and reform were stepped up.

A possible answer to the question whether internal measures should precede external remedies suggests itself when one closely examines the "food or famine" controversy. What causes famine, food shortage or something else? Some time ago the World Bank found that "famines are compatible with adequate food supplies within a country or within a large region." For instance, during the 1973 famine in parts of Ethiopia, according to the Bank "the national supply of food did not decrease [but] major groups of the poor, especially the landless, were extremely vulnerable to a sudden reduction in their earnings. In such cases, and particularly if prices rise suddenly, these are the people who starve."[3] This suggests that within certain areas famines may be prevented by appropriate internal distribution. (Whether the world as a whole actually faces a food shortage is another question.) Of course it can be argued that if poverty, not shortage, is the problem, foreign aid can attack the malady on that front as well as on the other. But that assumes a) that outside aid can be as effective internally as can measures taken by the governments affected and b) that it

Table 15-1. Leading Recipients of U.S. Aid (in million US$)[a]

Israel	3,000.000
Egypt	2,339.118
Pakistan	651.200
El Salvador	483.237
Philippines	275.294[b]
Honduras	231.206
South Korea	230.200
Costa Rica	190.075
India	178.890
Bangladesh	167.268
Morocco	138.225
Indonesia	133.545
Jamaica	132.716
Thailand	132.000
Peru	128.169
Dominican Rep.	122.592
Jordan	117.000
Total	8,650.735[c]

SOURCE: US Department of State (1985), Special Report No. 128, pp. 14–15.

[a] U.S. Administration Requests for Fiscal Year 1986 under the Foreign Assistance Program.

[b] In 1983, the Philippine Government demanded increased compensation from the U.S. for the use of certain military bases. In the event the U.S. failed to meet the demand, there was a veiled threat of a reorientation towards the Soviet Union.

[c] 65.5 percent of all country aid projected for 1986 and 78.1 percent of all aid to non-European LDCs. In addition, Turkey, Greece, Spain, and Portugal were scheduled to receive $939.000, $501.750, $415.000 and $218.000 million respectively or 15.9 percent of the total projected for all less developed countries in the Third World and in Europe.

can be effective in time to prevent the tragedy of famine. Experience shows that the answer to both questions suggests reliance on internal measures first.*

Most certainly not contributing to the narrowing, let alone the closing, of the viability gap was the pronounced shift from economic to military considerations as the deciding aid criterion. In 1985 seventeen countries were projected by the U.S. government to qualify for more than 100 million dollars each in military or economic aid. All had one thing in common: all played key roles in the United States' geostrategic designs to counter the Soviet Union and its allies.

A review of U.S. aid and assistance policies since World War Two indicates that outright grant and military assistance components of the overall U.S. aid program varied in direct proportion to worldwide tensions. The Korean and Vietnam wars caused grants to rise sharply along with military assistance to countries of immediate strategic value. As soon as tensions abated, grants and military assistance dropped sharply in favor of modest loans and nonmilitary development aid. For example, between 1950 and 1954 U.S. assistance grew 25 percent in the aggregate while the military portion grew from less than 5 percent to about 50 percent; the latter rose to 70 percent in the early 1970s, as the Vietnam conflict reached its peak.†(See Table 15-1.)

* Aside from emergency aid to starving people, giving away food surpluses on continuing basis could aggravate the problem in the Third World because it tends to remove any incentive for them to grow their own crops.

† U.S. Department of State (April 4, 1983), pp. 12-15. U.S. assistance of all types exceeded $40 billion during the postwar relief and Marshall Plan periods 1946-1952, of which some $30 billion was in economic aid (150 billion in 1983 dollars). The Marshall Plan (1947) was followed in 1949 by Point IV aid to LDCs; 1951 saw creation of the Mutual Security Agency, a response to the Korean war; 1954 brought the Food for Peace Act. Between 1950 and 1954, in response to perceived Soviet threats, U.S. aid grew some 25 percent in the aggregate, the military portion growing from less than 5 percent to about 50 percent. Vietnam accelerated that shift until it reached about 60 percent in the early 1970s.

In some respects U.S. aid and assistance to its neighbors to the South is symptomatic of North-South relations generally; in some respects it is unique, reflecting the special security interests the U.S. has traditionally pursued in the Western Hemisphere. On balance, one cannot say that the U.S. assigned high priority to measures designed to narrow the viability gap anywhere south of its borders. President Roosevelt's "Good Neighbor Policy," President Kennedy's "Alliance for Progress," and President Reagan's 1982 "Caribbean Basin Initiative" (CBI) failed to reflect that intent in practice. The "Good Neighbor Policy" was side-tracked by World War Two, the Alliance for Progress by the Cold War and the extension of Soviet influence to Cuba; the CBI was quickly overtaken by the general scourge of all aid programs, the primacy of military aid and by the threat of social revolution. The Caribbean and Mexico have been set back especially by the flight of capital, including loan capital from the U.S. which tends to flow back to U.S. safe havens, primarily in Florida and Texas. See *The New York Times* (February 2, 1982): "Frightened Central American businessmen are stashing their savings in Florida's banks and condominium market, causing an annual capital flight of more than $500 million. U.S. banks withdrew from January 1980 to June 1981, $200 million more. U.S. policies have tended to aid the 1-2 percent, who account for up to 50 percent of all income in South and Central America, more than the poor." See *Democracy* (July 1981), pp. 92ff.

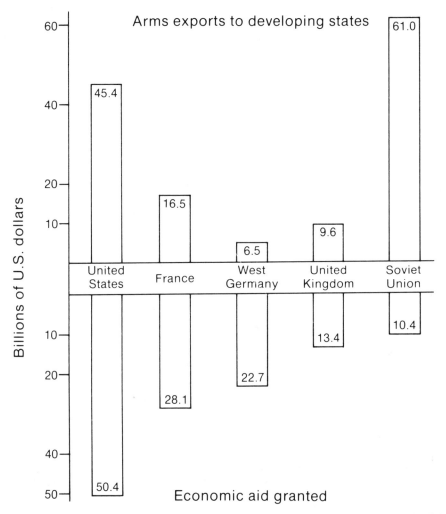

Fig. 15-1a. Economic Aid Granted and Arms Exports to LDCs, 1973–1982. (USACDA, *World Military Expenditures and Arms Transfers 1968–1977* and *1972–1982*, p. 11 and 9 respectively.)

Gradually it became clear to Western donors that unrest in Third World countries had military-strategic implications, as it provided opportunities for the Soviet Union and its proxies, especially in militarily sensitive areas such as the Middle East, Southeast Asia, East Africa, and Central America. That realization gave rise to "a new philosophy" on aid, leading in the United States to congressional passage of "new direction legislation" in 1973. A Department of State report gave the background for the new approach:

During the 1960s, it was commonly assumed that capital-intensive projects such as dams, railroads, and highways would guarantee an 'economic take-off' in the developing countries; that the benefits of such projects—jobs, food, education, and higher incomes—would inevitably 'trickle down' to the poorest people in those countries. The results, however, fell short of expectations, and today's working

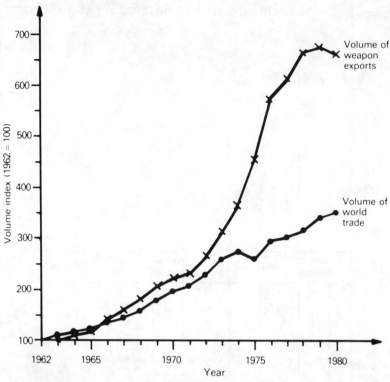

Fig. 15-1b. Export of Major Weapons to the Third World and World Trade, 1962–1980.
SOURCE: *SIPRI Yearbook 1982*, Fig. 1, p. xxvii. Reproduced by permission of SIPRI.

assumption is that it is equally important to improve the distribution of income and basic services to the very poorest people.

. . . Donor and developing countries have re-designed their development programs to raise the productivity and incomes of the poor and ultimately to help make Third World countries self-sufficient.[4]

As the world's leading donor, the U.S. set the tone, the major share of its aid flow being directed to secure "free access to the petroleum of the Persian Gulf." As revolutionary unrest and uprisings threatened to open Central America to hostile influences, Washington moved that region up on its priority scale. Multi-lateral aid from OECD countries, including the U.S., applied through a variety of outlets, took up the slack in strategically less critical areas.

At the outset of the first development decade (1960–1970) a UN resolution sponsored by the Southern group proposed that public sector "official" development aid from the industrial countries should amount to at least 0.7 percent of their GNP. By 1982, OECD countries' Official Development Assistance (ODA) had averaged only 0.35 percent with the Netherlands leading with 1.08 and the U.S. trailing with 0.27 percent; the Soviet Union, not an OECD member, contributed only 0.1 percent. In terms of total aid the U.S. continued to lead, accounting for 29.7 percent of all OECD-ODA aid in 1982.

Table 15-2. Official Development Assistance: Who Gives How Much?
1981

	ODA $ million	Share in world ODA %	ODA as per cent of GNP %	Per capita income US$
Arab Gulf States	7,317	20.5	3.85	16,120
Of which: Saudi Arabia	5,658	15.8	4.66	13,040
UAE[a]	799	2.2	2.88	36,040[a]
Kuwait	685	1.9	1.98	23,650
Qatar	175	0.5	2.64	26,520
Iraq	143	0.4	0.37	2,930
Libya	105	0.3	0.37	9,230
Algeria	65	0.2	0.16	2,120
Nigeria	149	0.4	0.17	1,000
Venezuela	67	0.2	0.10	4,790
Iran	−150	−0.4	−	(2,100)
Total OPEC	**7,696**	**21.6**	−	−
United States	5,783	16.2	0.20	12,730
EEC[b]	12,743	35.7	−	−
Of which: France	4,177	11.7	0.73	10,560
Germany	3,181	8.9	0.47	11,130
United Kingdom	2,195	6.1	0.44	8,980
Netherlands	1,510	4.2	1.08	9,770
Italy	665	1.9	0.19	6,090
Belgium	575	1.6	0.59	9,780
Denmark	403	1.1	0.73	10,820
Japan	3,171	8.9	0.28	9,580
Canada	1,189	3.3	0.43	11,320
Sweden	916	2.6	0.83	13,320
Norway	467	1.3	0.82	13,,890
Other OECD Donors	1,641	4.1	−	−
Total OECD	**25,910**	**72.1**	−	−
USSR	1,661	4.7	0.15	(4,240)
GDR (DDR)[c]	194	0.5	0.16	(7,390)
Other East European Countries	274	0.8	0.10	(3,330)
Total CMEA	**2,129**	**6.0**	−	−
Total ABOVE	**35,735**	**99.7**	−	−

SOURCE: OECD. *Aid From OPEC Countries*, Paris: OECD, 1983, Table 1.2, p. 15.
Figures in parentheses estimated.
[a] United Arab Emirates; per capita income as of 1980.
[b] Including Ireland and Luxembourg.
[c] German Democratic Republic.

Compared with OECD donors, members of OPEC, especially the four leading Arab members grouped in the Organization of Arab Petroleum Exporting

Countries or OAPEC, compiled a far more impressive record.* However, in 1980, a representative Arab publication hinting at probable cutbacks, reported that "In some cases now coming to light, for every $1 million of aid, less than $100,000 finds effective application in African countries like Zambia and Zaire."[5]

Finance and Trade

The loan capital solution: At one point, the more radical regimes had demanded a $300 billion transfer, "free and clear by the year 2000." Instead, by the early 1980s, several of the LDCs were awash with borrowed funds at cost to them well beyond their means. We discussed aspects of the debt tangle in earlier chapters. Here we want to examine specifically its impact on the viability gap.

To be sure, the concerted drive by the world's banking community, led by the major Western banking giants working in close cooperation with the IMF and the IRBD, to recycle surplus funds to the LDCs did provide in many cases the impetus for economic development envisaged in earlier UN and Group 77 resolutions. Several developing states on the verge of industrialization used the borrowed funds to attempt a leap forward toward that cherished goal. Others like Brazil, Mexico, and Argentina expanded existing industries as rapidly as possible. If one did not examine reported progress too closely, prospects seemed good that two or perhaps three dozen LDCs would by that means graduate into the developed class by the end of the century, if not earlier. Unfortunately, reality fell far short of that goal.

From 1976 and 1985, LDC borrowing rose from about $200 billion to $800 billion. It soon became apparent that borrowers as well as lenders had overestimated their respective capacities, the former misjudging their management skills, the latter their ability to subject the more imprudent among their clients to customary bank-imposed constraints. As borrower after borrower approached insolvency, the leading banks and with them many Western governments found themselves locked in, not unlike a would-be rescuer locked in the grasp of a potential drowning victim. That is one reason why LDC lending continued in the face of threatening disaster. For example, between 1975 and 1979, when oil price increases clearly reduced LDC capacity to pay interest on their debts let alone repay the loans, "bank lending to twenty-one of the major LDC borrowers grew at an annual rate of over 30 percent."†

---

* It is debatable whether OPEC should be regarded as part of the capitalist North or as part of the South. One might consider it part of the South-South self-help effort, but only to an extent.

† Griffiths (1983), p. 31. Other explanations, touched upon earlier, are profits earned by banks from interest payments and commissions from rescheduling. Also oil revenue available for recycling increased the banks' capacity to lend.

In their defense, bankers noted that not all borrowers sank deeper into debt.* Moreover, the U.S. secretary of the Treasury argued, the entire lending operation was merely a temporary measure to put swollen oil revenues to work at a time when the prime engines of LDC progress, the industrial countries, were in the the throes of recession. It was hoped that U.S. recovery would eventually trigger recovery in the Western world in general which would "help debtors off the rock."[6]

In chapter 12 we discussed the steadily rising debt-service/export-earning ratio which threatened to strangle some of the major LDC borrowers. That was the "rock" the secretary had in mind.† Whatever analogy one used, the loan approach could not by itself produce a permanent solution. Massive infusions of finance capital produced in the borrowing LDCs a dangerous euphoria, generating a false sense of progress, relieving both borrowers and lenders of immediate pressure to address more fundamental needs. The vagaries of international money markets were far too unpredictable, generally far too erratic to serve as a basis for rational economic planning.‡ According to the U.S. State Department, "Every 1% shift in world interest rates translates into roughly a $2 billion net increase in interest payments by the non-oil [exporting]

Table 15-3. Public and Private Debt of Developing Countries
1973 and 1978–1983
(in billions of U.S. dollars)

	1973	1978	1979	1980	1981	1982	1983
All Developing Countries							
Debt disbursed and outstanding	109.2	299.9	353.0	406.5	464.6	517.8	575.0
Debt service	16.0	48.2	63.4	71.1	82.8	93.0	96.0
Major Borrowers[a]							
Debt disbursed and outstanding	71.7	196.3	230.9	261.8	300.1	330.5	360.0
Debt service	10.3	32.3	46.0	50.7	58.5	65.5	67.0

SOURCE: World Bank, *Debt and the Developing World*, 1984, Table 1, p. ix.

[a] Major borrowers: Algeria, Argentina, Brazil, Chile, Egypt, India, Indonesia, Israel, Republic of Korea, Mexico, Turkey, Venezuela, and Yugoslavia; each owing at least $13.5 billion to external creditors. Between 1970 and 1983 Latin America's debt alone rose from $27 billion to $350 billion.

* For example, A.W. Clausen, President of the World Bank, noted in April of 1983 that 27 nations had graduated from being borrowers at the Bank's "soft loan window" (the International Development Association [IDA] established for low-income LDCs) to become clients of the Bank itself, now meeting tougher terms (1983), p. 4. The IDA was created in 1959 as an affiliate of the World Bank group. It lends money on soft terms, that is at no interest, for a low service charge, and for long repayment periods.

† See Chapter 12, p. 233 above. This is sometimes expressed as the debt service/hard currency earning ratio.

‡ As interest rose in the U.S., for example, the dollar strengthened, which improved many an LDCs export position, mainly because it caused imports into the U.S. to become less expensive. At the same time, however, higher interest rates drove up the cost of LDC borrowing.

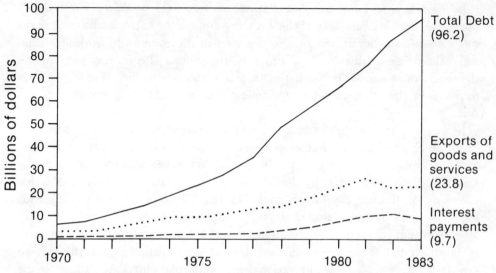

Fig. 15-2a.   Brazil's Debt (*World Bank Tables* and *Wall Street Journal*, May 16, 1984).

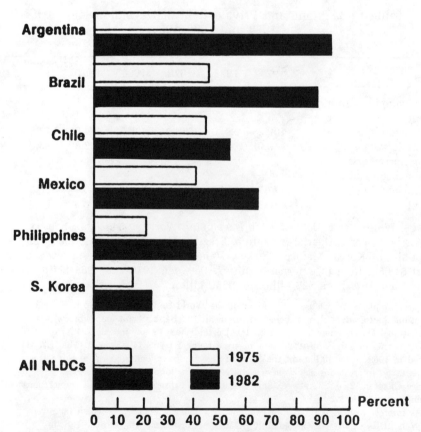

Fig. 15-2b. Debt Service Ratios for 6 Non-Oil-Exporting LDCs. (U.S. Congress, Senate (1983), *Hearings*, International Debt, Chart 12, p. 376.)

Nominal Interest Rate[1]

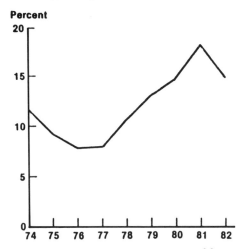

Real Interest Rate[2]

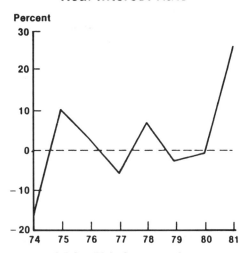

Fig. 15-2c. Interest Rates Faced by Non-Oil-Exporting LDCs. (U.S. Congress, Senate (1983), *Hearings*, International Debt, Chart 10, p. 374.)

developing countries." That offers yet another illustration of the difficulties capitalism encounters—or engenders—in attempting to manage global economic problems.[7] But capitalism is not alone to blame.

In mid-crisis heavily indebted Argentina embarked upon a military campaign to regain the Falkland Islands (Malvinas). Defeated in that effort, and while its debts continued to mount, it next embarked upon a costly rearmament program. It was reported that of the billions borrowed by Mexico a substantial share, immediately upon receipt, left for safe havens in lending countries, foremost as private investment in real estate in the United States.[8] On balance, whatever the causes the benefits of the entire lending operation failed to trickle down to the presumed real target, the steadily growing mass of the world's poor, which rendered the situation not merely economically critical but politically explosive, encouraging more radically inclined government leaders in the more heavily indebted LDCs to edge ever closer to outright debt repudiation. Insistence by the IMF on draconic austerity measures as a condition for further loans— we noted earlier that private bankers now pressed for internationalization of the burden, hence increased IMF involvement—merely fed that flame. So did suggestions by the World Bank that LDCs, including the major borrowers, not deviate significantly from existing trade relations with the North, relations, we have noted, regarded by structuralists and Marxists as basic causes of Third World economic retardation.*

---

* According to documentation captured by U.S. forces during the invasion of the Caribbean island of Grenada, the deposed Marxist government had planned to falsify its financial records to secure assistance from or endorsement by the IMF. *The Wall Street Journal* (November 16, 1983), p. 21. IMF endorsement of a debtor country's internal economic policies is a prerequisite for further loans from private banks or for rescheduling of current debts.

Ironically, especially in Latin America and the Caribbean, repercussions from the malfunctioning of the debt structure jeopardized two of the Western world's most cherished goals: to make the world safe for Western-style political democracy and to stabilize it militarily. The former was endangered as already unstable LDC governments were confronted with demands for internal reforms as a precondition for adjustment of their debts, the latter receded into the distance as, in the context of the East–West confrontation, all forms of social revolution or unrest including those of wholly indigenous provenance tended to assume global military-strategic implications. A change of government anywhere on earth favoring the left was interpreted by many American leaders as a strategic gain for the Soviet Union, a change bringing right-wing elements to power was presumed to benefit the West; both conditions inevitably precipitated military or social-revolutionary countermoves by the "losing" side.* It is clear that the loan capital formula was not working. Something had to be added to the package which would appeal not only to bankers and small ruling elites but to the steadily more disadvantaged masses. This brings us to the attempt to narrow the viability gap through trade and investment.

Mutual prosperity through trade: As a means of narrowing the viability gap, trade is at best a very long-term proposition. For LDCs in the lower per capita income group, long-term extends into the next century. But even for LDCs with reasonable chances for success, the future is far from encouraging, one reason of course being the fact that capital flow and trade are closely interrelated.

Whether because of economic stagnation or political impediments, world trade (which had grown significantly between 1963 and 1973) began flagging in 1981, possibly a delayed reaction to the oil price crisis. Perhaps the downward trend reflected a change in favor of investment capital, a consequence in turn of unfavorable economic conditions in the developing countries. As one U.S. official put it:

> As export growth slows down, the danger is that too many countries will succumb to the temptation to adjust imports to fit current earnings and thus accelerate the downward trend.
>
> The jeopardies in the field of capital are different but no less deadly. Heavily indebted countries may impose new capital controls—in an effort to retain the funds they have—or fail to meet payments and thus put all flows at risk. At a time when world competition for capital is intensifying, either can be disabling. In a capital-

---

* In 1983 for instance, Brazil faced a 1:5 unemployment rate, its rate of inflation approaching 200 percent per annum. IMF demands that the rate of inflation be cut by 75 percent, that the practice of indexing wages to inflation be abandoned or drastically modified, that a temporary wage freeze be instituted, that subsidies to workers be discontinued, that a sales tax be levied to improve the yield from state-owned corporations, and so forth, probably placed greater strain on Brazilian plans to embark upon another "experiment with democracy" than would have been the case had the Soviet Union or Cuba endeavored to interfere with these plans. Reports that the government was about to bow to IMF demands for austerity measures triggered riots in the Dominican Republic, Argentina, and Mexico in 1983 and 1984.

short world, the open economies will attract a disproportionate share of available funds.[9]

In short, debt-ridden LDCs were forced to reduce imports from the developed world, while the latter redirected its surplus capital to safer environments. A further downturn in world trade threatened both, as exports to LDCs and imports from them were in the former case essential to sustain the remaining sources of loan capital to prevent a total collapse of the debt structure and in the latter case equally essential to enable borrowers to service their debts. Still, the primary motivation for trade concessions to the South remained Northern self-interest, especially the interest of the EEC group and Japan, the latter importing more than 90 percent of its mineral needs from the Third World, the latter 75 percent; U.S. dependence hovered somewhere between 10 and 15 percent. The latter fact weighs heavily against LDC leverage as that places the world's most powerful economy beyond the retaliatory reach of most of the developing countries. It also serves to explain the slow pace of North–South negotiations.

In these negotiations the principal partner was, on the LDC side, the Group of 77, operating under the general sponsorship of GATT; the former European colonies operated within that framework and within the EEC, in close association with France and within the British Commonwealth. The leading Western industrial nations, whose consent was essential if any agreement was to be effective, negotiated on a bilateral basis or through ad hoc groupings within the several international organizational frameworks.

After years of seemingly unproductive discourse, some barriers to developing country exports were reduced first through the Generalized System of Preferences (GSP), a system approved by GATT in 1971 (adopted by the United States in 1976) and then under agreements reached in conjunction with the Tokyo Round of Multilateral Trade Negotiations (MTN). As a result of the former, among several concessions, manufactured and agricultural products from LDCs were allowed to enter participating DCs duty free; under the latter, to cite one example, the major industrial countries reduced their industrial tariffs by 33 percent "on a weighted averaged basis." In the eyes of Western negotiators, these agreements marked "an enormous step forward in North-South economic relations."[10] From the LDC point of view, foremost that of the non-oil-exporting ones, none of these concessions constituted progress sufficient to overcome their handicap. Certainly none sufficed as compensation for past injustices.[11]

The *World Bank Development Report,* 1983 indicates substantial increases in shares of world merchandise exports on the part of the high-income oil-exporters, moderate increases between 1965 and 1980 in the share of middle-income countries, but steady decrease experienced by developing countries overall. The relative lack of progress on the part of the middle-income countries becomes quite apparent if measured from their base in 1955, in the face of rising costs of energy and worldwide inflation generally.*

An alternate approach to the problem is to stabilize LDC earnings from commodity exports, typically the major if not sole source of foreign exchange. We shall address this subject in Chapter 16 in conjunction with an overall assessment of the struggle over the world's resources.

Direct foreign investment: A World Bank analysis of direct private investment in LDCs shows that even under most favorable conditions that source of capital for development will not begin to compare with loans or aid (see Figs. 14-4a, b).[12] Several reasons account for that: economically depressed conditions in the industrial countries, a resultant liquidity squeeze with accompanying high interest rates, increased risks facing investors because of threats of nationalization, frequent work stoppages, supply disruptions, and other negative factors arising from social and political instability; increasingly discouraging are costs of doing business in developing countries due to widespread graft and corruption on the part of host government, officials, or native entrepreneurs.

Direct private investment increased steadily during the first independence decade. Then came a period of reaction to the past when foreign investment and foreign aid as well were ever more vehemently denounced by potential beneficiaries as instruments of neoimperialism or neo-colonialism, denunciations often though coincident with requests for more aid and loans.[13] Eventually even the more militant advocates of social revolution and detachment from the capitalist world came to see the futility of their position. Loss of foreign investment capital, they now realized, also meant loss of needed technology and management skills. The changing posture, coupled with generous "overseas investment risk insurance" underwritten by donor governments, resulted in a modest increase. Still, no matter how attractively packaged LDCs invitations to foreign investors may be, they cannot hope to compete with far more attractive and far less troublesome invitations from more advanced and stable countries, including as already noted the members of the socialist bloc. Most certainly, the LDCs in greatest need, that is the low-income oil-importing countries, will not rank high on prudent investors' lists.

Socialist Practice

Unlike the Western, capitalist approach, socialist governments are nominally at least guided by ideological considerations. From that vantage point, the plight of the LDCs is attributed almost exclusively to abuse and neglect as-

* p. 25. One reason for the LDCs lack of progress is reflected in the following summary of their experience in the wake of the Tokyo Round:

The average tariff cuts affecting [the LDCs] . . . were less than those affecting products of industrial countries. In the case of the United States, the average tariff on developing countries' dutiable industrial products is almost twice as high as the average tariff on products from the European Community and Japan, and more than three times as high as those from Canada. Ibid., p. 156.

sociated with Western imperialism and colonialism. For that reason neither the Soviet Union nor its allies nor for that matter the Chinese communists consider it their duty to extend themselves and assume a proportionate share of the steadily mounting burden. Having gone on record that it is not their intent to bail out imperialist powers or save capitalism, they are prepared to derive from the rapidly deteriorating situation whatever propaganda or strategic advantage it may offer.

The Soviet Bloc*

In its posture toward the Third World the bloc, under the banner of revolutionary solidarity with the world's exploited and oppressed, underwent an interesting metamorphosis between 1954, the beginning of its campaign to penetrate the theretofore forbidden imperialist domaines, and the 1980s when new and different concerns called for a change of direction. By then the Soviet Union and its CMEA/COMECON partners had pressed forward with their own industrialization to a point where such matters as access to raw materials began to eclipse ideological considerations and self-interest began to replace socialist solidarity. Initially the burden of rendering whatever assistance could be spared fell almost exclusively upon the Soviet Union. Only gradually did other bloc members acquire the capacity to assume their share and, with Moscow's prodding, enter the field.

Aid and assistance: In keeping with its more limited interests and commitments—we recall that the Soviet perception of what is required by the LDCs and where or how that is to be applied differs vastly from the Western perception—Soviet bloc assistance to the Third World reflects four major policy objectives: First: limited financial, material, and technical resources are to be applied to strategically significant target countries, principally in the Middle East, North and East Africa, Southeast Asia, and Cuba. Should other "Cubas" develop in Central or Latin America, these might be included. Second: aid is to be directed to facilitate the overthrow or destabilization of weak regimes or shore up pro-bloc regimes where these are threatened. Third: following purely commercial and military-strategic interests, aid is to be directed where the bidding is open for critical mineral resources, including oil, or for other primary commodities currently in short supply within the bloc or likely to pose serious supply problems in the future. Fourth: where feasible, Chinese Communist influence is to be countered.[14]

Where the objective is to establish Marxist or Communist regimes, given the record of Communist rule in the bloc—in Cuba for instance or in Ethiopia—the impact of bloc aid on recipients' viability status is at best exceedingly long-range (unless, as was attempted under the Khmer Rouge regime in Kampuchea,

---

* Data here used are restricted to the Soviet Union and Eastern Europe. Cuba, also a bloc member but like the PRC a "developing country" as well, warrants separate consideration.

a country's development targets are artificially lowered by physicial liquidation of its more demanding upper and middle classes).[15]

Central economic planning and control advantages and disadvantages bloc aid. Since both trade and aid are under socialism the responsibility of central government, both being financed essentially out of the same public fund, both can therefore more readily be coordinated and adjusted to serve specific foreign policy objectives. In practical terms, if foreign policy goals so require, bloc trade can temporarily be conducted at a loss. On the other hand, relatively generous credits offered aid recipients are frequently only partially used because centrally planned, nonmarket economies set unrealistic prices for comparatively unattractive goods. It is not uncommon that delegations from LDCs commissioned to locate in bloc countries goods, especially equipment, suitable for their particular needs, return empty-handed.* For that reason recipients tend to prefer credits tied to specific projects, a dam or a plant, to be constructed for them by the socialist donor. Also preferred are outright grants, technical assistance, and exchange programs.

Technical assistance may extend to construction and initial operation of donated projects or to the training of native cadres who are expected to assume responsibility after the foreign instructors and advisors are withdrawn. Costs of training personnel are partly covered by credits, partly, and increasingly in recent years, by payment in hard currency. Where interests are charged, bloc loans offer relatively low rates, typically between 2 and 2.5 percent. (But as noted, what the recipient receives in return, frequently is overpriced).

Until recently, bloc donors gained a degree of popularity because loan repayment was possible with traditional exports, including products of projects constructed with bloc assistance. When repayment was demanded in hard currency, LDC enthusiasm waned. Moreover, several beneficiaries of the payment-through-traditional-export policy discovered to their dismay that their products were promptly sold to their traditional customers for hard currency, at prices below those the LDC could have obtained had they sold the commodities themselves.† Beyond that, critics of bloc, especially Soviet, tactics have pointed out that the apparently soft terms actually conceal hard-nosed practices, including cost and price manipulation similar to those which cause resentment among Moscow's East European client states.

Precise data on bloc aid and assistance are kept secret; data here used are compiled by Western, mainly U.S. and OECD, agencies. The reason for that secrecy is not difficult to fathom: the share of bloc aid of official development

---

* Of a total $57,104 million credits and grants pledged by the Soviet bloc between 1954 and 1978, only $24,340 million were actually drawn. The PRC, during the same period, pledged $4,756 million and $2,540 million were drawn. CIA (1979), Table 6, p. 11.

† See Bretton (1962), on the case of the Ghana cocoa crop transferred to the Soviet Union in exchange for aid, machinery, and technical assistance; that crop was sold to Ghana's previous customers below then current world market prices. In the 1980s, oil shipped by Libya to the Soviet Union in payment for arms aid was promptly sold by the Soviet Union to the Netherlands below levels set by OPEC, of which Libya is a member.

aid worldwide is embarrassingly small, amounting to about 10 percent of all official aid agreements with developing countries between 1975 and 1980, dropping to about 4 percent in 1981.* Also, in countries where consumers are hard pressed as are those in most bloc countries, aid to foreigners is even less popular than in the comparatively affluent West.

Secrecy at home stands in stark contrast to publicity abroad. Eager to extract maximum propaganda advantage from relatively limited aid, the Soviet Union concentrates its largess on "expensive, eye-catching heavy industrial public sector projects," according to Soviet media, accounting for about 75 percent of all Soviet economic aid.[16] Outstanding examples are the previously mentioned Aswan Dam project in Egypt and the Bokharo and Bhilai steel mills in India. For the same reason the Soviet Union eschewed for many years the anonymity of aid through international organization or multilateral agreements, preferring a highly publicized, one-to-one relationship. This changed with progressing bloc economic integration, the transferrable ruble facilitating a shift from bilateral to multilateral CMEA aid programs.[17]

Official protestations of bloc disinterest in political gain can safely be discounted. For one, the accent on public sector projects clearly is designed to provide the aid recipients with effective instruments of social change. Soviet and other bloc technicians quite frequently turn out to be more politically involved in host country internal affairs than meets the eye, a fact brought out by mass expulsions from numerous LDCs, foremost Egypt, Sudan, Somalia, and Guinea; and, increasingly, ulterior commercial motives and a quest for Third World resources, oil and phosphates for examples, inject themselves in bloc–LDC relations.[18] Still, it is an article of faith among bloc rulers that in its service to recipients their aid differs qualitatively from that provided by the West.†

Do Soviet leaders have a point when they claim that proprietary concessions sought and secured in LDCs by capitalist entrepreneurs, mainly MNCs interested in minerals, are detrimental to LDC interests whereas government-to-government aid, without proprietary claims, is beneficial? Only if reality is ignored, for bloc emphasis on the state sector has in case after case simply aided corrupt, incompetent, or power-hungry dictators to construct a power base, not so much to advance the cause of social revolution as to entrench

* In 1975 Soviet development aid amounted to 0.03 to 0.05 percent of its GNP compared with U.S. aid to the extent of 0.3 percent. *The New York Times* (August 20, 1976). see, CIA (July 1976), pp. 5–6; World Bank, *World Development Report 1982*, Table 16, p. 40. U.S. Department of State, Bureau of Intelligence Research (February 1983), Tables 4 and 5, p. 4.

† For example, Kostyukhin (1979), p. 125, who writes: "Socialist countries do not take advantage of the economic and political difficulties of other countries to obtain concessions or privileges for themselves, and consider political or economic conditions that infringe [sic] the interests of one of the parties to be inadmissible. . . . or, in the words of [Leonid] Brezhnev 'The Soviet Union does not look for advantages, does not hunt for concessions, does not seek political domination, and is not after military bases.' "

themselves.* What of the policy, also significantly different from the capitalist approach, of training, insofar as possible, native cadres to replace foreign technical assistance personnel? Numerically the bloc exceeds the West in this respect by a wide margin. In numerous instances, bloc technical assistance is more relevant and in that sense is qualitatively superior to what the West has to offer. Moreover, since bloc technical assistance typically addresses recipient countries' more basic needs, it is relatively easier to train native replacements. However, inevitably native cadres turn out to be politically indoctrinated to serve their foreign benefactors—another reason why bloc personnel are expelled so frequently.[19] Also, if bloc and Western technical assistance programs are to be compared, it must be noted that lately sharply increased bloc contributions in this sphere, rising to a record high of 115,000 personnel in 1981, constitute "one of their most profitable undertakings in the LDCs," as two-thirds of their technicians are paid in hard currency for their services.[20]

But the severest drawback with respect to LDC concerns and prospects stems from the aggressive and rapidly escalating bloc emphasis on military assistance and sales, neither of which is likely to contribute to the closing or even narrowing of the viability gap, especially as military sales, amounting to $14 billion in 1980, further drained precious hard currency from the LDCs' so "aided."[21] The West, not wishing to fall behind, further aggravates that hemorrhage. (Because neither effort is germane to the central concern of this chapter, the subject is discussed in Part Four).

For the first two decades of bloc participation in the competition, one argument frequently advanced by bloc spokesmen appeared valid: entry by the bloc into this field significantly improved the LDCs' bargaining position vis-á-vis the capitalist world, who now had to match the softer terms offered by the communist competition. When the Soviet Union and several other CMEA partners began to insist on repayment in hard currency, that argument lost its validity.[22] But most telling may be the fact that all OECD countries spent in one single year (1980) $27.2 billion compared with $34.2 billion which the entire Soviet bloc spent in 27 years of its participation in that form of assistance to the world's noncommunist poor.†

Trade: A U.S. Congressional study found that "the Soviet Union's trade pattern with the LDCs is remarkably similar to that of the highly industrialized

---

* Examples are the for Uganda catastrophic, rapacious, and murderous regime of Idi Amin Dada (1971-1979)—misrepresented to the Soviet public as the epitome of Third World "socialist heroism," Sekou Touré who ruined the economy of Guinea and brought its people close to perpetual poverty, and Nkrumah of Ghana who, though closer to the socialist model, also with Soviet bloc help set the stage for his country's descent into economic and social chaos.

† World Bank, *World Development Report 1983*, p. 182, and U.S. Department of State (February 1983), p. 17. If the approximately $12 billion in loans and disbursements by the World Bank and the $5.2 billion from the IBRD-IDA are added, the total non-communist aid is $44 billion in 1980 versus $34.2 billion Soviet bloc aid between 1954-1981. Soviet aid to Cuba represents an entirely different aid category and should therefore not be considered in this connection; see also C.I.A. *Handbook of Economic Statistics*, 1983, Table 79, p. 110.

Table 15-4. Soviet Bloc and PRC Aid to LDCs (in million US $)

| | 1954–81 | | 1954–78 |
	USSR	Eastern Europe	China (PRC)
Total	22,355	11,885	4,756
North Africa	3,250	980	331
Sub-Saharan Africa	2,870	1,990	2,368
East Asia	260	665	274
Latin America	1,420	2,135	154
Middle East	7,925	4,495	462
South Asia	6,625	1,370	1,153
Other		250	

SOURCE: US Department of State, *Soviet and Eastern European Aid to the Third World*, 1981, February 1983, Table 10 and CIA, National Foreign Assessment Center, ER 79–1041U, September 1979, Table 5, pp. 7–10. Not included in these compilations are Communist LDCs, that is Cuba, Mongolia, Vietnam and North Korea. During 1981/2 Cuba and Vietnam received 69 percent of all Soviet Aid and GO percent of East European Aid, OECD, *Development Co-Operation*, 1983, p. 90.

nations of the West. Food stuffs and raw materials make up the majority of the Soviet Union's imports from the Third World while manufactured goods—in particular machinery and industrial equipment—comprise a major portion of Soviet exports to the LDCs." To which another observer added that "this arrangement has the effect of perpetuating a trade pattern which is another context the Communists label 'imperialist.'"[23] In their defense, Soviet spokesmen point to the heavy emphasis on the Soviet bloc's part on exports to LDCs of material essential for their industrial development.[24] Overlooked in that explanation is the fact that an increasing share of Soviet and bloc trade with LDCs, similar to aid, is taken up by arms transfers, with unmistakable intent to incite wars likely to drain LDC resources even more.*

At the same time, mounting pressure from their own resource-starved industries has spurred the bloc to go beyond political—or even military—strategic considerations and earnestly engage the West in competition for Third World resources wherever these can be found, employing identical methods if that proves necessary. For example, as one report has it, "in Western multinational-style operation [the Soviet Union and its COMECON partners] have discreetly set up more than 600 companies."[25] By other accounts, the total is between 500 and 600. In any case, a majority of these companies located in OECD countries are set up to facilitate service, marketing, and manufacturing, partly using resources from LDCs economically associated with the OECD system. Between 180 and 200 of these establishments represent COMECON members

* In 1973, over 70 percent of Soviet-LDC trade was with Third World nations within the "national liberation zone" of the Near East and Southeast Asia. *Ibid.;* see also CIA (1979), pp. 1–6.

in LDCs, directing their attention almost exclusively to mining and mineral export.* In light of persistent Soviet protestations that it is not the socialist way "to hunt for concessions," it is interesting to note how these novel extensions of bloc economics are financed. Reflecting increasing sophistication, investments are diversified to expand their sweep of Western as well as LDCs goods and services, new corporations are formed through reinvestment of profits and local borrowing rather than with capital drawn from already strapped COMECON economies.[26]

Cuba's role: In return for substantial bloc (principally Soviet) aid, Cuba has gradually assumed the role of a proxy, providing technical including military personnel in areas where Soviet bloc personnel could not be introduced in large numbers. By 1978 about three-fourths of Cuba's contribution served in Angola. By 1981 large contingents had been added to serve in Libya, Ethiopia, Mozambique, Nicaragua, and Iran.†

The People's Republic of China (PRC)

Aid and assistance: Itself a Third World country in the lower income category, ranking next to some of the world's poorest countries in terms of per capita GNP, Communist China cannot for years to come be expected to play a significant role in the campaign to improve the lot of the LDCs.‡ Between 1954 and 1978, the PRC's total of economic credits and grants extended to LDCs amounted to about 15 percent of all Communist country aid. The real thrust of PRC aid and assistance seems to be assertion, on behalf of the Chinese Communist Party (CCP), of a preeminence over its rival the Soviet Union's CPSU. This is borne out both by the timing of Beijing's entry into the competition and by the targets selected. It seems that the Chinese Communists have convinced themselves that as non-whites representing a Third World state, a victim of imperialism like all the others, they rather than the caucasians who rule the Soviet Union are entitled to play a leading role in the emancipation and advancement of the world's oppressed and underprivileged.[27]

In form, PRC aid and assistance is similar to that offered by the other Communist states and for identical reasons: extension of credits and grants, provision of technical personnel, and exchange programs. One difference is that with more laborers to spare, at costs considerably below that required to maintain

---

* Some of these enterprises carefully conceal their bloc identity, which enables them to circumvent some of the barriers Western nations have set up to protect their interests. In at least one instance, several dummy corporations were established in neutral Switzerland to enable the Soviet Union and some of its partners to trade with Southern Rhodesia—now Zimbabwe—this at a time when bloc-supported resolutions in the UN had ordered a blockade of that then white-ruled African country because of its racist policies.

† U.S. Department of State, Bureau of Intelligence Research (February 1983), Table 11, pp. 20–21 and CIA (1979), Table 7, pp. 14–15. Smaller contingents served in such places as Grenada, locale of military action by the United States in 1983.

‡ The World Bank, *World Development Report 1984,* shows the PRC 12th from the bottom among 126 countries listed with reference to per capita GNP, Table 1, p. 218.

Soviet and East European personnel, the PRC can support labor-intensive projects more readily than can the bloc.* Overall, the pattern seems to be that the PRC either anticipates or follows Soviet bloc efforts.†

Trade: The People's Republic's trade with LDCs is still negligible. Goods offered on credit frequently prove unsuitable and choices are too limited, which renders credit arrangements unattractive for all but projects for which material is furnished by the donor. However, the PRC exceeds all other LDCs in manufactured exports to other developing countries, in other words within the North-South trading context, a subject we shall examine next.[28]

The LDC-Approach: Self Help

The foregoing discussion offers little support for optimism that either the capitalist or the socialist approach or the combination of these efforts will significantly boost the South's chances to catch up with the North. There is therefore no reason to assume that self-help on the part of the world's poor will do the job; the situation does not improve even if the high-income oil-exporting Arab group—whose aid, we noted, is considerable—is counted as part of the South. Still, it is worth noting that what might be termed "operation bootstrap" is under way. Basically, this takes two forms. First, modest aid begins to flow from some of the more fortunately positioned to those in greatest need. Second, over 7 percent of world trade and over a quarter of all of the South's exports flow within that group. However, this includes trade with high-income oil exporters and with relatively more advanced neighboring countries, geographically located in the South, who are involved peripherally, as processors of LDC commodities, for example.[29]

Capital flow within the South is no more encouraging, according to a Swedish study amounting to no more than 1 percent of all direct foreign investment. A large share of loan capital flowing into LDCs from industrially advanced market economies is, as noted earlier, derived from earnings by oil-exporters and deposited in Western banks before being recycled to LDCs. It would be

---

* By 1975, Beijing increased its already large force of economic technicians to 23,590, surpassing both the Soviet Union or the East European countries combined; the bloc as a whole supplied 31,700. The disparity in numbers was most striking in Africa and Southeast Asia. However, in Africa 90 percent of PRC personnel were working on the initially spectacular Tan-Zam railway, linking copper-rich Zambia with Tanzania's Indian Ocean outlet Dar-es-Salaam. Others were engaged in road construction in Somalia and the Sudan. By 1978, the Tan-Zam project still accounted for one-third of the PRC's total African contingent. The PRC share of total technical personnel had dropped, see CIA (1979), Table 7, pp. 14-15.

† For example, when in 1977 the Soviet Union shifted its support from Somalia to neighboring Ethiopia and 15,000 Cubans were sent to the latter in that connection, the PRC countered by sending 15 percent of its entire technical assistance personnel that year to Somalia, replacing the 6,000 Soviet "technicians" expelled by the Somalis. CIA (1976), Table 5, p. 8, and CIA (1979), Table 7, pp. 14-15. Leading recipients of PRC credits and grants, between 1954 and 1978 were Zambia, Tanzania—the Tan-Zam project—Pakistan, Sri Lanka, Bangladesh, and Nepal, all of the latter intended to counter Soviet courting of India.

far-fetched to classify that circuitious route as part of a Southern self-management system. For one, the Western banks and behind them their respective governments, and not the oil-rich countries, underwrite the debts incurred by LDC borrowers. But in any case even that source is diminishing. It remains true that the only method by which a country can lift itself up by its bootstraps is through investment from savings. The success story in that respect appears to be India's achievement. By 1982 that country recorded a gross investment equivalent of 25 percent of its GNP, 91 percent of which was financed from domestic savings.[30]

The extraordinary dependence of a majority of the LDCs on exports to advanced industrial countries and their overall gloomy and deteriorating position suggest that pending diversification of their economies, more likely as a precondition for such measures, the LDCs must substantially and promptly improve their bargaining position. Adverse terms-of-trade, a need for price stabilization, and so forth are not the only pressing reasons why action has become imperative. A potential economic catastrophe awaits countries whose principle source of outside revenue is a depletable resource, oil for example. In such cases, development of a strong bargaining position is mandatory before the bargaining chip has disappeared.

Realistically, autarky is not an option. Where this has been attempted, as in Tanzania, it has failed. Only three courses of action are available: (1) commodity agreements between producers and consumers, (2) commodity cartels imposing producers' terms on consumers, and (3) extracting maximum advantages, without recourse to formal frameworks, from East-West competiton, to a lesser extent from competition among members of the respective blocs (which pending increased friction within the Soviet bloc applies to the West more than to the East).

Which of these options is actually available and whether it will achieve desired results depends on a number of variables, mainly how critical a given resource is to the major consuming countries as a group. Because this aspect of the developing countries' future is inextricably linked to the global struggle for resources, it is considered under that heading in the following chapter.

Suggested Questions and Discussion Topics

In practical terms, concretely, how and by what means has the capitalist side approached the task of narrowing the viability gap?

What has been the socialist practice in that regard?

How and by what means has the "South" attempted to apply self-help?

What are the advantages, what the disadvantages of the "loan capital solution" and direct foreign investment, as a means of narrowing the gap?

Chapter 16
Resources: Joint Utilization or Conflict?

Those who see in certain resources the wedge needed by the South to break Northern resistance to their demands argue that with continuing expansion of industrialization and defense procurement, the industrial world's dependence on the South is rapidly approaching a critical point; the combined effect of population growth and resource scarcity further accelerates the process.[1] Rejecting the resource war hypothesis, others are inclined to doubt that the North is all that dependent on the South. In addition to the previously mentioned qualifications of essentiality and strategic necessity, skeptics note that renewable resources, agricultural products for example, can be produced in alternate locales, climatic and other environmental factors can be replicated, or the product can be adapted to different conditions by artificial means. With respect to strategic, nonrenewable resources, mineral oil for instance or any one of the other 26 critical ferrous and nonferrous minerals, current scarcity is measured only against known deposits or reserves. But the suspected deposits in most, if not all, nonrenewable resource categories are for practical purposes limitless, awaiting only the time when further exploration becomes technically and commercially feasible in the developed as well as the less developed countries. That point will be reached, so the argument goes, when the advanced industrial powers actually face absolute as distinct from artificially induced shortages.[2] OPEC, this analysis suggests, was made possible not so much because oil deposits were limited and reserves insufficient but because the major multinational oil corporations, the "Seven Sisters", conspired with the principal producers to keep supplies limited and to restrict further exploration.[3] For these reasons, denial to Western industrial states of access to strategic nonrenewable resources on the part of hostile LDCs, either on their own initiative or under pressure from the Soviet Union, even if reinforced by simultaneous disruption of the flow of supplies from the Soviet Union to the West, is not likely to be catastrophic.

Commodity Agreements

With respect to nonstrategic, nonessential resources—whether they are renewable or nonrenewable is of no consequence—the major industrial consumers clearly are in the driver's seat. Convinced that artificial restriction of international trade inevitably works to the disadvantage of both consumers and producers, the former have resisted and continue to resist formation of cartels in these categories. If concessions to producers were at all considered, preference has been for agreements protecting the interests of both. But given the decided edge consumers have over producers in such negotiations, it is not likely that the latter's interests are met even half-way. For instance, producers' demands that import restrictions on their exports be lifted is countered by consumers who will insist that this option be retained to protect them in the event demand for a given commodity declines. Similarly, no matter how urgently producers may seek price adjustment to compensate for market restrictions, or constriction, or for natural disasters such as drought or blight, consuming countries feel obliged to guard against price increases too steep for their processors or manufacturers to bear. For example, in the case of cocoa, chocolate manufacturers in the United States—which unlike Great Britain or France has no former cocoa-producing colonies to assure supply—will simply be driven out of business should the price of that commodity rise too precipitously for too long.

If formal agreement were to permit producers to hold up exports at their discretion, a proposal advanced from time to time, manufacturing in consumer countries could easily be thrown into turmoil, most likely compounding producers' economic problems. Given the volatility of politics in many of the LDCs, export hold-ups could well be a matter of a dictator's whim or could serve more sinister purposes intended to inflict serious harm on Western economies, as a matter of ideological principle perhaps. In light of these and similar concerns, producers' demands for a "fair price" for their products immediately evoke the response: What is a fair price and fair to whom? For these reasons only three commodities have seen any durable agreement: coffee, cocoa, and tin. This is best illustrated by the performance of the International Coffee Agreement (ICA) which, though seriously flawed, worked better than the other two.*

The International Coffee Agreement

Agreement became possible when the largest consumer, the United States, and the leading producer, Brazil, concluded that it was in their mutual interest to stabilize the price of coffee. Negotiated in 1962, administered by the International Coffee Organization (ICO), the agreement was suspended in 1972 when producers and consumers concluded that consumption was exceeding production—Brazil had experienced a serious blight, stocks were declining, and prices

---

* At first, attempts were made to create producer cartels or agreements on such commodities as bauxite, copper, rubber, bananas, iron ore, mercury, and cocoa. All of these fell short of producers' expectations. It was in response to that discouraging experience that UNCTAD IV (1976) proposed an "Integrated Commodity Programme (ICP)," under which commodities were to be "managed jointly" by producers and consumers. See Banks *et al.*, *Economic Handbook of the World, 1981*, pp. 9–10, and Julius L. Katz (April 1976).

received by producers seemed high enough. Had the U.S. accepted the higher prices demanded at that time, coffee consumption there, already declining for extraneous reasons, would have dropped even further, causing consumers to shift in even greater numbers to tea, milk, or soft drinks.

Following a severe frost in Brazil in 1975, a new agreement had to be negotiated, as the supply-demand outlook, compared to conditions underlying the earlier agreement, had not changed drastically. Accordingly the new version, negotiated the same year, dispensed with fixed prices or price indexing.* Instead, export quotas allocated to producers were to be adjusted automatically should prices drop or rise beyond set levels. However, when in 1983 a six-year extension was debated in the United States, it was noted that sharply deteriorating economic conditions in Brazil and in several of the lesser producers, for example Nigeria and the Philippines, had caused these countries to cheat and by means of forged and otherwise illegal documents ship coffee at substantial discounts to replenish their low foreign exchange reserves.[4]

Commodity Agreements in General

Attempts to forge lasting and binding agreements on cocoa foundered on essentially the same difficulties which impeded the coffee agreement from time to time. Producers of agricultural commodities cannot cut production at will. Projects designed to force price increases by storage in producing countries, seriously attempted by Ghana in 1960, are likely to fail for several reasons: damage to stock incurred under tropical conditions being only one of many, stiff competition from other producers being another.

Agreements were negotiated and ratified over the years between some producers and consumers, never by all on either side, on sugar, tin, copper, and bauxite. All had certain mechanisms in common to control price fluctuations, including export or production quotas and buffer stocks, the latter to be built up when prices fell below agreed minimum levels and to be released to the market when they rose above these levels. All fell far short of expectations by major consumers, the U.S. for example, hence became unworkable on that one count alone or proved unacceptable to major producers.

In the case of copper, an air-tight international cartel was out of the question as the four leading producers, Chile, Peru, Zambia, and Zaire, accounted for less than 50 percent of total world production—the Soviet bloc, the United States, Canada, and the Republic of South Africa accounting for the major share.[5] Still, with the Soviet bloc cooperating and not selling copper when agreement partners wished to withhold, the fact that the four did account for approximately 40 percent of "free world" production generated for them a degree of leverage. However their organization, the Intergovernmental Council of Copper Exporting Countries (CIPEC), Indonesia joining the other four, was afflicted

---

* The purpose of price indexing is to prevent sharp price fluctuations by establishing an average price over time as the base for current pricing.

by one of the major defects inhibiting international commodity agreements: the leading consumer, the U.S., also was the leading free world producer, hence was relatively invulnerable to world market price fluctuations and not susceptible to blackmail.[6] Moreover none of the free world copper producers had an interest in bringing about a recession in the industrialized countries, a possible outcome were they to exact too high a price for so critical a product. Not incidental to the LDCs producers' calculations was the fact that among the leading consumers were also the principal providers of foreign aid.

Export Stabilization Programs

Covering a broader range of exports from LDCs but addressing similar problems were a series of conventions between the European Economic Community, the British-led Commonwealth, and most of the former European colonies, the most notable being the one signed in 1975 at Lomé, Togo (Lomé I). The latter followed the Convention signed at Yaoundé, Cameroon, in 1963 and another signed at Arusha, Tanzania, in 1968, both establishing "associate" links between the EEC states and their former African colonies plus all other independent members of the Commonwealth should they wish to join. LDC participation in the system eventually included some 60 African, Caribbean, and Pacific former colonies, the so-called ACP states. Among other things, Lomé I provided for "the granting by EEC of duty-free access on a non-reciprocal basis to all industrial and to 96 percent of agricultural products exported from ACP countries and the setting up of a comprehensive export stabilization program (STABEX) guaranteeing income support to ACP countries for their primary products."*

Under the STABEX arrangement, the EEC set aside approximately $400 million to be paid out to LDC signatories when falling prices depressed earnings from EEC states. The poorer countries would receive cash, the higher-income ones loans repayable as prices improved. Yet, after four years of implementation of STABEX and the other features of Lomé I, the influential *Financial Times* of London commented: "What is there to show? In concrete terms, not much."[7] As is true of so many similar apparent concessions by the rich countries to please the poor, these were badly flawed: the agreements offered no surety that minimum levels of export volume would be maintained, bureaucratic delays held up funds while inflation eroded their real value and sales dropped, and relatively well-off LDCs were compensated for low prices of one commodity while two or three other exports from the same country boomed. About one quarter of the compensatory money was spent on studies, a blight afflicting welfare programs all over the world.

Under Lomé II, MINEX was added, covering minerals not included under STABEX, for example copper, cobalt, manganese, bauxite, phosphates, alu-

---

* Banks *et al. Political Handbook of the World, 1981,* p. 596. Lomé II (1979) further increased EEC aid and offered a plan to assist ACP producers of copper and tin. Lomé III (1984) included guarantees concerning private foreign investment in ACP states.

minum, and tin. Payments were to be made only if production was truly endangered, by insurrection or incursion. In addition EEC assistance was to strengthen the mining sectors in ACP states through technical aid and investment.

The Special Case Of Oil

Assessments vary as to why and how a group of oil exporting countries managed to succeed where exporters of other commodities have failed, especially why and how they succeeded so strikingly. Operating as the Organization of Petroleum Exporting Countries (OPEC), the group for several years appeared to have the industrial free market economies at its mercy, dictating prices, compelling incisive changes in the extraction and processing of their product, their decisions and nondecisions periodically sending deep shock waves around the globe. The following is a summary of the most plausible explanations centering on economic, military-strategic, and political aspects of that phenomenon.

Historical Background: Genesis of a Rebellion

In a way OPEC was the child of imperialism, the product of Western expansion in pursuit of cheap raw materials and of the manipulation of subject peoples which that pursuit entailed. The principal powers involved were Great Britain, France, the United States, and the Netherlands, Japan actively participating until its defeat in World War Two.* Major concentration of oil, aside from the substantial domestic deposits in North America and the Soviet Union, are those of the Middle East—mostly in the hands of Arabs, North, Central, and West Africa, the northern region of Latin America, Mexico, and the Asia-Pacific region. By far the largest share of the world's oil deposits are located outside imperialism's historic epicenter, industrially advanced Western Europe, which together with Japan today accounts for more than half of world oil imports. This set the stage for a confrontation: the oil-consuming, militarily powerful industrial countries versus the militarily and economically weak, less developed oil-producers.

* Shortly after oil was discovered in Mesopotamia, around the turn of the century, Imperial Germany and Czarist Russia were poised to participate in the race for that new source of power and wealth. The October 1917 Revolution eliminated Russia from competition for the time being; Germany and its ally Turkey (then the Ottoman Empire) were eliminated by their defeat in World War One. This left Great Britain and France in sole control in the Middle East. However, as beneficiaries of large-scale financial and military assistance from the U.S., during that war and afterward, both had to share their new-found wealth with their North American ally. Britain and France, with the U.S. now a tacit partner, unsuccessfully attempted to separate the young Soviet state from its oil-bearing region in the Caucasus during the Russian Civil War following the October Revolution. On the full-scale entry of U.S. oil interests in the Middle East, see U.S. Congress, Senate, 93rd 2d (1975), Chapter 1.

The idea of a common oil-exporters' front was originally broached to the Arabs and Iran by a Venezuelan petroleum expert in 1945.[8] His proposal was no more than a response to a powerful quasi-organization (some called it a cartel) consisting of seven giant multinational oil companies—dubbed the Seven Sisters—who ever since the late 1920s had seized and maintained control of world oil, including exploration, transport, refining, distribution, marketing and, most important, pricing. Their position was sufficient to force unwilling producer governments to accept their terms and remove challengers of their virtual monopoly from competition. Most frustrating to local interests was the group's iron-clad control of production and their ability to keep down the world market price of oil to accommodate their own corporate needs and those of the consuming countries at the expense of the product's rightful owners.*

Aside from constituting a response to collusion on the consumer or oil-importers' side, OPEC's *raison d'être* stemmed from the fact that oil is a non-renewable resource, hence deserving compensation considerably above that for resources which can be replaced. Concretely, OPEC's founders envisaged compensation at levels high enough to support diversification of their economies to prepare for the day when oil reserves approached depletion. If that goal proved unattainable, production would have to be curtailed, of course at commensurately higher prices, to prevent depletion before diversification had reduced dependence on oil. United action on the part of the less developed oil exporting countries seemed especially urgent when it was realized that the latter's oil resources were being drained so that reserves of developed countries, foremost those of the United States, could be preserved, partly for their national security, partly to build up economic and political leverage against the LDC producers. Especially disconcerting to struggling LDC producers was the discovery that the enormous profits earned by the major MNCs were being applied in part to develop alternate sources of supply to compete with oil pumped as rapidly

---

* In 1959 and 1960, the "majors" twice reduced the posted price. See *The German Tribune*, No. 958 (September 28, 1980), "Oil Companies' Pricing Policies Spawned OPEC Movement," p. 6; see also U.S. Congress, Senate, 93rd 2d *op. cit.*

Whether the Seven actually ever constituted a cartel in the full sense of that term is open to debate. Their critics insist that the designation is well deserved; the MNCs themselves of course deny it. The Seven certainly met one qualification: they did constitute "a group of firms which enter into Agreement to set mutually acceptable prices for their products . . . accompanied by output and investment quotas," a common definition of cartel. Debatable is whether they met two additional requirements, rules embodied in a *formal* legally enforceable document, including provisions for penalties in case of violation, and whether their grouping constituted "a formal system of collusion." Whatever the association may be called, it assumed concrete form with the Achnacarry Agreement of 1928 among three powerful groupings, each representing sets of small companies: Royal Dutch-Shell, Anglo-Iranian, and Standard Oil. There is no doubt that the agreement laid the foundations for *informal* coordination of pricing and of quotas on a global scale. Federal Trade Commission Report, 1952, *The New York Times* (August 25, 1952). Eventually the Seven Sisters emerged: Anglo-Persian, Socony-Vacuum, Standard Oil of New Jersey, Shell, Gulf, Atlantic, and Texas. By 1970, after take-overs, mergers, consolidations and reorganizations, the Seven were British Petroleum, Shell, Gulf, Exxon, Socal, Texaco and Mobil, one British, one Anglo-Dutch (Netherlands), and five American.

as possible from their soil. Examples cited were explorations in the Arctic and the North Sea.

As the organization acquired self-confidence, its more moderate members formulated demands for initial price increases in terms of estimates of what the market would permit. The radical members, foremost Libya and Iraq, urged increases in terms of what the industrially advanced and wealthy Western economies could stand, even if that should necessitate lowering of the latter's customarily high living standards. All agreed that the price prevailing at the time the rebellion got under way in earnest, $1.80 a barrel in 1970, was wholly insufficient from any point of view. Finally, since the development of all LDC oil exporting countries was likely to depend on the advanced economies for goods and services, it was felt that the price of oil should be in step with costs of imports from oil-consuming countries. As long as the latter was on the rise, and that was the prevailing pattern then, the price of oil had to be adjusted upward as well. Like all organizations about to extract concessions from an unwilling or recalcitrant adversary, OPEC timed its decisive moves when the consuming countries appeared most vulnerable.

Although the organization, at the time of its formation at Baghdad, Iraq, in 1960, included members geographically as far apart as Venezuela and Iran—eventually including Indonesia in Southeast Asia—four of its five founding members were concentrated in the Middle East: Iran, Iraq, Kuwait, and Saudi Arabia. The five possessed about two-thirds of known recoverable reserves,

Table 16-1. World Energy Reserves and Production[a]

Country	Estimated Reserves January 1985		Production est. 1984 Dec. 1983	
	Oil (1,000 bbl)[b]	Gas (10^9 cu ft)	Oil (1,000b/d)	Gas (billion cu ft)[b]
OPEC				
Latin America				
Ecuador	1,400,000	3,000	254	1.4
Venezuela	25,845,000	55,367	1,724	50.8
Africa				
Algeria	9,000,000	109,100	608	60.0
Gabon	510,000	550	150	0.4
Libya	21,100,000	21,200	1,090	12.5
Nigeria	16,650,000	35,600	1,414	14.5
Asia/Pacific				
Indonesia	8,650,000	40,000	1,332	47.0
Middle East				
UAE[c]	32,390,000	31,570	1,136	22.0
Iran	48,500,000	478,600	2,166	40.0
Iraq	44,500,000	28,800	1,218	1.5
Kuwait	90,000,000	32,500	925	12.0
Qatar	3,350,000	7,377	404	7.0
Saudi Arabia	169,000,000	123,270	4,545	35.0
Total OPEC	**470,895,000**	**966,934**	**16,966**	**304.1**

Table 16-1. *(Cont'd.)*

Country	Estimated Reserves January 1985		Production est. 1984 Dec. 1983	
	Oil (1,000 bbl)[b]	Gas (10⁹ cu ft)	Oil (1,000b/d)	Gas (billion cu ft)[b]
Non-OPEC Middle East				
Oman	3,500,000	7,377	404	–
North America				
Canada	7,075,000	92,300	1,430	265.0
Mexico	48,600,000	77,000	2,743	120.3
United States	27,300,000	198,000	8,750	1,546.0
Western Europe				
Norway	8,300,000	89,000	688	92.0
United Kingdom	13,590,000	27,800	2,452	160.3
Other W.E.	2,535,500	89,873	401	502.4
Total North America and Western Europe	**107,400,500**	**573,973**	**16,464**	**2,686.0**
Communist				
China (PRC)	19,100,000	30,900	2,250	31.0
Soviet Union	63,000,000	1,450,000	12,230	1,729.7
Other Comm.	2,000,000	16,500	490	175.0
Total Communist	**84,100,000**	**1,497,400**	**14,970**	**1,935.7**
World Total[d]	**698,667,400**	**3,402,025**	**54,090**	**5,310.6**
Major Groupings: Share of World Total (Per cent)				
OPEC	67.4	28.4	31.4	5.7
North America and Western Europe	15.4	16.9	30.4	50.6
Communist	12.0	44.0	27.7	36.4

SOURCE: *Oil and Gas Journal*, Vol. 81, No. 52 (December 26, 1983), pp. 80–81, Vol. 82, No. 14 (April 2, 1984), and Vol. 82, No. 53 (December 31, 1984), pp. 74–75.
[a] Only major producers listed by country
[b] bbl = barrels; b/d = barrels per day; cuft = cubic foot
[c] UAE = United Arab Emirates (Abu Dhabi, Dubai, Sharjah)
[d] World totals includes producers not listed

produced more than one-third of the world's then current output, and exported about 90 percent of all oil traded internationally.[9] At the zenith of OPEC's power, the Middle Eastern core group controlled over 56 percent of the world's proven reserves. To prevent dilution of the group's striking power, OPEC's charter stipulated that new members' product-related interests had to be "fundamentally similar to those of the founding members."[10] This explains why some oil-exporting states subsequently joined OPEC and others did not.* Nevertheless, it became necessary in 1968 to create the aforementioned Organization

* The five were joined by Qatar (1961), Libya and Indonesia (1962), Abu Dhabi (1967), Algeria (1969), Nigeria (1971), Ecuador (1973), and Gabon (1975). Abu Dhabi eventually joined other Arab sheikdoms to form the United Arab Emirates.

of Arab Petroleum Exporting Countries (OAPEC).* The central purpose of that step, taken in the wake of the 1967 Arab-Israeli war, was to prevent Arab oil from reaching countries directly or indirectly supporting Israel should another Arab-Israeli war become necessary. This signalled to the world that the Arabs were determined to employ oil as a political weapon in their struggle against the Jewish state in their midst. OAPEC's founding members were Saudi Arabia, Kuwait, and Libya.[11]

The Rebellion

The immediate precipitant of the rebellion was the outbreak of the Third Arab–Israeli war in October 1973. OPEC took action in three specific ways: sharp price increases, an oil embargo directed against the United States and the Netherlands, and a cutback in overall oil production levels. To be effective, threats of cut-offs or production cuts must be credible. OPEC proceeded to make its point by quickly driving the price of oil up to levels high enough to ensure its members reserves sufficient to withstand anticipated retaliation by consumers. The price hike was effective, the embargo viewed as an economic sanction was not.† Brief stoppages or temporary embargoes are relatively in-effective as a substantial share of all oil always is *en route* and can therefore readily be diverted to compensate for shortfalls.‡ Besides, many independent oil exporting countries failed to share the Arabs' preoccupation with Israel and were quite willing for that reason to assist embargoed countries.

The price increase and the production cutback could be enforced because initially, unlike the politically motivated oil embargo, it met with near unanimous acclaim on the part of the world's major oil exporters. Demand for oil at the time the move was made was primarily a Western problem, the Soviet Union being self-sufficient. Oil production in the U.S. had reached a peak. Generally in the West demand for oil had reached a level of addiction, a matter of sheer economic survival for some, especially continental Western Europe and Japan.

---

* OAPEC included radical Syria and at that time moderate Egypt, the latter suspended in 1979 following its signing of the Camp David Peace Accords with Israel.

† The embargo and long-standing Arab boycott of any country doing business with Israel plus the threat of further production cutbacks did have some political effect. Several Western governments, including the United States and the major oil companies, did move closer to the Arab position regarding the situation in the Middle East; see, for example, Standard Oil of California, *Letter to Stockholders* (July 26, 1973): "It is highly important that the United States should work more closely with the Arab governments to build up and enhance our relations with the Arab people." In 1975 Kuwait attempted to extend the anti-Jewish feature of the boycott—excluding persons of Jewish faith or identity from Arab business deals—to the United States. Violating U.S. Federal statutes, several companies complied. *The Wall Street Journal* (November 6, 1973) and *The New York Times* (October 22, 1981); on the "October [1973 OPEC] Revolution," see U.S. Congress, Senate, 93rd, 2d, *op. cit.*, Part III, Section VII.

‡ During the embargo, non-embargoed friends of the Netherlands, one of the oil-importers targeted by OAPEC, arranged to transfer to the energy-starved country oil purchased by them. Yergin and Hillenbrand (1982), p. 322; for an overall assessment of oil's value as a bargaining tool, see Feith (Winter 1981), pp. 19–39.

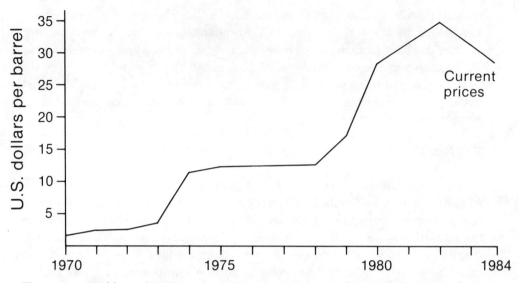

Fig. 16-1. World Crude Oil Prices (1970–1984). (*Oil and Gas Journal*; World Bank, *World Development Reports* 1982–1984.)

Great Britain and Norway found some relief in the North Sea deposits then beginning to yield results. Most vulnerable of course were the weaker and poorer oil-importing countries, some of whom were driven to near bankruptcy by the event. What rendered the advanced industrial states so vulnerable was the fact that ever since the product's industrial and military uses had first been discovered all had permitted their economies, their cities, their way of life, and their defenses to become overwhelmingly oil-dependent.* They had allowed this to happen on the strength of two assumptions: the inexhaustibility of cheap oil and retention in their hands, or those of the "Seven Sisters," of controls over notoriously corrupt, weak governments in the less developed oil-exporting countries. It was when the latter assumption lost its validity—the result mainly of the emergence in the oil-exporting states, of more assertive nationalistic, less corruptible and better trained elites—that the cheap oil assumption could be attacked.

It is possible that the rebellion had more progenitors, some of whom may well have come from outside OPEC. One suggestion is that the precipitant for action was advice from Moscow. The Soviet Union, so the argument goes, sometime around 1969, finding itself short of hard currency, was eager to raise the export price of its own crude oil. This in turn required matching price increase on the world oil market. Word was passed to the radicals among the Arab states, Libya, Algeria, and Iraq, that the "imperialist" ranks could be split by playing the oil-consuming states against one another, at a time, Moscow

* World-wide demand for oil had increased 7 percent per year for the two decades preceding the 1973 action.

advised, when their vulnerability was at an all-time high.* Another theory assigns immediate responsibility to American advisers to the Shah of Iran. Anxious to strengthen Iran as a block to Moscow's apparent southward thrust, the Shah was urged to drastically modernize and expand his armed forces. A substantial oil price increase should pay for that, help move Iran into the twentieth century, and coincidentally provide lucrative contracts for U.S. business, especially manufacturers of arms. A third party potentially interested in the price increase may well have been the multinational oil giants themselves.

As we have seen, at the time of its birth OPEC may have been less of a cartel than a veil for a real one, the "Seven Sisters."† Still, the latter may have been surprised. Be that as it may, indications are that as soon as they were aware that once pliable desert kingdoms and other once influenceable and controllable state entities now were threatening to break the hold, the major oil corporations were ready to make the best of a bad deal and seek mutually beneficial accommodation. It is conceivable, and their defenders insist that this was the case, that at first most or all attempted to resist, surrendering only when outmaneuvered by the Libyan dictator who had replaced the king and by the Saudis, both of whom employing the time-honored tactics by singling out the weakest company before moving against the rest.‡ Whatever the exact circumstances, oil eventually succeeded where other commodities failed, in part because of the MNCs. In the "Seven Sisters" and in the industrial and financial complexes with which these were associated, OPEC had what may be termed

---

* *Der Spiegel* (July 20, 1979). Ironically, the other members of the Soviet bloc eventually felt the economic consequences of that maneuver. When the world price of oil—including the price charged them by the Soviet Union which, if the value of the ruble was correctly evaluated, had all along been above the world price—began to rise at an ever more rapid rate, their already scant foreign exchange reserves now were being consumed even more rapidly; see also pp. 250–251.

† See Blair (1977). In their defense, the Seven have argued that they are not all that big or influential, that the term "the Seven Sisters" is derogatory, coined by a jilted competitor who failed to buy his way into "the club." It is possible that their political power has been exaggerated. However, in a statement seeking to counter Anthony Sampson's book *The Seven Sisters* (1975), Mobil Oil concedes that in 1949 the group "owned only 34.8 percent of non-Communist tanker capacity," and by 1972 no more than 28.5 percent. In refining capacity outside the U.S., "their share fell from 73 percent in 1953 to 49 percent in 1971." " 'The Seven Sisters': Another View," *The New York Times* Advertisement, (November 23, 1975). In any business 49 percent is controlling, if the remaining 51 percent are scattered and divided.

Indisputably, the group's share of OPEC oil dropped sharply from the near total ownership of OPEC output to somewhere around 45 percent in 1980. Their installations were nationalized or their ownership share reduced to shift nominal control to the producers. Still, as pointed out by one of the United States' foremost oil authorities, the majors "put OPEC" in the driver's seat, to their own considerable profit. M.A. Adelman, (1972-73), pp. 67-107; see also Hershey (1980).

‡ Libya succeeded, according to this explanation, by pressuring Occidental Petroleum, an American independent, the Saudis by using Aramco as their wedge. U.S. Congress, Senate, 93rd, 2d, *op. cit,* Part III, Section VI.

"hostage constituencies," located in the very heart of the industrial world, highly susceptible to pressure or even threats.*

The Consumers' Response and the Limits of Oil Power

Initially the Western industrial states were panic-stricken. Were the "oil sheiks" about to bring the industrial powers to their knees? Were they intent on causing a devastating global depression? Or, looking beyond the price of oil, was their intent, or that of their radical socialist associates, to compel the developed countries to adopt the New International Economic Order, shifting the world's wealth from "North" to "South?" Would they use their rapidly accumulating petrodollar surpluses to buy their way into key positions in the industrial states, possibly including seats on corporate boards of directors in sensitive defense industries? Were their mounting deposits in Western banks potential levers to be used, under threat of abrupt withdrawal, to compel key banks to do their bidding? Were they about to blackmail the United States and its allies to substantially alter their foreign policies, especially with regard to Israel?†

Objectively, the 1973-74 series of price increases and to an extent also the embargo demonstrated rather dramatically the industrial world's vulnerability to manipulation of its energy supply. Even if the overall damage eventually turned out to be less than at first feared, the initial impact on oil dependent sectors within exceedingly price—and cost—sensitive free market economies were severe. Countermeasures had to be taken urgently should OPEC decide on a repeat performance. Military action seemed out of the question under the circumstances.‡ More feasible were measures to coordinate responses of the industrially advanced oil-importing states in the event of another crisis, and reduce energy dependence. Accordingly, the major oil-importers in 1974 formed

---

* Allied with the major oil companies in all Western industrial states were the petrochemical industries, the vast network of gasoline dealers and distributors, and numerous other interests depending on oil imports.

† See U.S. Comptroller General (1980) and U.S. Congress, House, 96th, 2nd (1980), Committee on Government Operations. At the height of the crisis, Libya, Iraq, and Algeria sought to hitch far more ambitious, non-oil related causes to OPEC's power. But, encountering formidable resistance to their own comparatively moderate demands, OPEC's wealthier members saw no gain in a campaign to redistribute the world's wealth or further the cause of socialism on a global scale. Nor could the conservative capitalist core group in the organization be persuaded to expend oil's diminishing reservoir of power to advance the interests of other commodities.

‡ Western Europe and Japan, more dependent on oil imports from the Middle East than the U.S., would object strenuously. NATO might not survive such a move. The Third World, always fearful of imperialism's return, would band together with the oil producers in common cause, possibly triggering a violent reaction among Moslem populations throughout the world. United, the latter could severely damage Western interests, by scorched earth tactics for instance which could deny the oil to the invaders for extended periods. Possibly military moves so close to its borders could precipitate some kind of military response by the Soviet Union. See Yergin (1975). Officially, if any Western military action was contemplated, this was only in direct response to requests by the oil producers themselves or in response to Soviet moves beyond Afghanistan.

the International Energy Agency (IEA) to formulate a joint response to OPEC, should that become necessary, and develop an "aid-sharing mechanism" for use in times of "supply disruption."* Energy conservation and search for alternative sources of energy varied from country to country, depending in part on the degree of dependence on outside supplies.

As it turned out, more expensive energy slowed down the world economy, and overloaded world financial channels, as we noted, produced the worldwide debt crisis.† Neither accrued to OPEC's benefit. Rational oil exporters, it emerged fairly soon, could continue the pressure only if intent on committing economic suicide. Whether conservative or radical, their own prosperity hinged on their major customers' economic well-being as well as on that of their principal Western bankers. The industrial world, on the other hand, depended on continued social, economic, and political stability and on the military security of the major oil-exporting countries. If consumer economies falter, oil sales must decline and surplus proceeds from sales can profitably be invested only in expanding free market economies. Finally, the goods, services, technology, and loan capital required to diversify and modernize the oil-export-dependent economies can be obtained in sufficient quantity and of sufficient quality mainly, if not exclusively, from the advanced industrial oil-importing states. To be sure, and some OPEC members considered that option fleetingly, more of their oil could simply be left in the ground to be pumped and sold at some future date at even higher prices. This was rejected for the same reason the notion of extended or repeated embargoes was: the consuming states would accelerate their efforts to reduce their dependency on oil. Also, non-OPEC sources could be expected to take advantage of the opportunity and step-up production, thereby lowering the value of oil left in the ground.‡

OPEC has other sources of weakness. Most member states are militarily weak and hence depend upon foreign military assistance if not outright protection. Politically the organization is very fragile. Partly a consequence of deliberate imperialist design—all of the Middle Eastern states were creations of colonial offices in London and in Paris—partly for wholly indigenous reasons, Arabs are bitterly divided. There are feuds among the ruling royal families, jealousies

* Banks *et al., Political Handbook of the World 1981,* p. 603. In then U.S. Secretary of State Henry Kissinger's words, the agency was to serve either as an institutional framework for a long-term power struggle or for a long-term cooperative effort. *The New York Times* (September 30, 1974). The IEA was seen as an autonomous agency of OECD. Whether it would be a weapon in a power struggle or an instrument of cooperation, its founders felt, would depend on which of two major contending factions within OPEC would prevail, the moderate economically rational group centered on Saudi Arabia or the radicals, then heavily influenced by Libya's mercurial ruler. The IEA was the closest approximation to a formal counter-Organization of Oil Importing Countries OPIC.

† Feith (1981), p. 26, comments that "there are only four things that an oil state can do with its revenue: Buy goods or services, invest in foreign business enterprises, make deposits in banks, or bury the cash in the sand." The latter is no real option since inflation will erode its value rapidly.

‡ Similar results would obtain if excessive price pressure on the U.S. were to cause the U.S. dollar to fall in value, reducing the overall worth of OPEC holders of that currency.

and deadly feuds between political factions competing for preeminence within the Arab world. Concretely, it is most difficult to weld Egyptians, Saudis, Libyans, Iraqis, Syrians, and Persians into one cohesive political force. In addition, and increasingly lethal, is the conflict between mass-based Islamic fundamentalist and Westernized elites and among such Moslem sects as the Shi'ites and the Sunnis. Reflecting the global East–West struggle is the divergence between moderate regimes leaning towards the West and the radical socialists leaning towards the Soviet Union.

We have noted that OPEC members not from the Middle East do not fully share Arab preoccupation with Israel and are unwilling therefore to follow to extremes the Arab lead in that respect. Venezuela, Gabon, Ecuador, or even partially Islamic Nigeria view the Arab–Israeli conflict from entirely different perspectives. They certainly are not prepared to sacrifice their national economic interests on behalf of the Palestinians. But potentially most divisive is the disparity in *per capita* income, a function in part of population differential. More populous, low per capita income OPEC members, like Nigeria, Indonesia, or Iran, are under far greater pressure to sell their oil if need be at prices below OPEC levels than are low-population/high per capita income members like Saudi Arabia, Kuwait, or Libya.

Yet another peril arises from the existence of vast surpluses, namely surplus-driven, hurried, and ill-advised spending and overly hasty modernization, threatening the social and religious foundations upon which OPEC power has rested in the first place. Signs are mounting that governments which are expected to hold OPEC together in adversity and spearhead future moves, should these become necessary, are, under pressure from a variety of revolutionary influences, as one observer put it, "losing control of their own countries."[12]

OPEC at Bay?

The political edge of OPEC's sword proving to be quite dull, its economic edge, cutting deeply into the substance of the industrial world initially, lost its sharpness within less than a decade. One reason was a spreading glut caused in part by energy conservation measures in the industrialized countries, in part by stepped up sales by OPEC and non-OPEC exporters alike who needed to earn the cash to pay their spiraling debts or, in the case of Iraq and Iran, to pay for a costly war. That OPEC's strength was waning became especially clear when the organization proved unable to prevent some of its members from offering to selected buyers discount prices below the OPEC benchmark price. Saudi Arabia's commanding share of total OPEC production could have brought that practice to a halt by threatening to increase its production and drive the world market price to even lower levels, a move which should discourage the violators. The Saudis decided against that step because this would also have hurt friendly oil-exporting LDCs, some of whom were faced with staggering external debts, like Mexico. The end result was a retreat for OPEC, the benchmark price dropping from its all-time high of $34 per barrel to $29 in

1983, with prospects of further reductions in the years to come. The Soviet Union, incidentally, contributed to the weakening of prices by sharply increasing its exports to Western Europe, beginning in 1982.*

Will world market conditions once again favor the suppliers to the extent they did in 1973? Only if several developments occur. According to Western oil analysts, "the free world in . . . 1982 was consuming circa 43 million barrels a day of oil and natural gas liquids, non-OPEC sources supplying only about 23 million barrels per day, causing a shortfall of about 16 million which could

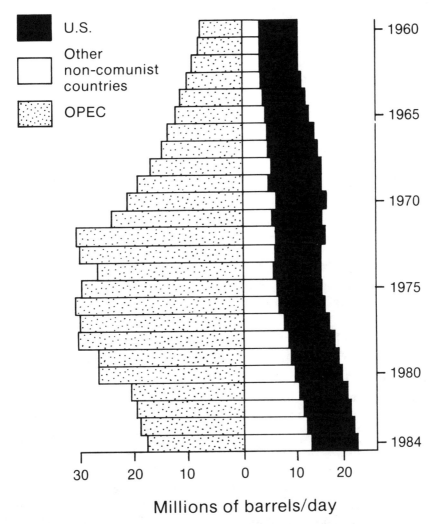

Millions of barrels/day

Fig. 16-2. Free Market World Oil Production (1960–1984). *(Oil and Gas Journal.)*

* *The China Daily* (April 4, 1983), reported an increase in Soviet sales from 200,000 to 1.1 million barrels per day. According to that source, after OPEC dropped its price to $29 a barrel, the Soviet Union "immediately lowered its price to $27.5 a barrel." An account in *The New York Times* (February 23, 1983) had the total increase at 400,000 barrels.

Box 16-1. Sources of Pressure on the Price of Oil

Downward Pressure:
Internecine conflicts within OPEC;

Increased oil production by OPEC members especially Saudi Arabia or outside OPEC;

Availability of alternate sources of energy in particular coal and nuclear; new oil fields;

Stockpiling in consumer countries; oil corporations draw on stocks;

Increased sales of oil stocks by the Soviet Union.

Oil companies increase their capacity to process lower quality, hence less expensive, crude oil.

Upward Pressure:
Increased demand due to economic recovery or boom conditions, or to war or acceleration of the arms race, or to profligate, wasteful consumption;

Production cutbacks, especially by the major producer, Saudi Arabia;

Anticipated OPEC action, e.g. price increase, causing run on available supplies including spot markets;

Oil corporations have depleted stocks;

War in oil-producing regions or supply disruptions for political or revolutionary causes.

only be met by OPEC."[13] If OPEC's share of world supply should increase, with the share of Gulf state oil within OPEC larger than ever but supplies from that region suddenly reduced for one or another reason, 1973 could be repeated; or, demand for oil might rise significantly in the wake of an upward swing in the world economy. According to one estimate, a 5 percent rise in energy demand in the United States could, under certain circumstances, translate into a 50 percent increase in demand for oil from the Persian Gulf.*

For their part, as the once fairly solid front began to splinter the Gulf states consolidated their position within OPEC. This became especially urgent when Iran showed indications of exporting not only oil but also its fundamentalist Islamic revolution and when Iran and Iraq seemed unable to conclude their war, brought on by Iraq's attempt to take advantage of turmoil in once powerful Iran and establish itself as the leading power in the Gulf region. In self-defense, in February of 1983 Saudi Arabia, Kuwait, Qatar, the United Arab Emirates,

* Causing a corresponding pressure on supplies available for Western Europe and Japan and adverse effects on the Western alliance system.

Bahrein, and Oman formed the Gulf Cooperation Council. At the same time, efforts were undertaken to establish more effective liaison with such non-OPEC exporters as Mexico, Great Britain, and Norway. The consumers were assured that all this was in their own best interest. Only an effective OPEC, it was argued, could be instrumental in stabilizing the world price of oil. For one, should the Gulf states lose control within the organization, OPEC and with it the industrial world would be at the mercy of the radicals. Throwing economic caution to the wind, they would once again hike prices, mainly to extract from the consumers the financial wherewithal to pursue their radical ambitions, Libya in Africa, Iraq and Iran throughout the Middle East. On the other hand price stability is needed as continuous downward pressure tends to dry up funds needed to sustain the IMF and prevent LDCs from collapsing under steadily mounting debts. (See Table 16-2.)

On balance, the case of "organized oil," so to speak, exemplifies the complexity and open-endedness of international resource politics as well as the multifaceted nature of international economics. If a strategic, to an extent actually indispensable, resource like oil cannot be organized to secure lasting advantages for its producers, the chances that less tightly disciplined producers' associations exporting less critical resources can prevail over major consumers are exceedingly slim. At best OPEC and, within OPEC, OAPEC will be able to exercise moderate influence to prevent a return to unbridled Western dominance, while maintaining price levels sufficient for their own most pressing developmental needs.

Critical Raw Materials In Global Strategy

The oil crisis served as a reminder of yet another threat to the stability and security of the industrial West: interruption in the supply of strategic nonfuel minerals.[14] Statistics on proven world reserves of fuel and nonfuel resources tend to support pessimists who see the industrial world either held up for ransom or brought to ruin under any one of numerous sets of circumstances. World stocks of one or more critical raw materials could deplete precipitously as a result of export stoppage by a major source torn by riot, civil war or revolution or because it becomes involved in international war. Important

Table 16-2. Gulf Cooperation Council: Oil Production est. 1984 ('000 b/d)[a]

Saudi Arabia	4,545
UAE	1,136
Kuwait	925
Qatar	404
Oman	404
Bahrain	41
Council Total	7,455
OPEC Total	16,966
World Total	54,090

SOURCE: *Oil and Gas Journal*, Vol. 82, No. 53 (December 31, 1984), pp. 74–75.
[a] b/d = barrels per day

mineral-bearing areas could be seized by a hostile power, or strategic trade routes or bottlenecks could be blocked. There is some concern that supply disruption may occur for ideological reasons, but few if any international trade experts take that seriously. As noted in the preceding chapter, predictions abound of coming wars between the capitalist and socialist systems or within competing blocs over one or more of twenty-seven minerals generally considered indispensable to the modern industrial state and society. (See Table 16-3.)

Some scenarios have the superpowers and their respective allies clash by the year 2000 if not earlier, when the Western oil producing states are expected to have exhausted mineral sources of energy under their direct control.[15] Others, predicting an energy crunch in the Soviet Union at about the same time, foresee a direct superpower conflict as Moscow moves to establish control over the Persian Gulf region to supplement its own diminishing supplies to meet Soviet as well as Warsaw Pact industrial and defense requirements. A spur to Soviet aggressiveness in that connection is the fact that dependence on Soviet energy supplies has for some time served as an effective lever for Moscow to ensure continued loyalty of its Warsaw Pact partners. The Soviet Union might seek to avoid loss of that source of leverage at all costs.[16] Most insistent that a resource war of global proportions is in the making are Western importers and consumers of scarce and critical minerals and raw material exporters with ulterior motives. The latter category is best exemplified by the Republic of South Africa.

While South Africa's share of the 27 critical minerals by no means approaches the level of monopoly, if the West discounts the Soviet share as potentially unavailable and that of certain LCDs, many of whom are in black Africa, as unreliable, South Africa's mineral wealth becomes strategically significant. Warned South Africa's Ambassador to the United States:

> If the Soviet Union could control the mineral resources of southern Africa, together with their own resources, the Russians would have available 80 percent of the world's gold production, 76 percent of its chrome production, 90 percent of its production of metals of the platinum group, 75 percent of the production of manganese, 80 percent of the production of vanadium and between 40 and 50 percent of the production of uranium.[17]

Overdrawn as that assessment may be in part, it strikes a sympathetic chord in Western, especially American military, circles. Certainly, if viewed against total U.S. reliance on imported critical raw materials, South Africa's strategic role cannot altogether be denied. According to some U.S. congressional observers, South Africa's importance increases if severe political disturbances reduce world supply causing astronomical price hikes, demands for a new international economic order assume more concretely threatening forms, or Third World anti-Americanism turns virulent diplomatically or militarily.[18] Whether directed at the United States or of a more generally anti-Western coloration, all pressures on world resources deepen the sense of insecurity among the allies, each seeing competitors in all the others. This gives rise to fears that "without South Africa

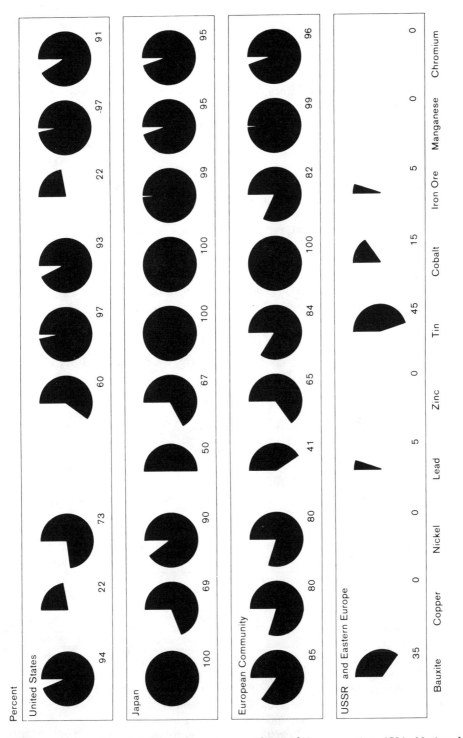

Fig. 16-3. Minerals and Metals: Imports as a Share of Consumption. (CIA, National Foreign Assessment Center, *Handbook of Economic Statistics 1984.*)

. . . the West [may] have no alternative but . . . depend upon the Soviet Union," meaning that under certain circumstances, some U.S. allies may drift out of the alliance into the arms of Moscow.[19] Or, as another analyst sees it: "The minerals vulnerability of Western Europe and Japan is the greatest strategic threat facing America." In other words, in addition to providing the nuclear shield for overall military security of its allies, the U.S. must also ensure their mineral security.[20]

But is South Africa actually as crucial to the West as the pessimists predict? At least one U.S. congressional committee arrived at a different conclusion:

> It is fortunate that in the case of each of the critical minerals imported from South Africa, means are available for dealing with an interruption without depending on the Soviet Union as an alternative supplier. These means may be costly, and they cannot in all cases be implemented without disruption. But in general, the disruptions can be minimized if preparations for a possible cut-off in South African supplies are made in advance.[21]

Of some relevance in this connection are the circumstances under which supplies from South Africa might be disrupted. Among possible causes, two are most likely to occur: either Western governments, especially the United States, apply intolerable pressure on the white South African rulers to change their universally condemned racist stance, or South Africa's black majority rebels, possibly with outside help. But even in the latter case, a black regime in South Africa would, like other such regimes on the African continent, find itself compelled to sell its resources on most advantageous terms and those will for some time to come be found mainly in the West.

In general, serious as loss of a particular supplier of any one of the more critical minerals would be to economic and military security interests on either side in the global contest, an impressive array of voices could be heard suggesting that like the oil crisis, which did not quite live up to worst case expectations, the mineral threat might also turn out to be more of a myth. Rebuttal of the

Table 16-3. The Twenty-Seven Critical Minerals: World Mine Production (In short tons; data are for 1978, both unless otherwise noted)

Mineral Commodity and Producing Country	Mine Production	Mineral Commodity and Producing Country	Mine Production
Ferrous Metals		New Caledonia	4,600
Chromite Ore:		CME	4,000
South Africa	3,700,000	Australia	3,800
CME[a] (principally USSR)	3,500,000	OME	3,700
OME[b]	1,800,000	Zambia	2,500
Turkey	700,000	Morocco	2,000
Zimbabwe	660,000	Philippines	1,200
Philippines	600,000	*Columbium:*	
Cobalt:		Brazil	9,300
Zaire	12,000	Canada	2,050

Table 16-3. The Twenty-Seven Critical Minerals:—Continued

Mineral Commodity and Producing Country	Mine Production	Mineral Commodity and Producing Country	Mine Production
Nigeria	350	Bolivia	3,300
OME	100	South Korea	2,750
Zaire	25	Australia	2,750
Malaysia	22	Thailand	2,500
CME	NA	*Vanadium:*	
Nickel:		South Africa	12,400
OME	197,600	Soviet Union	10,000
CME	150,000	United States	5,250
New Caledonia	70,000	OME	3,425
Cuba*	38,000	Chile	950
United States	11,600	**Nonferrous Metals**	
Silicon:		*Aluminum (Bauxite):*	
OME	990,000	Australia	29,150,000
CME	700,000	OME	24,090,000
United States	530,000	CME	13,420,000
Norway	280,000	Guinea	13,200,000
Tantalum:		Jamaica	12,540,000
Canada	125	*Copper:*	
Brazil	75	CME	1,660,000
Nigeria	75	United States	1,485,000
Australia	55	Chile	1,170,000
Mozambique	40	OME	967,000
Zaire	25	Canada	870,000
Iron:		Zambia	700,000
Soviet Union	269,000,000	Zaire	480,000
OME	106,150,000	Peru	370,000
Australia	101,200,000	Philippines	290,000
Brazil	96,800,000	South Africa	210,000
United States	88,550,000	Papua New Guinea	210,000
Canada	49,500,000	*Gold[c]:*	
India	46,200,000	South Africa	22.90
Manganese:		CME	8.20
CME	10,700,000	OME	5.80
South Africa	5,800,000	Canada	1.70
Gabon	2,100,000	United States	.97
India	2,000,000	*Platinum-group[c]:*	
OME	1,500,000	Soviet Union	3.0
Brazil	1,200,000	South Africa	2.9
Molybdenum:		OME	.4
United States	66,000	*Titanium (sponge metal):*	
Chile	13,000	CME	39,000
CME	11,000	Japan	9,000
Peru	500	OME	2,400
OME	350	United States	(W)
Tungsten:		*Zinc:*	
CME	21,500	OME	3,762,000
OME	11,100	CME	1,595,000
United States	3,600	Canada	1,408,000

Table 16-3. The Twenty-Seven Critical Minerals:—*Continued*

Mineral Commodity and Producing Country	Mine Production	Mineral Commodity and Producing Country	Mine Production
Lead:		OME	14,900
OME	1,237,500	Soviet Union	12,600
CME	1,232,000	*Petroleum*[f]:	
United States	584,100	OME	8,550
Australia	407,000	Soviet Union	4,000
Canada	396,000	Saudi Arabia	3,400
Magnesium (metal and compounds):		United States	2,987
Japan	4,200,000	Iran	2,200
United States	920,000	*Coal (bituminous and lignite):*	
Soviet Union	71,000	CME	2,030,000,000
OME	68,000	OME	777,000,000
Silver[c]:		United States	685,000,000
OME	100.0	South Africa	82,000,000
CME	70.0	*Thorium:*	
Mexico	50.0	Australia	300
Canada	41.0	India	200
United States	38.0	Malaysia	130
Peru	35.0	Brazil	100
Tin:		OME	40
Malaysia	66,000	United States	(W)
Soviet Union	36,300	CME	(NA)
Bolivia	33,000	*Uranium*[g]:	
Indonesia	28,600	United States	14,000
Thailand	28,600	OME	7,250
People's Republic of China	22,000	Canada	7,000
Fuels[d]		South Africa	4,000
Natural Gas[e]:		Namibia	1,500
United States	19,900	*Shale Oil*[h]:	

SOURCE: U.S. Congress, 96th, 2nd (1980), *Imports of Minerals . . .*, Appendix 4.

* Estimated.

(W) Withheld by the Bureau of Mines to avoid disclosing confidential information.

(NA) Not available.

[a] Central Market Economy nations. These are Albania, Bulgaria, People's Republic of China, Cuba, Czechoslovakia, German Democratic Republic, Hungary, North Korea, Mongolia, Poland, Romania, the Soviet Union, Vietnam, and Yugoslavia.

[b] Other Market Economy nations. These are market economy countries not otherwise listed.

[c] Data in million troy ounces of metal.

[d] Data on fuels are for 1977.

[e] Data in billion cubic feet measured at 14.73 psia at 60 degrees F. psia = per square inch airpressure.

[f] Data in millions of 42-gallon barrels.

[g] Uranium concentrate.

[h] Production negligible. The U.S. leads in estimated reserves with 2,200 billion of 42 gallon barrels, followed by South America with about 800 billion and Africa with 100 billion. (U.S.) Council on Environmental Quality and the Department of State, *The Global 2000 Report to the President*, Table 11–17, p. 199. Recoverable shale resources are estimated to be more than those of crude oil and natural gas together. *Ibid.*, Table 11-1, p. 187.

Table 16-4. South Africa and the Soviet Union: Production and Reserves of 5 Critical Minerals as a Proportion of Global Production and Reserves (1978, in percent)

	South Africa	Soviet Union	Total
Reserves:			
Chromium	68	< 1[a]	69[b]
Manganese	37	50[c]	87
Vanadium	19	74	93
Platinum-group metals	73	25	98
Gold	48	22[d]	70
Production:			
Chromium	34	32[d]	66
Manganese	23	43[c]	66
Vanadium	39	31	70
Platinum-group metals	46	47	93
Gold	58	21[d]	79

SOURCE: U.S. Congress, 96th, 2nd (1980), *Import of Minerals . . .*, p. xvi.

[a] Compared with Soviet production data, this percentage appears strikingly low. Indications are that the Soviet Union is indeed rapidly exhausting its reserve stock. In the opinion of two analysts: "The approaching depletion or deterioriation of chromite deposits in the Soviet Union may partly explain recent Soviet/Cuban initiatives in southern Africa." Bennett and Williams (1981), p. 8. The CIA, however, estimates reserves of ten percent with about 80 years to exhaustion, given current rate of production. CIA, Rowen (1982), Table 1 between pp. 14–15.

[b] An additional 30 percent of global chromium reserves are held in Zimbabwe.

[c] The manganese data are for the "Central Market Economies" as a group, reflecting the Bureau of Mines reporting method. According to the Bureau, "the USSR and the Republic of South Africa account for more than 80 percent of the world identified resources."

[d] Data are for the Central Market Economies as a group, again reflecting the Bureau of Mines reporting method.

prophets of doom commences with a challenge of statistics of proven and estimated world reserves, a challenge which incidentally also applies to ill-boding oil statistics.* Figure 16-4 illustrates the extreme elasticity of statistics on mineral reserves and of the political conclusions one may draw from them. Before statistics on reserves are accepted and chances of conflict over a given resource are assessed, it is advisable to determine first what portion or percentage of a country's *known* or proven reserves will actually be tapped under what economic, political, or technical conditions. As one analyst suggests, "[reserve statistics] are floating figures that rise with the mounting tide of geological knowledge."[22] These figures also rise with changing cost assessment and changing strategic considerations which may change or rearrange national priorities. Some resources believed to exist may never advance to the status of reserve,

* Nonetheless, a *Report* by the UN Secretary General (1983) predicts that the worldwide arms competition will significantly decrease the life expectancy of certain global fuel and nonfuel resources. p. 27.

some only if the incentive is there to go after them. For example, should Japan be willing to tie itself to the Soviet Union via an oil pipeline, Soviet Siberian deposits may suddenly expand statistically.

Resource dependency is equally adjustable. A nation's total dependency on import of a given mineral, U.S. reliance on tin import for example, can quickly change under certain circumstances, an unacceptable price increase for instance or new technology, both of which may render substitution feasible. If cost of import, transport, or processing so dictate, a nation will quickly review its dependency position. Increase uncertainty of a critical mineral being available when needed, in qualities required, and dependency on that resource will promptly be reduced. Under certain conditions, previously rejected lower quality imports will become acceptable. Untapped reserves will be explored, mines previously shut down will be reopened, or oil fields previously considered unprofitable will be given another look. Private inventories—which do not show up in dependency statistics—can be tapped for public purpose and national stockpiling can be stepped up and expanded. Industrial plants or equipment may be redesigned to dispense with raw materials difficult to obtain, and certain metals may be recycled for secondary use. Also nonessential use of critical materials can always be curbed.[23]

Tension over resources might be reduced by recourse to political and diplomatic options. For example, if the Soviet Union were to be allowed to acquire from the West the finance and technology to develop currently inaccessible oil

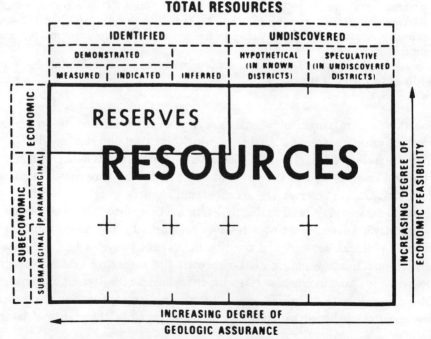

Fig. 16-4. Classification of Minerals: Reserves and Resources. (U.S. Congress, Senate (1980), *Imports of Minerals . . .*, Figure 1, p. 2.)

deposits, Moscow's incentive to enter into competition with the West in the Middle East might be reduced. In any case the West does have the option of resorting to "strategic supply diversification," that is, the identification and cultivation of alternate suppliers.[24] In that connection the natural gas pipeline from Soviet Russia to Western Europe might increase the latter's dependence on the Soviet Union, thus weakening the Western alliance.[25] Or the West could improve its resource position by making common cause with OPEC against the Soviet threat, provided, of course OPEC's Arab core could be appeased by progress in the Middle East peace process.

Managing the World's Food Supply

Whether the earth can produce sufficient food to support expanding populations is a question beyond the scope of this book. We referred earlier to the contention that there is no overall food shortage, only shortage of finance to pay for transportation and storage and shortage of will and managerial skill on the part of responsible authorities to distribute supplies actually available in the world at large including reportedly food-short countries. Where famines occur, so the argument goes, public authorities are unwilling or unable to so arrange national priorities as to meet minimal nutritional requirements.* In short it is contended that food, while certainly an agricultural production problem, assumes social and political significance mainly because of national or even global mismanagement in the face of man-made shortfalls or of natural disasters.[26] For example, a drought in the United States combined with a bad harvest in the Soviet Union will inevitably generate pressure on food supplies somewhere else on earth, if for no other reason than that food prices will rise.

Does food lend itself to exploitation as a weapon in world politics? The requirements of the world's most populous countries, for example the People's Republic of China, India, Pakistan, Bangladesh, and Indonesia, are of a magnitude too great for any power play to take effect. Their problems call for long-term measures devised internally in the first instance. In any case, indications are that progress is being made in this respect in all of these countries.[27] For a brief span, some circles in the United States believed that food might be used as a weapon to discipline the Soviet adversary and discourage OPEC from contemplating further pressure plays, mainly because the U.S. leads the world

---

* In 1984 the head of the World Food Council reported that the People's Republic of China wasted almost half of its food supplies because of "antiquated storage methods." *The New York Times* (January 10, 1984). Thus in 1984, while unable to meet all of its domestic food requirements, the PRC actually exported several hundred million metric tons of grain and soy beans. Famines, generally acknowledged to be caused by draught or desertification, may occur too unexpectedly or progress too rapidly for incompetent, corrupt LDC governmental bodies to handle. Preoccupation with ideological concerns also contributes to food shortfalls. See, for instance, John Walsh, *Science*, Vol. 224, No. 4648 (May 4, 1984), pp. 467–471. The CIA *Handbook for Economic Statistics 1983*, Fig. 14, p. 16, indicates that world wheat and coarse grain production and consumption rise and fall together, each leading the other periodically, at one time production at another consumption being ahead by several million tons.

in the production of grains and both the Soviet Union and key members of OPEC appeared to be dependent on food imports. Neither appeared to be able to meet all of their requirements from sources other than the United States. The notion was abandoned shortly after it was conceived. The grain embargo imposed on the Soviet Union following the invasion of Afghanistan failed to yield the results expected: Soviet forces were not withdrawn. Moreover, as noted earlier, in spite of a series of bad harvests, the Soviet Union was able to cover its needs by imports from Argentina, Canada, and other sources. The Arab food importers now had the financial means to buy on the open market whatever they required. In addition some American leaders argued, on humanitarian grounds that except in times of war food should not be used as a weapon.

In 1983 the United States signed a five-year agreement committing the Soviet Union to purchase at least 9 million metric tons of U.S. grain per year. In

Table 16-5a. Wheat, Rice, and Corn: Exports and Imports of 6 Leading Countries (1981) (In thousands of metric tons)

Leading Exporters	Exports 1981	Leading Importers	Imports 1981
Wheat		*Wheat*	
United States	43,909	Soviet Union	16,500[a]
Canada	15,472	China (PRC)	13,038
France	12,785	Japan	5,633
Australia	10,552	Brazil	4,360
Argentina	3,758	Egypt	3,949
Soviet Union	1,600	Poland	3,448
Rice		*Rice*	
Thailand	3,138	Korea, Rep. of	2,585
United States	3,133	Soviet Union	1,283
Pakistan	1,244	Nigeria	600
India	953	Indonesia	538
Japan	855	Iran	500
Burma	700	Saudi Arabia	427
Corn		*Corn*	
United States	54,856	Soviet Union	14,630
Argentina	9,112	Japan	13,590
South Africa	4,400	Spain	4,830
Thailand	2,549	China (PRC)	3,261[b]
France	2,355	Korea, Rep. of	3,051
Belgium-Luxem-bourg	1,486	Mexico	2,844

SOURCE: *U.S. Statistical Abstract* 1984, Table No. 1528, p. 878.

[a] In 1984–85, because of an exceptionally poor harvest, the Soviet Union was expected to import about 43 million tons of grain, 3 million less than in 1982, a record grain import year for the Soviet Union. The U.S. was expected to provide some 22 million of the 1984–85 requirements, *The New York Times* (August 28, 1984).

[b] A bumper corn crop in 1984 combined with inadequate storage facilities caused the PRC to export more than 2 million metric tons of corn.

Table 16-5b. World Meat Production: 10 Leading Countries (1981 est.)
(In thousands of metric tons)

World Total	110,079
United States	17,703
China (PRC)	19,512
Soviet Union	12,797
Germany, Fed. Rep. of	4,251
France	3,907
Argentina	3,377
Brazil	3,282
Italy	2,299
United Kingdom	2,233
Canada	1,886

SOURCE: *U.S. Statistical Abstract 1984*, Table No. 1529, p. 878.

return the U.S. agreed to drop an escape clause which under previous agreements had given it the option of reducing or suspending deliveries under certain circumstances. However, while the notion of using food as a weapon against the Soviet Union was abandoned, food remained a source of competition among suppliers. By signing a five-year agreement with the world's leading buyer of grains, the U.S. in effect foreclosed opportunities for Argentina, Canada, and others to resume sales to the Soviet Union as their agreements expired during that five-year period. The episode demonstrates that while not exactly a strategic weapon food does serve as a relatively subtle instrument of international politics: nations which had in effect defied the U.S. were reminded that the U.S. had the capacity to reciprocate.*

The Resources Of The Sea

Five factors combined in recent decades to intensify international competition for the resources of the sea: population increase, rising standards of living in the developed countries, progressive industrialization in all parts of the world, and major advances in technology. In particular, some maritime nations have enlarged and modernized their fishing fleets, and entirely new fleets have made their appearance. Some traditional fishing grounds appear to be exhausted, impelling nations accustomed to derive their protein from fish and other food from the sea to send their fleets farther afield, increasing conflicts over fishing rights. (See Table 16-6.)

Pressure mounted also to secure access to off-shore oil and gas deposits. Finally, as strategic reserves of critical nonfuel minerals dwindled in the leading industrial states, and access to supplies under national jurisdiction became problematic on political or military grounds, attention turned to resources recently discovered—though long suspected—on the bottom of the oceans. Thousands of feet

---

* Signing the agreement when it did, Moscow also came to the aid of the Reagan administration, which needed that sale to appease disgruntled supporters in the electorally pivotal American farm belt.

Table 16-6. World Fishery Statistics: Leading Countries (1980)

Fish Catches	'000 metric tons
Japan	10,410.4
Soviet Union	9,412.1
China (PRC)	4,235.3
United States	3,634.5
Chile	2,816.7
Peru	2,731.4
India	2,423.5
Norway	2,401.7
Korea, Rep. of	2,091.1
Denmark	2,026.8
Indonesia	1,853.2
Thailand	1,650.0
Philippines	1,556.6
Iceland	1,514.9
Korea, Dem. Rep. of	1,400.0
Canada	1,305.3
Mexico	1,240.2
Spain	1,240.0
Vietnam	1,013.5

SOURCE: *UN Statistical Yearbook 1981*, Table 105, pp. 557–560.

below national and international waters, it turned out, waiting to be scooped up by whoever possessed the requisite technology and finance, were trillions of dollars worth of potato-sized nodules of strategically important minerals.*

The Law of the Sea

We recall from our previous discussion of international law that at one time sovereign territoriality extented to three miles off-shore, the distance a cannon ball could travel. This was expanded to twelve miles until, with improved technology, oil and gas were discovered and rendered accessible for commecial exploitation all along the Continental Shelf, an area extending in some regions up to 350 miles from shore. To secure these, protect their fishing grounds, and stake out claims for nonfuel minerals, maritime nations promptly raised their sights to claim 200 miles of ocean floor, some claiming even more.†

A glance at a world map, especially where maritime nations are separated from each other by bodies of water less than 400 miles across or by narrow straits 20 or fewer miles wide, quickly reveals the chaos threatening world

* One estimate saw 22 billion tons of fine-grained oxides of copper, nickel, cobalt, and manganese reposing on the ocean floors. *UN Chronicle*, Vol XIX, 6 (June 1982), p. 6. Another estimate ran to 1.5 trillion tons, believed to be growing by 16 million tons a year. The finest (metal recovery rate from nodules between 80 and 98 per cent) were believed to be located in the Central Pacific.

† The U.S. claim to sovereignty over natural gas deposits and other resources along the Continental Shelf was first made by President Truman on September 28, 1945.

Table 16-7a. Seabed Nodules: Hypothetical Annual Mineral Production[a]
(in metric tons)

Potential Production Starting in 1985	Nickel	Manganese	Cobalt	Copper
Minimum Authorization[b]	175,000	1,300,000	23,000	150,000
Share of World Market ('85)	14.3%	7.9%	33.0%	1.0%
Maximum Authorization	350,000	2,600,000	46,000	300,000
Share of World Demand ('85)	28.6%	15.8%	66.0%	2 %
Estimated World Demand in 1985	1,220,000	16,400,000	70,000	14,900,000

SOURCE: United Nations, Third Conference on the Law of the Sea. *Economic Implications of Sea-Bed Mineral Development in the International Area.* A/CONF.62/25 (22 May 1974), Table 8, p. 56.

[a] Assuming 95% metallurgical recovery except for trace metals where an 80% rate is assumed; several recovery operations assumed.

[b] Authorization by the projected International Mining Authority.

Table 16-7b. Seabed Nodules: Initial Annual Production Projection by One
U.S. Company (Deep Sea Ventures, Inc.)

Nodules Total	Production (Metric Tons) 1,350,000	Net U.S. Imports (1972) as a Percentage of U.S. Consumption ————
Copper	9,150	9%
Nickel	11,300	71%
Cobalt	2,150	92%
Manganese	253,000	93%

SOURCE: U.S. Congress, Senate, 94th, 1st (1975), Committee on Interior and Insular Affairs, Subcommittee on Minerals, Materials and Fuels, Hearings, *Current Development in Deep Seabed Mining,* Part 1, p. 38.

shipping, fishing, and mineral exploitation if the 200 mile limit were to become law without modification or exception.* For example, imposition of territorial claims of 200 miles or more clashes with the behavior of fishing populations which migrate in response to subtle climatic changes, oblivious in their wanderings of restrictions set by international or national law. In any case, the entire subject turned critical when the United States and several other industrially advanced states prepared to exploit the minerals beyond the Continental Shelf, beneath the open international sea.

The United Nations Law of the Sea Treaty. The initiative to adjust then current international law to changed and changing conditions came from the

---

* We recall the international commercial and military strategic "choke points," such as the Strait of Hormuz through which much of the world's oil is shipped and which Iran and the United Arab Emirates could thus incorporate in their territorial limits or the Strait of Gibraltar which Spain and Morocco could then legally—though of course not realistically—close to the world.

Third World, mainly the Group of 77. Dependent as so many of them are on mineral exports, they feared drastic lowering of price and hence loss of income if the enormous wealth from the ocean floor was to be added to current world production. At the same time, they saw here another opportunity to press their demand for the New International Economic Order (NIEO). Numerically, within the framework of the United Nations, a clear majority existed to challenge the industrial powers' claim to the new sources of wealth. Consequently, on December 17, 1970, the General Assembly proclaimed by resolution that resources on the ocean bed beyond any nation's territorial jurisdiction are to be regarded as "the common heritage of mankind."* To endow that concept with international recognition and codify other changes in the law of the sea, a UN Law of the Sea Conference (UNCLOS) was convened in 1973. Following a series of such conferences (UNCLOS I-III), a Law of the Sea Treaty was signed in 1982 by 117 nations, 22 refusing to sign, and 24 declining invitations to attend the signing.

A list of groupings among the participants assembled at the time of signing, arranged by conflicting interests, offers a glimpse of the complexity of this and similar problem areas in world affairs:

   —less developed versus developed countries;
   —Third World versus Western world;
   —nations already possessing the financial, technical, and human resources
     to proceed with mining operations versus those of poor or no prospects
     of reaching that position;
   —maritime versus landlocked nations;
   —maritime nations with and without a continental shelf, and with and
     without gas or oil within 350 miles off shore;
   —maritime and naval powers interested in unrestricted transit rights versus
     states situated on either or both sides of narrow international straits;
   —nations with fishing grounds within or near their own territorial waters
     versus those compelled to go farther afield; within that category, major
     consumers of fish versus those whose populations derived their protein
     from other sources;
   —constitutional democracies versus "people's democracies" and other forms
     of dictatorship.

The United States, West Germany, and Great Britain cited many reasons why they could not sign. One was a concern that the Third World–Soviet bloc sponsored "common heritage of mankind" proposition was "the leading edge of the attempt to instill NIEO principles in all international organizations and institutions, and over other global problems, including energy, Antarctica, and outer space."[28] These states also found objectionable that the proposed decision-

---

* This pitted against each other proponents of *res nullius* and *res communis*, the former treating the ocean bed like the high sea, that is conferring *no rights*, the latter regarding both as within the right of *all nations*.

Box 16-2. Major Law of the Sea Provisions

Territorial Waters: Coastal states to exercise sovereignty over their *territorial sea* of up to 12 miles in breadth, but foreign vessels to be allowed "innocent passage" through these waters for purposes of peaceful navigation.

Straits: Ships and aircraft of all countries to be allowed peaceful "transit passage" through *straits used for international navigation.*

Exclusive Economic Zone (EEZ): Coastal states to enjoy a 200 mile *exclusive economic zone* with respect to natural resources and certain economic, scientific, and environmental-protection activities. All other states to enjoy freedom of navigation and overflight in the zone, and, with permission, may share in the zone's fisheries. Rights within overlapping zones to be apportioned by agreement among relevant states.

Continental Shelf: Each coastal state is given sovereign rights over gas, oil and other resources in or on the *continental shelf* for at least 200 miles from shore, and for 350 miles under specified circumstances.

Seabed Mining: The nodules of copper, nickel, cobalt, and zinc lying on the ocean floor under the high seas are "the common heritage of mankind" and are therefore to be exploited and administered under international authority.

Landlocked States: To have the right of access to and from the sea and enjoy freedom of transit through the territory of transit states by all means of transport.

Marine Pollution: All coastal, port, and flag states to be bound "to prevent and control *marine pollution* from any source."

Marine Technology: All states to be bound to promote the *development* and transfer of marine technology "on fair and reasonable terms."

SOURCE: *UN Chronicle,* Vol. XIX (June 1982), No. 6, p. 4.

making process underrepresented states possessing the requisite technology and finance while the cost allocation formula placed too heavy a burden on them, without giving them proportionate authority over the budgeting of the Treaty Authority's funds. Treaty amendment procedures, it was argued, would violate U.S. constitutional restrictions, while other provisions were contrary to U.S. statutory law on the rights and duties of private property—both sets of provisions incidentally reflecting an anti-free enterprise, anti-private property, anti-democracy consensus on such matters among Group 77 states and the Soviet bloc, itself a fact arousing strong opposition in the United States. Also causing concern in Washington were provisions on technology transfer which theoretically could enable a hostile majority to compel U.S. technology to be transferred to potential military adversaries or to economic competitors. Regarding treaty provisions unrelated to the seabed, the U.S. felt that existing international law served its commercial (including fishing), naval, and military-strategic interests more adequately than did the Treaty.[29]

Germany objected on somewhat different grounds. As one German observer put it: "After eight years of talk [the Federal Republic of] Germany has been allocated economic control over a section of the North Sea which is known to have no oil or gas deposits." On the other hand "every island . . . can lay claim to a 200 nautical mile sea around it in which it has exclusive economic rights."[30] That same observer's assessment of the long-range consequences if the Treaty were to be put into effect expresses succinctly the thrust which the leading industrial powers could not readily accept:

"The wars of conquest, starting with Persia and extending to the last czars of Russia, were nothing in terms of shifting power when compared with the Law of the Sea Conference," history textbooks in the year 2000 are likely to say, once all the provisions in the new Law of the Sea have been implemented.*

Suggested Questions and Discussion Topics

What practical steps have been taken by producers and consumers of critical resources to accommodate mutual interests? What have been, what are the major obstacles to agreement between producers and consumers and within each of these two groups?

What led to the oil producers' rebellion in the late 1960s and early 1970s?

Explain why OPEC succeeded where the other critical resource producers failed.

What economic and political conditions and forces combine to diminish OPEC's power-political effectiveness?

Outline the major implications of critical raw material demand and supply for global strategy in the East-West conflict.

Can food be used as a weapon to achieve foreign policy goals? Should it be so used?

* See note 30 for Chapter 16. In a way, the Law of the Sea Conference contributed to the Falkland (Malvinas) war of 1982, as under the terms of the treaty the sea around the island group and the various rock outcroppings farther out in the South Atlantic, which were considered part of the group, and their projection southward toward Antarctica potentially entitled its rightful owner to certain claims to that ice-covered region. Not insignificantly, if Great Britain retained possession of the island group and its extensions those rights would accrue also to West Germany in its capacity as a member of the EEC. The 200 mile Exclusive Economic Zone concept promised to trigger or aggravate numerous additional conflicts over resources throughout the world; see for example, The Heritage Foundation, Asian Studies Center, "Brewing Conflict In The South China Sea," *Backgrounder* No 17 (October 25, 1984).

What conflicting interests were represented at the Law of the
Sea Conference (UNCLOS)?

What are the principal provisions of the Law of the Sea
Treaty? Why did some industrial states find it difficult to accept
some of these terms? Offer arguments for and against the
position taken by some of the world's leading industrial powers
with regard to the Treaty's provisions on seabed mining.

Suggested Readings For Part Three: Managing The World Economy

Chapter 11

Cohen, Benjamin. *Organizing the World's Money. The Political Economy of
International Monetary Relations.* New York: Basic Books, 1977, Chapter
3.

Spero, Joan. *The Politics of International Economics.* Second Edition. New
York: St. Martin's, 1981, Chapter 1.

Chapter 12

Barnet, Richard J. *The Giants. Russia and America.* New York: Simon and
Schuster, 1977, Chapter 6.

Blake, David H., and Robert S. Walters. *The Politics of Global Economic
Relations.* Second Edition. Englewood Cliffs, N.J.: Prentice-Hall, 1983,
Chapter 3.

Friesen, Connie M. *The Political Economy of East-West Trade.* New York:
Praeger Special Studies, 1978, Chapters 2 and 3.

Hofheinz, Roy, and Kent E. Calder. *The East Asia Edge.* New York: Basic
Books, 1982.

Holzman, Franklyn D. *International Trade Under Communism: Politics and
Economics.* New York: Basic Books, 1976.

Keohane, Robert O. *After Hegemony. Cooperation and Discord in the World
Political Economy.* Princeton, N.J.: Princeton University Press, 1984.

Wilkinson, Endymion. *Japan Versus Europe. A History of Misunderstanding.*
Harmondsworth, Middlesex, England: Penguin Books, 1983, Part III.

Chapter 13

Friesen, Connie M., *op. cit.,* pp. 65–78.

Holzman, Franklyn D., *op. cit.*

Kostyukhin, Dmitry. *The World Market Today.* Moscow: Progress Publishers,
1979.

Chapters 14 and 15

Bauer, P.T. (Lord). *Equality, the Third World and Economic Delusion.* Cambridge, Mass.: Harvard University Press, 1981, Parts One and Two.

————. *Reality and Rhetoric. Studies in the Economics of Development.* Cambridge, Mass.: Harvard University Press, 1984; esp. Chapters 3, 4, 6.

Blake, David H. and Robert S. Walters, *op. cit.,* Chapter 5.

Cohen, Benjamin. *The Question of Imperialism. The Political Economy of Dominance and Dependence.* New York: Basic Books, 1973, Chapters IV–VI.

Hoogvelt, A.M.M. *The Third World in Global Development.* London: Macmillan Ltd, 1982.

Lewis, Sir W. Arthur. *The Evolution of the International Economic Order.* Princeton, N.J.: Princeton University Press, 1978.

North–South, *A Program for Survival.* The Report of the Independent Commission on International Development Issues. Cambridge, Mass.: The MIT Press, 1980, especially Chapters 1–4.

Spero, Joan, *op. cit.,* Part Three.

Turner, Louis. *Multinational Corporations and the Third World.* New York: Hill and Wang, 1973.

Chapter 16

Danielsen, Albert L. *The Evolution of OPEC.* New York: Harcourt, Brace, Jovanovich, 1982.

Pirages, Dennis. *Ecopolitics.* North Scituate, Mass.: Duxbury Press, 1978, Chapters 3–5.

Yergin, Daniel, and Martin Hillenbrand. *Global Insecurity.* Boston: Houghton Mifflin, 1982.

Selective Glossary of Key Arms Terms*

Antiballistic Missile (ABM): Missile capable of intercepting and destroying enemy missiles or their payloads in flight. ABM systems (ABMS) include radar and other control or guidance technology.

Arms Control: To curb the lethality and destructiveness of given weapons or weapon systems, prohibit use of certain weapon categories, for example biological and chemical, likely to produce fatal side-effects for the rest of humanity, such as poisoning of the atmosphere or rendering the seabed or outer space too dangerous for general use.

Arms Limitation: Limit the size, weight (throw-weight), range, number, and deployment of enumerated weapons or weapon systems. Negotiations mainly at two levels, strategic *Intercontinental (ICBM)* and *Intermediate-Range Nuclear Forces* (IRBMs or INFs).

Arms Reduction: Across-the-board quantitative reduction of certain weapon categories each side is permitted to have.

Anti-Satellite Talks (AST): Negotiations on limiting the ability to destroy satellites of any kind but especially those of military potential or use.

Ballistic Missile: A missile designed to follow the trajectory that results when it is acted upon predominantly by gravity and aerodynamic drag after thrust is terminated. Ballistic missiles typically operate outside the atmosphere for a substantial portion of their flight path and are unpowered during most of the flight.

Bomber: Aircraft designed or adapted to deliver bombs or nuclear missiles, also referred to as strategic aircraft.

CEP (Circular Error Probable): The radius of a circle around a target of such size that a weapon aimed at the target has a 50 percent probability of falling within the circle.

---

* Based on USACDA glossaries and Campbell (1982), pp. 267–284.

Cold-Launch: See *Rapid Reload.*

Cruise Missile (CM): A guided missile using aerodynamic lift to offset gravity and propulsion to counteract drag. Unlike a ballistic missile, the CM's flight path remains within the earth's atmosphere.

Countervailing Strategy: Includes the capability to survive a major nuclear attack, the capability to ensure destruction of the aggressor, and maintenance of a clearly evident capability to effectively engage in nuclear conflicts of a more limited nature.

Decapitation: Elimination or incapacitation, most likely by nuclear strike, of an enemy's entire central or supreme command, control, and communication (C^3) leadership.

Deterrence: Prevention or discouragement, mainly by nuclear retaliatory threat, of an enemy's first use of nuclear weapons.

Encryption: Encoding communications for the purpose of concealing information. In the SALT context, this term refers to a practice whereby one side alters the manner by which it transmits *telemetry* from a weapon being tested rendering the information deliberately undecipherable.

Fallout: Radioactive particles carried into the upper atmosphere as a result of a nuclear explosion, precipitating downwind from the explosion.

First Strike: Use of nuclear weapons against specific targets against an enemy before the latter has so used them; also referred to as *preemptive strike.*

Fixed ICBM Launcher: There are two categories of ICBM launchers, fixed and mobile. Fixed ICBM launchers have traditionally been referred to as either "soft," where the missile and most of its launch equipment remain above-ground, or "hard," where the missile and most of its launch equipment are contained in a hardened underground silo. In both cases, the launcher—the equipment which launches the missile—is in a fixed location.

Fission: The splitting of an atomic nucleus of certain heavy elements (such as uranium and plutonium), as by bombardment with neutrons resulting in the release of substantial quantities of energy.

Fractional Orbital Bombardment System (FOBS): A missile that achieves an orbital trajectory, but fires a set of retro-rockets before the completion of one revolution in order to slow down, reenter the atmosphere, and release the warhead it carries into ballistic trajectory toward its target. While a normal ICBM follows an elliptical path to target and is highly visible to defending radars, a weapon in low orbit, for example 100 miles altitude, can make a sharp descent to earth, cutting radar warning time substantially. A FOBS path accordingly would consist of a launch into low orbit, a partial circle to the earth target, and a rapid descent.

Fusion: The fusing or joining together of two atomic nuclei in a reaction which releases large amounts of energy and one or more neutrons. Alternatively defined as thermonuclear process, in which nuclei of light elements (deuterium or tritium hydrogen isotopes) combine to form nuclei of a heavier element releasing large amounts of energy.

Ground-Launched Cruise Missile (GLCM): A cruise missile launched from ground installations or vehicles.

Guidance System: The computer and other devices which guide a ballistic missile to the proper velocity and direction for booster (or postboost vehicle PBV) thrust cutoff. In the case of the CM, the guidance system takes the missile all the way to its target.

Hard Target: A target protected or strengthened against the blast, heat, and radiation effects of nuclear explosions.

Intercontinental Ballistic Missile (ICBM): A land-based or fixed or mobile rocket-propelled vehicle capable of delivering a warhead to intercontinental ranges; generally capable of a range in excess of 5,500 kilometers (km) or of 3,000 nautical miles.

Intermediate-Range Ballistic Missile (IRBM): A ballistic missile with a range between 1,000 and 3,000 nautical miles or about 1,850 and 5,500 km; missiles at the upper range of this category are longer-range IRBMs, those at the lower range are called Shorter-Range IRBMs.

Kiloton: Used as a measure of yield of nuclear weapons equivalent to 1,000 tons of TNT.

Laser (*L*ight *A*mplification by *S*timulated *E*mission of *R*adiation): Amplified light beams which can be focused to facilitate range finding, target illumination, and destruction.

Launch-Weight: Weight of a fully loaded missile at the time of launch; includes the aggregate weight of all booster stages, the postboost vehicle (PBV), and the payload.

Launch-on-Warning: Launch of nuclear weapons prior to actual verified impact on target on the basis of information provided by satellite or other electronic warning systems that an enemy nuclear attack is underway. Purpose is to use nuclear arms before losing them.

Medium-Range Ballistic Missile (MRBM): A ballistic missile with a range of 600 to 1,500 nautical miles.

Megaton (Mt): The yield of a nuclear weapon equivalent to 1,000,000 tons of TNT (1,000 kilotons Kt).*

Multiple Independently-Targetable Reentry Vehicle (MIRV): Multiple reentry vehicle carried by a ballistic missile. Each vehicle can be directed to a separate and arbitrarily located target. A MIRVed missile employs a postboost vehicle (PBV) or other warhead-dispensing mechanism.

Multiple Reentry Vehicle (MRV): The *reentry vehicle* of a ballistic missile equipped with multiple warheads all programmed to strike at the same target— as distinct from an MIRVed missile.

National Technical Means of Verification (NTM): Assets which are under control of the verifying nation for monitoring compliance with the provisions of an agreement. NTM includes photographic reconnaisance satellites, aircraft-based systems (such as radars and optical systems), as well as sea- and ground-based systems (such as radars and antennas for collecting telemetry). Distinct from means not under control of the verifying state, for example verification by international agencies or by agreement partners.

Overkill: Nuclear destructive capabilities in excess of those which should be adequate to destroy specified targets or attain specific military or political-military objectives. Overkill capability is sought because it can be diminished by appropriate defensive measures and by malfunctions.

Payload: Weapon components and *penetration aids (penaids)* carried by a delivery vehicle; in the case of a ballistic missile, the RV and antiballistic missile penetration aids placed on ballistic trajectories by the main propulsion stages or the PBV; in the case of a bomber, those bombs, missiles, and penaids carried internally or attached to the wings or fuselage.

Particle Beam Weapon: A device for producing an intense beam of atomic particles, usually electrons.

---

* The size of an area destroyed by nuclear blast increases with weapon explosive yield. However, megaton explosive yield does not increase by linear progression, that is 1 x 1Mt = 1Mt, 8 x ⅛Mt = 1Mt, 20 x 1/20 Mt = 1Mt. Instead, 1 megaton distributed three different ways, e.g. 1 x 1 Mt, 8 x 125 kt, and 20 x 50 kt produces explosive yields of 1, 2, and approximately 2.7 Mt respectively.

Penetration Aids (Penaids): Devices employed by offensive weapon systems such as ballistic missiles and bombers to increase the probability of penetrating enemy defenses. They are frequently designed to simulate or to mask an aircraft or missile warhead in order to mislead enemy defenses.

Preemptive Strike: See *First Strike.*

Post-boost Vehicle (PBV): Often referred to as a "bus," the post-boost vehicle is that part of a missile's payload carrying the *reentry vehicle(s),* a guidance package, fuel, and in the case of MIRVed missiles thrust devices for altering the ballistic flight path so that the *reentry vehicles* can be dispensed sequentially toward different targets.

Radar: A device which transmits and receives electromagnetic signals of radio wavelengths as a means of detecting ships, missiles, or aircraft.

Rapid Reload: The capability of a missile launcher to fire a second missile within a short period following initial firing. Capacity said to be enhanced by "cold" solid fuel, as distinct from "hot" liquid fuel launch; "cold launch" ejects ballistic missiles from silos or submarines using propellants that are separate from the delivery vehicle. Primary ignition of the vehicle itself is delayed until it is clear of the launcher, offering reload capability.

Reentry Vehicle (RV): Portion of the ballistic missile which carries the nuclear warhead. Called a reentry vehicle because it reenters the earth's atmosphere in the terminal phase of its trajectory.

SALT: See *Strategic Nuclear Systems.*

SAM: Surface-to-Air Missiles.

Sea Control: Employment of naval forces, supplemented by land and air forces, to destroy enemy naval forces, suppress enemy commerce, protect shipping lanes, and establish superiority in specific naval operation zones.

Sea-Launched Cruise Missile (SLCM): A cruise missile launched from a submarine or surface ship.

Second Strike: Nuclear response to a first-strike nuclear attack. Nuclear retaliation.

Soft Target: Target not protected against blast or the associated effects of nuclear or other unconventional weapons.

Strategic Nuclear Systems: Warheads and bombs targeted and deliverable on either the Soviet Union or the United States and intended to deter a nuclear attack or, if that is not possible, severely or critically cripple the opponent's warfighting capacity by retaliatory strikes. *Strategic Arms Limitation Talks (SALT)* are designed to limit these weapon systems.

Submarine-Launched Ballistic Missiles (SLBM): Ballistic missile carried in and launched from a submarine. Submarine-Launched Cruise Missile (SLCM) is also launched from a submarine.

Tactical Nuclear Weapons: Nuclear weapons used in support of battle formations in a particular battlefield or in similarly limited battle zones. See also *Theater Nuclear Forces (TNF).*

Telemetry: Data transmitted by radio to the personnel conducting weapons tests, which monitor functions and performance of the test; concealed by *encryption.*

Theater Nuclear Forces (TNF): Nuclear forces deployed in a particular "theater," for example the European or Pacific Theaters; Long–Range Theater Nuclear Forces or Long–Range-Medium or Intermediate–Range Missiles and bombers are weapons deployed to be effective only in a particular theater.

Thermonuclear Weapons: Nuclear weapons in which fission (A-bomb) provides high temperature for fusion of nuclei of hydrogen isotopes (H-bomb).

Throw-Weight: Ballistic missile throw-weight is the useful weight which is placed on a trajectory toward the target by the boost stages of the missile; for purposes of SALT II this was defined as the sum of the weight of a) the RV or RVs; b) any PBV or similar device for releasing or targeting one or more RVs; and c) any anti-ballistic missile penetration aids.

Verification: The process of determining, to the extent necessary to adequately safeguard national security, that the other side is complying with an agreement. This process of judging adequacy takes into account the monitoring capabilities of existent and future intelligence-collection systems and analysis techniques and the ability of the other side to evade detection if it should attempt to do so.

Warhead: That part of a missile, projectile, torpedo, rocket, or other munition which contains either the nuclear or thermonuclear system, the high explosive systems, the chemical or biological agents, or the inert materials intended to inflict damage.

Yield: The force of a nuclear explosion expressed in terms of the number of tons of TNT that would have to be exploded to produce the same amount of energy.

Part Four
Managing Military Power

Nuclear weapons serve no military purpose whatsoever. They are totally useless—except only to deter one's opponent from using them.

former U.S. Secretary of
Defense Robert S. McNamara

The unleashed power of the atom has changed everything except our modes of thinking; we thus drift towards unparalleled catastrophe.

Albert Einstein

There is a plethora of evidence now which when put together, calls into question the ability of modern armed forces to fight wars.

Kaldor (1981), p. 175.

Si vis pacem bellum para (If you want peace, prepare for war).

Roman wisdom

Introduction

For decades, while the United States and the Soviet Union held sway over their respective blocs of allies and/or satellites and no effective military or economic challenge to their hegemonic roles was in sight, bipolarity accurately described the prevailing global power distribution. Multipolarity seemed a more appropriate description when, in the early 1970s, the leading Western European industrial states, Japan, and a growing number of lesser powers appeared able to defy the two giants on occasion. As illustrated in Figures 1-2 and 17-1, bipolarity continued, however, to describe accurately the global distribution of nuclear military power. For that reason this Part devotes two chapters (17 and 18) mainly to the superpowers. Though increasingly ineffective, if not impotent, in many subnuclear conflict situations, the two will continue to play dominant roles in international relations generally for some time to come. The multipolar dimension of contemporary international politics is the theme of Chapter 19.

In 1984, agreeing with a comment in *The Illogic of American Nuclear Strategy* by Robert Jervis, Britain's Lord Zuckerman expressed the conviction that much of the strategic rationale put forward [by American Secretaries of Defense] "has never been anything but window dressing."[1] "The academic analysis of different so-called strategic nuclear policies," he added, "is already a sterile exercise." Indeed, indications are that no responsible civilian or military world leader actually believes that a nuclear war could be "won" or that one ever should be fought. To this one must add the insistence of physicists the world over who predict catastrophic environmental side-effects from which the world

345

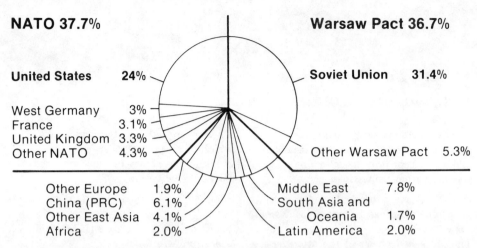

NATO 37.7%

Warsaw Pact 36.7%

| United States | 24% | Soviet Union | 31.4% |

West Germany	3%
France	3.1%
United Kingdom	3.3%
Other NATO	4.3%

Other Warsaw Pact   5.3%

Other Europe	1.9%	Middle East	7.8%
China (PRC)	6.1%	South Asia and	
Other East Asia	4.1%	Oceania	1.7%
Africa	2.0%	Latin America	2.0%

Fig. 17-1. Shares of World Military Expenditure (1982). (USACDA, *World Military Expenditures and Arms Transfers 1972–1982* (April 1984), Figure 3, p. 2.)

may never be able to recover. For that reason, the following two chapters will cover transparently unrealistic strategic considerations only briefly as background for more intensive analysis of contemporary nuclear strategic policies centering on the bedrock issue in the arms race, *nuclear deterrence.* Because nuclear deterrence has hard technical-military as well as soft propagandistic and diplomatic maneuvering and posturing dimensions, the latter aspects are not neglected.

Finally, in the succeeding chapters we continue to distinguish between nuclear and nonnuclear or conventional weapons. On the whole that distinction remains valid. The explosive yield of nuclear arms exceeds by far that of conventional weapons, using TNT for example. However, the destruction potential of chemical explosives also has been enhanced to a point where some "conventional" weapons have greater explosive yield than lesser or tactical nuclear ones. In other words, in some respects, at some levels, the distinction is becoming blurred.

Chapter 17
Soviet–U.S. Rivalry:
Deterrence or War?

Genesis of a Confrontation, or Of What Use are Nuclear Weapons?

It has all the appearances of a race, but no definite goal can be established and no clear starting point identified—which suggests that it may more appropriately be termed a contest or a competition. Whatever it is called, it has been under way for at least two, more likely three, decades. Given its lethality, potentially even its finality, the entire matter may strike an observer from another planet as a manifestation of an advanced form of insanity. Most difficult to comprehend might be the spectacle of two well-established venerable nations arming for a conflict they cannot possibly win, in the course of which the security they seek will most assuredly give way to anarchy, the values they seek to preserve cannot possibly be retained, and the integrity of the societies they seek to perpetuate will be a certain casualty. Yet, upon closer inspection of what might be termed the inner logic of this struggle, it becomes equally apparent that given the magnitude of the threat neither side can afford to abandon or compromise the sense of security which possession of tens of thousands of nuclear devices, with their thousands of megatons of destructive power, promises to convey. The reader of the following chapters should keep that paradox in mind.

Also to be kept in mind is the fact that to be useful nuclear military power need not be activated. It may effectively serve political, psychological, and diplomatic purposes solely as a force-in-being. In the Soviet-American confrontation, five of such purposes may be identified: (1) deterrence of a first-strike nuclear attack by one superpower directed at the other's territory or against one or more of its allies; (2) prevention of nuclear blackmail, that is defense against recourse by one power to nuclear threat, or "nuclear signaling" as some call it, as a lever to secure anywhere on earth certain foreign policy or military advantages detrimental to the other power's vital interests, for example blackmailing the other's allies; (3) compelling the other power to negotiate on a variety of outstanding issues, including arms control and limitations; (4) enhance each power's national prestige vis-à-vis allies, neutrals, and enemies; (5) provide a force of last resort in the event conventional military operations fail and an armistice must be secured.[1]

Of Cause and Effect in Nuclear Competition

The contest usually is described in cause and effect or action-reaction terms. But it actually is difficult to determine reliably whether a military advance scored by one side was designed to match a corresponding move by the opponent or whether the apparent success is pure coincidence. Both sides continuously develop plans, halt development of particular weapons, resume it, halt it again, or even scrap it. Is the opposing side's response—based on reports regarding the original design—the resumption, or is it that reports of a weapon having been abandoned are not believed? Then there is the matter of leap-frogging. When is the introduction of a new weapon or weapon system a reaction to a concrete advance in the same category by the other side? When is it the result of an initiative taken perhaps a decade earlier, in response to a totally different and perhaps forgotten stimulus? This problem arises in part because with modern weapon systems the process from idea to design, to production of a prototype, to testing, to mass production and deployment is quite protracted. In the case of the U.S. nuclear missile-bearing submarine, the Trident, this process consumed more than a decade.[2]

Nuclear Geostrategy

Although Soviet–American arms competition is conducted with strategic and nonstrategic, nuclear and nonnuclear weapons, the several categories are thoroughly intertwined. In the prenuclear era, strategic weapons were those which significantly weakened an enemy's war-fighting capacity—battleships, for example, aircraft carriers or swiftly moving, hard-striking armored battle formations, or fleets of submarines large enough to enforce massive blockades. But none of these could by themselves or even in combination decide the outcome of a war. Ballistic missiles and bombs armed with thermonuclear warheads, ranging partially or wholly around the globe and from pole to pole, capable of totally destroying a country's war-fighting capacity if used *en masse,* have lent the term *strategic* a new and entirely different meaning.

Because the survival of an entire nation may now hinge on the initial wartime performance of these weapons and their support systems, deployed both defensively and offensively, both the United States and the Soviet Union assign highest priority to attainment of a margin of safety in strategic capability on land, at sea, in the air, and now in space. Stubbornly both strive to achieve what their military leaders perceive to be absolute strategic superiority over their principal rival and for insurance also over all potential hostile combinations. Strategically the contest has two dimensions. The principal if not overriding competition is for a lead in weapon systems with global reach, sufficient to inflict upon any conceivable opponent decisive "unacceptable" damage to his military, industrial, and civilian war-fighting capacity.[3] Secondly, both powers compete for the lead in nuclear and conventional weapons with less than global reach to conduct traditional military operations in specific theaters of war. Representative of the first category are intercontinental ballistic missiles (ICBMs), long-range bombers, air-launched cruise missiles, long-range nuclear-powered submarines, and spacecraft. Examples of the latter are so-called theater nuclear weapons or forces (TNFs), e.g. intermediate or medium-range ballistic missiles (IRBMs or MRBMs) and missile-carrying cruisers, short-range bombers, certain surface-to-surface missiles and nuclear-capable artillery, and all conventional naval, air, and land weapons with related support and defense systems. (See Table 17-1.)

Emerging Nuclear Strategic Postures*

Phase I (1940s to 1960s): The U.S. Leads

Spy trials in Europe and the United States in the early 1950s indicate that from the moment the U.S. embarked upon its nuclear program during World War Two Moscow set out to share the secret and acquire the weapon for its own use.[4] The decision may be related to Stalin's plans to secure as much territory as possible in a post-World War Two settlement with the Western Allies, to make the world secure for communism, to protect the Soviet Union from yet another invasion, or both. Or it may have been to guard against nuclear blackmail, which any communist revolutionary will suspect imperialists may secretly plan, to undo the achievements of the October Revolution. After all, had not U.S. leaders demonstrated a readiness to use the bomb?[5]

Actually both sides had much to be concerned about. The wartime alliance between the United States and the Soviet Union began to break up before the last shots of World War Two were fired.[6] Thereafter, relations were but a series of confrontations. Almost immediately the two powers clashed over the unification of Germany and the reconstitution of nations overrun and occupied first by the German armies, then by their "liberators," the Red Army. The U.S. had not entered World War Two to enable Moscow to annex Lithuania, Latvia, and Estonia, or to establish Soviet-controlled Communist totalitarian regimes throughout the rest of Eastern and Southeastern Europe. A Soviet attempt to secure parts of Iran had to be repulsed, reportedly by subtle application of nuclear pressure.[7] From Washington's perspective, communism had turned militarily aggressive and had to be contained. Firm lines had to be drawn, backed by superior military power. To the west of the Soviet Union, including the northern borders of Greece and Turkey, this was to be the task of NATO. Elsewhere, containment was to be the responsibility mainly of the United States.

NATO, established in 1949, never was expected to bear the full brunt of a Soviet bloc attack in Central or Southeastern Europe. Instead it was to act as

---

* Time periods given are approximations. For a map of NATO and the Warsaw Pact see Fig. 13–1.

Table 17-1. Maximum Ranges of Strategic Ballistic Missiles (1983)
in km/nautical miles

ICBMs (a land-based missile capable of a range in excess of 5,500/3,000)

Soviet

SS–17	11,000/ 6,000
SS–18	11,000/ 6,000
SS–19	10,000/ 5,400

U.S.

Titan II	12,000/ 6,500
Minuteman II	12,500/ 6,800
MX	14,000/ 7,500

Long-range IRBMs (land-or sea-based missiles with a range between approximately 1,000 and 3,000 nautical)[a]

Soviet

SS– 4	2,000/ 1,080
SS– 5	4,100/ 2,200
SS–20	5,000/ 2,700

U.S.

Pershing II	1,800/ 970
GLCM	2,500/ 1,350

SLBM (submarine launched ballistic missile with a range in excess of 4,000/2,200)

Soviet

SS–N–18	8,000/ 4,300

U.S.

Poseidon (SLBM C–3)	4,000/ 2,200
Trident (SLMB C–4)	7,400/ 4,000

[a] By reducing the warhead load an IRBM such as the SS–20 can be converted into an ICBM, covering more than 3,125 natural miles. NATO does not regard LR-IRBMs as strategic missiles while the Soviet military do so regard them. Both powers are adding air- and sea-launched cruise missiles as strategic weapons.

a trip-wire, compelling westward moving Soviet bloc forces to attack U.S. contingents in their path, thus under the terms of the NATO treaty automatically bring into play the whole weight of U.S. nuclear might. In other words, NATO was to "couple" the United States firmly to its Western and Southeast European allies. A critical point in that respect, and one generating considerable controversy in later years, was the implicit threat on the part of the United States to respond to a *conventional* attack by Soviet bloc forces against Western Europe with a *nuclear* strike against the Soviet Union. It should be noted that this threat was never made explicit and therefore may well have to be regarded as mere bluff.[8] Others would point out that when the threat was first hinted at, in the early 1950s, the U.S. possessed the capacity to inflict unacceptable damage on the Soviet Union while the latter still lacked the means to retaliate in kind. NATO strategists calculated at the time that "massive retaliation" with U.S. nuclear weapons directed at the source of conventional attack on Western Europe was less expensive than trying to match Soviet bloc forces soldier for soldier and tank for tank.

Moscow should have felt reassured regarding Washington's nuclear intentions toward the Soviet Union, when the latter's armed invasion of Hungary in 1956 failed to provoke a Western military response, U.S. reaction being confined to vague rhetoric about a "roll back" of Communism and "liberation" of Eastern Europe. The U.S. also refrained from direct use of nuclear power during the Korean War (1950-1953).* Nonetheless, Moscow was concerned that West German participation in NATO augured a revival of German militarism, now reinforced by the United States, Great Britain, and France. In the Far East, Japan so it seemed was also being prepared to reclaim its possessions from Soviet occupation. Underscoring all of this, U.S. bombers and missile threats proliferated along an arc extending from Iceland, Greenland, and Norway through Central and Southeastern Europe and the Mediterranean to the Northern Pacific.

With the successful launch of Sputnik I in 1957, the Soviet Union demonstrated a capacity to lift into space heavy rockets armed with nuclear warheads developed in the late 1940s and early 1950s. That same year, the Soviet Union flight-tested land-based missiles capable of carrying nuclear warheads over a trajectory equivalent to the distance between the Soviet Union and the United States.† While enjoying clear nuclear superiority, U.S. leaders, especially then Secretary of State John Foster Dulles, had relied in rhetoric at least on "massive [nuclear] retaliation" to contain the Soviet Union within limits designated by the United States. Once Moscow had acquired the capacity to inflict crippling damage on the continental United States, U.S. doctrine had to be altered. Instead of "*massive* retaliation" the response now was to be "selective" or "appropriate," depending on the nature and extent of the provocation. Also to be reviewed was the question of first use of nuclear weapons by the United States, and if "first used" what the appropriate targets would be. One concept, "counterforce," called for appropriately limited nuclear response against conventional forces penetrating Western European defenses and for commensurate response against nuclear forces should these be utilized in a breakthrough attempt by the Soviet Union.

* However, to bring that war to an honorable end President Eisenhower is reported to have advised Communist China's rulers that he was prepared to use the atom bomb to achieve his purpose. A proposal to use the bomb against the Communist Chinese, recommended by General Douglas MacArthur, was rejected firmly by the same U.S. president who had authorized its first use, Harry S. Truman.

† During the contest's early stages, the Soviet Union lacked the industrial and technological wherewithal to produce missiles accurate and reliable enough to reach, hit, and destroy designated targets thousands of miles from their launching pads on Soviet soil. According to some analysts, it was to compensate for these deficiencies that for decades Soviet ballistics reflected a preference for greater throw-weight, hence greater destructive power, over precision. Fallows (1981), p. 60, writes: "American nuclear strategists . . . consciously decided that instead of following the Soviet pattern . . . they would concentrate on lighter smaller missiles by exploiting American technological advances in accuracy, warhead design, and propulsion systems." As a result, the U.S. now has the quantitative inferiority problem: Soviet throw-weight being greater than that of the U.S., the Soviet compensation for inaccuracy is greater than that of the U.S.

It was during this phase, mainly to thwart the feared Soviet thrust across Europe and to compensate for a rapidly growing conventional deficiency on the Western side, that NATO forces were equipped with thousands of low yield tactical nuclear weapons to be used over relatively short distances (between 50 and 500 km) should the need arise. But it was also during this period that both sides tested hydrogen weapons 200 or more times more powerful than the Hiroshima bomb, the Soviet Union developed the improved Bison long-range bomber with a range of approximately 6,000 miles, and both tested their first SLBMs. The appearance of the new Soviet bomber gave rise to the first of several "gap" crises in the United States; in this case, the U.S., it was alleged, was "behind" the Soviet Union as a result of a "bomber gap."

Phase II (1960s to 1970s): MAD

Now confronted by the threat of a potentially devastating attack on its own cities, the U.S. modified its nuclear strategy. Washington did not wish to be trapped in a situation where a conventional Soviet assault on Western Europe could only be answered by a nuclear strike against the Soviet Union, with now unforeseeable consequences for the U.S. itself. Accordingly, the U.S. added to its options "limited nuclear war," a "flexible" rather than a rigid response. This was to signal Moscow Washington's intent to respond to a conventional attack in Europe only gradually, escalating from conventional to tactical nuclear to a still restrained "counterforce" nuclear strike confined to appropriate military targets in the Soviet Union, all depending on the level of combat indicated by events on the scene.* If at all possible, damage to cities was to be avoided.

However, U.S. military planners soon became convinced that Soviet ABM capabilities now were adequate to protect sufficient numbers of its ICBMs to threaten the U.S. with unacceptable retaliation or with a devastating follow-up to a first strike of its own. Alternatively, Moscow could launch its entire strike force all at once, leaving no "counterforce" targets for U.S. weapons to hit. The appropriate remedy for this dilemma seemed to be to hold large Soviet population centers hostage to deter a Soviet bloc conventional attack against NATO or anywhere else.† In other words, as far as the superpowers were

---

* "Counterforce" represents a shift from "countervalue," that is city for city, population for population, oil fields for oil fields retaliatory response.

† The MAD doctrine assumed that U.S.-Allied strategic forces could reach a sufficient number of targets in the Soviet Union to cause losses of 25 percent of the population and 50 percent of Soviet economic infrastructure. Approximately the same damage was anticipated for the United States. Losses of that magnitude were presumed to be "unacceptable" to either side, hence MAD was deemed a sufficient deterrent.

The limited war concept was based on the following considerations: U.S. forces were to be armed with tactical weapons sufficient to cover attacking military targets within a given theater of war or combat zone but not beyond. Advised in advance that nuclear weapons might be employed at the tactical level, the Soviet Union would either not launch an attack in the first place or, if subjected to carefully placed tactical nuclear defensive strikes, would reciprocate only in kind, eschewing an all-out nuclear attack on the U.S. in retaliation for the limited nuclear action. This was called "flexible response,"

concerned, each was to be discouraged from attacking the other, or its allies, by the threat of Mutual Assured Destruction or MAD, that is, by an assured ability to absorb an attack on its nuclear forces while retaining the capacity to retaliate devastatingly against the other. To have any strategic validity MAD relied on neither side protecting all or most of its large population center with antimissile defenses.

At the beginning of this decade, Soviet Premier Nikita S. Khrushchev sought by diplomatic bargaining to secure removal of U.S. bases closest to Soviet territory, from Turkey for instance. Unsuccessful, he then attempted in 1962 to compel their removal by secretly introducing medium-range ballistic missiles into Cuba, threatening U.S. cities from an equivalent distance with equivalently shortened warning time. When under threat of U.S. retaliation the missiles had to be withdrawn, the arms race gathered momentum. Until then, and for another ten years thereafter, the United States had with some success employed nuclear diplomacy to have its will over the Soviet Union.[9] (Moscow too had used this ploy, but far less frequently and with less success). Now Soviet leaders swore never again to suffer such humiliation, never again to have to retreat under nuclear threat. Leonid Brezhnev, Khrushchev's successor, promptly embarked upon an accelerated arms program to raise the Soviet Union to the first-class world power status to which Soviet leaders thought it was entitled. But it was also toward the end of this period that both sides began to see some advantage if a cap could be placed either on weapon systems which they already possessed in sufficient quantity or on systems each suspected the other might soon develop and deploy. We shall turn to that subject in the succeeding chapter.

Phase III (1970s–1980s): Parity?

By 1973 Brezhnev was able to assure the communist world that a "decisive shift in the correlation of forces will be such that come 1985, we will be able to exert our will wherever we [require]." This put the world on notice that soon Moscow too would be in position to rely on nuclear diplomacy in pursuit of foreign policy objectives. To the West such remarks had offensive military overtones, quite in keeping with known and often reiterated communist revolutionary doctrine. We already referred to the accompanying Brezhnev doctrine which vowed unremitting struggle against "imperialism" via "national liberation." Moreover, in addition to a huge land army protecting Soviet borders, a capacity manifested in Hungary in 1956 and in Czechoslovakia in 1968 to

as the defenders would have several options. After first advocating it (Kissinger 1957), Kissinger repudiated the limited war strategy four years later. (1961), pp. 81–86. See also, The Comptroller General of the United States (1981). On U.S. Presidential Directive 59, 1980, see *ibid.,* pp. 11ff.

A major objective to the limited war concept was the probability that each side would be guided by the "use them or lose them" principle, that is, unless one fired off most of one's strategic weapons they might be destroyed in a surprise attack. The Soviets are said to have rejected the limited war concept from the outset as unrealistic, a ploy by Washington to reassure its European allies. Isby (1981), p. 209.

deploy these forces swiftly and resolutely, the Soviet Union now pressed forward with a matching expansion of its naval and airforces. The overall aim apparently was to acquire sufficient armed might to balance anything the West or the People's Republic of China could bring to bear against the Soviet Union, an objective which to many United States leaders at least translated into a drive for global military superiority.

Now, with both powers poised to launch nuclear strikes against each other, for whatever reasons and in whatever sequence, "destabilization" entered the nuclear vocabulary. It now became essential that neither side be permitted to achieve an advantage over the other sufficient to suggest to the potential loser that a preemptive nuclear strike was imperative to assure survival. Like parity or equivalence, destabilization did not lend itself to precise measurement. Even if parity could roughly be maintained in numerical terms, qualitatively it seemed impossible to prevent either side from attaining that theoretically fatal margin of superiority.* Inevitably, for that very reason each side has ever since explored ways and means to interdict and destroy the other's incoming nuclear missiles. But as with all military technological advances, each innovation is immediately countered by a response. Anticipating improved antiballistic missile defenses, both powers first increased the number of reentry vehicles to saturate enemy ABM systems (ABMS). This was accomplished by placing in each ICBM and SLBM additional warheads, converting single into multiple reentry vehicles (MRVs). When that seemed insufficient, the multiple independently targetable reentry vehicle (MIRV) made its appearance. (Not subject to controls or curbs, of course, is the improvement of missile capacity to deceive or foil enemy radar and ABMS). With that advance, enemy defenses could be saddled with the additional burden of trying to anticipate which of several possible targets an MIRV might be programmed to attack. MIRVing initially increased U.S. warheads from 1054 on ICBMs and 656 on SLBMs to a total of 7274.[10] On the Soviet side, if they performed at 80 percent reliability, 500 of their heaviest ICBMs, each armed with five independently targetted warheads, could in theory hit 1200 targets, stripping "the land-based Minuteman [retaliatory] core from the United States nuclear arsenal in a first strike."[11] It was the latter threat which, according to some U.S. critics of administration defense policy, opened a "window of vulnerability" through which Soviet power could be applied for nuclear blackmail purposes or for a preemptive strike sometime in the middle or later 1980s, unless of course the U.S. developed and deployed an antidote.†

* In 1969, then Assistant to the President for National Security Affairs Henry Kissinger spoke of "codification of parity" as a pressing U.S. objective. Safire (1975), p. 163.

† Safire (1975), p. 178, summarizes the hypothetical problem facing the U.S.: "Soviet ICBMs . . . attack the Minuteman ICBM force and eliminate it wholesale in a first strike while two-thirds of Soviet missiles still remain in their silos and [on] submarines. With the counterforce option knocked out, the one American response left would be a futile counter-city strike return. Surrender would be very attractive. The U.S. would have lost the war with the loss of its counterforce weapons (along with an estimated 10 to 20 million people)." See also Fallows (1981), p. 146, and graph, "The Open Window of

It was during this phase that *detente,* that is relaxation of East–West, especially Soviet–American, tension seemed possible and strategic arms limitation agreements could be negotiated and signed. Viewed from a different perspective, either or both sides were merely temporizing, each seeking to reassure the opponent of its good intentions until that definitive break-through in offensive or defensive capability was achieved. There is abundant evidence to support either interpretation.[12] In any case, *detente* came to an end about 1980 and the doomsday clock was moved several minutes closer to twelve.*

Phase IV (1980—): "Fine-tuning" Nuclear War

We do not know whether Soviet military planners are as inclined as are their U.S. counterparts to alter and discard strategic concepts, but the early 1980s saw a veritable flood of adjustments, modifications, and even abrupt reversals emanate from Washington. Berman and Baker offer a persuasive explanation of the apparent asymmetry between U.S. and Soviet strategic steadiness. "Soviet

Vulnerability," Committee on The Present Danger (1982), p. 19. Now both sides are known to have *Maneuvering* Reentry Vehicles (MaRVs) under development. For an updated version of the "window of vulnerability" syndrome see Committee on the Present Danger (November 30, 1984), pp. 14–16, especially Note 51, p. 15. One long-term means of narrowing the gap or closing the window is to shift to mobile ICBMs such as the Midgetman, deployable in the 1990s, *ibid.,* p. 17.

The "Open Window of Vulnerability"

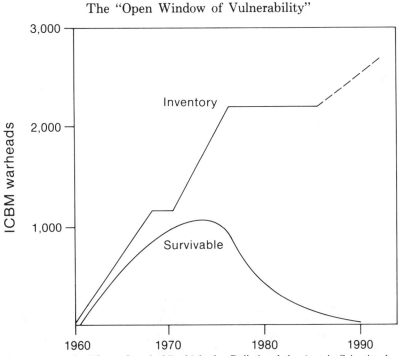

* Reference is to the "doomsday clock" which the *Bulletin of the Atomic Scientists* has included in each issue since 1947. The editors move the clock's hands back or forward depending on their estimate of how close the world is to a nuclear holocaust.

doctrine," they write, "has . . . been able to develop relatively free of concern for external alliances. The USSR's geographical proximity to and political dominance of the neighboring Warsaw Pact countries obviates the kind of nuclear commitment that the United States has been compelled to make to its overseas allies. For the United States, this relationship has been a critical influence in leading it to embrace such doctrinal concepts as limited nuclear war and selective strategic targetting."[13] In the 1980s, this relationship caused Washington to engage in a frenetic search for strategic syntheses designed to accomplish the well-nigh impossible: reassure the more vulnerable, hence increasingly nervous, Western European allies while maintaining its own nuclear credibility vis-à-vis Soviet military planners. From this concern stemmed such shifts as that from "limited nuclear war" to "countervailing strategy." Contained in the latter was a signal to both allies and the Soviet Union that the U.S. was determined as well as militarily able to respond to "a limited Soviet nuclear attack without losing the ability to respond in a controlled and deliberate manner," thus, it was hoped, preventing misreadings of Soviet intentions which could result in uncontrollable escalation. At the same time, the U.S. intended to "retain the ability to hold vital and valuable [Soviet] targets hostage while threatening their ultimate destruction."[14]

In 1982 the Defense Department (DOD) issued a defense guidance to form the basis for 1984–1988 budget requests which, going one step further, implied that the U.S. should be prepared to fight a nuclear war "over a protracted period."[15] To some observers this meant that Washington now expected a nuclear war to be fought in stages, each side probing carefully for a winning combination without immediately firing off all of its nuclear arsenal.* Yet a component of this new concept called for U.S. forces to advance beyond limited or restricted nuclear warfare and "render ineffective the total Soviet (and Soviet allies') military and political power structure." In other words, conducting protracted nuclear war required that the enemy was to be "decapitated," an objective made possible by greater accuracy of scaled-down nuclear weapons. At the same time, the U.S. C³ structure was to be protected to enable the president and his senior military advisors to control a nuclear exchange instead of being limited to an all-out "use it or lose it" spastic retaliatory blow.[16] Criticized for implying that the U.S. expected to "win" a protracted nuclear conflict, the DOD revised its position somewhat, a year later denying such intent.[17] Reflecting continued pressure from allies, from presumed Soviet moves,

---

* In 1984, the U.S. Army Chief of Staff told the Army War College that "the strategic requirements of the 1980s are to prepare for the 'Three Days of War': to deter the day before the war; to fight the day of the war; and to terminate the conflict in such a manner than on the day after the war, the United States and its allies enjoy an acceptable level of security." M.T. Owens, "The Utility of Force," The Heritage Foundation, *Backgrounder*, No. 370 (August 1, 1984), p. 9. Regarding a reported U.S. plan to ensure that in a Soviet-American nuclear exchange the U.S. "must prevail and be able to force the Soviet Union to seek earliest possible termination of hostilities *on terms favorable to the United States*," see Robert W. Tucker, "The Nuclear Debate," *Foreign Affairs*, Vol. 63, No. 1 (Fall 1984), p. 9, italics added.

and from hardliners at home and from ever advancing technology, U.S. planners produced such esoteric doctrines as "escalation dominance and control," "prompt hard-target kill capability," and "boost phase intercept," a term we shall examine shortly. Also considered during this period was "horizontal escalation," in which U.S. forces would strike back at Soviet interests not necessarily at a point chosen by Moscow, but one where U.S. forces were positioned more advantageously. Simultaneously, the U.S. ordered stockpiling of conventional supplies in order to prevent a situation from arising where superior Soviet bloc conventional forces might compel NATO to expend its conventional ammunition prematurely, leaving no choice but nuclear war. All of these and similar strategic variations concealed vast uncertainties compounded by weapon modernization, automation, miniaturization, and proliferation.

Balancing Arsenals, or Who is First?

The Credibility Problem

Whatever either side intended to do with its nuclear arsenal, it felt that it had to demonstrate that it not only had the ability if necessary to launch a first strike but could protect a sufficient number of weapons of all kinds needed for a follow-up second or even third strike and that somehow it could survive one, two, or three retaliatory responses. Put differently, to render a nuclear deterrent credible State B had to be convinced that in addition to absorbing a retaliatory attack in response to its first strike State A could retain sufficient weapons to launch a second strike inflicting unacceptable damage on the attacker. "Unacceptable" damage meant more than either combatant could tolerate if it wished to remain a viable state and more than it could accept if a follow-up strike was needed to punish the other for its nuclear attack. Neither side of course could determine with certainty precisely where the threshold of acceptability might be, which did not deter them from spinning out scenarios of first-second-third strikes and corresponding retaliation.

Key elements in the credibility contest are dispersal, partly through mobility, and concealment of a nuclear arsenal's principal components. U.S. deterrence has for sometime relied on a *triad* of weapons: land-based bombers, ICBMs, and submarines. The bombers, one-third of which were to be airborne at all times—thus out of reach of Soviet missiles, had to be capable of carrying nuclear weapons for delivery against specific Soviet targets, hence had to be capable to penetrate Soviet air defenses or launch missiles from a "stand-off position" outside the Soviet air defense perimeter. ICBMs launched from silos or platforms hardened against Soviet attack had to be capable of reaching their military targets quickly and surely enough to catch as many enemy missiles as possible in their silos or on their launching platforms. Submarines, preferably nuclear-powered, equipped with nuclear missiles were stationed at points close enough to key Soviet military and industrial centers to reduce the warning time to a point where defensive measures were possible only to a limited extent.

Submarines had to be quiet to avoid premature detection, accessible for alert and direction by high-speed communication wherever they were, and equipped to determine their exact position when preparing to launch their missiles. They also had to be well scattered, a segment of the entire force to be at sea at all times. Undergirding the entire system had to be listening and tracking stations located throughout the world, initially only on land, reinforced eventually by satellites. The overall strategic rationale for the *triad* was twofold: First, its purpose was to assure *survivability* of at least one-third of the total force in the event of an attack; secondly, if Soviet technology advanced to the point where one leg of the triad was rendered vulnerable, the other two legs would provide a margin of safety until the breech was closed.*

The Soviet Union, on the other hand, while technologically well behind the U.S. in sea power, especially submarines, and unable to match the U.S. bomber force, relied more heavily on land-based missiles, an imbalance, we shall note, which was to cause considerable difficulties in arms control and limitation negotiations and which contributed to apprehension among Soviet planners that their threat potential might lack credibility.

Counting Weapons

Threat and threat inflation. It is clear from the foregoing discussion that arms competition has reached its contemporary spiralling intensity for reasons similar to those which generated such contests in the past. But four incentives set the nuclear rivalry apart: 1) a more pronounced uncertainty with respect to performance under combat conditions of ever more sophisticated, complex, and intricate weapon systems; 2) greater uncertainties regarding the enemy's defensive capabilities, which, presumed to be equally sophisticated, are difficult to assess before they are activated in earnest; 3) arising from the two foregoing considerations, the need to produce sufficient nuclear weapons to overcome any conceivable defense system by saturation; and 4) the imperative to retain, following an enemy attack or a preemptive first strike, sufficient reserves (residual balance) for further nuclear combat.

Also contributing to escalation is the sheer magnitude of the nuclear threat with its megadestruction and potential megadeath. The global reach of nuclear and postnuclear weapons—more on the latter shortly—creates a need for greater versatility in design of offensive and defensive weapons; the accompanying technological advances enable planners and designers to make greater strides in weapon development than ever before in history. One aspect especially alarming to the respective high commands is the relative ease with which a system's delivery and destruction potential can be doubled and redoubled in virtually complete secrecy, always threatening to render a major defense com-

---

* In addition, the triad is designed to prevent concentration of Soviet resources, complicate Soviet attack planning, hedge against system failure in any one segment of the triad, and mutually reinforce all three. U.S. DOD (1983) *Annual Report*, Chart 1.B.2, p. 30.

ponent obsolete. Undeniably, there is a basic instability inherent in such competition.

We saw earlier that what appears to be an action-reaction pattern, that is, weapon system X stimulating production of weapon systems Y by the opposing side, may in part be an illusion; in this matter cause and effect are rather difficult to trace. There may, however, be something else at work: the spiral may be driven upward also by artificially contrived, militarily unwarranted, threat inflation. Basically this is not new. Military leaders, arms manufacturers, and chauvinists, most quite honestly and prudently but some self-servingly and some motivated mainly by greed, have always tended to inflate threats to their state's security. What is novel about this spur to armament is its apparently permanent nature, its stealth, its costs, and its potentially cataclysmic outcome. At least one U.S. president, Dwight D. Eisenhower, and one Soviet premier, Khrushchev, saw the danger clearly.* In fairness to the U.S. military, it has been noted that "with little information available on what the Soviets are doing, a natural tendency for American decision makers is to assume the worst and try to make sure that it does not happen."[18]

Deliberate threat inflation takes several forms and employs varying methods: mindless speculation without regard to real-life conditions, suppression of the fact that assertions regarding an opponent's capabilities have actually not been verified or are not verifiable or have been proven to be unwarranted, or that an opponent's stepped-up arms production is but a response to one's own overly ambitious goals. Reports on Soviet defense expenditures are a perennial source of threat inflation in the United States. U.S. intelligence agencies are known to have under- or overestimated Soviet military outlays by up to 100 percent.[19] Yet annually the U.S. Department of Defense seeks to justify its own requests for increased appropriations by presenting to the U.S. Congress the highest of several estimates.† Similarly, the overall Soviet strategic force, approximately 2400 missiles and bombers in the early 1980s, was suspected to have reached that level solely because such was the goal set by the U.S. military for their own production in the 1960s. The Russians "have simply copied it," commented

---

* According to Nincic (1982), p. 67, Khrushchev is reported to have quoted his own military commanders as telling him: "If you try to economize on the country's defenses today, you'll pay in blood when war breaks out tomorrow." Although he entertained doubts, in the end he gave "them the money they asked for"; see also Kaldor (1981), p. 117, on Khrushchev. Barnet (1977), p. 106, suggests that the military of both sides are in collusion, each providing the other with the arguments needed to overcome skepticism on the part of their civilian rulers; see also Pisar (1979), pp. 257-258.

† Cox (1982), pp. 103-104. It has been shown that Soviet military expenditures and rates of arms production were actually decreasing when official U.S. government assertions had them increasing. One source of error has been a complete misreading of Soviet efficiency in converting a given amount of rubles into military effectiveness. Contributing to *under*estimation may be a failure to treat as military outlay government-subsidized training of several hundred thousand engineers, half of whom enter the military services each year. Navrozov (1983); also, Holzman (1980), pp. 99-100, Nincik (1982), pp. 73-81; on "reciprocal threat inflation," see Zimmerman and Palmer (1983).

one U.S. defense analyst.* But that was not the official American explanation of the Soviet arms build-up. Then there is the "greater then expected threat" syndrome. Enthusiasts among the military on one side exaggerate to their political leaders the opponent's strength in one particular area. When the first exaggeration proves not to be persuasive, the "greater-than-expected" threat is presented, again most likely on very dubious foundations.

"Hawks continue to breed each other's hawks," comments a European critic of superpower rivalry.[20] Put differently, extremists, profiteers, diverse interest groups, and genuinely concerned patriots on either side thrive on each other's exaggerations. To make their case they credit the enemy with infallibility and absolute perfection, pointing with alarm only to their own side's deficiencies. A different strategy is followed when it comes to selling a new system or a new design to the respective publics or authorities. Thus, during the early stages of a novel system, its accuracy and reliability under all conceivable conditions is presented as tried and proven. Once funded and underway, it is made known that the enemy has solved his defensive problem, hence a new challenge must urgently be devised.†

Regarding deterrence itself, it has been argued that insofar as that strategy rests on the ability to "inflict relatively greater damage on the adversary," it is "less an expression of deep belief than an attempt to ensure continued defense expansion."[21] Comments another critic, "Strategic arguments [should be viewed] as disputes of faith rather than fact."‡ Yet faith or fact, real threat or threat

---

* Cockburn (1983), pp. 215–216; he also notes that as neither side advertises its errors, both may be copying each other's mistakes.

† For example, new weapon systems have been sold to the U.S. Congress and to the public on the strength of an argument that the missile in question has a circular error probable (CEP) of 0.1 of one nautical mile, that is, can hit its assigned targets within that small a radius. But myriads of factors must be expected to intervene between launch and arrival on target. When it is time to develop a new system, a new Soviet missile usually is credited with the identical degree of accuracy, again without regard to the high probability that neither CEP can actually be relied upon. To be remembered in that regard, estimates of CEP on both sides are based on telemetric data derived from pre-planned tests over familiar territory, usually in a West-East direction, under peacetime conditions. Commented former U.S. Secretary of Defense James R. Schlesinger: "The precision one encounters in paper studies of nuclear exchanges reflects the precision of the assumptions rather than any experience based on approximation-to-real-life test data" (quoted in Cockburn (1983), p. 211). As for these tests, they are often wholly artificial indeed, carefully planned to obtain predetermined results. While many such tests— artificial though they are—undoubtedly are conducted with the rigor called for in so deadly an undertaking, many are not. See also Kaldor (1981), pp. 183–184.

‡ Fallows (1981), p. 140. He continues:

Strategic arguments [should be viewed] as disputes of faith rather than fact. The "best" minds of the defense community have been drawn towards nuclear analysis, but so were the best minds to be found in the monastery arguing the Albigensian heresy, in the fourteenth century. A novel theory about how the Kremlin might respond to nuclear strike may be advanced, may make the author's name, and may lead to billions in expenditures without entering any further into the domain of fact than did the monk's speculations about the nature of God. Wars have been fought, empires built, heretics burned on the basis of theology, and so, on the basis of the nuclear theology, are missiles developed and war plans laid today.

inflation, the competition will not abate, the spiraling will not cease, and weapons inexorably increase in lethality. One single U.S. Poseidon sub carrying 16 missiles with 10 or more warheads each, or a total of at least 160 warheads, has a destructive power of at least 500 Hiroshima bombs. It has been noted that "a single [U.S.] sub would therefore be capable of simultaneously attacking such cities as Moscow, Leningrad, Kiev, Tashkent, Baku, Kharkov, Gorky, Novosibirsk, Kuibyshev, and Sverdlovsk, each having a population in excess of a million, and still have 150 warheads available to wipe out other cities, villages, and hamlets. This is the power of just one Poseidon sub, of which the United States has thirty-one."[22] If the Soviet Union cannot yet match the severity and immediacy of that menace, it soon will.

Because debates on strategy are, to an extent at least, public property in the United States, more is known about U.S. plans than about those entertained by Soviet leaders (incidentally a major contributing factor to the escalation). In that respect as well one can again not speak of symmetry. It is highly probable however, considering the uncertainties surrounding the entire subject matter, that Moscow is as much in the dark about actual U.S. intentions and capabilities as Washington is regarding Moscow's. One can assume therefore that the latter's vacillations between acceptance of the feasibility of fighting and winning such a war and declaring that such wars must never be fought, between counterforce, countervalue, and countervailing components of deterrence, and all the other concepts periodically taken up and then abandoned are for similar reasons replicated in the Kremlin.* Both antagonists appear to be locked into certain postures, both to an extent victims of what has been called "technology creep," the incremental pressure emanating from enthusiastic scientists, military officers, bureaucrats, and weapons systems which seem to generate their own momentum. Each political crisis ratchets the ambitions of the two military establishments several notches higher, boosting increments by several million or billion dollars or rubles and by batches of new ideas. Talk of first, second, and third strike continues while fewer experts believe either that offensive capabilities are accurate and reliable enough or defenses airtight enough to tempt one side or the other actually to take that risk.

Closing "windows" and inviting the holocaust. We already referred to the alleged bomber and missile gaps which proved to be nonexistent. Then there

* U.S. reading of Soviet intentions regarding nuclear war relied during critical stages of U.S. rearmament on a book edited by Soviet Marshall Vasily D. Sokolowskiy entitled *Military Strategy* but written, as another Soviet General pointed out, "at the dawn of nuclear weaponry." In an interview, Soviet Lt. Gen. Mikhail A. Milstein, on August 24, 1980, noted that Sokolowski's views had long been overtaken by other perceptions. Modern Soviet doctrine, he noted, "regards nuclear weapons as something that must never be used. They are not weapons with which one can achieve foreign policy goals." *The New York Times* (December 7, 1980); see also, Zuckerman (1982), pp. 74-75. A different view is cited in Gray (1982), p. 39, but the source is secondary, repeating someone else's speculation; see also Kaldor (1981), pp. 105-108. The Soviet military (Army) doctrine, however, seems prepared to resort to tactical use of nuclear weapons. Isby, *op. cit.,* pp. 209-210. See also Freedman (Recommended Readings), pp. 145ff and 257ff.

was the alleged "civil defense gap."* We also mentioned the "window of vulnerability" which was said to leave the U.S. virtually defenseless for the better part of a decade. One antidote to that presumed Soviet advantage was to be the MX (Missile Experimental). Heavier than the Minuteman III (successor to Minutemen I and II), hence more lethal and also advertised as more accurate, armed with ten warheads instead of the three carried by its immediate predecessor, and placed in "super-hardened" silos, this latest addition to the world's nuclear stock was to restabilize the dangerously unbalanced Soviet–American confrontation. But like all previous balancing acts, this too failed to achieve its purpose, for several reasons: 1) The MX was not the sole improvement on the U.S. side. The B-1 bomber promised to add to a standing U.S. advantage in long-range nuclear aircraft while the new D-5 Trident SLBM, scheduled for deployment about 1989, would strengthen the sea-leg of the U.S. triad. 2) At first, the MX was to have been protected against a Soviet first strike by an elaborate "race-track" basing scheme, a form of the well-known "shell game." About 100 MXs were to be moved about on the "race track," then installed in 100–200 of some 4000 silos leaving Soviet planners to guess precisely where the U.S. retaliatory ICBM force was based at any given time. When it was decided to abandon that scheme and deploy the missiles in existing but hardened Minuteman silos, which experts had declared to be vulnerable to a Soviet first strike, hardened or not, the "window of vulnerability" appeared to be as open as before. This, even though the missiles were to be "densely packed" to cause incoming Soviet missiles "fratricidally" to destroy each other. Indeed, U.S. defense planners now began to speak of the necessity to launch U.S. missiles "under attack," that is immediately after the first Soviet warhead had been detonated but before the full brunt of such an attack was determined. Some critics of this U.S. move argued that because the new missile left the U.S. as vulnerable as before, it could be spared a Pearl Harbor type surprise attack only by being launched *before* a Soviet attack was under way. In other words, not adding to U.S. defensive capabilities as was averred by its advocates the MX seemed to be a first-strike weapon, destabilizing an explosive situation even more.[23] On the other hand, and here was the next ratchet effect, anticipating first use by the United States, Moscow might be unable to resist the temptation to destroy 100 times 10 warheads deployed in vulnerable silos, very much as Japan found irresistible the pride of the U.S. Navy lying at anchor at Pearl Harbor.

---

* Barnet (1977), p. 118, reminds us of the "mine-shaft gap" satirized in the movie *Dr. Strangelove,* where the Russians were reported to have gained an edge over the U.S. by utilizing large numbers of available mine-shafts to protect a greater percentage of their civilian population than could the U.S., thereby enhancing their nuclear credibility in a confrontation. Another gap was said to have opened up in the 1980s when U.S.-Canadian northern regional air defenses (the Distant-Early-Warning [DEW] line) was allowed to develop openings through which Soviet bombers and air-launched cruise missiles might slip to "decapitate" U.S. C³ facilities, preparatory to a paralyzing all-out ICBM-SLBM attack on the U.S. nuclear arsenal itself. Gerald F. Seib, *The Wall Street Journal* (March 28, 1984).

The global strategic balance: Leaving threat inflation aside and taking official U.S. government data on face value, the Soviet Union is "ahead" at any given point. Accepting Soviet numbers and quality assessments of Western forces, the U.S. and its allies are "ahead." Actually, there is no reliable way to determine who leads in what respect. This for several reasons. None of the weapons critical to either side's success have been, nor can they be, tested in earnest without a war. Tests may be quite realistic in a simulated way. But no one really knows how these weapons will perform under nuclear combat conditions. For example, there is the just mentioned problem of weapon "fratricide." A first wave of missiles successfully delivered on target—a very risky matter this—may destroy or at least render ineffective the succeeding wave or waves. If they are fired in quick succession to prevent launching of a retaliatory volley, the same phenomenon could occur. None of the major strategic nuclear weapons has followed a trajectory over the magnetic pole. None has had to run the gauntlet of an imaginative, sophisticated defense whose secrets are wholly or substantially unknown to the attacker.[24]

Considering the risk in launching a first strike while not substantially or wholly eliminating the opponent's retaliatory capacity, accuracy is as important as surprise.* Strategists today speak of silo-killing capability. For example, SLBMs, to pose a real threat, must reach and destroy specific silos *before* retaliatory volleys can be launched. But submarines are far less accurate than land-based weapons. Even with satellite-assisted improvements it still is difficult to fix precisely a sub's position at time of launch.[25] Combat or flight-induced mechanical or electronic disturbances may throw many a ballistic missile off course; and, in any case, even the most sophisticated missile can be "spoofed" by tin foil, heat flares, or metallic camouflage.

Another unknown is "hardness," that is, a silo's capacity to actually withstand a multiple megaton explosion, directly on target or nearby. Warning time for the defender is equally difficult to pin down. Estimates of time available between awareness that an attack is under way and impact range from half an hour to 15 minutes, depending on the weapons involved and assuming that the strike originates in the other superpower's territory. If it originates off-shore or is delivered by suborbital bombardment system (SOBS), time available to activate defenses and retaliatory systems may be considerably shorter.

Much of the information upon which both sides base their best possible estimates of mutual strength and weakness is based on electronic monitoring of tests, testing of models of silos built on indirect information obtained from sources of greatly varying reliability, including satellite reconnaissance which can be misled. According to one writer, U.S. intelligence estimates of Soviet nuclear weaponry are "purely matters of conjecture, based on the size of Soviet underground tests and extrapolations from practice and experience with U.S.

---

* Cockburn (1983), p. 211, writes: "If you cannot be sure that you will be able to hit the enemy's silos, there is no point in even trying." Assessing the reliability of MIRVing, Cockburn comments: "The action of jettisoning each MIRV has the effect of throwing the postboost vehicle carrying the remainder slightly off course" (p. 215).

Table 17-2. Four Views of the Nuclear Strategic Balance[a] (1983–84 and 1986, Projected)

I (1983–84)

If all NATO, incl. all French, and all Soviet nuclear weapons are counted:[b]

NATO[b]		Warsaw Pact	
Weapons	Warheads	Warheads	Weapons
3,106	10,953	9,043	2,743

II (1983–84)

If only U.S. ICBMs and LR Bombers, U.S. and British SLBMs and Soviet ICBMs, SLBMs and LR Bombers are counted:

NATO		Warsaw Pact	
Weapons	Warheads	Warheads	Weapons
1,997	9,900–10,000	9,043	2,743

III (1983–84)

If only French Bombers, IRBMs and SLBMs capable of reaching targets in the Soviet Union are added to Count II:

NATO		Warsaw Pact	
Weapons	Warheads	Warheads	Weapons
2,116	10,025	9,043	2,743

IV (1986, Projected)

If ⅓rd of Soviet SS–20 IRBMs, altered to reach targets in the U.S. and NATO's Pershing II and GLCMs are added to Count III:

NATO		Warsaw Pact	
Weapons	Warheads	Warheads	Weapons
3,678	11,525	11,500[c]	3,400[c]

SOURCE: U.S. DOD (1984); IISS (1983/84); SIPRI (1984); NATO (1984); Nuclear Weapons Datebook Vol. I; USSR *Whence The Threat To Peace?* (1984). All totals are approximations.

[a] Limited to weapons capable of delivering nuclear warheads on targets in the Soviet Union from the U.S. and Western Europe, from land or sea, and in the U.S. from the Soviet Union or from submarines.

[b] Included all ICBMs, SLBMs, long-range bombers and intermediate-range region-based SLCMs, IRBMs and other NATO aircraft capable of delivering nuclear warheads on targets in the Soviet Union.

[c] By 1985 the Soviet Union was believed to have deployed about 410 SS–20s, each launcher equipped to fire five reloads, a potential of over 2500 missiles, carrying at least 7,600 warheads; although designed originally as IRBMs (see Table 17-1) ⅓ of these are expected to be deployed against the continental U.S., their intermediate range altered to reach targets more than 3000 miles from the northern Soviet Union; the remaining ⅔ are expected to be deployed against Western Europe and the PRC. Barring another arms agreement NATO is by then expected to have deployed the 572 IRBMs, targeted on points in the Western Soviet Union including Moscow.

warheads."[26] Or counts and estimates are based on information gleaned from spies or defectors and from analysis of published but possibly fabricated products of enemy "disinformation."[27]

Accurate or not, the numbers game acquires a reality of its own. Governments rely on numerical positions in calculating the concessions they may be prepared to make in arms control negotiations or in estimating their own needs, if they are to keep up with the other side.

Then there is the conflict over what to include and what to exclude in each national column. Are nuclear weapons built by U.S. allies for purely defensive purposes, their use under their own independent command, to be integrated with the U.S. arsenal and then balanced against all corresponding Soviet weapons? Or are Soviet ballistic missiles on nuclear subs deployed off the East and West coasts of the United States the full equivalent of U.S., British, and French nuclear weapons stationed in Western Europe, on firm ground, in hardened positions?

Are presumably more accurate missiles launched from land-based silos the full equivalent of less accurate missiles launched from nuclear submarines at sea? The Soviet Union in the early 1980s was presumed to have the capacity to reach and destroy 80 pecent of all of U.S. land-based missiles.* When the U.S. threatened to install the MX, said to have the identical capacity, the Soviets objected on the grounds that since 85 percent of all of their missiles were land-based, as against only 25 percent of the U.S. missile total, the added U.S. capacity would seriously destabilize what was at the time considered a condition of "balanced deterrence." In other words, Moscow argued that by destroying nearly all of U.S. land-based missiles, they would eliminate only 25 percent of United States retaliatory arsenal, whereas by eliminating all of the Soviet Union's land-based missiles the U.S. would virtually deprive the Soviet Union of any retaliatory capacity, opening the way for a U.S. first strike.†

Nonnuclear balance. Although they do not concede this in public, military leaders of both superpowers now appear to be convinced that a nuclear war—as distinct from a tactical nuclear exchange—cannot be "won." More than that, aside from its undoubted deterrent value nuclear force is rapidly becoming irrelevant to the pursuit of power. Recognizing this, both the Soviet Union and the United States are now also in a subnuclear competition to acquire the

---

* One problem with straight numerical count is highlighted by the Soviet ICBM (cold-launch) reload capacity, which enables them to reload and refire certain ICBMs. However, the process may take several days and a nuclear war is believed not to last that long; see U.S. Department of Defense, Second Edition, 1983, p. 21, hereafter cited as *DOD 1983* or Third Ed. *DOD 1984*. According to the DOD, certain "currently deployed liquid-propellent ICBMs" of the Soviet Union "are contained in a launch cannister within the silo." This too is believed to give the Soviet a reload capacity in the event the nuclear war is protracted *(ibid.)*.

† This assessment was based in part on a presumed Soviet preponderance in the throw-weight of about 10.3 million pounds to 2.3 million per missile, a 4:1 edge. That advantage was believed to "give the Soviets the ability to increase significantly their ICBM capability by deploying more warheads, decoys, or penetration aids on each missile, increasing the yield of the warheads, increasing the missile's range, or improving the missile's guidance system and accuracy." Committee on the Present Danger (1984), p. 15. On the other hand, miniaturization and other improvements in U.S. missilery, tended to compensate for the throw-weight gap.

most effective, most lethal, and most sophisticated nonnuclear means to prevail in a direct conflict substantially intact instead of being destroyed in the course of its resolution.* What is the balance in that respect? The problem breaks down into regional components, the European continent being strategically most critical.

Since Western nuclear strategy and tactics are based in part on the assumption that Soviet bloc general purpose forces are far superior in numbers to corresponding forces available to the West, it is appropriate to consider that argument briefly.† To U.S. planners, who do not entirely trust allies, the margin of Soviet forces, armored vehicles, and tanks, over those of the United States has always been alarming.‡ But the U.S. can count on its allies far more reliably than the Soviet Union can count on the rest of the Warsaw Pact. Regarding tanks, the U.S. and allies enjoy a substantial lead in combat electronics, their tanks for example, at least in theory, equalling several tanks on the opposing side. The same applies to combat aircraft and to all naval forces. In the latter case it would not be unreasonable to multiply the number of naval craft available to the West by a factor of 2 or 3, based on proven fighting ability and experience of the British and U.S. navies alone.

Overall military manpower balance *including reserves* calls for similar adjustment. In 1982, the respective grand totals for the U.S. and the USSR were said to be 2,901 and 9,250 million each.[28] But nearly one million of Soviet regular armed forces, totalling 5.8 million in 1983, are construction and railroad personnel. Additional rather substantial numbers are also not available for frontline combat, being assigned to internal security. In general, it has been estimated, four persons are needed in the Soviet armed forces to do the job performed by one in the U.S. military. If this 4:1 efficiency favoring the U.S. is applied to the above cited grand totals, the balance might arguably be closer to 2,900 million against 2,300 million in favor of the United States.

Measuring Quality

Leaving experience and efficiency ratio aside, Soviet armed forces appear to be weak in combat readiness, many of their division being far from combat strength. Whether the millions of graduates of the Soviet military conscription

* In a "1978 Military Strategy and Force Posture Review," U.S. military authorities estimated that in a nuclear war the United States would suffer 140 million fatalities and the Soviet Union 113 million. Almost three-quarters of their economies would be destroyed. In such a conflict, the report concluded, "neither side could conceivably be described as a winner." Richard Burt, *The New York Times* (January 6, 1978). Burt subsequently became Assistant Secretary of State for European Affairs. On the respective naval strategies, see Barnet (1977), pp. 122-124.

† General Purpose Forces: infantry, armored forces, airforce, and naval support forces. In the European theater alone, the advantage in divisions, in 1982, was approximately 2:1 in Warsaw Pact favor. DOD (1983), p. 63; see also, Committee on the Present Danger (hereafter cited as CPD) (1978), Chapter III.

‡ Main battle tanks (1981) 4:1; infantry fighting vehicles (armored carriers and so forth) (1981) 3:1. DOD 1983, p. 63, and NATO (1984).

system can be made combat ready and skeletal divisions brought up to full strength and deployed speedily is questionable.[29] Potentially affecting both conventional and strategic personnel are reportedly "abominable disciplinary and drunkenness problems" besetting Soviet armed forces. Ground forces are said to be critically short of non-commissioned officers, placing too heavy a burden on officers.[30] But, as former CIA Director William Colby points out, the weaknesses alleged to afflict Soviet forces "were there during the bloody campaigns against Hitler, whose brilliant officers, splendid non-commissioned officers and perfect discipline could not in the end withstand the raw power of the Soviet onslaught."[31]

The United States is said to place too heavy an emphasis on high technology (for example precision-guided munitions or PGMs), inviting critical breakdowns in combat against comparatively simpler Warsaw Pact arms and equipment, which, because less sophisticated, can presumably be repaired more readily under combat conditions.* If on the other hand the U.S. advantage in high technology is as pronounced and assured as generally assumed, an apparent decision by the U.S. to shift the weight of both nuclear and conventional competition with the Soviet Union from quantity to quality could prove decisive. According to one source, it is "the apparent [U.S.] intention . . . to develop a more sophisticated, more diverse U.S. strategic arsenal rather than a larger one and thereby . . . force major adjustments in the large Soviet deployments. The implied purpose is to force the Soviets to waste the heavy investment they so recently completed by making it technically obsolete." Another aspect of that plan is to offer the Soviets a choice between unrestricted *qualitative* competition in strategic weapons and negotiated arms control on the basis of approximate equivalence or parity giving neither side a decisive advantage or disadvantage.†

Where Strategic and Conventional Weapon Systems Merge

The European Theater of War. Whatever the actual state of balance, the new configuration of forces brought the European region into sharper military focus. Regarding forward Warsaw Pact defenses against yet another land invasion from the West neither militarily nor politically secure, Soviet leaders decided on backing Pact conventional forces opposite NATO with Theater Nuclear

---

* During World War Two, German officers at first scoffed at the Soviet practice of providing for breakdowns of rear axle assemblies by strapping spare differentials to the rear of their tanks. The practice however eventually contributed materially to the defeat of Germany's reputedly superior vehicles, by enabling Soviet vehicles to outlast German ones in the field of battle; see Kaldor (1981), pp. 183ff.

† Steinbrunner (1983), p. 8. U.S. generals asked by congressional committees "Would you rather have the U.S. or the Soviet military forces?" usually express a clear preference for the U.S. forces. However, as Fallows (1981) notes on p. 43, a similar question asked of U.S. pilots, "Would you rather fly a specific F-15 or a specific MiG?" might better be reformulated to reflect the numerical preponderance in fighter planes favoring the Soviet side: would you rather be the pilot of an F-15 or one of six MiG pilots attacking the former?

Table 17-3. The Nuclear Strategic Eurobalance[a]

I
Western Count 1983–84

| | NATO | | Warsaw Pact | |
	Weapons	Warheads	Warheads	Weapons
Landbased				
IRBMs				
U.S.[b]	40 +	40 +	1,400[c]	615[c]
France	18	18		
Bombers				
U.S.	150	150	635	635[d]
U.K.	56	56		
France	33	33		
Other NATO Aircraft[e]			Other Warsaw Pact Aircraft[e]	
	700[f]	700[f]	3,000	3,000
Seabased				
U.S.	44[g]	44		
U.K.	64	192[h]	–	–
France	80	80		
Totals	1,185	1,313	5,035	4,250
Soviet				
Count	1,978[i]	4,656[i]	2,215[i]	1,790[i]

II
Projected 1986 Balance

| | NATO | | Warsaw Pact | |
	Weapons	Warheads	Warheads	Weapons
Western				
Count	1,757	1,885	7,535	5,090
Soviet				
Count	2,550	5,228	-------	-------

SOURCE: NATO (1984); IISS (1983/84); SIPRI (1982); *National Security Record*, No. 71 (August 1984), pp. 3–4; USSR, *Whence The Threat To Peace?* (1984).
[a] Tactical nuclear weapons excluded.
[b] Pershing II and GLCMs excluded.
[c] Based on IISS estimates.
[d] Soviet Backfire bomber's range disputed.
[e] Nuclear-capable aircraft.
[f] Heavy load strike aircraft included.
[g] Poseidon SLBMs launched from European waters.
[h] Scheduled with 6 MRVs or 384 warheads.
[i] Included 572 Pershing II and GLCMs and ⅓ of Soviet SS–20s with 5 reloads per launcher. As noted, the other ⅔ are presumed to be targetted against the PRC and, after conversion from IRBM to ICBM, against the U.S.

Forces (TNF) as well as with the IRBM, just in case; U.S. strategists termed these Long-Range Theater Nuclear Forces or LR-TNFs. When French and British IRBMs made their appearance, threatening, as Moscow may have seen it, some western Soviet cities, ageing Soviet IRBMs (SS-4 and SS-5) were gradually replaced with a more formidable modern version, the reputedly more accurate SS-20, range 5000 km and armed with 3 MIRVs, subsequently further improved with reload capacity. When deployment of these weapons increased out of all proportion with respect to NATO's IRBM stock, West European capitals, but most of all Bonn, became alarmed.[32]

It now appeared possible that Moscow, convinced that it was dealing from strength, would attempt to subject Western Europe to nuclear blackmail over one issue or another. Or it would launch a preemptive conventional attack against presumably weaker NATO forces, resorting first to tactical nuclear weapons, then if resistance proved too strong to IRBMs. In either case, West European leaders began to wonder: would a U.S. president be prepared to retaliate with U.S. nuclear weapons and thereby risk Soviet nuclear attacks on American cities? Several answers suggested themselves. Those who favored de-escalation of the arms race argued that U.S. retaliatory capacity already was sufficient to deter any kind of Soviet bloc attack. Therefore, no additional measures needed to be taken. Others, foremost some West German leaders, fearing a U.S. retreat resulting in "decoupling" of Western Europe from the United States, long presumed to be a high priority Soviet objective, demanded some kind of nuclear insurance. The result was the Euromissile crisis of the early 1980s. Viewed from the West, the appropriate response to the Soviet threat and prevention of a U.S. nuclear retreat called for three mandatory steps: 1) NATO had to be equipped with land-based missiles capable of reaching an equivalent number of Soviet cities "to insure that the Soviet Union would not be a nuclear sanctuary in a European war"; 2) "these missiles had to be unambiguously owned and operated by the United States to make sure that the United States could not escape the consequences of their use"; 3) these weapons would have to be deployed in such a way as to force U.S. commanders "to use them early in a conflict or lose them."*

* Canby and Dorfer, p. 6. The situation possibly confronting a U.S. president is sketched most succinctly by Campbell, *op. cit.*, pp. 34–35:

> *Published Soviet doctrine envisages a war in Europe's Central Sector brought about by NATO adventurism. A massive land and air offense rolls back this aggression and penetrates deep into enemy territory destroying the opposing forces in the process. If the enemy should resort at the eleventh hour to nuclear tactical defense, either localized or theatre-wide, then any restraints on the use of theatre nuclear weapons are removed, becoming the main and legitimate means of destroying the enemy in battle, while hesitant half-measures would throw away the advantages of initiative. This implies pre-emptive attacks on counterforce targets, not just a single salvo but a sustained barrage until all targetable objectives are destroyed. The Soviets would employ their long arm, the SS-20s based in western Russian, which could blanket NATO's rear springboard for long-range theatre forces, the United Kingdom, which is dense with counterforce targets. In this gameplan, deterrence has signally failed for Britain and West Germany but the United States is still intact. Would the U.S. use their core strategic arsenal to save what's left of Europe?*

Even an exchange either side might regard as "tactical" would destroy much of central Europe, which of course was the major reason the Neutron Bomb was inserted into the equation.

In 1979 Washington responded by offering to deploy in several NATO countries, including West Germany, a sufficient number of modern, more accurate American IRBMs to counter the total Soviet IRBM force potentially available for deployment against NATO. Table 17-3 illustrates the conflicting versions of reality. The central issue over what became known as the European TNF tangle—actually a misnomer as globally deployable U.S. SLBMs and bombers were also involved—shaped up as follows: The Soviet Union insisted that its LR-IRBM total available for Europe was to equal the combined total of U.S., British, and French SLBMs and IRBMs and nuclear bombers. The French and British refused to have their nuclear forces included in any U.S.-Soviet counts, arguing that theirs were purely defensive and wholly insufficient in any case to pose as serious a threat to the Soviet Union as did the latter's IRBMs to Western Europe. The United States, arguing that Soviet LR-IRBMs, SS-20s mostly, one-third of which Moscow contended were deployed against the PRC, could all be redirected on short notice, as they were on mobile launchers. The U.S. therefore claimed the right to match whatever LR-IRBMs Moscow had at its disposal, not counting British and French nuclear arsenals. Moscow retorted that since these "forward based" American missiles threatened Soviet cities and strategic command positions within six minutes flying time, thus posing a potentially fatal threat of "surprise suppression" of Soviet retaliatory capability, this was a first strike and not a defensive move. If NATO persisted in this plan, NATO cities would be subjected to "an equivalent threat" from "analogous" positions, West European capitals from East Germany and Czechoslovakia and American cities from submarines, armed with SLBMs, and stationed off America's West and East coasts. Since this entire issue eventually and predictably became linked to arms control negotiations, we shall postpone further analysis until that discussion.* (See Fig. 17-2.)

Another issue arising over the presumed Soviet bloc conventional threat in Europe centered on the so-called Neutron Bomb. Because that weapon, through enhanced radiation but with reduced destructive yield, is said to kill tank crews while leaving buildings in nearby cities intact, its advocates viewed it as relatively low on the escalation ladder, thus not necessarily provoking a full-fledged nuclear exchange. On the other hand, it did seem to offer an effective defense against the thousands of blast-proof tanks which were expected to form the spearhead of the anticipated Soviet bloc assault.

Whither the Arms Competition

Unless ongoing negotiations yield concrete results, all signs indicate that the race will expand in lethality and destructiveness in scope and in technological

---

To further reduce the risk, NATO, especially U.S. planners, in the early 1980s developed the "deep-strike" or "deep interdiction" strategy. Employing the latest in "emerging technologies" (ETs), NATO would by aerial means seek to interdict and decimate Warsaw Pact "follow-on" forces, thus depriving enemy frontline forces of reinforcements. Soviet planners, of course, at once developed appropriate responses.

* Moscow also threatened to program its nuclear retaliatory weapons to be launched "on warning," not only *after* an attack was *confirmed*.

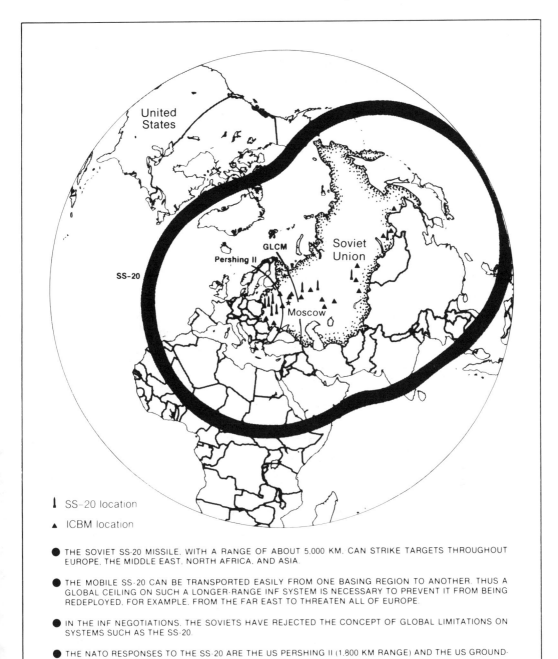

United
States

GLCM

Pershing II

Soviet
Union

SS-20

Moscow

❙ SS–20 location

▲ ICBM location

● THE SOVIET SS-20 MISSILE, WITH A RANGE OF ABOUT 5,000 KM, CAN STRIKE TARGETS THROUGHOUT EUROPE, THE MIDDLE EAST, NORTH AFRICA, AND ASIA.

● THE MOBILE SS-20 CAN BE TRANSPORTED EASILY FROM ONE BASING REGION TO ANOTHER. THUS A GLOBAL CEILING ON SUCH A LONGER-RANGE INF SYSTEM IS NECESSARY TO PREVENT IT FROM BEING REDEPLOYED, FOR EXAMPLE, FROM THE FAR EAST TO THREATEN ALL OF EUROPE.

● IN THE INF NEGOTIATIONS, THE SOVIETS HAVE REJECTED THE CONCEPT OF GLOBAL LIMITATIONS ON SYSTEMS SUCH AS THE SS-20.

● THE NATO RESPONSES TO THE SS-20 ARE THE US PERSHING II (1,800 KM RANGE) AND THE US GROUND-LAUNCHED CRUISE MISSILE (2,500) KM RANGE).

Fig. 17-2. Target Coverage of Major U.S. and Soviet IRBMs. (NATO, *NATO And The Warsaw Pact. Force Comparisons,* 1984, Fig. 15, p. 37.)

sophistication. To be sure much of today's futuristic literature is highly speculative. Still with the state of today's military arts it requires little imagination to see even the most far-fetched "star wars" creation emerging from weapon systems already deployed. The two frontiers already crossed in that regard are outer space and the world's oceans.

Outer Space*

Some planners believe that control of outer space promises the "winner" ultimate control over all military forces on land, at sea, and in the air. Current space technology already enables both superpowers to track all of the opponent's major surface naval vessels and to a limited extent most if not all nuclear-powered submarines entering or exiting from their ports. Predictions are that by the early 1990s few strategically significant military objects and no major military moves can be hidden from prying satellites. No major warship will be secure anywhere on the surface of the oceans; no major land- or airforce will move undetected and unopposed anywhere on earth. The tank will join the chariot as a historic relic and the plane will retain military value only as a vehicle to launch missiles at targets over the horizon. Only the more silent of the newer nuclear-powered missile-carrying subs may escape detection, hiding under polar ice, in a Scandinavian fjord, or in the opaque depth of oceans.[33]

Once outer space became accessible to nuclear weaponry, only costs, existing technology, and a sense of caution, perhaps even foreboding, prevented immediate full-scale extension of that aspect of the race to that dimension.[34] However, no matter how concerned political leaders in both Moscow and Washington may be that this step may spiral the competition out of control, it is difficult for them to resist military advice that the opponent has already tested a certain space weapon, is about to test one, or has already deployed one ready for instant action.

The surveillance potential over all land and all the oceans, coupled with the crucial if not decisive role space warfare can play during the first fifteen minutes of a nuclear conflict between the superpowers, has propelled armed forces' requests for such appropriations in both the Soviet Union and the United States to the top of the priority list.[35] Both powers have established space commands and both subordinate civilian and peaceful uses of outer space to military purposes.[36] Both powers are determined to anticipate and frustrate at once any breakthrough by the other side, the impenetrable space-based defense for instance or the unanswerable offensive capability.

In 1983 the United States Department of Defense estimated that the Soviet Union "on any given day" had between 70 and 110 satellites in orbit, 85 percent of which were said to be exclusively military or civilian with collateral military application. The payload the Soviets were said to lift into space and place in

---

* Outer Space is defined as being above and beyond the territorial jurisdiction of states. It is generally said to begin between 30 and 90 miles from ground level and includes all "celestial bodies."

orbit annually was said to be in the range of 600,000 pounds, carried on approximately 75 spacecraft per year, about four to five times the launch rate of the United States.*

Both powers increasingly made their military hardware and strategies dependent on satellite capability, each employing its orbital equipment for a variety of tasks: metereological, C³I (command, control, communication and intelligence), navigational, reconnaissance, surveillance, targeting, damage assessment, and antisatellite action (ASAT). Satellites were tracking all opposing surface ships, ready to provide guidance for bombers, missiles, or submarines.† Some U.S. satellites were designed to provide early warning of Soviet launches, others to provide nuclear-powered submarines with navigational fixes to improve accuracy of SLBMs. The Soviet Union was said to have repeatedly tested a fractional orbital bombardment system (FOBS). Taking the long way around the globe, such a system could reach targets in the United States by approaching from the South Pole, thus avoiding the North American radar "picket line," the Ballistic Missile Early Warning System (BMEWS) guarding the northern approaches to the United States. According to some experts FOBS "could rain nuclear warheads on the United States" virtually without warning, but others tend to discount this. Other spacecraft deployed were the manned Soviet Solyut space stations, all useable as weapons platforms, the U.S. space shuttle capable of lifting satellites and antisatellite weapons (ASAT) into space, and so-called "space-mines," silent satellite destroyers parked in orbit near opposing craft to be detonated by conventional explosive charges in the event hostilities break out.‡

---

* *DOD (1983),* pp. 65–66. The high rate of Soviet launchings was believed to reflect a correspondingly high satellite mortality rate.

† Soviet satellites (RORSAT) were believed to have provided Argentina with intelligence on British fleet movements during the Falkland war. On ocean reconnaissance, see Berman and Baker, *op. cit.,* pp. 162–165.

‡ Berman and Baker, *op. cit.;* DOD (1984), Chapter IV; DOD (1984), pp. 44–47. Satellites have been described as the "strategic nervous systems" of the superpowers. These craft circle the earth at varying orbits. Some are "geosynchronous" or "geostationary," that is they travel at precisely the same speed as the earth rotates, stationed at about 22,500 miles. Others are "semisynchronous," stationed at about 12,000 miles. Some orbit as low as 1,000 miles or, moving in elliptical orbit, rise higher and dip lower than these maximal distances. A Soviet antisatellite weapon (ASAT) tested and deployed or deployable by 1983 could only reach low orbit targets and had to go into full orbit itself to perform its mission. United States ASATs tested in 1983 ascended directly, carried by an F-15 fighter plane, then were boosted into space by a two-stage rocket, capable of going straight to its target with speeds sufficient to catch a low orbit object in space at that time. Nuclear explosions in outer space have been prohibited by two treaties, to be discussed in the following chapter. But in any case, it is doubtful that either side would resort to nuclear explosion to destroy or interfere with opposing space craft as such action would most likely affect their own craft and communication links as well. Assessment of the military significance of ASATs varies widely, one criticism centering on the controllability and accuracy of the electro-magnetic pulses generated by a nuclear explosion, which among other effects would indiscriminately destroy unprotected electronic circuits far from the point of its original impact.

A potential breakthrough in satellite control of outer space was sketched by the founder of the NASA Goddard Institute for Space Studies, Robert Jastrow. His scenario seemed not at all remote when in September of 1983 Soviet military authorities ordered a commercial airliner with 269 persons aboard to be shot down because it had strayed into Soviet airspace. According to Jastrow the Soviet Union, armed with killer satellites, could abruptly order all U.S. satellites to stay out of space above its territory. If the U.S. refused to comply, Moscow would order U.S. satellites orbiting over Soviet territory to be destroyed. In that event, all U.S. reconnaissance satellites needed to observe Soviet missile launches and verify whatever arms control or limitation agreements were still in force would suddenly become unavailable. With that the nuclear balance could be tipped decisively in Moscow's favor. The prohibition could next be extended to terrestrial zones which Moscow would declare to be within its "sphere of interest," probably the Middle or Far East. Soviet aggressive designs on either of these regions would then be effectively concealed from U.S. observation.[37]

Under the circumstances, interference by either side with the opponent's satellite capabilities would in effect be an act of war. The denial of access to space over military sensitive points would be serious enough. Equally destabilizing would be threats to interfere or actual interference with satellite missions essential for retaliatory nuclear capability of either power.* For example the Navstar system, a global satellite positioning system to be completed by the United States in the late 1980s, is expected to enable U.S. submarines to fix their position within one-hundredth of a mile or less, providing the sea leg of the U.S. triad with the long-sought ballistic accuracy needed in the event the other legs are decimated or incapacitated in a first strike.†

Closer to star war weaponry were several schemes advanced by the U.S. in the early 1980s, one the "high frontier", the other the Reagan administration's Strategic Defense Initiative (SDI) research program injected into the arms debate by the U.S. during the 1985 round of arms talks with the Soviet Union. Utilizing computer-directed satellite and ground surveillance and tracking systems, rocket interceptors and sensors, and such advanced technology as "directed energy" lasers and particle beam weapons to be projected from manned or unmanned space platforms or battle stations, or from the ground, the objective was to attack opposing satellites, defend friendly space craft, or provide the ultimate "impermeable" or near-perfect defense against long-range enemy bal-

---

* Current technology may not enable either power to determine with certainty whether malfunction of an ASAT system was due to technical flaws, caused by collision with space debris, an accidental collision with another satellite, or hostile action.

† The U.S. planned to deploy another system, the Milstar, equipped to detect anti-satellite weapons and able to escape attacks upon themselves.

listic missiles.* A "layered defense" system was to shoot such missiles down or otherwise render them harmless during the brief postlaunch boost phase, subsequently, with the aid of sensors locate warheads in mid-trajectory and cause their destruction with the aid of interceptor missiles, or destroy them with the aid of short-range missiles during the terminal phase as they descend to their targets.

In its research phase, SDI had several strategic objectives: It was to provide a hedge against a Soviet "breakout" from the ABM treaty—the Soviets were known to conduct research along similar lines and were believed to have already installed a radar facility in violation of that treaty—and counter still modest but potentially dangerous Soviet experiments with space weaponry. Second, it was to discourage the Soviet Union from making further investments in heavy ICBMs by threatening to render them virtually useless and, third, thereby set the stage for a possible shift from nuclear deterrence based on offense to one based on defense, i.e. from MAD to Mutual Assured Security (MAS). To assuage Soviet apprehensions, the U.S. offered to share research results with Moscow. Beyond the research phase, a deployed space defense system was expected to reduce U.S. vulnerability to a disabling nuclear first strike through a high-technology "end run" on Soviet advantage in heavy ICBMs and in any case deny Soviet leadership confidence in the outcome of a surprise nuclear attack on the United States. Eventually, it was hoped that the then presumably useless nuclear arsenals would follow the horse cavalry into technological oblivion.

Critics contended that the concept was badly flawed on several counts: Likely to consume staggering financial outlays it was probably unworkable, at best no more than 80 or 90 percent effective, leaving in any case enough room for devastating nuclear destruction—between 900 and 1000 Soviet warheads could then still reach their targets. The scheme also was believed to be highly destabilizing thereby inviting yet another upward turn in the nuclear arms spiral. Convinced that the U.S. might actually deploy such a system without sharing its technology with the Soviet Union, as a prelude to a first strike on Soviet targets from behind an effective defensive shield, the Soviet Union would most likely strive to develop an appropriate counter, strengthen its offensive nuclear capabilities or both. It probably could at once expect to be able to defeat the system at considerably less cost than would face the United States

---

* Lasers use a concentrated beam of radial energy to weaken the surface of a target, disable key components, or ignite fuel and explosives. Traveling at the speed of light they dissipate over relatively short distances in the lower atmosphere. See Deudney, *op. cit.*, p. 100. Also under development are "third generation" nuclear weapons, e.g. lasers powered by nuclear reaction. Particle beam weapons (PW) fire atomic or subatomic projectiles at close to the speed of light. Unlike the laser weapons, PWs are difficult to defend against. The third weapon category to be employed in this form of warfare are computer-guided or "smart" projectiles launched from the ground.

by underflying, overwhelming, or outfoxing it.* Or, concluding that once fully deployed the system might be virtually penetration-proof, Moscow could decide to attack its components during the extended transition phase when they still have the means to do that. Meanwhile, the prospect of America providing itself with a shield to protect its own missiles and cities would give rise to concern among U.S. allies in Western Europe and the Far East that they might then be left to fend for themselves against superior Warsaw Pact conventional forces. If not that, critics argued, reliance on space defense could divert the attention of U.S. allies from the urgent task of strengthening their critically weak conventional capabilities.

Partly dependent on space technology, partly on further advances in electronic warfare technology, was the defense planners' ultimate objective, the penetration-proof electronic or particle beam screen reaching from outer space to the ocean floor which would allow not one plane, missile, ship, or satellite to approach one's territory with hostile intent. Envisaged were systems linking "arrays of advanced electronic, accoustical, optical and other sensors with computers or enormous capacity and ultimately with precise[ly targetable] munitions such as missiles with homing devices so accurate that one shot would be as destructive as 10 would be today."[38] A proposal given some prominence in the United States envisaged a ballistic missile defense system (GBMD) consisting of 432 satellites covering the entire globe, theoretically enabling the U.S. to observe, track, and defend against any conceivable missile threat from any direction.[39]

Land-Based Electronic Warfare (EW)

Lasers aside, general electronic warfare technology also attained new heights. Aircraft-guidance, antiaircraft defenses, and related strategic and tactical measures steadily became more sophisticated and effective. During the 1973 Arab-Israeli War, Soviet-built integrated air defense systems—including radar jamming, and heat-seeking surface to air (SAM) missiles—enabled Egypt to parry the superior Israeli air force, inflicting unexpectedly heavy losses on the latter. Four years later in Lebanon, when once again SAM threatened to hinder its air operations, Israel neutralized the systems with electronic countermeasures (ECMs).†

---

* Hans Bethe *et al.*, Letter to the Editor The *Wall Street Journal* (January 2, 1985). The scheme reminded some observers of the Maginot Line, that state-of-the-art fortification system built by France in the 1930s to prevent forever another German invasion. In 1940 German armies successfully invaded France, obtaining its surrender six weeks later by circumventing the "impenetrable" line. On the other hand a limited ballistic missile defense (such as is permitted under the 1972 ABM Treaty) is feasible if restricted to defense against one or two missiles launched unintentionally. Such a defense could save a major city from being destroyed by mistake.

† The results of electronic intelligence (ELINT), obtained by radar and unmanned drones dispatched to test the enemy's electronic defenses, were integrated and programmed into electronic warfare (EW) jamming aircraft, enabling Israeli planes to blanket air defense frequencies, confounding the SAM systems deployed along the Syrian-Lebanese border or within Syria itself; see also, Campbell (1982), pp. 104ff.

During the same period the U.S. developed the concept of the "electronic battlefield" stretching under the ocean and into space. It begins with systems which can detect events many thousands of miles away and ends with radar which can track a sniper's bullet. We already referred to the hypothetically accoustically "transparent ocean" on or under which no craft can hope to hide, rendering SLBMs as vulnerable as ICBMs; we also encountered command, control, and communication (C^3) countermeasures combining EW (including electromagnetic pulses or EMP), highly and widely destructive nuclear weapons, deceptions, and conventional intelligence, all to "decapitate the enemy," that is to deprive him of effective leadership during the initial phase of nuclear attack.[40]

Chemical Warfare (CW)*

Hopefully World War One saw the last large-scale use of poison gas in combat. Like certain other weaponry, the use of chemical weapons was outlawed, but this by itself would not have prevented renewed recourse to gas in World War Two.† What deterred Hitler from making use of Germany's large stock of a

---

* In the early 1980s Biological and Biochemical Warfare (BW) was only a latent threat. Not yet solved was the problem, as one authority put it, of getting your "bug . . . from where it is to where you want it to go." Kucewicz (April 27, 1984). Likewise, the effect of the target environment on biological or biochemical agents still was sufficiently uncertain to discourage first use. However, breakthroughs in splitting and recombining genes, coupled with other advances in science and technology, raised the specter of Soviet-American, or worse, irrational and uncontrollable third party elements adding that genre of weaponry to their arsenals. One speculation was than an "aggressor armed with such . . . biological weapons could . . . vaccinate its own armed forces and population against this new disease, leaving them the only survivors of a world-wide plague." Also "economic warfare could be waged by unleashing new plant diseases attacking only certain crops, like rice or corn." William Kucewicz, "The Threat of Soviet Genetic Engineering," *The Wall Street Journal* (April 23, 1984); also *ibid.* (April 25 and 27, 1984).

The *Soviet Military Encyclopedia* notes that "achievements in biology and related sciences (biochemistry, biophysics, molecular biology, genetics, microbiology and experimental aerobiology) have led to an increase in the effectiveness of biological agents as a means of conducting warfare. Improved methods of obtaining and using them have resulted in a qualitative reexamination of the very concept of 'biological weapons'." The Soviet Institute of Molecular Biology near Novosibirsk is believed to be engaged in biochemical weapons research. The Soviet Union of course similarly suspects private and governmental U.S. installations and laboratories. To be sure aggression by such means entails risks also for the aggressor, but the potential is there and threatens to further becloud the world arms situation.

† The Italians in 1936 used poison gas against Ethiopian troops and civilians during the Italo-Ethiopian war, Soviet and Soviet allies are alleged to have used mycotoxins ("yellow rain") in Southeast Asia and in Afghanistan in 1979 and 1980, and Iraq is believed to have used poison gas against Iranian forces during the Iraqi-Iranian war in 1984; Egypt is said to have used Soviet-supplied gases in Yemen in 1967. See Isby (1981), p. 214. According to one source the British Chiefs of Staff seriously considered use of poison gas, even bacteriological warfare, to counter German rocket attacks on London in 1944. The gas warfare option was abandoned because it would have interfered with Allied movements on the continent, and bacteriological warfare was rejected because Britain would not be ready for another year. A.C. Brown (1975), pp. 726–727.

variety of poison gases between 1939 and 1945 was neither international law, existing treaties, nor fear of universal reprobation but fear of retaliation. Hitler and his advisors were aware that the Allies arrayed against him possessed superior poison gas delivery potential. Moreover chemical warfare technology was at that time far from pinpoint accuracy, creating the risk that a failed gas attack by Germany on Allied troops or cities would nevertheless result in clouds of poison gas released by Allied forces over Germany.

The central international instrument prohibiting use of poison gases and similar weapons is the 1925 Geneva Protocol.[41] The agreement does not prohibit research on or production of CW weapons. Indeed, today all major powers formally reserve the right to resort to CW if an enemy resorts to it first.

Both Washington and Moscow consider the other side capable of resorting to chemical weapons first and both therefore have equipped and trained their advance forces to defend against that threat and to respond in kind. Some Western observers believe that Soviet military doctrine, as far as the European theater is concerned and assuming nuclear weapons are not used, favors first use if rapid advance through NATO defenses cannot be achieved by conventional means.[42] Moscow, on the other hand, believes that the United States "flexible response" doctrine envisages first use of toxic gas as a rung on the escalation ladder, midway between conventional and nuclear response. This has prompted some European analysts to point out that signals by NATO, or by the United States in particular, of an intent to resort to CW as a counter to a Soviet bloc attack, could be interpreted by Moscow as "a diminishing resolve of NATO . . . to resort to nuclear weapons."[43] In any case, both sides are determined not to be caught unprepared. Both stockpile a variety of CW weapons, equip and train their troops, and work on rendering containers safer to transport and more effective in use, thereby enhancing their credibility in this respect as well.*

---

* One reason why the U.S. decided to proceed was the development of *binary* CW ammunition which answered two previous objections: unlike many of its unitary predecessors, it could safely be stored and transported and it was likely to be more effective and more accurate against combat forces. However, there also were contrary opinions. In any case, the principal product was a nerve gas, colorless, odorless, capable of attacking the central human nervous system within seconds, leading to death in minutes or hours. In any event, if delivered against armored forces, its most likely use, it would impede forward progress as forces would be compelled to change into protective mode. If used against defensively deployed forces, it would paralyze these, creating openings for the attackers. U.S. Comptroller-General of the (1983), pp. 68–71.

Unitary ammunition is stored and delivered to the target in "ready-mixed" state. For that reason, it tends to corrode or erode the walls of its containers and leak into the environment with deadly results for civilians as well as friendly military personnel. In binary ammunition, the second "precursor" is not joined to the first until it is about to be applied on a target. Arguments against binary weapons are, among others, that they are not as safe for friendly personnel as claimed and are less effective against soldiers, who can be protected, as against unprotected civilians. Also, the time required for an agent to eat through a diaphragm separating it from the second agent is about 10 seconds, posing serious problems in combat. For example, if it is used in artillery, targets must be located beyond the 10 second limit. If it is used in bombs, this too limits the range and altitude of delivering planes.

In the early 1980s, a U.S. administration had decided to intensify the competition to the point where a presumably economically and technologically weaker Soviet Union would be forced to the negotiating table. The Soviet Union, on the other hand, while agreeing to negotiate, seemed equally determined not to allow that strategy to endanger its security.

Appendix

Current Nuclear Strategic Force Levels (1983): Conflicting Interpretations

Given the extraordinarily sensitive nature of all data on questions of nuclear capability and security, it is small wonder that, in their interpretations of what published data signify, the two camps differ substantially. They of course also differ widely on questions of motivation, each attributing to the other a desire to achieve or maintain global nuclear superiority, one to make the world secure for capitalism, the other for communism. But the debate over numbers, relative quality of weapons systems, armed forces, and motivation is not wholly a matter of rhetoric. It assumes practical significance in the formulation of respective strategic goals and postures, and the conflicting interpretations serve as points of departure or premises in negotiations on limitation of strategic arms, arms control, and disarmament. They also are the substance around which propaganda campaigns are conducted. It is useful therefore to summarize briefly the most salient and strategically most consequential interpretations of the totals offered in current level calculations and of the respective positions with regard to non-nuclear conventional forces.

US	**USSR**

Strategic Interpretations (1984)

Warsaw Pact, homogeneous essentially under unified Soviet command, whereas NATO consists of truly sovereign and independent states. France, although cooperating with NATO, is technically not a part of its military structure or command system.	Soviet Union, frequently invaded, is compelled to defend 9.1 million square miles as against 800,000 square miles defended by NATO in Europe. USSR also faces 1 billion potentially hostile Chinese now also armed with nuclear weapons. U.S. directly threatens Soviet territory from a series of bases, close to the Soviet Union, with its nuclear submarines and from its aircraft carriers—of which they have 16 as against 2 on the Soviet side— positioned in European waters, in the Indian Ocean, the Persian Gulf, and in the Far East.

Soviet strategy is both defensive and offensive. Soviet ideology certainly is offensive, aimed to achieve world hegemony for communism.

Soviet strategy is purely defensive; offensive only if attacked, or vital interests are threatened. U.S. strategy, on the other hand, as stated in U.S. Presidential Directive 59 of July 25, 1980, envisages, first use of nuclear weapons in a "limited nuclear war."

Warsaw Pact has armed itself with nuclear and conventional weapons and forces far in excess of what is required for defensive purposes, measured against NATO capabilities.

Contention that Warsaw Pact enjoys conventional superiority is accepted but NATO has clear superiority in antitank weapons, including almost 200,000 antitank missiles.

Also NATO does not count civilian personnel performing duties which in Warsaw Pact countries are performed by uniformed personnel.

Quantitative and Qualitative Comparisons

In terms of sheer numbers, only U.S. and Soviet strategic weapons should be counted since all of Western Europe's weapons are purely defensive.

Many of NATO's weapons have strategic capabilities since they can reach targets in the Soviet Union. Moreover, while the USSR faces all of NATO plus China, NATO faces only the Warsaw Pact.

The Soviet nuclear force enjoys an overwhelming preponderance in throw-weight, that is in deliverable nuclear megatonnage. The hard core of Soviet ICBM force is mobile, whereas that of U.S. is stationary; missiles currently deployed against China can be deployed against NATO.

Only about two-thirds of SS-20s face West, the remainder facing China. Hence, U.S. should not count all of these weapons as part of the East-West strategic balance.

Whereas much of NATO military information is relatively easily accessible to trained Warsaw Pact observers, and much is publicly available, nearly all of the Pact's military data are shrouded in secrecy, which poses problems with respect to verification, among other difficulties.

The Soviet Union maintains tight controls over its nuclear arsenal, not allowing any independent nuclear force aside from its own, within the Warsaw Pact. On the NATO side, on the other hand, U.S. nuclear power has been enhanced by two additional threats to the Soviet Union, Great Britain and France.

Not publicly articulated by Moscow but explaining the drive for numerical superiority are such things as relative inefficiency, technological lag, unreliability of non-Soviet Warsaw Pact forces, lack of reliable overseas bases and allies, and relative inexperience in high sea naval confrontations and maintenance of long-range, transoceanic supply routes in times of war.

Suggested Questions and Discussion Topics

What technical-military and what military-strategic considerations have led the superpowers, and what considerations lead them to continue, to engage in arms competition? In that connection, what is meant by "threat inflation," and how does that affect the competition?

What have been the major milestones or turning points in the competition since 1945?

What are the roots of the "credibility problem?"

Considering the current balance of strategic and conventional arms, does it matter who is first?

Aside from the question of superiority or parity, compare and contrast the strategic arsenals (force levels) and the conventional forces of the superpowers, accounting for different interpretations of respective strength and weakness.

Why does one speak of the "European (TNF) Tangle" and what are the global strategic implications of the outcome of negotiations at that front?

Chapter 18
Curbing Weapons, Preventing War

Peril Points

Approaching the Point of No Return

What if the arms spiral already is out of control? What if neither Washington nor Moscow can bring themselves in earnest to slow down the competition or halt it altogether, because both feel threatened not only by the other's arms but also by arms limitation? Time may be running out on any kind of meaningful agreement. A point of no return can easily be passed without anyone being aware that it has been reached. Proliferation of nuclear weapons in the hands of the two principal contenders can alone render any thought of control, including verification, practically unattainable for the foreseeable future; proliferation worldwide may forever foreclose all such possibilities. It already is quite conceivable that the exponentially expanding arsenals of the superpowers, deployed on land, at sea, and now in space, are now so interlocked and interdependent that limiting one component will automatically weaken all others, causing panic in both military high commands.

Concern that a particular weapon is about to become technologically obsolete has always been the bane of efforts to render international conflict less lethal. It has been the root cause of military planners' reluctance to foreclose, by binding treaty, development of new weapons or designs. Miniaturization of weapons, made possible by the microchip and related advances in computer technology, their dispersal, and ever more sophisticated methods of deception defying available verification techniques do not help; extending nuclear competition into space poses a threat to arms agreement all its own.*

Triggering the Holocaust: The Deliberate and the Unforeseen

Ground Zero sketches "Four Simple, Easty-to-Use Scenarios for Killing 500 Million People." One centers on conflict in the Middle East, one in Europe,

---

* A powerful incentive to resist arms limitation and control arises from the previously mentioned "technology creep." As Mary Kaldor (1982), p. 134, has put it: "The acquisition of one weapons system begets the acquisition of another [and] the growth of one weapons system . . . infects whole families of weapons," and each remains militarily and technologically dependent on all others.

one is an updated version of the 1962 Cuban Missile Crisis, and one unfolds as a result of a technical malfunction.[1] How likely is it that any of these or similar events will actually come to pass? Three sets of circumstances suggest themselves as possible precipitants of an all-out nuclear conflict; 1) deliberate aggressive recourse to such weapons by one of the two superpowers against the other, 2) the so-called "third party" or catalytic threat, and 3) human, mechanical, or technical failure of a key link in the nuclear warning and launching chain.[2]

The "first" or "preemptive" strike. It is conceivable that the increasing sensitivity, hence vulnerability, of ever more complex weapon systems may in a crisis tempt Moscow or Washington to use all or most of their respective nuclear arsenals while they are still intact. However, on this point there is some room for optimism. Recent analysis indicates that for some time to come neither superpower will be able to eliminate more than a fraction of the other's retaliatory capacity. Neither may therefore rationally be prepared to assume the enormous risk inherent in an unprovoked first strike. Indeed, all the world seems to pursue their everyday tasks on the assumption that deliberate recourse to nuclear weapons by any government or leader is unlikely because of the persuasive power of deterrence. But then, human rationality has been shown to be a highly fragile commodity.[3]

The "limited war" scenario. Either Moscow or Washington attempts to resolve a crisis by low-yield, very short-range, nuclear weapons; the response escalates the exchange slightly, which may trigger further escalation but will probably not because the crisis will by that time have been resolved. Few experts can be found who believe that a nuclear war can actually be limited.[4]

The shrinking warning time threat. Steady improvement in missile propulsion and guidance systems, coupled with ability to move launch points ever closer to the opponent's more sensitive industrial and military targets, places a premium on ability to detect incoming missiles, arm defensive or retaliatory weapons, and launch these before they are destroyed. Both sides have begun to speak of "launch on warning" or "launch under attack." In the first case, the response is launched instantly and automatically upon verification that an attack is, or may be, under way; in the second, missiles are launched automatically following reports of a first hit. At best, both cases in all probability require delegation of decision-power from the commander-in-chief on either side to lower, perhaps very junior, command echelons. At worst, ultimate decisions will be by computer.

Warning time will certainly be too brief for prescribed command and control procedures, too brief perhaps for any human when space craft can attack space craft within seconds. Warns one concerned observer: "The Archduke Francis [sic] Ferdinand of World War III may well be a critical U.S. or Soviet reconnaissance satellite hit by a piece of space junk during a crisis."[5] The same writer, discussing "Cybernetically Initiated Annihilation" through "destruction entrusted automatic devices" or DEADS, notes: "A space laser would have about five minutes to knock out an ICBM in its slow moving vulnerable boost phase. It would have to respond to an attack from an orbiting laser system in fractions of seconds."[6] Chances that in a future crisis between the two rivals the nuclear war which neither wants can be averted are reduced even without "star war" scenarios. For instance, assume that a Soviet nuclear missile-carrying submarine has been located off the coast of the United States, has been identified, and is under surveillance. A Soviet-American crisis erupts. Will U.S. anti-submarine (ASW) forces wait for the sub to launch its deadly cargo, giving U.S. land defenses ten minutes or less warning time, or will they attack to kill? And if they do . . . .

War by time-table. The historian A.J.P. Taylor, in his book *War By Time Table: How the First World War Began,* attributes the outbreak of that war to pressure on the respective general staffs to follow railroad timetables in their decision on mobilization and troop deployment. Once that process had started, it seemed impossible to halt. Colin S. Gray suggests that similar pressures may be generated during a future great power crisis by timetables developed by missile commands.[7]

The "third party" or "catalytic threat." Could a nuclear attack by one "third party" against another or against a superpower trigger the warning mechanism in either the Soviet Union or the U.S.? Could, let us say, a North African or Caribbean dictator, or an erratic regime in the Far East, so direct a nuclear weapon as to cause either superpower to conclude that it was under attack by the other, thus triggering a global holocaust? At the time of writing this is not likely, since both Moscow and the United States have the capacity to obtain clarification from the other regarding origin, direction, and intent with respect to incoming nuclear weapons. But this problem seems manageable only because in the middle 1980s no third party disposes of the means of delivering a nuclear weapon in such a manner as to confuse either superpower.[8]

Mechanical or Technical Failure

"More than sensors and computers, said a NORAD (North American Aerospace Defense Command) operations officers, 'people are the key.' 'The entire system relies on people and the people who are here are trained to be suspicious.'"[9] The officer was referring to the principal North American command center, which is reported to have experienced 151 false alarms in one 18 month period.* According to a U.S. House of Representatives Report, in a typical year over one thousand military personnel had to be removed either for drunkenness or drug abuse from positions entailing some responsibility for nuclear weapons.[10] Regarding a particularly disturbing set of incidents involving false alarms, two leading U.S. senators sought to assure the public by stating that "[in] a real sense, the total system worked properly, in that, even though the mechanical electronic part produced erroneous information, *the human part correctly eval-*

---

* Pisar (1979), pp. 254–255, speculates whether after years of taut waiting, broken only by false alarms or practice alerts, missile crews and commanders may not regard an actual nuclear launch as a welcome release.

uated it, and prevented an irrevocable action."[11] What if the "human part" had evaluated the information incorrectly?

There are numerous additional inanimate links in the nuclear control and command chain whose potential to contribute to an accidental nuclear disaster increases in inverse proportion to each minute shaved off available decision time. One of these is the computer. Arthur May Cox, author of *Russian Roulette: The Superpower Game,* commenting on placement of U.S. missiles near the Soviet Union, writes: "Since no human decision-making system can be responsive in six minutes, the Russians will have to rely on computers. Their computers are not as advanced as ours, and ours make errors."* To which a U.S. under secretary of state added: "The tightening noose around our neck is the requirement for speed. The more certain one wants to be that [one's missile forces] could be launched within minutes, and under all circumstances, the more one has to practice the system and to *loosen safeguards.*"[12]

Computers are only as accurate and reliable as the information with which they are programmed. There is much room for concern regarding the accuracy and pertinence of the information on the strength of which computers in a hair-trigger warning and launch network, must record, analyze, and interpret data gathered by electronic, hence equally vulnerable, sensors thousands of miles away. In addition, high-altitude nuclear explosions could set off electromagnetic pulses, EMPs, which could cause an entire warning system to "go blind" at the most critical juncture.[13] In that case the survival of civilization might depend on that American or Soviet submarine commander, now out of touch with his command, who must then consider using his own authority to arm and fire his ballistic missiles.†

We are assured that "modern strategic systems possess many more safeguards to [prevent] accidental launch than did older systems. One protective feature are the *permissive action links* (PAL) which allow launch of weapons or arming of the warheads only under positive control."[14] Competent military advice is that in full recognition of the potentiality of these systems to malfunction, err, or break down, they are made secure by numerous redundancies, or back-up systems ("dual phenomenology"), that is, more than one sensor is relied upon before what appears to be an attack is treated as such. As for the much feared defective computer chip, which in at least one instance erroneously signalled

---

* "A War of Computers—For Nuclear Starters," *The New York Times* (May 27, 1982), Op. Ed. (1982), p. 160. In 1982 the world's largest and most modern ocean oil rig, the Ocean Ranger, located off the coast of Newfoundland, toppled and sank, killing dozens of oil workers, because of a computer malfunction caused by sea water pouring into a broken porthole where the computer was located; the flooding caused the computer to misdirect ballast distribution within the structure. Canada Broadcasting Corporation, October 24, 1982. This provides food for thought regarding the state of electronic components of nuclear warning and launch mechanisms before, during, and after a nuclear attack.

† According to Campbell, p. 160: "In certain circumstances each of the [U.S. nuclear] submarine commanders can arm and fire his weapons without coded instructions from the national command authority—even though such a launch would require the co-operation of practically the entire crew." See also Bracken (1983), pp. 229–30.

missile warnings, it is pointed out that a defective chip most likely produces gibberish. In the case at hand, all indicators were highly improbable combinations of 2's, alerting evaluators to the error.* Also, systems are being hardened against EMP. But the question remains whether all potential nuclear command centers on both sides are equally apt, especially under crisis conditions.

In any case, it is in the face of these risks, as well as to lighten the economic burden the nuclear competition has placed on both countries and their allies, and for some less honorable reasons, that both sides have been willing to negotiate.

If conducted in good faith, arms negotiations are in essence just a form of bargaining. Given a willingness to respect the opposing side's fundamental security concerns and to refrain from presenting totally unacceptable demands, there is ample room for compromise to mutual advantage. Each side can safely accept reduction in areas of its advantage for equivalent reductions in areas of advantage to the other. No progress will be made if each side stubbornly clings to its maximal position, seeking not loosely defined equivalent adjustments but precisely delineated matching concessions. Nothing will be accomplished if the object is merely to gain time in order to enhance an advantage, if for example the Soviets were to negotiate mainly to camouflage their drive to achieve nuclear superiority or the United States merely maneuvered to retain or recapture its lead.

Arms Agreements to Date

Whatever the rationale, a series of agreements have been signed covering the so-called ABC (atomic, biological, and chemical) group of weapons. These fall into two major categories, *multilateral* instruments of concern to the community of nations as a whole and *bilateral* ones negotiated exclusively between the superpowers. With regard to the former, the world has allowed itself to indulge in a bit of macabre irony. The purpose of one agreement—the 1925 Protocol, it is solemnly declared, is to prohibit the use of "barbarous" and "inhumane" weapons. Sadly enough, that prohibition has so far not been extended to barbarous and inhumane weapons of the nuclear variety. These are only to be "controlled" not banned. We noted in the preceding chapter that work continues to improve and expand chemical arsenals.[15]

Additional agreements signed between the U.S. and the U.S.S.R. designed to reduce tensions and minimize the risk of nuclear war were:

The Agreement on the Prevention of Incidents on the High Sea (1972).

Basic Principles of Relations between the two countries (1972).

For world peace, most consequential of course are agreements between the two nuclear giants, whose governments now hold in their hands the fate of civilization. For the sake of clarity this segment of the discussion is divided as follows: General Characteristics of the series of agreements, the Current

---

* The incident occurred in June 1980 and involved a 46 cent chip malfunctioning twice. Richard Halloran, *The New York Times* (May 29, 1983).

Table 18-1a. Multilateral Arms Control, Limitation, and Disarmament
Agreements and Treaties 1945–1984[a]

Agreement	Opened for Signature	Date Entered into Force	# of Signatories (1984)	# of States who have Ratified[b]
1. Protocol for the Prohibition of the Use in War of Asphyxiating, Poisonous or Other Gases, and of Bacteriological Methods of Warfare	6/17/25	2/ 8/28	128	
2. Antarctic Treaty	12/ 1/59	6/23/61	32	(12)
3. Limited Test Ban Treaty	8/ 5/63	10/10/63	111	(126)
4. Outer Space Treaty	1/27/67	10/10/67	92	(122)
5. Treaty Prohibiting Nuclear Weapons in Latin America	2/14/67	4/22/68	29	(33)
6. Nuclear Non-Proliferation Treaty	7/ 1/68	3/ 5/70	127	(131)
7. Seabed Arms Control Treaty	2/11/71	5/18/72	81	(109)
8. Biological Weapons Convention	4/10/72	3/26/75	104	(133)
9. Environmental Modification Convention	5/18/77	10/ 5/78	54	(72)
10. Convention on the Physical Protection of Nuclear Material	3/ 3/80		40	(12)[c]

SOURCE: USACDA (1982), and U.S. Congress, *USACDA 1984 Annual Report* (1985).

[a] The Final Act of the Conference on Security and Cooperation in Europe (CSCE), signed in 1975 at Helsinki, led to certain "Confidence-Building" Measures designed to reduce tension and minimize risk of accidental nuclear war.

[b] Incl. states which ratified or acceded with reservations, all by U.S. count. The U.S. considers signatures by the Ukrainian and Bylorussian Soviet Socialist Republics as included under the signature of the Soviet Union, whereas the latter counts both separately.

[c] Data on Agreement 10 as of July 1985.

State of Nuclear Arms Control and Limitation, especially SALT I and II, Major Obstacles to Progress in this matter, Major Proposals to Break the Deadlock, and Movement Toward SALT III.

General Characteristics of Agreements

Assuming a political will to compromise, agreements on some issues have been and remain theoretically possible between the two powers, for several compelling reasons: financial resources to cover steadily rising costs of nuclear

Explanation of Treaties and Agreements listed in Table 18-1a

1. Self-explanatory.
2. Freezes the legal status of the Antarctic Continent, ensures continuation of scientific cooperation, and restricts use of the region for peaceful purpose only.
3. In response to world-wide pressure, parties to the treaty undertook to refrain from carrying out nuclear test explosions in the atmosphere, under water, or in outer space, or anywhere else on earth "if the explosion would cause radioactive debris to be present outside the borders of the state conducting the explosion." USACDA (1982), p. 40. Not a party to the Treaty, France continued testing, causing fall-out problems in the South Pacific. Debris from a U.S. explosion at Bikini atoll in the Pacific contaminated a Japanese fishing vessel, and radioactive rain containing debris from a Soviet hydrogen bomb test fell on Japan. *Ibid.*
4. Among other things, declares signatories may not place "in orbit around the earth, install on the moon or any other celestial body, or otherwise station in outer space nuclear or any other weapons of mass destruction." Also demilitarizes space and the celestial bodies. (USACDA, p. 49.)
5. Restricts for all of Latin America use of nuclear energy to peaceful purposes and prohibits all parties "from engaging in, encouraging or authorizing directly or indirectly, or in any way participating in the testing, use, manufacture, production, possession or control of any nuclear weapon." (USACDA, p. 60.) Cuba had not signed and Argentina has not ratified as of 1982.
6. Seeks to prevent the spread of nuclear weapons beyond those countries already so equipped. Not signing among others were France, India, Pakistan, Israel, South Africa, the PRC, the Republic of China (Taiwan), Brazil, all aspirants to membership in the nuclear club or, if already members, interested in developing greater power or selling nuclear technology and fissionable materials.
7. Prohibits emplacement of nuclear weapons or weapons of mass destruction on the seabed and the ocean floor beyond a 12 mile coastal zone.
8. Parties agree "not to develop, produce, stockpile, or acquire biological agents or toxins 'of types and in quantities that have no justification for prophylactic, protective, and other peaceful purposes.'" All materials in the parties' possession at the time of signing were to be destroyed within 9 months. (USACDA, p. 122)
9. Parties agree "not to engage in military or any other hostile use of environmental modification techniques having wide-spread, long-lasting or severe effects as the means of destruction, damage, or injury to any other State party." (USACDA, p. 191)
10. Provides for certain levels of physical protection during international shipment of nuclear materials and establishes "a general framework for cooperation among states in the recovery and return of stolen nuclear materials." (USACDA, p. 278)

armament are not unlimited, world public opinion demands an end to the madness, and experts on both sides seem in agreement that existing "national means" of verification are adequate to detect treaty violations *within tolerable limits.** In the order in which they were negotiated, the agreements were designed

---

* Kissinger quoted by Safire (1975), p. 163: "A certain amount of cheating should be expected. The question was not whether but how much;" see also Deudney (1983-84), p. 95: "The current arms control regime is based on surveillance satellites."

Table 18-1b. Bilateral Agreements and Treaties Between the U.S. and the Soviet Union (1984) on Arms Control, Reduction, and Limitation

Agreement	Date Signed	Date Entered Into Force	Date Ratified[a]
"Hot Line" Agreement	6/20/63	6/20/63	
"Hot Line" Improvement Agreement	9/30/71	9/30/71	
Agreement to Prevent Accidental Nuclear War	9/30/71	9/30/71	
SALT I: ABM Treaty	5/26/72	10/ 3/72	10/3/72
SALT I: Interim Agreement to Limit Offensive Strategic Arms	5/26/72	10/ 3/72	10/3/72[b]
Agreement on the Prevention of Nuclear War	6/22/73	6/22/73	
Protocol to the ABM Treaty	7/ 3/74	5/24/76	7/6/76
Threshold Test Ban Treaty (and Protocol)	7/ 3/74		
Treaty on Underground Nuclear Explosions for Peaceful Purposes (and Protocol)	5/28/76		
SALT II Treaty on Limitation of Strategic Offensive Arms	6/18/79		
Agreement for Improving 1963 and 1971 Direct Communication Link (Hot Line)	7/17/84	7/17/84	

Source: USACDA (1982), and U.S. Congress, *USACDA 1984 Annual Report* (1985).
[a] Under the U.S. Constitution, Executive Agreements do not require Congressional consent.
[b] Congress "accepted" the Agreement; it expired by its terms 10/3/77.

to prevent misunderstandings leading to accidental nuclear war, establish a direct communication link between Moscow and Washington, the "hotline," limit strategic arms (the ABM Treaty and the Interim Agreement on Offensive Nuclear Arms, part of SALT I), spur mutual and cooperative efforts to prevent nuclear war entirely, limit underground nuclear testing to weapons of certain yield, limit the number of such tests, and strive to terminate all nuclear testing as soon as possible. The latter (Threshold Test Ban) treaty was to augment the previously signed multilateral Test Ban Treaty of 1963—confined to atmosphere, outer space, and underwater—and was accompanied by the Treaty on Underground Nuclear Explosions for Peaceful Purposes.*

---

* The [Bernard] Baruch Plan attempted as early as 1946 to forestall a nuclear arms race. So did the Eisenhower "open skies" proposal of the early 1950s. The Soviet Union rejected the Baruch Plan because to Moscow it implied control over its internal affairs which Stalin was not prepared to tolerate under any circumstances and his successors have rejected ever since. The "open skies" proposal was rejected on the grounds that it opened the skies to espionage. Bundy (1983), p. 3. A plan proposed by then Polish Foreign Minister Rapacki would have established a nuclear-free zone in Europe.

As the name implies, SALT II advanced the overall strategic arms limitation program to a second stage, preparatory, it was universally hoped, to placement of a firm cap on the panoply of doomsday weaponry.

Negotiations on various types and categories of weapons were of necessity conducted separately. Negotiations on intercontinental (strategic) arms seemed appropriate only between the two superpowers—a position modified in later years. Intermediate nuclear forces and Mutual and Balanced Force Reductions talks (MBFR) involved both NATO and Warsaw Pact, while chemical weapon and comprehensive test bans to be effective required at the very least concurrence of all members of the nuclear club. At the same time (and this created one of the major obstacles during the SALT talks) all arms negotiations but foremost those on limitation and reduction are intimately intertwined with East–West tensions generally and all the sensitivities these tend to conjure up.

SALT I

Background. Strategic weapons had been included in United Nations-sponsored General and Comprehensive Disarmament discussions. By 1964 it became apparent to Washington that progress seemed most unlikely on so broad a front.[16] Moreover, the Soviet Union was making giant strides in challenging the U.S. for the strategic nuclear lead, and a point had passed when it was no longer possible nor economically desirable to halt or reverse production of nuclear *materials* throughout the world. Prompted by these and similar considerations, Washington suggested in 1964 that the two principals as an attainable first objective "explore a verified freeze of the number and characteristics of their strategic nuclear offensive and defensive vehicles."[17] Only if progress could be made in these respects could a path be cleared for more comprehensive disarmament discussions involving the community of nations as a whole. By one count, the relative standing of the two competitors in 1972 at the outset of SALT I was as follows:

	U.S.	*U.S.S.R.*
ICBMs	1,054	1,607
SLBMs	656	740

(Bombers were not included in these talks)

The success or failure of SALT hinged on certain issues, all founded on a well-known but not always acknowledged asymmetry in the respective strategic forces. For example, relying on its superior technology the U.S. had begun to MIRV its ICBMs, which gave it the lead—only temporarily—in number of warheads. The U.S. also led in numbers of long-range bombers, surely offensive nuclear strategic vehicles. The Soviets had a limited ABM system to protect Moscow, while the U.S. was developing two such systems at two land-based ICBM sites to safeguard a portion of its retaliatory force.[18]

Most vexing, however, and confounding negotiations in years to come was Soviet insistence on defining as "strategic," hence as an appropriate subject for negotiations between the two superpowers, *any* U.S. or Soviet weapon system capable of reaching the other's territory. As viewed by the U.S., this "would have included U.S. 'forward-based systems', chiefly short-range or medium-range bombers on aircarft carriers or based on land in Europe, but it would have excluded, for example, Soviet missiles aimed at Western Europe. The United States held that SALT was to be confined to intercontinental systems. Its forward-based systems (FBS) served only to counter Soviet medium-range missiles and aircraft aimed at U.S. allies. To accept the Soviet approach would have prejudiced alliance commitments."* The Soviets countered that this was precisely one reason why the arms race had heated up: the NATO alliance system pointed at the heart of the Soviet Union whereas Soviet medium-range weapons cited by the U.S. did not threaten U.S. territory. If agreement was to be reached on strategic arms, then all arms with strategic potential had to be included in the discussions.

Terms of SALT I.

The product of SALT I was twofold: an Interim Agreement on ICBMs, and an Antiballistic Missile Treaty. The central purpose of the latter was to so restrict and locate two ABM systems and deployment areas for each power "that they cannot provide a *nationwide* ABM defense or become the basis for developing one." Each country thus was to leave unchallenged the "penetration capability of the other's retaliatory missile forces."† The intent was to obviate the necessity on either side to expand and improve offensive capabilities, at least on that account.

The Interim Agreement on Limitation of Strategic Offensive Arms was merely intended as "a holding action," to "complement the ABM Treaty by limiting competition in offensive strategic arms and to provide further negotiations."[19] But according to U.S. critics of SALT I, the Agreement, among numerous other flaws, provided the Soviet Union with sufficient loopholes through which

---

* USACDA (1982). Little is known of what actually was or is in the minds of Soviet leaders. On the U.S. side, some planners entertained high hopes while others approached the negotiations with extreme skepticism. On U.S. perception of the background of SALT, see U.S. Department of State (1979), p. 1.

† *USACDA (1982)*, p. 137 (italics added). An essential feature of this treaty, one causing problems a decade later, was the stipulation that while deployment of radar systems to provide early warning of strategic missile attacks was not prohibited, such systems had to be "located along the territorial boundaries of each country and oriented outward, so that they do not contribute to an effective ABM defense of points in the interior." *USACDA 1982*, pp. 137–138, and Article VI, *ibid.*, pp. 140–141.

Other provisions limited the number of ABM launchers each side could deploy in the designated and restricted areas and imposed restrictions on improvements, modifications, and construction of ABM weapons and systems. Anticipating continuous pressure resulting from technological change, provision was made for consultation should new ABM concepts and technologies render the system addressed in the Treaty obsolete. This Treaty limited each side to one ABM to defend its national capital and another to defend one ICBM field. A Protocol signed in 1974 restricted each side to one site only. *USCDA 1982*, pp. 161–163.

Moscow could surreptitiously introduce a vast array of improved, mobile land-based ICBMs. These critics viewed with extreme skepticism the defense offered by U.S. negotiators that the U.S. possessed the "national technical means" to verify Soviet compliance in this as well as in other respects and that, under the terms of the Agreement, the Soviet Union was prohibited from interfering with that process.[20]

The new strategic arms limits were to be as follows:

	U.S.	U.S.S.R.
Total Land-Based ICBM Launchers	1,054	1,618*
Total SLBM Launchers on Submarines	710 on 44 Submarines	950 on 62 Submarines

A harbinger of difficulties to come was Soviet insistence that a ceiling also was to be set for NATO as a whole, namely 50 submarines with a total of 800 SLBM launchers, and that should the NATO limit be exceeded by one or both of the United States' nuclear-power NATO allies, that is Great Britain and France, the Soviet Union would have the right to increase its forces correspondingly. The U.S. delegation noted the Soviet position but rejected it as inappropriate in a two-power agreement.[21] It was clear from the omissions and from statements made by the respective delegations and their governments on several disputed subjects that a second round was mandatory if the first one was to survive its anticipated five-year period.

SALT II

Preliminaries. Within a few months of the 1972 Agreement, discussions were underway toward a more comprehensive settlement. The U.S. objectives were "to provide for equal numbers of strategic nuclear delivery vehicles, to begin the process of reduction of these delivery vehicles, and to impose restraints on qualitative developments which could threaten future stability."[22] Both sides recognized that only a will to compromise on the most fundamental and potentially most destabilizing dimensions of the problem would clear the way for a more comprehensive agreement. Insistence by either side on dotting all i's and crossing all t's guaranteed failure, absolutely.

In November of 1974, at Vladivostok, Presidents Ford and Brezhnev agreed on a basic framework for SALT II featuring aggregate limits of strategic nuclear vehicles and MIRVs, a ban on construction of certain types of launchers, limits on deployment of certain types of strategic arms, and verification procedures

---

* The apparent quantitative Soviet advantage was balanced by U.S. advances in MIRVing its weapons including its SLBMs and as noted, long-range bombers, in which the U.S. enjoyed a decisive lead at the time, were not included.

better than those provided under SALT I. The new agreement was to expire in December 1985. As preliminary discussions got underway, two major points of dispute crystallized, the U.S. ground-launched cruise missile (GLCM) and the Soviet backfire bomber.* Basically, Washington approached this second round concerned mainly with protection of its triad-retaliatory capability, while Moscow appeared determined to use SALT II to ensure, at the very least, the coveted parity at two levels, which from their point of view were inseparable: intercontinental and European-Theater ballistic missiles.

Box 18-1. SALT II: Allotment of Strategic Nuclear Vehicles

Initial Total Delivery Systems:
  Each country was to be limited initially to 2400 strategic nuclear delivery vehicles of all types combined—that is, land-based ICBM launchers, SLBM launchers, air-to-surface ballistic missiles (ASBMs) capable of a range in excess of 600 kilometers, and heavy bombers. In 1981, the initial 2400 total was to be reduced to 2250. Within this overall ceiling there were to be sublimits imposed equally on both sides.

1982 Total	Combined strategic nuclear delivery vehicles of all types	2250
Sublimit 1	Of the 2250, neither side was to be permitted more than a combined total of 1320 of the following types: 1) launchers of MIRVed ICBMs 2) launchers of MIRVed SLBMs 3) heavy bombers equipped for long–range cruise missiles 4) MIRVed ASBMs	1320
Sublimit 2	Of the 1320 neither side was permitted more than a combined total of 1200 1) launchers of MIRVed ICBMs 2) launchers of MIRVed SLBMs 3) MIRVed ASBMs	1200
Sublimit 3	Of the 1200, neither side was permitted more than 820 launchers of MIRVed ICBMs	820

SOURCE: U.S. Department of State, *The Strategic Arms Limitation Talks*, Special Report 46 (revised May 1979), p. 7.

* The latter was a long-range plane believed to be capable of reaching the American Northwest unrefueled and all of the U.S. refueled. See U.S. State Department (1979) and Table 17-2.

The terms. Box 18–1 depicts the allotment of strategic nuclear delivery vehicles envisaged under the agreement. Briefly SALT II sought to ensure the following limits and accompanying safeguards:

- Equal aggregate limits on strategic nuclear delivery vehicles.
- Equal aggregate limits on total number of launchers of MIRVed ballistic missiles and heavy bombers with long-range cruise missiles.
- Ban on construction of additional fixed ICBM launchers and on increase in the number of fixed heavy ICBM launchers.
- Limits of warheads on ICBMs and on air-to-surface ballistic missiles (ASBMs) and of cruise missiles on planes.
- Ceilings on launch and throw-weight of strategic missiles.
- Ban on rapid reload ICBM systems.
- Ban on certain strategic weapons not yet deployed but feasible, for example ballistic missiles on surface ships and ballistic missiles launched from the seabed.
- Advance notification of certain ICBM test launches.
- An agreed data base for systems included in various SALT-limited categories.
- Modes of verification, including telemetry, both sides agreeing "not to engage in denial of telemetry information whenever such denial impedes verification of compliance with the provisions of the agreement."[23]

Even if SALT II had been confined to one or two simple propositions, it would have aroused considerable controversy in the United States. Given the actual scope of the undertaking, it should have surprised no one when the U.S. Senate refused ratification. The best the U.S. could offer was an assurance by President Reagan, on May 31, 1982, that the U.S. would "refrain from actions which undercut [SALT I and II] so long as the Soviet Union shows equal restraint." However, since even before SALT II had been concluded the U.S. president's top advisors had charged the Soviet Union with cheating on SALT I, and shortly after May 1979 the Soviet Union was charged with additional violations. SALT II was soon downgraded to a set of guidelines which either side could interpret as it saw fit.[24] If both sides nonetheless professed to abide by SALT II's quantitative limits, this was only as long as they felt that their strategic positions could be improved by other means.*

Security versus Control: The Hawks and the Doves

In the United States, the SALT process crystallized sharp divisions among professional military leaders, politicians, and intellectuals, not dissimilar from

---

* One of numerous soft spots in SALT II, as in similar agreements, was the exclusion of such IRBMs as the SS–20 which, as noted earlier could be, and probably was, converted into an ICBM.

such polarizations over arms control agreements within the leading military powers prior to World War II. Those who were convinced that national security could be achieved with the proper mix of weapons, backed by appropriately assertive strategies and foreign policies, tended to emphasize Soviet untrustworthiness and advocated continuous upgrading of U.S. nuclear capabilities. This school tended to bank on the United States' vastly superior economic strength and technological prowess to compel Moscow eventually to accept U.S. terms and conditions, all of which they of course considered eminently reasonable. Those were the "hawks." They were opposed by the "doves" who argued, with equal ardor and conviction, that given the infinitely complex near runaway nature of contemporary nuclear competition, no matter how devious communists might be, to seek further security in nuclear escalation was a dangerous illusion.[25] One must presume that similar divisions exist in the Soviet Union, though of course not as in a democracy in full public view.

The debate between hawks and doves is conducted at two levels, the technical-military and the ideological, one all too readily becoming enmeshed with the other. Technical arguments run the gamut from closely reasoned, cautiously advanced, and well documented assessments of the state of the military arts to highly exaggerated and tendentious versions of military reality. Both camps argue their case on selective evidence; regarding violations, for example, hawks focus exclusively on alleged, often unproven, violations by the other power. If hard data are not available to buttress an argument, the hawks simply intone that the other side is rapidly improving and narrowing or widening "the gap."[26] Ideologically, U.S. hawks are unable to accept cohabitation on this planet with communists and will not allow that, given its experience with war and given the horrors of a nuclear attack, the Soviet Union has perhaps a moral right to nuclear parity. Soviet hawks look forward to the day when the U.S. is eliminated as a military factor and capitalism can be buried at long last.

The epitome of respectable U.S. dovishness is George F. Kennan, whose now classic comment deserves to be repeated: "There is no issue at stake in our political relations with the Soviet Union—no hope, no fear, nothing to which we aspire, nothing we would like to avoid—which could conceivably be worth a nuclear war."[27] To which some hawks reply, in the U.S. as well as in the Soviet Union, that even a nuclear war is to be preferred to surrender; at the very least one must be prepared to "win," should such a war be forced upon a nation.[28] To which a leading U.S. arms control proponent, Paul Warnke, offered this rejoinder: "If we use our 10,000 warheads, and they use their 7,000, nobody will be king. 'By God, we beat them, we're now ahead of the Soviet Union. Of course, we're slightly behind the Fiji Islands.'"[29]

Positions Harden: Towards Accommodation or Armageddon?

It is an axiom of diplomacy that complex issues can be resolved only sequentially. This certainly applies to arms competition, and SALT I and II had been negotiated by both sides in full knowledge that those agreements represented no more than first steps, and very imperfect ones at that, in what all the world recognized would be a drawn-out and often painful process.[30] But a new U.S. administration, seizing upon apparent but inevitable shortcomings of all arms agreements negotiated previously, proposed in conjunction with ongoing Intermediate-Range Nuclear Force (INF) discussions to approach the entire subject from a different direction. While declaring its willingness to observe existing agreements as long as Moscow did likewise, Washington now focused on four new objectives: 1) to correct a perceived ICBM imbalance disadvantaging the United States; 2) to match Soviet intermediate-range advances in Europe; 3) to obtain, as a *sine qua non* for future agreements and ratification of old ones, Soviet consent to deception-proof means of verification; 4) to link arms agreements to improvement in Moscow's foreign policy conduct, especially in the Third World. All this rested on two basic assumptions: Moscow needed arms agreements more than the United States, and Kremlin leaders could be induced to make concessions only if approached from positions of strength, both highly debatable propositions. Overlooked was the distinct danger that arms negotiations pressed too hard too far, encompassing issues far less tractable than those already on the table, could well accelerate instead of slow down descent into the nuclear abyss.*

Especially detrimental to arms control was the threat that unless prevailing Soviet throw-weight advantages were reduced to a ratio of less than 2:1 the U.S. would reopen the "Comprehensive ABM" option, foreclosed for the time being by the ABM Treaty. (Under that option either side would be free to attempt to develop a total defense against incoming missiles, which could of course unravel all that had been negotiated up to that point.) To obtain from Moscow assurances that its what-is-ours-is-ours, what-is-yours-is-negotiable stance had been abandoned, was reasonable; but this injected into already far too complicated arms negotiations the politically and ideologically highly charged concept of "linkage," a thrust, as noted earlier, pointing directly at the heart of the Soviet system's revolutionary *raison d'être*.[31] The Euromissile segment of the American plan was no less controversial and no less detrimental to peace. As noted in the preceding chapter, that segment too had its technical-military and political dimensions.

Washington's European allies, more concerned than ever that they might be dragged into a nuclear war to be fought at their expense in Europe, insisted on a "dual track" approach: improved U.S. IRBMs, the Pershing II's and GLCMs, were to be installed in Western Europe only gradually, beginning late

---

* "Chips" in the bargaining then about to begin were, among other threats, the B-1 bomber, the U.S. MX (Missile Experimental), a weapon more accurate and more powerful than existing ICBMs in the U.S. arsenal, and the Trident II, and an SLBM hardened and heavier than its predecessor Trident I and extending the latter's range by 2,250 miles (3,600 kms). Equipped with a more accurate 8 warhead RV (the MK-12A) it had an expected CEP of 120 meters. According to its more enthusiastic proponents, it could hit "the Kremlin parking lot." Another "chip" was the continuing lead enjoyed by the U.S. in high technology, which could enable it to gain a crucial advantage in the ASAT competition then underway.

in 1983, the move to be cancelled if the Soviet Union agreed to modify its own arsenal so as to render deployment unnecessary. The second track required that Washington genuinely pursued agreement at the Intermediate-Range Nuclear Force talks (INF). Moscow rejected that approach. Here again was a demonstration that if too much is attempted nothing is achieved. Furthermore, there was doubt in some expert circles that the move was really necessary; the U.S., if it was so inclined, already had in hand the means to respond in kind to nuclear attacks on Western Europe and, by implied threat, deter a Soviet bloc conventional assault.

Arguably, the Soviet threat to Western European security had to be answered not by U.S. weapons stationed in the United States, carried on slow moving planes or positioned somewhere at sea, but by matching weapons firmly emplaced on West European soil. From Moscow's point of view, however, the move constituted an unbearable provocation. As noted in Table 17-3 counts differed substantially regarding respective theater as well as strategic nuclear missile strengths. Viewed from the Kremlin, the U.S. now made arms agreement conditional on Soviet consent to accept a position inferior to that of NATO. According to Moscow, unlike Washington's allies who had missiles capable of reaching Soviet cities, Moscow's Warsaw Pact allies had none with which to reach the U.S. Nor did the Soviet Union at that time have nuclear missiles at the doorstep of the United States, having withdrawn such weapons from Cuba in 1962 in response to U.S. pressure. Now Washington, as a bargaining ploy in arms negotiations, was about to introduce such missiles at the doorstep of the Soviet Union.[32]

What of NATO's contentions that British and French missiles were purely defensive, no match in any case for the steadily increasing SS-20 threat, and that none of the U.S., British, or French bombers, all of which Moscow counted in the balance, obsolete and slow-moving as they were, were actually capable of penetrating Soviet conventional air defenses? Certainly, whereas NATO bombers faced formidable in-depth air defenses flying East, Soviet bombers flying West could reach their targets more immediately. Moscow after all was more distant from NATO forward bases than were Western European capitals from Soviet bases in East Germany or Czechoslovakia. Thus NATO's demand that all of the Soviet Union's 2,700 bomb-carrying planes should also be counted had considerable merit. The tangle thickened substantially and agreement became more remote, if in addition to all bombing planes all tactical nuclear weapons were to be counted. Then all talk of arms reduction became hopelessly confused. In that connection NATO's argument that British and French nuclear weapons should not be included in Soviet-American arms negotiations had some merit. After all, they were not intended to defend other NATO partners. But, in response, Moscow could simply transfer—as it eventually did—a segment of its nuclear arsenal to Warsaw Pact allies, claiming that this was solely for their own defense.

Yet the greatest obstacle to an agreement at this level, as at the Strategic Arms Reduction Talks (START) and elsewhere, was the bane of all arms negotiations: the global web of interlocked, interdependent, offensive and defensive, conventional and strategic postures, coupled with the effects on all of this of internal political crosscurrents raging continuously within the United States and the Soviet Union.* In addition, technological advances constantly raised havoc with existing treaties and understandings; for instance, mutually accepted standards of measurement to determine weapon capability, which made agreements possible, tended to become obsolete before the ink dried on the treaties. Likewise, distinctions drawn between strategic and theater nuclear weapons seemed unreal if "Soviet weapons capable of hitting New York and Chicago could also be fired at London or Tokyo."[33] Then there always remained doubt as to what was action, what reaction. Was each side simply modernizing weapons, as they claimed? Or was it Washington's intent to deter a Soviet first strike by compelling Moscow to deplete its second-strike reserves in the initial attempt to destroy all or most of the United States retaliatory forces, now to be increased and positioned not only in the U.S. and at sea but also on land, closer to the Soviet Union? If Moscow's aim, as alleged, was to attain nuclear superiority to "paralyze the American nuclear deterrent by threatening to overwhelm it, and thus make Soviet aggression by conventional forces possible" then an American proposal to reduce Soviet advantages in the crucial European region was eminently fair.[34] If, on the other hand, Moscow sought preponderance at strategic and intermediate-range levels not to dominate but to check Western global domination at long last, the U.S. proposals to cut Moscow's IRBM stock targeted at Western Europe down to zero, while exempting from its count all of the other NATO nuclear weapons and all bombers, would seem provocative indeed.†

Late in 1983, purportedly in response to IRBM and GLCM deployment by the U.S., INF discussions came to a halt. Soon parallel talks on other arms

---

* Some initiatives were obvious nonstarters, even if termed START as was the case with the 1982 U.S. proposal to conduct not arms control or limitation but Strategic Arms *Reduction* Talks. Washington's aim apparently was to reduce the Soviet lead in land-based strategic missiles in return for certain reductions on the part of the United States. START proved wholly unproductive mainly because it failed to balance proposed reductions of the Soviet Union's principal defense arm (about 75 percent of their strategic weapons were land-based at the time) with truly reciprocal or equivalent reductions of the U.S. strategic arsenal.

† The central issue and the manner in which it was handled by both sides is instructive because it exemplifies the fate of numerous similar attempts to strike a balance: see Eugene V. Rostow (1982), pp. 13-14; also, Yuli Kvitsinsky and Paul H. Nitze (1984). The occasion was the "walk-in-the woods" (in July 1982) between the latter two, a tentative agreement formula worked out by them, and the prompt rejection of their "break-through" formula by their respective governments. According to Nitze, the formula's central feature "would have restricted each side to no more than 75 missile launchers and precluded deployment of American Pershing IIs in the European area, and would have frozen Soviet launchers at 90 in Soviet Asia." The U.S. would have been allowed to station in Europe no more than 75 cruise missiles. The proposal would have conceded the Soviet point that ballistic missiles were already stationed in Western Europe by Britain and France and that therefore no additional U.S. missiles were needed to counter Soviet defenses. The restriction on Soviet launchers in Asia was to prevent Moscow to shift missiles targeted on Western Europe to the Far East, there to threaten Japan or the PRC, both within the U.S. military interest zone.

issues also ceased. To be sure, as neither side was prepared to accept the onus of terminating ongoing negotiations, both went through the motions of offering apparent compromises. But too often they did so in public, to score propaganda points in the now ensuing battle for public opinion.* Moscow's objective clearly was less attainment of accords than manipulation of increasingly alarmed Western European and Soviet bloc publics. Indeed, mounting opposition to the U.S. move in European cities may have encouraged Moscow to believe that if it remained steadfast in its opposition to deployment the U.S. would eventually have to capitulate. This could open the way for complete removal of U.S. military presence from the European continent. In any case, it is most doubtful that, as charged by Moscow, deployment of U.S. weapons was the sole or even principal cause of arms talk interruption. What had been true when negotiations started in the 1950s remained true to this day: whenever one side seems prepared to make concessions, hawks and other interested parties on the other side urge their government to escalate demands.† In addition, in the absence of deception-proof arrangements to verify compliance with treaty terms there will always be grounds to suspect that the antagonist is cheating.[35]

Alternatives

The Freeze

Pending breakthroughs at the negotiating tables, various coalitions of peace advocates and other concerned citizens advanced alternatives to uncontrolled and uncontrollable arms competition. Among the least realistic proposals was unilateral disarmament in the West, advanced in the hope that the people under communist totalitarian rule would thereby become sufficiently aroused

---

* The Kvitsinsky-Nitze exchange was but one of numerous manifestations of the new "public [arms control] diplomacy."

† The sisyphean nature of this problem was captured concisely by Theodore Draper (1982), p. 41:

> The very subject of nuclear negotiations is enigmatic and tantalizing. The goal is always parity, but the Soviet and American systems are so different that a mythical parity can be achieved only by a process of "trade-offs." Each side must consider the needs and pressure of its own vested interests before meeting the needs and pressures of the other side. Two sets of negotiations are always going on, the internal and the external, with the former often more difficult and dreary than the latter. Once the trading starts, it can go on for months and even years, until a deal has been reached, if at all, so full of compromises and conditions that no side is finally prevented from doing what it really wants to do or made to give way what it really wishes to keep.

Contemplating two publications, the U.S. Department of Defense's *Soviet Military Power* and the Soviet Ministry of Defense's *Whence The Threat To Peace?*, the secretary general of the United Nations noted that together "these two publications provide a fairly clear idea of the intractability of matching launchers with warheads; warheads with speed, accuracy and damage potential; and of placing all these factors in a geo-political context with a view to arrive at mutually acceptable agreements about limiting the nuclear arms race." UN Sec. Gen. (1983), p. 17. See also Strobe Talbot, *Deadly Gambits. The Reagan Administration and the Stalemate in Nuclear Arms Control* (N.Y.: Knopf, 1984).

to compel their respective governments to reciprocate. Another was unconditional renunciation of nuclear force, resting on similar expectations. Taken most seriously in the United States and in Western Europe and pursued with unusual vigor and determination by segments of the public and elected officials alike was the proposal to (in a sense) shame the Soviet Union to agree to a nuclear freeze, by having the United States declare that it would forego all testing, production, and development of additional nuclear weapons (that is, aircraft and missiles but not submarines).* The proposal rested on the assumption that existing verification technology was adequate to monitor compliance. There were of course arguments on that, for and against.

For: 1) Inexorably advancing military technology threatens to remove any negotiated arms agreement from humanity's grasp on that count alone.† 2) Contrary to U.S. Defense Department assertions, the United States actually was ahead of the Soviet Union in critical respects, hence could afford to take the first step. The freeze would not be permanent—Soviet cheating would be detected soon enough—placing the U.S. on the side of the angels in the battle for world public opinion. 3) If the by now chronic upward spiral of nuclear arms competition was to be broken and the trend halted and eventually reversed, a start had to be made somewhere, sometime.

Against: 1) Moscow might agree but continue to arm in secret nevertheless; for while the U.S. under pressure from public opinion would be obliged to abide by the terms of the agreement, Soviet leaders, free of such impediments, could proceed as they saw fit as Soviet ability to cheat exceeded U.S. ability to monitor compliance.[36] 2) As the Soviet Union enjoyed a clear advantage in numerous respects, a freeze would lock the United States into a position where it had to accept and live with that fact. This could unnerve U.S. allies who, assuming that the Soviet Union would undoubtedly widen its lead, might reevaluate their posture and enter the arms race on a higher scale than theretofore, on their own behalf. This could in turn unhinge the entire Western alliance system.[37] 3) Historically, the Soviet Union has always shown an inclination to negotiate when confronted by a firm will. A freeze would undercut pending

---

* A Nuclear Freeze proposal was narrowly defeated in the U.S. Congress. *Congressional Quarterly* (June 26, 1982), p. 1515. One reason why the proposal was defeated, and one major reason why control negotiations are so difficult, was that a freeze "would stop production of new nuclear arms, would cut deeply into the work of some companies. For 39% of the nuclear arms work done by Martin-Marietta Corporation, which helps produce the MX and Pershing II missiles, is done on systems that would be affected by a freeze." From a report by the Investor Responsibility Research Center, Inc., Gerald F. Seib, *The Wall Street Journal* (January 9, 1984).

† Warned four leading U.S. citizens, long associated with the conduct of U.S. foreign affairs: "Without a freeze, within a few short years there will be thousands of nuclear-armed cruise missiles on both sides, small enough to be launched not from enormous, detectable complexes, but from the backs of large trucks or from ships and submarines. When these missiles are deployed in Soviet forests and on Soviet trawlers, verifiable limits on the number of nuclear weapons could be forever beyond the reach of humanity." W. A. Harriman, Clark Clifford, William Colby, Paul C. Warnke, Letter to the Editor, *The New York Times* (October 31, 1982).

efforts to compel Moscow to negotiate in earnest. To that end, it was argued, the U.S. must modernize its obsolescent weapons to match similar efforts on the Soviet side. 4) As long as nuclear weapons are part of the Western arsenal, they must be tested to determine their reliability.[38]

"No First Use"

In 1982 four prominent Americans, in a *Foreign Affairs* article "to start a discussion, not to end it," proposed that the U.S. unilaterally renounce first use of nuclear force.[39] To compensate for the resultant weakness in NATO's deterrent power, the four recommended strengthening NATO's conventional capabilities. This caused grave concern in some Western circles, especially in front-line West Germany where "the threat of first use [by NATO forces, that is by the United States] has always been regarded as an indispensable feature of the deterrent in as much as only the incalculable risk of nuclear war can definitely ensure a decision [by Moscow] to forego war in Central Europe."[40] But other Europeans and West Germans were not so sure.[41]

The Nuclear Test Ban Issues

As nuclear arsenals became permanent features of some armed forces, scientists as well as the military of all members of the "nuclear club" found it imperative to test the explosive capacity of their nuclear stock. Predictably, testing soon got out of hand, posing health hazards for all mankind. Following the March 1, 1954 tests of a hydrogen bomb by the United States in the Pacific, fall-out subjected numerous inhabitants on an atoll near point zero and some Japanese fishermen nearby, on a ship called the Lucky Dragon, to radiation. Scientists in various parts of the world had earlier and subsequently detected traces of radioactive strontium 90 in mothers' milk and in children's teeth. Hard pressed to assuage aroused public opinion but unable to negotiate a treaty, the United States, the Soviet Union, and Great Britain entered in 1958 into an informal agreement on a moratorium on weapons testing in the atmosphere. Partly because France would not go along, the Soviet Union felt impelled to violate that agreement in 1961. Eventually public pressure forced the three powers in 1963 to enter into a formal treaty agreement to limit such testing. The Limited Test Ban Treaty (LTBT), eventually signed by over 100 states, banned all tests in the atmosphere but permitted tests below ground. In 1974 the Soviet–American Treaty on the Limitation of Underground Nuclear Weapons Tests was signed, establishing a nuclear "threshold" by prohibiting tests of devices yielding in excess of 150 kilotons or 150,000 tons of TNT. Two years later another treaty was signed between the two powers limiting all nuclear testing for peaceful purposes below grounds.[42] Both governments expressed their intent to negotiate at the earliest possible time a Comprehensive Test Ban covering all types of weapons at all levels. Aside from benefitting humanity's health, a ban on testing was believed to have a stabilizing effect on the nuclear confrontation. As the United States Arms Control and Disarmament Agency put it: "Of particular significance is the relationship between explosive power of reliable tested warheads and first-strike capability."[43]

Unfortunately, the nemesis of all arms control agreements, mistrust, raised its ugly head in this respect as well. Skeptics in the United States, noting that available verification technology did not enable the U.S. "to distinguish with certainty a 300 kiloton explosion from a 150 kiloton blast," counseled delay in ratification of both treaties. Argued one U.S. military leader: "In the purest sense of the term, any agreement which limits the manner in which we develop our weapons systems represents a military disadvantage."[44] Others pleaded that ratification was worth the risk. In 1982 the Reagan administration decided not to proceed with a proposed comprehensive test ban treaty until verification methods appropriate for the partial bans were more reliable. But under a comprehensive ban prohibiting all types of tests, it would no longer be a matter of being unable to determine whether an explosion was above or below the threshhold; all nuclear explosions would be prohibited. Nevertheless the military, concerned about the reliability of untested nuclear warheads, and nuclear scientists as well as industrialists, fearful of loss of employment and of contracts, prevailed in the United States.*

Controlling Biological and Chemical Warfare

We noted in the preceding chapter that the Geneva Protocol did not actually prohibit military use of poison gas. Although chemical agents were not used in World War Two and biological warfare was never seriously considered by any of the belligerents, the mass destruction wrought during that conflict generated worldwide pressure to prohibit not only all atomic but also all biological and chemical weapons absolutely, for all time. But the *B* and *C* in the *atomic-biological-chemical* triad proved as difficult to cast into a binding treaty framework as did the *A*.

That the implements of biological warfare could not be totally prohibited did not at that time cause too much concern. It was practically impossible to prepare biological agents, germs for instance, for timely action, to ensure that such weapons would reliably cause immediate damage to a target and that they would not spread beyond control. Still the threat existed and some constraints had to be devised.[45] Here again, the principal obstacle to Soviet-American agreement was verification. When in 1979, in the Soviet city of Sverdlovsk, an accident provided a hint of possible large-scale preparation by the Soviet Union

---

* Daniel Ford believes that the test bans may have escalated the arms race by "sanitizing" testing, thereby alleviating public concern. Ford, *et al* (1982), p. 26. On the other hand, testing has enabled both sides to reduce nuclear stockpiles.

to wage biological warfare, on-site inspection became as critical in that respect as it had been previously with respect to nuclear and chemical control.*

The United States did not ratify the Geneva Protocol until 1975. However, in 1969, as part of President Nixon's comprehensive peace plan and in particular as a gesture toward the UN-sponsored Conference on Disarmament the United States unilaterally announced a moratorium on production of all CW agents, declaring that it would under no circumstances resort to chemical weapons first. Washington was confident that the Soviet Union could be discouraged from first use of chemical agents by the nuclear deterrent.

By 1982 a more skeptical U.S. administration, convinced that Moscow was taking advantage of the opportunity to achieve a decisive CW edge over the United States, ordered production resumed and proceeded to modernize its CW capability. There was a widespread feeling in U.S. military circles that the Soviet Union had in effect prevented the U.S. from improving its deteriorating and deficient chemical capability by merely sitting down at the negotiating table.[46] Concern turned into alarm when evidence was received of massive Soviet production increases and possible experimental use of toxic gases and other chemical agents by Soviet or allied forces in Kampuchea, Laos, and Afghanistan.[47] Early in 1984, probably in response to a U.S. initiative, Moscow appeared to soften its position regarding on-site inspection. To optimists, though vaguely formulated the offer opened the door to an agreement. Skeptics feared that what appeared to be a concession was perhaps just another propaganda move to score points at yet another security or disarmament conference.[48]

Mutual Balanced Force Reduction Talks (MBFR)

In 1973 NATO and Warsaw Pact representatives began to explore ways and means of reducing conventional armed forces facing each other across the dividing line in Europe.[49] By the middle of 1985 no progress had been made, partly because of the general stalemate in arms control and limitation talks, partly because no agreement could be reached on how a *balanced* force *withdrawal* could be implemented. NATO found unacceptable a Warsaw Pact proposal

---

* As with all other weapons, international agreements to prohibit or control biological or biochemical weapons are continuously rendered invalid or inoperative by advances in science and technology. Notes the 1983 Soviet *Military Encyclopedia:* "The rapidly developing industry in microbiology can be switched over from its peacetime [health and health-care related] mission . . . to the production of pathogenic microorganisms. This consideration complicates the capability for effective international monitoring of the ban on biological weapons." The same source then notes that because of developments in biotechnology "the boundaries between the biological and chemical weapons are erased, since all biological processes depend on chemical or physiochemical reactions." Therefore, the source concludes, bacterial toxins previously banned under the Biological Weapons Convention now should be classified as chemical—because biochemical processes produce them—hence they fall under the 1925 Geneva Protocol which prohibits *only their use, not their production.* The 1972 Biological Weapons Convention prohibited the production, development, and stockpiling of bacteriological weapons. Kucewicz (April 27, 1984), (italics added).

which pointed to an eventual equidistant withdrawal from Europe of both American and Soviet forces. Under the proposal, whereas Soviet forces would be removed only to positions along Europe's eastern edge, from which they could of course return in relatively short time, U.S. forces would have to be removed from Europe entirely. In 1984, Western estimates of Warsaw Pact ground and air forces exceeded Pact estimates by about 180,000. Again, the verification problem complicated matters, although in this respect it did not seem insurmountable. (See Table 18-2.)

The European Security Talks

In 1975, 35 nations, gathered at Helsinki, Finland, signed the Final Act of the Conference on Security and Cooperation in Europe (CSCE). The Act addressed three sets of issues of special concern to Europe, West as well as East. Grouped in "baskets" these included 1) military security measures, 2) economic, scientific, technological, and environmental cooperation, and 3) human rights, information, and education. Here we confine ourselves to military security.

Table 18-2. NATO and the Warsaw Pact

The North Atlantic Treaty Organization

Members (with year of accession)	Population (thousands, mid-year 1983)	Armed Forces (thousands, total active mid-1983)
Belgium (1949)	9,865	95
Canada (1949)	24,882	83
Denmark (1949)	5,115	31
France (1949)	54,604	493
Germany, Federal Republic of (1955)	61,543	495
Greece (1952)	9,898	185
Iceland (1949)	236	no forces
Italy (1949)	56,345	373
Luxembourg (1949)	366	0.7
Netherlands (1949)	14,374	103
Norway (1949)	4,131	43
Portugal (1949)	10,008	64
Spain (1982)	38,234	347
Turkey (1952)	49,115	569
United Kingdom (1949)	56,006	321
United States (1949)	234,193	2,136

Warsaw Pact

Members	Population (in thousands, mid-year 1983)	Armed Forces (in thousands, mid-1983)
Bulgaria	8,944	162
Czechoslovakia	15,420	205
German Democratic Republic	16,724	167
Hungary	10,691	105
Poland	36,556	340
Romania	22,649	189
U.S.S.R.	272,308	5,050

SOURCE: United States Department of State, Bureau of Public Affairs, Publication No. 9412, *Atlas of NATO*, 1985, pp. 2–3.

To Europeans who have experienced three major wars in less than 100 years, all military maneuvers have an ominous ring.[50] To reduce tension and build confidence, by reducing the possibility of surprise attack for instance, the Final Act among other things required signatories to give prior notification of "major military maneuvers [between the Atlantic Ocean and Soviet Russia's western region] exceeding a total of 25,000 troops, independently or combined with possible air and naval components." In addition, signatories were encouraged voluntarily to invite observers to maneuvers, participate in military exchange visits, and give prior notification of exercises involving fewer than 25,000 troops. At the Madrid talks on the Implementation of the Final Act (December 1, 1982–May 31, 1983), NATO members complained that whereas their side meticulously abided by the terms of the agreement Soviet bloc countries repeatedly had violated the Final Act in letter and in spirit.[51] Galling the West most of all was the fact that at Helsinki, in return for a Soviet undertaking to safeguard the peace on the European continent, that is disavow all aggressive plans, the Western powers had accepted as permanent the post-World War II boundary changes effectuated by the Soviet Union in Eastern Europe after the war to enhance its own security.

Future Prospects

The foregoing must make it painfully apparent that to bring the two-power arms rivalry under control, possibly even reverse the trend, is a gargantuan task, to say the least. Our discussion raises many disturbing questions: Do the complexities of the entire matter already exceed our grasp? Are the dynamics of civilian and military interest group struggles including military interservice rivalry, all pressing for more and better arms, too intense, the stakes too high, the principal players too powerful, to be brought under control? Are the punishment and reward systems within the two countries' political and military hierarchies such as to promote the nuclear warrior and penalize the advocate of genuine arms negotiation and of compromise? Is the constant need for modernization of nuclear weapons—the effect of "technology creep"—a further incentive to avoid firm treaty limits, evade test bans, generally to stall, procrastinate, and if all else fails, cheat? When is modernization cheating?* Is the joker in the arms control and limitation pack the nagging fear that unless nuclear redundancy—that is, backing existing weapon systems with more solely for insurance—is doubled and redoubled, all will be lost?

Is the inner logic of the arms race so muddled, so confused, so fudged by nebulous phrase-mongering, so fraught with deceit and ambiguity, that no one

---

* On alleged Soviet violations of existing treaties and understandings, see "A Quarter Century of Soviet Compliance Practices Under Arms Control Commitments: 1958–1983," a report by the (U.S.) President's General Advisory Committee (GAC) on Arms Control and Disarmament discussed in Colin S. Gray, "Moscow Is Cheating," *Foreign Policy,* 56 (Fall 1984), pp. 141–152; on violations of Chemical Warfare prohibitions generally, see SIPRI, *Yearbook 1982,* Table 10.6, pp. 340–341.

really comprehends or perhaps cares to comprehend its full dimensions? Or are things so complicated that a new type of weapon or a new strategy designed to prevent a nuclear war may actually bring it on more certainly? In the opinion of some observers, the latter possibility threatened to materialize when the U.S., in the 1980s, introduced the aforementioned Strategic Defense Initiative (SDI).

Yet neither side could afford to cease efforts to prevent the antagonist from achieving an unsurpassable lead in one or more respects, nor could either of them publicly concede that the arms spiral may have spun out of control. In addition Washington and Moscow were under severe pressure domestically and from their allies to try once more if for no other reason than to prevent an accidental nuclear war and bring relief to their own and others' hard pressed economies. Consequently talks were resumed in March 1985 mainly on strategic and intermediate weapons, and by choice of the U.S. on the concept of a strategic defense system utilizing outer space. Both obviously approached the renewed talks intent on preserving advantages and freedom to engage in "break-outs" from existing or future agreements should their national interests so dictate.

The U.S. had three major tactical objectives: 1) renegotiate those existing agreements which clearly placed the U.S. military at an unacceptable disadvantage; 2) with respect to existing and future agreements, secure Soviet consent to balanced and positively verifiable arms curbs, including restraints *on research* on ABC weapons; 3) if truly verifiable curbs could not be attained, acquaint Soviet leaders with Washington's determination to proceed with SDI in one form or another as the only reliable deterrent.* Pending availability of that option—a decade-long project at the very least—the U.S. would seek to match and if necessary more than match each and every Soviet advance on land, at sea, in the air, and in space. The Soviet Union, of course, would reciprocate.

The Soviet Union expected from these talks at least three concrete results: 1) if nuclear superiority could not be attained or secured in one or more categories, or U.S. superiority negated in others, then overall nuclear parity had to be assured; 2) to those ends and under all circumstances, U.S. advances in military space technology, in particular with respect to the SDI concept, had to be curbed, their military application prevented. (The U.S. of course suspected Moscow of wanting to sidetrack SDI and outlaw militarization of outer space because they had already made progress in those respects and were confident that this fact could be concealed until fully effective). Moscow's third objective was removal of U.S. IRBMs from the European continent in return for downward adjustment of Soviet nuclear missiles directed at Western Europe.

The resumed talks presented both sides with these options: 1) agree to piecemeal adjustment (e.g. updating and modernizing) existing agreements,

---

* Former U.S. presidential National Security Advisor Zbigniew Brzezinski, believing that "ams control as we have known it has come to the end of the road," and doubting that any U.S. President would actually order nuclear retaliation following a Soviet first strike, or be in position to do so, recommended a decisive shift from offensive to defensive nuclear strategy. *Wall Street Journal* (July 10, 1984).

including SALT I and II; 2) enter into new agreements either formally or informally to a) facilitate negotiations on a permanent basis, b) work out selective mutual reductions of strategically superfluous or redundant nuclear weapon systems, c) engage in mutual or reciprocal "builddown" that is, for each new warhead deployed two are to be retired, or d) accept temporarily a modified freeze whereby each side observes a moratorium with respect to one or more systems wherein it enjoys a clear advantage. If agreement could not be reached on the central issues, then perhaps a measure of agreement could be attained on such peripheral issues as Mutual Balanced Force Reduction or Prevention of Incidents on the High Sea. The hope was expressed by more cautious optimists that barring a breakthrough, over the long haul, both sides might agree to "mutual restraint," allowing deemphasis of systems not deemed essential for deterrence mainly to give world public opinion the impression that progress was being made. Alternatively, again without formal agreement, a state of affairs might be allowed to develop where each side would be permitted to shape its force structure in less dangerous ways while building a more secure deterrent force.[52] The latter formula promised reduced pressure on existing agreements when conditions changed.

Obstructing the path to any agreement, formal or informal, temporary or lasting, was the potentially fatal combination of domestic pressure and interest groups in both countries, "technology creep" and mutual distrust rooted in ideological, political-systemic, and technical-military commitments and interests. Perhaps the greatest obstacle to a meaningful accord was the ever more apparent fact that offensive and defensive, nuclear and conventional, space and terrestrial weapons, including high- and low-altitude surveillance and armed satellites now were integrally part of the same offensive and defensive national systems, hence control or limitation of one category could no longer fruitfully be considered in isolation from all others. Beyond that there was the old nemesis: arms agreements have always tended and always will tend to open up new competition in areas of weaponry not covered.

Suppose then that the nuclear genie cannot ever be returned to its bottle. Assume, as one must, that neither the Soviet leaders nor those of the United States, nor any other responsible leader in the world, really want any kind of nuclear war yet none seem able to rid the world entirely of that threat, what then? We shall attempt to provide a few rays of hope in the Epilogue.

Suggested Questions and Discussion Topics

What may trigger a nuclear holocaust?

What considerations have led to conclusion of a series of multilateral and bilateral agreements on arms prohibition, control, and limitation and on war prevention, and what have been the focal points of each of these agreements?

What objective considerations have led military leaders in the United States and the Soviet Union to seek, and may lead them in the future to seek and/or accept certain arms controls and limitations?

Why do some American and some Soviet military leaders counsel against entering into arms control and limitation agreements?

Why do some experts urge that in years to come the emphasis should shift from arms control, limitation, or reduction agreement to construction of total defense?

Discuss the merits and demerits of the so called "star wars" approach to the arms curb problem; can there be an ultimate, absolute defense and if so could that prevent a nuclear war?

Is the nuclear threat the only potentially catastrophic military threat facing the world?

Realistically what alternatives are or may be available to *formal* agreement between the superpowers on arms control and limitation?

Chapter 19
Under the Nuclear Threat:
Prelude to Anarchy?

Diffusion of Power

The threats of catastrophic nuclear destruction or just of nuclear blackmail continue to militate in favor of bipolarity in world affairs, causing allies in both camps to draw together, "follow the leader," and at least attempt to resist centrifugal inclinations. At the same time, the spreading conviction that nuclear weapons may actually never be used and seem in any case, as demonstrated in Vietnam and Afghanistan, quite irrelevant in peripheral military conflicts accelerates the shift from bi- to multipolarity; that shift, noticeable for some time in the realm of economics, is now about to extend to military affairs as well. One consequence is the emergence of a dichotomy between nuclear and subnuclear strategic patterns and pursuits. The trend is furthered politically by both superpowers, who in their intercontinental and regional confrontations must on the one hand seek to cultivate new allies and to accommodate and placate old ones and on the other hand try to destabilize the opposing coalition by promotion of rivalries, disaffection, and defection. Because it still constitutes a formidable military presence, Western Europe is a prime target in these respects for Moscow, which dangles before publics in that region the promise of permanent peace in return for defection from the North Atlantic alliance. A first step would be for Western Europe to accept the concept of a European nuclear-free zone. Japan is being similarly tempted. But among America's allies and many uncommitted states neither Soviet diplomacy nor propaganda seem able to overcome distrust of Soviet power and wide-spread distaste for the Soviet system.

But as we have seen in Part Three some rifts cannot be prevented, all Soviet overtures cannot be turned back. Ironically it has been the nuclear umbrella held over them by the United States which has enabled some of the U.S. allies and some neutrals to assume diplomatic postures in opposition to Washington. While remaining militarily committed, France opted out of NATO's integrated structure years ago. As U.S. economic power waned, the probability increased that some of the allies would step up their search for alternatives in conflict

411

situations between the superpowers *in which their own security was not directly threatened.*[1] If Moscow played its cards skillfully, such situations should increase in number in years to come.

Western Europe and to an extent Japan differ with Washington regarding the world strategic situation for several reasons: 1) Western Europeans and Japanese view Russian history and Soviet behavior and foreign policy differently than do most Americans; both claim to know Russians better and both generally subscribe to a less doctrinaire, less apocalyptic view of East-West relations.[2] 2) European and Japanese leaders and intellectuals tend to be less inclined than U.S. leaders to ascribe most of the world's troubles to machinations by Moscow or to communist conspiracies. 3) Militarily the U.S. is more distant from the Soviet Union than are either Western Europe or Japan. 4) Whereas U.S. military performance during World War Two was most impressive, the unsuccessful campaign in Vietnam and other military misadventures reduced allied confidence in American leadership, perhaps even in American military prowess and reliability as a military partner.* Political democracies all, the allies now had to respond to mounting criticism of U.S. foreign policy conduct and objectives within their own countries. 5) Now fully recovered, first France then the remaining allies began to see in the relative decline of the United States an opportunity to reassert their independence. 6) Unlike the Soviet Union, the United States is not inclined to discipline its allies by economic or

Table 19-1. The Changing Economic Position of the United States (1955–1980)

Country or Group	Share in World Population		Share in World GNP		Per capita in Current Prices as % of US GNP		Per Capita in Constant 1980 US Dollars	
	1955	1980	1955	1980	1955	1980	1955	1980
United States	6.0	5.1	40.3	23.7	100	100	7,030	11,560
Japan	3.3	2.6	2.4	9.5	11.0	77.9	1,600	9,010
Europe, Industrial Market Economies	9.2	6.5	26.6	27.9	43.2	92.8	4,640	10,720
Industrial Non-Market Economies	12.4	10.7	8.6	12.4	10.4	25.0	940	2,880
All LDCs	68.1	73.6	20.7	21.5	4.5	6.4	340	730

SOURCE: World Bank, *World Development Report 1982*, p. 22.

* For example, the aborted attempt in 1980 to rescue U.S. diplomatic hostages in Iran and the failed attempt in 1984 to bring peace to Lebanon on U.S. terms by insertion of U.S. Marines.

military pressure. 7) The nuclear as well as the conventional balance has shifted sufficiently to raise doubts in Western Europe capitals, in Tokyo, and elsewhere in the "free world" that Soviet power can be contained by military pressure. A belief is therefore spreading in allied capitals that if arms control and limitation talks fail to make progress—and the U.S. nuclear pledge might be a bluff—Moscow may have to be "disarmed" by diplomatic means, by offers of advantageous economic deals for instance.[3]

A political source of NATO weakness if not its disintegration is conflict among the allies over financial resources to be allocated to mutual defense. Proximity to the Soviet Union should increase resistance to strategies likely to result in a nuclear exchange. One effective means of reducing that hazard would be build-up of conventional forces opposite those of the Warsaw Pact. However, as soon as that subject is broached seriously, finance ministers of Washington's European allies—like those of Japan—plead financial and manpower inadequacy.[4]

Despairing of "the Europeans," Henry Kissinger noted as early as the late 1950s that "[o]ur European allies . . . have made just enough of a defense effort to induce us to keep our forces on the [European] continent but not enought to constitute an effective barrier to Soviet aggression."[5] Viewed from Europe, as a high French official put it, now that U.S. power definitely was on the wane, "The United States used to represent protection from risk. Now it represents protection *and* risk—or, to many Europeans, just risk."[6] Still, there were voices urging caution. Paris may stubbornly demur on some U.S. recommendation, London or Bonn may equivocate, Tokyo may politely drag its feet, or the Canadians assert their independence from their neighbor by some foreign policy initiative. In the final analysis, when the nuclear chips are down none of the United States' allies is as yet prepared to embark on a wholly independent course, for the global power structure still is such that any substantial move away from one superpower inevitably conveys the impression of intent to move closer to its rival; in any case, no Western power seems willing to risk permanent embrace by the Russian bear.

Emerging Subnuclear Geostrategic Patterns

The Western Posture

For the United States it remains imperative to frustrate a presumed Soviet plan to remove United States military presence from Europe and the Middle and Far East. Should Moscow succeed in that design, Mackinder's thesis (discussed in Chapter 2) would be borne out: the Heartland, that is the Euro-Sino-Soviet core of Eurasia, could then be consolidated and transformed into a base to conquer first the "Inner," then most of the "Outer Marginal Cresent," leaving the United States in a militarily untenable position. To forestall this, the U.S. must maintain both nuclear and subnuclear military capabilities to protect its interests in at least four major theaters: 1) Western Europe, 2) the

Far East, mainly Japan and the Philippines, 3) the Middle East, mainly the Persian Gulf and adjacent North and East African regions, and of course 4) the Western Hemisphere.[7]

Strategically, status quo-oriented powers seem at a disadvantage, mainly because they are committed to holding actions, resisting change throughout a changing world. Moreover as Kissinger noted a quarter of a century ago their challengers, ever prepared to employ unorthodox methods, shrewdly spread their moves so as not to provoke a severe military reaction yet achieve, little by little or slice by slice, their ultimate objective. Theirs, in Kissinger's words, is a strategy of ambiguous challenge, of subtle acts of aggression which do not appear as such. Such acts, like the downing of an unarmed passenger plane, in the prenuclear era might have evoked swift retaliation; under the nuclear threat, even deliberate provocations are downgraded to "incidents," calling for sanctions perhaps or for protests but never for direct military action.*

But if the Western alliance holds, it still has options. It can, following more conciliatory European precepts, enter into peaceful competition with the Soviet Union and its allies while holding its own resolutely, if necessary by conventional military means. Or it can, in keeping with more assertive U.S. policy, oppose revolutionary pressure with aggressive counterrevolutionary force. Simultaneously, their own regular armed forces, and those of friendly powers whose interests coincide with those of the United States, Great Britain, France or Japan—however tenuous such identification might be—are to be supplemented by Special or Rapid Deployment Forces. Designed to reach shores distant from Western Europe or the United States in shortest possible time, with sufficient strength to counter Soviet moves or those of Soviet proxies, these forces are to protect vital interests including critical raw materials supplies, to secure military bases, to keep open strategic sea lanes, and to assure passage through critical maritime or naval choke points. Of increasing importance in these respects are the countries of the Third World.

Since World War Two, U.S. armed forces alone have been used for peacekeeping and related tasks in some 185 incidents or conflict situations in less developed countries.[8] As the reach of Soviet and allied forces expands, so must of course the scope of Western military responses. With expanding responsibilities the costs of containing Soviet pressure increase commensurately. In

* "Against an aggressor skilled in presenting ambiguous challenges," wrote Henry Kissinger, "there will occur endless wrangling over whether a specific challenge in fact constitutes aggression and about the measures to deal with it. If the aggression is explicitly less than all-out or if it is justified as the expression of a "legitimate" grievance, at least some of the members of an alliance will be tempted to evade the problem by denying the reality of the threat. They will prefer to "wait and see," until the aggressor has "demonstrated" he is intent on world domination, and he will not have demonstrated it until the balance of power is already overturned." (1958), p. 207; see also Luttwak (1983), pp. 89–107, especially 109, who does not rule out surprise Soviet seizure of such strategically marginal areas as Northern Turkey, Northern Norway, Baluchistan, or Northern China; alternatively, Asiatic "Finlands" may be created, Iran for instance, or additional client states could be secured in the Middle East.

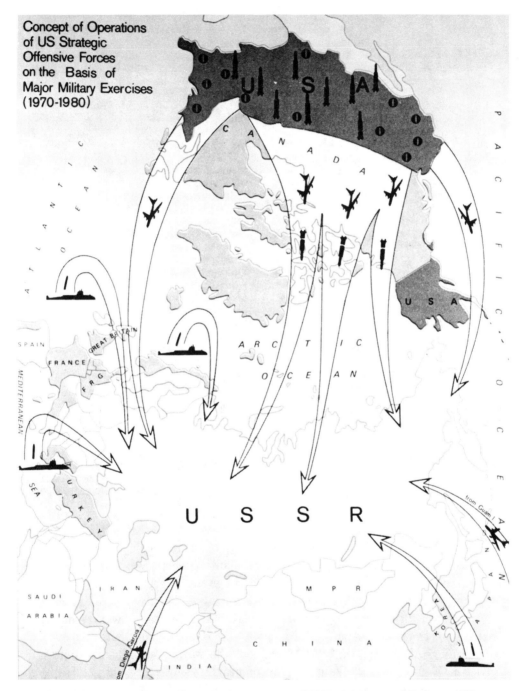

Fig. 19-1a. Map: Soviet Strategic Perceptions. (USSR, Ministry of Defense, *Whence The Threat To Peace?*, Moscow: 1982, p. 61.)

1983 the United States was paying with military and other aid packages—a form of rent—for the privilege of defending a wide arc of allies and friendly

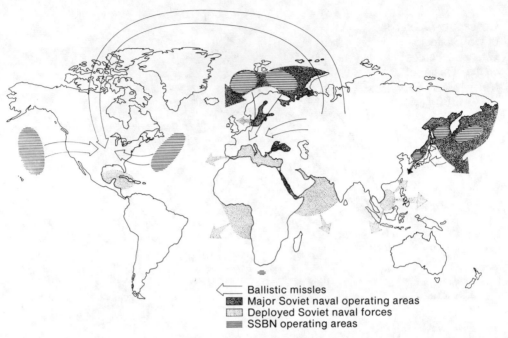

Ballistic missles
█ Major Soviet naval operating areas
░ Deployed Soviet naval forces
▬ SSBN operating areas

Fig. 19-1b. Map: U.S. Strategic Perceptions. (U.S. Department of Defense, *Soviet Military Power*, 1984, pp. 114–115.)

nations from 359 military bases located in Central America, Western and Southeastern Europe, North Africa, the Middle East, the Indian Ocean, the Far East, and the Western Pacific.

The strategic tasks confronting the U.S. armed forces, at the subnuclear level, are best illustrated by a summary of tasks assigned to the U.S. Navy. The ever expanding range of U.S. defense obligations predictably stretches resources of the U.S. Navy dangerously thin. Neither hardware nor personnel, especially of the technologically more highly skilled variety, nor effective battle groups can possibly be kept up to full strength as flash points multiply around the globe. Although probably still the world's best navy, mounting obligations threaten to create dangerous security gaps which substantially improved and expanded Soviet naval and air arms could exploit in the event of war.

Among a steadily lengthening list of lesser tasks, U.S. naval strategy calls for support of diverse land operations in a European theater of war, escorting convoys of troop and supply ships across the North and South Atlantic, safeguarding other vital sea lanes throughout the world, generally bottling up Soviet naval forces at "choke points" in or near Soviet waters and preventing closing of similar bottlenecks of strategic value to the West.*

---

* On Soviet naval strategy, see Barnet (1977), p. 123, and DOD (1984), pp. 61ff.

Among "choke points" of greatest strategic importance to the Soviet Union are the Bosporus and the Dardanelles in the eastern Mediterranean, the passage of Gibraltar at the western end, the narrows near Denmark and Norway through which units of the Soviet Baltic Fleet would have to travel to reach the North Atlantic, and outlets for the

To compensate for thinness, U.S. ships are being equipped with more sophisticated weapons. For example, by the 1990s about 60 battle cruisers are to be available for shore bombardment among other missions, each equipped with a total of 188 nonnuclear but exceedingly potent missiles. One of the vessels alone is expected to be able to disrupt a Soviet bloc advance in Central Europe. (Armed with nuclear warheads, two could obviate controversial deployment of nuclear weapons on European soil.) Similarly, because the Soviet navy seems designed to wear down the U.S. Navy by attrition, that is, to attack and sink it ship by ship, U.S. antisubmarine (ASW), especially electronic tracking capabilities are being substantially modernized and strengthened on land, at sea, in the air, and in space.*

It was in the wake of the Iranian revolution and the Afghanistan invasion, as a possible response to Soviet forces striking toward the Persian Gulf, that U.S. strategy began to consider "geographic escalation." Traditional doctrine called for engagement of the enemy where he attacked.† Under the changed concept, Western though still mainly U.S. forces would retaliate where Soviet forces were most vulnerable, not where they were strongest. Thus a response to a Soviet move toward the Arab oil fields could be directed against a Soviet ally or proxy, Ethiopia for example, or Cuba.

ally or proxy, Ethiopia for example, or Cuba.

U.S. conventional plans for the five-year period beginning in 1984 called for defense of the United States, including its vital interests in the Western Hemisphere, Western Europe, the oil resources of the Middle East, and only last, positions in the Western Pacific. Regarding the latter, Japan was to assume increased military responsibility not only for its own defense but for a widening arc in that region.[9] "Carefully measured" military assistance was to be given to the PRC to tie down Soviet forces along the extended Soviet-Chinese border. Special operations, including guerilla, sabotage, and psychological warfare units were to be upgraded, and pressure was to be increased on the Soviet economy to reduce its capacity to sustain the Soviet Union's presumed expansion plan.

Pacific Fleet from the Sea of Japan. See Cockburn (1983), pp. 253-254 and Garrity (1982). To protect North Atlantic sea lanes, U.S. and allied naval units, supported by air arms, will have to guard especially the Greenland-Iceland-Great Britain gap. Strategic narrows of special interest to the Western allies are Gibraltar, the Suez Canal, gateway to the Indian Ocean, the straits of Malacca along the shores of Southeast Asia, the Strait of Hormuz through which much of the industrial world's oil supplies are transported, and the Cape of Good Hope at the southern tip of the African continent, around which much of the world's commercial and naval traffic flows; see Fig. 19-1b.

* U.S. naval thinking attributes to the Soviet Navy a "sea denial" instead of a "sea controlling" strategy, a relatively limited mission requiring fewer outlays, the main purpose of which is to deny Western naval forces sea lanes and approaches from which the Soviet homeland could be threatened. Barnet (1977), p. 121.

† As noted in chapter 17 in 1984, this doctrine was revived when NATO began to consider responding to a Warsaw Pact attack in central Europe by "deep strikes" into Eastern Europe designed to prevent enemy reinforcements (follow-on forces) from reaching front lines.

*The Soviet Posture**

According to U.S. Defense Department analysis, Moscow's diplomatic and military subnuclear strategy appears to rest to a considerable extent on "the coercive leverage inherent in powerful nuclear forces, to induce paralysis [of will] and disarray in the free societies."[10] Contemporary Leninist perception of the changing strategic scene appears to arrive at an identical position:

> With the present world balance of power, superiority in armaments, and, particularly, the nuclear power of the United States and other countries, has practically lost its importance as an instrument of resolving local conflicts. Local anti-imperialist forces (the national liberation movement and the young national states), relying on socialist support, can successfully fight against both unstable puppet regimes and the American forces operating on land thousands of miles away from the United States.[11]

If "local antiimperialist forces" are in position to contest U.S. influence and that of other countries, it is because of a steady flow of arms, ammunition, equipment, and advisors from all Soviet bloc countries, a development we shall examine shortly under the heading Arms Transfer and Proliferation. The expanded Soviet navy backs that effort, lending effective moral as well as material support not only to client states and "liberation" movements far from the United States but now also at the very doorstep of the U.S. in the Western Hemisphere.[12]

The primary mission of Soviet armed forces is of course defense of the homeland and of client states Moscow regards as vital to that purpose, principally the states of Eastern Europe, Afghanistan, and the puppet state of Outer Mongolia. Beyond that, at a minimum, the combined Soviet forces are designed to support a future land war in Asia, mainly to deal with Communist China and "eliminate the United States' capability to conduct or support warfare beyond its own shores."[13]

More specifically, in the Western Theater of Operations the main goal is to weaken the North Atlantic alliance to the point where it either ceases to be a serious threat to Soviet defensive interests or an obstacle to westward expansion, should that become a serious strategic objective. To that end Soviet armed forces are assigned specific missions in the event of war, the Navy for instance the safeguarding of the previously mentioned strategic points of entry to or egress from the Baltic, the North Atlantic, and the Mediterranean. A primary naval and airforce mission will be to interdict movement of troops and supply from the United States to western and southern Europe. In the

---

* Concerning Moscow's basic strategic posture, Henry Kissinger's assessment is probably very close to the mark: "I believe that the Soviet Union . . . tends to believe very strongly in what they call the correlation of forces. If the correlation is favorable to them, then they must exploit it, and they do not even consider that an aggressive action; they consider that ratification of reality. Similarly if the correlation of forces is unfavorable to them, they must adjust to that, . . . they don't consider that a defeat; they consider that a tactical move." *Firing Line*, William F. Buckley, host, # 523 (July 15, 1982); see also Committee on the Present Danger [see above] (1984), pp. 1–4.

Southern Theater of Operations (the Northern Tier in the Middle East and South Asia), encompassing Turkey, Syria, Iraq, Iran, Afghanistan, and Pakistan, the overall diplomatic objective is to dislodge Western influence and replace it with Soviet power. The primary mission of Soviet strategic forces in Central and Southeast Asia is to counter the rising threat of Communist China and either compel withdrawal of U.S. military forces from the Asian continent and vicinity, from the Philippines for instance, or render them ineffective. Soviet nuclear forces are poised to neutralize the PRC's manpower advantage and back up Soviet conventional action should that become necessary. Another objective is to safeguard Soviet interests vis-à-vis a remilitarized Japan and possibly support North Korean plans to reunify the Korean peninsula under communist control. As a minimal objective, Soviet strategy is to ensure that the West recognizes the Soviet Union as a full-fledged world power. Toward that end alone Moscow is prepared steadily to increase military pressure wherever and whenever opportunities present themselves. Most certainly, Moscow expects to be accepted as an equal partner in discussions and negotiations involving countries situated along or near its borders.

One direct consequence of the apparent nuclear stalemate and the resultant diffusion of power is the creation of opportunities for militarily relatively weak or even inconsequential lesser states outside the respective major power blocs to pursue their own national interests in open defiance of either superpower or both, e.g. Iraq, Iran, Syria or Albania. Earlier examples were Ghana, Egypt, or Somalia, all of which abruptly expelled Soviet personnel and armed forces. Others are holding the U.S. up for ransom.

Arms Transfers and Proliferation

Who Transfers Arms, Who Proliferates?

To an extent, the outbreak of the First World War is said to have been expedited by the so-called "merchants of death," private arms dealers with powerful connections to Europe's and America's ruling circles and general staffs, who were said to have set out deliberately to sell ever more lethal arms to opposing camps to promote war to increase their profits.[14] Private trade in arms cannot be stopped. It may well be expanding with distinctly unsettling side effects; some fear that unless reduced in volume and slowed down, it may move the world closer to anarchy. But in the main, international transfer of large quantities of arms or of major weapon systems is today government business. Most likely, the occasional secret sale through private channels of large quantities of arms, equipment, or weapon systems, is conducted with full knowledge and consent of some government somewhere.

Governments have become active participants, some even prime movers, in what widely is regarded as a disreputable traffic, for several reasons: 1) In centrally planned and controlled economies, governments have of course always monopolized all production, military and civilian. Now, as noted in Chapter 2,

Table 19-2a. The Leading Major-Weapon Exporting Countries: Values and Respective Share (1979–1983). (Figures are SIPRI trend indicator values, as expressed in US $ million, at constant (1975) prices; shares in percentages. Figures may not add up to totals due to rounding.)

Country	1979	1980	1981	1982	1983	1979–83	Per Cent of total exports to Third World, 1979–83
USSR	6,921	6,486	4,962	4,736	4,070	27,174	
%	46.1	42.4	33.8	32.7	30.3	37.2	69.1
USA	3,901	5,512	5,519	5,704	5,264	25,900	
%	26.0	36.0	37.6	39.3	39.1	35.5	50.3
France	1,633	1,194	1,292	1,227	1,192	6,539	
%	10.9	7.8	8.8	8.5	8.9	9.0	79.3
UK	446	515	601	743	527	2,831	
%	3.0	3.4	4.1	5.1	3.9	9.0	77.3
Italy	483	377	526	579	458	2,424	
%	3.2	2.5	3.6	4.0	3.4	3.3	93.3
FR Germany	469	295	403	284	750	2,201	
%	3.1	1.9	2.7	2.0	5.6	3.0	55.4
Third World	349	271	396	438	332	1,785	
%	2.3	1.8	2.7	3.0	2.5	2.4	97.3
Others	810	660	989	792	856	4,106	
%	5.4	4.3	6.7	5.5	6.4	5.6	65.4
Total	15,011	15,310	14,688	14,503	13,449	72,960	

By permission, SIPRI *Yearbook 1984*, Table 7.1, p. 177.

rising costs of the vast quantities of mass destruction which twentieth-century warfare requires, and the high costs especially of ever more complex and sophisticated weapons, call for funding only government can procure, even in free enterprise economies. 2) For these reasons and as a corollary of sovereignty and national independence, as well as in the interest of national security, all governments routinely claim the right to license and control not only all military arms production but also all exports, the latter partly because certain types of modern weapons are too potent to be made available for universal and uncontrolled distribution.

Traditional sources of conventional arms have been the United States, the Soviet Union, Canada, the West European countries including perpetually neutral Switzerland and Sweden, Czechoslovakia, and Japan. Among new arrivals are Argentina, Brazil, Egypt, India, Israel, North and South Korea, Pakistan, Singapore, the Republic of South Africa, Taiwan, and Yugoslavia; Brazil and Israel are the leaders in that group.[15] By early 1985 possessing nuclear weapons

Table 19-2b. The 20 Leading Third World Major-Weapon Importing Countries[a] (1979–83)

Importing Country	Percentage of Total Third World Imports	Importing Country	Percentage of Total Third World Imports
1. Syria	11.8	11. Algeria	2.2
2. Libya	9.2	12. Morocco	2.2
3. Iraq	8.9	13. Viet Nam	2.0
4. Egypt	7.7	14. Korea, South	1.8
5. Saudi Arabia	7.0	15. Peru	1.8
6. India	5.5	16. Taiwan	1.8
7. Israel	4.7	17. Indonesia	1.7
8. Cuba	2.8	18. Jordan	1.5
9. Argentina	2.8	19. Pakistan	1.3
10. Yemen, South	2.2	20. Kuwait	1.2
		Others	19.9
		Total	100.0
		Total Value	$47,097 million

By permission, SIPRI *Yearbook 1984*, Table 7.2, p. 180.
[a] Percentages are based on SIPRI trend indicator values, as expressed in U.S. $ million, at constant (1975) prices.

Box 19-1. The Arms Tangle

Random arms transfers produce anomalies as illustrated in the Falkland (Malvinas) war of 1982. Argentina attacked the British-held islands with the aid of British-supplied aircraft carriers, a cruiser acquired from the U.S., two British destroyers, six from the U.S., corvettes sold by France, submarines from West Germany and the U.S., British Canberras, U.S. Boeing 707s, and French Mirage and Israeli planes. Several British ships were sunk or seriously damaged by French-produced Exocet missiles launched from French Super Etendard planes, both sold either directly or indirectly to Argentina by Britain's age-old ally and NATO partner, France.

---

technology and capable of exporting it if they were so inclined, were the two superpowers, Great Britain, France, the PRC, and India.

Policy Objectives

Most widely cited objectives are acquisition of *influence and leverage, security and stability,* and *economic benefits.* Andrew J. Pierre found that all reasons and explanations commonly offered to justify transfers fall short of being wholly persuasive. Indications are that arms transfers neither confer upon the supplier enduring influence or leverage, nor lasting security or permanent stability. Most are in any case of questionable economic value to both providers and recipients, if all aspects of production, sale, and use are taken into account.

Foreign political influence and leverage. A U.S. Senate report notes that because of the political symbolism stemming from close supplier–client arms relationship, "it is not clear who really has influence over whom in time of an ambiguous crisis situation."[16] It seems that generous arms contributions enabled neither the Soviet Union nor the United States to gain significant influence over clients' foreign policy in each and every instance. For example, Syria and Libya on the one hand, and Israel on the other, appear on occasion to have pursued foreign policy objectives in conflict with Moscow and Washington respectively. Massive contributions by the Soviet Union to the armed strength of Egypt and Somalia in the 1960s and early 1970s did not deter the two beneficiaries from expelling Soviet personnel unceremoniously when that seemed to be in their interest. In the late 1970s the Iranian revolution abruptly denied the United States the benefits expected from multibillion dollars arms deals with the late Shah's regime; Turkey and Greece, both major U.S. arms recipients, turn down from time to time Washington's foreign policy suggestions, and Israel, while presenting Washington with large arms requests each year, has compromised the U.S. time and again by its recalcitrance in Middle East peace negotiations.

Arms transfers are known to have followed in the wake of sudden shifts of allegiance, in Indonesia for example when Soviet and Communist Chinese influence was rejected by a strongly anticommunist regime, and in Egypt and Somalia when the latter two found Moscow unwilling to increase its transfers and support certain ambitious foreign policy objectives. In both instances the U.S. promptly moved into the breach. Moscow opened its arsenal of surplus weapons with alacrity to South Yemen and Ethiopia when revolutions there terminated pro-Western regimes. Or, arms are conveyed to induce a change of allegiance. France has asserted that its refusal to go along with U.S. arms embargoes against Libya contributed to a lessening of Soviet influence over Colonel Quadhafi. Similar arguments were advanced by France in defense of transfers of nuclear facilities and sophisticated weapons to Iraq, once a firm Soviet client and sworn enemy of Israel, the ally of the United States.*

The proliferation of states politically unstable, military weak, and economically deficient has precipitated international competition for dominance within these states. One way to gain a foothold under such conditions is to arm one faction, sometimes more than one. The need for replacement of weapons, spare parts, supplies including ammunition, and training does the rest. In some instances, transfers to militarily vulnerable LDCs can justifiably be regarded as bolstering their ability to resist outside aggression. In numerous cases such an explanation lacks credibility; if attacked, these states simply will not be able to use the arms received to good advantage. More likely the real purpose in such cases is to prop up an unpopular regime against internal opposition or to bring down a regime that is popular but independent-minded to make room for a more

---

* During the Iraq-Iran War (1980–) the U.S. joined the Soviet Union in supplying Iraq with arms.

compliant one.* A long-standing rationale for U.S. military aid in Latin America has been retention of the loyalty of powerful military factions for U.S foreign policy purposes.

There also is leverage in reverse, the buyer influencing the seller. Able to award extraordinarily lucrative arms contracts and pay in advance all or part of the costs of related research and development, Saudi Arabia has as of late granted and denied arms deals to the United States, France, and other Western suppliers on political and military-strategic grounds. Thus a $4 billion anti-aircraft missile system was developed in France with Saudi funds, then bought by the Saudis, with the understanding that no other country including France would use the technology without Saudi approval, a stipulation clearly directed at Israel, another potential customer of France. Specifically, Saudi Arabia and other oil exporters in the region use arms contracts routinely to pressure all Western powers to reconsider or modify their support of Israel. In addition these countries deliberately diversify their sources of arms supply to free themselves from undue dependence on the United States. As competition for arms deals with oil-rich Arab states increases, so will opportunities for the latter to extract foreign policy concessions.

Security and stability: Some arms transfers are genuinely intended to enhance recipient's national security or stabilize a potentially explosive political situation. Cuba has been converted into a giant Soviet arms depot mainly to steel it against U.S. invasion; another purpose, of course, as noted earlier, is to provide the hardware to enable it to function as a proxy in trouble spots throughout the world where Soviet military presence is inexpedient.

The United States has long regarded arms supply to a wide range of allies and otherwise friendly countries along the entire periphery of Soviet influence as integrally related to its own security. Both Moscow and Washington trade arms for military bases.[17] It is conceivable that the comprehensive capabilities of modern defense systems tend to act as equalizers within regions, thus reducing rather than exacerbating tensions. But, on balance, it is most doubtful that any substantial arms transfer contributes to military security anywhere; one state's concept of military adequacy or sufficiency will sooner or later be viewed by another state as a security threat. Indeed, many a regional arms race has its origins in one or more states' sense of insecurity, followed by contributions of arms and equipment from outside. The Middle East, of course, is a prime example.

Economic gain. The share of arms exports of total exports of the leading Western arms suppliers shows for France and Great Britain between 2 and 4 percent and for the United States from 4 to 5 percent. Low as these figures

---

* We noted earlier that Cuba, the East German Democratic Republic (DDR), and North Korea have apparently been assigned the internal security function under the Soviet bloc's arms export program. These Soviet allies provide newly established revolutionary regimes with entire internal security systems complete with weapons, secret police training programs, and regime bodyguards, as well as secure sophisticated internal communication systems.

may appear to be, they are significant.[18] A measure of what is at stake is indicated by the fact that between 1979 and 1983 the value of arms exports by the largest major weapon exporting countries was nearly $73 billion, at constant 1975 prices. To those who argue that arms sales are immoral, should be curbed for humanitarian reasons, and generally threaten world peace, defenders offer an impressive list of economic rationales. Arms sales, it is said, improve the balance of trade by earning foreign exchange, provide employment in the country of origin, and create economies of scale, thereby reducing per unit costs of arms which the country of origin requires for its own defense.* In that connection, the need for weapon modernization, an absolute in this age, inevitably creates surpluses; if disposed of at high enough prices these can help amortize the cost of the next generation of weapons.[19] Arms exports also are said to be "a way of spreading out, or recouping, some of the arms research and development expenses."†

If the stress is not on economic gains, then it is on cost. The West European NATO partners consistently cite, as one of the reasons for their aggressive arms export drives, their obligation to maintain for common defense ever more expensive armed forces. Or a 40 percent reduction in U.S. weapon exports is said to result in a minimum 2 percent depreciation of the American dollar, which among other adverse consequences would in turn raise the costs of imports such as oil.‡ In that connection, all oil-importing countries, less developed as well as developed, in response to the 1973–1974 oil price increase rushed to recover the added cost of energy by selling for cash or bartering for oil as many arms as the traffic would bear. Then there is the opportunity cost. British, West German, and U.S. exporters and their respective defense establishments can point to instance after instance when their refusal to provide arms for a potential customer, to make a diplomatic point or spare an ally's feelings, did not deter some competitor, most likely France, from promptly filling the rejected order.#

* According to the U.S. Department of Labor, every billion dollars in arms exports support 50,000 jobs directly or indirectly. Also the need for labor and staff, including research and development departments, to be retained between phase-out of one weapon system and commencement of production of the next one, provides yet another incentive for export of systems in the production line. The *German Tribune,* No. 964 (November 9, 1980), p. 7. Similarly, arming the soldiers of poorer nations may be cheaper. "A U.S. soldier in Egypt . . . would cost [U.S. taxpayers] $150,000 a year, while an Egyptian soldier costs $2,100 a year." *SIPRI Yearbook 1982,* p. 180.

† Pierre (1982), p. 24. That expense is shifted increasingly to the buyers. In 1984, it was reported that Saudi Arabia had financed development of an antiaircraft missile defense system, which it then purchased from France at a cost of more than $4 million. *The Wall Street Journal* (January 27, 1984). It is said that to cover the production costs of Kfir jet planes, militarily overburdened and financially strapped Israel must export about 25 percent of them.

‡ Pierre (1982), p. 27. An $8.5 billion deal with Saudi Arabia, involving sophisticated tracking and observation planes (the AWACs), helped reduce the U.S. trade balance in the early 1980s.

The defense was used by West Germany, when Israel demanded cancellation of a lucrative West German–Saudi Arabian deal in 1984 on the grounds that Germany, responsible for the anti-Jewish holocaust of the 1940s, still had to atone for that crime against the Jewish people.

Many of the economic arguments in favor of arms exports are questioned by critics or are refuted by statistics. For example, regarding its own contention that arms sales generate employment, the U.S. Department of Labor also found that in 1975, "[U.S.   ] arms exports accounted for only 0.3 percent of national employment."[20] With progressive automation, that figure is likely to decrease. While arms sales do earn foreign exchange, concomitant cost of raw material imports deplete that reservoir. Always looming in the background is the cost of yet another war.

Some financially unstable or otherwise hard-pressed LDCs have entered arms production and arms sales in the hope that this will bring relief, not only from the high cost of energy, but for the economy generally. They expect to save precious foreign exchange by reducing dependence on outside suppliers, improve the technical proficiency and training of their own industrial workers, and create financial as well as technical incentives for their engineering graduates to pursue careers at home instead of abroad.*

Whatever the rationale for arms exports by the industrial countries, because their national security is firmly believed to depend on the viability and readiness of the arms industry, representatives of that sector weigh more heavily in the contest for government attention than do most other competing interests. Moreover, as national treasuries, aid and assistance agencies, defense industries labor unions, and the banks, become progressively more involved in international arms transfers, it becomes ever more difficult to determine whether a given transaction reflects a country's political, military, or financial foreign or domestic policy.

The Transfer Format

Official arms transfer may take the form of sale, donation, lend-lease, or storage on the receiving nation's soil under the donor's continuing control and supervision; or arms and equipment are introduced, then left behind for local use, in conjunction with training programs for the receiving state's armed forces. Package deals are negotiated exchanging weapons for goods, natural resources, military bases, or pledges of mutual assistance in the event of war. Both the Soviet Union and the United States, while their respective allies were still recovering from World War Two, provided substantial arms, training facilities, and equipment either free of charge or on low interest-bearing loan. As economic pressure mounted and allies as well as certain LDCs now could afford to pay, the U.S. phased out its more generous and comprehensive Mutual Assistance Program (MAP) in favor of a Foreign Military Sales Program (FMS). Eventually, in need of hard currency to support its own military efforts, the Soviet Union also shifted the emphasis to sales. Donation of course is less altruistic than it

---

* Several LDCs have progressed "from buying, to assembling, to producing, to selling." Some are known to buy only limited quantities of new arms wherever they can copy these, then mass-produce their own version for profit. U.S. Department of State (1980), "Arms Coproduction," p. 2.

seems. In the Third World, where there is no shortage of conflict situations, if some weapons are transferred free of charge tensions will rise soon enough in the area to induce receiving governments to acquire additional supplies through purchase, now to defend themselves against neighbors who consider themselves threatened and who therefore also purchase arms. Or, as is typical in the poorer LDCs, sales follow donation as the underequipped military develop an appetite for more.

As Western Europe acquired a capacity not only to produce but also export arms in competition with its original benefactor, the United States, the latter was compelled to choose between alternatives: either engage in cutthroat competition with close allies, endangering NATO in the process, or expand existing military integration to encompass industry and finance as well. The result was a shift to *coproduction.* Such cooperation commended itself especially to an alliance of 15 different armed forces whose combat effectiveness depended in part on familiarity with weapons they were expected to use and on interchangeability of ammunition, fuel, and spare parts. Thus, to satisfy the requirement of weapon *rationalization, standardization,* and *interoperability* (RSI), arms transfer among the allies now also involved transfer of funds, resources, and know-how.* The Soviet Union could meet the RSI requirement either by simply insisting that all Warsaw Pact members use only weapons produced in the Soviet Union or that weapons produced by allies meet Moscow's specifications.

Regional Nuclear Threat Proliferation†

The Threat. Some 31 countries, many of them embroiled in long-standing regional disputes, are expected to be able to produce nuclear weapons by the year 2000. It is not inconceivable that several of these, if hard pressed, may actually make use of nuclear arms.‡ In any case, the inability of the superpowers to come to terms, and of producers of surplus nuclear energy to eschew high profits associated with that trade, threaten a gradual erosion of existing controls

---

* U.S. Department of State (1980); arms coproduction was one answer to U.S. demands for greater defense outlays by NATO partners. Great Britain and France in particular argued that one way to entice them to increase their contribution to the common defense was to shift more arms contracts, in whole or in part, to their industries. Examples of joint production were the British, Italian, West German Tornado all-weather "multirole" combat aircraft, a British-West German-French fighter plane, the TFK-90, several multinationally-built and-financed helicopters, the F-16 fighter plane built in the U.S. but assembled in Belgium and the Netherlands, the Anglo-American Harrier "jump jet," and the West German-U.S.-Belgian M-1 tank.

† A distinction must be drawn between horizontal and vertical proliferation; the former reflects an increase in the number of states with nuclear weapons, the latter growth of weapon stockpiles now held by nuclear powers.

‡ Relevant is the following word of caution: "A nuclear explosive is not necessarily useable as a weapon. To perform a military as well as diplomatic role, a nuclear explosive device must be designed and constructed so that potential users will have confidence in its performance, and mated to a means for delivery to a potential target appropriate to its predicated role." J.J. King (1979), p. 1.

to prevent spread of the nuclear threat to regions as yet unaffected. Already there are signs of incipient nuclear arms races among lesser powers. For example, when Brazil noted that Argentina was striving to acquire nuclear know-how, it became nervous, joined Argentina and Cuba in refusing to sign the 1967 Tlatelolco Treaty to establish a nuclear-free zone in South America, and proceeded to cast about for the requisite technology. Today, with the help of Italy and West Germany, possibly also from communist countries, both Argentina and Brazil, whether their governments intend this or not, are nearing the nuclear threshold.

If Pakistan and India do not produce the first peripheral nuclear confrontation, the Middle East may. Probably already capable of producing nuclear weapons, and ready to proceed as soon as one of its Arab neighbors does, Israel may eventually see no alternative to reliance on a nuclear deterrent. It may do so because it exists in a region where it soon may be overwhelmed by conventional military standards, yet where none of its more virulent enemies are likely to acquire a penetration-proof antimissile defense system, or, if they should acquire one, may be unable to operate it effectively. (Saudi Arabia, recipient of the French defense system, is not likely to participate directly in an attack on Israel.)

At least one Israeli strategic specialist finds in the nuclear option the answer to Israel's defensive needs: "The punishment involved in nuclear retaliation," he speculates, "makes it very likely that the Arabs would recognize the extent

Table 19-3. Prospects of Nuclear Proliferation (1984)

Believed to have acquired or to be developing nuclear weapon capability, though not necessarily proceeding to production:

Argentina	Israel
Brazil	Libya (in cooperation with another Islamic state)
Chile	Pakistan
Egypt	South Africa
India	Korea, Republic of
Indonesia	Taiwan
Iran	

Also capable of acquiring a nuclear arsenal, should they be so inclined:

Australia	Japan
Austria	Netherlands
Belgium	Norway
Canada	Spain
Denmark	Sweden
Finland	Switzerland
Greece	Thailand
Iraq	Turkey
Italy	Yugoslavia

Based on SIPRI, *Nuclear Energy and Weapon Proliferation.* (London: Taylor and Francis, 1979), p. 387 and King (1979), pp. 11–12.

to which this punishment removes any challenge to Israel's survival from the range of alternatives open to them."[21] Should Israel be provoked to defend its existence with nuclear weapons, in most states involved "three to five targets encompass all their hopes for a better future. Almost everything that enables them to participate in the twentieth-century marketplace is concentrated in those few targets: their entire business, technical, industrial, intellectual, military and political elites reside there."[22] The rationale then is that, thus threatened, the Arab elites will cease exerting pressure on their governments to seek Israel's destruction.[23]

Threat Containment.* Although we encountered aspects of this problem earlier, it is useful to summarize at this point international efforts to contain the threat of nuclear proliferation. In 1946, the memory of Hiroshima and Nagasaki still fresh, it seemed eminently sensible to place nuclear energy under international control and thus head off a universal nuclear race. A substantial number of states stood ready to accept a concrete proposal to that effect, advanced by Bernard Baruch of the United States (the Baruch Plan). Unfortunately, as is the case with all disarmament and arms control proposals, unless the leading powers without exception are genuinely committed to abide by them even the best laid plains will be stillborn. The Baruch Plan was to create a United Nations Atomic Development Authority empowered to administer and enforce requisite controls, allocate benefits of nuclear production equitably among all nations, and, most importantly, terminate all nuclear arms production then and there; it ended up on the same burial ground as did the arms control and disarmament proposals and treaties which were to have prevented World War Two. This may well have been the first and last opportunity to direct nuclear power exclusively and securely into peaceful channels, for neither the UN's International Atomic Energy Agency (IAEA) founded in 1957, nor the Nuclear Non-Proliferation Treaty (NPT) of 1970, nor any other less formal undertaking has so far managed to accomplish that feat.†

Several factors and developments have contributed to this potentially tragic failure: 1) Always a bar to progress in such matters is preoccupation with national security. With the entry of the Soviet Union into nuclear competition in 1949, nothing could prevent other fearful nations capable of entering the race from following suit. Accordingly Great Britain joined "the club" in 1952, followed by France in 1960, and the People's Republic of China in 1964. Eventually, the growing list of other nations, mentioned earlier, joined for identical reasons. 2) Production of nuclear energy as well as weapons turned

---

* For an optimistic assessment of this problem, see Kenneth N. Waltz, "The Spread of Nuclear Weapons: More May Be Better," *Adelphi Papers*, No. 171 (Autumn 1981), who proposes that "the slow spread of nuclear weapons will promote peace and reinforce international stability," p. 28. See also Freedman (Recommended Readings), p. 316.

† The IAEA was to "accelerate and enlarge the contribution of atomic energy to peace, health, and prosperity throughout the world," and to ensure that such assistance "is not used in such a way as to further any military purposes." Banks *et al.*, *The Political Handbook of the World, 1981*, p. 664.

out to be less costly and technically less formidable than had been thought at first, enabling less well-endowed and less developed states to cross the nuclear production threshold. 3) Anticipated or actual shortages of mineral fuels or in some cases their total lack, coupled with the theoretical certainty that all of the known nonrenewable sources of energy will some day be exhausted, created an additional spur for conversion to nuclear energy production: when the price of oil quadrupled between 1973 and 1974, conversion to nuclear power acquired special urgency. 4) As noted earlier, the Western powers, fearful of being overwhelmed by Soviet bloc conventional forces in Europe in 1964, introduced the Multilateral Nuclear Force (MNF) concept, which Moscow viewed as a provocation, partly because under that plan West Germany appeared to become once again a threat to the Soviet Union—armed with nuclear weapons, far more menacing than ever. 5) Acquisition of large-scale, multiple nuclear production facilities by the leading industrial nations, for commercial as well as military reasons, spawned a separate competition among them, and on their part against newcomers, to sell nuclear technology, including complete facilities, on the world market to the highest bidder. 6) Engaged in high-stake commercial competition, some governments suspect that restrictions imposed by international agreement, but at Washington's initiative, may be designed to accrue to the advantage of their U.S. competitors in nuclear and related fields.[24] 7) As exemplified by Israel, failure to achieve general, universal, and comprehensive disarmament motivates states not able to field conventional forces, adequate to protect their borders, to look to nuclear weapons as an attainable substitute.[25]

Prospects of bringing this phase of the universal arms race under control diminished sharply in the early 1980s. Whereas in 1966 nuclear reactors for generation of electric power were in operation in only five countries, it was estimated that "by 1985 more than 300 nuclear power reactors would be operating, under construction, or on order," in a substantially larger number of states. By that time, "the quantity of plutonium being produced would make possible the construction of 15 to 20 nuclear bombs daily, depending upon the level of technology employed."[26]

To be sure, not all signs were negative. By 1981, 115 nations had ratified the Non-Proliferation Treaty, including all major industrial states with the exception of the nonsignatories among states already producing weapons, that is France, the PRC, Israel, South Africa, and India.[27] Also, as of 1982 no nuclear weapons had been transferred by NPT signatories who possessed such arms and "no non-nuclear weapon state party to the Treaty [had] acquired or manufactured a nuclear explosive device."[28] Moreover, the IAEA had developed sophisticated safeguards and monitoring capabilities to ensure that "nonnuclear materials located in non-nuclear weapon states party to the Treaty are used solely for nonexplosive purposes."[29] But again, soon evidence was received that these precautions also were in danger of being circumvented on a potentially massive scale.

The sheer volume of nuclear energy produced by the United States, coupled with its high motivation as a status quo power to contain the spread of nuclear arms, has assigned to Washington a leading role in this campaign. The Soviet Union appears to take a similar position. Both powers seem to be mindful of the obligations assumed under the NPT. In addition, both have stakes in the prevention of transfer of nuclear arms to nations which for one or another reason could trigger a nuclear exchange involving them as well. Committed to regard nonproliferation as "a fundamental national security and foreign policy objective," the United States continued to abide by the terms of the NPT, the Treaty of Tlateloco (the 1967 Treaty for the Prohibition of Nuclear Weapons in Latin America), and the purposes and objectives of the IAEA. Under that policy, Washington seeks to coordinate exports by the major producers, to persuade states not yet party to one or another international pact to accede, and generally to work to reduce tensions in all regions where nuclear weapons already are available or are in process of being produced. Ominously, in 1983 U.S. intelligence reports indicated that one or more states might be able to circumvent the constraints imposed upon them by external suppliers such as the U.S., West Germany, Switzerland, or Canada by developing their own nuclear fuel cycle capable of producing bomb-grade material in plants not subject to international safeguards.[30]

Suggested Questions and Discussion Topics

Why, and on what specific grounds, do some allies differ with U.S. assessment of the East-West military strategic situation? What are some of the practical consequences of such disagreements?

Outline the emerging "Subnuclear Strategic Patterns."

Why are arms transferred from nation to nation? What form do such transfers take? What is the likely impact of such transfers on world peace?

What has been the experience with attempts to contain nuclear proliferation? Should nuclear proliferation be contained? What militates against its containment?

Epilogue
Preventing World War Three and Beyond

> War is a relation not between man and
> man, but between state and state, and
> individuals are enemies only accidentally,
> not as citizens but as soldiers.
>
> Rousseau. *Social Contract*

The full extent of what a nuclear war will do to this planet may be in doubt. There may be room for argument whether those scientists are correct who predict that in addition to megadeaths and megadestruction the world will also be subjected to devastating ecological disaster or whether, as the optimists contend, following some setbacks the environment will shortly return to normal. Realistically, prospects are not good that the world we know will survive an unrestricted nuclear exchange.[1]

We noted earlier that the United States and the Soviet Union possess at least the destructive power of 800,000 to 1 million Hiroshima bombs and that in World War Two all of the weapons used by all sides are said to have had 3-4 megatons of destructive capability.[2] By 1985 the two superpowers are believed to dispose of combined equivalent nuclear megatonnage of more than 13,000. Today both powers are capable of detonating the World War II explosive tonnage every hour for 200 hours. A single U.S. missile, the Titan II, is believed to have a greater explosive power than all weapons used by all sides in World War II, and the U.S. can destroy one third of the Soviet people and three-fourth of Soviet industrial capacity ten times over. In a simulated attack on Boston, USA, a city of 2,875,000 people, 1 million were killed outright, but of doctors needed to administer aid to the survivors only 10 percent remained alive. On that basis, if each doctor spent 10 minutes with each patient, the first patient would be seen again in 12 to 14 days, assumed that the doctor worked 20 hours per day, this without blood, without x-ray, without diagnostic equipment, and without communication; and in all areas affected, the pathological and the criminal elements would be at large.[3] Even if some of these estimates should prove somewhat exaggerated, it may well be, as a Soviet leader once predicted, that following a nuclear war the living may envy the dead. Modern conventional wars of mass destruction have been called slaughter. It is difficult to find a term doing justice to what a nuclear war will do to human beings.[4]

431

What is to be Done?

Short-Term Measures

Needed: nuclear realism. To their credit, most contemporary political leaders appear to be convinced that a nuclear war should never be fought and, if fought, cannot be won. But, considering what now is in store, that is not sufficient. In addition to being vaguely appraised of quantitative losses incurred in a nuclear exchange, today's leaders need to be realistically briefed and conditioned to comprehend the full human, social, and political consequences should the weapons they command be used.[5] In past wars, to ensure clarity of military thought and professional detachment, supreme military and civilian leaders were screened off from the gore and horror of the battlefield; it also was considered essential for national survival if the stark realities of war remained concealed from public view. Today, the magnitude of nuclear destruction demands a radically different approach. Past practice of covering up hundreds of thousands of dead and maimed with a blanket of euphemisms or statistical abstractions was bad enough. Any attempt to obscure the probability of tens or hundreds of millions of fatalities by subterfuge should be rejected. The question must be asked *exactly what* do public officials have in mind when they speak of "acceptable damage" or the need "to prevail" in a nuclear war.[6] People are entitled to ask: acceptable to whom, precisely who is expected to prevail in what kind of a world and to what purpose?

Although as we have shown it is by no means certain, we must assume that humans and not electronic controls make ultimate nuclear decisions. Assuming further that no monster, no absolute madman, can attain, let alone maintain, a position of power in Moscow or Washington, we still are left with extremely fragile links in the nuclear decision chain. Irrationality in high places can never be ruled out; too many world leaders are known to have become detached from reality, and the human capacity to suppress unpleasant, embarrassing or vexatious subject matter is too well established.[7] Can the world be assured that sane and responsible leaders will not, at the moment of decision, either banish from their minds concrete thoughts about the human consequences of the nuclear war they are about to trigger or cease to think about the event in terms acceptable to them and their next of kin? In that connection, it is understandable that nuclear powers are compelled to provide for the personal safety of their principal decision-makers and commanders-in-chief. The integrity of C^3I must be maintained. But that concern now must urgently be balanced by the need to discourage leaders from lightly embarking upon the holocaust because they themselves may be able to escape the physical consequences of their act.

Bowing to reality. Whatever one may think of their merit, prudence demands that the perceived vital military and political security interests of *both* superpowers be understood, appreciated, and respected. As we have seen, it may be too late on the nuclear clock to expect either power to abandon or substantially reduce its nuclear arsenal. No formula for reduction of tensions will be adopted if it fails to take into account internal political, economic, and military pressures and political dynamics in either the U.S. or the Soviet Union. By all appearances, both powers have the capacity and the determination to attempt to prevail in a future conflict, even if they themselves and the world at large should be the losers.

To many Westerners, communism is a bankrupt and evil ideology and the Soviet brand a thoroughly undesirable manifestation. Committed communists view the West in identical terms. What if the more pessimistic assessment of the Soviet system, its leaders, and of the Soviet threat to our way of life turns out to be well founded? According to that view, an ever more insecure and ideologically bankrupt regime—though still bent on promoting world revolution—has convinced itself that only the U.S. stands in the path of communism's ultimate triumph or of their own regime security. Now militarily at least the equal of the United States, therefore no longer in need to placate foreign communist parties for political insurance against capitalist attack, Moscow can afford to proceed from a primarily defensive posture to offense against U.S. and allied interests throughout the world. What should be the West's response?[8] It would seem that, considering the consequences of failure, there may realistically be no alternative to a rapprochement between the two camps. But that calls for an extraordinary degree of tact and circumspection. Certainly, diplomatic civility must replace hostile and offensive rhetoric, especially among the leaders.[9] It should be possible to apply to that purpose the concepts and rules utilized in ordinary conflict resolution.[10] Among other things, facts need to be established to dispel myths; for instance, the Soviet Union may actually not be a monolith. To be avoided under all circumstances are attacks on the negotiating partners' personal integrity, national pride, or self-esteem. Each side must endeavor to genuinely understand the fears and apprehensions of the other. Once serious and constructive dialogue becomes possible, discussion focuses first on issues which seem readily resolvable, then proceeds to more difficult negotiations; following success at the negotiable end of the issues spectrum, previously intractable problems tend to become manageable.

Both Washington and Moscow have for some time explored common or overlapping interests. Since Stalin's death, Soviet and allied Communist leaders have made considerable progress in giving their political systems a more human face. They have demonstrated a willingness to proceed quite far along that road, provided their political systems and their national security are not threatened. This could of course be deceptive, but the world can ill afford not to explore these prospects and possibilities more earnestly than has been the case so far. For instance, although in practice Soviet policies in the Third World appear to be diametrically opposed to those of the United States, there is a common denominator: a commitment to aid the world's poor. In addition, there are the mounting threats to the planetary environment, from causes other than nuclear explosions and the wasting of the world's resources through arms competition or aimless industrialization. In addition there are the myriads of tasks arising from steadily advancing global economic interdependence, a development Soviet leaders once thought their system could escape but which they now realize is inescapable.

Militarily, if the nuclear weapons competition is not halted, there soon will be no area on earth which does not directly impinge on the perceived security of either superpower. A slow-down or reversal of the rivalry should clear the way first for establishment of limited nuclear-free zones, then for their extension. Initially, highest priority should be accorded areas of vital mutual security concern: eastern and central Europe, southwest Asia and the Middle East, the Far East, and Central America and the Caribbean. This should be possible if it is recognized that, aside from their mutual deterrence value, nuclear weapons serve no military purpose whatsoever. Because in their deterrence strategy both superpowers are inclined to regard outer space as essential, permanent denuclearization of that region will prove more difficult. Nevertheless, once it is recognized that should nuclear and postnuclear weapons be allowed to be deployed in outer space no nation will be secure, agreement may be possible in this respect as well. Beyond that, neither Moscow nor Washington should expect tensions to be reduced if proposals for arms reduction or limitation cut to the core of the opponent's basic military or political security concerns: if, for example, the United States offers a formula which would in effect require a major restructuring of Soviet armed forces, or the Soviet Union proposes to deprive the U.S. of a weapon category regarded by U.S. military leaders as a most highly prized security guaranty.

Finally, if the United Nations is to survive and perform its function as the peacekeeper of the world, its structure and procedures must be revised to reflect more accurately the distribution of economic and military power in the world. Within the UN and outside, given the current configuration of forces in the world, only cooperation between the two superpowers can create conditions permitting the myriads of local and regional conflicts now proliferating throughout the world to be contained.

Long-Term Measures

"Rid the world of the scourge of war." The list is long of prescriptions on how to avoid war and what might be its causes. We cited some in our previous discussion. But nothing can improve on the steps outlined in the Preamble to the UN Charter:

> . . . to reaffirm faith in fundamental human rights, in the dignity and worth of the human person, in the equal rights of men and women and of nations large and small, and to establish conditions under which justice and respect for the obligations arising from treaties and other sources of international law can be maintained, and to promote social progress and better standards of life in larger freedom, and for these ends to practice tolerance and live together in peace with one another as good neighbors, and to unite our strength to maintain international peace and security, and to ensure, by the acceptance of the principles and the institution of methods, that armed force shall not be used, save in the common interest, and to

employ international machinery for the promotion of the economic and social advancement of all peoples. . . .

Towards a planetary perspective. The world has undergone decisive changes since 1917 when the socialist-capitalist confrontation first assumed international dimensions. It certainly has changed since Karl Marx wrote *Das Kapital* and Adam Smith his *Wealth of Nations.* Under the circumstances, aggressive advocacy of either Western or opposing socialist prescriptions may prove as detrimental to world peace as aggressive insistence always did if the aim was to defend the status quo. While the majority of the people of the world still lack the military strength to enforce their will, they increasingly find ever more troublesome ways and means to make their frustration known. What in the West is termed terrorism and in the East national liberation is one form of that expression. Already challenged are the superpowers' claims to a right to consume the world's resources in self-centered but universally destructive pursuits, for their own national self-preservation, to maintain high standards of living, for private profit, or to perpetuate ideologically rigid and archaic oligarchies.[11] In short, drastically new ideas and certainly new perspectives are required to manage a world vastly different from that which sparked the American, French, or Russian Revolutions.

A planetary perspective eschews stereotyped images of people and their leaders and casts aside the acrimony, the distortions, and the misrepresentations with which centuries of human conflict have encrusted fundamental human aspirations. Most dangerous among these encrustations are unrestrained ethnocentrism, nationalism, racism, and religious or ideological fanaticism. An example of what is needed is George F. Kennan's advice to Americans. Alarmed over the widening chasm between the United States and the Soviet Union and in particular over the American tendency to demonize Soviet leaders and the people of the Soviet Union generally, Kennan urged his countrymen to recognize that there is "another great people, one of the world's greatest, in all its complexity and variety, embracing the good with the bad—a people whose life, whose views, whose habits, whose fears and aspirations, are the products, just as ours are the products, not of any inherent inequity but of the relentless discipline of history, tradition, and national experience."[12] A planetary perspective extends the wisdom contained in that advice to all peoples on earth without exception.

Focus on human values. A millenium of preoccupation with the nation-state, usually personified by more or less humane leaders, has created an illusion which always had its perils but which in the nuclear age escalate peril to assured disaster. It is the illusion that the state accurately reflects the sumtotal of the aspirations of the individuals within. From that have followed several propositions. One being that it is humanity's overriding purpose in peace and war to serve a state's interests and only those. But something happens to human aspirations in the process of conversion into foreign and military policy; as history has demonstrated again and again "the national interest" may but does not necessarily serve the best interest of the individuals who make up the nation.

The consequences of ignoring or downplaying the primacy of the human factor were tragic enough prior to the nuclear explosion over Hiroshima. Toward the end of his life, Adolf Hitler was prepared to let the entire German nation perish along with him as punishment for its failure to win the war he started.[13] Fortunately, in his day the destruction of a culture would have required the cooperation of an undoubtedly unwilling multitude of administrators and soldiers. Not so today. In the past, raising national and international politics and especially war to high levels of abstraction made it easier for rulers so inclined to engage with impunity in ill-conceived and murderous adventures resulting in millions of deaths and maimings and in property losses too vast to be assessed. Emphasizing state over people enables diplomats and war-games strategists to pretend that they are engaged in games of chess, the figures on the board representing not humans but inanimate legal, political, and military pawns. For identical reasons military and strategic technologists speak and think of systems, targets, or objectives.

The emergence of participatory democracy made it mandatory in the past to couch international power contests, including wars, in terms acceptable to "the public" and their representatives. Wars now were said not to serve the interests of monarchs but "the people's will;" of course, rarely if ever did the people have a choice between war and peace. Given the infinitely higher price humanity may have to pay in the event of another major war, the time has come for human values to be accorded their rightful place. This will not be easy, for the practice, if not the habit, of concealing the human element beneath layers of social myths and euphemisms is deeply rooted in our past.

Since the beginning of recorded history humans have been described in terms designed to obscure their universal, in all essential respects identical, human characteristics. They have been labeled tribes, peoples, races, or nationalities or were classified as members of religious, ethnic, or language groups. With the emergence of the modern nation-state, sometimes genuinely for its defense, sometimes for less honorable purposes, notions of universal human commonality have been disparaged and frequently suppressed. In its place, insistence on "blood," "racial," or national identity and similar abstractions has been at times zealously, in many instances brutally, enforced.

At the same time, while such secondary human characteristics as speech, mode of reasoning, culture, attitudes, and so forth have undergone significant change since our species began to walk upright, innate traits such as killing fellow humans as a mode of conflict resolution have not yet been shed. Humans still remain capable of murdering or torturing each other without much thought. But war, torture, and murder are unpleasant—and they raise questions of legality. Hence, in this respect also euphemisms are employed to justify the deed. Wars of mass destruction and aggression are fought only for "noble" or even "sacred" causes; genocide, lesser massacres of innocents, and torture are said to be committed not against humans but against hateful objects such as

Box 20-1. Partial List of Politically Motivated Mass Killings by
Governments[a]

Country	Period	Estimated Total
Afghanistan	1978–1980s	thousands
Argentina	1976–1978	6,000–7,000
Burundi	May–June 1972	50,000
CAE[b]	1979	50–100 school children
Chile	1973–1979	thousands
China (PRC)	1966–1977	1,000,000
East Timor	1975–	hundreds
El Salvador	1979–1980s	6,000–22,000
Ethiopia	1974–1978	thousands
Guatemala	1966–1980s	tens of thousands
Guinea	1969–1976	2,900
India	1960s–1970s	hundreds
Indonesia	1965–1966	500,000–1,000,000
Iran	1982–1984	more than 4,500
Kampuchea	1975–1979	300,000–1,000,000
Korea, Rep. of	1980–	1,000 or more
Syria	1980–1982	more than 10,000
Uganda	1971–1979	100,000
	1979–1985	50,000–100,000

Estimates from Amnesty International, *Political Killings by Governments*
(New York: 1983) and *New York Times* (1984–85).
[a] Killings of civilian non-combatants deliberately illegally ordered or encouraged by government authority; war or civil war casualties not included.
[b] Central African Empire, now Central African Republic.

"traitors," "threats to national security," "subversives" and now "terrorists."
Typically, to enable forces of military aggression, as well as executioners,
torturers, and death squads to proceed against fellow humans, the victims are
first rendered impersonal. They are not depicted as feeling, thinking human
beings entitled to compassion and empathy but as "vermin," "excrement," or
"kooks." To facilitate conquest, subjugation, even extermination of the Soviet
people, Nazi German propaganda termed them *Untermenschen* (subhumans).
It was easier to exterminate "bolshevists" than Russians, or, in another theater
of the same war, "Japs" could be exposed to the ravages of nuclear explosion
more readily than Japanese. In their once frequent wars, the French and Germans
devised similar means to obscure the fact that both are members of the human
race; the French were taught to call the Germans *"boches"* (swine) and German
children were encouraged to think of their fellow Europeans as degenerate,
depraved, unmanly species deserving to be conquered and subdued. Today, one
speaks of communists to obscure their actual ethnic origin, "imperialists" make
more acceptable targets than Americans, and it is easier to incite masses to
fight "satan" than United States Marines. What is at work here is a process

of conversion. One converts real, live human beings into abstractions with attributes conveniently designed to facilitate first hate, then extermination. In the quotations cited at the outset of this chapter, Rousseau was mistaken. Organized violence by humans against humans is never an accident. It always is a matter of design.

Now cities crowded with wholly innocent men, women, and children are transformed into "targets" to be programmed into missile guidance systems, to be "taken out" in a nuclear "strike." It would seem that little has changed since Genghis Khan ordered the sacking of towns and the massacre of entire populations, without considering the individual tragedies and the suffering resulting from such deeds. Today, we are still incapable of feeling precisely what tragedies ensue with the death by starvation of tens of thousands in a place called Ethiopia or what really happens to the human body and soul when thousands of humans perish in Iran, Uganda, or Sudan, or a million Cambodians, Moslems, or Chinese are murdered by rampaging mobs or by uniformed thugs dispatched by ruthless ideologues or power hungry and frightened dictators, or when several thousand members of a religious minority are bludgeoned to death in India. We *learn* that torture led to the death of thousands in Argentina, that sons and daughters are murdered in front of their parents in Lebanon, but do we *understand*? Do we really care what the father feels who finds his son's mutilated body lying in the gutter in El Salvador?

We can assess in detail the human consequences of an event which we are able to observe directly, within our immediate environment. With distance and large numbers, the inclination and the ability to appreciate fully what is involved decreases, until at the level of entire nations, regions, or continents only the vaguest, grossest, most inaccurate and sterile impressions will be formed. Thus, at the height of persecution of the Jews in Nazi Germany, every German is said to have known at least one "good Jew," typically the Jew or Jewish family within their immediate circle of acquaintance. But to the multitude, abstractly, Jews in general were not worth saving from the Holocaust. In a nuclear war, the technician servicing the missile destined to erase a Soviet or American city will probably make a conscious effort to wipe from his memory the image of friendly Americans or Russians he may have known.

We are inclined to worship "national security" as a good, losing sight of the now distinct possibility that an all-out nuclear war, perhaps even a conventional war fought with weapons of greater-than-ever destructive power, will release on earth forces which humanity has sought to contain since the beginning of time. We seek to achieve "collective security" in order to contain and punish aggression, not expending much thought on the fact that among the states made "secure" are many whose leaders do not shrink from torturing, maiming, and murdering their own subjects at will. The same applies to sovereignty. Posited as an unqualified "good," the right to sovereign independence is defended all too often, if necessary by force of arms, not to protect citizens from danger to life and limb, but to exploit or harass them beyond the limits of endurance or to prevent them from escaping a tyrant, a corrupt dictatorial regime, or a greedy, corrupt, and dissolute ruling class.

To be sure, governments invoke and enforce national security, collective security, and sovereign independence also for unquestionably humanitarian purposes. But overall the rules of international conduct have all too frequently been invoked not to protect the individual but to maintain political, social, military and economic systems not worth maintaining if *human* values and interests were genuinely at issue. It would seem that the time has come to protect the individual from the dubious protection by the state.

Human Rights: shield of civilization. The cause of human rights has progressed considerably since the American and French Revolutions, two events purporting to center on "the rights of man." No society which has abolished slavery has reintroduced it and few have gone the way George Orwell envisaged in his *1984.** Before 1945, vast segments of humanity were excluded from consideration in matters of human rights. Now at least in principle no people are exempt. On the opposite side of the ledger, slavery survives in some parts of the world and humanity has yet to rid itself of genocide, of government-induced or encouraged massacre of social, religious, racial, or political minorities, of brutal elimination of political opponents, and of gruesome and barbaric torture, and millions of human beings still are not assured enjoyment of the most fundamental attributes of human dignity.[14] Now the ultimate indignity faces all or most of humanity: megadeath, megadestruction in a nuclear war, followed by desolation and extinction of human civilization as we know it.

If the overall human rights record seems discouraging, this has not been for want of trying. Since 1926, twelve separate international accords on that subject have been signed. The United Nations has elevated the cause of human rights to central importance in its declared commitment to reduce conflict and human suffering. In addition, numerous private and semipublic organizations have sprung up to augment that effort.† Most promising, in Western Europe under certain conditions human rights take precedence over the rights of states.[15]

Among other obstacles to progress in this regard are the contrived though substantial differences in cultural and religious value systems within individual states and in the world at large, the well-known ideological juxtapositions, all exacerbated by spreading social, economic, and military insecurity. A powerful incentive to resist concessions in this respect stems from the insecurity of regimes established and maintained by force. To insecure and frightened regimes or ruling classes, the cause of human rights will always be anathema.

From the Western perspective, human rights are said to fall into two major categories:

---

* Contemporary North Korea and Albania appear to come close; so did the People's Republic of China during the "Cultural Revolution," 1966-1977.

† Foremost, Amnesty International and the International Commission of Jurists; see Forsythe (1983), pp. 62-70, and Jacobson (1984), pp. 313-315.

Box 20-2. Selected International Human Rights Agreements

Slavery Convention of September 25, 1926

Inter-American Convention on the Granting of Political Rights to Women of May 2, 1948

Convention on the Prevention and Punishment of the Crime of Genocide of December 9, 1948

Geneva Convention Relative to the Protection of Civilian Persons in Time of War of August 12, 1949

Geneva Convention Relative to the Treatment of Prisoners of War of August 13, 1949

European Convention for the Protection of Human Rights and Fundamental Freedoms of November 4, 1950

Convention on the Political Rights of Women of March 31, 1953

Supplementary Convention on the Abolition of Slavery, the Slave Trade, and Institutions and Practices Similar to Slavery of September 7, 1956

International Convenant on Civil and Political Rights of December 16, 1966

International Covenant on Economic, Social and Cultural Rights of December 16, 1966

Protocol Relating to the Status of Refugees of January 31, 1967

American Convention on Human Rights of November 22, 1969

SOURCE: U.S. Department of State, Bureau of Public Affairs, 1981. *Human Rights Report Bulletin* Reprint.

1. The right to be free from governmental violations of the integrity of the person—violations such as torture, cruel, inhuman or degrading treatment or punishment; denial of fair public trial; and invasion of the home;
2. The right to enjoy civil and political liberties, including freedom of speech, press, religion and assembly; the right to participate in government; the right to be free within and outside one's own country; the right to be free from discrimination based on race or sex.[16]

Doctrinaire communists and some independent socialists, committed to a radically different view of the role of the individual in state and society, and subscribing to different priorities generally, attach less value to rights cherished in Western political democracies; to them, far more important are such things as right to a fair share of the world's, or a country's, wealth, a right to meaningful employment, health care, education, and social security in old age. Theorists of social revolutionary systems such as the Soviet Union, while not oblivious to the concept, rank individual and collective human rights below those of the state "until the ultimate objectives of the revolution have been realized."[17]

Thus what may be regarded as an inalienable right in one country may be viewed as an offense against society in another; for example, granting women equal treatment under the law is viewed as a form of blasphemy by fundamentalist Moslems. Similarly, the rights to freedom of speech and free assembly, constitutionally guaranteed in Western democracies, are seen as openings to insurrection and dissolution of the state by totalitarian leaders. In less developed countries, where governments are always under pressure to provide for their citizens the most basic amenities, goods, and services, housing and employment, certain rights highly prized in economically better situated countries are regarded as luxuries the state can ill afford. In general, to persons who have no home and are starving, freedom of speech and assembly weigh far less heavily than food and a place to sleep.

Implementing disputed and ill-defined principles. Recognizing that sharp divisions among member-states would guarantee defeat of a comprehensive and binding human rights convention, the UN divided the entire complex into two separate covenants, one politically more sensitive, hence less likely to attract majority support than the other. The former confined itself to civil and political, the latter to economic, social, and cultural rights. Underlying that strategy was the hope that while the first set would most likely not be enforceable the second, conceivably less controversial, might be so at least in part. Several circumstances combined to frustrate both efforts.

Within the United Nations, the formation of ideologically opposed blocs quickly politicized the entire matter. Soon rhetoric triumphed over substance, *promotion* of human rights beyond one's borders took precedence over *protection* of these rights at home. Governments with poor records in this respect (and their number is growing) and in particular those engaged in terrorist, inhuman acts against their own population, displayed a tendency to take a "hands-off approach," even in the face of conclusive evidence of wholesale slaughter.[18] Generally, the majority, itself an expedient coalition of fundamentally opposed world views, measured human rights violations by a double standard; one nation or group would be judged "by the Sermon on the Mount and all other nations on [a] curve."[19]

Another illustration of how human rights should *not* be handled is the strategy pursued by the United States in the late 1970s when the issue was used as a battering ram against the Soviet Union. Whatever the political-strategic merits of the approach may have been, it does not require mastery of psychiatry to predict the consequences: it provoked the ire of an already paranoid regime which held in its hands all means necessary to safeguard its interests. More a scattershot approach than a carefully designed and measured set of proposals covering the entire spectrum of political, social, economic, and cultural rights, the strategy provided little room for concessions by a system where dissent is tantamount to treason. If the intent was to embarrass Soviet leaders—in a world where thousands can disappear without a trace, tens of thousands can be massacred, and millions subjected to disease and starvation—denial of free speech and incarceration of a relatively small number of political dissenters in the Soviet Union, though arousing a segment of elites in Western countries, will not greatly agitate public opinion in the world at large.*

Efforts by the U.S. and allies, under the 1975 *Helsinki Final Act,* to trade guarantees of East European–Soviet bloc security for a broad range of human rights concessions are commendable in principle. They are suspect if the same or similar demands were not also pressed with regard to the People's Republic of China during the devastating Cultural Revolution, or with regard to the Republic of South Africa, El Salvador, Nicaragua while it was virtually a U.S. protectorate, the Philippines, South Korea, or Chile.† Under those circumstances, Soviet bloc leaders are inclined to view the campaign not as a genuine effort to improve the status of human rights in their countries but as a stratagem to soften their ideological and sociopsychological defenses, merely another propaganda move by the "imperialists" to undo the achievements of the October Revolution.[20] By the same token, cynically selective human rights debates, votes, and resolutions, initiated by the Soviet bloc/Third World/Non-Aligned coaliton in the United Nations solely to embarrass the United States, encourage violations of human rights in countries protected by that process: members of that grouping have for decades depended on their coalition partners to keep accusations against them off the UN agenda.[21]

If first things are to be accomplished first, protection of truly basic and fundamental rights should take precedence over secondary considerations. Highest priority should be accorded protection of rights bearing directly on physical, physiological, and mental integrity of the individual. Conceived that narrowly, yet focussing on concerns every human being values most highly, the cause can attract universal, crosscultural, crossideological support. Neither arbitrary death nor torture are essential to the survival of state or society. As for other

---

* It should perhaps have been realized that totalitarian regimes, confident that they can effectively prevent genuine monitoring of compliance on their part, readily sign agreements guaranteeing human rights. They simply imprison the monitors. See U.S. Department of State, Semiannual Reports, Fifteenth Report (1983), pp. 6ff.

† See Forsythe (1983), Chapter Three. A major shortcoming of the 1975 Helsinki Final Act, the product of the Conference on Security and Cooperation in Europe (CSCE), 35 states signing the Act, was the inclusion of the entire spectrum of rights and claims on behalf of individuals and minorities within states as well as states themselves. The ten principles which were to "guide" relations among nations under the Act were: "sovereign equality [an escape clause, since it rules out any kind of outside intervention]; territorial integrity of states; peaceful settlement of disputes; nonintervention in the internal affairs [of states; another escape clause]; respect for human rights and fundamental freedoms, including the freedom of thought, conscience, religion, or belief; equal rights of and self-determination of peoples; cooperation among states; and fulfillment in good faith of obligations under international law." See U.S. Department of State, Bureau of Public Affairs, Semiannual Reports on the *Implementation of Helsinki Final Act,* Twelfth Report, p. 5. All of these objectives of course completely duplicated the principles already enshrined in the UN Charter. The Final Act made theoretically impossible what eventually did occur in Poland in 1981. See *ibid.,* Thirteenth Report and Fourteenth Report.

"rights" many are but claims, to be discussed discreetly if international tensions are to be reduced.

The State of the World: Finite or Expansive

Much of the human rights agitation and promotion in the West, and to an extent also in the East, reflects concerns mainly by the economically, socially, and physically secure. But in a world where 250 million people lack housing fit for human habitation, two billion have no access to sanitary water, 40,000 children are estimated to die each day for want of food, and untold millions of youths grow up without prospect of regular employment in their lifetime, the self-centered preoccupations of the world's rich and semirich pale into insignificance.[22] Under such conditions, more needs to be done, more urgently, if global chaos even anarchy are to be averted.

What of the thesis that the earth's resources are finite, that the "tragedy of the commons" must inevitably engulf the world? Is Lester Brown's *Twenty-Ninth Day* prognosis accurate, which predicts that the world population will in the not-too-distant future double in one single year, filling up this planet's available living space completely? Brown uses the analogy of the lily pond where lilies, having doubled in number steadily and inexorably, fill the pond eventually in only thirty days, after filling half the pond only one day before the last one. Is our planet analogous to a finite lily pond?[23] This is not the place to resolve the dispute between those who forecast irreversible ecological and other global disasters even without a nuclear war and those who see grounds for hope. In any case there are ample grounds for concern.[24]

Whether food production will or will not suffice to support exploding populations, whether finite resources will or will not sustain economic growth, if the West—especially the United States—feels committed to resist social and economic change by force and the East feels equally committed to promote it, World War Three is a near certainty. We have seen that in such a war the security interests of the superpowers cannot possibly be served. Neither will those of the rest of the community of nations. It would seem therefore that there is actually no alternative to East–West, especially Soviet–American, cooperation. First in the order of priorities should be the discarding in both camps of the ideological baggage accumulated from another age. Once that is done, the different social and economic approaches and systems can enter into truly peaceful competition, not to serve their own interests but to advance the interests of humankind. A conflict-ridden world will thereby not become entirely peaceful. But it may become more manageable.

By harnessing the computer, the atom, other as yet only imagined but attainable alternative sources of energy, expanding our resource base to include the ocean bed, as yet unexploited frozen wastes, the desert, and outer space, it should be possible to alter the message conveyed by limits-to-growth cassandras. But new frontiers, of which there are many, cannot be reached without new perspectives and new approaches. Privileged positions carved out by wars of conquest in past centuries cannot be perpetuated. To uncover hidden strength among the world's planners and thinkers, these human resources obviously must be freed from national and ideological restraints and constraints. Ours is an imperfect but the only world. It remains difficult to manage, but if it is to remain livable the old management, having performed so disastrously until now, must give way to new forms. To give concrete expression to that imperative must be the focus of the study of international relations from now on.

The Study of International Relations and World Peace

As stated in the Preface to this book, nothing, absolutely nothing is more important to this and the coming generation than to do all that can be done to prevent World War Three. It is appropriate therefore that an introduction to the study of international relations end with a brief assessment of the contributions it can make to world peace.

The study of international relations can be said to have as its overall objective creation of intellectual order in a progressively or even permanently disorderly if not chaotic world and to that end the development of theories, concepts, and explanations useful for statesmen, other practitioners of international relations, and the educated public throughout the world. Since its inception as a modern academic discipline, it has implicitly or explicitly addressed itself to the need for world peace or world order. Specifically, the study serves five purposes: 1) to identify, classify and delineate forces, factors, and patterns in international relations; 2) to analyze those, determining their cause and effect relationships and interaction; 3) to develop and present options and guidelines for policy-makers as well as for ordinary citizens who merely wish to be informed; 4) to develop formulae to solve specific problems and offer solutions to specific conflicts or conflict situations, 5) to predict probable developments and probable outcomes in international affairs. To that end or in the course of that work, theories, theorems, and methodologies are developed, refined, and—if proven to be unproductive or irrelevant—abandoned to be replaced by more promising intellectual and scientific tools.

Like all intellectual endeavors, but more so than in the natural and physical sciences, theory-building in international relations has tended to follow ascertainable, discoverable events rather than to lead or anticipate; and it has historically tended to focus more on the dramatically apparent than on obscure or hidden subject matter. Thus, with regard to modern international relations, the first notable focal points were the traumatic experiences of World War One and the post-World War One movement to outlaw war and raise international law to new heights; then the objective was to return to the relatively peaceful order which had lasted from 1815 to 1914. This phase understandably gave way to an even greater concern with the causes of the second global war and the politics surrounding its outbreak, its course, and its conclusion. Following that war, concern with war prevention was once again accorded highest priority, first because the Second World War was bloodier and more destructive than the first, then because nuclear power threatened yet another global catastrophe overshadowing all that went before. Other developments attracting special attention were the collapse of the great empires, emergence of former colonies to statehood and the attendant proliferation of independent states, economic interdependence, the arms race, and the steadily expanding threat of a nuclear holocaust.

The First World War, occurring toward the nadir of what became known as *Die Grosse Politik* (the politics among great powers), inspired diplomatic history, the study of records and official acts of statesmen whose countries had become involved in that international disaster and some of whom now were expected to prevent another.* After 1918 concern with war prevention spawned the idealist school, and the first modern arms race, at the time mainly restricted to naval power, gave rise to *geopolitics.* The phenomenon of one hundred years of relative peace inspired search for an explanation. This was found with the discovery that Great Britain had manipulated Europe's powers and entities in parts of Asia, to serve its ends by balancing one group of nations against others. This principle—the Balance of Power—then was raised to a theorem believed to govern relations between major and lesser powers generally. To an extent it did so. Failure of the idealist school between the wars to save the League of Nations, render more effective international law and collective security, and prevent the rise of fascism and militarism and their product, wanton and cynical military aggression, gave rise to the realist school, of which Hans J. Morgenthau remains to this day the most notable exponent.† That school was opposed in turn by another generation of idealists, this one motivated to make the United Nations, its agencies, and international organization generally, succeed where the League of Nations and the peace structure which it spawned had failed so dramatically. Not unrelated, the appearance on the Western world's intellectual horizon of the masses of Asia, Africa, and the southern regions of the Western Hemisphere directed the discipline at last to concern itself also with their needs and aspirations.

Enrichment of the social sciences through theoretical and methodological infusions and adaptations from the harder sciences enabled the study of international relations to link up with subject matters such as micropolitics, human behavior, decisions and policy-making, conflict and conflict resolution. This thrust seemed appropriate especially because concentration of great-power politics had manifestly failed to bring the discipline closer to its objectives. At

---

* Diplomatic history received a major boost with the release of previously secret archives by revolutionary regimes in Moscow and Berlin.

† For Morgenthau, the central issue to be addressed and the basis for his still definitive study was "the contest between two schools that differ fundamentally in their conception of the nature of man, society and politics. One believes that a rational and moral political order, derived from universally valid abstract principles, can be achieved here and now. . . . The other school believes that the world, imperfect as it is from the rational point of view, is the result of forces inherent in human nature. To improve the world one must work with those forces, not against them." This was the "realist" School. Morgenthau, p. 3.

the same time, technological mastery of complex systems outside the social and political universes, in physics mainly, suggested application of system or systemic theory to international relations. Successes with game theory in strategic planning and in some practical military respects during World War Two inspired recourse to gaming, eventually to simulation along with model-building.[25] Social psychology contributed such foci as group dynamics and interpersonal relations.

The break-up of the great empires, followed by the imposition on world politics and economics of demands generated by rising expectations in the former colonies, directed attention to problems of dependency and domination, development, and independence. Different political positions manifested by the new Third World leaders produced a change of emphasis from exclusively Western or North Atlantic to non-Western perspectives; eventually this encouraged, in the 1960s, non-Western area or regional studies, leading inevitably to fragmentation of whatever degree of global coherence decades of international and global studies had achieved.

Aided by improved methods and facilities for data collection the field proceeded to attack problems of war and peace and of want at yet different levels. It did so by concentrating on the more basic causes of human, hence national behavior, for example underdevelopment, maldistribution of the world's wealth, public opinion surveys, and the like. Improved statistical capacity and skill, coupled with greater awareness of cultures other than one's own, and generous funding, brought about crosscultural analysis of the relations among nations. Partly to emulate the hard sciences, partly because data accumulation, storage, retrieval, and analysis were now greatly facilitated, the field saw the rise of an entirely new breed of scholars, empirically and quantitatively inclined survey and computation specialists, applying their new tools to the entire range of international concerns, from great power politics, the causes of war, and voting in international organizations, to the physical quality of life.

When it became apparent that the world monetary system, laboriously constructed during and immediately following the Second World War, had begun to crumble, and evidence mounted that economic forces influence politics at least as much as politics influences economics, the field placed greater emphasis than ever before on the place of trade, aid, and finance in the affairs of nations. (Given the actual role of economics in national and international affairs since antiquity, it is remarkable how little emphasis on economic factors and forces can be found in some of the most seminal works of the interwar and immediate postwar periods, including studies of imperialism and related subjects so thoroughly permeated with economics.) With the collapse of Bretton Woods, the sharp increase in international trade, and international economic interdependence, political-economic thought began to replace pure or predominantly political analysis. This, in turn, drew special attention to the multinational corporations, some of whose assets exceeded those of an impressive number of nation-states, and whose "global reach" seemed to vie with that of some of the world's more powerful governments.

Worsening East-West relations, the Cold War, and the nuclear threat invited topics like bipolarity, security, the arms race and proliferation. Soon the "high frontier" of outer space beckoned and so did another dramatic development, international terrorism.

Throughout its life, the discipline has been subjected to the push and pull of idealists and realists, believers in a well-ordered world that could, given the correct attitude, be brought back from impending chaos and pessimists who saw only anarchy if force was not employed judiciously. There always were the firm believers in world order, morality, and world government as the sole alternatives to universal cataclysm and their antagonists, convinced that balance of power, wielded firmly, coupled with deft diplomacy could save the world from self-destruction.

To summarize this brief discourse on theory and practice: It has not been, nor is it now our intent to choose among the very large and steadily growing number of contending theories of international relations.[26] Considering the depth and breadth of our subject matter, diversity in theory and practice should be regarded as a virtue. As noted in the Preface, it was not the purpose of this volume to add to the discipline's theoretical foundations but to provide students of international relations with the raw material needed to gain a sense of direction and order in a seemingly disorderly world, a world seemingly hurtling to disaster. In the process, we have inevitably relied on some theories more than on others. If some important theories appear to have been underutilized or neglected, that does not necessarily signify lack of appreciation or disdain. The present writer, whose study and teaching career in international relations spans forty years, came to appreciate and use for profit even some outlandish theories. The same experience also imbued him with a sense of caution, seasoned with a dose of skepticism, not to accept or follow every new focus or fad. In general, every major theoretical construct and every methodological thrust has something of value to offer our discipline, and none can therefore be totally rejected. Relevance, or pertinence, of theory or method depends ultimately on the level of analysis selected.

The present author's career spans the transition from traditional diplomatic history, as a point of departure for international political analysis, to geopolitics, realism, behaviorism, and empiricism including analysis by computer. Along that road he inevitably encountered oddities. All approaches offer something of value, all fall short of the maximal claims advanced by their more enthusiastic proponents. Over the decades, he has learned that it is imprudent to ascribe too much order or subscribe to too much theoretical rigidity with respect to history, which Zbigniew Brzezinski (the practitioner, not the scholar) described as "neither the product of design nor of conspiracy but . . . rather the reflection of continuing chaos."[27]

Diplomatic historians in some respects quite superficially have drawn attention to a critical stage in the conduct of international relations, foreign policy. Idealists, less objective than they are prepared to concede, have prevented us from falling victim to cynical existentialism, to realism devoid of any moral or ethical content. Realists on the other hand have chosen to be quite selective, indeed somewhat arbitrary, in what they wanted the world to be realistic about. Still, that school produced works of enduring value, directing our attention to the hazards of incautious pursuit of high-sounding but pragmatically unsound and unproductive foreign policy objectives; realists labored to save us from attempting policy designs serving the enemies of peace more than its defenders. Idealists, of course, contended that realism not tempered by idealism is the surest road to war.

Behaviorists enabled us to look beyond the state, dissect government, and explore the anatomy of power to greater depth and in detail. In the process some of them opened the door to infinite regression, to total immersion in detail which may or may not have any bearing on what truly matters in international affairs. System theory, helpful in some respects, lent too much order, too much structure, too much mechanical regularity and predictability to the disorder which is the world of international affairs. It also can be faulted for covering up vast areas of pronounced uncertainty. Empiricism, as of late enhanced by quantification and computers, brought degrees of precision where blunt judgment had reigned, broadened the base upon which generalizations can be formulated, and rendered intelligible and manageable masses of data the existence of which could theretofore only be surmised, the significance of which could only be estimated; it drew attention to information which, for want of accessibility, had been totally ignored. But here too, errors of judgment and excessive zeal produced false leads and unwarranted expectations as well as claims. Among other problems, in order to compress vast arrays of data into quantifiable form, reality was adapted and at times grossly distorted. Boundaries between what is and what is not quantifiable, what can and what cannot be rigidly programmed into computers, were all too readily crossed; phenomena of substantially unequal character and weight were indiscriminately cast into seemingly precise mathematical molds. As a result injustice was done too often to variety, diversity, and the infinite potential of the human spirit for good and evil, for efficiency and inefficiency, for rationality and irrationality or madness. Some theories were developed not because hard data comprehensively and systematically gathered tended to support them but, the reverse, to find a home for truncated snippets of reality. Yet no one can deny that thanks to these pioneers we know more today about war and peace, conflict resolution, and economic development than would have been possible without their contributions.

Occasionally a concept is advertised as novel, a theory as revolutionary, which strike the seasoned student as quite familiar. To cite one example, the dependency theory appearing in the late 1960s (see our discussion of the viability gap) replicated in substance the well-known Marxist/Leninist and Schumpeterian theories of imperialism; the sudden concern with multinational corporations tended to gloss over the fact that large commercial and financial empires or concentration of power had, as theory of imperialism had amply demonstrated, influenced world politics for more than two centuries; or, with respect to another key concept: "The trouble with the balance of power," wrote Inis L. Claude, Jr., "is not that it has no meaning, but that it has too many meanings."[28] This, of course, can be said of many more concepts employed in international relations. In the final analysis, given the nature of our universe it would seem most prudent if a degree of intellectual flexibility and a sense of modesty were to be added to dedication in an endeavor now more than ever demanding our attention.

For the future, needed first of all is a sense of urgency. Whether one focuses on macro- or micropolitics, on aggregate or fragmentary social, political, economic, or military power, or on the mindset of a group of leaders in one country, does not matter as long as one realizes that time may be running out on intellectual pursuits related to the world as one would like it to be, not the world that is.

Suggested Questions and Discussion Topics

What short-term, what long-term measures might prevent World War Three?

What if any considerations, values, or interests, might justify a first-strike nuclear attack by either superpower against the other?

What is the place of human rights and aspirations in international politics, what should it be, and what are the reasons human rights and aspirations are generally not accorded in international politics the priority they deserve?

Why and how do human rights today more than ever relate to the question of war prevention?

How should the cause of human rights protection and promotion be approached to prevent regression to barbarism?

Identify the major approaches to the study of international relations discussed in the epilogue.

Suggested Readings for Part Four: Managing Military Power

On Nuclear War

Ground Zero. *Nuclear War. What's in it For You?* New York: Pocket Books, 1982.

Bracken, Paul. *Command and Control of Nuclear Forces.* New Haven: Yale University Press, 1983.

Katz, Arthur M. *Life After Nuclear War. The Economic and Social Impacts of Nuclear Attacks on the United States.* Cambridge, Mass.: Ballinger Publishing Company, 1982.

McNamara, Robert S., "The Military Role of Nuclear Weapons: Perceptions and Misperceptions," *Foreign Affairs* (Fall 1983), pp. 59-80.

Riordan, Michael, ed. *The Day After Midnight. The Effects of Nuclear War.* Palo Alto, Cal.: Cheshire Books, 1982.

U.S. Congress, House 98th, 1st (1983). Committee On Science And Technology. *The Consequences Of Nuclear War On The Global Environment.* Washington, D.C.: GPO, 1983.

Chapter 17

Barnet, Richard J. *The Giants. Russia and America.* New York: Simon and Schuster, 1977.

Cockburn, Andrew. *The Threat. Inside the Soviet Military Machine.* New York: Random House, 1983.

Fallows, James. *National Defense.* New York: Random House, 1981.

Freedman, Lawrence. *The Evolution of Nuclear Strategy.* New York: St. Martin's Press, 1981.

Green, Philip. *Deadly Logic: The Theory of Nuclear Deterrence.* New York: Schocken, 1968.

Holloway, David. *The Soviet Union and the Arms Race.* New Haven: Yale University Press, 1983.

Kaldor, Mary. *The Baroque Arsenal.* New York: Hill and Wang, 1981.

Kennan, George F. *The Nuclear Delusion. Soviet-American Relations in the Atomic Age.* New York: Pantheon, 1982.

Lebedev, N.I. *A New Stage in International Relations.* Oxford: Pergamon Press, 1978.

Luttwak, Edward N. *The Grand Strategy of the Soviet Union.* New York: St. Martin's Press, 1983.

Mandelbaum, Michael. *The Nuclear Revolution: International Politics Before and After Hiroshima.* New York: Cambridge University Press, 1981.

Wieseltier, Leon. *Nuclear War, Nuclear Peace.* New York: Holt, Rinehart and Winston, 1983.

Zuckerman, Solly. *Nuclear Illusion and Reality.* New York: The Viking Press, 1982.

Chapter 18

Allison, Graham T. *et al,* eds. *Hawks, Doves, And Owls. An Agenda For Avoiding Nuclear War.* New York: W.W. Norton, 1985.

Ford, Daniel, Kendall, Henry, Nadis, Steven. *Beyond The Freeze. The Road to Nuclear Sanity.* Boston: Beacon Press, 1982.

Drell, Sidney. *Facing the Threat of Nuclear Weapons.* Seattle: University of Washington Press, 1983.

U.S. Arms Control and Disarmament Agency. *Arms Control And Disarmament Agreements. Texts and Histories.* Washington, D.C.: USACDA, 1982.

Chapter 19

Lowenthal, Richard, "The Diffusion of Power and the Control of Force in a New International Order," *Adelphi Papers,* No. 134 (Spring 1977), pp. 9–16.

Luttwak, Edward N., *Grand Strategy of the Soviet Union,* 1983.

Pierre, Andrew. *The Global Politics of Arms Sales.* Princeton, N.J.: Princeton University Press, 1982.

Stanley, John and Maurice Perton. *The International Trade in Arms.* London: Chatto and Windus, 1972.

Epilogue

Theory of International Relations

Bull, Hedley. *The Anarchical Society: A Study of Order in World Politics.* New York: Columbia University Press, 1977.

Butterfield, Herbert and Martin Wight. *Diplomatic Investigations. Essays In The Theory Of International Politics.* Cambridge, Mass.: Harvard University Press, 1966.

Claude, Inis L. *Power and International Relations.* New York: Random House, 1962.

Dougherty, James E. and Robert L. Pfaltzgraff, Jr. *Contending Theories of International Relations.* Philadelphia: Lippincott, 1971.

Garnett, John C. *Commonsense and the Theory of International Politics.* Albany, N.Y.: State University of New York Press, 1984.

Hoffman, Stanley H., ed. *Contemporary Theory in International Relations.* Englewood Cliffs, N.J.: Prentice-Hall, 1960.

Keohane, Robert O. and Joseph S. Nye. *Power and Independence. World Politics in Transition.* Boston: Little, Brown and Company, 1977.

Knorr, Klaus and James Rosenau, eds. *Contending Approaches to International Politics.* Princeton, N.J.: Princeton University Press, 1969.

Mitchell, C.R. *The Structure of International Conflict.* New York: St. Martin's Press, 1981.

Morgan, Patrick M. *Theories and Approaches to International Politics.* San Ramon, Cal.: Consensus Publishers, 1972.

Morgenthau, Hans J. *Politics Among Nations. The Struggle for Power and Peace.* Revised by Kenneth W. Thompson. Sixth Edition. New York: Knopf, 1985.

Thompson, Kenneth W. *Masters of International Thought. Major Twentieth Century Theorists and the World Crisis.* Baton Rouge: Louisiana State University Press, 1980.

Waltz, Kenneth N. *Theory of International Politics.* Reading, Mass.: Addison-Wesley Publishing Company, 1979.

Human Rights

Forsythe, David P. *Human Rights and World Politics.* Lincoln, Neb.: University of Nebraska Press, 1983.

Hoffman, Stanley. *Duties Beyond Borders. On the Limits and Possibilities of Ethical International Politics.* Syracuse: Syracuse University Press. 1981.

Jacobson, Harold K. *Networks of Interdependence.* New York: Knopf, 1984, Chapter 13.

Van Dyke, Vernon. *Human Rights. The United States and World Community.* New York: Oxford University Press, 1970.

Endnotes

Chapter 1. The Community of Nations

1. See Walker Connor (1972).
2. For different explanations, see Bull (1977) among others. Bull attributes whatever degree of world order prevails to such things as Balance of Power, common interests, or national and international institutions.

Chapter 2. Power And Its Sources

1. See Bretton (1972).
2. Kaiser, Robert G. (1976), pp. 301–302.
3. Spykman (1944), pp. 8–18.
4. Mackinder (1919); Spykman (1944); Gyorgy (1944).
5. Spykman, *op. cit.*, p. 55.
6. Gray (1977).
7. See Chapter 16.
8. The distinction is made by Knorr (1973), p. 78.
9. Thoughtprovoking attempts to cast complex economic, military, and other data into a framework for prediction were undertaken by Mesquita (1981) and Organski and Kugler (1980). Both seem to undervalue the role of economic forces. Milward (1977), pp. 21-22, analyzing aspects of World War Two, presents an interesting formulation expressing nations' "war potential," a formulation which can more broadly be applied to analysis of power generally: $x = p + r + s + e - f$, x representing war potential, p the national product in a peacetime year, r economic reserves, s savings realized from not maintaining the peacetime rate of capital replacement, e the volume of resources external to the economy which can be drawn on, and f the reduced efficiency caused by "administrative friction" due to war. From that premise alone, the U.S. should have appeared unbeatable to war planners in Hitler's Germany or in Japan.
   Germany, Japan, and Italy fare equally poorly if the second principle of war potential developed by Milward is applied: $W = x - c - i - d$ "where W is the second concept of war potential, c is the amount of civilian consumption which it is not necessary to forego, i is the amount of new investment for non-war purposes which it is not necessary to postpone, and d is the amount of disruption of the political and social systems which it is not necessary to suffer;" x of course is the first concept of war potential in that scheme.
   Mesquita's "expected utility-theory" encourages him to predict when and why nations may go to war. Milward's formulation, in the present writer's opinion, is

453

the more reliable basis because it focuses on the central source of state power in international affairs, the economy.

10. The phrase is ascribed to Mao Zedong, who actually was referring to political power.
11. See Brodie and Brodie (1973); in 1946, believing that the nuclear bomb made any further weapon development superfluous, a group of scholars published *The Absolute Weapon: Atomic Power and World Order.* Brodie ed. (1946).
12. The relationship between costs and strategy is discussed by Fallows (1981), pp. 11–12.
13. On the place of strategy in military affairs, see Gray (1982).
14. See Kaldor (1981), p. 4.
15. See Fallows (1982), pp. 51–52, and Kaldor (1981), p. 4.
16. Rostow, Eugene V. (1982).
17. Servan-Schreiber (1980).
18. Speer (1970), Chapter 16.

Chapter 3. Foreign Policy

1. Zbigniew Brzezinski, quoted by George Urban (1981), p. 13.
2. Smith, D. Mack (1982), p. 209, indicates that Mussolini came to believe his own bombast.
3. James A. Robinson and Richard C. Snyder in Kelman (1965), pp. 435–463.
4. Wiseman (1966), p. 153.
5. Kelman, *op. cit.;* see also Frankel (1967).
6. For example, Robins (1977), Rivera (1968), Waite (1977), and Smith, D. Mack (1982).
7. Miller, James G.; see also his "The Individual As An Information Processing System," in Singer (1965), pp. 202–212.
8. The present author has repeatedly demonstrated these effects for the benefit of students in a course built around Internation Simulation; see Guetzkow et al (1963).
9. See Hoffman, Stanley, on Brzezinski, *The New York Review of Books* (September 29, 1983), p. 54.

Chapter 4. Communication And Information

1. *The New York Times* (October 2, 1981).
2. Nimetz (1980).
3. See Cherry (1971).
4. See Herzenstein (1978).
5. U.S. War Department (1976), p. 211.
6. *Ibid.*
7. U.S. Department of Defense (1983), Chapter VI, and (1984), Chapter VII.
8. U.S. War Department *op. cit.*
9. *Ibid.,* p. 216.
10. U.S. Department of State (October 1981 and July 1982); see also U.S. Department of Defense (1983), pp. 86–87.
11. U.S. Department of State (October 1981), p. 1.
12. Powers (1979) and U.S. Congress, Senate, 94th, 1st, (Report 94-465); also Cline (1976).
13. Smith, D. Mack (1982), p. 92.

Chapter 5. Finance

1. Cohen (1977), p. 3.
2. *Ibid.,* p. 4.
3. Bretton (1980), Chapters 6 and 11.
4. (1969), p. 141.
5. Leopold (1962), pp. 257-258.
6. Bretton (1980).
7. See, for example, Ruggie (1981).
8. See James P. Hawley and Charles I. Noble, "The Internationalism of Capital and the Crisis of the Nation State." Unpublished paper, n.d.
9. Marchetti and Marks (1974), pp. 60-61.
10. See discussion of "expatriate" funds, for example Euro- and petrodollars, Chapter 12 below.
11. Bretton (1976); U.S. Congress, House, 96th, 2nd (1980).
12. U.S. Congress, Senate, 94th, 1st (1975) *Direct Investment Abroad,* p. xi.

Chapter 6. Trade And Aid

1. National Association of Manufacturers (n.d.).
2. See Bretton (1970), pp. 292-293.
3. Tomashevsky (1974), pp. 200ff.
4. Stadnichenko (1975), pp. 80-93; also see Chapters XIV and XV below.
5. Bretton (1970), pp. 277-299.
6. Kindleberger (1970).
7. See, for example, Public Law (US) 480, Westerfield (1963), pp. 365-371.
8. See Chapter 16 below.
9. Bretton (1980), p. 258.
10. *Ibid.,* p. 161. The General was discouraged by his financial advisors who reminded him that such a move would hurt France more than the United States.
11. Carter, Jimmy (1982), p. 465.
12. On sanctions and international enforcement, see Doxey (1980).
13. See Bennett and Williams (1981).
14. Sampson (1974), pp. 230-257; also U.S. Congress, Senate, 93rd (1973). Parts 1 and 2. *Multinational Corporation and U.S. Foreign Policy.*
15. Based on U.S. Congress, Senate, 96th, 2nd (1980), *Imports of Minerals,* p. 46.
16. Milward (1979), pp. 326-327.
17. *Ibid.,* Chapter 9.

Chapter 7. Armed Force And Intelligence: Non-Violent Aspects

1. Kaplan, Stephen S., "Diplomacy of Power: Soviet Forces as a Political Instrument," published March 1981, cited in Jerry F. Hough, "Soviet Perspectives," *The Brookings Bulletin,* Volume 17, No. 3 (Winter 1981), p. 12; see also Blechman and Kaplan (1978), on U.S. usage.
2. Bemis (1946), Chapter XXXVI; also Churchill (1948), Chapters 6-9.
3. U.S. Department of State (1947), Part V: Military, Naval, and Air Clauses; also Bretton (1953).

Chapter 8. Armed Force And Intelligence; Violent Uses

1. For a comprehensive definitional effort, see Alexander and Gleason (1981), Part I; an unconventional definition is offered by Herman (1982); for an official US definition, see CIA (1980), p. 8.
2. In 1984, the U.S. began to treat terrorist acts sponsored by governments as acts of undeclared war against the U.S. and considered taking preemptive steps, Sec. of State Shultz *Department of State Bulletin,* Vol. 84, 2086 (May 1984), pp. 13-14.
3. U.S. Congress, Senate, 96th, 2nd (1980), Committee on the Judiciary, p. 18; see also Colley (1981), pp. 74-93; CIA (1980), p. 9; and Weintraub (1976).
4. The closest former CIA Director William E. Colby would come to accusing the Soviet Union directly was to say "we are entitled to draw natural conclusions from circumstances [details regarding which] we do not know," U.S. Congress, Senate, 97th, 1st (1981), Committee on the Judiciary, Subcommittee on Security and Terrorism, Hearings, (Washington, D.C.: GPO, 1981), p. 30. No direct link has as yet been established; see CIA, National Intelligence Estimates 1980, *New York Times* (March 29, 1981) and CIA (1981), pp. 8-9. Seeing a Soviet connection is Harry Rositzke, *The New York Times,* op. ed., (July 20, 1981).
5. Herman (1982), links the U.S., mainly the CIA to an international terrorist network of right-wing coloration.
6. See *UN Chronicle,* Volume XVII, No. 1 (January 1980), pp. 5-13.
7. For a discussion of this problem, see Norton and Greenberg (1979); see also U.S. Congress, House, 98th, 2nd (1984), *Binary Weapons.*
8. U.S. Congress, Senate, 94th, 1st (1975), Select Committee to Study Governmental Operations . . .; Herman, *op. cit.,* offers a far more extensive list.
9. See Rositzke (1981), Chapter VI. Following the 1941 partition of Poland, Soviet security troops executed between 10,000 and 20,000 members of Poland's military, political, professional, and cultural elites in the forest of Katyn, Bylorussia. After World War Two, additional Polish leaders were murdered on Stalin's orders.
10. See Wright (1965) throughout but in particular pp. 1515-1518. Singer and Small (1972), whose purpose was "to identify variables that are most frequently associated with onset of war during the century and a half since the Congress of Vienna," hoped in particular "to ascertain which factors characterize those conflicts which terminate in war, and which ones accompany those which find less violent resolution," p. 4.
11. See Waite (1977).
12. See Milward (1979), Chapters 1 and 2 and Mesquita (1981), Chapter 2.
13. See Chapter IX, pp. 000.
14. See Wright (1965), p. 158.
15. V.I. Lenin, quoted in Tomashevsky (1974), p. 109; see also *Marxism-Leninism On War and Army* Moscow: Progress Publishers (1972), pp. 62-72.
16. Tomashevsky (1974), p. 111.
17. *Ibid.,* p. 112.
18. *Ibid.,* p. 129.
19. *Ibid.,* pp. 129-130.
20. *Ibid.,* p. 141.
21. See Chapter 19 below.
22. Katz, Arthur M. (1982) and Riordan (1982).

Chapter 9. International Law

1. See Epilogue, below.

2. See Chapter 4, above.
3. Resolution 3314 (XXIX Session), Article 1.
4. Schwarzenberger (1976), pp. 16–17.
5. *Ibid.*, p. 19.
6. Akehurst (1977), pp. 23–26.

Chapter 10. International Organization

1. Claude (1964), p. 4.
2. Jacobson (1984), pp. 22–24.
3. Claude (1967), Chapter 2, especially pp. 26ff and 39ff.
4. Abrams (1981).
5. See Claude (1967), Chapter 2, especially pp. 26ff and 39ff; see also a sharp critique in The Heritage Foundation, A United Nations Assessment Project Study, "U.N. Peacekeeping."
6. See Chapter 16, the Law of the Sea.
7. See Department of State (1978).
8. Bennett, A. LeRoy (1980), p. 368.
9. (1984), pp. 4–5.
10. See Chapter 16, below.
11. Kegley and Wittkopf (1981), pp. 134–135, Table 5.3; see also Hoogvelt (1982), pp. 56ff.
12. For instance, U.S. Congress, Senate, 93rd (1973). (MNCs and U.S. Foreign Policy).

Chapter 11. Postwar Recovery

1. Cohen (1977), p. 95.
2. *Ibid.*, p. 97.
3. *Ibid.*, p. 103.
4. *U.S. Power and the Multinational Corporation: The Political Economy of Foreign Direct Investment* (N.Y.: Basic Books, 1975), cited by Cohen (1977), p. 106.
5. *Ibid.*, p. 82.
6. Vernon (1971).
7. Blake and Walters (1983), Chapter IV; Turner (1973).
8. Vernon (1977).
9. For a convenient overview of the U.S. perspective, see Department of State, Special Report No. 17 (July 1975) and *ibid.*, No. 273 (April 8, 1981).

Chapter 12. The Advanced Capitalist Sector: A House Divided Against Itself

1. Monson and Walters (1983) and the review of that book by Robert L. Heilbroner, "The Coming Invasion," *The New York Review of Books* (December 8, 1983), pp. 23–25.
2. For example, Hallstein (1962), pp. 1–29.
3. Harrington (1976).
4. Thurow (1981).
5. For example, Kostyukhin (1979), p. 48.
6. See Blake and Walters (1983), Chapter Two.
7. See Chapter 6, above, footnote p. 115.

8. See Clyde Farnsworth "Trade War . . . Over Food Export," *The New York Times* (February 21, 1983).
9. Dam (March 21, 1983), p. 3.
10. Burns (1982).
11. Bretton (1955), pp. 107–118.
12. Levitt (1970); Sykes (1973) Roussopoulos (1973).
13. Wilkinson (1983), pp. 202–203.
14. *Ibid.*, p. 202.
15. Nishihara (1982).
16. Wilkinson, *op. cit.*, pp. 208–221.
17. CIA (December 1, 1982).
18. See footnote Chapter 13, p. 251.
19. Nixon (1982).
20. Wallis (March 20, 1983), p. 3.
21. John Tagliabue, *The New York Times* (June 23, 1982).
22. World Bank, *World Development Report 1982*, Table 3.4, p. 26.
23. Sheng (1981); Shouyi (1982), Chapter X; also Liao, "Decline of Antiforeignism in Chinese Foreign Policy," in Liao (1981), pp. 13–20.
24. Chun-to-Hsueh, "Modernization and Revolution in Liao (1982), pp. 1–2; aware of investors' fears of another political upheaval, the PRC, in 1983, began to sign agreements with Western countries designed to protect foreign investments.
25. Liao (1981), Appendix 1, p. 80.
26. Cooper (August 29, 1977), p. 1.
27. U.S. Congress, House, 96th, 2nd (1980), *The Adequacy of the Federal Response* . . . .
28. "The Debt Crisis: No Need For IMF Bailout," *The Wall Street Journal* (April 27, 1983).
29. Jahnke (1982), pp. 9–12.
30. U.S. Department of State (January 27, 1982), p. 1.
31. The Heritage Foundation *Backgrounder* No. 154 (October 19, 1981).
32. Felix Rohatyn, *The New York Review of Books* (November 4, 1982), p. 6.
33. Harold Lever, "International Banking's House of Cards," *The New York Times* (September 24, 1982), op. ed.
34. Dam (1983), p. 3.
35. Rostow, W.W. (1978), pp. 36–37.

Chapter 13. The Advanced Socialist Sector: Unity or Fragmentation?

1. Tomashevsky (1974), pp. 266–268.
2. Spero (1981), p. 291.
3. Holzman (1976), pp. 51–52.
4. Möller (1968), pp. 61–62.
5. *Ibid.*
6. Banks *et al.*, *Political Handbook of the World, 1979*, p. 372.
7. Holzman (1976), p. 114; also on the subject of Soviet dominance and intra-bloc tension, see Friesen (1976), especially pp. 70–78.
8. Kostyukhin (1979), pp. 87ff.
9. John F. Burns, *The New York Times* (May 10, 1983); Friesen (1976), p. 65.
10. See Friesen (1976), Chapter 3; also Luttwak (1983), p. 162.
11. Holzman (1976), p. 26.
12. Kostyukhin (1979), p. 124; see also Lebedev (1978), Chapter 5.
13. CIA (December 1, 1982), pp. 14–19; see also Shafer (1982), pp. 154–171.

14. CIA *op. cit.,* p. 14.
15. See Chapter 16, below, pp. 314–315.
16. Goldman (1975) and CIA, Statement by Henry Rowen (December 1, 1982), p. 11.
17. Lee, Edmund (1983), p. 31.
18. Waller (1981).
19. Huichan (1982), pp. 46–73; also Peter N.S. Lee in Liao (1981), pp. 29–42.
20. Tomashevsky (1974), p. 273 and North (1969), pp. 106–107; also Waller (1981), p. 183.
21. Lee in Liao (1981), pp. 36–37.
22. Commentary in *Renmin Ribao* (January 12, 1983) reprinted in *Beijing Rundschau,* Volume 20 (February 8, 1983), No. 6, pp. 19–21; also Xiang (1983), pp. 45–47.
23. Tomashevsky (1974), p. 273 and Holzman (1976), p. 90.
24. *Beijing Review,* Volume 26 (March 21, 1983), No. 12, pp. 11–12; also Suryadinata in Liao (1981), pp. 117–126.
25. See, for example, Fengmin (1982), pp. 98–123; also Machetzki in Liao (1981), pp. 67–76 and Appendices 1 and 2, pp. 77–93.
26. *South China Post* (Hong Kong, April 13 and 16, 1983).

Chapter 14. Closing the Viability Gap: The Problem and Proposed Solutions

1. Tjulpanov (1969), pp. 344ff. For an example of the earlier approach by Soviet academicians to the socio-political problems facing the LDCs, see Potekhin (1968).
2. U.S. Congress, House, 95th, 1st (1977), p. 61.
3. Spero (1981), p. 140.
4. For its recommendations, see North-South (1980), Annex 1, pp. 282–292.
5. On the origin of the term see Hoogvelt (1982), p. 92.
6. (1978), p. 74.
7. Spero (1981), p. 190.
8. UN General Assembly, XVIII Session, *Official Records,* Supplement No. 7 (A 5507), p. 24 cited in Spero (1981), pp. 19–20.
9. Declaration On The Establishment Of A New International Economic Order, May 1, 1974, UN General Assembly, Res. 3201 (S–VI), and Charter of Economic Rights and Duties of States (December 12, 1974), UN General Assembly Res. 3281 (XXIX).
10. Turner (1973).
11. For a critical assessment of UNCTAD see Michalak (1983).
12. One of the more skeptical among Western development specialists has been P.T. (Lord) Bauer; see for example his *Realty and Rhetoric* (1984), especially Chapters 3, 4, and 6, and *ibid.* (1981), Chapters 3–4.
13. Tetzlaff (1983), p. 9.

Chapter 15. Closing the Viability Gap: Practice

1. See Bretton (1973), Chapter 2.
2. Offergeld (1982), p. 3.
3. World Bank, *World Development Report 1982,* Box 7.5, p. 89.
4. U.S. Department of State (April 4, 1983), pp. 13–14.
5. *Voice of the Arab World* (London) as reported by Ray Vicker, *The Wall Street Journal* (September 4, 1980).
6. U.S. Secretary of the Treasury, Donald Reagan, Public Broadcasting System (PBS), *Frontline* (July 18, 1983), rebroadcast.
7. Department of State (March 3, 1983), p. 3.

8. See footnote Chapter 15, p. 286.
9. Enders (1982), p. 2.
10. Cooper (May 15, 1980), p. 11.
11. Ehrlich and Gwin (1981), pp. 155-158.
12. World Bank, *World Development Report 1982*, Table 4.3, p. 35.
13. For example, Nkrumah (1965).
14. See Friedrich-Ebert, Stiftung (1964). On Soviet-PRC rivalry, see U.S. Congress, House, 95th, 1st (1977), pp. 49-59.
15. Reference is to the regime of Pol Pot; see Banks *et al., Political Handbook of the World*, 1977, p. 212.
16. CIA (1976), p. 7; also U.S. Congress, House, 95th, 1st (1977), p. 61.
17. *Ibid.*, p. 131.
18. CIA (1979), pp. 12-13.
19. U.S. Congress (1977), *op. cit.*, pp. 63-64.
20. U.S. Department of State, Bureau of Intelligence Research (February 1983), p. 6.
21. *Ibid.*, Tables 1-3, pp. 2-3.
22. U.S. Congress (1977), *op. cit.*, pp. 71, 130-132.
23. *Ibid.*, p. 66.
24. *Ibid.*
25. Peter O'Neill, *The Christian Science Monitor* (June 10, 1981).
26. *Ibid.*
27. Friedrich-Ebert-Stiftung (1964), pp. 23-30 and U.S. Congress, House (1977), *op. cit.*, pp. 49-50.
28. World Bank, *World Development Report 1982*, Tables 11 and 12, pp. 130, 132.
29. *Ibid.*, p. 32.
30. Shultz (May 26, 1983), p. 4.

Chapter 16. Resources: Joint Utilization or Conflict?

1. Spero (1981), p. 200; Bergsten (1973), pp. 103-122.
2. For example, Shafer (1982), pp. 154-171.
3. See footnote, Chapter 16, p. 310.
4. Katz, Julius (1976).
5. U.S. Congress, Senate, 96th, 2nd (1980), *Imports of Minerals . . .*, Appendix 6 and Table 3, p. 4.
6. Katz, Julius (1976), p. 5.
7. October 31, 1979.
8. Danielsen (1982), pp. 151-152.
9. *Ibid.*, p. 151.
10. *Ibid.*
11. *Ibid.*, pp. 153-154.
12. I. Niblock, Department Director, Center of Arab Gulf Studies at Exeter University, quoted in Ibrahim, Youssef M., "Ill-Advised Spending of Oil Funds Hurts Arab Societies," *The New York Times* (January 28, 1980); also Hottinger (1980), pp. 23-24.
13. William P. Tavoulareas, Mobil Oil Stockholder Meeting, *The New York Times* (May 7, 1982).
14. U.S. Congress, Senate, *op. cit.*, p. ix.
15. Rocks and Runyon (1972), p. 21. The reference, in this instance, was to oil. For a contrary assessment, see Kahn and Schneider (1981).
16. Pirages (1978), pp. 128-129.

17. *Backgrounder* (issued by the South African Embassy to the U.S.), No. 9 (1980), p. 3; however, the Ambassador included in his total for "southern Africa" the production of several black African states.
18. U.S. Congress, Senate, *op. cit.*
19. *Ibid.;* see also Bennett and Williams (1981).
20. Shafer, *op. cit.,* p. 158.
23. On a proposal to reduce U.S. resource vulnerability, see U.S. Congress, *op. cit.,* p. 4.
24. Goldman and Schroeder (1981), p. 96.
25. *Ibid.,* pp. 109-113. Coupled with the pipeline are mutually binding credit arrangements, sales and purchasing obligations, and pricing agreements. A matter of great sensitivity within the Western alliance system is the fact that the U.S. expends approximately one-third of all industrial power generated on earth, that is, less than 6 percent of the earth's population use 33 percent of its energy, Rocks and Runyon, p. 8.
26. Kahn and Schneider (1981), pp. 141-143.
27. World Bank, *World Development Report 1983,* Table 6.
28. The Heritage Foundation, *Backgrounder,* No. 188 (1982), p. 5; see also Burke and Brokaw (1982), pp. 75-76. Indications are that the several CMEA/COMECON members also entertained serious reservations.
29. The Heritage Foundation, *op. cit.,* pp. 6-14. On the U.S. "Exclusive Economic Zone" (EEZ) within 200 miles of its coast and overseas possessions, see U.S. Department of State, Bureau of Public Affairs *gist* (April 1983). For the official U.S. view on the entire subject, see Malone (1984).
30. Wolfgang W. Schöhl in *Die Zeit* (May 21, 1982).

Chapter 17. Soviet American Rivalry: Deterrence or War?

1. Blechman and Kaplan (1978), pp. 47-49; also the Harvard Nuclear Study Group (1983), pp. 150-151 and Chapter 7.
2. See, for example, Kegley and Wittkopf (1981), Box 10.1, p. 339 or Sivard (1981), p. 14.
3. Katz, Arthur M. (1982), pp. 6ff.
4. Traces of a nuclear competition may be found as early as 1940. Halloway (1983), p. 20; also Campbell (1982), pp. 180-181. Kaldor (1981), p. 99, suggests the 1930s as the starting point.
5. Gray (1982), p. 39.
6. Leopold (1962), pp. 600 and 640ff; Barnet (1977), p. 69.
7. For other incidents involving "nuclear signalling" see Blechman and Kaplan (1978), pp. 47-49.
8. See, for example, Ball (1983).
9. Harvard Nuclear Study Group (1983), pp. 140-143; there may have been at least 17 instances of "nuclear signalling" by the U.S. between 1945 and 1965; *ibid.,* pp. 150-152.
10. Campbell (1982), p. 172.
11. *Ibid.,* p. 173 and Fallows (1981), p. 146.
12. Campbell, *op. cit.,* p. 176.
13. Berman and Baker (1982), p. 33.
14. U.S., The Comptroller General of the (1981), p. 12 and Harvard Nuclear Study Group (1983), p. 95.
15. Congressional Quarterly Inc. (1983), pp. 27-28.
16. Steinbrunner (1981-82) and Cox (1982), pp. 8-11.

17. U.S. Department of Defense, Fiscal Year 1984–85 "Defense Guidance."
18. Harvard Nuclear Study Group, *op. cit.,* p. 105.
19. Navrozov (1983) also CIA Report to U.S. Congress, Joint Economic Committee and NATO Economic Committee indicating that Soviet defense spending has slowed. *The New York Times* (January 30, 1984).
20. Thompson (1982), p. 111.
21. Nincic (1982), p. 97.
22. Ford, Kendall, and Nadis (1982), p. 7.
23. On the MX, see Kaldor (1981), pp. 185–189.
24. Cockburn (1983), pp. 210ff.
25. Deudney (1983–84), p. 96 writes that "geodetic satellites" are said to "have mapped gravitational anomalies in [strategically critical] areas and trajectories have been adjusted." For a contrary view, see A.G.B. Metcalf, Chairman U.S. Strategic Institute, *The Wall Street Journal* (April 2, 1984) Letters to the Editor.
26. Cockburn, *op. cit.,* p. 211.
27. See Fallows (1982), pp. 146ff, and Cockburn, pp. 205ff.
28. Committee on the Present Danger (CPD) (1982), Chart 4, p. 27.
29. Cockburn, *op. cit.,* p. 104, describes some of these as "paper divisions;" see also Halloran and Austin (1980).
30. For an "inside" assessment, see Suvorov (1982).
31. Former CIA Director Colby's review of Cockburn, *The New York Times Book Review* (June 26, 1983).
32. "Less-than-ominous reasons" were cited for the SS-20 deployment by a defense analyst Raymond L. Barthoff. *The New York Times* (May 13, 1983), *Letters to the Editor.*
33. See Allen and Polmar (1984), pp. 13ff.
34. See Zuckerman (1982), pp. 49–50.
35. Deudney, *op. cit.,* p. 92.
36. The U.S. Airforce has a Space Command and the Soviet Union appears to treat space warfare as part of its Strategic Defense System. U.S. Department of Defense (DOD), *Soviet Military Power 1983,* pp. 65–69; and DOD, *ibid.,* 1982, Chapter III; also Berman and Baker (1982), p. 150.
37. Jastrow (1982).
38. Richard Halloran, *The New York Times* (August 23, 1983); see also Karas (1983), Chapter Eight.
39. Graham (1982); see Zuckerman (1982), pp. 52–53 on the technical futility of the "astrodome" concept.
40. Campbell (1982), pp. 106–110 and Berman and Baker (1982), pp. 162–165.
41. See Chapter 18, pp. 403–404.
42. Isby (1981), pp. 214–219.
43. Hamm (1983), p. 15.

Chapter 18. Curbing Weapons, Preventing War

1. Ground Zero (1982), pp. 102–121; also see Harvard Nuclear Study Group (1983), Chapter 3.
2. For other possible "unintended risks" see Frei (1983).
3. Green (1966).
4. Writes one of Great Britain's foremost military scientists, Zuckerman (1982), p. 68: "My experience of generals and air marshals in the Second World War . . .

does not lead me to suppose that if unlimited force were available, less rather than more would be used in order to secure some objective."

5. Deudney (1983-84), p. 101.
6. *Ibid.,* p. 104.
7. Gray (1982), p. 40.
8. Frei (1983), pp. 172-173, and Harvard Nuclear Study Group, *op. cit.,* pp. 64ff.
9. Richard Halloran, *The New York Times* (May 29, 1983) and Kaldor (1981), pp. 181-183.
10. Tom Wicker, "War By Accident," *The New York Times* (November 21, 1982), and Sivard (1981), p. 15; another report shows over 2000, *ibid.* (September 23, 1985).
11. Wicker, *op. cit.*
12. Fred C. Iklé, quoted by Cox, *The New York Times* (May 27, 1982), Op. Ed.
13. Campbell (1982), pp. 155-156.
14. Barlow (1982), p. 10.
15. Grey (1982), pp. 14ff.
16. Claude (1971), Chapter 13 and United States Arms Control and Disarmament Agency (hereafter cited as UACDA), (1982), pp. 3-8.
17. USACDA (1982), p. 132.
18. *Ibid.,* p. 134. The U.S. envisaged 12 ABMs at that time.
19. *Ibid.,* p. 148.
20. Committee on the Present Danger (1978), Part II. The verification provisions are found in Article V of the Interim Agreement.
21. Agreed Statements with respect to the Interim Agreement, Section 3D (b), USACDA (1982), p. 157; also Harvard Nuclear Study Group, p. 94.
22. USACDA (1982), p. 239; also U.S. Department of State, Special Report No. 46 (1979), p. 5.
23. USACDA (1982), pp. 246-277.
24. For example, SALT II banned production, testing and deployment of the Soviet SS-16. By April 1982, reports circulated in Washington that the Soviet Union actually had "fully deployed" 200 of these banned weapons. On the reasons for the ban, see USACDA (1982), pp. 244-255; for further discussion of alleged Soviet violations, see USACDA (1984), pp. 10-12 and The Heritage Foundation, *National Security Record* No. 63 (December 1983) and No. 66 (March 1984).
25. See, for example, "A Debate: Warnke and Rostow Work the Nuclear Equation," *The New York Times* (March 21, 1982).
26. Committee on the Present Danger (1978), Table 8, p. 39.
27. (1976), p. 194-195.
28. Harvard Nuclear Study Group, Chapter 7.
29. *The New York Times* (March 21, 1982).
30. Carter, Jimmy (1982), pp. 251-253.
31. On Kissinger and "linkage," see Safire (1975), p. 436.
32. See discussion of Euromissiles, Chapter 17, pp. 000.
33. Rostow, Eugene V. (1982), p. 5.
34. *Ibid.,* p. 27 and 13-14.
35. USACDA (1984), *op. cit.*
36. Brown, Harold (1983), Chapter 11.
37. The Heritage Foundation, National Security Record No. 44 (April 1982).
38. See Sigal (1982) and Brown, Harold (1983), p. 189.
39. McGeorge, Bundy, *et al.* (1982); for a critique, see Draper (1982), pp. 35-36 and Kaiser *et al.* (1982), pp. 1157ff.
40. Czempel (1983).
41. Bahr (1982).
42. USACDA (1982), pp. 164ff.

43. *Ibid.,* p. 164.
44. Brown, Harold (1983), pp. 190-191.
45. On Kissinger and biological warfare, see Safire (1975), pp. 162-163.
46. U.S., Comptroller General of the (1983), p. 86.
47. William Kucewicz, "Beyond 'Yellow Rain'," *The Wall Street Journal* (April through May 1984).
48. U.S., The Comptroller General of the (1983), p. 79.
49. North Atlantic Treaty Organization (1982), p. 26. France, Portugal and Iceland did not participate.
50. 1870-71, 1914-1918, and 1939-1945.
51. U.S. Department of State, Bureau of Public Affairs, Semi-Annual on the Implementation of Helsinki Final Act, Fourteenth Report, p. 14. On the Human Rights provisions, see Epilogue, below.
52. See Kenneth L. Alderman. "Arms Control With and Without Agreements,"*Foreign Affairs,* Vol. 63, No. 2 (Winter 1984/1985), pp. 240-262.

Chapter 19. Under The Nuclear Threat: Diffusion of Power

1. U.S., Comptroller General of the (1981), p. 9.
2. Lord *et al.* (1981), pp. 15ff.
3. See Haseler and Kaltefleiter (1981) and Dankert (1983-84).
4. Congressional Quarterly Inc. (1983), p. 170.
5. Nuclear Weapons and Foreign Policy (1958), p. 201; see also Kissinger, "A Plan to Reshape NATO," *Time* (March 5, 1984), pp. 20-24 and Helmut Schmidt, "Saving the Western Alliance," *New York Review of Books* (May 31, 1984), pp. 25-27.
6. *The New York Times* (July 12, 1981).
7. For an adaptation of Mackinder's thesis to the nuclear age, see Gray (1977).
8. U.S. Department of State (February 16, 1983), p. 2.
9. Pillsbury (1978-79).
10. DOD (1983), p. 13.
11. Tomashevsky (1974), p. 144.
12. For an official U.S. view, see Sanchez (1983).
13. DOD (1983), p. 13.
14. After that war, widespread revulsion in the U.S. resulted in legislation to curb such dealings, see the Nye Committee (1934-1936); Leopold (1962), pp. 501-508; see also McCormick (1965) and Brockway (1933).
15. U.S. Department of State (July 15, 1989), p. 2.
16. Pierre (1982), p. 18.
17. DOD (1981), pp. 83-93 and Stanley and Pearton (1972), Chapter Four.
18. Pierre, *op. cit.,* pp. 25-26.
19. U.S. Department of State (August 1982), p. 10.
20. U.S. Department of Labor.
21. Feldman (1982), p. 54.
22. *Ibid.,* p. 56.
23. *Ibid.,* p. 22.
24. USACDA (1982), pp. 85-86.
25. *Ibid.,* p. 82ff.
26. *Ibid.,* p. 82.
27. *Ibid.,* pp. 96-98; Banks *et al., Political Handbook of the World, 1981,* p. 665. In 1984, the U.S. and the PRC signed an agreement for cooperation in the peaceful uses of atomic energy. The agreement was accompanied by a verbal undertaking

on the part of the PRC to observe the terms of the Non-Proliferation Treaty, U.S. Department of State *Bulletin.*

28. USACDA (1982), p. 89.
29. *Ibid.*
30. *The New York Times* (September 7, 1983).

Epilogue. Preventing World War III and Beyond

1. U.S. Congress, House, 98th, 1st (1983), The Consequences of Nuclear War on the Global Environment; see also Katz, Arthur M. (1982), Riordan, Michael, ed. (1982); *Science,* Vol. 222, No. 4360 (23 Dec. 1983), pp. 1283–1300, and *Scientific American,* Vol. 251, 2 (Aug. 1984).
2. U.S. Congress, *op. cit.,* p. 3.
3. *Ibid.,* p. 8; also Corporation for Public Broadcasting (1983), p. 9.
4. U.S. Congress, *op. cit.,* pp. 7–8.
5. *Ibid.,* p. 19; also Thomas (1981), p. 6.
6. Katz, Arthur M. (1982), who focuses in the main on the question of "acceptability."
7. Philip M. Boffey, "Social Scientists Believe Leaders Lack a Sense of War's Reality," *The New York Times* (September 7, 1982) *Science Supplement.*
8. Luttwak (1983), especially pp. 63–66.
9. Bialer (1984), pp. 6–10.
10. For example, Fisher (1981) and *ibid.,* three articles "On Negotiating," *The New York Times* (September 24, 25, 26, 1981), op. ed.
11. For instance, India's Prime Minister Indira Gandhi. U.N. General Assembly, September 28–29, 1983.
12. Dartmouth College, November 17, 1981. *The New York Times* (November 18, 1981).
13. Fest (1973), pp. 724–750.
14. See *Amnesty International Report 1983.*
15. Akehurst (1977), pp. 79–82; also Weston, Falk, D'Amato (1989), pp. 498ff.
16. U.S. Department of State, Bureau of Public Affairs (1981) Human Rights Report, p. 1 and *ibid.* (1985); see also Van Dyke (1970), Part II.
17. Forsythe (1983), pp. 78–87 and 170–172.
18. Weston, Falk, D'Amato, *op. cit.,* p. 496; also see International Commission of Jurists (1977).
19. Kirkpatrick (November 24, 1981), p. 2.
20. Forsythe, *op. cit.,* pp. 208–209.
21. Kirkpatrick (December 1983), p. 12.
22. Sivard (1981), pp. 20–23.
23. Brown, Lester (1978), p. 15, discussing the modern-day implications of the "Tragedy of the Commons."
24. See Meadows *et al* (1972), Walter (1981), North-South (1980) and Kahn and Schneider (1981).
25. For example, von Neumann and Morgenstern (1944); also Gray (1982), Chapter 7, Guetzkow *et al* (1963), and Zinnes (1976).
26. Dougherty and Pfaltzgraff, Jr. (1971); Knorr and Rosenau (1980); Hoffman (1960); Butterfield and Wright (1966); Waltz (1979).
27. Urban (1981), p. 337.
28. (1962), p. 13.

BIBLIOGRAPHY

Academy of Sciences of the U.S.S.R. *Marxism-Leninism On War and Army.* Moscow: Progress Publishers, 1972.

Abrams, Eliot. "General View of the UN System." U.S. Department of State, *Current Policy,* No. 287 (June 5, 1981).

Adelman, Kenneth. "Speaking of America: Public Diplomacy In Our Time." *Foreign Affairs* Vol. 59, No. 4 (Spring 1981), pp. 913-936.

Adelman, M.A. "Is The Oil Shortage Real? Oil Companies As OPEC Tax Collectors." *Foreign Policy,* No. 9 (Winter 1972-73).

Akehurst, Michael. *A Modern Introduction to International Law.* Third Edition. London: Allen and Unwin, 1977.

Alexander, Yonah, and John M. Gleason. eds. *Behavioral and Quantitative Perspective on Terrorism.* New York: Pergamon Press, 1981.

Allen, Thomas B. and Norman Polmar. "The Silent Chase: Tracking Soviet Submarines." *The New York Times Magazine* (January 1, 1984).

Allison, Graham T. *Essence of Decision. Explaining the Cuban Missile Crisis.* Boston: Little, Brown, 1971.

Amnesty International. *Political Killings By Governments.* London: Amnesty International Publications, 1983.

Andelman, David. "Space Wars." *Foreign Policy,* No. 44 (Fall 1981).

Aspin, Les. "Misreading Intelligence." *Foreign Policy,* No. 43 (Summer 1981), pp. 166-172.

Ball, George W. "The Cosmic Bluff." *The New York Review of Books* (July 21, 1983).

Bahr, Egon. "'No First Use'." *The New York Times* (May 10, 1982), Op. Ed.

Bamford, James. *The Puzzle Palace: A Report on America's Most Secret Agency.* New York: Houghton Mifflin, 1982.

Banks, Arthur S., *et al.,* ed. *Economic Handbook of the World, 1981.* New York: McGraw-Hill, 1981.

———, *Political Handbook of the World 1977-1981.* New York: McGraw-Hill.

Barlow, Jeffrey G. "The Hard Facts The Nuclear Freeze Ignores." The Heritage Foundation, *Backgrounder,* No. 225 (November 3, 1982).

Barnet, Richard J. *The Giants. Russia and America.* New York: Simon & Schuster, 1977.

———, *The Alliance: America, Europe, Japan, Makers of the Postwar World.* New York: Simon & Schuster, 1985.

Bauer, P.T. (Lord). *Equality. The Third World and Economic Delusion.* Cambridge, Mass.: Harvard University Press, 1981.

———, *Reality and Rhetoric. Studies in the Economics of Development.* Cambridge, Mass.: Harvard University Press, 1984.

Bemis, Samuel Flagg. *A Diplomatic History of the United States.* New York: Henry Holt, 1946.

Bennett, James T., and Walter E. Williams. *Strategic Minerals. The Economic Impact of Supply Disruptions.* Washington, D.C.: The Heritage Foundation, 1981.

Bennett, A. LeRoy. *International Organization.* Second Ed. Englewood Cliffs, N.J.: Prentice-Hall, 1980.

Beres, Louis Rene. *Apocalypse. Nuclear Catastrophe in World Politics.* Chicago: The University of Chicago Press, Phoenix Edition, 1982.

Berman, Robert, and John C. Baker. *Soviet Strategic Forces: Requirements and Responses.* Washington, D.C.: Brookings Institution, 1982.

Bernstein, Richard. "The United Nations vs. The United States." *The New York Times Magazine* (January 22, 1984), pp. 18ff.

Bialer, Seweryn. "Danger in Moscow." *The New York Review of Books* (February 16, 1984).

Blair, John M. *The Control of Oil.* New York: Pantheon Books, 1977.

Blake, David H., and Robert S. Walters. *The Politics of Global Economic Relations.* Second Edition. Englewood Cliffs, N.J.: Prentice-Hall, 1983.

Blechman, Barry, and Stephen S. Kaplan. *Force Without War.* Washington, D.C.: Brookings Institution, 1978.

Bracken, Paul. *Command and Control of Nuclear Forces.* New Haven: Yale University Press, 1983.

Brandt, Willy. "The Future Under Threat." *Die Zeit* (February 15, 1980), reprinted in *The German Tribune,* Third World Review No. 1 (May 11, 1980).

———, see *North-South.*

Bretton, Henry L. *Stresemann and the Revision of Versailles.* Stanford, Cal.: Stanford University Press, 1953.

———, "The European Coal and Steel Community (Schuman Plan)," in Andrew Gyorgy and Hubert S. Gibbs, eds., *Problems in International Relations.* New York: Prentice-Hall, Inc., 1955, pp. 107–118.

———, "Problems of Underdeveloped Nations: The Emergence of Ghana," in Andrew Gyorgy and Hubert S. Gibbs, eds., *Problems in International Relations.* Englewood Cliffs, N.J.: Prentice-Hall, 1962, pp. 227–243.

———, *The Rise and Fall of Kwame Nkrumah. A Study of Personal Rule in Africa.* New York: Praeger, 1966.

———, "The Overthrow of Kwame Nkrumah," in Andrew Gyorgy et al., *Problems in International Relations.* Third Edition. Englewood Cliffs, N.J.: Prentice-Hall, 1970, pp. 277–299.

———, *Patron-Client Relations. Middle Africa and the Powers.* New York: General Learning Press, 1971.

———, *Power and Politics in Africa.* Chicago: Aldine, 1973.

———, *Direct Foreign Investment in Africa: Its Political Purpose and Function in Patron-Client Relations.* Morristown, N.J.: General Learning Press, 1976.

———, *The Power of Money.* Albany, New York: State University of New York Press, 1980.

Brockway, Fenner. *The Bloody Traffic.* London: Gollancz, 1933.

Brodie, Bernard, ed. *The Absolute Weapon: Atomic Power and World Order.* New York: Harcourt, Brace and Company, 1946.

Brodie, Bernard, and Fawn M. Brodie. *From Crossbow to H-Bomb.* Bloomington, Indiana: Indiana University Press, 1973.

Brown, Anthony C. *Bodyguard of Lies.* New York: Harper and Row, 1975.

Brown, Harold. *National Security.* Boulder, Colo.: Westview Press, 1983.

Brown, Lester R. *The Twenty-Ninth Day.* New York: Norton, 1978.

Bryant, Ralph C. *Money and Monetary Policy in Interdependent Nations.* Washington, D.C.: The Brookings Institution, 1980.

Brzezinski, Zbigniew. "The Perils of Foreign Policy." *Encounter* (May 1981).

Bull, Hedley. *The Anarchical Society: A Study of Order in World Politics.* New York: Columbia University Press, 1977.

Bundy, McGeorge, George F. Kennan, Robert S. McNamara, and Gerard Smith. "Nuclear Weapons and the Atlantic Alliance." *Foreign Affairs,* Vol. 60, No. 4 (Spring 1982), pp. 753-768.

Bundy, McGeorge. "The Bishops and the Bomb." *The New York Review of Books* (June 16, 1983).

Burke, W. Scott, and Frank S. Brokaway. "Law at Sea." *Policy Review,* No. 20 (Spring 1982).

Burns, Arthur F. "Economic Health of the Western Alliance." U.S. Department of State, Bureau of Public Affairs *Current Policy,* No. 445 (December 9, 1982).

Butterfield, Herbert, and Martin Wight. *Diplomatic Investigations. Essays In The Theory Of International Politics.* Cambridge, Mass.: Harvard University Press, 1966.

Calleo, David P. *The Imperious Economy.* Cambridge, Mass.: Harvard University Press.

Campbell, Christy. *War Facts Now.* Glasgow: Fontana, 1982.

Canby, Steven and Ingemar Dorfer. "More Troops, Fewer Missiles." *Foreign Policy,* No. 53 (Winter 1983-84).

Carter, Jimmy. *Keeping Faith, Memoirs Of A President.* New York: Bantam Books, 1982.

Cherry, Colin. *World Communication: Threat or Promise?* London: Wiley Inter-science, 1971.

Churchill, Winston. *The Gathering Storm.* Boston: Houghton Mifflin, 1948.

C.I.A., *Communist Aid to Less Developed Countries of the Free World 1975.* Publication No. ER10372U. Washington, D.C.: C.I.A., Director of Public Affairs, July 1976.

C.I.A., National Foreign Assessment Center. *Communist Aid Activities in Non-Communist Less Developed Countries 1978.* Publication No. ER79-10412U. Washington, D.C.: C.I.A., Director of Public Affairs, September 1979.

———, *International Terrorism in 1979.* Washington, D.C.: C.I.A., Director of Public Affairs, 1980.

———, *Patterns of International Terrorism: 1980.* Washington, D.C.: C.I.A., Director of Public Affairs, 1981.

C.I.A., Statement by Henry Rowen Before The Joint Economic Committee, Subcommittee On International Trade, Finance, and Security Economies. *Central Intelligence Agency Briefing On The Soviet Economy.* Washington, D.C.: Joint Economic Committee (December 1, 1982), mimeographed.

Claude, Inis L. Jr. *Power and International Relations.* New York: Random House, 1962.

———, *The Changing United Nations.* New York: Random House, 1967.

———, *Swords Into Ploughshares.* Fourth Edition. New York: Random House, 1971.

Clausen, A.W. "Accelerating Growth and Reducing Poverty: A Multilateral Strategy for Development." Remarks prepared for delivery before Atlantik-Brücke and Deutsche Gesellschaft für Auswärtige Politik. Bonn (April 18, 1983), mimeographed.

Cline, Ray S. *Secrets, Spies and Scholars. Blueprint of the Essential C.I.A.* Washington D.C.: Acropolis Books, 1976.

Cochran, Thomas B., William M. Arkin, and Milton M. Hoenig. *Nuclear Weapons Databook.* Vol. I. *U.S. Nuclear Forces and Capabilities.* Cambridge: Mass.: Ballinger Publishing Co., 1984.

Cockburn, Andrew. *The Threat. Inside the Soviet Military Machine.* New York: Random House, 1983.

Cohen, Benjamin J. *The Question of Imperialism. The Political Economy of Dominance and Dependence.* New York: Basic Books, 1973.

———, *Organizing the World's Money. The Political Economy of International Monetary Relations.* New York: Basic Books, 1977.

Colley, John K. "The Libyan Menace." *Foreign Policy,* No. 42 (Spring 1981), pp. 74-93.

Collins, M. *U.S.-Soviet Military Balance 1960-1980.* New York: McGraw-Hill, 1980.

Collins, John M. *United States/Soviet Military Balance.* Washington, D.C.: The Library of Congress, Congressional Research Service, September 26, 1980.

Committee on the Present Danger (CPD). *Is America Becoming Number 2?* Washington, D.C.: C.P.D., October 5, 1978.

———, *Has America Become Number 2?* Washington, D.C.: C.P.D., June 29, 1982.

Congressional Quarterly, Inc. *U.S. Defense Policy.* Third Edition. Washington, D.C.: Congressional Quarterly, Inc., 1983.

———, *World Economy, Changes and Challenges.* Editorial Research Reports. Washington, D.C.: Congressional Quarterly, Inc., 1983.

———, *Can America Catch Up? The U.S.-Soviet Union Military Balance.* Washington D.C.: C.P.D., November 30, 1984.

Connor, Walker. "Nation-Building or Nation-Destroying." *World Politics,* Vol. 24 No. 3, (1972), pp. 319-355.

Cooley, John K. "The War Over Water." *Foreign Policy,* No. 54 (Spring 1984), pp. 3-26.

Cooper, Richard N. "International Debt: Current Issues and Implications." U.S. Department of State, Bureau of Public Affairs, *Statement* (August 29, 1977).

———, "North-South Dialogue." U.S. Department of State, Bureau of Public Affairs, *Current Policy,* No. 182 (May 15, 1980).

———, "World Monetary System in the 1980s." U.S. Department of State, *Current Policy,* No. 239 (November 1980).

Corporation for Public Broadcasting. Inside Story. Special Report. *Nuclear War: The Incurable Disease.* A discussion among International Physicians for the Prevention of Nuclear War (IPPNW), October 13, 1982, Kent, Ohio: PBS, 1983.

Cox, Arthur Macy. *Russian Roulette. The Superpower Game.* New York: New York Times Books, 1982.

Czempel, Ernst-Otto. "The Future of the Atlantic Alliance." *Das Parlament* (April 2, 1983).

Dam, Kenneth W. "Looking Toward Williamsburg: U.S. Economic Policy." U.S. Department of State, Bureau of Public Affairs, *Current Policy,* No. 479 (March 21, 1983).

Danielsen, Albert L. *The Evolution of OPEC.* New York: Harcourt Brace Jovanovich, 1982.

Dankert, Pieter, "Europe Together, America Apart." *Foreign Policy,* No. 53 (Winter 1983-84), pp. 18-33.

Deudney, Daniel. "Unlocking Space." *Foreign Policy,* No. 53 (Winter 1983-84), pp. 91-113.

Deutsch, Karl W. *The Analysis of International Relations.* Englewood Cliffs, N.M.: Prentice-Hall, 1968.

Dore, Isaak I. *International Law and the Superpowers.* New Brunswick, N.J.: Rutgers University Press, 1984.

Dougherty, James E., and Robert L. Pfaltzgraff, Jr. *Contending Theories of International Relations.* Philadelphia: J.B. Lipponcott, 1971.

Doxey, Margaret P. *Economic Sanctions And International Enforcement.* Second Edition, New York: Oxford University Press, 1980.

Draper, Theodore. "How Not To Think About Nuclear War." *The New York Review of Books* (July 15, 1982).

Drell, Sidney. *Facing the Threat of Nuclear Weapons.* Washington University Press, 1983.

Ehrlich, Thomas, and Catherine Gwin. "A Third World Strategy." *Foreign Policy,* No. 44 (Fall 1981), pp. 145-166.

Einzig, Paul. *Foreign Exchange Crises.* London: Macmillan, 1968.

Ellsworth, Robert, and Kenneth L. Adelman. "Foolish Intelligence." *Foreign Policy,* No. 36 (Fall 1970), pp. 147–159.

Emmerson, John K. *Arms, Yen, and Power.* New York: Dunellen, 1971.

Enders, Thomas O. "Maintaining Momentum Toward an Open World Economy." U.S. Department of State, Bureau of Public Affairs, *Current Policy,* No. 393 (May 13, 1982).

Epstein, E.J. *The Rise and Fall of Diamonds. The Shattering of a Brilliant Illusion.* New York: Simon & Schuster, 1982.

Fallows, James. *National Defense. New York: Random House, 1981.*

Feith, Douglas J. "The Oil Weapon De-Mystified." *Policy Review,* No. 15 (Winter 1981), pp. 19–39.

Feldman, Shai. *Israeli Nuclear Deterrence: A Strategy for the 1980's.* New York: Columbia University Press, 1983.

Fengmin, Guo. "West European Countries-The Canons of Their Foreign Policy." *China and the World.* (*Beijing Review* Foreign Affairs Section), Vol. 2 (1982), pp. 98–123.

Ferris, Paul. *Men and Money. Financial Europe Today.* Harmondsworth, Middlesex, England: Penguin Books, Ltd., 1970.

Fest, Joachim C. *Hitler.* New York: Harcourt, Brace, Jovanovich, 1973.

Fischer, Dietrich. *Preventing War in the Nuclear Age.* Totowa, N.J.: Rowman and Allanheld, 1984.

Fisher, Roger. *Getting To Yes. Negotiating Agreement Without Giving In.* Boston: Houghton Mifflin, 1981.

Ford, Daniel, Henry Kendall, Steven Nadis. *Beyond The Freeze. The Road to Nuclear Sanity.* Published by the Union of Concerned Scientists. Boston: Beacon Press, 1982.

Forsythe, David P. *Human Rights and World Politics.* Lincoln, Neb.: University of Nebraska Press, 1983.

Francis, Samuel. *The Soviet Strategy of Terror.* Washington, D.C.: The Heritage Foundation, 1981.

Frankel, Joseph. *The Making of Foreign Policy. An Analysis of Decision Making.* London: Oxford University Press, 1967.

Frei, Daniel. *Risk of Unintentional Nuclear War.* Allenheld, Osmun, 1983.

Friedrich-Ebert-Stiftung, Forschungsinstitute der. *The Soviet Bloc and Developing Countries.* Hanover: Verlag für Literatur und Zeitgeschehen, 1964.

Friesen, Connie M. *The Political Economy of East-West Trade.* New York: Praeger Special Studies, 1978.

Garnet, John C. *Commonsense and the Theory of International Politics.* Albany, New York: State University of New York Press, 1984.

Garrity, Patrick J. "Soviet Policy in the Far East: Search for Strategic Unity." *Military Review,* Vol. LXII, No. 12 (December 1982), pp. 26–38.

Goldman, Marshall I. "The Russians and Oil." *The New York Times* (January 20, 1975).

Goldman, Steven C. and Wayne A. Schroeder. "The Geopolitics of Energy." *Policy Review,* No. 17 (Summer 1981).

Goldsborough, James O. *Rebel Europe.* New York: Macmillan, 1982.

Graham, Lt. Gen. (Ret), Daniel O. *High Frontier.* A Heritage Foundation Project, Washington, D.C.: High Frontier, 1982.

Gray, C.S. *The Soviet-American Arms Race.* Lexington, Mass.: Saxon House-Lexington Books, 1976.

Gray, Colin S. *The Geopolitics of the Nuclear Era: Heartland, Rimlands, and the Technological Revolution.* New York: Crane, Russak, 1977.

———, *Strategic Studies. A Critical Assessment.* Westport, Conn.: Greenwood Press, 1982.

Green, Philip. *Deadly Logic: The Theory of Nuclear Deterrence.* Columbus, Ohio: Ohio State University Press, 1968.

Green, Timothy. *The World of Gold Today.* London: Arrow Books, 1973.

Grey, Robert T. "An Explanation of START, INF, MBFR, and CW Issues." *Remarks* before American Legion National Security and Foreign Policy Study Group, Chicago, August 12, 1982.

Griffin, Brian. "Banking On Crisis." *Policy Review,* No. 25 (Summer 1983), pp. 28–35.

Gross, Feliks. *Foreign Policy Analysis.* New York: Philosophical Library, 1954.

Grosser, Alfred. *Germany in Our Time: A Political History of the Postwar Years.* New York: Praeger, 1971.

Ground Zero. *Nuclear War: What's In It For You?* New York: Pocket Books, 1982.

Guetzkow, Harold et al. *Simulation in International Relations: Development For Research and Teaching.* Englewood Cliffs, N.J.: Prentice-Hall, 1963.

Gyorgy, Andrew. *Geopolitics. The New German Science.* Berkeley, Cal.: University of California Press, 1944.

Hackett, Sir John. *The Third World War. August 1985.* New York: Macmillan, 1978.

Halloran, Richard and Anthony Austin. "The Soviet Military: Its Power and Limits." *The New York Times* (December 9, 1980).

Hallstein, Walter. *United Europe, Challenge and Opportunity.* Cambridge, Mass.: Harvard University Press, 1962.

Hamm, Manfred R. "Deterring Chemical War: The Reagan Formula." *Backgrounder,* No. 272 (June 15, 1983).

Harrington, Michael. *The Twilight of Capitalism.* New York: Simon & Schuster, 1976.

Harvard Nuclear Study Group (Albert Carnesale *et. al.*) *Living With Nuclear Weapons.* New York: Bantam Books, 1983.

Haseler, Stephen and Werner Kaltefleiter. "NATO and Neutralism." *The Heritage Lectures,* 8. Washington, D.C.: The Heritage Foundation, 1981.

Heritage Foundation, The. "The Economic Roots of the Polish Revolt." *The Backgrounder,* No. 133 (February 17, 1981).

———, "The Polish Dilemma: Soviet Vulnerabilities and Western Opportunities." *Backgrounder,* No. 154 (October 19, 1981).

———, "The Law of the Sea Treaty: Can The U.S. Afford to Sign?" A United Nations Assessment Project Study. *Backgrounder,* No. 188 (June 7, 1982).

———, "Revitalizing The U.S.-Japan Partnership." *Backgrounder,* No. 244 (January 25, 1983).

———, "Soviet Treaty Violations and U.S. Compliance Policy." *National Security Record,* No. 63 (December 1983).

Herman, Edward S. *The Real Terror Network. Terrorism in Fact and Propaganda.* Boston: Southend Press, 1982.

Hershey, Robert D. Jr. "The Shrinking Power of Big Oil." *The New York Times* (February 26, 1980).

Herzenstein, Robert E. *The War That Hitler Won.* New York: Putnam's Sons, 1978.

Hoffman, Stanley H., ed. *Contemporary Theory in International Relations.* Englewood Cliffs, N.J.: Prentice-Hall, 1960.

———, *Duties Beyond Borders.* On the Limits and Possibilities of Ethical International Politics. Syracuse: Syracuse University Press, 1981.

Hofheinz, Roy, and Kent E. Calder. *The East Asia Edge.* New York: Basic Books, 1982.

Holloway, David. *The Soviet Union and the Arms Race.* New Haven: Yale University Press, 1983.

Holzman, Franklyn D. *Financial Checks on Soviet Defense Expenditures.* Lexington, Mass.: Lexington Books, 1975.

———, *International Trade Under Communism: Politics and Economics.* New York: Basic Books, 1976.

————, "Are the Soviets Really Outspending the U.S. on Defense?" *International Security*, No. 4 (1980).

Hoogvelt, Ankie M. M. *The Third World in Global Development* London: Macmillan, 1982.

Hottinger, Arnold. "The Rich Arab States in Trouble." *The New York Review of Books* (May 15, 1980), pp. 23-24.

Hsueh, Chun-tu. "Modernization and Revolution in China" in *Liao*, ed. (1981), pp. 1-28.

Huichan, Li. "The Crux of the Sino-Soviet Boundary Question." *China and the World*, (*Beijing Review* Foreign Relations Series), Vol. 1 (1982), pp. 46-73.

Ibrahim, Youssef M. "Ill-Advised Spending of Oil Funds Hurts Arab Societies." *The New York Times* (January 28, 1980).

International Bank for Reconstruction and Development, see World Bank.

International Commission of Jurists (ICJ). Reports to the UN Commission on Human Rights. *Uganda and Human Rights*. Geneva, Switzerland: ICJ, 1977.

Independent Commission on International Development Issues, Chairman Willy Brandt. *North-South: A Program of Survival*. Cambridge, Mass.: M.I.T. Press, 1980.

Isby, David C. *Weapons and Tactics of the Soviet Army*. London: Jane's, 1981.

Jacobson, Catherine. "The Technology Transfer Issue." *Business America*, Vol. 5, No. 11 (May 31, 1982), pp. 2-5.

Jacobson, Harold K. *Networks of Interdependence. International Organizations And The Global Political System*. Second Edition. New York: Knopf, 1984.

Jacobson, Harold K. and Susan Sidjanski. *The Emerging International Economic Order: Dynamic Processes, Constraints and Opportunities*. Beverly Hills, Cal.: Sage Publishers, 1982.

Jahnke, Joachim. "The East Bloc and Western Credit." *The German Tribune* (September 19, 1982), pp. 9-12.

Jastrow, Robert. "The New Soviet Arms Buildup in Space." *The New York Times Magazine* (October 3, 1982).

Jeffreys-Jones, Rhodri. *American Espionage. From Secret Service to CIA*. New York: The Free Press, 1977.

Kahn, Herman and Ernest Schneider. "Globaloney 2000." *Policy Review*, No. 16 (Spring 1981), pp. 130-157.

Kaiser, Karl, et al. "Nuclear Weapons and the Preservation of Peace: A German Response." *Foreign Affairs* Vol. 60, No. 5 (Summer 1982), pp. 1157ff.

Kaiser, Robert G. *Russia. The People and the Power*. New York: Pocket Books, 1976.

Kaldor, Mary. *The Baroque Arsenal*. New York: Hill and Wang, 1981.

Karas, Thomas. *The New High Ground*. New York: Simon & Schuster, 1983.

Katz, Arthur M. *Life After Nuclear War. The Economic and Social Impacts of Nuclear Attacks on the United States*. Cambridge, Mass.: Ballinger Publishing Company, 1982.

Katz, Julius L. U.S. Department of State, Bureau of Public Affairs, *News Release: International Commodity Policy* (April 1976).

Katz, Mark N. *The Third World in Soviet Military Thought*. Baltimore, Md.: Johns Hopkins University Press, 1982.

Kegley, Charles W., Jr. and Eugene R. Wittkopf. *World Politics; Trends and Transformation*. New York: St. Martin's Press, 1981.

Kelman, Herbert C., ed. *International Behavior: A Socio-Psychological Analysis*. New York: Holt, 1965.

Kennan, George. *The Nuclear Delusion. Soviet-American Relations in the Atomic Age*. New York: Pantheon, 1982.

Keohane, Robert O. *After Hegemony, Cooperation and Discord in the World Political Economy*, Princeton, N.J.: Princeton University Press, 1984.

———, and Joseph S. Nye. *Power and Interdependence. World Politics in Transition.* Boston: Little, Brown and Company, 1977.

Kindleberger, Charles P. *Power and Money, The Economics of International Politics and the Politics of International Economics.* New York: Basic Books, 1970.

King, John Jerry. ed. *International Political Effects of the Spread of Nuclear Weapons.* Washington, D.C.: GPO, 1979.

Kirkpatrick, Jeane J. "Double Standards in Human Rights." U.S. Department of State, Bureau of Public Affairs, *Current Policy,* No. 353 (November 24, 1982).

———, "Human Rights and Foreign Policy." U.S. Department of State, Bureau of Public Affairs, Selected Documents No. 22 (December 1983).

Kissinger, Henry. *Nuclear Weapons and Foreign Policy.* New York: Doubleday Anchor Books, 1958.

———, *The Necessity for Choice.* New York: Harper and Brothers, 1961.

Knorr, Klaus. *Power and Wealth. The Political Economy of International Power.* New York: Basic Books, 1973.

———, and James Rosenau, eds. *Contending Approaches to International Politics.* Princeton, N.J.: Princeton University Press, 1969.

Kostyukhin, Dmitry. *The World Market Today.* Moscow: Progress Publishers, 1979.

Krause, Lawrence B. "The Crisis in the World Economy." *The Brookings Review,* Vol. 1, No. 3 (Spring 1983).

Kucewicz, William. "The Threat of Soviet Genetic Engineering." *The Wall Street Journal* (April 23, 25, and 27, 1984).

Kvitsinsky, Yuli. "Soviet View of Geneva." *The New York Times.* (January 12, 1984), Op. Ed.

Lebedev, N.I. *A New Stage in International Relations.* Oxford: Pergamon Press, 1978.

Lee, Edmund. "Beijing's Balancing Act." *Foreign Policy,* No. 51 (Summer 1983), pp. 27–46.

Lee, Peter N.S. "The Sino-Soviet Dispute Re-Examined," in *Liao* (1981), pp. 29–42.

Leopold, Richard W. *The Growth of American Foreign Policy.* New York: Knopf, 1962.

Levi, Werner. *Contemporary International Law: A Concise Introduction.* Boulder, Colo.: Westview Press, 1979.

Levitt, Kari. *Silent Surrender. The Multinational Corporation in Canada.* Toronto: Macmillan, 1970.

Lewin, Ronald. *Ultra Goes To War.* New York: McGraw-Hill, 1978.

Lewis, Sir W. Arthur. *The Evolution of the International Economic Order.* The Eliot Janeway Lectures on Historical Economics. Princeton, N.J.: Princeton University Press, 1978.

Liao, Kuang-sheng, ed. *Modernization and Diplomacy in China.* Hong Kong: Public Affairs Research Centre, The Chinese University of Hong Kong, 1981.

———, "Decline of Antiforeignism in Chinese Foreign Policy," in *Liao,* ed. (1981), pp. 13–29.

Lider, Julian. *The Political and Military Law of War. An Analysis of Marxist-Leninist Concepts.* Westmead, Farnborough, Hants., England: Saxon House, 1979.

Lindblom, Charles E. *Politics and Markets. The World's Political-Economic System.* New York: Basic Books, 1977.

Lissakers, Karin. "Money and Manipulation." *Foreign Policy,* No. 44 (Fall 1981), pp. 107–126.

Lord, Winston, Karl Kaiser, Thierry de Montbrial, and Davitt Watt. *The West's Security. What Has Changed? What Should Be Done? New Dimensions and Tasks.* New York: Council On Foreign Relations, 1981.

Lowenthal, Richard. "The Diffusion of Power and the Control of Force in a New International Order." *Adelphi Papers,* No. 134 (Spring 1977), pp. 9–16.

Luttwak, Edward N. *The Grand Strategy of the Soviet Union.* New York: St. Martin's Press, 1983.

Machetzki, Rüdiger. "China-EC Economic Development in Perspective," in *Liao* (1981), pp. 67–76.

Mackinder, Sir Halford J. *Democratic Ideals and Reality: A Study in the Politics of Reconstruction.* London: Constable, 1919.

———, *The Geographical Pivot of History.* New York: The Cooper Union, Division of Social Philosophy, 1943.

Malone, James L. "Who Needs The Sea Treaty?" *Foreign Policy,* No. 54 (Spring 1984), pp. 44–63.

Mandel, Ernest. *Decline of the Dollar, A Marxist View of the Monetary Crisis.* New York: Monad Press, 1972.

Mandelbaum, Michael. *The Nuclear Revolution: International Politics Before and After Hiroshima.* New York: Cambridge University Press, 1981.

———, *The Nuclear Future.* Ithaca: Cornell University Press, 1983.

Marchetti, Victor, and John D. Marks. *The CIA and the Cult of Intelligence.* New York: Knopf, 1974.

Marsh, David, and Bernard Simon. "Russia's Discreet Gold Chain." *The Financial Times* (London) (March 31, 1981).

Meadows, Donella, Dennis L. Meadows, Jorgen Randers, and William W. Behrens III. *The Limits To Growth.* A Report for the Club of Rome's Project of the Predicament of Mankind. London: Potomac Associates, 1972.

Mesquita, Bruce Bueno De. *The War Trap.* New Haven: Yale University Press, 1981.

Meyer, Arno J. "The Cold War Is Over." *Democracy* (January 1982).

Meyer, Stephen. *Soviet Theatre Nuclear Forces.* Part II: *Capabilities and Implications.* Adelphi Papers, No. 188 (Winter 1983–1984).

Michalak, Stanley J. Jr. *UNCTAD. An Organization Betraying Its Mission.* Washington, D.C.: The Heritage Foundation, UN Studies Series, 1983.

Middleton, Drew. *Crossroads Of Modern Warfare.* Garden City, N.Y.: Doubleday and Company, 1983.

Miller, James G. "The Individual As An Information Processing System," in J. David Singer, ed. *Human Behavior and International Politics.* Contributions from Social Psychological Sciences, Chicago: Rand McNally and Company, 1965, pp. 202–212.

Milward, Alan S. *War Economy and Society 1939–1945.* Berkeley, Cal.: University of California Press, 1977.

Mitchell, C.R. *The Structure of International Conflict.* New York: St. Martin's Press, 1981.

Möller, Alex. *Währung und Aussenpolitik.* Hanover: Verlag für Literatur und Zeitgeschehen, 1968.

Monson, Joseph, and Kenneth D. Walters. *Nationalized Companies: A Threat to American Business.* New York: McGraw-Hill, 1983.

Morgan, Patrick M. *Theories and Approaches to International Politics.* San Ramon, Cal.: Consensus Publishers, Inc., 1972.

Morgenthau, Hans J. *Politics Among Nations. The Struggle for Power and Peace.* Revised by Kenneth W. Thompson. Sixth Edition. New York: Knopf, 1985.

McCormik, Donald. *Pedlar of Death.* New York: Holt, Rinehart and Winston, 1965.

McNamara, Robert S. "The Military Role of Nuclear Weapons: Perceptions and Misperceptions." *Foreign Affairs* Vol. 62, No. 1 (Fall 1983), pp. 59–80.

National Association of Manufacturers. *The Many Faces of Non-Tariff Barriers.* New York: N.A.M., n.d.

Navrozov, Lev. "Why the C.I.A. Undershoots Soviet Arms Expenditures." *The Wall Street Journal* (December 6, 1983).

Neumann, John von, and Oscar Morgenstern. *Theory of Games and Economic Behavior.* Princeton, N.J.: Princeton University Press, 1944.

Nimetz, Mathew. "International Communication Policy." U.S. Department of State, Bureau of Public Affairs, *Current Policy,* No. 245 (October 6, 1980).

Nincic, Miroslav. *The Arms Race. The Political Economy of Military Growth.* New York: Praeger Special Studies, 1982.

Nishihara, Masashi. "Stop Buffetting Japan." *The New York Times* (May 14, 1982).

Nixon, Richard. "On Economic Power." *The New York Times* (August 19, 1982), Op. Ed.

Nkrumah, Kwame. *Neo-Imperialism, The Last Stage of Capitalism.* London: Nelson, 1965.

Noble, Charles L. "The Internationalization of Capital." Unpublished paper, n.d.

North Atlantic Treaty Organization (NATO). *NATO Handbook.* Brussels: NATO Information Services, 1982.

———, *NATO And the Warsaw Pact: Force Comparisons.* Brussels: NATO Information Service, 1984.

North, Robert C. *The Foreign Relations of China.* Belmont, Cal.: Dickenson Publishing Company, 1969.

North-South. A Program For Survival, see Independent Commission on International Development Issues.

Norton, Augustus and Martin H. Greenberg, eds. *Studies in Nuclear Terrorism.* Boston, Mass.: G.K. Hall, 1979.

Offergeld, Rainer. "Economic and Political Warning Signs." *The German Tribune* (October 3, 1982).

Organski, A.F.K., and J. Kugler. *The War Ledger.* Chicago: Chicago University Press, 1980.

Pierre, Andrew. *The Global Politics of Arms Sales.* Princeton, N.J.: Princeton University Press, 1982.

Pillsbury, Michael. "A Japanese Card?" *Foreign Policy,* No. 33 (Winter 1978–79), pp. 3–30.

Pines, Burton Yale. "The U.S. and the U.N.: Time For Reappraisal." *Backgrounder,* No. 293 (September 29, 1983).

———, ed., *A World Without A U.N.: What Would Happen If The U.N. Shut Down?* Washington, D.C.: The Heritage Foundation, 1984.

Pirages, Dennis. *Ecopolitics.* North Scituate, Mass.: Duxbury Press, 1978.

Pisar, Samuel. *Coexistence and Commerce. Guidelines for Transactions Between East and West.* McGraw-Hill, 1970.

———, *Of Blood And Hope.* New York: Macmillan, 1979.

Pond, Elizabeth. "Nuclear Weapons: Where Is The High-Tech Race Taking The World?" *The Christian Science Monitor* (June 24, 1982).

Potekhin, I.I. *African Problems.* Moscow: Nauka Publishing House, 1968.

Powers, Thomas. *The Man Who Kept The Secrets. Richard Helms and the CIA.* New York: Pocket Books, 1979.

———, "The Ears of America." *The New York Review of Books* (February 3, 1983).

Riordan, Michael, ed. *The Day After Midnight. The Effects of Nuclear War.* Palo Alto, Cal.: Cheshire Books, 1982.

Rivera, Joseph de. *The Psychological Dimension of Foreign Policy.* Columbus, Ohio: Charles E. Merril Publishing Company, 1968.

Robins, Robert S., ed. *Psychopathology and Political Leadership.* New Orleans: Tulane Studies in Political Science, Vol. VI, 1977.

Robinson, James A. and Richard C. Snyder. "Decision-Making in International Relations," in Kelman (1965), pp. 435–463.

Rocks, Lawrence and Richard P. Runyon. *The Energy Crisis.* New York: Crown Publishers, 1972.

Rose, Richard, and Guy Peter. *Can Government Go Bankrupt?* New York: Basic Books, 1978.

Rosenau, James N. *The Scientific Study of Foreign Policy.* Revised Edition. New York: Nichols Publishing Company, 1980.

Rositzke, Harry. *The KGB—The Eyes of Russia.* New York: Doubleday, 1981.

Rostow, Eugene V. "The Future of Soviet-American Relations: Where Are We Going in the Nuclear Arms Talks?" *Arms Control Bulletin* (September 10, 1982), pp. 1-12.

Rostow, W.W. *Getting From Here To There. America's Future in the World Economy.* New York: McGraw-Hill, 1978.

Roussopoulos, Demitrios I., ed. *The Political Economy of the State. Quebec/Canada/U.S.A.* Montreal: Black Rose Books, 1973.

Ruggie, John S. "The Politics of Money." *Foreign Policy,* No. 43 (Summer 1981), pp. 139-154.

Safire, William. *Before The Fall.* New York: Belmont Tower Books, 1975.

Sampson, Anthony. *The Sovereign State of ITT.* London: Coronet, 1974.

———, *The Seven Sisters: The Great Oil Companies and the World They Made.* New York: Viking, 1975.

Sanchez, Nestor D. "The Communist Threat." *Foreign Policy,* No. 52 (Fall 1983), pp. 43-50.

Schmidt, Helmut. "After Deployment: Avenues Towards A Reduction In World Tensions." *The German Tribune,* No. 1111 (December 11, 1983).

Schwarzenberger, Georg. *The Dynamics of International Law.* Milton near Abington, Oxon, England: Professional Books, 1976.

Scott, Andrew M., and Raymond H. Dawson, eds. *Readings In The Making Of American Foreign Policy.* New York: The Macmillan Company, 1965.

Seeler, Hans-Joachim. "The Role of Economic Sanctions." *The German Tribune* (Political Affairs Review), No. 41 (December 5, 1982), pp. 7-10.

Servan-Schreiber, Jean-Jacques. *The World Challenge.* New York: Simon & Schuster, 1980.

Shafer, Michael. "Mineral Myths." *Foreign Policy,* No. 47 (Summer 1982), pp. 154-171.

Sheng, Hu. *Imperialism and Chinese Politics.* Beijing: Foreign Language Press, 1981.

Shouyi, Bai, ed. *An Outline History of China.* Beijing: Foreign Language Press, 1982.

Shultz, George. "The U.S. and the Developing World: Our Joint Stake in the World Economy." *Current Policy,* No. 487 (May 26, 1983).

Sigal, Leon V. "Warming To The Freeze." *Foreign Policy,* No. 48 (Fall 1982), pp. 54-65.

Singer, J. David, ed. *Human Behavior and International Politics. Contributions from Social Psychological Sciences.* Chicago: Rand McNally, 1965.

———, and Melvin Small. *The Wages of War, 1916-1965. A Statistical Handbook.* New York: Wiley, 1972.

Sivard, Ruth Leger. *World Military and Social Expenditures 1981.* Leesburg, Va.: World Priorities, 1981.

Smith, Denis Mack. *Mussolini.* New York: Knopf, 1982.

Sokolowskiy, V.D., ed., *Military Strategy.* Third Edition. A Translation Analysis And Commentary. Menlo Park, Cal.: Stanford Research Institute, January 1971.

Sorensen, Theodore G. "Test Ban and Epitaphs." *The New York Times* (July 25, 1982), Op. Ed.

Speer, Albert. *Inside The Third Reich.* New York: The Macmillan Company, 1970.

Spero, Joan Edelman. *The Politics of International Relations.* Second Edition. New York: St. Martin's Press, 1981.

Spykman, Nicholas J. *The Geography of Peace.* New York: Harcourt, Brace and Company, 1944.

Stadnichenko, A. *Monetary Crisis of Capitalism.* Moscow: Progress Publishers, 1975.

Stanley, John and Maurice Pearton. *The International Trade in Arms.* London: Chatto and Windus, 1972.

Steinbrunner, John O. "Nuclear Decapitation." *Foreign Policy,* No. 45 (Winter 1981–82), pp. 16–28.

———, "Arms and the Art of Compromise." *The Brookings Review* (Summer 1983).

Stern, Fritz. *Gold and Iron: Bismarck, Bleichröder, and the Building of the German Empire.* New York: Knopf, 1977.

Stoessinger, John G. *Why Nations Go To War.* Second Edition. New York: St. Martin's Press, 1978.

Suryadinata, Leo. "ASEAN Relations With China. Problems and Prospects," in *Liao* (1981), pp. 117–126.

Suvorov, Victor. *Inside the Soviet Army.* New York: Macmillan, 1982.

Sykes, Philip. *Sellout. The Giveaway of Canada's Energy Resources.* Edmonton, Canada: Hurtig, 1973.

Taylor, A.J.P. *War by Time-Table. How the First World War Began.* London: MacDonald, 1969.

Tetzlaff, Rainer. "Utopias and Reality." *The German Tribune, Third World Review,* No. 3 (October 3, 1983).

Thomas, Lewis. "Unacceptable Damage." *The New York Review of Books* (September 24, 1981).

Thompson, E.P. *Beyond the Cold War. A New Approach to the Arms Race and Nuclear Annihilation.* New York: Pantheon, 1982.

Thompson, Kenneth W. *Masters of International Thought. Major Twentieth Century Theorists and the World Crisis.* Baton Rouge: Louisiana State University Press, 1980.

Thorp, Willard Long. *The Reality of Foreign Aid.* New York: Praeger, 1971.

Thurow, Lester C. *The Zero-Sum Society. Distribution and the Possibilities of Change.* New York: Penguin Books, 1981.

Tjulpanov, S.I. *Politische Ökonomie and ihre Anwendung in den Entwicklungsländern.* Frankfurt/Main: Verlag Marxistische Blätter, 1969.

Tomashevsky, D. *Lenin's Ideas and Modern International Relations.* Moscow: Progress Publishers, 1974.

Trepper, Leopold. *The Great Game.* New York: McGraw-Hill, 1977.

Trezise, Philip H., ed. *The European Monetary System: Its Promise and Prospects.* Washington, D.C.: The Brookings Institution, 1979.

———, "Industrial Policy is Not the Major Reason for Japan's Success." *The Brookings Review,* Vol. 1, No. 3 (Spring 1983).

Turner, Louis. *Multinational Companies and the Third World.* New York: Hill and Wang, 1973.

Union of Soviet Socialist Republics, Academic of Science of the, see Academy of Science of the USSR.

United Nations, UNCTAD. *The International Monetary Situation: Impact on World Trade and Development.* TD/140/Rev. 1. New York: U.N., 1972.

———, Third Conference on the Law of the Sea. *Economic Implications of Sea-Bed Mineral Development in the International Area:* Report of the Secretary General. A/Conf. 62/25 (May 22, 1974).

———, Department of Political and Security Affairs, Centre for Disarmament. Report to the Secretary General. *Comprehensive Study on Nuclear Weapons.* A/35/392 House. New York: U.N., 1981.

————, Secretary General. *Economic and Social Consequences of the Arms Race and of Military Expenditures.* Report. New York: U.N., 1983.

Urban, George. "A Long Conversation with Dr. Zigniew Brzezinski." *Encounter* (May 1981), pp. 13ff.

United States Arms Control and Disarmament Agency (USACDA). *Arms Control And Disarmament Agreements. Tests and Histories.* 1982 Edition. Washington, D.C.: USACDA, 1982.

————, *Arms Control. U.S. Objectives, Negotiating Efforts, Problems of Soviet Noncompliance.* Washington, D.C.: USACDA, 1984.

United States, Central Intelligence Agency, see C.I.A.

United States, Comptroller General of the. *Despite Positive Effects, Further Acquisitions of U.S. Banks Should Be Limited Until Policy Conflicts Are Fully Addressed.* Report GGD-80-66, August 26, 1980. Washington, D.C.: GAO, 1980.

————, *Countervailing Strategy Demands, Revision of Strategic Force Acquisition Plans.* Report to the Congress, MASAD-81-55. Washington, D.C.: GAO, August 15, 1981.

————, *Chemical Warfare: Many Unanswered Questions.* Report to the Committee on Foreign Affairs of the House of Representatives (GAO/IPE-83-6). Washington, D.C.: GAO, April 29, 1983.

United States Congress, House of Representatives, 95th Congress, 1st Session, Committee on International Relations. *The Soviet Union and the Third World.* Washington, D.C.: GPO, 1977.

————, 96th Congress, 2d Session, Committee on Government Operations. Twentieth Report. *The Adequacy of the Federal Response to Foreign Investment in the United States.* Washington, D.C.: GPO, 1980.

————, 97th Congress, 1st Session, Committee on Science and Technology, Hearings *National Materials and Minerals Policy Research and Development Act of 1980.* (July 28, 1981). Report No. 44. Washington, D.C.: GPO, 1981.

————, 98th Congress, 1st Session. Committee on Science and Technology. Report. *The Consequences of Nuclear War on the Global Environment.* Washington, D.C.: GPO, 1983.

————, 98th Congress, 2nd Session. Committee on Foreign Affairs. Subcommittee on International Security and Scientific Affairs. Report. *Binary Weapons: Implications of the U.S. Chemical Stockpile Modernization Program for Chemical Weapons Proliferation.* Washington, D.C.: GPO, 1984.

United States Congress, Senate, 93rd Congress, Committee on Foreign Relations, Subcommittee on Multinational Corporations. Hearings. *Multinational Corporations and United States Foreign Policy.* Washington, D.C.: GPO, 1973, Parts 1-11.

————, 93rd Congress, 1st Session. Committee on Interior and Insular Affairs. Subcommittee on Minerals, Materials, And Fuels. *Current Development In Deep Seabed Mining.* Part I. Washington, D.C.: GPO, 1975.

————, 2nd. *Mineral Resources Of The Deep Seabed.* Part II. Washington, D.C.: GPO, 1974.

————, 2nd Session, Committee on Foreign Relations. Report. *Multinational Oil Corporations and U.S. Foreign Policy.* Washington, D.C.: GPO, January 2, 1975.

————, 94th Congress, 1st Session, Select Committee to Study Governmental Operations with Respect to Intelligence Activities. *Alleged Assassination Plots Involving Foreign Leaders.* Washington, D.C.: GPO, 1975.

————, Committee on Foreign Relations, Subcommittee on Multinational Corporations. *Direct Investment Abroad and the Multinationals: Effects on the United States Economy.* Committee Print. Washington, D.C.: GPO, 1975.

————, 96th Congress, 2d Session, Committee on Foreign Relations, Subcommittee on African Affairs. Report. *Imports of Minerals from South Africa by the United States and the OECD Countries.* Washington, D.C.: GPO, 1980.

————, Committee on Governmental Affairs, Permanent Subcommittee on Investigations. Hearings. *Transfer of Technology to the Soviet Bloc.* February 20, 1980. Washington, D.C.: GPO, 1980.

————, Committee on the Judiciary, Subcommittee to Investigate the *Activities of Individuals Representing the Interests of Foreign Governments.* Hearings. Washington, D.C.: GPO, 1980.

United States, Department of Commerce, International Trade Administration. *China's Economy and Foreign Trade 1979-81.* Washington, D.C.: GPO, May 1982.

United States, Department of Defense (DOD). *Soviet Military Power.* Washington, D.C.: GPO, 1981, 1983, 1984, 1985.

————, *Annual Report For The Fiscal Year 1985.* Washington, D.C.: GPO, 1983.

United States, Department of State. *The Treaty of Versailles and After. Annotations of the Text of the Treaty.* Publication 2724. Conference Series 92. Washington, D.C.: GPO, 1947.

————, Bureau of Intelligence Research. *Soviet and East European Aid to the Third World, 1981.* Publication No. 9345 (February 1983).

————, Bureau of Public Affairs. *Semiannual Reports on the Implementation of the Helsinki Final Act, 1981-1984.* Special Reports No. 100, 105, 109, 113, 119.

————, Bureau of Public Affairs, Media Services. *Toward a Strategy of Interdependence.* Special Report No. 17 (July 1975).

————, Bureau of Public Affairs, Office of Public Communications. *Reform and Restructuring of the U.N. System.* Selected Documents No. 8 (July 1978).

————, Bureau of Public Affairs. *World Court Rules on Hostage Case.* Selected Documents No. 15 (December 1979).

————, *The Strategic Arms Limitations Talks (SALT).* Special Report No. 46. Revised (May 1979).

————, "Arms Coproduction." *Current Policy,* No. 200 (July 15, 1980).

————, *1981 Human Rights Report. Bulletin.* Reprint.

————, *Soviet Active Measures. Forgery, Disinformation, and Political Operations.* Special Report No. 88 (October 1981).

————, Bureau of Public Affairs, Media Services. *Global Economic Interdependence.* Special Report No. 273 (April 8, 1981).

————, Bureau of Public Affairs. *"Poland: Financial and Economic Situation".* Special Report No. 96 (January 27, 1982).

————, *Conventional Arms Transfers in the Third World, 1971-1981.* Special Report No. 102 (August 1982).

————, *Patterns of International Terrorism: 1982.* (September 1983).

————, Bureau of Public Affairs. "Our Development Dialogue With Africa." *Current Policy,* No. 462 (March 3, 1983).

————, *Report to Congress on Voting Practices in the United Nations.* Submitted Pursuant to Public Law 98-151 and Public Law 98-164, February 24, 1984.

————, *International Security and Development Cooperation Program.* Special Report No. 108 (April 4, 1983).

————, *Soviet Active Measures: An Update.* Special Report No. 101 (July 1982) and Special Report No. 110 (September 1983).

————, *1983, 1984 Human Rights Reports.* Special Report No. 14 (Febryary 1984) and No. 121 (February 1985).

————, Bureau of Public Affairs. *Realism, Strength, Negotiation: Key Foreign Policy Statements of the Reagan Administration.* Washington: May 1984.

United States War Department. *War Report of the OSS* (Office of Strategic Services). New York: Wacker, 1976, Vol. I.

Van Dyke, Vernon. *International Politics.* New York: Appleton, Century, and Crofts, 1957.

———, *Human Rights, The United States and World Community.* New York: Oxford University Press, 1970.

Vernon, Raymond. *Sovereignty At Bay. The Multinational Spread of U.S. Enterprise.* New York: Basic Books, 1971.

———, *Storm Over the Multinationals. The Real Issues.* Cambridge, Mass.: Harvard University Press, 1977.

Waite, Robert G.L. *Adolf Hitler. The Psychopathic God.* New York: Basic Books, 1977.

Waller, Derek J. *The Government and Policies of the People's Republic of China.* Third Edition. London: Hutchison, 1981.

Wallis, Allen. "Meeting the Global Challenge: Leadership in the 1980s." U.S. Department of State, Bureau of Public Affairs. *Current Policy,* No. 474 (March 20, 1983).

Walter, Edward. *The Immorality of Limiting Growth.* Albany: State University of New York Press, 1981.

Waltz, Kenneth N. *Theory of International Politics.* Reading, Mass.: Addison-Wesley, 1979.

———, "The Spread of Nuclear Weapons: More May Be Better." *Adelphi Papers,* No. 171 (Autumn 1981), pp. 28–30.

Weintraub, Bernard. "Libyans Arm and Train World Terrorists." *The New York Times* (July 16, 1976).

Weintraub, Robert E. *International Debt: Crisis and Challenge.* Fairfax, Va.: George Mason University, April 1983.

Westerfield, H. Bradford. *The Instruments of American Foreign Policy.* New York: Crowell, 1963.

Weston, Burns H., Richard A. Falk, and Anthony A. D'Amato. *International Law and World Order.* St. Paul, Minn.: West Publishing Company, 1980.

White, Ralph K. *Fearful Warriors. A Psychological Profile of U.S.-Soviet Relations.* New York: Free Press, 1984.

Whiting, D.P. *Finance of Foreign Trade.* Second Edition. London: MacDonald and Evans, 1969.

Wieseltier, Leon. *Nuclear War, Nuclear Peace.* New York: Holt, Rinehart and Winston, 1981.

Wilkinson, Endymion. *Japan Versus Europe. A History of Misunderstanding.* Harmondsworth, Middlesex, England: Penguin Books, 1983.

Wiseman, H.V. *Political Systems.* New York: Praeger, 1966.

World Bank. *1980 Atlas: Population, Per Capita Product and Growth Rates.* Washington, D.C.: The World Bank, 1980.

———, *1983 Atlas.* Washington, D.C.: The World Bank, 1983.

———, *World Development Reports 1981, 1983, 1984.* Washington, D.C.: 1981, 1983, 1984.

Wright, Quincy. *A Study of War.* Second Edition. Chicago: The University of Chicago Press, 1965.

Xiang, Huan. "China Is Its Own Master In Foreign Affairs." *China and the World,* (*Beijing Review,* Foreign Affairs Series), Vol. 3 (1983), pp. 40–47.

Yergin, Daniel. "The Economic Political Military Solution." *The New York Times* (February 16, 1975).

Yergin, Daniel and Martin Hillenbrand. *Global Insecurity.* Boston: Houghton Mifflin Company, 1982.

Zhongyun, Zi. "US Policy Toward Taiwan." *China and the World,* (*Beijing Review,*
    Foreign Affairs Series), Vol. 2 (1983), pp. 51-79.
Zimmerman, William and Glenn Palmer. "Words and Deeds in Soviet Foreign Policy:
    The Case of Soviet Military Expenditures." *American Political Science Review,*
    Vol. 77, No. 2 (June 1983), pp. 358-367.
Zinnes, Dina. *Quantitative International Politics: An Appraisal.* New York: Praeger, 1976.
Zuckerman, Solly. *Nuclear Illusion and Reality.* New York: The Viking Press, 1982.

Index

See also the Comprehensive Table of Contents and List of Illustrations. For additional references to individual countries, organizations, or events, see Figures, Tables, and Boxes.

Footnotes are indexed as such only when text above does not cover the same material or covers it inadequately.

483